Introduction to Social Work

ELEVENTH EDITION

O. William Farley
University of Utah

Larry Lorenzo Smith
University of Utah

Scott W. Boyle
University of Utah

PEARSON

Boston • *New York* • *San Francisco*
Mexico City • *Montreal* • *Toronto* • *London* • *Madrid* • *Munich* • *Paris*
Hong Kong • *Singapore* • *Tokyo* • *Cape Town* • *Sydney*

Senior Series Editor: *Patricia Quinlin*
Editorial Assistant: *Carly Czech*
Marketing Manager: *Wendy Albert*
Production Editor: *Pat Torelli*
Editorial Production Service: *Connie Strassburg*
Manufacturing Buyer: *Debbie Rossi*
Electronic Composition: *GGS Book Services*
Interior Design: *GGS Book Services*
Cover Administrator: *Kristina Mose-Libon*
Cover Designer: *Jennifer Hart*

For related titles and support materials, visit our online catalog at www.ablongman.com

Between the time website information is gathered and published, it is not unusual for some sites to have closed. Also, the transcription of URLs can result in typographical errors. The publisher would appreciate notification where these errors occur so that they may be corrected in subsequent editions.

Library of Congress Cataloging-in-Publication Data

Farley, O. William
    Introduction to social work / O. William Farley, Larry Lorenzo Smith,
      Scott W. Boyle.—11th ed.
      p. cm.
    Includes bibliographical references and index.
    ISBN-13: 978-0-205-62576-5
    ISBN-10: 0-205-62576-2
      1. Social service. 2. Social case work—United States. 3. Social service—United States.
  I. Smith, Larry Lorenzo. II. Boyle, Scott W. III. Title.
  HV40.S59 2009
  361—dc22
                    2008010412

Printed in the United States of America

10 9 8 7 6 5 4 3 2 1   RRD-VA   12 11 10 09

Credits appear on page 449, which constitutes an extension of the copyright page.

New to This Edition

New material on **International Perspectives** to the profession (The profession is expanding to countries around the world.) (Ch. 1)

New information on the **plight of children** in the U.S. (13 million of America's children live in poverty.) (Ch. 2)

Introduction of the concept of "**best practices**," stressing the importance of empirical research in the delivery of services. (Ch. 3)

Coverage of a **strengthening generalist practice** with the inclusion of the strengths-based perspective. (Ch. 4)

Inclusion of the **integrated systems theory** as one of the prominent paradigms used in the profession today. (Ch. 5)

New section on "**evidence-based practice**" and why it is important to the social work profession and especially to social work practice. (Ch. 8)

New section on "**Clients Experiencing Poverty**" that includes how to work with these clients and how to involve them in their own treatment. (Ch. 9)

New section on "**Client with Disabilities**" including a list of dos and don'ts in working with these clients. (Ch. 10)

New section on "**Motivational Interviewing**" and how this technique is used in working with clients who lack motivation to change troublesome behavior. (Ch. 11)

New section on "**Medicare Drug Program**" that includes a discussion of costs, coverage, and limitations (i.e., the "doughnut hole"). (Ch. 12)

Coverage of the effects of **marriage and divorce** on the individual's economic, interpersonal, psychological, and physical well-being. (Ch. 13)

New material introduced regarding the "**Keep Children in Families Safe Act**" (2003). (Ch. 13)

New section on **depression and the elderly**. (Ch. 15)

New information on the **effects of marijuana**. Updated information on adolescent drug abuse in the U.S. and the most effective prevention programs. (Ch. 16)

Summary and discussion of the **NASW standards** on culturally competent practice. (Ch. 17)

Discussion of the importance of the re-emergence of **case management services** to the social work profession. (Ch. 19)

Added information about **Afghanistan and Iraq** and how the war is affecting the social work profession. (Ch. 20)

Analysis of the attempt to pull all social work organizations together by 2012 to form a **more unified profession**. (Ch. 22)

Contents

Preface   xiii

PART I   •   *Introduction*

1   *What Is Social Work?*   *1*

Social Welfare   *3*

Social Work   *4*

Distinguishing Characteristics of Social Work   *7*

Sociology and Social Work   *11*

Psychiatry and Social Work   *11*

Psychology and Social Work   *12*

Counseling and Social Work   *13*

Social Work in the World Today   *13*

Summary   *15*

Selected References   *16*

2   *The Evolution of Social Welfare and Social Work*
in the United States   *17*

Echoes of the Past   *19*

European Roots   *20*

Beginnings in the United States   *22*

Public Assistance and Social Welfare Emerge   *25*

Services of Volunteers   *27*

Social Workers Appear   *28*

Summary   *30*

Selected References   *31*

3 *Education for Social Work*   *33*

Social Work Education   *35*

Council on Social Work Education   *46*

Summary   *46*

Selected References   *47*

PART II • *Social Work Practice*

4 *Generalist Practice and Introductory Theory*   *48*

Need for a Theoretical Framework   *52*

Introductory Inner and Outer Forces Paradigm   *53*

Additional Model Definition   *56*

The Life Cycle and the Inner and Outer Forces Model   *57*

Social Functioning   *60*

Levels of Social Functioning   *60*

A Base for Generalist Social Work Practice   *61*

Summary   *62*

Selected References   *63*

5 *Social Work Practice with Individuals*   *64*

Work with the Individual—A Generalist Approach   *64*

Clinical Social Work Defined   *66*

History of Social Casework and Clinical Social Work   *67*

Trends in Casework and Clinical Work   *69*

The Practice Framework   *71*

Methods of Clinical Social Work   *74*

The Clinical/Direct Practice Process of Social Work   *76*

The Multisystems Approach   *85*

Summary   *86*

Selected References   *86*

6 *Social Work Practice with Groups*   *87*

Historical Developments   *89*

Group Work Defined   *91*

Group Work Models   *93*

Formation of Groups   *97*

Selection of Group Members   *99*

Preparation of Group Members   *101*

Structuring the Group   *102*

Stages of Groups   *105*

Group Work Settings   *106*

Summary   *109*

Selected References   *110*

7 *Social Work Practice with Communities*   *112*

What Is Community Organization?   *113*

Beginnings of Community Social Work   *116*

Underlying Principles in Community Organization   *119*

Community Social Work Processes   *121*

Roles of the Community Organizer   *125*

Case Summaries   *126*

Summary   *127*

Selected References   *127*

8 *Administration and Research*   *129*

Administration   *130*

Research   *143*

Summary   *149*

Selected References   *150*

PART III • *Social Work Services*

9   *Mental Health Services*   152

Beginnings in Mental Health   153

Elements of the Mental Health Network   154

Essential Elements of Comprehensive Mental Health   156

Special Problems and Issues in Mental Health   164

Summary   173

Selected References   174

10   *Social Work in Health Care*   176

Definition of Social Work in Health Care   178

The Meaning of Illness   181

The Role of Social Work in Health Care   183

The Future of Social Work in the Health Care Services   191

Prevention and Social Work   193

Summary   193

Selected References   193

11   *Social Work in the Schools*   195

The Education Delivery System: New Approaches   197

Problems Plaguing the Public Schools   198

Beginnings in School Social Work   202

Social Work Practice in the Schools   203

Social Work Using a Group Approach   205

School Social Work and the Community   207

Working with Minorities   207

When the System Fails   208

Summary   211

Selected References   211

12 *Social Security and Public Welfare*   *213*

Government's Responsibility for Welfare   *214*

The Social Security Act   *216*

Aid to Families with Dependent Children   *220*

Government and Public Welfare   *233*

Summary   *234*

Selected References   *235*

13 *Family and Child Welfare Services*   *237*

Marriage and Family Counseling   *238*

Child Welfare Services   *246*

In-Home Care of Children   *247*

Foster Care of Children   *249*

Adoption Services   *255*

Child Protective Services   *260*

Summary   *265*

Selected References   *265*

14 *Correctional Services*   *267*

The Social Problems of Delinquency and Crime   *267*

Social Work and Corrections   *270*

Social Work Practice in Corrections   *271*

Processes and Principles   *273*

Social Services and Case Examples   *277*

Social Work in Institutions   *279*

Summary   *285*

Selected References   *286*

15 *Services for Older Americans*   *288*

Older Americans Act of 1965   *289*

White House Conference on Aging, 1971   *291*

Adequate Income   *292*

Appropriate Living Arrangements   *293*

Institutional Responsiveness and a New Attitude toward Aging   *294*

Independence and Dignity   *302*

Summary   *306*

Selected References   *307*

16 *Drug Abuse and Social Work*   *308*

Misused Drugs and What They Do   *312*

Extent and Cost of Drug Abuse   *321*

Programs for Control, Prevention, Treatment   *322*

Role of Social Work in Treatment   *330*

Summary   *334*

Selected References   *335*

17 *Services with Minorities*   *337*

Minority Problems   *338*

Social Services   *346*

Educational Developments   *349*

Summary   *351*

Selected References   *352*

18 *Social Work in Rural Areas*   *354*

Beginnings in Rural Social Work   *356*

Rural Social Work Practice   *357*

Roles of the Rural Social Worker   *359*

Rural Social Service Agencies   *362*

Distance Learning for Rural Social Work   *363*

Summary   *363*

Selected References   *364*

19 *Case Management*   *366*

Historical Developments   *369*

Case Management Defined   *371*

Case Management Research   *374*

Summary   *375*

Selected References   *375*

PART IV • *Professional Development*

20 *Social Work: A Maturing Profession*   *377*

Criteria of a Profession   *377*

Historical Background   *379*

Social Work Today   *383*

Summary   *394*

Selected References   *395*

21 *Social Work Prevention and Enrichment*   *397*

Social Work Focus on Prevention   *399*

Problems Involved   *402*

Examples of Prevention   *402*

Implications of Prevention   *409*

Social Work Enrichment   *411*

Summary   *412*

Selected References   *412*

22 *Social Work and the Future*   415

Professional Maturation   417

Increase in Services   418

Professional Identification and Visibility   419

Certification and Licensing   420

Spirituality in Social Work Practice   421

Changing Continuum in Social Work Education   423

Development of the Role of Consultant   424

Status of the Social Worker   424

Private Practice   425

The Aging of Our Population   426

Advocacy Role   426

Improved Public Relations   426

Rural Social Work   427

Technology   427

Expansion of Leadership Roles   428

Increase in International Social Work   429

Prevention   430

Enrichment   430

Movement for Higher Quality   430

Summary   431

Selected References   431

Name Index   *433*

Subject Index   *437*

Preface

The authors are pleased to present this eleventh edition of *Introduction to Social Work*—thanks to the wide use of the tenth edition by students, social work educators, and practitioners. Many of their suggestions have been incorporated in this current version.

We live in a world that seems to change constantly. Technology has become so advanced that nothing seems impossible. A few years ago we learned that scientists had cloned a sheep. Now recent advances in stem-cell research may unlock the mysteries behind such devastating genetic disorders as Parkinson's disease, multiple sclerosis, and diabetes. We also have learned that a technique called *gene splitting* may make it possible in the next decade to grow vital organs in a test-tube environment for patients in need of transplants. Just when it seems that "the world is our oyster," we are brought "down to earth," so to speak, by the Columbine school tragedy, foot-and-mouth disease, ethnic cleansing in Kosovo, the worldwide AIDS epidemic, the September 11, 2001, terrorists' attack on the World Trade Center and the Pentagon, and the war in Iraq. As advanced as our world has become, "people problems" still confront our globe and challenge the social work profession every day.

Since the first edition of this book, advancements in knowledge have exploded in nearly every field of human endeavor. Our high-tech/high-touch society opens swinging doors for communication and meaningful human relationships, but people are still having difficulty in communicating and in getting along with each other. For example, a person may be in a room mingling with others but feel abject loneliness for lack of ability to interact effectively with those present. Human relationships can bring satisfaction and joy, but also—for many people—suffering, insecurity, and other difficulties. Social work is one answer to challenges related to communication, feelings, and human actions.

The purpose of this book is to help students understand social welfare and social work. It presents a comprehensive, highlighted view of social work. It focuses on the *why,* the *what,* the *who,* the *when,* the *where* and describes beginnings of the *how* of social work. The book is for (1) college undergraduate students who want to increase their general understanding about social welfare and social work and (2) those who have a professional interest in social work. It can also be used in social work philosophy classes and as a reference on the graduate level.

Social welfare depicts human beings as the center of the universe. In their associations with others their lives are enriched, but they also encounter numerous problems. Social work is a professional attempt to help people solve and prevent problems in social functioning, strengthen their social relationships, and enrich their ways of living.

Social work is both a field *and* a method. This book presents an introductory, integrated, overall view of both. Special consideration is given to such perplexing problems as

AIDS, gangs, youth suicide, drugs, battered women and children, welfare reform, the Social Security crisis, and distance learning for rural social work. The country is struggling with many health care concerns, the economy, and the difficult war in Iraq. Social work is continually being called upon to render services and expertise in all of these problem areas. This book encompasses the history and breadth of social work practice. Readers will hopefully come to appreciate that the need for professional social workers is ever expanding and we encourage students to strongly consider joining the ranks of the profession.

Several areas have been given special emphasis to update and enrich this edition. New materials and references on drug courts, school violence, drug treatment and prevention, new programs for aging, welfare reform, the Social Security crisis, distance learning for rural social work, and President Bush's faith-based social service initiative have been added. In one sense, this book encompasses the sociology of social work. Case glimpses and case histories are used to illustrate traditional and innovative social work settings and services.

The authors want to thank and acknowledge the reviewers of the previous editions: Stephen M. Aigner, Iowa State University; Patricia Albaugh, Southwest Oklahoma State University; Lessie Bass, East Carolina University; William C. Berleman, University of Washington; Scott Burcham, Arkansas State University; George W. Caulton, Western New England College; Nancy Chavkin, Texas State University; Shirley Clark, Chattanooga State Technical Community College; Mary A. Dowery, Ball State University; Ginger Edwards, Charles Stewart Mott Community College; Sharon Eisen, Mott Community College; Charles E. Grenier, Louisiana State University; Martin Hope, Winthrop College; Joan M. Jones, University of Wisconsin–Milwaukee; Johnette G. McCracken, West Liberty State College; Thomas D. Oellerich, Ohio University; Gwenelle O'Neal, West Chester University; and Paul Sanzenbach, Louisiana State University.

We also want to thank our reviewers for their helpful suggestions and kind remarks for this new edition: Barrett Michelle Horton, University of Tennessee at Martin; Anita Sharma, University of Louisiana; and Saman Yaghmaee, San Diego Community College.

The authors want to thank Karen Hanson, Editor-in-Chief, Social Science; Patricia Quinlin, Senior Series Editor; and Carly Czech, Editorial Assistant, at Allyn and Bacon. These individuals have been a great help and support throughout the revision process. Also, a special thanks goes to Connie Strassburg and GGS Book Services, who kept us organized and moving forward throughout this process.

The authors deeply appreciate the caring support and encouragement of their wives, Mary and Jane, and other family members, who made many helpful suggestions and devoted their time and talents to reading, editing, and typing the manuscript. Also, Cathy Garber, an MSW student, should be thanked for her library research on the manuscript.

O. William Farley
Larry Lorenzo Smith
Scott W. Boyle

1

What Is Social Work?

At 3:00 A.M. an ambulance pulled up to the medical center emergency room. Attendants rushed to get a 17-year-old Hispanic teenager into the hospital and onto life support systems. The teenager had desperately, but resolutely, driven his car into a solid brick wall.

The social worker on duty during those early hours was called to be there when the boy's parents arrived. The look of desperation on their faces told the whole story. This couple had come to the United States from Mexico some three years ago, bringing their boy and his three younger sisters with them. The language, the school system, and the entire community had created subtle barriers for this family. The father and mother both obtained low-paying jobs and tried to begin a new life.

The 17-year-old tried to fit in. His grades weren't bad, but he just didn't have friends. He couldn't get a sense of who he was. His dad saved some very hard-earned dollars to buy the young man a car. Perhaps the car would help his son find a place. It was that same car that now was a twisted wreck.

The boy died that night. The social worker tried to comfort the parents. Over and over again the social worker asked himself the questions, "Why couldn't this tragedy have been prevented? What can I do now to help this family?"

A second case glimpse illustrates community problems. Riots rocked Los Angeles after the acquittal, Wednesday, April 29, 1992, of four white police officers in the videotaped beating of a black motorist, Rodney King. In less than twenty-four hours mobs attacked police headquarters, motorists were dragged from their cars and beaten, and hundreds of businesses and homes were looted or burned in South Central Los Angeles. A night of arson, looting, and gunfire killed nine persons. By the following Tuesday when life was "back to normal," the rioting had resulted in fifty-five dead and 5,500 fires. More recently, Cincinnati has suffered from severe riots brought on by the shooting of a young black man by a white police officer. What might have been done to prevent such disasters? Can social work play a part in facing and helping solve community problems?

We live in a challenging, fascinating world. We have learned how to travel to the moon and sent a millionaire son of a retired U.S. astronaut on a Russian rocket to live on the orbiting international space station, yet we often have difficulty reaching someone in the same room. We live in a fast-moving, push-button space age, yet we find that people are still the center of the world and its values. Mars and the rings of Saturn are important, but humans

1

are more important. As people live together, problems of relationship and interaction emerge. Personal problems, family problems, and community problems appear on the horizon of everyday living. Drug abuse, homelessness, crime, delinquency, mental illness, suicide, school dropouts, AIDS, and numerous other social problems abound at every turn.

Every day new scientific and technological discoveries enlarge our knowledge and skills. We not only travel in space and have space stations but also have one or more cars in the garage for personal travel. We carry iPods, iPhones, video cell phones, laptop computers, and TV sets that bring instant news twenty-four hours a day, shrinking the world to a small community. Fifteen-second ads channeled into our homes are common. Wonder drugs are used by millions everywhere searching for peace of mind as well as for treatment. Genetically-engineered foods are reaching dining tables for distinctive eating. Digital cameras, VCRs, computer chips, Internet, DVDs, and computer banking are altering our recreational, educational, and business endeavors at every turn.

Medical triumphs surprise the imagination with use of lasers and miniature instruments under high magnification to restore eyesight, use of an artificial arm that gives amputees lifelike dexterity, and test-tube babies.

On the negative side, all kinds of difficult situations exist. Terrorism is rampant; the Iraq War has cost much in human lives and money; no place on the globe is any longer free from attack. Single mothers are raising children in many women-dominated homes with no fathers around. Use of drugs is on the increase around the world, bringing bizarre, uncertain behavior into the lives of people, their families, and their communities. "Computer criminals" are on the scene. Movies, TV, radio, and current literature are continuing to increase in negativism and violence. The average child views TV about four hours a day. By the age of sixteen he or she has watched more than 200,000 acts of violence—50,000 of which are murders.

In this high-tech uncertain world, personal, family, and community problems exist as never before. Emotional difficulties are rife. Teenage and senior citizen suicides are on the increase. There seems to be an overall ebb in meaningful human relationships—people enjoying people and helping each other.

When serious difficulties in human relationships arise, the question immediately becomes, "Can we get help?" The answer is usually, "Yes." Many professions, one of which is social work, are ready and eager to help. What is social work? What is social welfare? What part do they play in this satellite age?

Social work and social welfare are based on three premises: (1) that the person is important; (2) that he or she has personal, family, and community problems resulting from interaction with others; and (3) that something can be done to alleviate these problems and enrich the individual's life. An introductory glimpse of two particular cases illustrates all three premises.

Joe had been in a state hospital for nineteen years, confined to one of the back wards. Hospital personnel were unsuccessful in getting him involved in any type of interaction with staff or fellow patients.

Then came a change. As a part of a new program, a social worker was assigned to meet with Joe for thirty minutes daily with the goal of encouraging him to be more active in his own treatment. The worker explained to Joe that she was going to see him regularly and that she was genuinely interested in him. For the first two weeks, he uttered not a word. Then one day he surprised the worker by saying, "I like you."

The worker continued to spend about thirty minutes daily with Joe. She was sympathetic, interested in him, warm, friendly, and accepting. He responded steadily to her interest and efforts. Within six months he was discharged from the hospital; and with the follow-up help of the local community mental health center, Joe was placed in an independent-living situation where his quality of life improved dramatically over the next several years.

When Joe was asked by a close friend what had happened to make the difference in his life, he eagerly replied with much seriousness, "The worker was just like a magnet—drawing me out of my shell. I couldn't resist her."

A second case further illustrates these three premises.

A school of social work and a local businessman formed a partnership to bring both volunteer and professional social services to a small inner-city neighborhood that contained many senior citizens who were not being served adequately to meet their needs. Neighborhood residents were helped to form a "neighbor-to-neighbor" volunteer effort. The volunteers, assisted by social work students, became the "eyes and ears" of the local community and began to address the needs of many of the seniors. The needs ranged from having a friendly visit to the replacement of brokendown furnaces and roofs. The funding for these repairs came from the local businessman. Many of the services were provided by volunteers who lived in the neighborhood whereas others were provided by volunteers recruited from the larger community. The social work students were also able to link senior citizens with professional services already available. The quality of life and the independence of these senior citizens were improved by this social work approach.

Social Welfare

The terms *social work* and *social welfare* are often confused and sometimes used synonymously. Actually, *social welfare* has a broader meaning and encompasses social work, public welfare, and other related programs and activities. Social welfare, according to Friedlander,[1] "is the organized system of social services and institutions, designed to aid individuals and groups to attain satisfying standards of life and health, and personal and social relationships that permit them to develop their full capacities and to promote their well being in harmony with the needs of their families and the community." Long and Holle state: "Social welfare is a necessary thread in the fabric of social structure, and society has a responsibility for the plight of its members."[2]

Social welfare, in a broad sense, encompasses the well-being and interests of large numbers of people, including their physical, educational, mental, emotional, spiritual, and economic needs. Economically it is big business. For example, in August 1985, the Old Age, Survivors, Disability, and Health Insurance (OASDHI) program in the United States was paying $15.3 billion in monthly cash benefits to 36,787,000 beneficiaries. By July 1999 monthly benefits in the amount of $31.96 billion were sent to 44,335,030 beneficiaries.

As reported in the *Social Security Bulletin*, expenditures for social welfare under public law amounted to $1,434.6 billion in fiscal year 1994, an increase of 5.0 percent over the previous year. The 1994 amount represented 21.8 percent of the national output of goods and services as measured by the gross domestic product (GDP). Federal and state governments spent $407.9 billion on health and medical care alone in 1994.[3] A 2006 news article reported that the Medicare trust fund will run out of money in 2018. The same article reported that the Social Security trust fund will be exhausted in 2040. The United States will have major social welfare problems if these trusts are allowed to run out of money.[4]

Many professionals deliver social welfare services, but social workers have always been prominent welfare service providers. In fact, they have played such a central role that the terms of *social welfare* and *social work* have been interchanged over the years. In 1970 according to the U.S. Bureau of the Census, there were 216,000 social workers in the United States—136,000 female and 80,000 male. In 1995 there were more than 500,000 social workers in the United States, two-thirds of whom were women. The National Association of Social Workers (NASW) estimates that there are currently some 600,000 people who hold social work degrees. It predicts the profession will grow by 30 percent by 2010.[5]

Social welfare includes the basic institutions and processes related to facing and solving social problems—problems that affect large numbers of people and that require some kind of concerted group effort to resolve. In this sense, social welfare includes not only qualified social workers, but also untrained personnel employed in public welfare, probation, and other areas where social problems are being faced and resolved. Minimum traditional standards required a Master of Social Work degree for the professional social worker, with at least two years of work experience under adequate supervision.

However, action by NASW, the Council on Social Work Education (CSWE), and schools of social work has provided for recognition of undergraduate programs in social work; students who have completed these programs satisfactorily are recognized as the first level of "professional" social workers. Their training includes supervised field experiences as well as classes in methodology and basic knowledge. In addition, many two-year programs have been introduced in community and other colleges that provide two-year certificates in social services and training for paraprofessionals as social work technicians or aides to help people with problems.

A glance into the history of social welfare reveals that services have been provided across the centuries for disadvantaged persons and groups. Examples of such services include the care of the sick and the poor administered by the early Christian Church, and the provisions of the Elizabethan Poor Laws of the sixteenth and seventeenth centuries. Social services came first, and methods of social work developed out of social welfare. At the turn of the twentieth century, social work was becoming more formalized, and within the next several decades emerged into a profession—a specialized, modern segment of the totality of social welfare.

Social Work

The next question that follows is, "What is social work?" An answer appeared in an editorial in *The New York Times:*

> A new profession has been growing to maturity under our noses. It is social work. Once thought of as basket-on-the-arm assistance to the poor, it now is a discipline, scientific in method and artful in manner, that takes remedial action on problems in several areas of

Social worker developing a relationship.

society. It ministers to families in economic or emotional difficulty. It helps communities to bring their welfare and related services into good balance. It works in medical, group, and school situations. It seeks to correct the causes underlying delinquency and adult criminality.

A much-used historical definition of social work appeared in the 1959 Curriculum Study sponsored by CSWE: "Social work seeks to enhance the social functioning of individuals, singly and in groups, by activities focused upon their social relationships which constitute the interaction between man and his environment. These activities can be grouped into three functions: restoration of impaired capacity, provision of individual and social resources, and prevention of social dysfunction."[6]

The underlying assumptions of social work are:

1. Social work like all other professions has problem-solving functions.
2. Social work practice is an art with a scientific and value foundation.
3. Social work as a profession came into being and continues to develop because it meets human needs and aspirations recognized by society.
4. Social work practice takes its values from those held by the society of which it is a part. However, its values are not necessarily or altogether those universally or predominantly held or practiced in society.
5. The scientific base of social work consists of three types of knowledge: (a) tested knowledge, (b) hypothetical knowledge that requires transformation into tested

knowledge, and (c) assumptive knowledge (or "practice wisdom") that requires transformation into hypothetical and thence into tested knowledge.

6. The knowledge needed for social work practice is determined by its goals and functions and the problems it seeks to solve.
7. The internalization of professional knowledge and values is a vital characteristic of the professional social worker since he is himself the instrument of professional help.
8. Professional skill is expressed in the activities of the social worker.[7]

The basic functions of social work—restoration, provision of resources, and prevention—are intertwined and interdependent. Restoration of impaired social functioning may be subdivided into curative and rehabilitative aspects. Its curative aspects are to eliminate factors that have caused breakdown of functioning, and its rehabilitative aspects, to reorganize and rebuild interactional patterns. Illustrations of restoration would include assistance in obtaining a hearing aid for a partially deaf child or helping a rejected lonely child to be placed in a foster home. The rehabilitative aspect might be helping the one child to psychologically accept and live with the hearing aid and supporting the other child as he or she adjusts to the new foster home.

Provision of resources, social and individual, for more effective social functioning may be subdivided into developmental and educational. The developmental aspects are designed to further the effectiveness of existing social resources or to bring to full flower personal capacity for more effective social interaction. An example would be the services of a Family Service Society that help Mr. and Mrs. X, through individual and conjoint interviews, to understand each other better and to open the channels of meaningful communication between them. The educational spectrum is designed to acquaint the public with specific conditions and needs for new or changing social resources. Again, this could be illustrated by public talks given by staff members of a Family Service Society, in which counseling services are described as a resource in alleviating marriage and family problems.

The third function, prevention of social dysfunction, involves early discovery, control, and elimination of conditions and situations that potentially could hamper effective social functioning. The two main divisions are prevention of problems in the area of interaction between individuals and groups, and second, the prevention of social ills. Premarital counseling would be an example of an attempt to prevent individual and social problems in relation to social functioning. It is hoped that through this process couples will be able to anticipate possible difficulties in marital interaction and, through adequate consideration and understanding, avoid the problems that might ensue otherwise. Prevention of social ills ordinarily falls within the area of community organization. An example of this function is the Community Services Council approach to the reduction of juvenile delinquency through the utilization of all community organizations and economic resources (for example, to build a new Youth Center and provide it with a professionally trained staff to work with boys and girls who are near-delinquent or who live in "delinquency areas"). An overall conclusion in the Curriculum Study states that "the focus on social relationships, however, is suggested as the *distinguishing characteristic* of the social work profession."

Harriet Bartlett claims that social work is "a configuration of elements none of which is unique but which, in combination, represent a contribution quite distinct from that rendered by any other profession."[8] The 1992 CSWE Curriculum Policy Statement indicates that "the profession of social work is committed to the enhancement of human well-being and to the alleviation of poverty and oppression. The social work profession receives its sanction from public and private auspices and is the primary profession in the provision of social services." The 1995 edition of *The Social Work Dictionary* defines social work as "the applied science of helping people achieve an effective level of psychosocial functioning and effecting societal changes to enhance the well-being of all people."[9]

A Current Definition

Social work may be defined as an art, a science, a profession that helps people solve personal, group (especially family), and community problems and attain satisfying personal, group, and community relationships through social work practice (see Figure 1.1). Social work practice today is often generic, involving all three of the traditional methods. The major focus is on reducing problems in human relationships and on enriching living through improved human interaction.

Certainly the main focus of the social worker is on helping people improve their social functioning, their ability to interact and relate to others. On the other hand, there are many in the related helping professions who also assist with interactional problems. In addition, social workers sometimes help individuals solve individual and personal problems.

Social work is an art; it requires great skills to understand people and to help them to help themselves. It is a beginning science because of its problem-solving method and its attempt to be objective in ascertaining facts and in developing principles and operational concepts. It is a profession because it encompasses the attributes of a profession.

Distinguishing Characteristics of Social Work

Comprehension of social work may be enhanced by considering its distinguishing characteristics that follow:

1. Focus is on the wholeness and totality of the person—encompassing the person, environmental factors, and behavior. Social work stresses the total person in the total environment.

2. Emphasis is on the importance of the family in molding and influencing behavior. Social workers attempt to understand the principles underlying family interaction and to work with the family as the basic unit for improving social functioning, recognizing that most social problems inhere in inadequate or imbalanced family relationships. The family is often regarded as the *case* in social work. Although the modern family is changing and many new forms of marital and family living have appeared, the family is still the basic institution in society and as such is a focal factor in social work.

3. Utilization of community resources in helping people solve problems is very important. Social workers have a comprehensive knowledge of community resources and are able to tap them to meet the needs of their clients. They help get "Mr. or Mrs. Jones to the

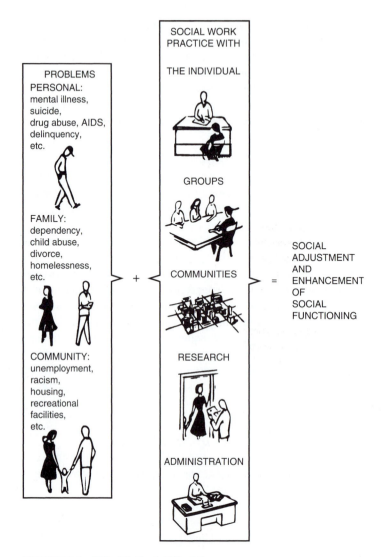

FIGURE 1.1   What Is Social Work?

clinic," to the agency that can help the most in the solution of his or her particular problems. Making referrals is a major service of social workers. They also make significant contributions to the larger community, utilizing their skills in planning and organizing, helping governmental and private organizations and agencies be more effective.

4. Use of the supervisory process provides for guidance and direction of inexperienced workers and for continuing growth of the experienced. Both in academic study and in practice, social work provides supervision by qualified, professional personnel to help the worker continue to grow professionally and acquire increased understanding and skill.

The supervisor is available regularly to help the worker do a better job and increase his or her understandings and skills in working with people. This process is particularly important because social workers themselves are the tools in helping troubled persons, and they need to grow professionally, keeping abreast of new knowledge and skills.

Patterns of supervision have been changing so they are less rigid today than previously. The general trend is toward more self-direction and less formalized supervisor–supervisee relationships. Participatory supervision, self-supervision, and peer supervision are being used extensively.

5. Social work has a unique educational program involving classwork and practical field work experience, which go hand in hand. To obtain a Master of Social Work (MSW) degree requires two years of graduate training—or its equivalent—in one of the 168 (2004) Master of Social Work Education programs in the United States. This program includes both academic classes and live field experiences working with clients, which gives an integrated combination of theory and practice.

Provision has been made for undergraduate programs in social work and/or social welfare to be accredited by CSWE. Thus, graduates in these programs with a Bachelor of Social Work (BSW) degree are recognized as beginning social workers, qualified to start in professional practice.

6. Traditional social work emphasizes three basic processes: clinical work, group work, and community organization. Clinical work involves a close, face-to-face relationship—mainly on an individual-to-individual basis—in working with people and their problems. Group work utilizes the group as the tool to bring about desired changes in social functioning with troubled persons. Community organization is the intergroup approach toward facing and solving social pathologies. It aims to increase understanding of community needs and helps provide for them. Social workers often play an advocate role to strengthen and improve community resources and bring desired social changes.

Some social workers believe there is only one social work process—that of problem solving related to social relationships. They state that the method is basically the same whether working with individuals, groups, or communities. This new approach is called *generalist social work practice.*

7. Social work has distinctive professional bodies: the National Association of Social Workers (NASW) and the Council on Social Work Education (CSWE). NASW was established in 1955, after careful study, and brought together several smaller professional social work groups in a unified, dynamic organization. Its membership has increased rapidly, and in 2004 it enrolled more than 150,000 social workers. This organization is doing much to raise the standards of social work practice, recruit qualified persons for professional training, and interpret practice and values of social work to the public. CSWE, which originated in 1952, is helping improve training facilities, standards, and programs as well as helping with recruitment, public relations, and strengthening social work practice.

8. The *relationship* is the key in the social work process. Everything that is a part of the interview is important, but to the social worker, the feeling tones between the worker and client are particularly important. The social worker attempts to make it possible for the client to face and solve his or her problems by sharing knowledge and helping with understanding and acceptance in an emotionally-supportive relationship.

9. Social work has an orientation in psychiatric concepts and places considerable stress on understanding people. The social worker is particularly interested in how clients feel about themselves and their relationships with others. The social worker possesses considerable understanding of the basic knowledge and concepts of psychiatry and dynamic psychology that assist him or her in dealing with human behavior.

10. The *social* in social work emphasizes stress on social interaction and resultant social functioning and malfunctioning. Significant principles from sociology and social psychology, as well as from group dynamics, are woven into the artful fabric of social work, and are utilized in understanding relationships of people and in helping them resolve their conflicts.

11. Social work recognizes that social problems and human behavior inhere to a considerable degree in the social institutions of humanity. To understand these problems and behavior, it is necessary to understand the institutions of humans. Social problems may be reduced by working with individual personalities or by changing social institutions. For example, a particular boy may be helped to turn from delinquent behavior through individual therapy; on the other hand, social work recognizes that perhaps thousands of delinquent acts may be prevented through sensible changes in political or economic institutions.

12. Most social workers are employed in agency settings. Although the number of social workers in private practice is increasing, most operate within the framework and policies of agencies; this gives them structural backing and support that strengthens their services in many ways. Supervision, consultation, and collaboration, inherent in agency settings, provide many positive resources for the workers.

13. The basic aim of social work is to help clients help themselves or to help a community help itself. Contrary to what many people believe, the social worker does not listen to a client and then prescribe a "social-psychological pill"—even though many clients ask for this. The social worker endeavors to help a person improve his or her understanding of oneself and relationships with others and tap his or her own and community resources in solving personal problems. The social worker operates under the premise that most people have the ego strength to solve their own problems when they really bring them out into the open and understand what they are. Whereas several professions are primarily concerned with pathological problems, social work endeavors to stress and utilize strengths—both individual and community—to effect desired changes. Social work also makes a major thrust to understand community resources and to help solve community problems, thereby bringing desired changes.

14. Because most social workers are employed in agencies and are on fixed salaries, fees are utilized for the welfare of the agency rather than for increased incomes for the workers.

15. Traditionally, social workers have provided services and therapy for individuals and families. Within the past two decades, prevention has received considerable emphasis, and recently a focus on enrichment in living, for all people, has surfaced.

16. A social worker is particularly effective in developing and using the team approach and in bringing about coordination of services and activities. Many professional workers regard the social worker as the catalyst who has the ability and responsibility to help the professional team work together and function in optimal fashion. The social worker often acts as coordinator and integrator for the team effort.

Sociology and Social Work

How are sociology and social work related to each other? Admittedly, they share much in common but are also different in many ways. Sociology has been defined by early American sociologists as follows: by L. F. Ward as the "science of society," and by F. H. Giddings as "the scientific study of society." A. W. Small said that sociology "is the study of men considered as affecting and as affected by association."

Sociology and social work are both interested in people, their interactions, and understanding these interactions. The sociologist is particularly concerned about the *how, when,* and *why* people behave as they do in association with others. He or she aims to pinpoint the social problems, conduct research, and do everything possible to understand interaction in human associations. The sociologist is particularly interested in the *why* of human interaction.

The social worker is interested in understanding people and how they behave in association with others; but he or she is particularly concerned about helping these same people solve the problems they have and improve their social functioning. Whereas the sociologist generally spends most of his or her time in study and in ferreting out the facts, the social worker tries to understand the client or the community, to make an appropriate diagnosis, and to proceed with treatment, helping solve the problems and change the situations to bring about better adjustment.

Psychiatry and Social Work

The roles of the social worker and psychiatrist are different but are of coordinate status. The psychiatrist and the social worker are frequently both members of the same professional team and each has unique contributions to make.

The founding of the American Psychiatric Association, first known as the Association of Medical Superintendents of American Institutions for the Insane, took place in 1844. Great strides have been made during the intervening years, and today more than 40,000 psychiatrists practicing in the United States are making significant contributions in increasing understanding of the dynamics of family life, of human personality and how it functions, and in helping many individuals with various kinds of personal and emotional disturbances.

One psychiatrist states that the major difference between psychiatry and social work is that the psychiatrist deals with the treatment of illness and the medical model, whereas the social worker focuses on problems and strengths in human relationships. The psychiatrist places stress on intrapersonal dynamics, often delving into and handling unconscious motivation and related factors, whereas the social worker utilizes environmental and community resources, usually operating within the conscious level of behavior.

Psychiatry and social work have many things in common. Both professions involve work with people who possess personal and social problems. Both help people improve their relationships with others. Both have considerable interest and sensitivity in the ability to understand and direct feelings and emotions.

Several differences stand out between social work and psychiatry. The social worker tends to utilize the total community resources, sometimes tapping many material resources, economic and otherwise, in improving social relationships. The psychiatrist deals with patients on a medical basis, prescribes medication and hospitalization, if needed, and tends to focus on the unconscious, intrapsychic factors, working particularly with individual personality reorganization. With the advent of new drugs, drug therapy has become common to the psychiatrist in the treatment of people with emotional illness. The social worker often works with the marriage and/or family as a whole, rather than just the individual. Ordinarily, serious mental disturbances are handled by the psychiatrist; yet social workers use psychiatric understandings in diagnosis and treatment, and sometimes work directly with individuals and families who are seriously disturbed.

Psychiatry tends to focus on pathology and the healing of illness; social work concentrates on strengths and the development of potential. The psychiatrist is particularly interested in the internal dynamics of individual and group behavior. The social worker is especially concerned about social functioning involving social and community factors and interactions.

Psychology and Social Work

The psychologist and social worker are often members of the same professional team, particularly in treatment clinics and related settings. Nevertheless, many people raise questions about the overlapping and the differences between the two.

Psychology is the science of the mind; it seeks to study, explain, and change behavior of people. The psychologist is particularly interested in understanding the individual and his or her behavior.

Psychology and social work operate on some common grounds. Both are interested in the behavior of people, in their interactional patterns in particular, although the psychologist focuses mainly on individual behavior and the social worker on social functioning. They both seek the thinking and feeling processes of people.

In regard to differences, psychologists have an area entirely unto themselves in the field of testing and measurements. Psychologists study biological factors as well as social factors related to individual behavior. The psychologist is particularly interested in the individual attributes of people, and aims to understand their characteristics and behavior. On the other hand, some psychologists, particularly clinical psychologists, go beyond the study phase and work directly with people in the helping process. These activities overlap some with social work, and yet the focus seems to be different when considered as a totality. The psychologist usually works with individuals on a rather intensive basis and sometimes becomes a psychotherapist. Conversely, the social worker is particularly interested in the social functioning and relationships of clients and in utilizing community resources to meet clients' personal and social problems.

A clarifying tribute was paid to social work by a graduate student who reported:

> It may sound naive, but I was most impressed by the philosophy underlying the principles used in social work. I am in psychology, and while I am certain psychology operates from the same philosophy, this had never been spelled out. What I am referring to is emphasis on human worth and dignity which would seem to stem from a Judeo-Christian ethic and also the belief in democratic processes and an attempt to make this work at the community level—not only in community organization, but in case and group work as well.

Counseling and Social Work

Some people confuse the role and functions of the counselor with that of the social worker. There are many kinds of counselors, but only three are mentioned here: the school counselor, the marriage counselor, and the rehabilitation counselor.

The school counselor is usually trained in educational psychology. He or she ordinarily works with students on a short-term basis, helping them particularly with vocational choices and academic problems. The school counselor and the social worker share much in common. The social worker tends to be more intensive, works with the client longer, focuses more on the family constellation, and utilizes community resources. The school counselor also uses testing to advantage in many situations.

The marriage counselor may receive basic training from any of several graduate fields of study, only one of which is social work. He or she is then required to have clinical experience under supervision. In one sense, then, social work is a part of marriage counseling. In another sense, marriage counseling is one particular emphasis in social work. The differences arise across the variations in graduate training and professional experiences.

The rehabilitation counselor is one who usually is trained in educational psychology, is skilled in the use of testing, and focuses attention and abilities on the individual and his or her immediate problems of vocational rehabilitation. In situations where both a counselor and social worker are part of the team in rehabilitation, the counselor ordinarily helps with the testing, the short-term counseling, and related activities. The social worker usually assists with the emotional and/or family problems, has fewer cases, and works with clients more intensively.

Social Work in the World Today

Social work is emerging as an important profession in the modern world. As we noted earlier, the National Association of Social Workers has 150,000 members. In December 1961, provision was made for professionally trained and experienced social workers to become members of the Academy of Certified Social Workers, which gave them additional professional status; more than 20,000 qualified. By 2004, some 64,000 were certified.

Social work today is utilized in a variety of settings and agencies. Some of the important ones are psychiatric, medical, marriage, and family counseling; the school; rehabilitation; corrections; public welfare; workplace; drug abuse; and child welfare. Schools of social work train a student to work in any agency, giving him or her the generic understandings, skills, and attitudes that make it possible to function adequately.

Social work is becoming more important because thousands of persons are benefiting from its services and are telling their friends and associates who have problems of its many values and services. People are not only being helped with personal and family problems but also with neighborhood, national, and even international difficulties. A prominent American, on returning from a trip abroad, made the statement that what the United States needs most of all to improve its foreign policy and relations is to have trained social workers as State Department attachés where each of the official government representatives works and lives. Trained social workers in foreign countries would understand the people and work with them where they are, helping them help themselves and interpreting the United States in a much more favorable light than in the past.

One area in which social work services are expanding is in international social work. For many years, the social work profession has been an important part of both the American Red Cross and the International Red Cross. International social work services have been an important part of the United Nations' efforts to rehabilitate war-torn Kosovo and to bring aid and comfort to sub-Saharan Africa and their fight against AIDS. Social work services are also becoming an even more important part of international adoption services. Starting in 2004, the State Department is requiring all foreign adoption agencies to have full-time social workers on their staffs before the State Department will certify these agencies and permit them to provide adoptive services to American citizens.

This expansion in international social work services provides new and challenging opportunities for the social work profession. For the past decade, the University of Utah College of Social Work and the American University of Bulgaria have been working together to improve the quality of social work services at the Bulgarian campus. By utilizing in-service training, educational workshops, consultation, and faculty and student exchanges, the quality of social work services has been improving at the American University of Bulgaria. One of the more unique and challenging components of this joint program has been creating summer field placements in Bulgaria for students from the University of Utah College of Social Work. These summer internships have enriched the programs of both universities and helped establish a student counseling center at the American University of Bulgaria.

International social work provides a new challenge for schools of social work. At the University of Utah College of Social Work, student interest has increased to the point that a practice emphasis in international social work has been created for second-year MSW students. The international social work practice emphasis requires students to complete six semester hours of course work that focuses on international social work along with an optional practicum or internship in a social service agency that works with international clients and their families. One such social service agency is the Hartland Partnership Center in Salt Lake City, Utah, that serves 1,000 apartment residents including adults and children, 75 percent of whom are nonnative English speakers and half of whom are refugees from all over the world including Eastern Europe, Africa, and Asia. MSW students also have the

Social work plays an important role in international relations.

option of completing a summer practicum or internship in a number of international settings including Bulgaria, Japan, Mexico, Nicaragua, Romania, Scotland, South Africa, Botswana, and the Czech Republic.

Current evidence indicates that social work is here to stay and that in the decades ahead it will likely grow and expand its services, helping more people with personal, family, and community problems, especially related to adequate social functioning.

Summary

However fast-moving and uncertain today's world may be, people are still at its core. People have problems that invite professional assistance: personal, family, and community. Social welfare is an important aspect of the modern way of life. Social work is a profession that focuses particularly on helping people solve their personal, family, and community problems through enhancing social functioning. It emphasizes human values and also the value of humans.

The basic functions of social work are (1) restoration of social functioning, (2) provision of social services, and (3) prevention.

Social work shares some knowledge and skills with sociology, psychiatry, psychology, and counseling, but it possesses distinguishing characteristics that set it apart from these disciplines.

Social work is moving ahead as a progressive profession in the helping services arena.

Selected References

BRIELAND, DONALD, "Social Work Practice: History and Evolution," in *Encyclopedia of Social Work,* 19th ed., Vol. 3. Washington, DC: NASW Press, 1995, pp. 2247–2258.

FARLEY, O. WILLIAM, BOYD E. OVIATT, REX A. SKIDMORE, and MILTON G. THACKERAY, "Social Work— Professional Mediocrity or Maturation," *Social Casework,* 58 (April 1977), 236–242.

GARVIN, CHARLES D., and JOHN E. TROPMAN, *Social Work in Contemporary Society,* 2nd ed. Boston: Allyn & Bacon, 1998.

HAGEN, JAN L., "Women, Work, and Welfare: Is There a Role for Social Work?" *Social Work,* 37 (January 1992), 9–13.

HARPER-DORTON, KAREN, and JIM LANTZ, *Cross-Cultural Practice: Social Work with Diverse Populations*, 2nd ed. Chicago: Lyceum Books, 2007.

KARGER, HOWARD JACOB, and DAVID STOESZ, *American Social Welfare Policy,* 3rd ed. New York: Addison-Wesley Longman, 1998.

KLEIN, WALDO C., and MARTIN BLOOM, "Social Work as Applied Social Science: A Historical Analysis," *Social Work,* 39 (July 1994), 421–431.

LONG, DENNIS D., and MARLA C. HOLLE, *Macro Systems in the Social Environment.* Itasca, IL: F. E. Peacock, 1997.

MEYER, CAROL H., and MARK A. MATTAINI, eds., *The Foundations of Social Work Practice.* Washington, DC: NASW Press, 1995.

MORALES, ARMANDO, and BRADFORD W. SHEAFOR, *The Many Faces of Social Workers.* Boston: Allyn & Bacon, 2002.

SKIDMORE, REX A., *Social Work Administration, Dynamic Management and Human Relationships,* 3rd ed. Boston: Allyn & Bacon, 1995.

Notes

1. Walter A. Friedlander, *Introduction to Social Welfare,* 2nd ed. (Englewood Cliffs, NJ: Prentice Hall, 1961), p. 4; see also 5th ed., 1980, p. 4.

2. Dennis D. Long and Marla C. Holle, *Macro Systems in the Social Environment* (Itasca, IL: F. E. Peacock, 1997), p. 5.

3. *Social Security Bulletin*, 62 (Fall 1999), 40, 60.

4. Robert Pear, "Finances of Social Security and Medicare Deteriorate," *The New York Times,* May 2, 2006.

5. *NASW Website Homepage*, "The Power of Social Work," November 2007.

6. Werner W. Boehm, *Objectives of the Social Work Curriculum of the Future,* Curriculum Study I (New York: CSWE, 1959), p. 54.

7. Ibid., pp. 41–42.

8. Harriet M. Bartlett, *50 Years of Social Work in the Medical Setting, Past Significance/Future Outlook* (New York: NASW, 1957), p. 24.

9. Robert L. Barker, *The Social Work Dictionary,* 3rd ed. (Washington, DC: NASW Press, 1995), p. 357.

2

The Evolution of Social Welfare and Social Work in the United States

It was evening in the city. Couples were arriving at the theater to attend the opening night of a new musical. Crowds were pressing the box office, and ushers were busily engaged in tearing tickets and guiding the theater-goers to their seats. Not more than thirty steps from the well-lighted entrance was a blind man, with tattered clothes and wrinkled brow, playing a beat-up violin with *a weathered plate before him. A few passersby stopped and dropped coins on the plate. Most glanced quickly and kept moving. In almost every storefront homeless individuals were setting up cardboard shelters to get some protection from the bitter cold wind. What systems do we have for taking care of those in need? Which are most effective?*

In 1962, for the first time in history, a president of the United States gave a message to Congress devoted solely to public welfare. President John F. Kennedy declared to the 87th Congress: "Our basic public welfare programs were enacted more than a quarter century ago. Their contribution to our national strength and well-being in the intervening years has been remarkable.

"But the times, the conditions, the problems have changed—and the nature and objectives of our public assistance and child welfare programs must be changed, also, if they are to meet our current needs."

President Kennedy, in his statement to Congress, stressed the importance of the family unit and its preservation. He indicated that a united attack needed to be made on the problem of family breakdown, and then continued, "unless such problems are dealt with effectively, they fester and grow, sapping the strength of society as a whole and extending their consequences in troubled families from one generation to the next."

Each president of the United States since Kennedy has taken messages to Congress with recommendations and interpretations regarding social welfare programs for this country. These programs have varied philosophically and in regard to specificity, but most have underlined a vital concern for the welfare of the American people. President Ronald Reagan proposed many curtailments and restrictions of social welfare programs while maintaining that those in need who could not help themselves would be given welfare. Subsequently there were many cutbacks and elimination of some social work services. In his inaugural address, President George Bush talked about a kinder nation, to "secure a more just and prosperous life for man on Earth," and the need for greater tolerance of "each other's attitudes and way of life."

At his inauguration, President Bill Clinton emphasized the importance of change: "We must do what no generation has had to do before. We must invest more in our own people, in their jobs and in their future. . . . We must do what America does best: offer more opportunity to all and demand more responsibility from all." The 1994 Republican U.S. Congress came in to office with "Contract with America" commitments both to reduce the costs of public welfare services and to improve their effectiveness.

President Bill Clinton's signing of the Personal Responsibility and Work Opportunity Reconciliation Act of 1996 ushered in sweeping changes to the nation's public welfare system. The most dramatic changes were the loss of individual entitlement and the loss of an economic safety net for children and their families. The philosophy of the act was based on the notion that the old welfare system had failed by creating an entire class of people in our society who would perpetuate dependency and an unproductive lifestyle. As the title of the act declared, "personal responsibility" and "work opportunity" would be the themes of public welfare for at least the next decade.

As President George W. Bush began his presidency, he immediately declared his hope in a faith-based social service initiative to help address the human service needs in the country. Many organizations, including the National Association of Social Workers, shared some skepticism in the initiative. The tax cut that was passed also added to the worry that our government would move away from its responsibility to serve the needs of its people. NASW stated

> NASW supports efforts of faith-based organizations to provide the necessities of life to people in need. However, individuals and families in crisis often face multiple, complex problems and issues. Staff should be trained, competent and qualified to deliver social services to those facing life crises. NASW believes that all social service agencies must adhere to accreditation standards, licensing laws and other regulatory mechanisms that protect consumers and ensure quality service delivery.
>
> *Maintaining government responsibility*—NASW reaffirms the essential role of government in developing policies and programs that expand opportunities, address social and economic justice, and enhance social conditions of the nation's communities. The association reaffirms its commitment to the promotion of the positive role of government as guarantor of the social safety net. The faith-based initiative should not create the expectation that private charity will substitute for public service funding, nor result in a reduction of currently supported programs, said NASW's position paper.[1]

In a recent *NASW News* article, Ram Cnaan, a professor at the University of Pennsylvania School of Social Work and a recent immigrant from Israel to the United States, made the following comments: "When I came, I [didn't know] anything about religion and social work. Nobody told me anything, I didn't find it in any texts. When I realized that a lot of social services—caring for the homeless, caring for the poor—was done by religious organizations, I was surprised by the lack of social work [attention to this issue]." Cnaan said he developed a course on religion for social work practice, which has been very successful. "Social workers are usually not trained for [approaching] religion as a source of strength," he said. The course covers subjects ranging from "what do you do when a client asks to pray, all the way to policy issues."

Other social workers, such as members of the North American Association of Christian Social Workers, also have worked to increase the profession's attention to the spiritual needs of the communities served. Social work as a profession "down-plays religion in professional and political life," Cnaan said. "But in our personal lives, the majority of us have a strong connection with our religion." Cnaan said educators must "prepare students for a new reality. They will have to collaborate with faith-based organizations."[2]

As Bush finishes his term as president, there are many problem areas that seem to be surfacing in our social welfare systems. NASW quoted a report from the Every Child Matters Education Fund that identified the following problem areas for children:

- Over 8 million children have no health insurance in the United States.
- Nationwide, 3.5 million children were reported abused and neglected in 2005.
- Millions of children are left alone every day after school.
- Almost 13 million of America's children live in poverty.
- Millions of children have a parent in prison.[3]

Inhabitants of the United States live in a land of freedom wherein democracy and democratic processes are prevalent. Stress is on the interdependence of people in society, and it is generally recognized that the well-being of one person affects the well-being of neighbors and others. The preamble of our Constitution, spelled out by the Founders, contains the immortal words "to promote the general welfare."

The worth of the human personality and the importance of individual adjustment and well-being are significant aspects of the American way of life. The pages of American history, past and present, reflect that in a given society there are many disadvantaged persons. What has been done in the United States in the past to help them? What is being accomplished at present? Social welfare and, more recently, social work have arisen on the American scene and provide some answers to these questions. Social welfare, according to *The Social Work Dictionary,* is "a nation's system of programs, benefits, and services that help people meet those social, economic, educational, and health needs that are fundamental to the maintenance of society."[4]

Echoes of the Past

The beginnings of social welfare were probably coexistent with the beginnings of human life and humans' association with others. It is not difficult to imagine that even in the days of the cave dwellers, neighborliness and helping one another with problems, both personal and family, were part of the daily living pattern. In all probability some of the wiser of these inhabitants had paths beaten to their dwellings by people seeking someone who would listen and help.

In primitive societies numerous kinds of plans and programs have often been in operation for helping people with social problems. Tribal customs and mores have provided for care of the sick, the aged, and others who needed to be nurtured and given special attention. There has been a recognition of the necessity to help one another promote the welfare of all.

In ancient civilizations various and sundry attempts were made to care for the destitute, the poor, the sick, the unfortunate, and the disabled. Many of these were handled on a family, neighborhood, or religious basis.

Social welfare was rooted in the distant past.[5] In ancient China there were refuges for the aged, the sick, and the poor, free schools for poor children, free eating houses for weary laborers, associations for the distribution of secondhand clothing, and even societies for paying expenses of marriage and burial among the poor and destitute. In India, especially after the time of Buddha, considerable activity was related to giving to beggars. A saint with his bowl was one of the traditions of the Orient, and the emphasis in the religious teachings on the obligation of almsgiving not only made the holy men of that country a nuisance but also encouraged imposters. The Greeks had no regular charitable organizations, but they did have institutions for the unfortunate and the sick. Gifts and assistance were publicly distributed at the time of the great festivals by men who were candidates for public office. There were asylums for wounded soldiers and for abandoned children; and in Athens a poor tax was levied and collected to help the destitute. The religion of the Hebrews laid great stress on charity and helping those in need.

In the medieval period the Church played a significant role in giving relief and in helping distressed persons. Monks and monasteries provided services to care for indigent, lame, halt, and other unfortunate individuals. The monasteries were utilized to provide food and housing for pilgrims, soldiers, and beggars, as well as medical and hospital facilities for those in need. Orphaned or deserted children were also cared for by the monks and nuns.

Across the centuries there has been a shift from individualism to collectivism in helping those in need. Mutual aid has come to the fore particularly as populations have increased and moved into concentrated areas, and there has been additional need for societal programs to aid disadvantaged persons.

European Roots

The roots of social welfare, and in a general sense of social work, reach a long way into the past. However, several significant developments in Europe have been particularly important in setting the stage and patterns for development of social welfare and social work in the United States. In 1536 a law was passed in England stating that alms collected by local authorities and by churches on Sundays were to help relieve the sick and the poor. This act, which is often regarded as the beginning of the English poor law system, superseded the merely repressive measures of earlier legislation in an attempt to work out specific and definite provisions for relief. To deter people from openly begging, the law stipulated that "the mayor of every town and the Church wardens of every parish were to collect alms every Sunday, holiday or festival in common boxes," which were then to be utilized by those in need. Accounts were to be kept of the money collected and dispersed. The income was to be allocated so that poor, sick, and diseased persons, not able to work, might be helped and relieved. This law marked the shift in poor relief from an ecclesiastical to a secular system. The act had several significant provisions, including the illegality of begging, responsibility of society to help, assistance by and through the local community, and voluntary alms, with clerical assistance, but under the direction of the state.

In 1572 overseers of the poor were appointed as civil officers. The Parliamentary enactment at this time provided for a direct public tax to assist the poor and destitute.

During the reign of Queen Elizabeth several laws were enacted that have been designated as the Elizabethan Poor Laws. Toward the close of the sixteenth century a civic sense of responsibility on a nationwide basis had developed in England. An act was passed in 1598 and revised in 1601 that provided a systematic plan for helping the poor and established a system of public responsibility implemented through local care. The main provisions of the law remained in operation basically until 1834, and have played important roles in the development of social welfare in Europe, in the United States, and elsewhere. The act of 1601 established legislation that differentiated three classes of the poor: the able-bodied poor, who were to be provided with work, or with punishment in prison or the stocks if they refused to work; the impotent poor, who were to be kept in almshouses; and dependent children, who were to be apprenticed unless parents or grandparents could support them. For the dependent children group, the boys were to be apprenticed until they were twenty-four years old and the girls until they were either twenty-one or married. Monies to finance these laws were provided by taxes levied on lands, houses, and tithes, from money left for charitable purposes, and from fines levied for the breaking of certain laws. To carry out the administration of the system, the justice of the peace appointed civil officers in each parish, although nominations for these positions were made at a meeting of the parish church.

Many other laws have been passed in England and on the Continent to help the poor, and to provide other services for children, families, and individuals in trouble. The industrial revolution of the eighteenth century, accompanied by urbanization, slums, and anonymity in living brought numerous situations resulting in many persons with problems that called for help. Begging, almsgiving, charity, workhouses, orphanages, insane asylums, and jails became part of the culture of the times. Attempts to help people in a dignified manner were instigated, and various programs, both public and private, came into existence.

The Elizabethan Poor Laws provided the basis for public social welfare in England with only minor changes until the Poor Law of 1834 was passed. This act provided for centralized administration with a pattern of uniformity throughout the country. It established a central authority consisting of three Poor Law Commissioners, who were given regulatory powers over the local authorities. They could divide the country into districts, which were called Poor Law Unions, to replace the parishes as units of administration. Each unit was a district with an elective Board of Guardians with salaried officers who were responsible for the administration of relief. The law also stipulated that the Guardians of each district were authorized to build or provide at least one workhouse, and all relief to able-bodied persons outside the workhouse was abolished.

In England in the 1860s, there was a considerable increase in the number of applicants for aid that focused attention on welfare and helping the poor. As a result there was revived concern in social reform, and some individuals became interested in bringing about innovations and change. Such persons as Octavia Hill and Edward Denison pioneered in social welfare at this time. As a result of their efforts and those of others, a new type of social work organization emerged. In 1869 the "London Society for Organizing Charitable Relief and Repressing Mendicancy" was established and has generally been referred to as the London Charity Organization Society (COS). The name of the organization is descriptive of its purpose—the organization of relief rather than its creation or multiplication. It proposed, in other words:

> (1) the coordination of the work of the various charitable societies in London so as to prevent duplication; (2) an acquaintance by each of the work of other agencies; (3) a bureau of registry for all cases; (4) personal service to promote independence of spirit rather than the giving of material aid; and (5) a devotion to measures for the prevention of pauperism.[6]

Beginnings in the United States

No attempt is made here to give a historical coverage of social welfare in the United States. Nevertheless, some highlights and examples of such developments are considered.

In colonial days in America the basic pattern for assisting the poor and unfortunate followed the poor laws and activities of the mother country. Town and local governments provided services somewhat similar to those that had been instigated in the homeland. "Outdoor relief" was administered to the poor in their own homes initially. Placement or boarding out of dependents was also utilized both for children and adults. Almshouses were established as a means of "indoor relief." Extreme examples of the "farming out" procedure involved public auctions where orphans, neglected children, or disabled individuals were passed on to those who were willing to support them at the lowest cost to the community. The first almshouse for the care of the poor and indigent was established in Massachusetts in 1662. In 1685 it began to function both as an almshouse for the disabled and as a workhouse for the able-bodied poor. Another indication of community interest in providing services for the poor and needy was the establishment in 1644 of the Boston Latin School, which was supported in part by a land grant from that town. This was the beginning of free or charity schools in this country, and was the foundation underpinning free public education, which developed decades later. In 1691, in Boston, the town leaders appointed the first "overseers of the poor," which was an initiatory step toward governmental centralization in the care of the destitute.

Beginnings in the child welfare movement go back many years. In 1729 in New Orleans an institution was established by the Ursuline Sisters for children of parents killed by Indians. In 1790 an orphanage was begun in Charleston, South Carolina, for children who had no living parents. By 1817 a school for the education of the "deaf and dumb" was in operation in Connecticut.

In early nineteenth-century America people who were mentally ill were treated harshly, inhumanly, and often regarded as persons who had no sense of feeling either mentally or physically. In March 1841, the famous Dorothea Lynde Dix by chance visited the East Cambridge, Massachusetts, jail and was shocked at the deplorable treatment of the insane inmates. She visited other jails and almshouses throughout the state and found all kinds of brutalities being practiced within them. On the basis of these experiences, she devoted the rest of her life to improving services for those who were mentally ill. She gave speeches, wrote letters, and contacted community and political leaders and others at home and abroad. As a result of her relentless campaign many state hospitals for the insane were established or enlarged and great improvements in treatment in poorhouses and jails took place. Through her activities and those of other dedicated leaders, the treatment of individuals with mental illness has shifted so that now they are more respected as other persons who are ill, and attempts are made to treat them and return them to their families and to society as quickly as possible.

Likewise, in the area of the treatment of the juvenile delinquent and the criminal, the pages of history show significant developments related to social welfare and social work. In the latter part of the eighteenth century, in the very shadows of Independence Hall in Philadelphia, a new system of prison discipline, called the Pennsylvania System, was established. This innovation provided for individualized attention and treatment of prisoners accompanied by housing in separate cells. Prior to this time inmates were held in congregate rooms, sometimes twenty or thirty or even forty of them, day in and day out, often both men and women confined together. The new philosophy and practice were an attempt to treat and rehabilitate rather than merely to punish or seek retribution.

With the depression of 1873, after the Civil War in the United States, came chaos and many personal, family, and community problems. The charity organization movement in America was started, patterned in the main after European innovations. Across the decades this movement has resulted in the establishment of numerous private agencies and community welfare councils in most of the large population centers of this country. These councils, increasingly staffed by competent social workers, attempt to understand community needs, involve community leaders in studying these needs, make plans regarding them, and bring these plans to fruition.

The first Charity Organization Society (COS) in the United States was established in Buffalo, New York, in 1877. The coordinating function of this type of agency was urgent because of the numerous independent welfare agencies that were springing up and mushrooming in the population centers. In 1909 in Pittsburgh and Milwaukee the first community welfare councils—called Councils of Social Agencies—were established. These have grown and developed so that today one such council in a large metropolitan area has thirteen full-time people working in research—collecting and interpreting information pertinent to community needs, problems, and solutions.

The charity organization movement in the United States was a significant one because it provided for private agencies that were interested in finding ways and means of organizing help to the poor through individualized services. These services included investigation of need, a registration bureau for charitable agencies for clearance to avoid duplication, friendly visiting, and other related activities.

Closely allied to the community welfare council movement has been the one for federated drives, collecting money for several agencies at one time. Historically the first such drive took place in Liverpool, England, in 1873, and the original one in the United States occurred in 1887, spearheaded by the Associated Charities in Denver. The latter involved twenty-three agencies, which joined together and raised a total of $20,000. After World

War I federated drives in this country were organized under the name of the Community Chest. By 1950 more than 1,400 such organizations existed in the United States. In the last forty years the trend has been toward establishment of united fund agencies (now called United Way in many communities), which have been organized on a broader base than Community Chests, the aim being to bring together as many of the local and national health and welfare agencies as possible in the collecting of funds.

Another significant development in social services in America has been that of the social settlement house. The first American settlement was organized in New York City in 1886; and three years later the most famous one, Hull House, was established by Jane Addams in Chicago. Similar neighborhood centers were instigated in many of the large cities in this country. Today these centers play a significant role in providing for the recreational, health, and welfare needs of boys and girls, youth, men, and women, particularly in deprived areas. They are also being used by the total citizenry, including the middle and upper classes, as centers for providing social experiences, for taking care of recreational needs, and for solving personality problems.

There have been several pioneers in this country in social welfare. Many of these people have come from the upper classes and many have devoted their lives to helping disadvantaged people.

Jane Addams was such a person. She was born in Cedarville, Illinois, in 1861 and died on May 21, 1935. She traveled extensively in Europe, where she was impressed with Toynbee Hall in England. She decided to establish a similar settlement house in this country, which was located on Chicago's west side. Hull House provided many educational opportunities and social services for those with limited economic means and was patronized by immigrants who had come to make this country their homeland. This settlement was established particularly for the working people and those in meager circumstances.

Jane Addams talking to children.

Jane Addams was also a leader in international women's and children's movements and wrote extensively. Two of her best known books were *Democracy and Social Ethics* (1902) and *Twenty Years at Hull House* (1910).

Social welfare services have developed so that today they reach out to practically every personal, family, and community need. As a result, research in welfare is being sponsored as never before.

Public Assistance and Social Welfare Emerge

Almost from the beginning of the colonization of America there have been various attempts to provide governmental assistance to the poor and needy. For example, following the patterns of the Dutch, and later the English, New York City had a city physician for the poor as early as 1687. Various other programs were established by towns and local communities in colonial America to provide for those who required different services.

Later laws were passed in states of the Union helping provide financial and other services for the indigent, poor, destitute, and those with personal and family problems.

With the financial collapse of 1929 and the Great Depression that followed, numerous attempts were made to assist the poor and the unemployed and to bolster the economy. The Federal Emergency Relief Administration (usually known as ERA), the Works Progress Administration (WPA), the Civilian Conservation Corps (CCC), and other federal programs were established to provide work and assistance for millions. Social workers played an important role in the creation of some of these agencies and in their implementation. Many men and women gained their first interest in social work during those difficult times.

On the federal level the monumental Social Security Act of 1935 altered the total plan of helping persons in need. For the first time the federal government assumed a major role and responsibility in assisting those in need. The major provisions of the original act are summarized as follows:

1. A national old-age insurance system (OASDHI), to be supported through taxes on payrolls, equally shared by the employers and employees. The survivorship provision was instituted in 1939.
2. A federal–state unemployment insurance system, to be financed by a federal tax on payrolls. Liberal provisions were offered that encouraged the states to become partners in this system, and all states adopted unemployment acts soon after the law was passed.
3. Grants-in-aid to the states for old age assistance, aid to families of dependent children, and aid to the blind.
4. Services for aiding maternal and child health, crippled children, child welfare, vocational rehabilitation, and public health measures.

Major significant changes were made in social security legislation in the enactment of Public Welfare Amendments of 1962—Public Law (P.L.) 87-543. For the first time the importance of preventive, protective, and rehabilitative services in public welfare was significantly recognized by a new formula that provided 75 percent of the costs of such services from federal funds.

As President Kennedy said when he signed the legislation, "This measure embodies a new approach—stressing services in addition to support, rehabilitation instead of relief, and training for useful work instead of prolonged dependency. . . . Our objective is to prevent or reduce dependency and to encourage self-care and self-support—to maintain family life where it is adequate and to restore it where it is deficient."[7]

A major development in social welfare began on July 1, 1966, when the health insurance program for the aged under Title XVIII of the Social Security Act went into effect. Commonly called Medicare,[8] it provided a compulsory hospital insurance plan and a voluntary supplementary medical insurance. This program helps provide economic security and protection against the high costs of hospital and medical care for the elderly. It is for everyone aged sixty-five or over who is entitled to social security or railroad retirement. Others over sixty-five may enroll by paying monthly premiums.

The 1972 amendments expanded Medicare to extend the coverage to certain disabled workers, disabled widows and widowers, and childhood disability beneficiaries.

Medicaid, medical care for low-income people, was enacted under Title XIX of the Social Security Act. Administered by the states, it provides direct payments to providers of services. Persons who qualify for assistance under the federally financed income maintenance program are eligible for assistance. Medicaid may be used to provide hospital and medical care for people who have no regular income from employment and for others whose income is so low that they are unable to provide payments for medical and health care for themselves and their families.

On the volunteer level, two programs were developed that have been significant in the areas of education and social welfare. The Peace Corps, established under President Kennedy, invited persons, particularly the young, to enlist for a two-year period to provide much needed services, particularly in underdeveloped countries throughout the world. The Volunteers in Service to America (VISTA) program was established to use volunteers to help their own country and citizens in disadvantaged areas—educationally, economically, vocationally, and otherwise—to improve their situations in life.

In 1972 there was a basic separation between maintenance and social services provided in public welfare and by divisions of family services. Many social workers were shifted from helping with maintenance into the specific areas of social services that are attempting to assist individuals and families with personal, family, and community problems.

Social welfare has expanded rapidly in the United States. Federal spending for what the Social Security Administration defines as "social welfare purposes" rose from $14 billion in 1950 to nearly $1,434 billion in 1994. By July 1999 Social Security benefits (OAS-DHI) alone provided more than $31.96 billion in monthly benefits to beneficiaries.[9] In 2007 the first "baby boomer" accepted her Social Security check. A whole new set of problems will emerge as the large numbers of boomers receive Social Security benefits.

In the last two decades there has been a major development among social workers individually and in agencies to become more concerned about protecting the rights of clients, being advocates for them, and also in helping alter our basic institutions to provide better aid for poor and disadvantaged persons. Social workers as never before are using a two-edged approach: helping individuals and families clinically and focusing on improving society's institutions and programs.

A historic event took place on May 4, 1980, with the creation of a cabinet-level U.S. Department of Education, taken from the parent Department of Health, Education, and Welfare (HEW). The health and welfare sectors of HEW are now called the U.S. Department of Health and Human Services (DHHS); the change has been accepted positively by social workers and others who believe this dual partnership may prove advantageous to both areas and the United States as a whole.

The 1983 and 1988 amendments to the Social Security Act were particularly significant. Ozawa suggests the 1983 amendments reflected that the country is willing to face the challenge of meeting social security's enormous financial crisis, and reported, "Through a complex, sweeping, reform package, Congress established an actuarial balance between the cost rate and the income rate in social security for the coming seventy-five years."[10] For recent amendments and policy changes see Chapter 12.

The Personal Responsibility and Work Opportunity Reconciliation Act of 1996 offers both promise and challenge for the social work profession. Certainly social workers must be constantly vigilant to ensure this social welfare direction will not harm families and children. On the other hand, if our society opens meaningful work opportunities to all of our citizens, this legislation may restore dignity and a sense of purpose to those populations in our country who have lost hope.

Services of Volunteers

Over the years many dedicated and interested individuals have provided their time and money to help people in need. They have done this as individuals or as families rather than as citizens in a city, state, or federal community. These services have increased so that today thousands of volunteers are assisting in social welfare services in almost every kind of setting.

Examples of volunteer services include the following:

Twenty-five members of a Junior League in a middle-sized city spend half a day a week in assisting with activities in the local Comprehensive Mental Health Center. They provide their own cars and transport clients to and from the center. They "care" for the children in the waiting rooms and also spend time with some of the clients, on a friendship basis, helping them with routine problems and decisions.

Volunteers from churches and religious groups minister to the sick, the poor, the destitute, and unfortunate in numerous ways. They cooperate with the professional disciplines to bring total, effective services.

Working as a volunteer is characteristic of the American way of life. From the young to the old, volunteers help other people through various social work and welfare agencies and on an individual basis. In 1965 the U.S. Department of Labor estimated that 16 percent of persons over fourteen years of age, or 22 million individuals, made contributions to some health, education, or welfare service on a volunteer basis. More than half of these persons were in the twenty-five to forty-four age group. In 1974 some 37 million men and women, one of every four Americans over age thirteen, did some form of volunteer work.[11]

Volunteer assisting in social welfare services.

In 1973 the United Way of America made a quantitative study of volunteer activities. It revealed that United Way and its member agencies average an estimated 2.4 billion volunteer person-hours per year and that the largest percentage of volunteer activities (over 80 percent) is in the area of direct program activity rather than in setting policy and raising funds.[12] In the 1978 United Way campaigns more than 32 million people made contributions to help others. The nation's 2,200 United Way campaigns, in 1985, collected a recordbreaking $2.33 billion, a gain of 9 percent over 1984. Giving in the United States was on the increase and United Way was not the only philanthropy enjoying a boom in giving. In 1980 total giving in the United States stood at $49 billion; in 1985 total giving was more than $75 billion—up more than 50 percent over 1980.[13] In 1988 contributions to voluntary organizations in the United States exceeded $100 billion, and 80 million people volunteered a total of 14.9 billion hours, worth at least another $150 billion.[14] By 1995 it was reported that more than a third of the U.S. population—89 million people—were participating in voluntarism.[15]

Social Workers Appear

In the eighteenth and nineteenth centuries, with industrialization, greater mobility, and the increase in population and the accompanying social problems, it became apparent that both public and private social services needed to be increased if the problems and needs of the public were to be met.

Social welfare has developed slowly over several centuries. It is only within the past few decades, however, that social work has entered the scene as a major aspect of social welfare. In the latter part of the nineteenth century humanitarians and other dedicated persons, especially women, devoted their time and talents to helping the underprivileged, and began to lay the groundwork for the development of social work as a profession. In 1898 education for social work was initiated in a summer training course given by the COS of New York at Columbia University. This was a beginning impetus toward providing trained social workers. This course developed into a one-year program in 1904 within the New York School of Philanthropy at Columbia. Other schools of social work developed and before long many men and women were calling themselves *social workers*. These were people who had obtained special training and experience to help people help themselves. By 1921 the American Association of Social Workers was established, the first major professional social work body. In 1955 the National Association of Social Workers was created based on the amalgamation of seven smaller specialized social work associations. This professional body has grown in stature and in numbers so that it now enrolls 160,000 members. In 1995 NASW celebrated its 40th anniversary and recognized it had made many contributions to social work but still had many challenges ahead. In 1998 social work celebrated the profession's centennial anniversary.

Social workers today are employed in every kind of setting of social welfare. They are given, ordinarily, the more difficult tasks to perform and many gravitate to administrative and supervisory positions. They are also used as consultants in helping guide the work and activities of less trained social welfare aides and associates. Numerous county and state welfare departments now have many on their staffs who have received Bachelor of Social Work or Master of Social Work degrees, and the work being accomplished in these agencies is taking on a professional demeanor that was unknown in the past.

In 1974 the Council on Social Work Education approved the accreditation of the undergraduate programs in social work or social welfare with the understanding that they would be upgraded and would provide the first level of practice in social work. At the other end of the continuum is the increasing number of doctoral programs being offered by schools of social work aimed at developing leaders in the top echelons of social work and social welfare.

The last ten years has brought a number of significant changes to social work master's degree programs. Beginning in the early 1980s, many schools of social work adopted a generalist perspective format for their master's programs. This generalist format focused on preparing social work students to practice with a variety of systems including individuals and groups, couples and family, and communities as well as providing training in administration and supervision. A few years later some schools also began offering what was called an advanced generalist perspective for the second year of master's programs. This advanced generalist perspective built on the generalist foundation of the first-year curriculum. As social work educators moved into the 1990s, some revisited the concentration or specialization or domain focuses that many social work programs had used for their second year curriculum in the 1970s. Moving into the 2000s, many schools of social work now offer a generalist perspective for the first-year curriculum and a concentration or specialization or domain focus for the second year. This shift to specialized social work education during the second year of the master's program is in keeping with the specialization focus that other professional schools have adopted, especially in law, business, nursing, and pharmacy.

One recent development in social work education has been the growth of joint degree graduate programs. At the University of Utah College of Social Work, a joint master's degree in social work and public administration was started in 2006. Although both degrees are conferred separately, students take a significant number of required and elective courses in both programs. Separately, the MSW program requires sixty semester hours of credit whereas the public administration program requires forty-five hours. Together, students complete eighty-one semester hours for both degrees which is twenty-four semester hours fewer than if the two programs were completed separately. The University of Utah College of Social Work is also working on joint graduate degree programs with the College of Law and the College of Public Health. Joint graduate degree programs with social work and other professional schools make sense. For decades professional programs have stressed the importance of interdisciplinary training and teamwork. Joint graduate degree programs go a step further by offering students not only the interdisciplinary training and teamwork, but also a joint degree that enriches both professional programs. It is clear that this trend in joint graduate degree programs will continue to grow and develop in social work education.

Summary

The American way of life with its democratic emphasis has been conducive to the initiation and development of social welfare services. The pages of history reflect that, almost from the beginning of the colonization of this country, humanitarian men and women, both in public and private agencies and situations, have been interested in establishing and supporting services and activities to help distressed and unfortunate individuals and families.

The roots of social welfare in America had their beginnings in Europe, particularly related to the Elizabethan Poor Laws of England. Towns and local communities assumed responsibilities for aiding unfortunate and disadvantaged persons.

Most of the other beginnings in social welfare were private in nature and involved philanthropic programs and activities. Gradually, civic-minded individuals and leaders proposed welfare programs financed by the tax dollar. Various state programs were started.

In 1935 the Social Security Act was passed in the United States, revolutionizing the total social welfare scene. The act provided public assistance, social insurance, unemployment insurance, aid to dependent children, aid to the blind, and other special services.

In 1962 major modifications were made in the Social Security Act. These provided for additional federal participation, liberalization of grants, and safeguarding the rights of children and families. They also placed considerably greater emphasis on rehabilitation and preventive social welfare.

Medicare, which encompasses a compulsory hospital insurance plan and a voluntary supplemental medical insurance, and Medicaid, which provides medical care for low-income people, were both established in 1965 as amendments to the Social Security Act and are forming a foundation for an expanding medical and health care system in the United States.

The signing of the Personal Responsibility and Work Opportunity Reconciliation Act of 1996 ushered in a new public welfare system. The effects of this direction will not be known for several years to come. Many argue that the new incentive for people to work will help our citizens become more independent, whereas others worry about families and children losing their safety net.

As the new millennium began, the Republican administration seemed to begin the process of trying to move the responsibility of social welfare needs back to the private/nonprofit sector through its "faith-based" social service initiative. Perhaps, the country will find a proper balance between the private/nonprofit and public sectors in meeting the social welfare needs of its citizens.

A major step in the development of social welfare has been the rise of the profession of social work. Since the turn of the twentieth century the number of trained social workers has increased rapidly. Social work now has a central professional body, the National Association of Social Workers, and a national educational body for setting standards, the Council on Social Work Education.

Selected References _____

ABBOTT, EDITH, *Some American Pioneers in Social Welfare.* Chicago: University of Chicago Press, 1937.

DIGGINS, JOHN, *The Promise of Pragmatism.* Chicago: University of Chicago Press, 1994.

DOLGOFF, RALPH, and DAVID FELDSTEIN. *Understanding Social Welfare*, 6th ed. Boston: Allyn & Bacon, 2003.

EDIN, KATHRYN, and LAURA LEIN, *Making Ends Meet.* New York: Russell Sage Foundation, 1997.

GARVIN, CHARLES D., and JOHN E. TROPMAN, *Social Work in Contemporary Society.* Englewood Cliffs, NJ: Prentice Hall, 1992.

JOHNSON, LOUISE C., CHARLES L. SCHWARTZ, and DONALD S. TATE, *Social Welfare: A Response to Human Need.* Boston: Allyn & Bacon, 1997.

KARGER, HOWARD JACOB, and DAVID STOESZ, *American Social Welfare Policy*, 3rd ed. New York: Addison-Wesley Longman, 1998.

KLEIN, WALDO C., and MARTIN BLOOM, "Social Work as Applied Social Science: A Historical Analysis," *Social Work*, 39 (July 1994), 421–431.

MARX, JERRY D., *Social Welfare: The American Partnership.* Boston: Allyn & Bacon, 2004.

PAYNE, MALCOLM. *What Is Professional Social Work?* Chicago: Lyceum Books, 2006.

POPPLE, PHILLIP R., and LESLIE LEIGHNINGER, *Social Work, Social Welfare, and American Society*, 5th ed. Boston: Allyn & Bacon, 2002.

REID, P. NELSON, "Social Welfare History," in *Encyclopedia of Social Work*, 19th ed., Vol. 3. Washington, DC: NASW Press, 1995, pp. 2206–2225.

SKIDMORE, REX A., *Social Work Administration, Dynamic Management and Human Relationships*, 3rd ed. Boston: Allyn & Bacon, 1995.

Notes _____

1. National Association of Social Workers, *NASW News*, 46, no. 4 (April 2001).

2. National Association of Social Workers, *NASW News*, 49, no. 7 (July 2004).

3. Lyn Stoesen, "New Report Challenges 2008 Candidates," *NASW News*, Washington DC (Vol 52, #9, October, 2007), p. 9.

4. Robert L. Barker, *The Social Work Dictionary*, 3rd ed. (Washington, DC: NASW Press, 1995), p. 357.

5. For a highlighted description of historical developments, see James H. S. Bossard, *Social Change and Social Problems*, rev. ed. (New York: Harper & Row, 1938), pp. 673–678.

6. Ibid., p. 697.

7. Wilbur J. Cohen, "The New Public Welfare Legislation," News Release, U.S. Department of Health, Education, and Welfare, September 24, 1962.

8. See Chapter 12 for details.

9. *Social Security Bulletin*, 62 (Fall 1999).

10. Martha N. Ozawa, "The 1983 Amendments to the Social Security Act: The Issue of Intergenerational Equity," *Social Work*, 29 (March/April 1984), p. 131.

11. Violet M. Sieder and Doris C. Kirshbaum, "Volunteers," in *Encyclopedia of Social Work*, Vol. 2 (Washington, DC: National Association of Social Workers, 1977), p. 1583.

12. United Way of America, *A Study of the Quantity of Volunteer Activity of United Way and Its Member Agencies* (Alexandria, VA: United Way of America, 1974), p. iv.

13. *The Wall Street Journal*, December 24, 1985.

14. Brian O'Connell, "Our Open Hearts and Open Wallets," *Deseret News* (Salt Lake City, UT), January 26, 1989.

15. *Deseret News* (Salt Lake City, UT), May 14, 1995.

3

Education for Social Work

From his Pacific island home, Luis applied to one of the 168 accredited graduate programs of social work offering the MSW degree in the United States. In that year he was one of 36,475 successful applicants. Why was Luis accepted as a student? Would he be a good social worker? What did the admissions committee find in his application to put their stamp of approval on him? His autobiographical sketch contains material schools look for. Luis wrote: "In the Jesuit high school I attended, religion classes were often spent in discussing the condition of the slum dwellers on our island, and what we could do to help them. I belonged to clubs that were encouraged to work with the poor, the elderly, and juvenile delinquents. In high school I was a volunteer with social service agencies. . . . In my first year in college I trained in the juvenile justice system,

and for the next several years I combined full-time work as a counselor with my night classes at the University. . . . For the past three years I have worked in the prevention division of a substance abuse agency. My efforts have been directed at developing an educational curriculum in the schools as a drug abuse prevention approach. I have observed that young people who have positive self-esteem, who can communicate with their peers and their elders, and who have problem-solving skills are less likely to turn to drugs and other self-destructive practices. . . . I intend to return to my Pacific island home upon completing my degree in social work, and I hope to acquire the skills to plan and implement programs that will meet the unique cultural needs of my people, and at the same time help me realize my full human potential."

Social work education is a phenomenon of the twentieth century. Social work's prominence among the professions results from community demands for trained staff to administer a multibillion-dollar human service system. Society has declared that the work of helping people with personal and social problems must be handled with professional competence and subjected to rigorous tests of accountability.

The first agencies trained their own staffs in the "fundamental theory and practice of charity." The early schools of social work, the outgrowth of pressures and demands from agencies for competent personnel, were sponsored by the agencies themselves. Classwork was practice-oriented and intended to prepare staff for work in particular agencies.

Through the efforts of the Charity Organization Society (COS) of New York, the first course of instruction was established in 1898 with thirty students enrolled for three months. This summer school of "philanthropic workers" continued until 1904, when the course was reorganized on an eight-month basis to become the New York School of Philanthropy, now the Columbia University School of Social Work.

At the turn of the century, an Institute of Social Science was established as a part of the Extension Division of the University of Chicago. In response to efforts of practicing social workers, the institute became an independent School of Civics and Philanthropy and was later incorporated into the University of Chicago and the School of Social Service Administration. In Boston a school was established jointly by Harvard and Simmons College, and in Pennsylvania the Philadelphia Training School for Social Work was begun. These institutions have become schools of social work at Simmons College and at the University of Pennsylvania.

An Association of Training Schools for Professional Social Work was formed through which schools could "gain recognition and exchange views and experience." The association was a forerunner of the American Association of Schools of Social Work and the present Council on Social Work Education. Membership in the first association was open to any school that maintained a course of training covering at least one academic year with substantial fieldwork and classwork. A minimum curriculum, adopted by the schools in 1932, was association policy until 1944 and set forth the standard for one year of training.

During the Great Depression new demands were made on the social work profession, and opportunities were offered by the social legislation enacted to meet the growing needs of society. To meet these demands, social work education was greatly expanded.

Early schools trained workers for jobs in specific agencies. But in a mobile society, social work graduates are on the go, and their education needs to be applicable to all

Social work students in computer lab.

situations. Mobility places a premium on flexibility and the free exchange of personnel, intelligence, knowledge, and skill. In planning curriculum, schools consider the fact that their graduates will be employed in agencies widely dispersed throughout the country, representing not one, but many fields of practice. Fortunately, because of the timely and forward-looking action on the part of schools, graduates completing their training have the assurance that their professional skills can be utilized. Moreover, it is possible for graduates who receive part of their training in one school to transfer to another school.

Social Work Education

Social work education provides excellent opportunities for students in undergraduate, master's, and doctoral programs. Community colleges also offer course work in human services.

The master's degree has been acclaimed in the past as the basic professional social work degree. Programs for this degree are the heart of education for social work and are among the best in American universities. Doctoral programs, developed by an increasing number of schools, have taken their place among the strong professional schools of the country.

In response to mounting pressures for manpower in the human services, practice degree programs have been instituted at the bachelor's degree level. These programs have been given official recognition and sanction by the profession as the first professional practice degree in social work. Undergraduate social work programs have become very popular, and the number of programs has increased dramatically. Today there are some 463 baccalaureate social work programs in the United States.

In May 1982 the board of directors of the Council on Social Work Education (CSWE) adopted a new curriculum policy statement for both the MSW and BSW programs. This policy statement was the first time that the BSW education program's expectations were included in this seminal document.

In 2001 the board of directors of CSWE adopted an Educational Policy and Accreditation Standards (EPAS) that defined the purposes of social work education as follows:

> The purposes of social work education are to prepare competent and effective professionals, to develop social work knowledge, and to provide leadership in the development of service delivery systems. Social work education is grounded in the profession's history, purposes, and philosophy and is based on a body of knowledge, values, and skills. Social work education enables students to integrate the knowledge, values, and skills of the social work profession for competent practice.[1]

The preparation of effective social work professionals is expected at both the baccalaureate and master's level. The baccalaureate programs prepare students for generalist social work practice whereas the master's programs prepare students for advanced social work practice in a specific concentration. The concentration can be in a social work method, such as direct practice or community organization and planning, or in a field of practice such as mental health, family services, health, and child welfare.

Although the focus and theoretical depth may be different between the BSW and MSW level, the following material from the 2001 EPAS gives the basic parameters of the foundation areas:

A. VALUES AND ETHICS

Social work education programs integrate content about values and principles of ethical decision making as presented in the National Association of Social Workers Code of Ethics. The educational experience provides students with the opportunity to be aware of personal values; develop, demonstrate, and promote the values of the profession; and analyze ethical dilemmas and the ways in which these dilemmas affect practice, services, and clients.

B. DIVERSITY

Social work programs integrate content that promotes understanding, affirmation, and respect for people from diverse backgrounds. The content emphasizes the interlocking and complex nature of culture and personal identity. It ensures that social services meet the needs of groups served and are culturally relevant. Programs educate students to recognize diversity within and between groups that may influence assessment, planning, intervention, and research. Students learn how to define, design, and implement strategies for effective practice with persons from diverse backgrounds.

C. POPULATIONS-AT-RISK AND SOCIAL AND ECONOMIC JUSTICE

Social work education programs integrate content on populations-at-risk, examining the factors that contribute to and constitute being at risk. Programs educate students to identify how group membership influences access to resources, and present content on the dynamics of such risk factors and responsive and productive strategies to redress them.

Programs integrate social and economic justice content grounded in an understanding of distributive justice, human and civil rights, and the global interconnections of oppression. Programs provide content related to the implementing strategies to combat discrimination, oppression, and economic deprivation and to promote social and economic justice. Programs prepare students to advocate for nondiscriminatory social and economic systems.

D. HUMAN BEHAVIOR AND THE SOCIAL ENVIRONMENT

Social work education programs provide content on the reciprocal relationships between human behavior and social environments. Content includes empirically based theories and knowledge that focus on the interactions between and among individuals, groups, societies, and economic systems. It includes theories and knowledge of biological, sociological, cultural, psychological, and spiritual development across the life span; the range of social systems in which people live (individual, family, group, organizational, and community); and the ways social systems promote or deter people in maintaining or achieving health and well-being.

E. SOCIAL WELFARE POLICY AND SERVICES

Programs provide content about the history of social work, the history and current structures of social welfare services, and the role of policy in service delivery, social work practice, and attainment of individual and social well-being. Course content provides students with knowledge and skills to understand major policies that form the foundation of social welfare; analyze organizational, local, state, national, and international issues in social welfare policy and social service delivery; analyze and apply the results of policy research relevant to social service delivery; understand and demonstrate policy practice skills in regard to economic, political, and organizational systems, and use them to influence, formulate, and advocate for policy consistent with social work values; and identify financial, organizational, administrative, and planning processes required to deliver social services.

F. SOCIAL WORK PRACTICE

Social work practice content is anchored in the purposes of the social work profession and focuses on strengths, capacities, and resources of client systems in relation to their broader environments. Students learn practice content that encompasses knowledge and skills to work with individuals, families, groups, organizations, and communities. This content includes engaging clients in an appropriate working relationship, identifying issues, problems, needs, resources, and assets; collecting and assessing information; and planning for service delivery. It includes using communication skills, supervision, and consultation. Practice content also includes identifying, analyzing, and implementing empirically based interventions designed to achieve client goals; applying empirical knowledge and technological advances; evaluating program outcomes and practice effectiveness; developing, analyzing, advocating, and providing leadership for policies and services; and promoting social and economic justice.

G. RESEARCH

Qualitative and quantitative research content provides understanding of a scientific, analytic, and ethical approach to building knowledge for practice. The content prepares students to develop, use, and effectively communicate empirically based knowledge, including evidence-based interventions. Research knowledge is used to provide high-quality services; to initiate change; to improve practice, policy, and social service delivery; and to evaluate their own practice.

H. FIELD EDUCATION

Field education is an integral component of social work education anchored in the mission, goals, and educational level of the program. It occurs in settings that reinforce students' identification with the purposes, values, and ethics of the profession; fosters the integration of empirical and practice-based knowledge; and promotes the development of professional competence. Field education is systematically designed, supervised, coordinated, and evaluated on the basis of criteria by which students demonstrate the achievement of program objectives.[2]

In addition to the foundation areas, the MSW program offers students the opportunity to select concentrations. Each graduate program determines which areas it will make available to students. The following concentration frameworks are outlined in the EPAS Statement:

ADVANCED CURRICULUM CONTENT

The master's curriculum prepares graduates for advanced social work practice in an area of concentration. Using a conceptual framework to identify advanced knowledge and skills, programs build an advanced curriculum from the foundation content. In the advanced curriculum, the foundation content areas are addressed in greater depth, breadth, and specificity and support the program's conception of advanced practice.[3]

The Master's Program

There has been an increase in the number of schools offering the master's degree. There were 63 schools in 1963 compared with 168 in 2004. The number of MSW students graduating in 2004 was 15,473.

The pattern for the master's degree had been a two-year program of class and field instruction. However, in 1971 the board of directors of CSWE adopted standards that provided for advanced standing for students, making it possible for schools to opt for a master's degree to be completed in one year.

The master's program prepares students for professional service and leadership. Curricula include diversified bodies of knowledge, professional skills, and value orientations as requisites for practitioners to serve individuals, families, small groups, communities, and organizations. Master's programs provide opportunity for mastery of concentrations as can be seen in Tables 3.1 and 3.2 in selected social work methods and social problems. Education is

TABLE 3.1   Master's Degree Students Enrolled on 11/1/04, by Primary Methods Concentration*

| | Concentration Framework | | | | | | | |
| | Methods Only | | Methods Combined with Field of Practice or Social Problems | | Field of Practice or Social Problem Only (No Methods) | | Total | |
Methods	#	%	#	%	#	%	#	%
Direct practice or clinical	5,307	59.7	14,671	54.5	—	—	19,978	54.8
Community organization and planning	303	3.4	820	2.9	—	—	1,123	3.1
Administration or management	218	2.5	700	2.8	—	—	918	2.5
Combination of direct practice with C. O. and planning or administration or management	0	0.0	1,610	10.1	—	—	1,610	4.4
Combination of C. O. and planning with administration or management	427	4.8	420	2.0	—	—	847	2.3
Advanced generalist	730	8.2	3,974	13.7	—	—	4,704	12.9
Other	441	5.0	1,291	3.3	—	—	1,732	4.7
Not yet determined	1,468	16.5	3,215	10.6	—	—	4,683	12.8
None (field of practice or social problem only)	—	—	—	—	880	100.0	880	2.4
Total	8,894	100.0	26,701	100.0	880	100.0	36,475	100.0

*Column totals may not correspond among tables within this report due to variance in response rates.

Source: Council on Social Work Education, Statistics on Social Work Education in the United States: 2004 (Alexandria, VA: CSWE, 2007), p. 41. Reprinted with permission of the publisher.

TABLE 3.2   *Master's Degree Students Enrolled on 11/1/04, by Primary Field of Practice or Social Problem Concentration*[*]

Type of Concentration	#	%
Aging/gerontological social work	1,332	3.7
Alcohol, drug or substance abuse	938	2.6
Child welfare	2,695	7.4
Corrections/criminal justice	471	1.3
Developmental disabilities	148	0.4
Family services	2,337	6.4
Group services	194	0.5
Health	1,449	4.0
Occupational/industrial social work	174	0.5
Mental health or community mental health	4,274	11.7
Public assistance/public welfare	194	0.5
Rehabilitation	55	0.2
School social work	1,643	4.5
Other	2,934	8.0
Combinations	2,338	6.4
Not yet determined	6,405	17.6
None (methods concentration only)	8,894	24.4
Total	36,475	100.0

[*]Column totals may not correspond among tables within this report due to variance in response rates.

Source: Council on Social Work Education, *Statistics on Social Work Education in the United States: 2004* (Alexandria, VA: CSWE, 2007), p. 42. Reprinted with permission of the publisher.

structured to provide opportunity for the application of skills and knowledge acquired in the classroom to actual social work situations through an integrated fieldwork experience.

Students are also given opportunities to participate in school governance, to involve themselves in school policy and procedure formulation and implementation, and to engage in all dimensions of the learning process.

Social work education is an open system with different patterns of education encouraged. Illustrative of schools' conceptions of what is to be achieved by their training programs are the following educational objectives, assumed to have been attained when students:

1. Understand and incorporate the basic values, concepts, and methods of social work, recognizing some significant variations by method and field of practice.
2. Acquire and utilize understanding of human behavior and the social environment, of social policy and services, of institutional reconstruction, and of forces shaping public policy.
3. Achieve competence and basic skill through study and practice in one method, or in a combination of related methods by which services are provided.
4. Understand the unique features of minority and disadvantaged peoples, the significance of their problems, and of their contributions to the resolution of issues in effecting social change.

5. Acquire mature and sensitive attitudes toward one's self and others, which result in becoming an accountable and a disciplined helping person.
6. Develop a commitment to the spirit of inquiry and to research methods through which inquiry can be pursued in advancing professional knowledge and practice.
7. Establish an identification with the profession of social work and the need to integrate knowledge, feeling, and responsible action in becoming a professional person.
8. Become oriented to the contribution of the professional social work association and develop a conviction that the student will carry responsibility for specifying the dimensions of its concerns and practices.
9. Gain the ability to work with and support other professional disciplines and volunteer and paraprofessional groups in the belief that many of the social and personal ills of our time can be overcome by intelligent and cooperative intervention.

Admission to the Master's Program

Candidates admitted to the master's program have received their undergraduate degrees and possess the requisite qualifications for practice in the profession of social work. Men and women who can meet the personal and academic qualifications are accepted for training irrespective of race, creed, or color. Qualifications usually include:

1. Evidence of superior ability, character, and personality.
2. Academic credentials attesting above-average scholarship and satisfactory completion of four years of college work with a baccalaureate degree from an accredited college.
3. Suitable undergraduate background in the arts and sciences with some emphasis in the social sciences—sociology, psychology, political science, social ethics, anthropology, economics, education.
4. A bachelor's degree from an approved undergraduate college or university.

The policy of schools of social work, which is reflected in their admission procedures, is to select only those college graduates who combine native endowment, relationship capacity, maturity, imagination, industry, motivation, and such other physical, social, emotional, and spiritual qualities that lend themselves to excellence in helping others.

Numbers of students are admitted from foreign countries representing cultures radically different from American communities. Special problems often ensue in the training of foreign students, and this matter has received searching study from the profession, which has guidelines for schools admitting and training students from other countries. The profession is zealous of maintaining and improving its public image. It is constantly upgrading and seeking to improve the quality of its services to the public. Schools of social work are often the vanguard of this striving and have made notable advances in their educational contributions.

Evaluating Master's Programs

If the quality of social work master's programs is to improve, social work educators must constantly evaluate the curriculum and the impact it is having on students and the profession. It can be argued that the human behavior sequence in master's programs establishes an important foundation for the other sequences including practice, social policy, research, and field education. Theories of human behavior have always been a vital part of the social work profession. In the 1940s and 1950s, human behavior theories focused on Freud, psychoanalysis, and dysfunctional behavior. The civil rights movement of the 1960s produced a shift in human behavior content to include conflict, power, and social injustice. By the 1980s, a wide range of human behavior theories were being promoted and taught in master's programs. This wide range of human behavior theories continued to expand into the 1990s and now includes behavior modification, cognitive therapy, and systems theory.

Recently, social work educators have begun to question whether the wide range of human behavior theories being taught in master's programs might be creating more confusion than understanding among students. In reviewing the MSW human behavior foundation course outlines of sixty-one schools of social work, Farley et al. uncovered some interesting findings.[4] The results of their study indicated that 70 percent of the schools of social work used a "life span," "ecological perspective," "bio-psychosocial," or "social systems" approach as their primary theoretical focus, whereas only 3 percent included a major theoretical focus on "disorder," "dysfunctional behavior," or "abnormal behavior." This theoretical shift from "disorders" to a "life span" or "ecological perspective" was needed, but probably not to the degree it has been incorporated. Social work students still need instruction and training in dysfunctional behavior, diagnosis, and treatment. This is especially true for those students who deal with clients with a variety of mental illnesses and disorders. In making this shift away from dysfunctional behavior, social work educators may be "throwing the baby out with the bath water." There is clearly still a need to educate social work students about mental illnesses and mental disorders. Farley and colleagues' review of the human behavior curriculum is a excellent example of why social

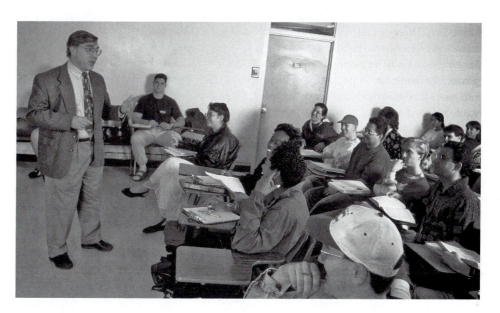

Students in a master's program of social work.

work educators must continue to evaluate the curriculum of master's programs if the quality of graduate education is to improve.

The Baccalaureate Program

In 1970 CSWE initiated a plan to "approve" undergraduate educational programs whose objective included the preparation for practice in the field of social work. Since that time baccalaureate degrees have been awarded to an increasing number of students who are considered professional and are employed in social welfare positions. In addition, students enroll in the programs to enrich their general education, to prepare for graduate social work study, or to prepare for graduate study or employment in one of the other human service occupations.

Of the 463 undergraduate programs reporting in September 2004, a total of 25,715 junior and senior students were matriculated with 9,889 having graduated the previous school year of 2002–2003. Each "accredited" undergraduate program must demonstrate that it

1. builds on, and is integrated with, a liberal arts base that includes knowledge in the humanities, social, behavioral, and biological sciences;
2. provides content in the areas of (a) social work practice, (b) social welfare policy and services, (c) human behavior and social environment, and (d) social research; and
3. requires educationally directed field experience with engagement in service activities for at least 300 clock hours, for which academic credit commensurate with the time invested is given.[5]

Building on the broad base of prerequisite course requirements, individualized study programs, and careful coordination of required and elected social work courses, students are assured of a foundation in the liberal arts, research, human behavior and social environment, social welfare policies and services, social work practice skills, and practical experience in the field.

The practice portion of the curriculum makes possible not only the opportunity for students to integrate and internalize their understandings into practice skills, but also allows field- and campus-based faculty a chance to evaluate and determine whether the educational content given to students is being developed, utilized, and translated into practice. A learning atmosphere can be created in which a student can share any inadequacies, fears, or experience of an educational gap.

In many undergraduate programs the field seminar and practice sequence classes are limited in numbers of students enrolled to encourage the kind of in-depth exchange and resultant learning that can occur within the context of a supportive group. Built into the curriculum is the provision for ongoing, individualized educational direction for accomplishing the program's educational objectives with each student.

Undergraduate programs include the following desired educational goals:

1. Analytic and research skills that enable students to evaluate critically the complex social problems and issues that confront America today, including knowledge and understanding of the resources and strategies that have been used—or may be used—to meet these problems and issues in the future.

2. Basic knowledge, skills, and values related to problem solving in social work practice regardless of the particular position a student may occupy on graduation. These include an understanding of

   a. the philosophical values that underlie practice in the field of social welfare;
   b. social welfare institutions and their relationship to other institutional structures in society;
   c. social welfare policies and the ways in which they are developed;
   d. social work as a profession;
   e. individuals in society, including an understanding of human behavior and development; and
   f. basic social work treatment techniques and skills employed in working with individuals, groups, and communities, including educational opportunities to participate directly in service programs through field experience.

Students are exposed liberally to the many disciplines and professions concerned with the welfare and behavior of people. Social work courses, whenever possible, integrate and apply concepts learned in the related basic sciences and disciplines to the field of social welfare and the profession of social work.

Admissions

Students are admitted into social work undergraduate programs under procedures compatible with those of the parent institution. The first interview with students is given particular emphasis, with the faculty member pointing out the requirements and helping students assess their motivations, interests, and abilities to perform successfully in this profession. These interviews are part of an ongoing advisement process, which allows for periodic evaluation of the students' performance.

A fieldwork placement center is necessary for each student, and this often places a limitation on the number of students who can be accepted into the program. Fieldwork instructors and supervisors are necessary to maintain the close liaison between faculty and students. Imaginative faculty, cooperating with fieldwork placement centers, often are able to create field placements that offer opportunities to the students and fill a need for the community.

An example of involvement of undergraduates in field placement is in foster care of children. Students work with small groups consisting of a set of natural parents, the child in placement, and the foster parents. This gives an opportunity for the natural parents to share as equal partners in the planning for their child, and to meet and relate to the foster parents on a basis of respect and mutual admiration. Students plan for conferences of foster parents and assist in the program planning. In an analysis and building program dealing with foster care, the information gained by the students may produce a composite picture of foster children, natural parents, and foster parents. Students can review the strengths as well as gaps in the social service delivery system. This provides an experience in operational research when they present the material to the agency involved.

Other students work through YWCAs and YMCAs to develop volunteer programs for various groups, such as women at state prisons, minority youths, or divorced women.

These programs help a student become tuned in to personnel and human needs, and to realize the potential for help in creating a better society.

The Doctoral Program

The doctoral program in social work has as its primary objective the preparation and development of selected professional social workers for leadership positions. In offering this advanced degree, the sixty-six available schools are responding to the need for qualified social work educators, researchers, social planners, and administrators. Requirements for admission to the program are usually the MSW degree, with some practical work experience. In 2004 approximately 313 students received doctoral degrees.

The aims of the doctoral program are to enable students to (1) develop and demonstrate their capacities as social work scholars and to acquire the requisite knowledge, background, and skill to teach, conduct research, write, and speak with authority about social work; and (2) achieve an advanced understanding of the methods employed in social work practice and of the broad range of social welfare services, and to study the social and behavioral sciences and to assess their relevance to social work practice.

Curriculum

Schools vary in the curriculum offered, but typically there is emphasis on continuing scholarship, with students expected to develop their abilities in organizing, extending, testing, communicating, and applying knowledge of the field of social work and social welfare. Study centers on social work theory and practice, research and statistics, social and behavioral science theory, social welfare policy and planning, and educational theories and methodologies.

A recent shift in the curricula of bachelor's, master's, and doctoral programs in social work education has incorporated the concept of "best practices." Best practices simply means stressing the importance of empirical research in selecting interventions and designing social service programs. For example, what is the best way to help clients who are suffering from a major depressive disorder? Most treatment programs for clinical depression emphasize either medications or talk therapy or a combination of both. Empirical research studies have determined that by themselves medications and talk therapy can help clients overcome their clinical depression. Best practice studies have shown that the benefits of combining medications with talk therapy are even more successful in treating clinical depression.[6] Another example of best practice is social service programs for poor persons. Best practice research suggests that they should be consulted as services are planned and developed and also made an important part of the delivery, evaluation, and improvement of these services.[7] A best practice focus will improve the social work curriculum in bachelor's, master's, and doctoral programs and bring the social work profession more in line with other professional schools such as medicine, nursing, and business.

To enrich the educational program, courses from other departments of the university are usually recommended. There also is opportunity for the pursuit of individualized interests.

Continuing Education

With the vast accumulation of knowledge in the social work field, workers continually need to reevaluate their habits of thought, concepts, values, and methods of practice. Those who say "That's it! I'm educated" when they receive a degree are only saying "I have stopped learning."

Continuing education (CE) is an essential part of social work education, designed to qualify practitioners to meet the demands of an ever-changing social service kaleidoscope. It prepares workers to accept change. It is recognition by the profession that degree-producing programs can provide only entry-level qualifications for practitioners.

The point of entry of community college workers, with no previous practice, demands knowledge and underpinning. Seeking professional identity to provide direction and purpose to their practice, they look to continuing education provided by social work schools and professional associations.

The bachelor's degree practitioner looks ahead to movement along the continuum. Moving up the ladder of practice, meeting new challenges, developing new skills, and building a knowledge base are imperatives. CE is an important means for fulfilling these demands.

The master's degree holder who understands the knowledge explosion, who increasingly relates to practice in collaboration with prestigious disciplines and the decision makers, and who reads the professional literature ensures against obsolescence by continuing education.

CE makes it possible for workers to update their knowledge and skills, acquire new knowledge, advance on the job, and prepare for new roles and responsibilities.

Social work is an open and ever-changing system. It is constantly being renewed, added to, and improved. CE is a major component of social work education, serving all curricular sequences and all levels of practice through sharing of research, empirical findings from practice, and new knowledge from the sciences and humanities. It is an essential part of the continuum, an imperative in a rapidly developing profession.

CE is a network of learning associations, arrangements, and resources designed to improve practice and the quality of services. It aids in the formulation of ideas, keeps the mind alert to new and exciting developments in social work and related disciplines, and helps one become a "wise man" as defined by André Gide, the French novelist who won the Nobel Prize for literature in 1947: "The wise man is he who constantly wonders afresh."

Student Participation in Social Work Education

In the 1960s students often complained of powerlessness, that their views were not heard, and that the schools served not students, but the faculty and the Establishment. Education, they said, was not relevant.

Students in the new millennium have become more involved and identified. They are serving on the board of directors of the National Council on Social Work Education and as members of the House of Delegates, where they participate in policy formulation and decision making. They are appointed to national committees and commissions. In the universities they are elected or appointed to college councils and to executive and policy-making committees, including the important curriculum and student review committees.

In these positions students not only offer a student point of view, but have voting power and impact decisions having to do with their education. In some universities they serve on university-wide committees and participate in university government.

Students in social work in many ways are the architects of their learning, and they contribute to the system as they take from it.

Stipends and Scholarships

Financial assistance is available to qualified students at all levels of training. Students planning to attend school may contact the school of their choice for detailed information on stipends, scholarships, and work-study arrangements administered by the educational institutions and social agencies. A list of accredited colleges and universities for training social workers may be obtained from the Council on Social Work Education.

Council on Social Work Education

Schools guided by the Council on Social Work Education have improved their offering to students by raising their standards of training, tightening admission requirements, and shifting to a common core, concentrations, some specialties, and a continuing emphasis on basic principles, values, and philosophy.

The CSWE reviews the programs of schools and accredits training. It also actively assists colleges and universities in implementing their programs and offers consultation services to both undergraduate and graduate programs.

In 1998 CSWE adopted the following mission statement:

> CSWE is a national association of social work education programs and individuals that ensures and enhances the quality of social work education for a professional practice that promotes individual, family, and community well-being, and social and economic justice. CSWE pursues this mission by setting and maintaining national accreditation standards for baccalaureate and master's degree programs in social work, by promoting faculty development, and by advocating for social work education and research.[8]

Moreover, CSWE sponsors an annual meeting attended by faculty members and by leaders of voluntary and government agencies at local, state, and national levels.

Colleges and universities are the source of well-educated social workers to meet the needs of agencies concerned with the many social problems of the country. The CSWE helps schools maintain standards, so that a social worker graduating from an accredited school will be able to function in his or her role in working with those who need social services.

Summary

Social work education is a phenomenon of the twentieth century and resulted from the nation's demand for trained staff to administer a multibillion-dollar human service system. It has moved from practice-oriented, agency-focused training to colleges and universities having status with other professional schools and academic colleges.

Curricular models have been developed for professional education at the doctoral, master's and bachelor's degree levels. All programs have enjoyed significant growth, but the bachelor's level programs have increased their numbers dramatically.

The Council on Social Work Education, the only official accrediting body, addressed itself to the important problems of structure and quality in social work education. Because of the complexity of modern society, CSWE has required schools on all levels to stress generalist practice and a generalist perspective. The social worker needs to understand and be able to work with the interaction of multiple human systems.

Continuing education has developed on a broad front in recognition of the need for practitioners to keep current in the rapidly expanding and changing field of practice.

Selected References

BELCASTRO, BONNIE ROWAN, and GARY F. KOESKE, "Job Satisfaction and Intention to Seek Graduate Education," *Journal of Social Work Education*, 32 (Fall 1996), 315–327.

BISNO, HERB, and FRED COX, "Social Work Education: Catching up with the Present and the Future," *Journal of Social Work Education*, 33 (Spring/Summer 1997), 373–387.

COMMISSION ON ACCREDITATION, *Handbook of Accreditation Standards and Procedures*, 4th ed. Alexandria, VA: CSWE, 1995.

FARLEY, O. WILLIAM, LARRY L. SMITH, SCOTT W. BOYLE, and JOHN RONNAU, "A Review of Foundation MSW Human Behavior Courses," *Journal of Human Behavior in the Social Environment,* 6, no. 3 (2002), 1–12.

JARMAN-ROHDE, LILY, JOANN MCFALL, PATRICIA KOLAR, and GERALD STROM, "The Changing Context of Social Work Practice: Implications and Recommendations for Educators," *Journal of Social Work Education*, 33 (Winter 1997), 29–45.

JOHNSON, LOUISE G., and STEPHEN J. YANCA, *Social Work Practice: A Generalist Approach*, 8th ed. Boston: Allyn & Bacon, 2004.

KOERIN, BEVERLY, JANE REEVES, and MICHAEL SHERIDAN, "BSW Autonomy Issues in Combined BSW/MSW Programs," *Journal of Social Work Education*, 37 (Spring/Summer 2001), 309–319.

MEHR, JOSEPH J., and RONALD KANWIS CHER, *Human Services: Concepts and Intervention Strategies*, 9th ed. Boston: Allyn & Bacon, 2004.

MILEY, KARLA KROGSRUD, MICHAEL O'MELIA, and BRENDA L. DUBOIS, *Generalist Social Work Practice*. Boston: Allyn & Bacon, 1995.

RIPPLE, LILLIAN, *Report to the Task Force on Structure and Quality in Social Work Education*. New York: CSWE, 1974.

RUSSELL, MARY NOMME, *Clinical Social Work: Research and Practice*. Newbury Park, CA: Sage, 1990.

TICE, KAREN, "Gender and Social Work Education: Directions for the 1990's," *Journal of Social Work Education*, 26 (Spring/Summer 1990), 134–144.

Notes

1. Council on Social Work Education, *Educational Policy and Accreditation Standards* (Alexandria, VA: CSWE, 2001), p. 5.

2. Ibid., pp. 9–11.

3. Ibid., p. 11.

4. O. William Farley, Larry L. Smith, Scott W. Boyle, and John Ronnau, "A Review of Foundation MSW Human Behavior Courses," *Journal of Human Behavior in the Social Environment*, 6 (2002), pp. 1–12.

5. Lillian Ripple, *Report of the Task Force on Structure and Quality in Social Work Education* (New York: CSWE, 1974), p. 12.

6. Harold I. Kaplan and Benjamin J. Sadock, *Concise Textbook of Clinical Psychiatry*, 2nd ed. (Baltimore: Williams & Wilkins, 2004), pp. 171–172.

7. Bradford W. Sheafor and Charles R. Horejsi, *Techniques and Guidelines for Social Work Practice*, 7th ed. (Boston: Allyn & Bacon, 2005), pp. 513–517.

8. *Social Work Education Reporter*, 46, no. 1 (Alexandria, VA: CSWE, Winter 1998), p. 1.

4

Generalist Practice and Introductory Theory

Jimmy was failing in school; his sister, May, was in and out of correctional homes; their father never seemed to be able to keep a job; and the mother was always "sick." The family got by— they lived mostly on public assistance—but they never had enough money. Food stamps helped. Neighbors and the local church unit had tried, but this family was "undeserving"—they just wouldn't try to help themselves. Actually, the entire family didn't perform, or performed poorly at best, all their various social roles. The parents

failed at parenting; the children failed in school; parents and children were failing as a family.

Multiproblem families epitomize family disorganization and breakdown, and in their failure to perform in their various roles, they illustrate problems of social functioning, or more appropriately, the failure to function. Functioning or dysfunctioning individuals, families, or communities in their many socially determined roles become the objects of the social work profession.

Because of the complexities of modern society, the profession of social work has chosen to emphasize the generalist practice perspective. The profession was actually founded on a generalist premise that social workers needed to consider and work with both the individual and the environment as they attempted to improve the life quality and functioning of individuals, groups, and communities. This basic premise compelled the profession toward a holistic and comprehensive knowledge base that honors diverse value systems and possesses a wide range of professional skills.

Over the years the social work profession partially left the commitment to generalist principles in an effort to specialize and develop specific methodologies designed to work in "direct practice" (i.e., individuals, families, and groups) or "indirect practice" (i.e., community organization and administration). The Council of Social Work Education suggested in its 1992 Curriculum Policy Statement that the undergraduate program teach a strong generalist practice core and that graduate programs also teach a generalist perspective, combined with an advanced concentration of some type. The advanced concentration could be in working with individuals, groups, or communities or in a field of practice such as mental health or child welfare. Schools of social work were encouraged to develop their curriculum in a flexible way within basic guidelines.

One of the strong basic themes of all social work education today is the generalist conceptualization. Miley, O'Melia, and DuBois offer the following definition:

> Generalist social work provides a contemporary approach for meeting the purpose of social work. This view moves beyond the confines of individually focused practice to the expansive sphere of intervention with multiperson systems. Broadly defined, generalist social work considers the interplay of personal and collective issues and works with a variety of human systems—societies, communities, neighborhoods, complex organizations, formal groups, informal groups, families and individuals—to create changes which maximize social functioning.[1]

In his new text on generalist practice, Derezotes makes the following statement:

> In summary, although there is still no agreement on the definition of generalist, an emerging consensus suggests that the generalist perspective includes an eclectic base of practice, a multimethod approach, and a focus upon social justice. Thus, in a generalist curriculum, the student becomes familiar with the basic, generic knowledge, skills, and values necessary to practice with a variety of social work populations.[2]

When a person comes into a social worker's office requesting help or when the social worker visits an individual in a homeless shelter, the purpose of the meeting is to enhance the person's well-being or social functioning. Also, when the social worker meets with a state legislative committee or a local school board, the professional purpose is to help them design programs that will alleviate poverty and oppression and meet basic human needs. The professional social worker is expected to perform difficult and complex tasks. To help conceptualize the role of social workers, CSWE defined the foundation program objectives in the 2001 EPAS for both the baccalaureate and master's programs as follows:

1. Apply critical thinking skills within the context of professional social work practice.
2. Understand the value base of the profession and its ethical standards and principles, and practice accordingly.
3. Practice without discrimination and with respect, knowledge, and skills related to clients' age, class, color, culture, disability, ethnicity, family structure, gender, marital status, national origin, race, religion, sex, and sexual orientation.
4. Understand the forms and mechanisms of oppression and discrimination and apply strategies of advocacy and social change that advance social and economic justice.
5. Understand and interpret the history of the social work profession and its current structures and issues.
B6. Apply the knowledge and skills of generalist social work practice with systems of all sizes.[*]

---

[*]Items preceded by a *B* or *M* apply only to baccalaureate or master's programs, respectively.

Social workers assisting homeless persons.

M6. Apply the knowledge and skills of a generalist social work perspective to practice with systems of all sizes.

  7. Use theoretical frameworks supported by empirical evidence to understand individual development and behavior across the life span and the interactions among individuals and between individuals and families, groups, organizations, and communities.

  8. Analyze, formulate, and influence social policies.

  9. Evaluate research studies, apply research findings to practice, and evaluate their own practice interventions.

  10. Use communication skills differentially across client populations, colleagues, and communities.

  11. Use supervision and consultation appropriate to social work practice.

  12. Function within the structure of organizations and service delivery systems and seek necessary organizational change.[3]

Kirst-Ashman and Hull explain why the generalist approach is so appropriate for the social work profession. They state

> Social workers don't pick and choose what problems and issues they would like to address. They see a problem, even a very difficult problem, and try to help people solve it. They must prepare themselves to help people with individualized personal problems on the one hand and very broad problems that affect whole organizations and communities on the other.[4]

Kirst-Ashman and Hull go on to say that, in generalist practice, the social worker is involved with four systems: (1) client system; (2) change agent system; (3) action system;

and (4) target system. The client system includes those people who benefit from the change process whereas the change agent system is the individual who initiates the change process. The action system includes those people who are working to make the situation better whereas the target system is the individual, group, or community to be changed or influenced. In working with these four systems, the social worker who uses a generalist model can assume a number of different roles including the following:

1. Enabler
2. Mediator
3. Integrator/coordinator
4. General manager
5. Educator
6. Analyst/evaluator
7. Broker
8. Facilitator
9. Initiator
10. Negotiator
11. Mobilizer
12. Advocate[5]

Although there are many important parts to generalist practice, one of the most crucial is the part that empowers the client. In helping the client in the empowerment process, the focus moves toward the strengths of the client and away from the client's weaknesses or pathology. Rather than exploring what the client can't do, the therapist emphasizes what unique strengths and abilities the client brings to counseling. By building on the strengths and resources of the client, the therapist encourages the client to use his inner skills and resources to deal with personal problems and concerns. One way to begin the empowerment process is for the therapist to review with the client what problems and concerns have occurred in the past and how the client has dealt with these issues. As the client describes in detail what has happened and what was done to meet each challenge, the therapist identifies the strengths and resources that the client used and how these strengths and resources can be used again.

According to Miley and colleagues, the following assumptions characterize an empowerment and strengths perspective in generalist practice:

1. Acknowledge that clients have existing reservoirs of resources and competence to draw on.
2. Recognize that each client has a distinct capacity for growth and change.
3. Define problems as occurring within the transactions between systems rather than residing in deficient system functioning.
4. Hold that collaboration augments existing strengths to build new resources.
5. Affirm that clients know their situations best and, given options, can determine the best solution for their challenges.
6. Maintain that positive change builds on a vision of future possibilities.
7. Support a process to magnify mastery and competence rather than correct deficits.[6]

Need for a Theoretical Framework

Because of the inclusive professional purpose statements, the wide variation of client groups, and the intense interaction among and between these groups, the profession of social work has struggled to develop a theory base that would provide an adequate foundation for the knowledge needed to carry out its mandate. The profession of social work has borrowed heavily from academic disciplines dealing with human biological, social, psychological, and cultural systems. Theories stressing the impact of economic forces on individuals and communities have added another important dimension in understanding how systems promote or deter people from achieving optimal health and well-being. The study of political processes and policy formulation has recently been incorporated into the social work knowledge base.

To address the wide-ranging theories from other academic disciplines and to help make these theories understandable to social work practitioners, CSWE has required that schools of social work teach a series of classes under the title of Human Behavior and the Social Environment. The council has defined the HB and SE sequence in the recent Educational Policy and Accreditation Standards (EPAS) as follows:

> **D. HUMAN BEHAVIOR AND THE SOCIAL ENVIRONMENT.**
>
> Social work education programs provide content on the reciprocal relationships between human behavior and social environments. Content includes empirically based theories and knowledge that focus on the interactions between and among individuals, groups, societies, and economic systems. It includes theories and knowledge of biological, sociological, cultural, psychological, and spiritual development across the life span; the range of social systems in which people live (individual, family, group, organizational, and community); and the ways social systems promote or deter people in maintaining or achieving health and well-being.[7]

The HB and SE sequence has been a basic mechanism to help the professional focus on the perspective of the person and the environment with a proper understanding of the important interaction that goes on between people and the context in which they live. This perspective has assisted social workers to incorporate theories into practices that explain how individuals grow and develop socially, biologically, emotionally, and spiritualistically. Also, the dual perspective has encouraged an understanding of social structures, systems, and cultural norms that play such an important part in the lives of all people.

In the early days of social work the interactive perspective was evidenced in the Charity Organization Societies (COS) and the Settlement House Movement (SHM). The COS focused on changing the individual, whereas the SHM chose to change social systems. There was an important shift toward more emphasis on the individual with social work's adoption of Freud's psychodynamic model. However, as different theorists broke away from Freud, the environmental perspective began to again claim more prominence. The profession of social work accepted theoretical constructs from such theories as ego psychology, behavioral and cognitive models, humanist and existential models, social psychological, and communication models. Since the 1970s, the profession has added the systems and ecological models as a way of again stressing the importance of balancing the focus of social work practice between the "person" and the "environment."

The systems and ecological models also give the social work practitioner theoretical constructs to thoughtfully analyze interactions between and among social systems and to visualize how these interactions influence people's behavior.

Systems theory addresses the impact that organizations, policies, communities, and groups have on individuals. Individuals are thought of as being involved in constant interaction with various systems in the environment. The aim of social work is to improve the interactions between clients and systems. Barker defines a system as follows:

> A combination of elements with mutual reciprocity and identifiable *boundaries* that form a complex or unitary whole. Systems may be physical and mechanical, living and social, or combinations of these. Examples of social systems include individual families, groups, a specific social welfare agency, or a nation's entire organizational process of education.[8]

Ecological theory is a subset of systems theory that makes some important contributions to social work. One contribution of this theory is the definition of the following three levels of systems:

1. **Micro:**   This system refers to an individual and incorporates the biological, psychological, and social systems that impact on the individual.
2. **Mezzo:**   This system refers to small groups that impact the individual such as the family, work groups, and other social groups.
3. **Macro:**   This system refers to groups and systems that are larger than families. Four important macro systems that impact individuals are organizations, institutions, community, and culture.

Both systems theory and ecological theory have assisted the profession by giving the practitioner an organizing framework to analyze the ever-shifting, volatile interaction of people in their environments. Also, these two theoretical constructs facilitate the process of linking concepts from traditional theories such as "psychodynamic" and "behaviorism" together, enabling practitioners to visualize the human process as an eclectic whole. After the linkage has been established, practitioners can then sort out the concepts they subscribe to and utilize them in their practice in an organized and disciplined fashion.

Introductory Inner and Outer Forces Paradigm[9]

The following paradigm has been developed to introduce the interactive perspective of social work to students who anticipate becoming social work practitioners. The paradigm is simple and straightforward, and yet it incorporates elements of systems and ecological theory. The paradigm is basic, but it allows for additions of the more sophisticated theories of human behavior.

The inner and outer forces paradigm attempts to explain why people seem to act at times in strange and unpredictable ways. Some people get excited thinking about a golfing vacation, whereas others prefer the ocean. Some like to work with their hands, and others enjoy paper work behind a desk. The reasons behind the selection of mates, too, have often been a great mystery.

Outer forces play a role in the human drama.

Although there is seemingly no chance in the foreseeable future to fully explain and predict the human drama, we propose a conceptual model to assist the social worker in bringing some kind of order to the human scene. The basic assumption in the inner and outer forces model is that there are forces developed both within the person and from the person's environment that cause him or her to behave in certain ways. The real origin of the forces may never be identified, but the recognition that the forces exist and continually interact to produce behavior is significant.

We have chosen the terms *inner* and *outer* to identify the two major forces that shape human behavior. An example of the inner and outer framework can be observed when a child begins to walk. One important inner force is created by the neurological development of the child that produces a force which incites the child to try to walk, as well as creates the capacity to walk. The important outer force of mother's rewarding the child with pleasant smiles and hugs further encourages the continuation of this new behavior. Thus, the child's walking is a product of the interaction of inner and outer forces.

Figure 4.1 illustrates the inner and outer forces model in a simplified format. The arrows indicate that force is being exerted on the individual from within and without, which produces a resultant behavior.

Social workers can utilize the inner and outer forces framework in several ways. The framework can assist in assessing and treating problems of a troubled person. The following case history illustrates the assessment and treatment use of the model.

John, a 17-year-old high school student from a small rural community, was referred to the mental health center because he was continually fighting, had received numerous speeding tickets, was doing poorly in school, and had beaten up his stepfather. As John described his

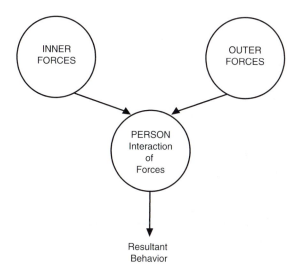

FIGURE 4.1

problems, it was apparent to the worker that the outer forces in John's life were overpowering him. The school officials seemed to be set on removing him from the school and the local police watched constantly for him to drag Main Street so they could give him a ticket. John's stepfather, an aggressive, anxious person, was trying to help John by, in his words, "tightening the screws" to make him perform better.

Although the worker was able to recognize the outer forces precipitating the present referral, consideration was also given to the inner forces influencing John's life. John admitted that he felt insecure because he had no plans for earning a living. He felt he was a failure in so many areas that he was almost panicked. These feelings of inferiority and insecurity were strong inner forces that required attention from the social worker.

Recognizing that the outer forces needed to be relieved before anything could be done to work on John's inner forces, the worker called meetings with school officials, police personnel, and John's family. After the worker explained the great negative pressure brought to bear on John by the outer forces, all the people involved agreed to work toward the goals of realistically reducing the outer pressure on him. Teachers set up tutorials for him and gave him positive support. The police officers agreed to overlook the fact that sometimes John drove two miles over the speed limit on Main Street. This was the same consideration they gave to boys who weren't in the "troublemaker" category. The stepfather, too, relaxed his controls on John.

As the outer forces were reduced, John's behavior began to change. He functioned better in the community. The worker then helped him work on some of his negative inner forces, such as feelings of inferiority, and brought about additional changes. John completed high school and opened an auto body shop.

The inner and outer forces model utilized in John's case is shown in Figure 4.2. The social worker reduced the negative outer forces and increased some positive inner forces, producing more functional behavior in John. The inner and outer forces framework helped the worker assess John's problems and suggest a successful treatment course.

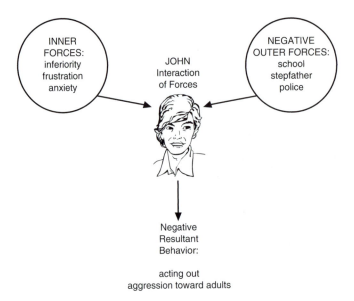

FIGURE 4.2

Another use of the inner and outer forces framework is in prevention. If the worker can recognize what impact outer forces have on people, it will be possible to remind communities and other social systems of the effect they have on the behavior of people. There is a growing recognition in all systems of our society that meaningful planning has to be done to help the social systems create positive outer forces. Recently there has been a push in industry to recognize and work with the outer forces created in the important area of employment.

A third use the social worker can make of the inner and outer forces framework is creating a classification system for the new theories that are developing in the area of human behavior. The worker can place the new theories from sociology, psychology, social work, psychiatry, and anthropology in the inner and outer forces framework, thus helping the learning process and increasing the understanding of those in the field of social work.

Additional Model Definition

To be more specific, the inner and outer forces have been divided into the micro, mezzo, and macro systems. It should be recognized that these systems overlap and are not all-inclusive. With the expanded definition (see Figure 4.3) of the inner and outer forces model, the social worker can sharpen assessment abilities. The following case illustrates the use made of the micro, mezzo, and macro designations.

George, an 18-year-old high school senior, was referred to the social worker because of his refusal to do any work in class. He presented himself in a belligerent, negative fashion, stating that he did not enjoy school and did not want to work.

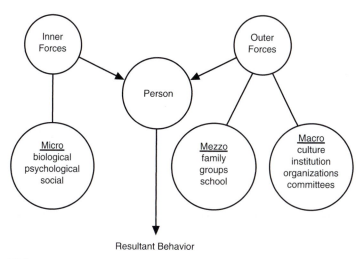

FIGURE 4.3

In the initial interviews the social worker explored along the lines of the micro, mezzo, and macro systems. There were no problems in the macro system. George and his family had lived in the same community for many years and had accepted the mores of the group. In the micro and mezzo systems, however, there were problems: George did not feel good about himself and had aggressive impulses that he couldn't control; and school personnel were pressuring him to make sure he would graduate. The worker discovered what he considered the most difficult problem, however, in the micro system. George was suffering from a learning disability and couldn't read. His inability to perceive and organize the written word was striking. George had struggled through all his classes in a small rural school not having the capacity to read.

The social worker proceeded to help George understand his reading problem as a biological failure and one that was not due to his laziness. Teachers were asked to modify their teaching techniques to allow George to do more verbal work than the rest of the class. The science teacher refused to go along with the social worker and continued to try to force him to read several chapters a day. George was hopeless in the class and responded with aggressive behavior. After intervention by the principal and the social worker, George was transferred into another class where the teacher was willing to cooperate.

George graduated from high school, although he still could not read. However, because of the efforts of the social worker and the school personnel, he felt less ashamed of himself and had less need to fight the world. The social worker discovered that the most important force in this young man's life at this particular time was his learning disability; the worker used the inner and outer forces model, focusing on the micro system of the inner force classification.

The Life Cycle and the Inner and Outer Forces Model

An important addition to the inner and outer forces model is the life cycle concept. Theorists in behavior recognize that there are stages of human development that seem to be universal. One simple developmental classification is childhood, adolescence, adulthood, and old age. Erik Erikson, who adapted his formulation of a life cycle from basic Freudian theory, developed an eight-stage classification that he felt identified the main life crises or stages, which are: (1) trust (0–1 year); (2) autonomy (1–3 years); (3) initiative (4–6 years); (4) industry (7–11 years); (5) identity (12–17 years); (6) intimacy (18–22 years); (7) caring (23–45 years); and (8) integrity (45+ years). The age ranges appearing next to the stages have been added to give the reader an approximation of the person's age at a given stage of development. Erikson's formulations are especially useful when combined with the inner and outer forces model in Figure 4.4.

The representation of Erikson's eight stages of life, utilizing the step configuration, gives one a sense of climbing and also moving ahead one step at a time. The step diagram is used to illustrate Erikson's epigenetic approach.

With the superimposition of the life stages diagram on the inner and outer forces model, the social worker can consider a person's problem from an organized, total approach. For instance, a child in the third grade is reported to be daydreaming too often

FIGURE 4.4

and not completing her assignments. The child has been referred to the social worker. Utilizing the model, the worker can ask the following questions.

1. What stage of life is the child in? What are the most important developmental tasks for the child at this time?
2. Is it an inner or an outer force that seems to be causing the problems? Is there a combination of pressure from both inner and outer forces?
3. If it seems to be the inner forces, is the main problem in the psychological or biological area within the micro system? Does the child have feelings of inferiority that prevent her from working or does she have something wrong with her eyes that prevents her from reading?
4. If the problem is mainly in the outer force area, is it in the mezzo or macro system? Perhaps the child has been having trouble in the family because of tremendous conflict between her mother and father. In the cultural area it could be discovered that the child's Hispanic parents speaking Spanish in her home makes it difficult to relate to class material written or spoken in English.

The previously stated questions that a social worker could ask about a client are shown in Figure 4.5. Stage 4, Industry, is highlighted. As the diagram is followed horizontally, the main systems of inner and outer forces are considered. This diagram can help

FIGURE 4.5

social workers assess the problems in a logical fashion. Also, it can assist the worker in looking across the individual's total experience (i.e., micro, mezzo, or macro).

Social Functioning

The inner and outer forces framework is a tool to help the social worker explain some of the reasons why individuals may not function well in their environment. The behavior that is produced by the inner and outer forces can be defined as being on a continuum from functional to dysfunctional.

The intervention and aid of social work are indicated when people unaided cannot cope with social obligations and commitments, and when problems interfere with relationships that exist within the family, at school, on the job, or in other social groupings. The aim of social work is to improve and enhance social functioning.

During the history of social work, many attempts have been made to describe its nature and purpose and to differentiate social work from other helping professions. Social work has determined that "social functioning" is its central purpose. Intervention by social workers is to give prominence to the restoration, promotion, and enhancement of social functioning.

Levels of Social Functioning

In their various roles—in the home, on the job, and in the neighborhood—individuals are not always at their best. Social workers have long since learned that individuals differ in their role performances, from moment to moment, and from other individuals. Nevertheless, the functioning of some people can be so grossly impaired as to preclude their doing anything for themselves.

A group—for example, a family—may be said to function in a rewarding and functional manner when its several members have more or less agreed-on goals; the transmission of ideas among members is clear and unclouded; individuals reciprocally contribute to their own needs and to the interests of each other; activities are mutually supported with an adequate resource base; and disorganizing influences from the outside are effectively checked and held to a minimum. A community, or social system, is functional or dysfunctional depending on how responsive or unresponsive it is to the needs of the people who created it. For example, a school system that is constructively educational for *all* the children of all the people can be described as a functional system. Conversely, one that consistently records a 50 percent dropout rate and does not promote the curiosity and mental growth of pupils is dysfunctional to some degree.

All professions take cognizance of the *wholeness* of individuals. However, because life is complex and science is specialized, each profession must confine itself to some aspect of the human condition. Medicine, except for the fields of public health and preventive medicine, confines itself largely to work with those who are ill. Education is focused on teaching methods, learning theory, motivation, and other aspects of pedagogy. The rites and ordinances of the church and scriptural exposition are functions of the ministry.

Social work places its primary attention on an individual's relationships with other human beings. It focuses on how and with what effectiveness the person performs various social roles. Threats to, or actual impairment of, role function are the situations to which the profession addresses itself. The social worker analyzes the social relationships, works with clients to find solutions to the factors that interfere with social functioning, and also gives direction to the enrichment of human association.

A typical example of a problem is an illness causing inability of the wage earner to work or to work efficiently. Illness can result in loss of employment and income for the family and in breakdown in family as well as employee–employer relationships. Social work, when called on to intervene, concerns itself with the fact of unemployment, rehabilitation of the wage earner, the family's income-maintenance needs, and the shift in role relationship within the family due to the individual's illness.

A second illustration involves a mother suffering from "nervous exhaustion." She spent several days in a hospital. In a few weeks following her release, her symptoms reappeared, and it was necessary for her to be readmitted. A social study disclosed that her home was literally making her sick, and that her marital and family relationships would have to improve before she could derive any lasting benefit from medical treatment.

Social work is an enabling profession that helps with problems of living and human relationships and with the dysfunctional complexities of various social institutions. Social work assumes humanity's worth and preeminence and takes the position that people inherently have the potential for dealing with their problems. However, at times and under stressful circumstances, people often need help. Social work addresses itself to this need and has systematically developed a helping philosophy and the knowledge and skill to implement this philosophy.

Social work is not antiseptic. It does not aim to make life free from stress-producing problems or to relieve people of their responsibilities. Problems can be building blocks. Crises are frequently the mainspring of adaptive behavior.

Generally, people struggle successfully, often with imagination and ingenuity, with their everyday concerns. Many people learn to cope with stress and to take minor crises in stride. Some, spurred on by disabilities, rise to great heights. In other situations, however, people are faced with problems they cannot solve by themselves. Some of these are personal, resulting from weak egos or poor native endowment; some are family induced and conditioned; and others result from community pressures and failures.

Abandoned, neglected, and deprived children may be incapable of functioning independently. As people grow old, many rely on their families or society to meet their basic needs. No age group, economic class, or society is ever completely free of difficulties that interfere with the role performance of some of its members.

A Base for Generalist Social Work Practice

The interactive perspective or inner or outer forces paradigm can be a basis for generalist social work practice. Generalist social work practice requires the worker both to be able to explain human behavior and to decide on a course of intervention to improve social functioning. The paradigm assists the practitioner to continually assess behavior across the micro, mezzo, and macro systems and to understand the tremendous forces that are brought to bear on the individual by these systems. The paradigm also utilizes the notion of systems theory, which recognizes the continual interaction of the systems and helps the worker understand the constant reconfiguration of the systems.

Because the generalist social worker must work with the micro, mezzo, and macro systems, it is important that each new social worker be grounded in the traditional social work methods. The rich history and methodology of social work practice with individuals, groups, and communities should be understood by the generalist social work practitioner. The following three chapters define each of the traditional social work methods that offer the generalist practitioner a base on which to build a practice.

In addition to the three traditional methods, the social work profession has always been interested in the methodology of administration. Because of social work knowledge, skills, and values, most social workers become administrators in their agencies. Also a profession is required to develop its knowledge base, and there has been an increased effort by social work to stress the importance of research. Social workers must evaluate their own practice to see if they are doing effective work and to improve their skills. Recently, the public has been pressuring for more accountability in all areas of social services. This text includes a chapter on administration and research, because these basic processes are so important for the beginning generalist practitioners to understand.

Summary

The social work profession is emphasizing the generalist perspective to deal with complexities of modern society. The generalist perspective helps the social work practitioner deal with multiperson systems and gives direction in assessing the interplay of personal and collective issues with a variety of human systems. Both baccalaureate and master's programs are focusing their curriculum on generalist practice.

The inner and outer forces paradigm is an introductory framework that helps generalist practitioners both explain behavior and plan meaningful intervention. The paradigm is based on social systems and ecological theory. It also includes a developmental component that places the human growth process in perspective.

Social work is an enabling profession that helps with problems of living and human relationships and with dysfunctional complexities of individuals and social institutions. The profession has determined that social functioning is the central purpose of its existence and sets about to enhance or restore social functioning of individuals, groups, or communities.

Because the social work generalist practitioner works with individuals, groups, and communities, the person who chooses this profession should know and understand the traditional social work methods as well as the overall generalist perspective. The traditional methods of working with individuals, groups, and communities have a rich history and have provided the means of helping many people. Administration and research have also played a major role enabling the development and maintenance of the profession. The remaining chapters of this book offer the new generalist practitioner and others an overview of traditional social work methods and fields of practice.

Selected References

BRILL, NAOMI, and JOANNE LEVINE, *Working with People: The Helping Process*, 7th ed. Boston: Allyn & Bacon, 2002.

DAY, PHYLLIS, SANDRA M. SHELLY, and HARRY J. MACY, *Social Working: Exercises in Generalist Practice*, 2nd ed. Boston: Allyn & Bacon, 2000.

DEREZOTES, DAVID S., *Advanced Generalist Practice*. Thousand Oaks, CA: Sage, 2000.

EDWARDS, RICHARD L., ed., *Encyclopedia of Social Work*, 19th ed., Vol. 12. Washington, DC: NASW Press, 1995.

KIRST-ASHMAN, KAREN K., and GRAFTON H. HULL, JR., *Generalist Practice with Organizations and Communities*. Chicago: Nelson-Hall, 1998.

KIRST-ASHMAN, KAREN K., and GRAFTON H. HULL, JR., *Understanding Generalist Practice*. Chicago: Nelson-Hall, 1995.

MILEY, KARLA KROGSRUD, MICHAEL O'MELIA, and BRENDA DUBOIS. *Generalist Social Work Practice: An Empowerment Approach*, 4th ed. Boston: Allyn & Bacon, 2004.

ZASTROW, CHARLES, and KAREN K. KIRST-ASHMAN, *Understanding Human Behavior and the Social Environment*, 3rd ed. Chicago: Nelson-Hall, 1994.

Notes

1. Karla Krogsrud Miley, Michael O'Melia, and Brenda L. DuBois, *Generalist Social Work Practice* (Boston: Allyn & Bacon, 1995), p. 10.

2. David S. Derezotes, *Advanced Social Work Practice* (Thousand Oaks, CA: Sage, 2000), p. x.

3. Council on Social Work Education, *Educational Policy and Accreditation Standards* (Alexandria, VA: CSWE, 2001), p. 8.

4. Karen K. Kirst-Ashman and Grafton H. Hull, Jr., *Generalist Practice with Organizations and Communities* (Chicago: Nelson-Hall, 1998), p. 4.

5. Karen K. Kirst-Ashman and Grafton H. Hull, Jr., *Generalist Practice with Organizations and Communities*, 2nd ed. (Belmont, CA: Brooks/Cole, 2001), pp. 21–26.

6. Karla Krogsrud Miley, Michael O'Melia, and Brenda DuBois, *Generalist Social Work Practice: An Empowering Approach*, 4th ed. (Boston: Allyn & Bacon, 2004), p. 80.

7. Council on Social Work Education, *Education Policy*, p. 10.

8. Robert L. Barker, *The Social Work Dictionary*, 3rd ed. (Washington, DC: NASW Press, 1995), p. 385.

9. Some of the following material is adapted from Milton G. Thackeray, Rex A. Skidmore, and O. William Farley, *Introduction to Mental Health: Field and Practice* (Englewood Cliffs, NJ: Prentice Hall, 1979), pp. 155–166.

5

Social Work Practice with Individuals

Suzanne stepped into the office of the clinical social worker and was offered a seat. She was an attractive young woman in her early thirties. She appeared neatly dressed and well groomed. Her affect seemed appropriate and her responses were very polite, causing the practitioner to initially wonder why she was seeking help. After an exchange of pleasantries, the worker asked how she might be of assistance. Suzanne responded by saying she felt so foolish for being there. She said she had everything a person could want—a wonderful husband, two beautiful children, a nice home in a great neighborhood, and the ability to stay at home because of her husband's employment. Then, her affect quickly changed and her eyes welled up with tears when she said, "I'm so miserable. I'm in a state of panic most of the time and I can't stand it. I don't want to be around my husband and that's not right. He's a good person and hasn't done anything wrong." As the session passed, Suzanne revealed the reason behind her change in mood. As a child she had been sexually

molested by her stepfather. She assumed she had gotten over the effects from it when she moved out, the summer following high school graduation. She finished her college education, had worked a couple of years, then married the "man of her dreams." They were able to purchase a home and together decided to start a family. They were delighted when she gave birth to their son. A couple of years passed and they felt right about having a second child. She reported that "things couldn't have been better" when she delivered a daughter. She had felt like their family was complete until a few months ago. Their daughter, Megan, now a toddler, had full range of the house. But when little Megan began climbing up into her father's lap, that brought on a flood of memories from Suzanne's past. She thought she was over the effects of being abused by her stepfather, but now it was all coming back and she didn't know how to deal with it. Most of all, she feared for her daughter, believing it would happen to her. She sat sobbing, then she asked, "Can you help me?"

Work with the Individual—A Generalist Approach

From its inception, the profession of social work has been vitally interested in helping individuals help themselves. The worth and dignity of the individual charts the course of modern social work practice. The goals of the individual are embedded in the theory and practice of social work and are exemplified in its values and traditions.

Systems theory is widely accepted and applied as a paradigm within the profession of social work. A system is made up of interconnected parts from different levels. These parts come together to make a functioning whole. Over the years, social work has adopted concepts from systems theory and applied them to a working model for the study of people, groups, and organizations as well as developing methods for assisting or intervening at various levels within the system. Common terminology in the profession is to use three broad levels within the system to describe points of study, entrance, assessment, and/or interventions. The three levels are known as micro, mezzo, and macro, as discussed in Chapter 4. In each level, specific components or groupings have been identified. For example, the "micro system refers to an individual. In a broad sense, a person is a type of system that entails biological, psychological, and social systems. All of these systems interact. A micro orientation to social work practice involves focusing on an individual's needs, problems, and strengths. It also stresses how that individual might address issues, generates solutions, and make the best, most effective choices possible."[1] The mezzo level includes any small group such as a family, a treatment group, or a task-oriented group. The macro level includes larger components of systems such as an entire organization, a community, or a nation.

Social work with individuals, at the micro level of a system, has been one of the three main thrusts of generalist practice. In the main, however, levels of practice are often combined to maximize the services provided to clients. For example, a worker may engage and intervene with a client as an individual (*micro* level) or as a member of a family (*mezzo* level), as is often the case when providing clinical social work or direct practice services. Yet, the practitioner may also choose to include additional interventions such as a treatment group at the *mezzo* level as well as helping communities organize their resources in dealing with a social problem at the *macro* level.

Using the case study at the beginning of the chapter to illustrate how this is likely to play out in the world of the practitioner, the clinical social worker would have met Suzanne in an outpatient clinic of a community mental health center. Because of her training, the practitioner is prepared to work directly with Suzanne to help her with her anxious, angry, guilty, and depressive feelings. To do this she spends time trying to understand the feelings and thoughts expressed by the client as they relate directly or indirectly to those experiences resulting from the years of abuse. The practitioner also sees the need to help Suzanne and her husband with their relationship that is currently suffering due to Suzanne's general fear and mistrust of men. In addition, the practitioner may recommend to Suzanne that she attend a support group she sponsors for survivors of childhood sexual abuse. This will allow her the opportunity to meet with others and learn that she is not an isolated victim. It will also provide her an opportunity to learn valuable coping skills from others as they too have learned to deal with their own pain. Plus, the social worker may also be actively involved in her community by sitting on a board at the YWCA. There she is able to provide her clinical expertise and input into awareness programs provided by the organization to identify and assist victims of abuse early as well as establish programs for the prevention of sexual abuse in the community. Thus, generalist practitioners are knowledgeable and skillful in the application of methods at all three levels (micro, mezzo, and macro) of a system, yet may choose to focus or concentrate their practice primarily in one of the three areas.

This chapter focuses on the working individuals at the micro level of practice. The approach is commonly referred to today as *clinical social work* or *direct practice*.

Clinical social work[*] is a method of practice employed by thousands of social workers in a wide variety of social services, institutional settings, and private practice. We have chosen to use the term *clinical social work* because of its development as a primary method of practice in recent years and because the term is indigenous to the practice of social work.

Before the term *clinical social work* appeared, *social casework* was used in the literature. However, its beginnings were neither smooth nor well accepted. As far back as 1909, Mary K. Sinkovitch declared at the conference on Charities and Corrections: "I believe that this paper will interest nobody, for I think that the modern emphasis is so strongly on preventative work of a social character, that casework is secretly, if not openly, despised. The general feeling is that casework is a small affair, unimportant, a necessary evil, a depressing piece of business, a practically hopeless job."

Since at least 1982, clinical work is virtually the antithesis of Sinkovitch's earlier characterizations. Its emphasis is primarily on the provision of services to individuals who are receiving social work services. Clinical work is no longer despised, although most people would like to see a diminution or disappearance of personal and social problems addressed by practitioners. The literature, however, attests to support for the inclusion of clinical work among clientele receiving services. An assortment of public institutions recognize and support clinical work as viewed by licensure laws and third-party reimbursement.

A great deal of back-and-forth jockeying takes place among professionals on the issue of effectiveness of treatment and applied modalities. This subject has been tested and researched, yet most will agree that clinical practice needs ongoing validation. Social workers insist that practice be subjected to critical review. They believe that practitioners should be held accountable for what they do and for their social work competence.

Knowledge and skills derived from clinical social work have also been applied to mezzo and macro levels of social work. In a society of rapid change, clinical work is a mitigating influence for individuals who experience psychological, interpersonal, and social problems.

Clinical Social Work Defined

Clinical social work is an outgrowth of what was formerly recognized as social casework. *Social casework,* the preferred term for the greater part of the first half of the twentieth century, when one's primary method of intervening was with individuals and families, has been defined as "the orientation, value system, and type of practice used by professional social workers in which psychosocial, behavioral, and systems concepts are translated into skills designed to help individuals and families solve intrapsychic, interpersonal, socioeconomic, and environmental problems through direct face-to-face relationships."[2] A more

---

[*]The term *casework* was widely used during the first half of the century and has been replaced by *clinical social work, direct practice*, or the broader term *micro/mezzo practice*. Currently, *clinical* or *direct social work practice* are the preferred terms when working with individuals, along with families and small groups. The terms *micro, mezzo*, and *macro* are descriptions of practice approaches at different levels within a system and are associated with the generalist model of practice. For this chapter, we selected the term *clinical social work* to represent practice with individuals.

recent definition for *clinical social work,* as accepted by NASW's board of directors in 1984, and revised in 1989, reflects principles and ideas similar to social casework, that of improving people's functioning through the implementation of interventions, yet it has been expanded and is more comprehensive.

> Clinical social work shares with all social work practice the goal of enhancement and main-tenance of psychosocial functioning of individuals, families, and small groups. Clinical social work practice is the professional application of social work theory and methods to the treatment and prevention of psychosocial dysfunction, disability, or impairment, including emotional and mental disorders. It is based on knowledge of one or more theories of human development within a psychosocial context.
>
> The perspective of person-in-situation is central to clinical social work practice. Clinical social work includes interventions directed to interpersonal interactions, intrapsy-chic dynamics, and life-support and management issues. Clinical social work services consist of assessment; diagnosis; treatment, including psychotherapy and counseling; client-centered advocacy; consultation; and evaluation.[3]

All of this is implemented in compliance with the values and ethical standards set forth by the profession.

In recent years, the incorporation of culturally sensitive practice has been added. Race, ethnicity, and culture are important factors that influence a person's identity, choices, and opportunities. To more effectively serve people from differing backgrounds and minority groups, Jackson writes that we need to incorporate the following professional beliefs and practices:

- an appreciation of clients' identities and worldviews;
- attention to contextual factors that influence clients' needs, concerns, and problems; and
- anticipation of clients' initial suspicion or lack of trust.[4]

Clinical social work, as a method of practice, is about helping people solve prob-lems. It is individualized, scientific, and artistic. It helps individuals with personal as well as external and environmental matters. It is a method of helping by developing a relation-ship with the client that taps personal and other resources for coping or solving problems. Interviewing and assessment are major tools of clinical work. Changes in attitudes, thoughts, and behaviors are affected by the dynamics of the client–social worker relation-ship. The possible need for the person to obtain help from one or more community services is also facilitated by the process. This method of practice also involves an understanding of the potential influences of the biological, psychological, environmental, and cultural ele-ments on the behavior of the individual.

History of Social Casework and Clinical Social Work

Stereotyping, making broad generalizations about individuals and situations, is the antithe-sis of modern direct or clinical practice. Yet, the past has been punctuated with efforts to lump categories of individuals together for convenient classification, if not for study and favorable attention. The "workhouse test" and the "less eligibility" clauses of the infamous

English Poor Laws are based, in part, on naive and unfounded general assumptions, namely that *all* the poor are poor because of ignorance, willful refusal to work, shiftlessness, and depravity; that assistance to all of them should be made noxious, given in small amounts, extended for short periods of time, and only for emergencies. For only in this way can *poor* people be made to work, sense their responsibility, and be protected from the evils of relief.

The Association for Improving the Conditions of the Poor (AICP), founded in America in 1843, approached the problem of poverty individually. The aims of the AICP were to "combat poverty primarily through 'character building' activities." Volunteers tried to get poor people to abstain from alcohol, become more self-disciplined, and acquire the work ethic. Many of the methods and goals of AICP were later adopted by some Charity Organization Societies (COSs) and by friendly visitors.[5]

The COS, established in the United States in 1877, gave additional impetus to individualization and casework. The main plan of this organization included an investigation of applicants to determine need, central registration, recording, relief-giving, and the use of the volunteer family visitor.

It was probably through the efforts of the family visitor that the concept of *scientific charity* evolved and the seeds of social casework were sown. The visitors discovered that all poor people are not alike and that they should not be treated in the same manner. Various papers presented at the National Conference of Charities and Corrections during this period enunciated the principle of individualization. They affirmed that the aim of the COS was to reach the individual, and that its broad purpose was restoration of function, not detection of imposters on relief. "The poor, and those in trouble worse than poverty, have not in common any type of physical, intellectual or moral development, which would warrant an attempt to group them as a class."[6]

With the development of schools of social work at the turn of the century, *visitors in training* received instruction in methods of investigation, diagnosis, and treatment from experienced social workers. Developing out of the COS movement the first family welfare association was organized in 1905. Pioneered by Mary Richmond and Frances H. McKlean, family service societies, numbering over 300, offered specialized casework services to thousands of clients. *Social Casework,* journal of the Family Service Association of America, grew out of the efforts of this great pioneer movement.

Preoccupation with social conditions external to the individual was characteristic of casework during the early part of the twentieth century. Finding work for families in distress, getting all children to school, and placing children in institutions when abused, neglected, and abandoned were natural products of this type of practice. The thinking was that if the environment could not be changed, the individual should be removed from the environment, even if it meant separating families.

A shift in emphasis from external *sociological* factors to the individual's conscious social attitudes marked an important shift in the development of social casework. Problems were considered as the outgrowth of real-life experiences, such as neglect and rejection, and dealt with at the conscious level. This shifting of emphasis posed a need for new knowledge about the individual, and it was at this time that the impact of dynamic psychology and psychoanalysis was felt. Dynamic psychology shed new light on the importance of instinctual drives as part of psychobiological growth, in addition to life experiences and the part played by repression and the unconscious in personality makeup and problems.

As new schools of psychology, sociology, and psychiatry began to emerge, starting in the early 1900s, their influence on the study and treatment of individuals and families had an impact on schools of social work and on professional practice. Prominent schools of thought included those such as the aforementioned dynamic psychology, including Freud and those who followed him (Erikson, Anna Freud, and Adler); behavioral (Pavlov and Skinner); humanistic (Rogers and Pearls); the cognitive movement (Ellis and Beck); family therapies (Minuchin, Haley, and Ackerman), and the research on human biology. (The names identified with each of the prominent schools is not meant to be a complete list. It is provided so that students will recognize some of the individuals associated with each school.) Although our profession has borrowed from these schools, the difference between social work and the other professions is that the individual is viewed from a broader perspective, as more than only their biological and psychological makeup. The influence of social or environmental forces are deemed to be just as important and in need of change, depending on the nature of the problem, as the client.

With the emergence of skills necessary for the practice of social work with individuals, families, and groups, and the acceptance of social workers as health care providers as well as recipients of third-party payments from insurance companies, in the 1970s states began licensing social work practitioners. The title most often identified with state licensure acts is "Licensed Clinical Social Worker."

Clinical social work was formally recognized by NASW, as a method of practice, when it established a task force on the topic in 1978. The task force became the Provisional Council on Clinical Social Work in 1982. The Provisional Council established NASW's standards for the practice of Clinical Social Work in 1984, with the standards being revised in 1989. "Historically, the social work profession has focused on both people and their social environment. Clinical social work, whose focus is on individuals, families, and groups, has its roots in social casework, which always has been a primary method for the delivery of social work services. . . . Clinical practice continues to be an integral part of the services delivered in agency settings. At the same time, an increasing number of clinical practitioners have been moving into independent private practice."[7]

Trends in Casework and Clinical Work

G. Stanley Hall, who invited Sigmund Freud to this country in 1910, and William White, who later presented Freud's work, paved the way for the introduction of psychoanalytic theory and *depth** psychology into the casework movement. This was the mental hygiene and psychiatric era of social work. In the decade following World War I, the psychosocial component of the problem-solving method in social casework became the focus. There had been a decided shift in interest from sociological improvements to those in which psychology predominated, placing the individual and inner forces squarely in the center of the stage.

---

*By "free association" and "dream analysis" Freud learned that certain ideas, mental images, and emotions hidden away in the unconscious were often driving forces of behavior. By helping patients become aware (making conscious) of these "depth" elements, the individual could often learn to deal with disturbing intrapsychic forces.

Deluged with psychoanalysis and *depth psychology,* caseworkers struggled to retain their social work identity in the twenties; nevertheless, it was during this period that individual therapy came into its own. Whereas the friendly visitor of the prepsychoanalytic era more or less intuitively relieved the patient's feelings in the last five or ten minutes of the interview, by "dwelling upon hopeful and cheerful things," the caseworker consciously handled anxiety, helped the client to help himself or herself, and used relief as a tool of treatment. Emotions, attitudes, repressed conflicts, and the struggle within the unconscious became an integral part of social casework understanding and method.

The social and economic needs of the Great Depression refocused sociological and reality considerations for social work and compelled action on the part of the federal government. This was the period of the many work programs such as the Federal Emergency Relief Act, the Works Progress Administration, and Public Works Administration, and the Civilian Conservation Corp, culminating in the Social Security Act of 1935. The Depression resulted in a healthy turnaround from emphasis on psychological causation to the renewed study of economics, budgets, and environmental factors. Actually the pendulum swung from one extreme to the other, and over the years the two have come closer together.

According to Helen Perlman:

> A growing rapproachment between the social sciences and dynamic psychiatry has yielded a number of ideas of potential usefulness for caseworkers. Consonant with casework's focus upon the social environment are concepts such as these: role performance, as index of social functioning and as cause as well as effect of personality disturbances; culture identifications as affecting personality, behavior, interpersonal conflicts, caseworker-client relationships; class differences in behavior standards and values, as determinants of responses to given situations; social stability in its relation to personal stability; and so on. Practice has yet to test the actual value and import of these ideas for casework.[8]

There has also developed a renewed interest in the family, family dynamics, and the interaction of family members with the result that families are "better understood today and therefore potentially better dealt with. . . . Thus 'family diagnosis' and 'family treatment' are theoretical and methodological problems in casework today" and there is a greater interest than ever before in the "hard-to-reach" individual and family, in efforts to conceptualize practice, in research and evaluation.

The problem-solving method widely applied in social work today, combining work with individuals, families, small groups, and organizations, marks a shift from the much narrower focus of practice utilized in traditional casework approach. The trend in clinical work today views the "person" (with biological and psychological traits) in the context of his or her "environment" (family, neighborhood, ethnic and cultural as well as economic and political influences). This person-in-environment or systems perspective is now a fundamental paradigm that guides social work practice and posits that the continual and reciprocal interaction between the two (individual and his or her environment) is an ongoing process that shapes both. Although clinical work primarily intervenes on the individual and/or the family (micro, mezzo) levels, assessment and interventions more likely take place at multiple levels. Thus the practitioner today must be trained in more than just theories of psychology or sociology because assessments and planning for interventions using a person-in-environment model as a guide will expand the practitioner's view to incorporate multiple areas of influence on the individual. The scientific base, the search for new knowledge, and philosophical assumptions regarding the worth and value of the individual will, however, remain.

The Practice Framework

Purpose, values, sanctions, knowledge, and methods are at the heart of social work practice with individuals. Purpose is the *raison d'être* of practice. Values determine worker attitudes and approaches. Sanctions are society's mandates and provisions of social work expressed in structural arrangements, the law, and policy statements. The knowledge base provides the facts, concepts, and principles for practice, whereas the methods are both the science and art of applying theory to practice.

Purpose

The purpose of social work practice is to prevent or ameliorate those conditions which contribute to the breakdown of a healthy relationship between an individual and his or her family, other associates, or the environment. It helps people to identify and resolve problems in their relationships or, at least, to minimize their negative effects. In addition, social work seeks to strengthen the maximum potential in individuals, groups, and communities.

Social Work Values

Social work assumes the inherent worth and importance of the individual and the interdependence between the individual and society. In the democratic tradition, powers not delegated are reserved to the individual and to the people. Social institutions are the creation of people, acting as individuals or with others, and are subordinate to their desires and wishes. They were formed by individuals and exist to serve them. They can be changed, constantly renewed, allowed to decay or even dismantled; but the individual remains and enjoys the right to self-determination. Emphasis is placed on the importance of respect for the dignity of the individual and on his or her ability to make important decisions.

Basic assumptions about people profoundly influence professional practice. The following value postulates are examples of influences in the practice of social work and social work with individuals.

Value Assumption on Individual Worth and Capacity

The dignity and worth of a person is believed to be such a significant element in the provision of services, as well as the professional relationship with clients, that it is recognized as one of the six core values of the profession of social work. A "worth" value places the individual in a position of eminence. He or she is above objects and institutions, worth caring for because he or she is an individual. This is one of the entitlements a person does not have to deserve. Others include respect, dignity, and opportunities to express individuality.

The value of worth suggests that the individual has the ability to guide his or her actions and the potential for determining goals and their achievement. The person's worth is validated equally by his or her decision to achieve potential or to permit it to lie unused, by a decision to achieve or merely vegetate.

Uniqueness Value

Belief in a person's uniqueness and individuality guide social workers toward acceptance of individual's differences, even to viewing them as assets. Strength in role relationships is viewed as coming from differences. Marriage, for example, is enhanced by the contributions of husband and wife who combine their separate qualities of mind, feeling, and performance. Enhancement in human associations is recognized as deriving from differences organized for the good of the group. The perception of uniqueness, as a part of the social worker armamentarium, guides the application of the casework process.

The Value Postulate of Self-Determination

As applied to the process of clinical social work this value concept clearly recognizes that the client is his or her own person. Whether to accept or decline a service is the client's decision. The client, not the worker, makes the choice among alternatives. As part of this process the worker may discuss and consider options, elaborate these, and help weigh their pros and cons. The worker may suggest preferences and cite evidence for them, but still retains awareness of what he or she is doing and clearly communicates that these are the client's prerogatives.

Self-determination means that the client will decide whether or not to engage in the therapeutic process. Self-determination is affirmed, explicated, and implemented at the beginning, in the middle, and at the end of the process. It is part of each component and guides the interaction from moment to moment. Self-determination implies questioning and answering questions. It implies giving and taking, struggle, risk, pain, suffering, failing, and self-fulfillment. In all stages of service delivery the client remains free to withdraw or to continue.

The social worker remains effectively and mentally neutral, but may share ideas, feelings, experiences, along with expressing interest, concern, sympathy, and empathy.

Impositions that remove free choice and self-determination may damage the relationship and weaken the client's problem-solving resolve and capacity. Furthermore, they are likely to be perceived as unwelcome intrusions. The social worker applies knowledge, understanding, and skill, with discipline and intelligence and with the basic value assumption that the individual has the need and the right to make his or her own choices and decisions.

Sanctions

Social work practice with individuals, like all other methods of practice, is directly or indirectly under the auspices of various governmental and/or private agencies that sanction the work. Governmental agencies are intended to express the will of the people. Private voluntary associations are also mandated by the people to serve human needs. The authorization for services is provided by law or by policy-making bodies in bylaws and constitutions of agencies reflecting the wishes of the people who support the services of the agencies.

A working definition of *social work practice,* as defined by NASW, states that it "consists of the professional application of social work values, principles, and techniques to one or more of the following ends: helping people obtain tangible services; counseling and psychotherapy with individuals, families, and groups; helping communities or groups provide or improve social and health services; and participating in legislative processes.

The practice of social work requires knowledge of human development and behavior; of social, economic, and cultural institutions; and the interaction of all these factors."[9]

For years, social work has been recognized at local, state, national, and international levels as a profession that provides services to help meet the needs and improve the conditions of people. Authority is derived from government sanctions and laws recognizing those who are trained by the profession as having legitimate knowledge and skills, along with a value base and ethical standards, to provide services to numerous people, agencies, communities, or groups. State licensure or certification laws require social work practitioners to obtain a level of educational competence that is recognized by both the Council on Social Work Education (CSWE) and NASW. At the BSW and MSW levels, this includes obtaining knowledge and skills in five core areas (human behavior and the social environment, policy, research, practice, and a practicum). Those who wish to be licensed as clinical social workers must continue to receive supervision for the equivalent of two years of full-time employment in clinical social work–related practice following the completion of an MSW degree. Along with obtaining supervision, the applicant must obtain a minimum of 70 percent on a state-approved exam that tests for knowledge (assessment and theories of practice) applicable to clinical practice. Those who are not licensed, but working in direct practice or clinical settings, are supervised by those who are more experienced, both by education and practice, whereas all social workers are required to adhere to the ethical standards of the profession as well as the laws and guidelines for practice set forth by the federal and state governments, in addition to the policies of the agency.

Knowledge

The theories applied to clinical social work are derived basically from the profession of social work, other social and behavioral science fields, as well as practice. Research contributes to the knowledge base and appears to be growing in sophistication and importance.

The profession continues to recognize the contributions from the behavioral, social, and biological sciences. Among the more important contributing disciplines are humanistic psychology, ego psychology, cognitive and behavioral psychology, and the various theoretical developments in family therapy, sociology, social psychology, psychiatry, biology, and cultural anthropology.

Classical and operant psychologies are well-integrated theories and readily apply to clinical practice, especially with children and certain behavioral and affective disorders. Behavior modification does not use a theory of personality. It proceeds from assumptions about operant behavior and practice focused on observable behavior that can be researched and explicated.

Clinical social work applies role theory to practice. Role theory illuminates understanding of people using the services of social agencies, who frequently believe they have failed in one or more of their social roles or in society's expectations of them. Practitioners understand that social roles are culturally ascribed or achieved. Everyone chooses from among many roles within the group or culture to which he or she belongs. The performance or behavior of the individual in these roles, with some leeway, can be fairly accurately predicted. Social role becomes a determinant of behavior and cuts across a wide variety of situations in which individuals find themselves. Knowledge about these forces and their culturally determined influences support practice with the individual.

Learning theory, adult socialization, small group, cognition theory, general systems theory and the ecological perspective, and discoveries in biology and endocrinology are other strains that have been adapted for use in clinical work and help broaden the theory base of practice.

Although social work "borrows" from psychology, sociology, and from the biological sciences, the profession itself orders, arranges, adapts, and determines the emphasis it will make of these contributions. Theories of psychology are integrated into the several models of practice. Theory applied becomes practice theory. Theory from the disciplines becomes less and less biopsychological-social-cultural and more social work practice theory. The contribution of social work to the integration and adaptation of theories takes on a dimension of major proportions and of itself is a major contribution to theory building.

Knowledge of the various services of the community is basic to the practice of social work. Knowledge from social work about social service agencies—legally mandated agencies sanctioned by the community, their organization and function—is an important part of the knowledge base of the profession. The function and purpose of agencies and referral procedures, and increasingly the legislative process, all provide essential underpinning for the delivery of services.

Services require community sanction and support. Laws when implemented by administrative policy become the framework in which a particular program operates. Knowledge of the constitutions and bylaws of voluntary organizations, and agency policy statements, serve a similar purpose for these organizations and are binding on the directors and administrative officers. They must be understood for sound social work practice with individuals.

Methods of Clinical Social Work

Methods of working with individuals and families have remained open. In the 1950s there was much discussion of the diagnostic and functional methods of casework. Since then, many models of practice have been identified: psychosocial, functional, task-centered, problem-solving, behavior modification, family group treatment, crisis-oriented brief treatment, and adult socialization. The most recent model focuses on generalist practice with an emphasis on clients' strengths as well as acknowledging and respecting the importance of diversity.

Social workers tend to be guided in practice by the theories of one or another model, by a method that combines principles from several theories and their own individual styles—which, in some particulars, may bear little resemblance to any of the existing models. New theories and new models of practice develop in response to the experience of practitioners to the many situations they encounter. Thus, theory building continues and practice is enriched by diversity as different methods are validated and guided by the values of the profession.

The trend in the new millennium appears to be what has been appropriately labeled a *multidimensional or integrative model:* (1) a greater utilization in practice of elements from a variety of theories and a blending of models, (2) selective interventions that are empirically grounded, (3) a solution orientation with less of a focus on the inner problems,

(4) direct practice embracing more than work with the individual, and (5) a greater utilization of interventive approaches that can be measured and validated.

Brief mention is made of several models of clinical casework over the past century. The *psychosocial* model was one of the first models to be developed and applied to the practice of social casework. Its psychological origins date back to the 1920s when psychoanalytic principles and theory were incorporated into the then largely sociological approach to casework. Conceptualizations, and refinements, of the psychosocial model are based on the pioneering work of Gordon Hamilton and her associates at the New York School of Social Work, now known as the Columbia University School of Social Work. Professor Hamilton referred to her work as an organismic approach to casework. Cause and effect relationships are identified between the individual and environment. Ego psychology and the behavioral sciences provide important underpinning for practice. Essentially this model has a Freudian theory base modified and adapted for use in social work practice.

The *functional* model was developed at the Pennsylvania School of Social Work in the 1930s. Emphasis was on the relationship, the dynamic use of time, and the "use of the agency" function. The psychology of Otto Rank provided underpinning as adapted for use by proponents of the functional school. Diagnostic categories have tended to be avoided as having limited usefulness in social work practice. For instance, how does one reconcile the concept of individuality and uniqueness with a pigeonholing of individuals into several classifications?

The *problem-solving* method is identified with the work of Perlman at the Chicago school. This model is formulated and made articulate in *Social Casework,* written by Perlman and published in 1957. A few characteristics of the problem-solving method include the identification of the problem by the person, subjective aspects of the person in the situation, the centrality of the person with the problem, the search for a solution to the problem, decision making, and action. The purposes of the process are to free the client for investment in tasks related to the solution of the problem, involve the client's ego in work designated to deal with the problem, and to mobilize inner and outer forces in the service of satisfactory role performance.

The *behavioral model* is Pavlovian and Skinnerian, and it began to be incorporated in the social work literature in the 1960s. Practice applying to this model lends itself to research because behavior to be modified is observable. This may be one of the chief values of behavior modification.

Behaviorists agree that symptoms are the same as other responses in that the behavior is mainly respondent or operant. Problematic behavior learned through the processes of conditioning reacts in the same way to laws of learning and conditioning as does "normal" behavior. It can be modified by applying what is known about learning and modification.

Task-centered casework, a "general service model" developed at the University of Chicago, first appeared in publications early in the 1970s. Designed to solve specific psychosocial problems of individuals or families, this model is a short-term, time-limited form of practice. Together the caseworker and client reach an explicit agreement on the particular problems to be worked on and also the probable duration of treatment. Organized around problem-solving actions developed collaboratively by the practitioner and client, the tasks assigned will state a general direction for the client's action or a specific behavior the client is to follow. By concentrating his or her effort in helping the client follow the program, the caseworker makes use of various interventions.

The *generalist practice model,* currently embraced by the profession, is influenced by the efforts of Gordon, Bartlett, and other social work educators to broaden the perspective of social work practice.[10] The Council on Social Work Education responded to their call for commonalities within the profession by implementing accreditation standards requiring the Bachelor of Social Work (BSW) and foundation year of the Master of Social Work (MSW) curriculum to contain courses designed to prepare students for generalist practice. Generalist practice is based on a problem-solving model from a systems or person-in-environment perspective. This model is applied with the unique qualities, values, and ethics espoused by social work.

The psychosocial, functionalist, behavioral, task-centered, problem-solving, and generalist models have been cited as trends of thought in the profession. In addition to these overarching models are approaches and methods utilized in the provision of clinical services with specific populations or areas of practice. Other approaches are identified as *family preservation, crisis intervention,* and *adult socialization.* These developments seem to be treatment approaches with an increasingly strong theoretical base. They are options of treatment in different developmental stages and have been tested in practice long enough to emerge as theoretical positions. They are examples of theory-building in process. What happens to them in the future will depend on what use is made of them in practice. Social work is a profession of practice, and theory is always subjected to application.

The Clinical/Direct Practice Process of Social Work

Study, assessment, intervention, and termination are main divisions of the clinical social work process (see Figure 5.1).

Study

In the study phase, the client is engaged in presenting the problem. The key is engagement. Frequently, clients seeking help have the expectation that the agency or the social work will take over. This is an erroneous conception of the therapeutic process, which may have resulted from the client's previous life experiences—with doctors, lawyers, the clergy, educators, and others whose help-giving models tend to be that of prescribing for, preparing briefs for, performing marriages for, and teaching by telling students what they are to learn. Engaging the client meaningfully begins with the study phase. It is one of the threads of the process that will continue to be interwoven throughout. Interaction and client participation are emphasized, not because of their special relationship to the beginning phase, but for their importance throughout the process as a setting for the process.

In the study phase, the client makes the important decision of whether to enter treatment. If the decision is not to accept the service, the initial contacts should be constructive and not diminishing experiences. The worker's attitude is an important controlling factor in what the client decides. Respect for the worth and dignity of the client and his or her right to self-determination will be communicated by interested concern, listening to statements of the problem, and by assurances that the views of the client are of paramount concern. Guided by social work values in each phase of the process, the worker will optimally

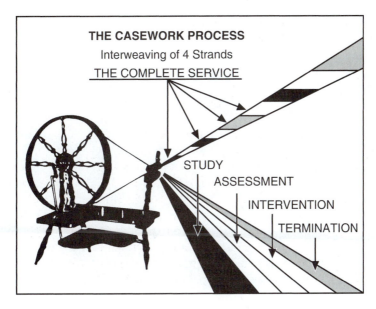

FIGURE 5.1

develop a helping relationship by cooperation and collaboration in addressing the problem and the tasks associated with it.

The emphasis on the interaction is on the here-and-now and on the problem not as might be perceived by the worker, but as experienced at the moment by the client. The problem, as presented in the initial phase, is either *the* problem for which help is sought or that part of it the client chooses at the moment to focus on. In later phases, as the relationship is tested by the client and proved to be sustaining, other aspects of the problem and possibly other problems will be focused on. The client's view and the worker's view remain fluid in the study phase.

During this phase, data-gathering and history-taking concentrate on relevance. There is no requirement for a complete longitudinal history. A sufficiency of facts may be required to satisfy the demands of the agency. If so, this consideration should be communicated to the client. Of greater importance, data and feelings as these are communicated in the interview provide important clues regarding the problem, the client's perception of the problem, and the way in the past he or she has handled the problem. Such data are useful for assessment purposes and for decisions on treatment goals. Data-gathering is not an end but a means and is justified only as it serves the purposes of assessment.

Assessment and intervention are phases that sometimes are mistakenly believed to occur in a fixed time frame, namely, following the study or initial phase. Actually, "hunching" on a problem begins in the study phase, often with the making of appointments or in the contacts with the referral source. Contacts during the initial phase may be among the most dynamic of the entire process. During this phase the client is likely to feel most helpless and vulnerable, hence most available to the helping process. At this point of crisis, sympathetic listening, demonstration of acceptance, reassurance, demonstration of confidence in ability,

Social worker talking to a client.

and judicious stroking can all be powerful tools in the hands of the skilled worker and can be highly therapeutic. The interventive potential of early encounters is inestimable. In fact, beginning social workers often underestimate the dynamic healing qualities of early encounters and misinterpret client's "dropping out of treatment" as rejection of the worker or the services when actually he or she has already received the help needed for a crisis.

The study-assessment-interventive phases blur and may proceed simultaneously. However, there tends to be an emphasis on time in one or the other, and although discrete stages are not the rule, it seems helpful in discussing the processes to recognize their separateness.

Evaluation and termination are also phases of the clinical process, which, although receiving an emphasis near the end of the process, are introduced early in the helping process, in the study phase, during the period of assessment, and in the interventive process itself. In each interview, the worker will ask himself or herself, and the client, to consider the importance of that interview in relation to goals. Also, terminal considerations are given as to how the client will function with greater satisfaction and self-reliance as a result of the interview and the steps taken to implement the problem-solving process. Transferability of gains in the interview to real-life situations is always uppermost in the process at the beginning, in the middle, and at the end. Termination occurs when the client has gained the strength, the understanding, and the problem-solving know-how necessary for successful coping with problems and life situations.

Assessment

Assessment provides a differential approach to treatment based on individual differences and needs. It clearly recognizes the uniqueness of every situation, the importance of treatment planning related to a particular problematic situation, area of family dysfunction, system breakdown, or trouble within a life situation. In addition, an individual's strengths need to be identified and utilized as part of the change process. Defining the problem is clearly a way of individualizing the person.

Assessment is fluid and dynamic. It is ever-changing, beginning at intake and continuing to termination. It is likely to be the emphasis of the worker–client effort to understand the problem in the situation. Assessment begins with a statement of the problem by the client. It is guided by what the client indicates to be the major problem and may penetrate a range of somatic, psychological, social, cultural, spiritual, and environmental forces. Assessment results in an understanding of the problem. It includes initial impressions that are confirmed, modified, or even rejected in the light of additional information as the case moves from moment to moment. There is a circular quality about assessment. It never ceases during the clinical process. It includes judgment about the strength and limitations of the individual in coping with the situation. Assessment addresses itself to strengths, capacities, limitations, motivation, and opportunity. Treatment planning and treatment itself are guided by assessment.

The functioning person, the person with mastering ego capacity, can be expected ordinarily to say what brings him or her to the agency. This becomes the interface between the worker and the client. The worker will apply his or her knowledge of forces, knowledge of life situations, problem-producing stresses, and understanding of people to the helping role by questions, comments, and many nonverbal ways. He or she will help achieve elaboration of the problem as may be required for treatment. Because of the ever-changing diagnostic nuances, this may be repeated during the process.

Assessment and diagnostic work should not result in the categorization of individuals, or in the application of labels to their problems, particularly when labels are likely to be misused and create a static situation where fluidity is called for. Social workers use psychosocial classifications but with a tentativeness that recognizes the dynamic and changing life situation. There is mutual agreement of the worker and the client in assessment. Goals must be congruent with the client's needs and the availability of services. These goals are respected, supported, and reinforced.

Intervention

Intervention or treatment begins with the first contact. The study process *is* treatment when it helps the client clarify the problem for himself or herself and make changes in his or her life situation resulting from this understanding. Interventive goals are determined by the client and the worker together. Intervention is determined by the client's need, and when the agency does not provide the service indicated the worker has the responsibility to help the client tap other sources.

The relationship is the mainspring of social work with individuals or any type of client, but it is extremely critical when directly working with a person. Warmth, genuineness, and congruence have been identified as essential qualities the worker must bring to the relationship. Combined with interviewing skills, the worker helps the client tell his or her story and make a partial approach to treatment so as not to be overwhelmed.

Interventive skills include interviewing, recording, letter writing, referrals to other agencies and services, and helping the client use personal and other resources. Interventive

efforts support and strengthen the client's ego through emotional catharsis, reassurance, clarification of the problem, and sympathetic listening. Intervention, geared to the worker–client
relationship, is guided by such basic principles as:

1. The client's right to determine his or her own course of action within the limits of his or
   her capacity to make sound choices. The client may have no more ability than to button
   a shirt or blouse; nevertheless, the decision to function to the limits of his or her capacity,
   or to button the shirt or blouse, is respected and encouraged, with the worker knowing
   that one small achievement can be the mainspring of an expanding capacity to achieve.
2. Acceptance of a client as is, implying acceptance of his or her capacity to change,
   and that he or she can and will utilize his or her resources to improve. In a nonjudgmental way, social work seeks to understand the individual or family, the reasons for
   their behavior, and to help them develop their potential for more satisfying social and
   personal adjustments.
3. Social work traditionally relates to strength rather than to pathology. Limitations are
   recognized and handled realistically, but the worker seeks to assess and develop
   strengths within the individual and his or her family.
4. The social worker seeks to understand the person and to help him or her plan for constructive change. He or she collaborates with the client on goal-setting and assessment, and supports the values of society.
5. Knowledge about the client's family and its situation is used responsibly for the welfare of the family and society. This permits sharing pertinent information wherever
   possible and appropriate and with the knowledge and consent of the client.
6. The family worker has a professional responsibility for the welfare of the total family. Social work is constantly evaluating the effect of treatment of one member of the
   family upon other members. A family-centered focus is maintained where intervention is carried out through work with one or several family members or through individual or joint interviews.
7. The family worker is responsible not only to the client but to himself or herself, the
   agency, the community, and the profession.
8. Innovations of professional activities, determined for the worker by various principles and concepts, must be consistent with the client's goals.
9. As mobilizers of material, environmental, and psychological resources, social workers array themselves with efforts to develop, improve, change, and strengthen services and to facilitate their constructive use by the client in need.

Termination

A decision to accept a "case," to intervene professionally, to provide help to an applicant
carries with it the assumption that at some point in the process the intervention will end.
Termination as used in social work means the ending or limiting of a process that was
commenced when the agency (worker) agreed to enter into the interventive process aimed
at delivering a service to a client with a problem. The processes of study, assessment, and
intervention do not continue forever. Termination plans need to be considered, and these
should be understood alike by the worker and the client.

Termination can be a dynamic of change and growth, a time when the client can look back with satisfaction on what has been accomplished. Most often initiated by the worker, termination that outlines realistic goals will affirm the importance of what the client can do and is expected to do in resolving problems and in achieving goals. Termination in effect signals that the worker has confidence in the client's ability to learn to cope with situations and to grow and that the role of the worker is enabling; he or she will serve as a resource for the client in the present situation.

Termination planning will avoid the fostering of crippling dependence and the false hope by some clients that in some magical way there can be a shifting of responsibility to the agency or to the worker. Termination, understandably, will receive the greatest emphasis as the ending of the relationship nears and will be a summation of gains made in the interventive process. This summation will be more than a recitation of the worker's observations; it will be a process entered into by both the worker and the client and includes self-assessment as well as worker contributions. Reassurance of the client's readiness to function more effectively will highlight this phase of the interventive process. When there are doubts and fears, these can be allayed by a review of realistic accomplishments and the readiness of the client to perform his or her various roles with greater self-assurance and adequacy.

Case Examples

The three case examples that follow are illustrative of three aspects of the clinical process—the interweaving phases of study, assessment, and intervention as they relate to the psychosocial model; task-centered casework; and the behavior modification model.

Psychosocial Model

Study.   *Such factors as the following, revealed in the initial interview, are noted and considered for assessment and intervention:*

Jessica, the only daughter in a family of six children, grew up having her parents always protecting her, limiting and controlling her activities, and often thinking for her. Even though she was married with three small children, not much had changed in her relationship with her parents since she was a child. They continued to be oversolicitous of her welfare, gave her money and gifts so that she wouldn't have "to go without anything."

Jessica liked to receive gifts, and the money always came in handy, but she didn't like the strings the parents attached their generosity. Mother always called Jessica for help if she was ill, or if she needed someone to run an errand. Mother also took it for granted that Jessica would do her ironing and her weekly cleaning. Father was sure Jessica would love to do the bookkeeping for his small business. When Jessica did not volunteer her services to her parents, they would ask her to do what they wanted.

Assessment.   *Jessica, excessively dependent on her parents, resented this dependency, and wanted to break out of the box she felt she was in. She also was resentful of the demands of her own children, even though this dependency was age appropriate. Much of the time she was angry with her husband because he didn't take more responsibility with the children and* *because he took her for granted. She complained that he assumed how she felt, what she liked and didn't like, and made decisions for her. She became furious when he said, "Come on, you'll like it," when he wanted to make love. She wanted to decide matters that affected her, although she admitted to indecision and being unable to make up her own mind.*

Her feelings of helplessness in social situations, with her children, her husband, and sometimes with neighbors and friends, appeared to be referable to the long period of time when the choices she made in myriad family matters were minimal.

Intervention.   *The goal was to support Jessica in efforts to become more self-reliant and to help her become less dependent. She was encouraged to make decisions affecting her life. She was helped to question her relationship with her mother. She was aided to understand why she resented her children's dependency and how to cope with this by encouraging them to be self-reliant. She learned, for example, that it was not necessary to continue to tie the shoelaces for their 5-year-old, but that she could teach this skill to the child.*

She was helped to understand her dependency and how to handle her relationships with others without feeling helpless and rejected. She was supported by the caseworker in the positions she took with her parents. For example, she was helped to say "no" to them when they asked for favors in return for the money they gave and to refuse the gifts if this meant that she couldn't be her own person.

Task-Centered Model

Study.   *Quanah, a 17-year-old pregnant girl, sought help at the Children's Service Society, a teen pregnancy program.*

She told the social worker that she was three months pregnant, frightened, and didn't know what she wanted to do. Although her parents were extremely upset, they were concerned about her and had urged her to come to the agency.

In interviews with the girl and her mother, the following list of significant options surfaced; Quanah listed the options in terms of priorities approximately as follows:

1. *Have the baby and give it up for adoption. She preferred to keep the baby, but realized that she was not ready to be a parent.*
2. *Have the baby, keep it, and marry the father when he is released from the army in two years. She is willing to get married, but the putative father is not, and for a variety of reasons her parents were adamantly opposed to the marriage.*
3. *Continue in high school while she is pregnant and prepare for graduation. She had one year to complete her high school work. An "A" student, she is highly motivated in academic studies and extracurricular activities. She sang in the school's chorus, played the violin, and participated in school plays. She definitely wants to finish high school and go to college.*
4. *Have an abortion. Her mother opposed this on religious grounds. Quanah, somewhat opposed to this, was not as strong in her view on abortion as her mother. Nevertheless, abortion was low on the list.*

Assessment.   *The problem was planning for an unwanted pregnancy. From the standpoint of the caseworker, the problem was one of assisting a young, immature woman make a decision*

Social worker discussing issues with a pregnant teenager.

about an unborn child, and possibly helping the girl's parents accept her decision. Quanah's feelings about what to do were mixed—she would like to keep the baby, but questioned her readiness to care for a child. She first thought of getting married, but discovered that the father was not ready for this step. She needed practical help, such as where to live, where to get a job so she could have some income, medical care including hospitalization, and a chance to finish high school.

Intervention.   *Specific interventive tasks that were addressed:*

1. *Quanah was allowed to discuss and weigh her options as she made her decision to have her baby.*
2. *Arrangements were made for her to attend a high school for pregnant teens within her school district.*
3. *She was scheduled for regular clinic checkups with an obstetrician who worked with the society.*
4. *She was paid a wage for light housekeeping in the foster home.*
5. *Provision was made for her to discuss her plans for the baby with the caseworker. Quanah learned the policies of the agency and was assured that as far as possible her wishes regarding the baby would be respected.*
6. *The putative father was included and he helped financially and in other ways to assist Quanah in her decision and with her plans.*
7. *At the end of six months, her case was terminated. She continued on with her education and earned her high school diploma and made plans to attend the local community college, having obtained grants to subsidize her tuition.*

This list of tasks illustrates only what specifically was done to solve a psychosocial problem. This outline fails to show the skill and technique employed to accomplish these and related tasks. It fails to indicate the sustaining nature and importance of the relationship between the worker and the client. Nor does it begin to suggest the support provided by an agency and its staff to the girl and her parents that made it possible for her to make sound decisions and choices.

We have attempted to illustrate in an oversimplified manner something of the nature of clinical work that is time limited, problem focused, and organized on the basis of a specific task to be accomplished. The social worker's role in carrying out the tasks is more implied than explicated in the outline, and the way the client and the worker collaborate is not fleshed out. Clinical social workers can be expected to use an array of interventive, often integrative modes, including tangible sociological reinforcers—a place to live, provisions for income, medical care, hospitalization, and transportation.

Behavior Modification Model

Study.   *In behavior modification, the therapeutic process is problem-focused and involves the observation of the behavior to be changed. Jacques had a behavior problem whose most objectionable aspects were hitting the other children, kicking various objects in the classroom, and swearing when the other children hit back or when the teacher corrected him.*

Assessment.   *The assigned clinical social worker[11] didn't look for the underlying causes of Jacques's behavior or try to get at the whys of it. Taking a "social history" was not the object of her efforts. Much more important was the charting of Jacques's behavior to determine its frequency and severity. During the observation and behavioral assessment period, it was noticed that the attention and response of the teachers and his classmates maintained Jacques's behavior. The way they conveyed attention was reinforcing.*

Intervention.   *The following brief statement by the social worker describes her effort to change Jacques's behavior:*

> *The expression "pay no attention" is perhaps closest to what must be done to discourage the patient's behavior. When we say "do not reinforce a behavior" we are actually saying "ignore the behavior." That is what I did. Every time Jacques would say crude words, kick the blocks around or express any form of aggressive behavior, I would ignore that behavior. I felt social reinforcement would be very important in modifying Jacques's behavior. Children repeat behavior if it is rewarded and avoid behavior if it is punished or ignored.*
>
> *Continuous social reinforcement was given to Jacques for any approved activity that took the place of his aggressive behavior. For example, prior to treatment, Jacques would kick and throw the building blocks when asked to clean up his mess and was reinforced by peers laughing when the teacher scolded him. After the treatment was started, I would ignore Jacques's aggressive behavior and socially reinforce the other children who were cleaning up their blocks by saying "Thank you, Bobby, for being such a good helper; your blocks look so straight and nice." Soon all the children were trying to get praise by putting away their blocks. After a while no one paid any attention to Jacques and he started participating in the cleanup. I would reinforce him verbally as I did the other children.*

By using behavior modification I was able to perform my therapy with a direct application of conditioning principles and techniques, which can be used to alter or remove specific undesirable, maladaptive, or abnormal behavior.

Behavior modification, as is true of other approaches discussed in this chapter, has been treated somewhat superficially. Anyone wanting to use the approaches now extant will want to avail himself or herself of detailed and excellent texts on the subjects.

In the case of Jacques one might observe that quality reinforcers will affect the increase or decrease of behaviors and the performance of other behaviors, that one or more of these would likely be used as reinforcers of behavior that was not disruptive, as soon as it occurred. Abused children may be vulnerable to further abuse because this is the only attention they have been getting and that they know. Also they may continue to remain silent about the abuse rather than tell on their parents for fear of being removed from their families. The case of Jacques is a good example of a beginning student's use of "inattention" that in this instance seemed to work.

The Multisystems Approach

Several traditional methods and "approaches" of working with the individual have been identified. More recently a multisystems approach[12] has been mentioned in such fields as child welfare and mental health. As the name implies, this approach affirms the inter-relationships of the individual to an interlocking network of systems each influencing the other.

Treatment using this approach takes into consideration the importance of the systems—the individual, family, school, neighborhood, culture, and welfare institutions—impacting and being impacted by each other. Treatment may and often does enlist the support of others for the purpose of bringing about desired change in the individual. A multisystems approach is not a method but an *approach* and will need study and research for refinement. This approach is a far cry from an era when the theoretical view was that only understanding intrapsychic dynamics by the therapist and client was needed to bring about problem resolution.

Social work methods and approaches need to be proved and validated. Fortunately, social work is developing an effective and sophisticated evaluation and research base for guiding practice.

Summary

Intrapsychic forces, the psychodynamics of behavior, interpersonal relations, and the impact of family, small groups, school, and the workplace are identified with the practice of social work with individuals.

The roots of casework and clinical work are deep and date back over a hundred years to society's efforts to help people with relationship problems.

Psychoanalysis and Freud have contributed theories of personality and intrapsychic determinants of behavior that radically brought about a shift of emphasis from outer to inner forces of behavior. Current practice combines both inner and outer forces or the person-in-environment paradigm (see Chapter 4).

The knowledge base of practice includes the scientific work of a wide variety of disciplines, social work's adaptations of this knowledge, and its own theoretical and scientific formulations and findings.

The processes of clinical social work embrace study, assessment, intervention, and termination. The application process is designed to aid the client in the discovery of what is functional and dysfunctional and to lead to solutions of personal, family, and other problems.

Brief examples provide clues to the application of such theories and models of practice as the psychosocial theory, functional theory, task-centered theory, problem-solving theory, behavior modification, and to a multisystems approach.

Selected References

ALLEN-MEARES, PAULA, *Social Work with Children and Adolescents.* New York: Longman, 1995.

BALGOPAL, PALLASSANA R., ed., *Social Work Practice with Immigrants and Refugees.* New York: Columbia University Press, 2000.

BRANDELL, JERROLD, R., ed., *Theory and Practice in Clinical Social Work.* New York: Free Press, 1997.

CORSINI, RAYMOND J., *Current Psychotherapies,* 5th ed. Itasca, IL: F. E. Peacock, 1995.

DILLER, JERRY V., *Cultural Diversity: A Primer for the Human Services.* Pacific Grove, CA: Brooks/Cole, 1999.

DORFMAN, RACHELLE A., *Clinical Social Work: Definition, Practice, and Vision.* New York: Brunner/Mazel, 1996.

EWALT, PATRICIA, and NOREEN MOKUAU, "Self-Determination: A Pacific Perspective," *Social Work,* 40 (March 1995), 168–175.

FARLEY, O. WILLIAM, KENNETH A. GRIFFITHS, REX A. SKIDMORE, and MILTON G. THACKERAY, *Rural Social Work Practice.* New York: Free Press, 1982.

JENZEN, CURTIS, and OLIVER HARRIS, *Family Treatment in Social Work Practice.* Itasca, IL: F. E. Peacock, 1997.

PROCTOR, ENOLA K., and LARRY E. DAVIS, "The Challenge of Racial Difference: Skills for Clinical Practice," *Social Work,* 39, no. 3 (1994), 314–323.

SATIR, VIRGINIA, *Conjoint Family Therapy.* Palo Alto, CA: Science and Behavior Books, 1983.

TOLSON, ELEANOR REARDON, WILLIAM J. REID, and CHARLES GAVIN, *Generalist Practice: A Task-Centered Practice.* Irvington, NY: Columbia University Press, 1994.

ZASTROW, CHARLES, and KAREN K. KIRST-ASHMAN, *Understanding Human Behavior and the Social Environment,* 4th ed. Chicago: Nelson-Hall, 1997.

Notes

1. Charles Zastrow and Karen K. Kirst-Ashman, *Understanding Human Behavior and the Social Environment,* 7th ed. (Belmont, CA: Brooks/Cole, 2007), pp. 19–20.

2. Robert L. Barker, *The Social Work Dictionary,* 5th ed. (Washington, DC: NASW Press, 2003), p. 402.

3. National Association of Social Workers, *Standards for the Practice of Clinical Social Work.* Definition accepted by the Board of Directors at its January 1984 meeting and revised in 1989. Retrieved from www.socialworkers.org/practice/standards/clinical_sw.asp.

4. Aurora P. Jackson, "Diversity and Oppression," in Carol H. Meyer and Mark A. Mattaini, eds., *The Foundations of Social Work Practice* (Washington, DC: NASW Press, 1995), pp. 42–58.

5. Barker, *The Social Work Dictionary,* p. 30.

6. *Proceedings of the National Conference on Charities and Corrections* (Boston: George H. Ellis, 1886), p. 187.

7. National Association of Social Workers, *Standards for the Practice of Clinical Social Work*, revised 1989. Retrieved from www.socialworkers.org/practice/standards/clinical_sw.asp.

8. Helen Perlman, "Social Casework," in *Social Work Year Book,* 1960 (New York: NASW, 1960), p. 538.

9. National Association of Social Workers, *Social Work Practice.* Retrieved from www.socialworkers.org/practice/default.asp.

10. Dean A. Hepworth, Ronald H. Rooney, Glenda Dewberry Rooney, Kimberly Strom-Gottfried, and JoAnn Larsen, *Direct Social Work Practice: Theory and Skills,* 7th ed. (Belmont, CA: Brooks/Cole, 2006), p. 23.

11. JoAnna Jones was a volunteer worker in a Head Start program. The material is adapted from an unpublished recording of her work.

12. Rocco A. Cimmarusti, "Family Preservation Practice Based upon a Multisystems Approach," *Child Welfare* (May–June 1992), pp. 241–254.

6

Social Work Practice with Groups

Patients from the community mental health center summarized their perception of the benefits of group therapy. Supatra had learned to express her feelings. Anne, not unscathed, was glad that members honestly told her what they thought of her. Jeremy and Ibrahim learned that ultimately they had to take responsibility for their own lives; that blaming others, or dependency on others for a sense of direction, ended in being "driven and tossed." The discovery that they had similar ideas with others, and that their own diffidence and malaise were shared, was reassuring. Jordan was *especially helped to learn that he really was obnoxious to others, though he was pained by this disclosure. Having others accept the unacceptable in themselves helped them to be less self-critical. For Jim, having the leader respond with understanding when he was attacked by the group seemed to open the door for him to take a second look at his real enemies. Almost all members of the group benefited from the chance to handle anger, to experience the relief from saying what bothered them, and to learn that one does not always have to hold back to be accepted.*

Over the years social workers have understood the power of the group process in helping individuals improve their social functioning. "Social work with groups, one of the three [historical] foundation methods that make up the trinity of practice (casework, group work, and community organization), has played an important role in transforming the way we think about clients and about the helping process."[1] The generalist practitioner can utilize group work methodology in many productive ways. One only has to observe the number of support groups prevalent in our society to see the importance of group dynamics and methodology.

People are gregarious, and the more they discover themselves, the more they discover the group and society. They do not live by themselves; they are not islands. Their welfare, in fact, their existence, is tied to the success or failure of other humans and to an ever-growing number of group associations.

There was a time when people's interests were mainly self- and family-centered; the clan, the tribe, and then the nation, in succession, received the spotlight of concern. But today the world is the stage and people are the center of it. Their existence on this globe can be secured depending on how well the lesson is learned that human beings are social and must learn to live in society regardless of ethnic origins, national ties and loyalties, or even personal preferences.

To his daughter, Thomas Jefferson wrote

> I am convinced our own happiness requires that we should continue to mix with the world, and to keep pace with it as it goes; and that every person who retires from free communication with it is severely punished afterwards by the state of mind into which he gets, and which can only be prevented from feeding our sociable principles. . . . From 1793 to 1797 I remained closely at home, saw none but those who came there, and at length became very sensible of the ill effect it had upon my own mind, and of its direct and irresistible tendency to render me unfit for society and uneasy when necessarily engaged in it. I felt enough of the effect of withdrawing from the world then, to see that it led to an anti-social and misanthropic state of mind, which severely punishes him who gives into it; and it will be the lesson I shall never forget.[2]

Science has made the discovery that infants who are isolated from other human beings, however well cared for otherwise, succumb to inattention. Children find loneliness intolerable. Psychologists have observed that learning can actually be enhanced by association with others. A parent can tell whether his teenage son or daughter has been driving the family car—the radio begins to play the moment the key is turned on; for youth is impatient with solitude, and the human voice, albeit on radio, is a welcome intrusion.

It is a well-documented fact that many of the physical and mental illnesses of people are caused by social and emotional malaise and that social needs bring people to the office of social workers, psychologists, and marriage counselors.

People not only need to be loved, they need to know that they are wanted and understood. A patient, about to be discharged from a mental hospital, voiced anxiety about leaving because the hospital had become "my home" and she was not sure that the future she faced in the community would be friendly. In talking to the social worker, she was reassured as she remembered, "Mrs. Jones will be my neighbor. I can talk to her and she will understand." Anne Frank wrote in her diary, "A person can be lonely even if he is loved by many people, because he is still not the 'One and Only' to anyone."[3]

A patient who was a registered nurse hospitalized in a mental hospital, when greeted perfunctorily, "How are you?" defended her delusion by falsely claiming that she had been *asked* to come to the hospital to head the nursing services—thus affirming self-importance and worth. The fear of being unloved and devalued exists in the mind of this chronically mentally ill person along with yearning for intimacy and friendship. The behavior of individuals who are delinquents, developmentally disadvantaged, shut-ins, and many others may be marked by social dysfunctioning and failure.

Isolation may not be physical. One knows that one can be lonely in the midst of a crowd. Members of families, living under the same roof, sometimes become isolated one from another. No sense of loneliness is more painful than that which exists between friends and loved ones because they are unable to communicate. Yet each of us seeks some form of connection with others. "Whether people are struggling to save a marriage, to cooperate in a family crisis, or to build rapport with a difficult boss, they usually have one thing in common: they need to share emotional information that can help them feel connected."[4] The poet Matthew Arnold captured this universal dilemma with the words:

Alas, is even Love too weak
To unlock the heart and let it speak?
Are even lovers powerless to reveal
To one another what indeed they feel?
I knew the mass of men conceal'd
Their thoughts, for fear that if reveal'd
They would by other men be met
With blank indifference, or with blame reproved:
I knew they lived and moved
Trick'd in disguises, alien to the rest
Of men, and alien to themselves—and yet
There beats one heart in every human breast.[5]

Human relations are blocked by many influences—physical disability, illness, jealousy, pride, racial prejudice and discrimination, religious intolerance, class superiority and preference, and others.

Human beings are strongly dependent on interactions with other human beings at all levels. Almost everything that is done in life is done in some form or context with other people. Social work practice with groups builds on the important impact that groups have on individuals, other groups, communities, and organizations and utilizes group processes to accomplish individual, group, agency, and community goals. Toseland and Rivas state:

> As one prepares to become an effective social work practitioner, it is important to realize the effect that groups have on people's lives. It is not possible to be a member of society without becoming a member of numerous groups and being influenced by others (Falek, 1988). Although it is possible to live in an isolated manner on the fringes of groups, our social nature makes this neither desirable nor healthy.
>
> Groups provide the structure on which communities and the larger society are built. They provide both formal and informal structure in the workplace. But more important, they provide a means through which relationships with significant others are carried out. Participation in family groups, peer groups, and classroom groups helps members to learn acceptable norms of social behavior, to engage in satisfying social relationships, to identify personal goals, and to derive a variety of other benefits that result from participating in closely knit social systems. Experiences in social, church, recreation, and other work groups are essential in the development and maintenance of people and society.[6]

Historical Developments

Groups are as old as the history of the people of this world. "From the beginning of humankind, individuals have gathered together to rebel, create, and achieve in ways not possible otherwise. . . . groups are a natural way for people to communicate and interrelate with one another."[7] Group work began as a form of *social service* with various kinds of activities under the auspices of the church. In the 1855–65 decade, the YMCA and YWCA were organized and became formalized, independent associations that provided group programs, activities, and opportunities.

During the latter part of the nineteenth century the settlement movement developed. The Industrial Revolution had brought considerable social disorganization and the breakdown of the primary group in many situations. Dedicated leaders believed that social improvement could be accomplished by having members of the more fortunate classes live or visit among and with the underprivileged groups, sharing their ideas and ways of life. Certain philanthropists donated money as well as time to help sponsor settlement houses in the underprivileged districts, especially in the large cities.

Toynbee Hall was established in London in 1884 in an attempt to help, with a group program, the underprivileged in that huge, milling city. The Neighborhood Guild was established in 1886 in the United States and was the first settlement house in this country. Jane Addams's Hull House, begun in Chicago in 1889, and other settlement houses were not long in developing and have become part of the American tradition. The basic aim of these settlement houses was to provide a place for the underprivileged to go and, through the two-way process of association and interaction, to develop their personalities and enrich their living.

In 1935 a group work section of the National Conference on Social Work was established to give additional emphasis and focus to this rapidly developing movement. In 1936 the National Association for the Study of Group Work was organized, with a representative coordinating committee of about 100 from all sections of the United States and an executive committee of 10. The association was established to further the interest of group work practice and to help in recruiting and getting more people professionally trained. In 1939 its name was changed to the American Association for the Study of Group Work.

In 1955 several different professional associations of social workers joined together to create a single professional organization, the National Association of Social Workers. The American Association of Group Workers, formed in 1946 as the successor to the American Association for the Study of Group Work, joined with the new organization, declaring itself an integral part of the new, unified social work professional organization.

In addition to the developments in areas of service, there have been several significant developments in regard to training of people interested in social work practice with groups. Apparently it was in the United States that the first major emphasis on training in group work was established. The first systematized class in a school of social work was offered in the School of Applied Social Sciences of Western Reserve University in the 1920s.

By the early 1930s the words *social group work* were used to distinguish it from social casework, the other main social work practice method at that period of time. The National Conference of Social Work in 1935 included group work as a division at its annual program meeting, and several people joined together in sharing their thinking about this relatively new development. In 1939 a committee concerned with professional education began a study of the courses in group work offered by the schools of social work on both graduate and undergraduate levels. As a result of this study, an official statement, "Professional Education for Group Work Practice," was accepted by the American Association of Group Workers in 1947.

During the 1940s the American Association of Schools of Social Work (AASSW) encouraged and recommended the inclusion of group work courses in the graduate curriculum of its member schools, of which less than half offered a sequence in group work. The emphasis in groups during this period of time was on remediation and therapy. This occurred because of the influence of ego psychology and psychoanalytic theory on the profession.

In the 1960s, group work lost its popularity. This was due, in part, by a trend within the profession toward a more generalized view of social work practice that was being taught in schools. It was a movement away from specializations in casework, group work, and community organization. Those working with youths placed more emphasis on educational and training programs for work rather than the use of groups to battle delinquency. This trend continued into the 1970s.

The 1980s and 1990s have seen a resurgence of group work within the profession. The Association for the Advancement of Social Work Groups (AASWG) has enlarged and has been able to appoint one of its members as a liaison to the Council on Social Work Education (CSWE). AASSW has also enacted standards for group work education. Today all schools of social work offer one or more classes or curriculum units in working with groups, and several of them offer a basic sequence or concentration including class, field instruction, and related experiences in the group method. To illustrate, in 1962 there were 448 students enrolled in group work sequences in the schools of social work in the United States and Canada. Of the 36,475 master's degree students enrolled in training in 2004, nearly 62 percent were listed in "direct practice, clinical, or advanced generalist"—all of which include group work methodology and skills as part of their expertise.

Group Work Defined

Group work is a method of working with people in groups (two or more people) for skill development, personal growth through insight, the enhancement of social functioning, the achievement of socially desirable goals and the accomplishment of tasks. Group work is based on the knowledge of people's needs for each other and their interdependence. Group work is a method of reducing or eliminating roadblocks to social interaction and for accomplishing socially desirable purposes. Helen Northern gives the following definition of group work:

Social worker in group work with teenagers.

Within the general purpose of the profession, social work with small groups may be directed toward helping the members to use the group for coping with and resolving existing problems in psychosocial functioning preventing anticipated problems, or maintaining a current level of functioning in situations in which there is danger of deterioration. Further, it may be directed toward developing more effective patterns of group and organizational functioning and removing environmental obstacles. With any group, the specific outcomes sought vary with the desires, needs, capacities, and situations of the members who comprise the group and with the purpose and nature of the group itself.[8]

Konopka explains that "group work is an approach consciously directed toward developing the individual's greatest capacity while relating him to the group and learning when he has to contribute and when he has to withdraw."[9]

Reid writes that group work, when provided by a competent and well-trained practitioner, has become an accepted form of practice. The purpose is to help improve the well-being of the members and relieve personal suffering. This is accomplished because groups have the "power to enhance problem-solving capacity, prevent the development of serious social problems, and restore and maintain the social functioning of members."[10]

Toseland and Rivas define group work as follows:

Goal-directed activity with small treatment and task groups aimed at meeting socioemotional needs and accomplishing tasks. This activity is directed to individual members of a group and to the group as a whole within a system of service delivery.[11]

Toseland and Rivas suggest their definition is broad and functional in that it allows for both generic and specialized group work practice:

This definition describes group work as goal-directed activity, which refers to planned, orderly worker activities carried out in the context of professional practice with people. Goal-directed activity has many purposes. For example, group workers may aim to support or educate members, help them socialize and achieve personal growth, or provide treatment for their problems and concerns. . . . Workers may also help members of a group develop leadership skills so that they can take increasing responsibility for the group's development. Workers should also enable their groups to change the social environment. This includes helping members gain greater control over the organizations and communities that affect their lives.[12]

Almost all social service agencies use group work. Group work is being utilized in many fields of practice including, but not limited to, stepfamilies,[13] bereavement for children,[14] addiction disorders,[15] adolescent parents, battered women, personality disorders, eating disorders, families of schizophrenics,[16] batterers, elderly,[17] and problem-solving task-oriented and organizational work groups.[18] Zastrow reports

Every social service agency uses groups, and every practicing social worker is involved in a variety of groups. Social work with groups is practiced in adoption agencies, correctional settings, halfway houses, substance abuse treatment centers, physical rehabilitation centers, family service agencies, private psychotherapy clinics, mental hospitals, nursing homes, community centers, public schools, and many other social service settings. To effectively serve clients in human service systems today, social workers in generalist practice positions must be trained in group methods. Often, social workers serve as leaders and participants in myriad groups requiring skills ranging from the simple to the complex. The beginning social worker is likely to be surprised at the diverse groups in existence and excited by the challenge of practicing social work in such settings.[19]

Social workers apply knowledge of group organization and functioning to affect the performance and adjustment of the individual, as defined by Toseland and Rivas, within *treatment groups.* (Enhancement of socioemotional functioning through the use of groups is the primary aim of treatment groups.) The individual remains the focus of concern; the group is the vehicle of growth and change. Programs and facilities are used as dynamics of interaction and change. Because of the importance of the individual in all group work, the worker equips himself or herself with the knowledge of the individual. As with treatment groups, social workers equally apply their skills and knowledge of group functioning with *task groups.* The difference between treatment and task groups is that in task groups, the focus is less about the socioemotional needs of the individual and more about achieving the task that the group has been charged with. "They are used to find solutions to organizational problems, to generate new ideas, and to make decisions." [20]

Barker has summarized several theoretical paradigms of social group work in the definition he included in *The Social Work Dictionary* (1999). He states that social group work is

> an orientation and method of social work *intervention* in which small numbers of people who share similar interests or common problems convene regularly and engage in activities designed to achieve certain objectives. In contrast to *group psychotherapy,* the goals of group work are not necessarily the treatment of emotional problems. The objectives also include exchanging information, developing social and manual skills, changing value orientations, and diverting antisocial behaviors into productive channels. Intervention techniques include, but are not limited to, controlled therapeutic discussions. Some groups also include education and tutoring; sports; arts and crafts; recreational activities; and discussions about such topics as politics, religion, sexuality, values, and goals. Although social group work draws on the theoretical perspectives of *existential theory, learning theory, psychoanalytic theory,* and *social exchange theory,* its major theoretical perspective to describe group functioning is *social systems theory*. This orientation provides workers with a way to conceptualize the effect of group dynamics and interrelationships outside the group.[21]

Group Work Models

Humans are richly endowed with the potential for high achievement. Group work is a method and a process developed to assist people to improve the quality of their lives and to maximize their potentials. Applied skillfully, with imagination and intelligence by a competent, caring person, the group method can assist the group (1) in achieving mutually determined goals; (2) in achieving desirable change for individuals experiencing personal, family, occupational, and adjustment problems; (3) in developing self-enhancement and individual enrichment; and (4) by using a combination of treatment, self-enhancement, and personal fulfillment.

Social work with groups is especially relevant for many individuals who find themselves disempowered by our society. Gitterman and Shulman state

> Social workers in practice today deal with profoundly vulnerable and disempowered populations. People dealing with such life conditions and circumstances as AIDS, homelessness, sexual abuse, and community and family violence, are overwhelmed by oppressive lives, circumstances, and events they are powerless to control. Their life stressors often appear intractable because they are chronic and persistent or acute and unexpected. Their overwhelming stressors often overwhelm them. When they lack community and family supports, they are often at risk of physical, psychological, and social deterioration. Moreover, when their internal resources are impaired as well, they become extremely vulnerable to social and emotional isolation. Yet, in spite of the numerous risk factors and overwhelming odds, a surprisingly large number of people somehow—miraculously at times—manage their adversities. They adapt, cope, overcome, and meet challenges of physical and mental conditions, severe losses and traumas, and chronic discrimination and oppression. The group modality offers a powerful counterforce, a potential to empower vulnerable populations. A group mutual support system has the inherent potential to help members acquire a sense of greater personal, interpersonal, and environmental control over their lives.[22]

Group goals and objectives, or purposes, will determine the group work model employed. Three such models have been pioneered by Papell and Rothman: (1) the social goals model, (2) the remedial goals model, and (3) the reciprocal goals model.[23]

Social Goals Model

Groups serving the social goals model are formed, and continue, because of socially determined interests, which, if attained, bring about important social gains for the group. This model is closely identified with the group interest and effort. It is likely to address itself to problems within communities and is practiced in settlement houses, PTA organizations, and community service and neighborhood councils. More recently this model has been used in addressing social problems accompanying community development and growth. Principles guiding practice involving the social goals model include

> Clarification of agency policy, positive use of limitations, identification with agency goals, determination of appropriate issues for collective action, and the weighing of alternatives for action and their consequences.
>   . . . The principles of democratic group process that are fundamental to this model have become the hallmark of all social group work practice. Every practitioner, regardless of his theoretical loyalty, tends to work toward the adoption and institutionalization of democratic procedures in small groups.[24]

Remedial Goals Model

The remedial goals model, a model of treatment, tends to be clinically oriented. The group is used as an agent of change. The group worker facilitates the interaction among members of the group to achieve change for the individual. He or she applies knowledge and skill in helping individuals gain self-awareness and improve social functioning. The group supports the member, encouraging new, more appropriate modes of functioning. Intervention is reality focused and addresses the problem of dysfunction in the group and within the full range of the individual's relationships. The treatment group is widely used in mental hospitals, correctional institutions, family service organizations, counseling services, schools, health care facilities, and in many other agencies.

Example 1

Group process was initiated to improve a dysfunctional child–parent relationship. A mother noticed that her son took greater interest in his schoolwork and was more responsive to the family after he became a member of a Boy Scout troop. What she did not fully realize was that her attitude about her son had changed as a result of her membership in a group, and that this was an important dynamic of improvement in her son's behavior. She recalled her tears of joy at a court of honor, when she said, "It is wonderful to have my boy do something good for once, rather than something for which he is always getting into trouble." The change in him was brought about because of his activity in the troop and because, for the first time, he had his mother's approval and acceptance.

Example 2

A group of overweight adults wanted to lose weight. The approach that proved effective in bringing lasting results for most members consisted of medical information, diet, exercise, a system of rewards and punishments, greater self-awareness, and the support from the group. Similar results were obtained by a treatment approach with cardiac patients in adhering to a salt-free diet, exercise, rest, and in accepting the medical regimen. The group provided the means for diagnosing emotional problems related to physical difficulties, which were then approached by the group and individuals.

Reciprocal Goals Model

The reciprocal goals model serves both the individual and society. It sees the individual largely as an abstraction that can be studied, understood, and treated only in relation to the many systems and subsystems of which he or she is a part. It views the individual as being created, influenced, and modified by his or her relationships, social institutions, and the interdependency between society and the individual. Papell and Rothman write

> The reciprocal model presupposes an organic, systemic relationship between the individual and society. . . . This interdependence is the "focus" for social work and the small group is the field in which individual and societal functioning can be nourished and mediated. . . .
>
> Unlike the remedial model, the reciprocal model does not begin with a priori prescriptions of desired outcomes. However, it does conceive of an ideal group state, namely a system in mutual aid. Such a system is not dependent upon the specific problem to be resolved by the group but is a necessary condition for problem solving. To state it in still another way, the reciprocal model has no therapeutic ends, no political or social change programs to

which it is addressed. It is only from the encounter of individuals that compose a reciprocal group system that direction or problem is determined. Emphasis is placed on *engagement* in the process of interpersonal relations. It is from this state of involvement that members may call upon each other in their own or common cause.

The reciprocal model views the individual primarily in terms of his motivation and capacity for reciprocity. . . . Diagnostic considerations or structural descriptions of the individual are not regarded as significant predictors of behavior in the group. Therefore they do not serve as a basis for selection of members for a group or assessment by the worker.

The image of the worker projected by this model is that of a mediator or enabler to the needs system converging in the group. The worker is viewed as a part of the worker-client system both influencing and being influenced by it. In the terminology of social work, he neither does *to* the client nor *for* him, but *with* him."[25]

Theoretical sources of this model come from systems theory, field theory, social psychological theories of behavior, and the practice principles that are a part of generic methodology for social work.

In the example to follow, the group had no preconceived purpose. The outcome of the association was not a major concern. Their emphasis was on engagement. The leader would influence the group behavior and be influenced by it.

Organized in a YWCA, the "Young Mothers" learned that it was good mental health to bring their children to a well-staffed nursery to be cared for while they joined others in a morning swim, an hour of "slimnastics," a few hands of bridge, an arts and crafts program, in a discussion of foods, fashions, child rearing, or in talking to those who had similar worries, concerns, and problems with their young families.

Their program usually included refreshment or lunch arranged by their committee. Young Mothers provided an outlet for social contacts and relieved the stress and strain of caring for the children.

One mother who was enrolled in the TANF program was helped to make an adjustment to divorce. The group assisted her to find new purposes in life, to accept and enjoy her children rather than to see them as a burden. Before joining the group she thought there was nothing to look forward to but dirty dishes, soiled diapers, and runny noses. By talking to others who were also going through periods of adjustment she drew strength from them and at the same time contributed her talents to the group.

A group of seven- and eight-year-old boys, formed for an engagement group, became a socialization tool under the leadership of a group worker.

The group was reconvening in the group room from an outdoor activity. Calvin pushed Stephen as they entered. Stephen retaliated and a brief fistfight ensued. The group worker separated the boys and stated that it was hard to wait for a turn through the door. Calvin did not say anything, but Stephen said, "It was all his fault. He pushed me first." Calvin looked at the floor, and Stephen added that he didn't like Calvin. The worker indicated that sometimes when we get in fights we really don't like the person at that particular time. Calvin looked up and caught Stephen's glance and then looked back down again.

The group worker asked, "What do we do when we have problems, or fights, or disagreements with one another?" The entire group got involved and offered ideas and suggestions about what happens in the process of fighting. Their focus was on resolving the immediate conflict. The group worker continued to discuss what happens when people fight and how difficult it often is for people to say "I'm sorry" or "I didn't mean to do that."

Both boys were looking up and the worker asked Calvin how he was feeling. He said he had been really mad at Stephen, but it wasn't that important, and he wished he could learn how to prevent fights from happening. (This was one of his problems, and he had discussed it before.) The group members talked about ways in which they could handle their enthusiasm and energy and have positive experiences and ways in which they could handle their feelings when a fight did occur. The worker asked for suggestions about how to make up, and the group wanted Stephen and Calvin to shake hands immediately. The boys thought about it, jumped up, and shook hands.

Without a therapeutic goal or program for social change, a group of adolescents was helped to evolve a method of mutual aid.

The girls came to the group individually. Everyone that day was very quiet and nonresponsive. The group worker tried a number of ways to get them to share their thoughts. No one wanted to say anything. The worker asked if something had happened outside the group. No one responded. She asked if there were problems about which anyone wanted to talk. No one spoke. When she commented that it was going to be a very quiet session a few girls nodded. After approximately five minutes of silence, the worker stretched out on the floor and said, "Some days it helps if you can just relax. Anybody wanting to relax on the floor may do so." One by one the girls relaxed on the rug and gradually began to talk about some of their feelings and the problems they were having with schoolwork, pressure from parents and teachers, and general nonachievement. At the end of the period the girls were responding with greater effect and understanding.

Formation of Groups

Groups come into being in a variety of ways. The existence of a social problem or need will often result in groups forming almost spontaneously to solve the problem. Social workers in treatment centers organize groups from their caseloads and from the clientele of the agency. Lonely people who want friendship, those on weight-watching diets, and parents troubled by the behavior of their children actively seek group membership.

Regardless of the reason for a group forming or the mechanics of bringing people together, the agency, group member, and worker goals are at the heart of the process.

Agency Goals

Agency goals, having to do with social consciousness and public concern for social welfare, are likely to reflect community interest. Usually they are related to identified needs, are likely to be fairly general, and often are given public utterance at the time the agency or new service mode comes into existence. The goals of agencies should be systematically reviewed for relevance, especially in times of rapid social change.

Group Goals

Group purposes are often general in nature. However, they must be explicated for individual group members. Group purposes will ordinarily incorporate (1) the agency's purpose, (2) the goals of the group members, and (3) the goals and objectives of the group worker. In addition to being realistic and clearly definable they must be within the reality of attainment. They should be transferable to other social situations in which group members would be expected to function.

Member Goals

Member goals are defined as those wishes and desires of each member that motivated the attainment of group member status. These are not to be confused with worker goals, and a distinction between the two is necessary.

The group worker in an agency should be aware that members join groups in order to achieve goals that may be secondary to the purpose for which the agency was established. An example: A member may join a group because he or she wants to participate in "fun" activities or test his or her reasoning ability with others of similar age and circumstances. The attainment of social skills and acceptance of differences in others, which are group purposes, become important to the individual only as he or she finds fulfillment of personal needs and is influenced by the group and the worker to consider meaningful reasons for participation.

The group is enhanced considerably when members and workers share compatible goals aimed toward the members' resolution of personal difficulties, the attainment of problem-solving skills, or personal improvement. This mutual agreement is often referred to as a "contract," and it identifies goals and purposes as well as methods to achieve objectives. The group worker commits himself or herself to responsibility for the group process, and members commit themselves to an investment in goal achievement.

Worker Goals

The group worker goals include the plans, methods, means, and programming developed and used to help members accomplish their goals and purposes. Unless the worker is clear about group purposes and member goals, he or she will be ineffectual and unable to validate group success. Only when goals and purposes are clearly explicated, understood, and accepted can the process of attainment be actualized. The group worker is responsible for the organization, the treatment process, and termination. He or she must be engaged in a continual process of self-evaluation and understanding to avoid "hang-ups" that would militate against group process. Clarity of purpose, goal formulations, and purpose are essential in group process.

The examples in Tables 6.1 and 6.2 illustrate group, member, and individual goal explication for a treatment group of thirteen-year-old boys.[26]

TABLE 6.1 *Group and Worker Goals*

Group Goals	Worker Goals
Improve self-image.	Provide opportunities for successful experiences in sports, arts, crafts, or discussions.
Expand self-awareness and understanding.	Provide leadership experiences.
Achieve a group status.	Encourage expressions and opinions related to self with opportunities for analysis for each individual and other group members.
	Encourage looking at behavior and feelings and coming to terms with weaknesses and strengths.
	Develop research proposals to evaluate the program.
Improve peer relationships.	Offer experiences in sharing, give-and-take considerations of others.
Accept peers as individuals.	Provide social experiences at appropriate levels.
Develop friendship-building skills.	Encourage practicing of skills. Reinforce goal attainment tangibly and with praise when appropriate.
	Provide role-model identification and opportunities for discussion of friendship roles, expectations, rewards, satisfactions, and responsibilities.

Selection of Group Members

How are individuals selected for the group? It depends on the purpose of the group. Some leaders may prefer participants who are more homogeneous whereas others may select a more heterogeneous membership. Conducting a treatment group for adolescent survivors of sexual abuse would likely be established with participants having more homogeneous characteristics whereas a community task group invited to make recommendations for a new recreation facility would be better represented by a diverse group of people. The following are factors to consider when selecting group members.

   1. *Age.* Chronological age seems to be more important in the younger age group than the maturity of the individual. In adolescence, for example, where age enjoys greater status and additional freedom privileges, it may be extremely important to strive for homogeneity of age in the group. With adult groups, age seems much less important than other social or economic factors.

   2. *Value System.* Some differences in value system can be tolerated and stimulate discussion in interaction. If the differences are too great, however, they may present problems. A group with more or less common values can work together, whereas a group with extremely diverse values can be expected to run into difficulty and to lose cohesion because of the differences. For example, in a group of girls who had been placed together to assist each other with an adjustment problem, some may become very destructive because the girls were physically attacking each other across a different value system.

TABLE 6.2 *Worker and Member Goals*

Worker Goals	*Member Goals*
Discuss the expectations of appropriate behavior.	Bobby wants to be accepted as a member of the group and manage his anger; wants to be liked by both boys and girls.
Provide support and reinforce other members' support of him.	
Supply casework as necessary to maintain him in the group until he can function more appropriately on his own.	
Determine with help of speech therapist speech limitations.	Jose wants to learn how to express himself without stuttering.
Provide support.	Wants to belong and feel more at ease in a group.
Recognize feelings of difficulty and achievement.	Wants to find out who he is and where he fits in.
Plan activities and short discussions around Joe's interest and previous experience.	Wants friends.
Help him present an activity to the group providing individual help with preparation as necessary.	
Verbalize understanding of his feelings and difficulties.	Ben wants to eliminate his "tough" and "mean" image.
Call his attention to reactions of the group.	Wants to improve his vocabulary and eliminate crude and rude remarks.
Place limits on offensive behavior.	
Program for areas of his interest and strengths, such as swimming and hiking.	Wants to settle down to accomplish important activities and tasks.
Support his abilities.	
Discuss his lessened need to act aggressive.	
Increase attractiveness of group by programming activities of interest.	Jung Woo wants acceptance for his identification as a nonconformist.
Allow discussion of present group.	Would like to expand his friendship to include others outside his gang.
Bring members of his gang if the group can tolerate them.	Would like to bring members of his gang to group meetings.
Increase skills in areas other than current interest.	Wants to identify with good workers.
Avoid criticism of dress, but encourage discussion thereof.	

    3. *Common Problems.* Sometimes participants who have common problems are grouped together. Adult men arrested for domestic violence and anger may be sentenced to a treatment facility while specifically addressing the behaviors, beliefs, laws, and consequences of their actions. It would be of value to men just entering into treatment to learn from those who are more experienced in how to manage their behavior appropriately and how to deal with relationships. They are also more likely to be confronted and expected to deal with manipulative behaviors by those who know their "games."

    4. *Enjoyment Patterns.* Common interest, although not always of the greatest importance, can help bring about groupness among individuals. Groups find a common interest in activity. The base of interest can always be broadened and used to assist in better social adjustment in peer groups and in proper male and female identification.

5. *Intelligence.* Intellectual differences do not appear to be of prime importance, but where the extreme is great, difficulty may be encountered unless this factor is considered.

6. *Tolerance of Structure.* Sometimes groups do not congeal simply because the members of the group are unable to accept the structure or the leader. Treatment does not take place when clients are not interacting or relating to one another. There is nothing very therapeutic about listening to the "gastric rumbles of the other members of the group." In other words, an important part of skill is to foster therapeutic relationships that will result in integration.

7. *Sex.* Depending on the purposes of the groups, the sex of the members may or may not be important. Mixed-gender groups have been quite successful in working with relationship problems of adolescents and adults. Adolescents and adults have also found success when some of the work has been done separately and then the subgroups are brought together to integrate what has been addressed during the session. Social workers in schools and in the juvenile justice system and those working in the field of addictions have recognized that single-sex groups have greater freedom for intimacy in their discussions and greater support and encouragement around the expression of common problems.

8. *Ego Strengths.* There is almost unanimous agreement that group members must have sufficient ego strengths to stand exposure, because group reactions cannot be controlled in the same way individual work is controlled.

Other variables might be considered, but those touched on briefly here seem to be of the greatest importance and are more or less recognized by most workers in the field.

Preparation of Group Members

Principles to be applied to the preparation of members are directly related to (1) the purposes for which the group is established; (2) the goals of the members and the worker; (3) the reason for the agency's existence; and (4) the knowledge, skill, and individual preferences of the worker.

The worker will usually become acquainted with the members of the group in individual interviews. This may be a shared experience with the member and the worker learning about each other. Special knowledge, interest, skill, experience, and caring for the members are the worker's main contributions to the group.

In preparatory sessions, a working relationship will be achieved among the members and between them and the group worker. The group will define its purpose and continue the diagnostic and goal-setting process. Preparation will also be facilitated by the use of information prepared by the group leader with important input from group members.

Some groups will not predetermine their objective except in a tentative way. In their views of the ever-emerging quality of the human condition, they see the group as an experience in becoming. For groups who feel the excitement of anticipation, "the road is better than the inn." They exist to explore and to discover their potentials. Preparation includes setting the stage and creating a climate for discovery within the framework of democratic values and agency goals.

Structuring the Group

Structuring aspects of the group process include the setting; group size; rules and norms; open or closed groups; time limits; meeting days and times; male, female, or mixed groups; leadership; and programming.

The Setting

The setting is related to purpose. For children with limited self-control, activities in a gymnasium or on a playground do not provide essential boundaries for group programming. Lounges may not be conducive to activity groups. However, in some agencies one may have to learn to do with less and to help the members work within the available areas. Furnishings should not be so comfortable or formal as to detract from a "working" atmosphere. Privacy should be provided; the group should not disturb others. The use of a table may represent a psychological barrier to interaction for some groups, but for groups serving refreshments, a table may be helpful.

Group Size

Although there is no optimal size for task and treatment groups, the number of participants ought to be determined by the objectives of each group. Seven to nine members are most often thought to be small enough to allow for open discussion and attention given to individuals in order to accomplish tasks, yet large enough to have adequate diversity, ideas, skills, and resources to assist in reaching the purpose and objectives of the group.

A day camp for children who are emotionally disturbed or have inadequate social skills requires a small group. A group of ten or more may be difficult to manage where the focus is on recreation. It is important to keep the group small enough to maintain optimal member–worker relationships. Awareness of what is going on is enhanced when the group is small and limited as it becomes larger. The recommended size for educational groups is larger and varied according to purpose. These groups may be as small as twelve or as large as thirty.

Group Rules

A group that makes its own rules is more likely to abide by them and to apply sanctions as needed to enforce them. Individual beliefs and values should be considered in relation to group rules. Religious days, respected by some members of the group even though meaningless to others, need to be considered. Rules should not apply sanctions to norms of behavior peculiar to an individual member. Rules should be few in number and include only those deemed essential to achieve the purposes of the group. If they are appropriately chosen and enforced, they lead to the establishment of group norms. Capricious rules and those that make no sense will have little support from the group.

Some members may attempt to impose inappropriate rules on the group. The worker will need to remain active to avoid situations where coercion is attempted to meet the power needs of individuals at the expense of group cohesiveness.

Open or Closed Groups

Designations of "open" and "closed" pertain to the timing of admission to the group. Open systems take new members at any time during the group's existence. Closed groups include only those members selected at the group's formation. In closed groups, a modus operandi is set up at the beginning. Group purpose, individual goals, and group norms tend to be established early. Open groups are like a slice of life—birth, separation, marriage, and death. Open systems tend to simulate reality and provide transferability to real-life situations. Decisions related to this area are determined by the purpose and goals of the group.

Short-Term or Long-Term Groups

Adults and mature adolescents usually can accept a time limit on the number of meetings to accomplish their goals. Youngsters who have experienced repeated rejections may see time limits negatively and try to negotiate for more sessions rather than invest themselves in the area of goal attainment.

Meeting Days and Time

The day and time of meetings will be adapted to the needs and wishes of the members as part of initial planning. It is unrealistic to expect members to radically alter their patterns of living to participate in the group. Consideration should be given to distances, travel expenses, and the need for babysitters. For children who are mentally retarded and are very young children, arrangements may need to be made for transportation.

Groups usually meet weekly for one or two hours. Groups living in institutions may meet more frequently; "marathon" groups may literally continue around the clock for days. Nothing is magical about once-a-week meetings and experimentation is encouraged. One meaningful encounter can have lasting influence and be the dynamic for a succession of changes.

Flexibility of time and meeting days as well as duration of the group seem warranted. As goals are achieved and as members successfully transfer learning from structured group meetings to practical everyday experiences, meetings can be tapered off.

Male, Female, or Mixed Groups

Many young children, older adolescents, and adults may be members of male–female groups. They can be expected to work cooperatively toward the attainment of their goals. Older children and younger adolescents often prefer all-male or all-female groups, especially when they are working toward the acquisition of skills or tasks related to more specific male or female problems. The group worker should be aware of the meaning that membership in the single-sex or mixed group has for the individual members. Will these feelings contribute or hinder to the attainment of goals and objectives?

Leadership

Many group workers advocate the development of leadership ability in all group members. Most do not recommend a system of elected leaders at the beginning of the group's origin, for they are often chosen more for their initial display of power than for leadership ability. Some workers advocate a revolving leadership system, particularly in activity groups with children and adults.

Group workers continually must assess the leadership development of their group as well as the members' ability to share leadership functions and participate as both leaders and followers.

Programming for Goal Attainment

The use of resources should be geared to objectives and goals. If plans include discussion on health or problems of children, a health nurse may be invited. If dealing with an eating disorder, someone who is successfully managing her problem with bulimia may be helpful. The group worker will have knowledge about resources in programming a particular activity. The worker should be concerned with the following: (1) the components of the activity to be emphasized; (2) the competence of the group to handle the program; (3) the needs of the group; (4) the developmental stage of the group (beginning, middle, and end); (5) the physical, social, emotional, and intellectual development of group members; (6) the rewards and threats involved in participation; and (7) the overall effect on group and member goal attainment.

Programming is the means of goal attainment. It includes educational topics, games, crafts, discussions, tours and field trips, and all activities the group engages in during their

Social worker talking to a mixed group.

group sessions. Appropriately developed, the program will stimulate and free individuals to behave and release their feelings in acceptable ways.

In discussion groups, themes reoccur. Minority groups may discuss poverty, anger toward the majority race or authority figure, hunger and disease, and the futility of their present existence. Married couples often discuss their partner's emotional unresponsiveness, poor communication, undependability of mates, or lack of good parent–child relationships. The group worker needs to be aware that these themes are representative of many basic questions. His or her knowledge is essential to the facilitating of the activity of the group.

Stages of Groups

As groups meet for a period of time, researchers have found that the groups go through a growth and developmental process. Although many writers over the years have described this process in multiple stages, Toseland and Rivas (1998) summarized them into three stages: beginning, middle, and end. Group workers must continually assess the stage and understand the dynamics associated with each when planning and supervising groups.

Beginning

In the first meeting the group worker sets the stage. It is essential for the group worker to take time to identify the purpose(s) of the group. He or she should clearly commit to the goals and procedures considered to be part of the group worker's role. Members need to know what they can expect from the group worker, what the purpose of the group is and how it relates to them, and what will be expected of them.

For participants, this stage is characterized as a time to convene, to organize, and to set a plan. Typically, members want to become part of the group, but they are likely to remain somewhat distant or removed until they have had time to develop relationships. They will explore their roles and determine if it is viable for them to retain their roles or change them.

Middle

Almost all of the group's work will occur during this stage. In the beginning stage, most of the participants' energy is invested in establishing relationships and defining each person's role. In this stage, relationships are strengthened as a group so that the tasks can be worked on. *Problem solving* is a term often used to describe this stage. For task groups, ideas are presented and decided on, plans for implementation are made, and assignments are given. For treatment groups, the socioemotional needs of individuals are seen as paramount. Members' problems are disclosed and confronted, plans for change are discussed, and they are encouraged to practice new behaviors both inside and outside the group.

During this stage, group leaders are usually less involved. They often back out of the process as long as the group is on task and then move back in to help the group regain its focus and direction if it veers off task. The leader may remind the group of its goals and rules and confront relationships that may be interfering with the overall purpose of the group.

End

The last stage is marked by the accomplishment of the goal(s) of the group, production of results, and the evaluation of the group's work. It is also a time when members begin to separate from each other.

Evaluation begins for the worker with the formation of the group and continues on until the group is terminated. Evaluation needs to consider the gains made by the group members and their ability to function within the purpose and boundaries of the group.

Preparation for termination should begin with the first session. When members know that a finite amount of time is provided for the achievement of their goals, they may be likely to focus and function in ways to accomplish the goals and to maximize the use of their time.

The worker will help members deal with their feelings associated with the termination of the group. They will also help participants plan on ways to maintain and generalize the gains each member has made.[27]

Group workers need to understand the stages of groups and the roles they play in order to help groups achieve their goals. One of the most important tasks is for workers to be able to clearly articulate for themselves and group participants the purpose(s) of the group.

Group Work Settings

Traditional Settings

The YMCA and YWCA are examples of agencies that focus on the use of group processes in helping youths and adults. Through its various programs and facilities, the YWCA is helping meet the needs of 2 million girls, women, and families in the United States. In the year 2006, the YWCA was operating out of nearly 300 associations in the United States. Since its inception, the organization has expanded to over 100 countries and estimates that it represents 25 million women worldwide.[28]

In the 2000s, groups in the YWCA have been guided by a mission statement that states

> The Young Women's Christian Association of the United States of America is a women's membership movement nourished by its roots in the Christian faith and sustained by the richness of many beliefs and values.
>
> Strengthened by diversity, the YWCA draws together members who strive to create opportunities for women's growth, leadership, and power in order to attain a common vision: peace, justice, freedom and dignity for all people.
>
> The YWCA will thrust its collective power toward the elimination of racism wherever it exists and by any means necessary.[29]

Again, residential accommodations are provided for women and girls in crisis situations as well as for those who need temporary living facilities.

Latoya came from a home broken by divorce. She felt alone in the world and left a small rural town to take a job in the "big city." She fortunately arranged to stay at the

YWCA. There she mingled with other girls in their teens, some of whom had similar problems. She became an active member in one of the girls clubs sponsored by the "Y." This club, although organized primarily for recreational activities, planned and accomplished many other worthwhile things. Once a week it had meetings of intellectual and spiritual interests. Guest speakers were invited and there was a social worker who assisted in organizing and supporting the club and its activities. After several lecturers had been asked to make presentations, one evening the members informally decided to have some group discussions limited entirely to themselves and their social worker to talk about some of their own problems and questions about life.

These group sessions were most interesting and effective. Latoya shared with the other girls some of the emotional hurts that she had experienced. She discovered that other girls had problems and psychological scars also. As they shared these experiences, and particularly feelings regarding them, many of the emotional hurts were lessened, and Latoya, in particular, changed from a frightened, uncertain girl, bewildered by the perplexities of life and social interaction, to a girl who felt more comfortable in her daily living and more secure in her associations with others. Frank, informal discussions on an intimate group basis had unlocked some of the fears, uncertainties, and anxieties that had welled up within her. The group process had opened the door to a new outlook and perspective on life and to new patterns of behavior.

Another well-known organization that utilizes group workers is the Girl Scouts of the United States of America. This organization, established in 1912, had a membership in 2007 of over 2.7 million girls, with more than 50 million women in the United States having been members at one time. Membership is open with no restrictions regarding race, creed, or color to girls aged five through seventeen and to adults over eighteen. The purpose of the organization is to "inspire girls with the highest ideals of character, conduct, patriotism, and service that they may become happy and resourceful citizens." This program provides group activities for girls, planned democratically and carried out in accordance with a code of ethics embodied in the Girl Scout Promise and Law. It offers a variety of kinds of practical training opportunities for service to others in such fields as agriculture, arts, crafts, community life, health and safety, homemaking, international friendship, literature and dramatics, music, dancing, nature, outdoors, sports, and camping.

Alyssa, a girl of twelve, was not only shy, but did not have the ability to share with others. Through encouragement and support of her parents she joined the Girl Scouts. Gradually, through the various camping and social activities of this organization, she began to think more of others, to share her ideas and personality with friends. With the support and understanding of a group worker, she developed her personality in many ways, gaining confidence and an improved self-image. After two years' association with the Girl Scout group, she was elected, by vote, as one of the leaders. People who knew her before and after her membership in this organization could hardly believe the changes that had taken place.

Numerous other youth organizations also provide group work activities, including Boys' Clubs of America, Girls' Clubs of America, Camp Fire Girls, the Catholic Youth Organizations, Jewish Community Centers, and Young Men's and Young Women's Hebrew Associations (YMHAs and YWHAs). These agencies, and others, offer various recreational, health, and welfare opportunities, many of which are related to group endeavors.

Group Services in Host Agencies

Group process is being used considerably in the field of corrections. The influence of group action is illustrated in this case glimpse from a juvenile correction facility. A new boy who had just been introduced to a group in a delinquency center was questioned by his peers. He was in legal trouble for stealing. They asked why he stole and he said "to get even with my dad." He had taken a gun and killed a goat belonging to his father. They asked him why he did this, and he again replied "to get even with my old man." The boys questioned him further, and it was apparent that they were helping him bring out some of his feelings as well as their own. Through these group discussions the youths shared with each other what they had done, why they had done these things, how they felt about their behavior and society, and what they thought they should do in the future.

In hospitals, clinical social workers often help patients in groups understand some of their medical and emotional problems. To illustrate, a small group of elderly cardiac patients met together to discuss their heart conditions, their feelings about their health, and the reaction of their families to their medical problems. As they shared their fears and anxieties, the social worker was able to guide their thinking to ways they could solve some of their problems. After a few sessions together their total adjustment to both medical and psychological conditions improved.

In psychiatric hospitals groups of patients join together on a group basis under the guidance of a group leader. They meet once or twice a week and discuss themselves, their difficulties, their hopes, their aspirations, and their plans. In one such hospital, the patients were even given the opportunity and responsibility to discuss and help with the planning of group members regarding their leaving the institution. The doctor who reported this experience said that the patients did an effective and fair job in helping people plan for and carry out departure from the hospital. In other words, through the use of the group as a tool, many patients were influenced and assisted in planning for release.

Many school districts utilize group process in working with boys and girls who have various kinds of personal and family problems. Under guidance of a qualified social worker, eight to twelve boys and/or girls meet together regularly. They discuss themselves, their problems, adjustments, relationships in school, and family situations and help each other understand their difficulties and that effective action can be taken regarding them. Many boys and girls today are adjusting well in school because the group has been utilized as a tool to assist them to understand themselves better, to face personal and family problems, and to actively work toward improvement. The group has helped free them of the problems that have shackled them and kept them from achievement in school.

Group process is used in the areas of marriage and family relations. John and Mary Smith were having serious marital difficulties that involved lack of affection and the inability to communicate. After individual interviews at a family service society they were invited to join a group of six couples who had similar or related difficulties. The social worker, Luwanda, who directed the sessions helped the group share their problems, hopes, and plans. Through this interaction they developed an understanding of themselves, of each other, and their marital relationship. After several sessions John and Mary discovered they were ineffectively communicating on several levels, and through successful attainment of out-of-group asssignments they also became aware that each had become more affectionate.

An example of a newer service utilizing group process is that of Joe Girardi, a 19-year-old who had been using drugs for three years and had decided he wanted to quit. He went to a residential drug treatment center. He paid $50 a month and lived there for six months. During that time, he was helped to become aware of other people's needs as well as his own and was assisted back to meaningful relationships with others. The group process was utilized as a major tool in achieving these goals.

Joe belonged to a group of about thirty who were living in the residential center and who shared meals and other living experiences. He joined with the total group in management and other discussions almost on a daily basis. He also participated at least weekly in small-group discussions, in which there were five to eight members and one or two group workers. In these meetings they shared and discussed their own feelings, needs, plans, decisions, and hopes. These weekly conferences ordinarily lasted about ninety minutes. Occasionally Joe participated in a marathon group, again involving a small group of five to eight persons, in which there was a deeper kind of group process utilized to help him and the others become more aware of their own needs, the needs of others, and to return to meaningful interpersonal relationships.

A third kind of group experience included recreational activities where the residents of the center became active in the local Y, attended sports events, or participated in other recreational activities. The power of the group was effective in helping bring about changes in Joe, in his attitude, his philosophy of life, and way of living. At the end of six months he walked out the front door of the living center with a firm conviction that use of drugs was a thing of the past for him.

In recent years group treatment has been emphasized in the area of spouse and child abuse. Groups have been formed to assist victims of childhood sexual abuse, perpetrators of sexual and physical abuse, and neglectful parents.

Summary

Everyone soon discovers social needs, interests, and imperatives basic to the individual's effort to survive. Social hungers are the common lot of humankind. People need association with other human beings, to be nurtured, loved, wanted, and understood.

Group work is based on the assumption that individuals have a need for each other. Personality enhancement and social functioning are tied to considerations related to the group. Group work is a method of working with the individual, of treating him or her, of helping him or her adjust, achieve his or her potential through the vehicle of the group, and of helping the group as a whole toward achievement of goals approved by society.

The social worker uses the knowledge of the individual and group association to effect change and uses program and various media such as crafts, games, and other creative activities to produce change within the individual.

As an open system, the group process is identified with several models of practice including the social goals model, the remedial model, and the reciprocal model. Goals and purposes of the group determine the model to be used.

Selection of individuals for the group is determined by such factors as age, value system, common problems, enjoyment patterns, intelligence, tolerance of structure, sex, and ego strengths.

In planning group process, consideration is given to setting; group size; group rules; open or closed groups; short-term or long-term groups; meeting days and time; male, female, or mixed groups; leadership; and programming. Workers also need to understand and be able to evaluate group development based on the stages.

Group work, one of the basic social work processes, is utilized in providing services both in traditional group work agencies and in various host and treatment centers. It is being used effectively to help individuals and families face their problems and solve them through utilization of the power of the group and group interaction.

The principles of group work include recognition of the fact that it is an enabling function based on scientific knowledge and understanding. It is guided by such principles as the use of relationship, use of self, use of the agency, acceptance, starting where the group is, individualization, personal involvement and responsibility, and the use of verbal and nonverbal techniques for achieving communication. Principles of group selection lead to more effective results in working with groups.

Selected References

ALISSI, ALBERT S., *Voices from the Field: Group Work Responds.* New York: Haworth Press, 1997.

ANDERSON, JOSEPH, *Social Work with Groups: A Process Model.* New York: Longman, 1997.

BALGOPAL, PALLASANNA R., and THOMAS V. VASSIL, *Groups in Social Work, An Ecological Perspective.* New York: Macmillan, 1983.

BEAVER, MARION L., and DON A. MILLER, *Clinical Social Work Practice with the Elderly,* 2nd ed. Belmont, CA: Wadsworth, 1992.

BROWN, LEONARD N., *Groups for Growth and Change.* New York: Longman, 1991.

COREY, GERALD, *Theory and Practice of Group Counseling,* 4th ed. Monterey, CA: Brooks/Cole, 1995.

GARVIN, CHARLES D., *Contemporary Group Work,* 3rd ed. Englewood Cliffs, NJ: Prentice Hall, 1996.

GITTERMAN, ALEX, and LAWRENCE SHULMAN, eds., *Mutual Aid Groups, Vulnerable Populations, and the Life Cycle,* 2nd ed. New York: Columbia University Press, 1994.

JOHNSON, DAVID, and FRANK P. JOHNSON, *Joining Together: Group Therapy and Group Skills,* 8th ed. Boston: Allyn & Bacon, 2003.

KOTTER, JEFFERY, *Learning Group Leadership: An Experiential Approach.* Boston: Allyn & Bacon, 2001.

NORTHERN, HELEN, *Social Work with Groups,* 2nd ed. New York: Columbia University Press, 1988.

REID, KENNETH E., *Social Work Practice with Groups: A Clinical Perspective,* 2nd ed. Pacific Grove, CA: Brooks/Cole, 1997.

TOSELAND, RONALD W., and ROBERT F. RIVAS, *An Introduction to Group Work Practice,* 3rd ed. Boston: Allyn & Bacon, 1998.

YALOM, IRVIN D., *The Theory and Practice of Group Psychotherapy,* 3rd ed. New York: Basic Books, 1986.

ZASTROW, CHARLES, *Social Work with Groups,* 2nd ed. Chicago: Nelson-Hall, 1992.

Notes

1. Benjamin L. Stempler, Marilyn Glass, and Christine M. Savinelli, eds., *Social Group Work Today and Tomorrow: Moving from Theory to Advanced Training and Practice* (New York: Haworth Press, 1996), p. 1.

2. John Day, *Jefferson Profile* (New York: John Day, 1956), pp. 136–137.

3. Anne Frank, *Diary of a Young Girl* (New York: Doubleday, 1952), p. 139.

4. John Gottman and Joan DeClaire, *The Relationship Cure* (New York: Three Rivers Press, 2001), p. 3.

5. Frederick William Roe, ed., *Essays and Poems of Arnold* (New York: Harcourt, Brace & World, 1934), p. 411.

6. Ronald W. Toseland and Robert F. Rivas, *An Introduction to Group Work Practice,* 5th ed. (Boston: Allyn & Bacon, 2005), p. 3.

7. Samuel T. Gladding, *Group Work: A Counseling Specialty* (New York: Macmillan, 1991), p. 3.

8. Helen Northern and Roselle Kurland, *Social Work with Groups,* 3rd ed. (New York: Columbia University Press, 2001), p. 18.

9. Gisela Konopka, "Group Work: A Heritage and a Challenge," in *Selected Papers in Social Work with Groups* (New York: NASW, 1960), p. 8.

10. Kenneth E. Reid, *Social Work Practice with Groups: A Clinical Perspective,* 2nd ed. (Pacific Grove, CA: Brooks/Cole, 1997), p. 4.

11. Toseland and Rivas, *An Introduction to Group Work Practice,* p. 12.

12. Ibid., p. 12.

13. Lynn T. Billenberg, "A Task-Centered Preventive Group Approach to Create Cohesion in the New Step Family," *Research on Social Work Practice,* 1 (October 1991), pp. 416–433.

14. Robert F. Schilling, Nina Koh, Robert Abramanitz, and Louisa Gilbert, "Bereavement Groups for Inner-City Children," *Research on Social Work Practice,* 2 (July 1992), pp. 405–417.

15. Beatrice Rogoff Plasse, "Parenting Groups for Recovering Addicts in a Day Treatment Center," *Social Work,* 40, no. 1 (January 1995), pp. 65–74.

16. Alex Gitterman, ed., *Handbook of Social Work Practice with Vulnerable Populations* (New York: Columbia University Press, 1991).

17. Jerrold R. Brandell, ed., *Theory and Practice in Clinical Social Work* (New York: Free Press, 1997).

18. Karen K. Kirst-Ashman and Grafton H. Hull, Jr., *Understanding Generalist Practice* 4th ed. (Chicago: Nelson-Hall, 2006).

19. Charles Zastrow, *Social Work with Groups,* 2nd ed. (Chicago: Nelson-Hall, 1992), p. 4.

20. Toseland and Rivas, *An Introduction to Group Work Practice,* p. 29.

21. Robert L. Barker, *The Social Work Dictionary,* 5th ed. (Washington, DC: NASW Press, 2003), p. 404.

22. Alex Gitterman and Lawrence Shulman, eds., *Mutual Aid Groups, Vulnerable Populations and the Life Cycle,* 3rd ed. (New York: Columbia University Press, 2005), p. xi.

23. Catherine P. Papell and Beulah Rothman, "Social Group Work Models: Possession and Heritage," *Journal of Education for Social Work* (Fall 1966), pp. 66–77. Reprinted with permission of the Council on Social Work Education.

24. Ibid., pp. 69–70.

25. Ibid., pp. 74–75.

26. Case examples and ideas on group formation adapted from unpublished papers by Margie E. Edwards, Professor of Social Work, Graduate School of Social Work, University of Utah.

27. Toseland and Rivas, *An Introduction to Group Work Practice,* p. 88.

28. YMCA, *About US, FAQ.* Retrieved from www .ymca.org/annualreports/2006.

29. YWCA, *Mission Statement.* Retrieved from www.ymca.org/site/pp.asp?c=djISI6PIKpG&b= 281372.

7

Social Work Practice with Communities

In a western city juvenile delinquency was rampant. Boys and girls in their early years were getting into trouble with the law, and both youths and adults were becoming apprehensive about being out on the streets at night. Newspapers reported robberies, burglaries, drug abuse, rapes, and occasional murders. What should be done? Could the citizens band together to do something?

Various citizens and community leaders began to think seriously about their local situation. Leaders in the Community Welfare Council met and discussed this social problem. A committee was appointed in the council under the direction of a social worker who was skilled in community organization to make a study and recommendations. From several months of study the committee ascertained that juvenile delinquency and youth violations had definitely been on the increase in this locality during the previous decade and warranted concerted action by citizens and community leaders. Another committee was appointed by the council to formulate plans and recommendations for alleviating this problem. This committee devised an overall plan with many recommendations for action. Members invited some of their youths to serve on the planning and action committees. The teenagers presented many ideas the adults had never thought about. Together they formulated sound plans and began to put them into operation. These plans called for informing the public about juvenile delinquency on a local level and inviting their cooperation in facing this problem. Professionally trained social workers were hired to work with the street-gang groups and to use their abilities in other ways. Paraprofessionals were also drafted. Local clubs and organizations, after discussing the problem of delinquency and the plans of action, gave support to the positive program for reducing antisocial behavior. Two recreational centers were established in temporary quarters to provide more opportunities for youths in their leisure-time hours.

What was the outcome? Within two years the amount of delinquency in this community was reduced by one-half. Parents and youths were communicating with each other and helping each other. Why had the change come about? Simply because people within a community faced a problem and worked together, helping each other confront and reduce it.

What Is Community Organization?

Working with the community requires the generalist practitioner to be able to assess community functioning and design specific intervention techniques. Community work can be very satisfying if the generalist worker understands both the knowledge and process variables needed to be effective in this area.

Community organization has been recognized for many years as one of the main methods of social work. In fact, the Curriculum Policy Statement of the Council on Social Work Education, issued back in 1962, included community organization, along with casework and group work, as the three major methods of social work.

Additionally, through the influence of systems theory and the ecological perspective, along with the generalist model of practice, many schools have since chosen to use the broader term *macro practice* to refer to work done with communities, along with organizations and those skills applied to administration. Barker writes that macro practice is "aimed at bringing about improvements and changes in the general society. Such activities include some types of political action, community organization, public education campaigning, and the administration of broad-based social services agencies or public welfare departments."[1]

Although macro practice is still based on such basic theoretical concepts as social action, social planning, and locality development, there has been considerable debate regarding which direction macro practice should take in the social work profession. Zastrow and Kirst-Ashman state

> National and world politics have changed since the three traditional methods of community organization were enthusiastically espoused. Resources continue to shrink and hard decisions must be made regarding where they should be focused. Many postulate that macro practice today is substantially different than it was a few decades ago.
>
> Macro practice, which involves effective interventions with large systems and organizations on behalf of people, is still a major thrust of generalist social work. Systems and their policies need changes and improvement. Oppressed populations need advocacy on their behalf. The focus of change must not be limited to changing the behavior of individual clients or client groups. Rather, there is a cluster of macro practice skills that social workers can use to effect change. Today most macro practice takes place within an organizational context.
>
> The basic concept of community is no less important now than it was years ago. It remains just as critical to focus on the benefits of large groups of people, their overall well-being, their dignity, and their right of choice. The community concept provides a global perspective with which social workers can view the world, assess problems, and set goals.[2]

In the past, Dunham suggested that community organization was "a conscious process of social interaction and a method of social work concerned with any or all of the following objectives: (1) the meeting of broad needs and bringing about and maintaining adjustment between needs and resources in a community or other area; (2) helping people to deal more effectively with their problems and objectives by helping them develop, strengthen, and maintain qualities of participation, self-direction, and cooperation; (3) bringing about changes in community and group relationships and in the distribution of decision-making power."[3]

Brager and Specht indicated that community organization was "a method of intervention whereby individuals, groups, and organizations engage in planned action to influence social problems. It is concerned with the enrichment, development, and/or change of social institutions, and involves two major related processes: planning (that is, identifying problem areas, diagnosing causes, and formulating solutions) and organizing (that is, developing the constituencies and devising the strategies necessary to affect action.)"[4]

Kettner, Daley, and Nichols[5] defined community organization in the context of a planned change model. The three components of their model include the change process, arenas for practice, and types of interventive effort anticipated. The change process includes the following nine steps:

1. Identifying the change opportunity
2. Analyzing the change opportunity
3. Setting goals and objectives
4. Designing and structuring the change effort
5. Resource planning
6. Implementing the change effort
7. Monitoring the change effort
8. Evaluating the change effort
9. Reassessing and stabilizing the situation

Thus, the two arenas for practice, at this level of intervention, are defined as organizations and the community itself. In other words, the community organization social worker or macro practitioner may be asked to provide new or better services to people by helping change the organization or the community.

In terms of modes of intervention, Kettner and colleagues stated: "Approaches or types of interventive effort are the creation of modification of policy, the creation or modification of a program, or the initiation of a project."[6] Kirst-Ashman and Hull, utilizing the generalist social work practice model, define macro practice as applying skills that "include changing agency and social policies, planning and implementing programs, and initiating and conducting projects within agency and community context."[7] In Zastrow and Kirst-Ashman's writings, they identify current models most often employed by community trained social workers as falling into one of three major categories. "A variety of approaches have been developed for community practitioners to bring about community change. Rothman (2001) has characterized them into three models: *locality development, social planning,* and *social action.* These models are 'ideal types.' Actual approaches to community change have tendencies or emphases that categorize them into one of three models; yet most approaches also have components characteristic of one or both of the other models."[8] Thus, the community organization social worker must have an understanding of how policy guides human service programs—both in organizations and communities—and must be able to change those policies and programs to be more responsive to human needs, whether it be by developing a program that strives to fulfill a need in the community or enacting some form of social change.

Certain basic factors underpin a definition of community social work practice. The community is the client. The needs of the community are paramount. These needs are spelled out in problems that affect large numbers of people. The resources of the community are considered and are tapped. Clinical social work stresses the individual-to-individual relationships. Group work uses the group as the tool to help with socioemotional needs to solve personal and/or family problems, or to accomplish a specific task as a group. Community organization is the intergroup process that utilizes community agencies and resources to ferret out its social problems and take appropriate action to remove them. Fellin states

> Competent practice at both micro and macro levels requires that the social worker understand communities as a major element of the social environment. Knowledge about communities is needed for assessing the impact of the environment on the individual's development and behavior. The social worker must know about resources located in the various communities to which the client relates (such as national helping networks), and about community conditions which might constrain an individual's personal and social opportunities.[9]

Social work practice with communities is sorely needed in our society today. The 1992 riots in Los Angeles are a grim reminder that many of our communities are fragmented and in serious disarray. As Rivera and Erlich state:

> There is little doubt that the struggle to bring about significant social change at the community level is a Herculean task. Despite widely-heard political rhetoric to the contrary, the gates to social justice are sliding further shut—not open. Increasing numbers of people of color continue to be thrown into disadvantage and poverty—homeless, drug addicted, alcoholic, imprisoned, AIDS-infected, underemployed and unemployed, pushed out of deteriorating schools without marketable skills.
>
> Community organization and development with people of color offers one small vehicle for battling to reverse this trend. The editors join the authors in the belief that organizers

Community action group meeting.

can make a difference. The work is not lucrative and is rarely romantic, but it can be critical in helping to meet people's needs. Perhaps above all it is about empowerment, an empowerment that organizer and community can share.[10]

Beginnings of Community Social Work

The first attempts to coordinate community activities and actions stemmed from the London Charity Organization Society, begun in 1869, which tried to eliminate duplication and fraud in relief administration. Its aim was to improve total services in the community through better cooperation and coordination. The first organized attempt to coordinate and systematize social services in the United States was made in 1877 with the establishment of the Buffalo Charity Organization Society. The need was great because many private agencies had been established and this brought about much duplication, with many gaps in total services, as well as unnecessary competition.

In 1909 in Pittsburgh and Milwaukee, the first community welfare councils in the United States were established. They were called Councils of Social Agencies. They have since spread and been extended so that most of the larger population centers now have community welfare councils. There are over 450 of them in the United States today. A few have developed to the extent that they have several persons on their staffs who spend full-time in research helping locate and interpret information that will be of value to the community.

These councils, organization-wise, generally focus on three main areas: health, welfare, and recreation. Most of them have a council delegate body representative of all the agencies in the community that join the council. This membership body is the basic authority for carrying out the council's activities. Usually a board of directors, elected by the delegate body, is the operating authority. The board of directors appoints various administrative committees, which consider such matters as membership, personnel, and budgets. It also sponsors project committees or task forces that deal with particular problems; for example, a committee to work on the problem of transients, services to the aged, drug abuse, or school dropouts. Social policy and action committees often play important roles.

Historically, the development of federated financial drives was also an important aspect of community social work. Originally private social service agencies conducted individual drives for money to maintain themselves and their services. As additional agencies came into being, various leaders suggested that it might be best to join hands to collect money and then divide it among the several agencies. In 1873 in Liverpool, England, the first such federated drive took place. In 1887 the first federated drive in the United States originated under the auspices of the Associated Charities in Denver. Twenty-three agencies joined together and raised a total budget of about $20,000. After World War I the name Community Chest became popular in designating federated fund driving. Expansion has taken place in these drives to the extent that in 1958 United Funds and Community Chests in 2,100 American communities raised $427,262,622 for the support of services of the 27,700 participating agencies during 1959. These united campaigns enlisted the efforts of 3,300,000 volunteers and secured 26,700,000 contributions.

Currently, many fundraising agencies are gathered under the umbrella of the United Way. The figures from 1958 are contrasted with current figures that illustrate the growth in the United Way funding through financial support as well as volunteerism. As of 2007, the United Way maintained approximately 1,300 organizations in communities throughout the United States. It is currently generating about $4 billion that are used to provide services in those communities with more than one million volunteers helping each year.

United Way is a national network of more than 1,300 locally governed organizations that work to create lasting positive changes in communities and people's lives. Building on more than a century of service as the nation's preeminent community-based fundraiser, United Way engages the community to identify the underlying causes of the most significant local issues, develops strategies and pulls together financial and human resources to address them, and measures the results. United Way of America is the national organization dedicated to leading the United Way movement. While local United Ways tackle issues based on local needs, common focus areas include helping children and youth succeed, improving access to health care, promoting self-sufficiency, and strengthening families.[11]

Community organization has been the last basic social work method to emerge. Casework gained status and recognition in the 1920s, as group work did in the 1930s. In 1909 the first section meeting of a national conference, The National Conference of Charities and Corrections, was held on the theme "Neighborhoods and Civic Improvement." This appears to be the beginning of specific interest in community organization in social work. In 1939 significant discussions on community organization as a field and method were held at the National Conference of Social Work. In 1944 the curriculum for the schools of social work included community organization as one of the "basic eight." By 1946 enough interest had developed in community organization so that, at the annual meeting of the National Conference of Social Work in Buffalo, the Association for the Study of Community Organization was founded. Its purpose was "to increase understanding and improve professional practice of community organization for social welfare." From its beginning until it merged with six other associations in 1955 to form the National Association of Social Workers, it had a membership that varied from about 500 to 1,000 individuals.

In 1950 representatives at the National Conference of Social Work at Atlantic City presented several papers on community organization topics and agreed that community organization was one of the basic processes in social work. In 1950 there were about 100 fieldwork placements in community organization in some sixteen of the accredited schools of social work. On November 1, 1962, there were 116 students in training in community planning services in the United States and Canada. As of 2001 there were 3,310, or 10.4 percent, of the total 31,847 full-time or part-time master's degree students who were taking community organization as a separate concentration or in combination with administration and planning as a method of practice.

The 1962 Curriculum Statement of the Council on Social Work Education reaffirmed the importance of community organization in both training and practice by specifying it as one of the basic methods of social work. The 1982 Curriculum Policy Statement made a significant change and no longer listed the three historical modes of intervention (casework, group work, and community organization), instead allowing for MSW programs to provide specialized training based on concentrations. Many schools of social work have chosen to continue to offer a concentration in community social work, and over the years they have been listed by a variety of titles including: community organization, social development, locality development, and social planning.

The 2001 Educational Policy and Accreditation Standards (EPAS) continue to support community practice as a fundamental skill and knowledge base critical to the profession. Broad guidelines pertaining to social work practice are identified but content must include work with individuals, families, groups, communities, and organizations. In other words, CSWE is recommending that every social work student should have some understanding of the knowledge, values, and skills of community organization practice and that some students should have the opportunity to pursue a community organization concentration.

The 2001 EPAS recommends that concentrations, offered in the second year of the MSW program, prepare graduates with advanced knowledge and skills built on the foundation content. The advanced curriculum is to be addressed in greater depth, breadth, and specificity from that content offered during the foundation year. Schools generally offer MSW concentrations according to fields of practice (mental health, child, welfare, community organization, international social work, administration) or populations at risk (children, elderly, persons who are developmentally disabled, mentally ill, and economically disadvantaged). Both the foundation and concentration curricula are to be based on the values and ethics of the profession as well as historical traditions.[12]

Social work educators are beginning to reaffirm the necessity for all social workers to understand the interconnectedness between micro and macro practice. By definition, the social worker needs to understand and work with both the individual and the environment. Netting, Kettner, and McMurty summarize the need for a connecting link between micro and macro as follows:

> Social work practice is broadly defined and allows for intervention at the micro (individual, group, or family) level, and at the macro (organization and community) level. Given this division of labor, some professional roles require that the social worker be involved full-time in macro practice. These professional roles are often referred to by such titles as *planner, community organizer, manager,* or *administrator.* The direct service worker or clinical social worker, however, also bears responsibility for initiating change in organizations and communities. The direct service worker is often the first to recognize patterns indicating the need for change. If one or two clients present a particular problem, the logical response is to deal with them as individuals. However, as more persons present the same situation, it quickly becomes evident that something is awry within the systems in which these clients are interacting. It then becomes incumbent upon the social worker to help identify the system(s) in need of change and the type of change needed. The nature of the system(s) in need of change may lead to communitywide intervention or intervention in a single organization.
>
> Given these statements, practitioners may begin to feel overwhelmed. Is it not enough to do good clinical work? Is it not enough to listen to a client and offer options? Professional practice focusing only on an individual's intrapsychic or interpersonal concerns does not fit the definition of social work. Being a social worker requires seeing the client as part of multiple, overlapping systems that comprise the person's social and physical environment. If the social worker is not willing to engage in some macro-practice types of activities relating to these environments, then he or she is not practicing social work.
>
> Similarly, social workers who concentrate in macro practice must understand micro practice, which may be defined as intervention directed primarily at the individual or group level. Without this understanding, macro practice may be carried out in the absence of an adequate grounding in the nature of client needs. MBA and MSW administrators would act similarly in all situations, and cost alone—rather than an understanding of client need balanced

with cost—would drive community planning. The interconnectedness of micro and macro roles is the heart of social work practice. In short, it is as important for social workers in macro-practice roles to understand the importance of individual and group interventions as it is for social workers in micro-practice roles to understand the importance of organizational, community, and policy change.[13]

Underlying Principles in Community Organization

First, it is important to understand, from a general perspective, the fundamental purposes of communities. Warren identified five basic functions of communities that serve its members:

1. **Socialization:** This function helps new members learn the norms, what is valued, the commonly held beliefs, and the culture.
2. **Production, distribution, and consumption of goods:** People in communities help make products and services available such as food, clothing, housing, transportation, and other services. Codes and ordinances are enacted in a attempt to regulate, to a certain extent, how and where these services are made available to its citizenry.
3. **Social control:** Laws are formulated that specify the behaviors considered acceptable and nonacceptable. These laws are based on what the community values and the norms that are held to be important.
4. **Mutual support:** This function is broadly defined and ranges from an individual helping a neighbor fix a broken sprinkler to the establishment of community services such as fire protection and law enforcement.

Community organizers can work on local needs.

5. Participation of residents: Various events and services, including community festivals, recreation programs, such as organized baseball and soccer, outreach programs that check up on shut-ins, and events held at local schools, allow members of the community to interact with one another.

Having grasped the importance of these basic functions of communities, social workers are then prepared to look more closely at the underlying principles that shape community organization as it relates to the provision of social services.[14]

McNeil, in a pioneering effort, observes that there are several principles that seem universally applicable:

1. Community organization for social welfare is concerned with people and their needs. Its objective is to enrich human life by bringing about and maintaining a progressively more effective adjustment between social welfare resources and social welfare needs.
2. The community is the primary client in community organization for social welfare. The community may be a neighborhood, city, county, state, or nation. Rapidly, too, there has emerged the international community.
3. It is an axiom in community organization that the community is to be understood and accepted as it is and where it is.
4. All the people of the community are concerned in its health and welfare services. Representation of all interests and elements in the population and their full and meaningful participation are essential objectives in community organization.
5. The fact of ever-changing human needs and the reality of relationships between and among people and groups are the dynamics in the community organization process. Acceptance of the concept of purposeful change and John Dewey's philosophy of the "ever-enduring process of perfecting, maturing, refining" as goals in community organization is basic.
6. Interdependence of all threads in the social welfare fabric of organization is a fundamental truth. No single agency can usefully "live unto itself alone," but is constantly performing its functions in relation to others.
7. Community organization for social welfare as a process is a part of generic social work.[15]

Community social work is based on and related to certain fundamental assumptions. Ross epitomizes these as follows:

1. Communities of people can develop the capacity to deal with their own problems.
2. People want change and can change.
3. People should participate in making, adjusting, or controlling the major changes taking place in their communities.
4. Changes in community living that are self-imposed or self-developed have a meaning and a permanence that imposed changes do not have. "Man, insofar as he acts on nature to change it, changes his own nature," says Hegel.
5. A "holistic approach" can deal successfully with problems with which a "fragmented approach" cannot cope.

6. Democracy requires cooperative participation and action in the affairs of the community, and people must learn the skills that make this possible.
7. Frequently communities of people need help in organizing to deal with their needs just as many individuals need help in coping with their own individual needs.[16]

Community Social Work Processes

Although there are various classifications and descriptions regarding the processes utilized in community social work practice, those most commonly discussed and utilized are presented in the following pages.

Research

Social research is the process of obtaining facts regarding social phenomena, social problems, and their solutions. Scientific research is regarded as basic to community social work. For example, a community recognizes that it has a problem in juvenile delinquency. The newspapers report a sensational account of a young girl being attacked in a dark alley. What can the community do about it? What does it do about it? How much delinquency is there? Where are the areas of greatest delinquency? These and other questions can be answered by capable and properly trained individuals ferreting out the facts and studying the total situation.

Various research methods are utilized in community social work practice. Statistical studies, surveys, and case studies are used in particular. The underlying idea is that a community, to act wisely and fairly, must know what the realities are and what the facts show.

Planning

Planning is purposeful formulation of future action and ways of procedure. In community social work it is used extensively. It is usually carried out by representatives of various community groups meeting together and making decisions regarding social difficulties and their solutions.

In a southern community, a canal in an old dilapidated part of the city was wide open, with no fencing or protection. Several children had wandered to the banks of the canal, fallen in, and drowned. What happened? Finally, enough parents and irate citizens voiced their opinions to the extent that the community welfare council studied this problem. Representatives from various professions and organizations met many times and formulated plans for alleviating the problem. Through careful planning and other activities, they proposed to the city planners that an allocation be made for fencing the dangerous areas. With support of the community welfare council, the press, radio, and TV, enough momentum was gathered so that the desired action was accomplished.

Coordination

Coordination is the process of working together to avoid unnecessary duplication, effort, and conflict. On the positive side, it is the joining of people, agencies, and forces to support and strengthen each other, making possible increased effective services that surpass what could be done unilaterally. This process is easily exemplified by federated drives for financing, such as those accomplished by united funds. It is also illustrated by activities of community welfare councils, which have as one of their basic aims the avoidance of unnecessary duplication of social services in a community as well as alleviating service deficits.

Coordination is more than cooperation. Cooperation is a working together to accomplish a given end. It is usually utilized positively to bring about effective activities. Ordinarily, it involves a specific, single goal. Coordination generally encompasses a combination of goals and affects several people or groups. In community organization it means that various peoples and agencies in the community join hands to support each other and help each other to attain better individual and mutually shared goals.

Organization

Organization is the process of establishing a structure to accomplish certain goals. In community social work it is the method of formulating a structure to consider community needs, resources, and the utilization of the resources to satisfy the needs. Various kinds of organizations exist in this area. United funds, community welfare councils, coordinating councils, community information services, state conferences on social welfare, and national and international agencies are established to understand social problems and to help meet them. A formal organization usually gives substance to a movement. Without it, activities, even though some are significant, often take place on a hit-or-miss basis. (See Figure 7.1.)

An example of an organization that is effective in relation to community problems is a state-formed association of citizens. It was organized to bring together representative individuals to become well acquainted with social problems in the state, study them, talk

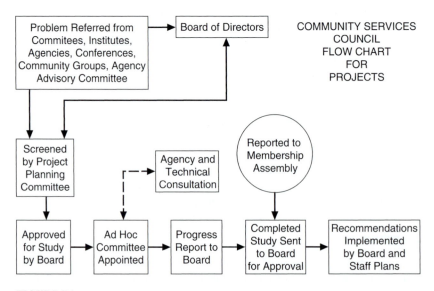

FIGURE 7.1

about them, and attempt to make specific recommendations to legislative bodies to do something about them. This association was organized as an action group. It has helped bring about many worthwhile changes in its particular state. The organization has been a tool that has opened one avenue to accomplishing social goals.

Financing

Financing is the process of collecting, budgeting, and spending funds in relation to community needs and resources. Collection is usually carried out by a combination of professional persons and volunteers. United Way drives are examples of this kind of activity. Millions of dollars are collected each year. Appeals are made to touch the heartstrings as well as the minds of people.

Most united funds, welfare councils, and other community social work bodies have committees on budgeting. These committees try to study the needs and make proper allocations so that the total community welfare is best served. This most challenging aspect of community organization requires dedication and careful thought and consideration.

The spending part of this process is done by the specific agencies, most of which have finance committees. These committees prepare budgets prior to fund drives and then work out detailed plans for the best use of the money that is available after the annual allocation has been received. Again, this process is a challenging one requiring careful consideration and planning. Frequently the trained social worker on the staff can be most helpful in assisting the finance committee to work out a fair and appropriate budget, with specific listings of expenditures.

Administration

Social work administration can be defined as the process of transforming social policy into social services. It is the process of carrying out plans and implementing the actions on which decisions have been reached. It is a particularly important process in community organization.

Effective administration includes all the staff, not only the executive, but the janitor, the assistant secretary, and the board. Where all staff members are a part of the total venture and make suggestions and contributions to the total effort, the best results ensue. In the next chapter we will present a more detailed discussion of administration.

Committee Operation

Committee operation is the essence of social work community practice. Through committees most of the planning and action takes place, decisions are made, and ideas and feelings are brought into the open, making it possible for appropriate action to follow. The social work community processes are effective when committees function on a democratic basis; otherwise complications arise. For adequate committee operation there needs to be adequate representation for all of the groups that may be interested and involved in relation to a particular project. Committees do most of the planning for community action. Ordinarily it is best for committees to be small; otherwise they bog down and become ineffective.

Experts in the field recognize that it is difficult for a group of more than ten to fifteen to work together effectively. Usually even smaller groups are better.

Committee members should be selected for their interest in a given problem, for their knowledge and abilities to help with a problem, and for their willingness to use their time and talents in working on the problem to bring about appropriate action. Ordinarily, it is not best to pressure people into accepting committee assignments; rather it is more effective to appeal to their civic pride and to stress that their services are needed for important tasks ahead.

Within the work of the committee, the community organizer has to know how to resolve conflicts through negotiation. A good record must also be kept of the actions of the committee as a reminder of the thinking and planning of the past and as a tool for opening the door for appropriate action in the present and the future.

Advocacy and Social Action

One of the significant developments in community social work has been the increasing emphasis on client advocacy. Earlier only a few social workers went "all out" to back up and champion their clients and groups of disadvantaged persons, trying to bring about social action and social change to help fulfill their needs and improve society. Today advocacy and the social action model of community organization are a well-accepted part of social work practice. Examples of social action can be seen in the civil rights movement, the Grey Panthers, and the National Association for the Mentally Ill (NAMI). These movements were able to create action in our society because they generated "power" by forcefully educating our country about their legitimate problems. As a result of the efforts of NAMI, every state was bound by law to have a case management plan for each chronically mentally ill person in the state by 1991. This case management law is designed to ensure that chronically mentally ill individuals will have a coordinated and comprehensive service delivery system to help them cope and maintain their human dignity.

Advocacy and social action in social work practice and education are gaining momentum. Many social workers in community settings and agencies are assisting their clients with support and guidelines in facing social problems and in trying to change strong debilitating situations and patterns. Social workers must be willing to learn and use principles of advocacy when they encounter dehumanizing conditions or abusive treatment within service agencies or societal institutions.

An example of community work is illustrated in the concept of the Neighborhood Team.[17] The concept developed as a result of the need for change felt by social workers within the Division of Child and Family Services. The basis for the concept is to build relationships with key community partners and families for the purpose of strengthening families and protecting children. It is a community-based system of care. Teams are set up to work in specific areas of the county in order to be close to local community members and agencies (schools, community leaders, health care). The goal of the team is to join together in a partnership with at-risk families to help in accessing and utilizing community services within a neighborhood. By moving services out of a main central office and back into the community, families are able to build relationships within their community partners and avoid the breakup between parents and children.

Roles of the Community Organizer

Social workers in community organizations should have good technical skills and be able to get along well with people. Much of community organization is done to change systems, and many times the system resists change. The resistance usually comes in the form of anger or hostility from people who are going to be affected by the change. The community organizer needs to be able to systematically apply a relevant body of knowledge that is guided by social work values. Rubin and Rubin have defined four key roles in community organization as follows:

ORGANIZERS AS TEACHERS

Consistent with the ideal of community development, it is fundamental for a community organizer to believe in the objectives of increasing human capacity. One way of doing so is through the creation and encouragement of local leadership, that is, the activation of potential partisans into roles in which they directly confront authorities. Building capacity is teaching people that they can be leaders.

ORGANIZERS AS CATALYSTS

A community organizer is also a catalyst, a person who stimulates actions in others. Organizers start community organizations by finding common problems that community members feel to be important, bringing together people who may not know each other, or working to create a sense of community that can become the basis for organizing. Organizers try to target initial actions so that they bring about victories to keep people interested and active. Organizers gradually enlarge people's vision of what is possible and thereby get them active on a range of issues.

ORGANIZERS AS FACILITATORS

Community organizers do more than start people on solving a problem; they also act as facilitators. Too often, community actions fail because members lack the experience or patience to keep an organization going. Probably, more organizations fail from lack of follow-through than from lack of original enthusiasm. The community organizer facilitates keeping an organization going and ensures the follow-through.

A LINKING ROLE

The fourth role often played by organizers is in bridging the gap between the organization, its members, and the community. There are many ways in which linking is accomplished.

Sometimes, linking involves a broad search for information: What is the political climate? How much support will the group receive for its cause? At other times, linking is limited to a very specific task. For example, one person in a woman's rape counseling center may work as a liaison with police to discuss testimony, protection, or training police to deal with victims.[18]

The community organizers should have the ability to relate to people, analyze problems, locate resources, see potential for change, and create effective structures for problem solving. These abilities combined with skill in the roles of teacher, catalyst, facilitator, and a creator of linkages are essential for community organization effectiveness.

Case Summaries

Current action in community social work is illustrated by the two case summaries that follow.

Older Citizens' Center

Concern for problems of and services for older citizens prompted the Community Services Council to appoint a representative committee of aging to consider what needed to be done in the community. Based on a study of need made by the department of sociology of the university and information from other communities, the committee surveyed the community resources and exist-ing programs for senior citizens. These responses indicated that many organizations and agen-cies were interested and that several had projects underway. However, the survey results revealed that, for the most part, these activities were fragmentary in nature and sorely in need of coordi-nation and direction with respect to the overall needs of older persons in the community.

In developing its plan, the committee agreed that it would be most effective if the various pro-grams were developed one by one, as resources and support became available. Several factors con-tributed to the selection of leisure-time services as the first area of focus by the committee. These included (1) the recognition that leisure-time activities represented a major need for older persons, (2) the need for a focal point around which a number of activities might be supplied, (3) the lack of a coordinated leisure-time program, and (4) identification of the inadequacies of facilities and pro-gram in the largest recreation program in the county, the County Recreation Department.

The committee involved others in its next steps. Census material was studied. Program experi-ence was sought from other communities. A visit was made to the Los Angeles area to see develop-ments firsthand. Out of this investigation came the recommendation for a new facility in a central location. The story of need was presented to the county commissioners, who agreed to erect the building if the city would supply the land. The city commission asked the committee to recommend a location and considerable effort was expended in listing possible spots and an ideal location. Finally, after some disagreement in the community, the location was agreed on and the building program set into motion. Result is that a new senior citizens' center has become a reality.

Protective Services

At a meeting of the Community Services Council, representatives of several community agen-cies expressed concern over the large number of child neglect complaints that regularly came to them. It was reported that many children who were waiting for possible placement in foster homes were lodged in the county detention home, which was considered unsatisfactory and undesirable from the standpoint of both child and agency.

In discussing the situation, several questions were raised: How many complaints of child neglect were received by the agencies? What were the nature and source of such complaints? How many agencies were offering protective services? How adequate were the services? What consti-tutes a sound protective service program? As a result of the discussions a committee was formed to find answers to these questions based on an agreed-on definition of protective services.

Questionnaires were distributed to agencies to gather information concerning agency pro-tective service activities during the previous year and protective service complaints. During the year the committee studied the responses and deliberated on a proposed plan of procedure. It was finally recommended by the committee and approved by the council's board of directors that a unit of protective services be established in the county department of Public Welfare's Child Welfare Division. Negotiations with the state and local departments culminated in the unit being established with the provision that the council cooperate in appointing an advisory committee to aid in getting the program underway and in helping set up a plan of procedure and referral system with the other agencies. As a result, the State Conference on Social Welfare adopted "protective services" as the theme of its annual conference a year after the program was started, and other counties have requested assistance of the council in organizing such a service.

Summary

Community social work is one of the main approaches in social work. It is the intergroup process that attempts to help communities understand social problems that exist and utilize available community resources to bring about solutions that will strengthen the total community and enrich the lives of its members.

Community social work is one of the newer thrusts in social work and one that has great potential for preventing and solving social problems.

Many of the principles basic to community organization are shared with clinical and group work, but there are several that are unique.

Basic processes in community social work practice include research, planning, coordination, organization, financing, administration, committee operation, and advocacy and social action.

The four main roles of the community organizer are teacher, catalyst, facilitator, and a person who creates linkages between organizations and communities. These roles must be carried out with skill and an understanding of the importance of human relationships.

Selected References

AUSTIN, MICHAEL J., and JANE ISAACS LOWE, eds., *Controversial Issues in Communities and Organization.* Boston: Allyn & Bacon, 1994.

BRAGER, GEORGE, and HARRY SPECHT, *Community Organizing,* 2nd ed. New York: Columbia University Press, 1987.

EWALT, PATRICIA L., EDITH M. FREEMAN, and DENNIS L. POOLE, *Community Building. Renewal, Well-Being, and Shared Responsibility.* Annapolis JCT, MD: NASW Press, 1998.

FAURI, DAVID, STEPHEN WERNET, and F. ELLEN NETTING, *Cases in Macro Social Work Practice,* 2nd ed. Boston: Allyn & Bacon, 2004.

LONG, DENNIS D., and MARIA C. HOLLE, *Macro Systems in the Social Environment.* Itasca, IL: F. E. Peacock, 1997.

MONDROS, JACQUELINE B., and SCOTT M. WILSON, *Organizing for Power and Empowerment.* New York: Longman, 1993.

NETTING, F. ELLEN, PETER M. KETTNER, and STEVEN L. MCMURTY, *Social Work Macro Practice.* New York: Longman, 1993.

RIVERA, FELIX, and JOHN L. ERLICH, *Community Organizing in a Diverse Society,* 3rd ed. Boston: Allyn & Bacon, 1998.

ROTHMAN, JACK, ed., *Reflections on Community Organization: Enduring Themes and Critical Issues.* Itasca, IL: F. E. Peacock, 1998.

ROTHMAN, JACK, and JON SIMON SAGER, *Case Management: Integrating Individual and Community Practice,* 2nd ed. Boston: Allyn & Bacon, 1998.

RUBIN, HERBERT J., and IRENE RUBIN, *Community Organizing and Development,* 2nd ed. Boston: Allyn & Bacon, 1992.

WEIL, MARIE, ed., *Community Practice: Models in Action.* New York: Haworth Press, 1997.

Notes

1. Robert L. Barker, *The Social Work Dictionary,* 5th ed. (Washington, DC: NASW Press, 2003), p. 257.

2. Charles Zastrow and Karen K. Kirst-Ashman, *Understanding Human Behavior and Social Environment,* 4th ed. (Chicago: Nelson-Hall, 1997), pp. 38–41.

3. Arthur Dunham, *The New Community Organization* (New York: Thomas Y. Crowell, 1970), p. 4.

4. George Brager and Harry Specht, *Community Organizing* (New York: Columbia University Press, 1973), pp. 27–28.

5. Peter Kettner, John M. Daley, and Ann Weaver Nichols, *Initiating Change in Organizations and Communities* (Monterey, CA: Brooks/Cole, 1985), p. 25.

6. Ibid., pp. 25–26.

7. Karen K. Kirst-Ashman and Grafton H. Hull, Jr., *Generalist Practice with Organizations and Communities,* 3rd ed. (Chicago: Nelson-Hall, 2006), p. 20.

8. Charles H. Zastrow and Karen K. Kirst-Ashman. *Understanding Human Behavior and the Social Environment,* 7th ed. (Belmont, CA: Brooks/Cole, 2007), p. 33.

9. Phillip Fellin, *The Community and the Social Worker* (Itasca, IL: F. E. Peacock, 1987), pp. 2–3.

10. Felix G. Rivera and John L. Erlich, *Community Organizing in a Diverse Society* (Boston: Allyn & Bacon, 1992), p. 25.

11. United Way of America, *About United Way, Mission and Vision: Basic Facts about the United Way.* Retrieved from http://national.unitedway.org/about/index.cfm

12. Council on Social Work Education, *Educational Policy and Accreditation Standards* (Alexandria, VA: CSWE, 2001).

13. F. Ellen Netting, Peter M. Kettner, and Steven L. McMurty, *Social Work Macro Practice* (New York: Longman, 1993), pp. 4–5.

14. Roland Warren, "Introduction," in *The Community in America,* 3rd ed. (Chicago: Rand-McNally, 1978), pp. 1–20.

15. C. F. McNeil, "Community Organization for Social Welfare," in *Social Work Year Book,* 1954 (New York: American Association of Social Workers, 1954), p. 123.

16. Murray G. Ross, *Community Organization, Theory, Principles, and Practice,* 2nd ed. (New York: Harper & Row, 1967), pp. 86–93.

17. Patti Van Wagoner, Rock Boyer, Megan Wiesen, Deb DeNiro-Ashton, and Hal A. Lawson, "Introducing Child Welfare Neighborhood Teams That Promote Collaboration and Community-Based Systems of Care," in Alvin L. Sallee, Hal A. Lawson, and Katherine Briar-Lawson, eds., *Innovative Practices with Vulnerable Children and Families* (Dubuque, IA: Eddie Bowers, 2001).

18. Herbert J. Rubin and Irene Rubin, *Community Organizing and Development* (Columbus, OH: Merrill, 1986), pp. 45–47.

8

Administration and Research

The supervisor sent a stinging memo to Ron, a caseworker with three years' successful experience in a mental health agency. The supervisor was incisive, blunt, and critical of Ron's work and his reports. Ron responded with a retaliatory memo, stating he resented what had been written and asking for a chance to see the director. The supervisor sent another memo, avoiding talking with Ron in person; then the sparks really flew. Finally, the agency administrator heard of the conflict that had begun to divide the staff and invited the two workers to her office.

The director asked each one to state what he thought the situation was and what should be done about it. Although differences were wide, as they discussed their ideas and feelings, changes began to emerge. The director encouraged them to get together more often to discuss their work with understanding and acceptance. Gradually they learned to communicate with each other and carry out their assignments with effectiveness and satisfaction.

Traditional practice in social work has encompassed direct practice, group work, and community organization, with administration and research as enabling processes. Generalist practice today provides an integrative approach with these processes intertwined and utilized to help provide a perspective and focus that are comprehensive and effective in bringing about appropriate changes in individual and group behavior. Generalists need basic knowledge of the administrative process as well as its skills in utilizing its facilitative resources.

Generalist practice reaches for increased knowledge about human behavior, especially social relationships, and recognizes the essential need for more scientific research. Again, social workers need an introductory knowledge of significant research and an ability to read and understand research literature. This chapter considers briefly the administrative and research processes that are vital to the social work profession.

Administration

Some social work educators have advocated that the administrative process is the very heart of social work education and practice. For example, the University of Chicago's graduate school of social work was named the School of Social Service Administration when it was established in 1908.

Administration is one of the major aspects of social work practice. Certainly every agency program requires an able administrator to be effective.

The demand for trained workers for administrative positions is definitely on the increase. Salarywise, many attractive opportunities exist for social work administrators.

Historically, administration has been utilized through the centuries, but has not been recognized in a formal way as it is today. More than 2,500 years ago a poem, written by Laotse in the *Book of Tao,* illustrated goals for leaders:

> A leader is best
> When people barely know that he exists . . .
> But of a good leader, who talks little,
> When his work is done, his aim fulfilled,
> They will say, "We did this ourselves."

At the meeting of the Council on Social Work Education in Detroit in 1958, a study was reported that indicated only 1 percent of full-time students in graduate schools of social work in 1957 were majoring in administration; yet 54 percent of the students suggested that within 10 years they hoped to be in administrative positions. In 1960 about one-third of all social welfare workers in practice in the United States were performing as administrators, either as supervisors or executives.

Today most master's graduates move into administrative positions on graduation or within a few years of practice. They become supervisors, assistant executives, consultants, or directors of agencies.

In 1962 there were only twenty-four students enrolled in administration in graduate schools of social work in the United States, representing eight schools. In 1974 there were 604 students enrolled in a concentration of "administration, management, social policy," representing twenty-eight schools of social work. In November 1979, there were 309 first-year master's students and 619 second-year students enrolled in the "administration, management, social policy" concentration, amounting to 3.8 percent and 6.7 percent of their respective groups. In 1994 there were 1,044 MSW students enrolled in the administration and management concentration. In addition, there were 1,384 MSW students enrolled in a concentration involving a combination of direct practice with community organization and planning or with administration or management.[1]

A study of NASW members by Chess, Norlin, and Jayaratne[2] presented a positive statement about social work administration. A significant finding of this study was that between 1981 and 1985 the percentage of practitioners in social work administration increased from 27.8 to 36.5. These authors concluded that "given the economic and political climate and its implications for the practice of social work administration, the data presented here are generally quite positive. In short, these data suggest that social work administration in 1985 is alive, happy and prospering."[3] Data compiled by NASW in the 1990s show that social work administration remains a vital part of social work practice.

Definition

John Kidneigh states that social work administration is "the process of transforming social policy into social services . . . a two-way process: (1) . . . transforming policy into concrete social services, and (2) the use of experience in recommending modification of policy."[4] This definition, of course, encompasses the idea that administration is the process of implementation, of translating policies into action programs. Stein defines the concept of administration as a "process of defining and attaining the objectives of an organization through a system of coordinated and cooperative effort."[5]

The Social Work Dictionary, 1995 edition, defines administration in social work as "methods used by those who have administrative responsibility to determine organizational goals for a *social agency* or other unit; acquire resources and allocate them to carry out a program; coordinate activities toward achieving selected goals; and monitor, assess, and make necessary changes in processes and structure to improve effectiveness and efficiency. In social work, the term is often used synonymously with management."[6]

Skidmore summarizes the various definitions of administration as follows: "social work administration may be thought of as the action of staff members who utilize social processes to transform social policies of agencies into the delivery of social services. It involves executives—the leaders—and all other staff—the followers or team members. The basic processes most often used are planning, organizing, staffing, directing, and controlling."[7]

That administration is relatively new in social work is illustrated by the fact that it was only in 1946 that the National Conference of Social Work sponsored a section on administration for the first time in its seventy-two years. This program included consideration of the following: process of administration, dynamics of leadership, salaries, job classification, boards, public relations, organized labor, civil service, program development, and retirement planning.

In the early days of social work, administration was not thought of as distinct from services and functions. By 1914 a course in administration was established in at least one school of social work and the content was borrowed mainly from adjoining fields. World War I, the Great Depression, and World War II—with their numerous problems and tensions—gave considerable focus and emphasis to the administrative process. Technical literature began to appear. For a while the Cooperative Committee on Administration was in operation. Further interest in administration was developed through a special department in the magazine *The Survey* and through the activities of leaders in the YWCA, YMCA, and Family Welfare Association of America, whose organizations were beginning to set standards for their administrators. In 1944 the Curriculum Committee of the American Association of Schools of Social Work included social welfare administration as one of the *Basic Eight* for training students.

The 1962 and 1969 curriculum statements did not emphasize administration as a specific required methodology. Nevertheless, these statements provided flexibility and opportunity for emphasis in this area. Administration is included as a possible concentration in the 1982 Curriculum Policy Statement. The guidelines state: "Practice Roles and

Interventive Modes: Practice with individuals, families and groups, consultation, training, community organization, social planning, program planning and development, administration, policy formulation, implementation, and analysis, and research."[8] Most schools now have a concentration in administration or in an administration focus related to social planning or other aspects of social work practice. By 1977 interest in social work administration had developed to the extent that a new journal appeared, *Administration in Social Work,* a quarterly "devoted to the theory and practice of management and administration in social work and related human services fields." In 1978 CSWE issued a communication that indicated administration in social work was being given "high priority." Currently, many social workers are being hired as administrators in large social service systems such as state hospitals and state divisions of family services. This trend will continue.

Basic Assumptions and Principles

One of the basic principles in administration is that all levels of staff participate in the administrative process. This includes executives, subexecutives, supervisors, consultants, direct practitioners, group workers, community organizers, secretaries, attendants, and others. Traditionally, people have thought of administration only as involving those at the top, the directors or the executives. Today, if we are to be realistic, it is essential to recognize that all staff members are involved, directly or indirectly, in the administrative process. It is also apparent that some of the major contributions toward improving administration come from persons in the lesser status categories of staff.

Spencer, in the pioneering *Curriculum Study,* suggests that several underlying assumptions should be kept in mind in relation to administration:

1. Administration of social agencies is the process of securing and transforming community resources (human and financial) into a program of community service. This process involves active participation of the board, executive, staff, and volunteers or constituency in varying degrees.
2. Administration in social work is concerned in a major way with enterprise determination, which includes goal formation. This means that the agency itself has the primary responsibility for the creation and control of its own destiny and community planning bodies exercise only a secondary role.
3. Administration in social work is concerned in a major way with "provisioning" the service. It has to do with the logistics of the program and activities of the particular agency.
4. The executive is not a neutral agent. This means that creative leadership is needed in all phases of the agency's operation.
5. The executive's functions within the agency combine the following: (a) to provide a seeing-the-enterprise-as-a-whole quality, (b) to participate in a leadership capacity and policy formulation, (c) to delegate, coordinate, and control the work of others to promote and enhance the work of board and staff, (d) to provide for board, staff, and community an executive who represents in personal attitudes, abilities, and activities a person with whom they can identify positively.
6. Administration is involved with the creative use of human resources—board, staff, and volunteer. The social agency is a group enterprise.

7. The parts of the enterprise are interrelated and interacting. This principle is basic to the operation of a social agency and means that a part of the executive function is to establish roles, relationships, rules, and regulations that will produce the optimum of good effects and the minimum of bad effects.
8. What one does not do has effects as well as what one does do.[9]

Within the past few years, social work administration has incorporated many of the principles and approaches utilized in business, particularly in improving efficiency and effectiveness in the delivery of social services.

Newman and Turem indicate that accountability is an issue of high visibility, high priority, and considerable controversy in the social work profession. At the same time, they describe the need for understanding what accountability is and for utilizing it to advantage for social work. They suggest

> A sound system of accountability goes beyond honesty and is based on results. The techniques oriented to relationships and processes, which are the heart of the social work profession, are the most "soft" and most in need of being put in proper perspective. If credible professional accountability is to occur, casework and group work must be viewed as inputs that may or may not reduce the incidence of definable social problems, and the profession must develop a new orientation based on outputs that can be measured objectively.[10]

It is suggested by Rapp and Poertner that "not to monitor client outcomes substantially and use that data to improve operations is tantamount to managerial irresponsibility, incompetence, and unethical conduct."[11] We live in an era of accountability and diminishing resources where human services agencies must continually demonstrate the efficacy of their programs. Recent developments in business management and computer technology will help social work administrators become more accountable. Cost-accounting, zero budgeting, information services, and other business advances can assist social work administrators. The unprecedented growth in computer technology and its application to business is a case in point. This is especially true of expanded telecommunications systems in which data from field offices can be transmitted in seconds to regional offices for analysis and evaluation.[12]

Supervision

Supervision, a major part of social work administration, is concerned with helping staff *use* their knowledge and skill in getting the job done efficiently and well. In the etymological sense, the word *supervision* means "oversight, control, surveillance." In social work it is more commonly used to define the function that one individual, the supervisor, assumes in relation to another, the supervisee. Supervision can be thought of as an administrative process that assists staff development and performance. The agency will function with the optimum of efficiency, conserving human values in work with clients, when the staff responsible for the operation of the agency is qualified, and when its capacity to render service is aided by effective agency policy and procedures that emphasize the preeminence of the worker in the helping process. Supervision focuses on the acquisition and use of knowledge and the application of skills to practice. It is a teaching–learning situation, educational as well as administrative and enabling.

A social worker meeting with staff.

In the public and private welfare agency the position of supervisor enjoys status and respect. The qualified and competent supervisor is a key person in a staff organization with responsibility for both administration of services and staff development.

Supervision in social work is a response to the needs of clients and the mandate of the community to relieve suffering and to restore people to greater usefulness. Social problems are always a challenge and decisions aimed at relieving stress and rehabilitation are among the most difficult on the spectrum of human experience. The supervisor's role is one of support, encouragement, the imparting of information, and of listening to the worker, particularly to the new and inexperienced staff. Supervisors point out knowledge gaps and deficiencies in skill and assist workers to control their biases. They give psychological support by allaying anxiety and by their interest and understanding; they are professional models for new workers and a bridge to the agency for the experienced worker new to the particular job or agency.

Supervision Is Teaching

Supervision is essentially a teaching job, and its theory is derived from education as well as social work. Some of the important educational principles of supervision are mentioned in the following paragraphs.

The supervisee participates actively in his or her own learning. He or she is involved in the planning for his or her function in the agency and not a receptacle of a "ready-made, hand-me-down plan" devised by someone else. This person must think through and make decisions relative to clients, which will be implemented in his or her interviews and social study. Supervision is based on the assumption that the worker learns best when taking responsibility for one's own learning. Hence, the supervisor resists the temptation, however great, to impose personal standards, values, and methods of helping. He or she encourages, gives information, and even offers advice, but will not preempt the learning role. The supervisor would agree with Emerson that "Nothing is . . . sacred but the integrity of our own mind."

The assumption is that the worker learns by doing. This individual must be given the opportunity to carry responsibility for the work performed in the agency. If mistakes are made, they will be viewed as learning opportunities and used by the supervisor to call attention to better ways of doing things. They will not be an excuse for the supervisor to take over the service function. In a Veterans Administration (VA) psychiatric hospital, a social worker was promoted to supervisor but continued his direct service function until supervisees objected because they were not permitted to do their work. One learns by doing, in part through identification. A worker, however, may be driven by fear to identify with his or her supervisor and to accept that which is imposed from without. When this occurs, learning may not be integrated, only falsely imitated, used ambivalently, and later rejected.

The worker learns by using his or her whole self. Learning is more than an intellectual exercise. It involves the integration of feelings, intellect, and performance. Frequently, learning fails to take place because of a worker's excessive anxiety, which often results in stereotyped behavior, excessive dependency, passivity, submission, and intellectualization. A friendly working atmosphere and acceptance of a supporting relationship with one's supervisor are safeguards to performance and a protection against immobilizing anxieties. Feeling and intellect are one in learning in social work.

The worker–supervisor relationship is the main dynamic in learning. It is predicated on the greater knowledge and skill of the supervisor, his or her regard for the worker, willingness to share, and on the capacities and desires of the worker. Positive learning takes place through a positive relationship. When the relationship is negative and destructive, learning is resisted or occurs under conditions inimical to good practice. The relationship can be facilitated by the supervisor who has confidence in the worker, who believes in the worker's capacity and worth. He or she builds on the worker's strengths and emphasizes those qualities that make for competence and efficiency on the job. He or she freely acknowledges the superiority of the worker in those situations where it is demonstrated. Honesty and integrity must characterize the relationship if the purpose of the agency is to be served.

One beginning worker, whose relationship with the supervisor was one of mutual respect and trust, was heard to say that she had been enhanced by (1) the knowledge her supervisor shared with her, (2) the kind of a caring person the supervisor was, and (3) in knowing that if she needed help, her supervisor was available.

Techniques of Supervision

Records of supervisory conferences are used for teaching, for improving practice, and for identifying areas of need in the training of the worker. Evaluations are also dynamic, continuous, and are discussed freely in worker–supervisor conferences that may be regularly scheduled.

Evaluation conferences at times reveal fear on the part of the worker of his or her ability to control the situation, a loss of self-esteem, a threat to the worker's self-image, and fear of punishment. Evaluations, too, become sources of satisfaction when used realistically to appraise and assess the performance of the worker by his or her superior.

The supervisor has feelings about evaluations as well. If the person lacks self-confidence and has a desire to be liked it may lead him or her to cover up the worker's weaknesses and inadequacies. To avoid conferences too charged with feeling the supervisor keeps in mind that the evaluation is a means of promoting the supervisee's learning and self-awareness and a process in which the supervisor and the worker both participate.

The subject matter of evaluation is the worker's feelings about people, his or her method of handling feelings, understanding of behavior in social situations, as well as ability to express oneself. He or she will be helped to relate to the client's needs and to the *what* and *how* of resources and will be taught to participate in the agency's program for staff development—institutes, classes, workshops, and regularly scheduled staff meetings.

One caution needs to be kept in mind—the danger of too much supervision. Some leaders in social work suggest that their supervisory system makes the inexperienced workers too dependent on the administrators and senior workers. Certainly care should be taken so this does not happen. A basic goal in supervision should be helping a worker become independent in planning and implementing the worker's practice.

Basic to successful supervision are enabling qualities of personality that make it possible for the worker and for the supervisor to be essentially giving persons. Supervisors need to bring to their jobs a readiness to live beyond themselves and a concern for people. Giving and a regard for people, combined with a trained and disciplined mind, make supervision a constructive and dynamic force in the life of the learner, enabling him or her to meet obligations to the client and the agency.

Supervision and Licensing Laws

Every state has passed legislation that requires social workers to be licensed before they can practice. An important part of this legislation requires social workers to be supervised by licensed social workers before they can be licensed themselves. In the State of Utah, for example, a social worker with an MSW degree must practice under the supervision of a licensed clinical social worker for two years before he or she can be licensed as a clinical social worker. During this two-year period, the social worker must complete 4,000 hours of general counseling, 1,000 hours of which must be in psychotherapy, pass two licensing examinations, and complete 100 hours of face-to-face supervision.

The supervision that social work students receive in their undergraduate and graduate training is an important part of social work education. The supervision that social workers receive when they become employed is equally important. In fact, many social workers believe that the supervision that BSW and MSW social workers receive as part of their employment is the critical factor in maintaining and improving social work services. Because supervision is such an important part of a social worker's growth and development, it is essential that social work agencies provide the best supervision for the social workers they employ regardless of whether they are new to the profession or seasoned professionals.

Consultation

Another important part of administration is consultation, which is the means by which agencies are able to extend and improve their services to clients. Consultation is an interaction between professional persons who explore a problem to find a solution that will best serve the needs of a client.

As a process, consultation is a technique for improving and expanding services. This method provides specialized help and technical information from a variety of disciplines by bringing together competent persons in an exchange of information, making it possible to provide greater service to troubled individuals and families.

Consultation is not the province of any one discipline. The knowledge, skill, and the scientific base it rests on is that of the professional discipline of the consultant. Social work consultants derive their competence from social work.

Consultation is predicated on three main assumptions:

1. That the consultant has a greater knowledge than the consultee in the areas of agency and worker needs, which can be communicated in usable form.
2. That the consultant can help the consultee improve on the use of his or her skills or to acquire new ones for the better performance of the job.
3. That the consultee can use the process to enhance his or her caretaking function by clarifying thinking, elaborating his or her own ideas, and defining treatment goals and purposes. Consultation may result in the confirmation of the soundness of what the consultee is doing and identify gaps and weaknesses in his or her efforts. Psychological support, selective testing of the worker's thinking, and the results of creative interaction of professional people when goal-focused are important products of the consultation process.

Principles of Consultation

The consultant organizes and arranges knowledge and skill for a specific consultation purpose, namely, that of helping someone else do the job that he or she is hired to do and do it better.

Consultation is a helping process involving the use of technical knowledge and a professional relationship with one or more persons. This is a relationship of mutual respect and confidence, which the consultant develops, enhances, and maintains by employing sound principles of social work. These include beginning where the client is, the use of a nonjudgmental approach, emotional support, acceptance, defining the situation, role clarification, and confidentiality.

Essentially, the consultant has a conviction that the consultee can do the job he or she is assigned to do. The egocentric person who attaches a magic quality to his or her own self fails in consultation for the reason that the consultant must be an enabler of others. The consultant does not evaluate or make judgments about the work of the consultee.

The consultant–consultee role is task-oriented and is concerned with only certain aspects of the consultee's function. The consultant helps with problems experienced by the consultee, although he or she may recognize that the main problem is something other than that for which help is requested. In the process of clarification the consultant may assist the consultee to encompass the broader, more vital elements of the problem. Unless this is done, however, no shift is made in the area identified by the consultee.

The consultee must be free to accept or reject the services of the consultant. The consultant never carries the force of administration and the consultation role is destroyed when the consultant tries to prescribe the use that will be made by the consultee of the service offered. The confidentiality of communication between the consultant and the consultee is the cornerstone of consultation. Consultation is facilitated when the worker's relationship with the consultant is one of trust and when he or she knows that the consultant does not evaluate personnel or report conversations to administration.

The heavily laden consultee, burdened by the pressures of the job, responds to the emotional support that comes from intelligent listening and understanding of his or her problems.

It has been generally observed that a crisis in life can serve as an impetus toward getting things done. Crises may mobilize individuals, families, and even larger groups to more thoughtful, creative behavior, and to action that may lead to constructive change and progress. Thinking behavior can be the product of crises.

Major and minor crises occur in the lives of all people and the staffs of social agencies are often confronted with crises in the lives of their clients. Sometimes workers, unaided, are powerless to give effective help in a crisis; but it is a known fact that a crisis can motivate the worker to seek and use the help of a consultant. Sometimes the inadequacies of the worker result from feelings of helplessness stemming from the magnitude of the task to be accomplished and sometimes because of gaps in training or lack of preparation and experience. Regardless of the reality, when a need exists the worker who can mobilize independently to array the various forces at his or her disposal to meet the demands of the situation is particularly favorable at that moment for consultation.

Social agencies and their workers have long recognized the benefits resulting from the contributions of psychiatrists, psychologists, cultural anthropologists, sociologists, and others who have been retained by agencies in consultant capacities. Social workers confronted with difficult and perplexing social and personal situations have been among the first to recognize and to use the knowledge of the specialist. In turn, social workers serve as consultants to other professions and on staffs in the fields of health and welfare in local, state, regional, and national offices. Services to clients are thus improved and extended. Consultation often can be particularly helpful in the schools where social workers help teachers understand human behavior and child growth and development. In addition, they help teachers develop skills in dealing with children and in evaluating their behavior.

The use of social work consultants by other helping professions and by administrators of health and social service departments and units is increasing. Their knowledge and skills related to human behavior and practice skills in helping persons with personal, family, and community problems are being utilized as never before. Also, they are often asked to provide a gestalt view of problems and solutions that is helpful to professional workers outside the social work arena.

Collaboration

Collaboration is a device for making treatment as total and as effective as possible by a wide and discriminating use of resources and by combining professional competences. At its best, collaboration is an orchestration of agency services, professional talents, and client needs.

Collaboration in the social service system becomes a shared experience in which the knowledge of professionals, paraprofessionals, and indigenous workers is shared in the various processes of service delivery.

Interagency collaboration is achieved formally and informally by cooperation and community planning, communication of information, case conferences, and referral of clients. Agencies are only loosely federated. Collaboration among them results from their common purpose of relieving suffering and restoring clients to more helpful and satisfying ways of functioning. Thus, a hospital, for example, may, through proper use of medication, nursing care, and rest, succeed in relieving a patient of distressing symptoms that are due to severe stress situations in the patient's home environment. Knowing this, the hospital, through its social work department, refers a client to a family agency for counseling, helps with family finances, and aids in the budgeting of the family income. Or again, an adoption agency whose program is to provide food, shelter, clothing, and casework services to unwed mothers refers these mothers to their own physicians for obstetrical care and uses the hospital services available in the community. If the agency takes relinquishment from the natural mother and makes plans to adopt the baby, the adopting parents are directed to lawyers who handle the legal technicalities of adoptions.

The clinic team is the best known of the formal arrangements for collaboration. It is a closely knit working group in contrast with the looseness of the organization of a community of agencies. A more rounded service is available to the client when the knowledge, skill, and training of several disciplines are pooled in deciding objectives, building programs, and planning services.

The clinic team functions under one administrator. It has a common budget, and shares the same office and work space with clients whose needs can be served by the efforts of the team working individually or in concert. Historically, the team created by the child guidance movement was somewhat proscribed. The social worker did the social study and worked with the parents, generally the mother, with a parent–child focus. Representing other disciplines were the psychiatrist, who treated the child, and the psychologist, who did the testing. These somewhat arbitrary divisions of labor have been relaxed in the child guidance clinic and community mental health center, and team concepts have been modified and adapted to a rather wide variety of clinic settings and agencies.

Teamwork Concepts

Teamwork derives its meaning and validity from the democratic tradition; it is incompatible with an authoritarian ideology. The authority is largely that of knowledge and competence, which asserts itself at each encounter with the client, or of the work to be done in the agency at that moment when it is needed.

A team is a cooperative democratic group of professional individuals who work together to provide diagnosis and treatment. They think and contribute as a whole, and no important action is taken without the consent of the group.

The team is a fellowship of people and ideas. The bond that unifies a clinic team is a bond of service—each member of the team has and shares a common purpose, a common objective, and each is desirous of providing a maximum of service for the individual who comes to the agency for help.

The team is a union of interdependent inquiry. Different team members approach the problem from the standpoint of their particular disciplines and from the framework of their body of knowledge, their philosophy of working with individuals, and their skill; yet at the same time they respect the independence, the skill, and the competence of other team members. Respect and regard for the competences of others is a cornerstone of successful teamwork. The common denominator of a team is the conception of humans as products of a biological, psychological, social, and spiritual continuum, and the method pervading the efforts of the team is that of scientific inquiry jointly pursued or of collaboration.

Teamwork is predicated on the individuality of the participating disciplines. It derives its strength through the preservation of differences. For social work this implies that before one can become a useful clinician he or she must first have established identity as a social worker. It is true, however, that individuals on the team surrender some of their independence. Team members are obligated not only to deliver their professional functions, but also to be aware of what is going on in other phases of treatment. In addition, a member must keep others on the team informed about his or her own progress, for other professions depend on him or her for the success of the case.

Teamwork does not just happen; it is a dynamic process that develops from the discovery of self and others. It implies a capacity for growth and change.

There must be conviction at the administrative level of the validity of the common purpose. There must be executive conviction that the team purpose is as important as any other. Teamwork cannot exist by administrative decree alone and structure cannot make a team. The administration should acquaint other services with, and define responsibility for, each service. The chief of the individual service defines his or her service and explains how it is given. This individual is responsible for the standards of performance and the quality of services given.

To illustrate the importance of teamwork, Skidmore has coined the term "teamship." He explains the concept as follows:

> Considerable emphasis has been placed on the importance of leadership in the administration process. However, teamship, or lack of it, is also vital. Teamship means teamwork plus the ability to work effectively in a joint endeavor. *The New Twentieth Century Webster's Dictionary* states that teamwork is "joint action by a group of people, in which each person subordinates his individual interests and opinions to the unity and efficiency of the group; co-ordinated effort."
>
> The ability of staff members to work together effectively is part of teamship. A total team effort in social work practice, involving leaders and workers, is particularly significant since social work involves people, their relationships and their feelings. Competent leadership and supportive teamwork can make a major difference in the services offered.
>
> The contributions of individual staff members to an agency can equal more than the sum of their efforts. They can be synergistic, with joint efforts and combined actions enhancing the significance of individual efforts. Staff members working cooperatively together can bring results that surpass in quantity and quality the mere addition of the contributions of each. When they do not work together, the results may be negative or diminished. As in football, cooperative, unified action brings the team's efforts and forces together; individual competition, inaction, or showing off by players may do the opposite.[13]

Overall collaboration of team members is a continuous process. Collaboration begins with a group leader, the one who coordinates all services in the setting, who must recognize the positive and negative feelings that he or she brings to the collaborative process. Such an individual must value oneself as a professional person and be clear about the way in which the service entrusted is to be offered. In social work, stress is placed on the need for the individual to be clear about individual responsibility and relationship to the patient. Unity of purpose within the organization is basic and can be reached best through the planned conference, the formal method by which the team is put together and comes into existence. However, there are informal methods through which teamwork is enhanced, and the informal methods are often equal in importance to the more formal ones.

Life Management Strategies

One of the more recent developments in social work is the application of life management strategies to social work administration and supervision. A case in point is Stephen Covey's best seller *The 7 Habits of Highly Effective People.* Covey presents a principle-centered approach to solving personal and professional problems that can be applied to social work administration and supervision. Covey's list of seven essential habits is designed to bring the character ethic back into our personal and professional lives. According to Covey, "habits are powerful factors in our lives. Because they are consistent, often unconscious patterns, they constantly, daily, express our character and produce our effectiveness . . . or ineffectiveness."[14] By developing these seven habits of highly effective people, social work administrators and supervisors and their staffs can become even more successful in serving the public. The seven habits of highly effective people include

1. Habit 1: Be Proactive.
2. Habit 2: Begin with the End in Mind.
3. Habit 3: Put First Things First.
4. Habit 4: Think Win/Win.
5. Habit 5: Seek First to Understand, Then to Be Understood.
6. Habit 6: Synergize.
7. Habit 7: Sharpen the Saw.[15]

In *The Black Book of Executive Politics by Z,* Lenson lists the rules that he considers essential if a person is to work successfully with other people, rules that can be applied to social work administrators and supervisors and their staffs:

1. Good communication and cooperation gets more work done.
2. There are two sides to every question. (Variant: Everybody's entitled to an opinion.)
3. Behave consistently if you want other people to respect you.
4. Always insist on getting credit for your ideas—and on giving it where it's due.
5. To get people to do things for you, you first have to get them to like you.
6. The best way to deal with other people is to treat them as you would like to be treated. (Did anybody ever ask you to treat them the way you like to be treated? Sure it's the golden rule, but nine times out of ten it's just as bad for others as it is for you—or worse.)
7. Nonconformity has no place in business—you have to fit in and be a team player.[16]

Another life management strategy that can energize social work administrators and supervisors and their staffs is found in Spencer Johnson's best seller *Who Moved My*

Cheese? If there is a constant factor in life and work, it is that life and work constantly change. Johnson believes change is a given in life that should be accepted and embraced rather than avoided and feared. In his book, "cheese" is a metaphor for what people want in life such as a good job, fame, money, or a vacation home. The "maze" is where people look for what they want in life and includes our spouse, children, family, friends, and work. In Johnson's story, he describes how two mice search the "maze" looking for "cheese." He offers the following suggestions for dealing more effectively with change:

1. Change happens—they keep moving the cheese.
2. Anticipate change—get ready for the cheese to move.
3. Monitor change—smell the cheese often so you know when it's getting old.
4. Adapt to change quickly—the quicker you let go of old cheese, the sooner you can enjoy the new cheese.
5. Change—move with the cheese.
6. Enjoy change—savor the adventure and the taste of new cheese!
7. Be ready to quickly change again and again—they keep moving the cheese.[17]

Shifting Power in Social Work Administration

Traditionally, social work administration included an agency director at the top with considerable authority and jurisdiction. Assistant directors and supervisors had authority to direct staff and provide services. Planning and decisions were made mainly by the administrators. Clients had little opportunity for input, to offer suggestions, or to raise questions.

There has been considerable shifting taking place, allowing for redistribution and sharing of administrative power. Three groups are involved in agency services: executives, staff, and clients. Today the leaders share more power with their staffs and with clients. In one sense, symbolically, this move leaves an authoritative power triangle behind, shifting to an open circle, which allows for interaction and sharing of ideas, feelings, and actions among all three groups. Joint discussions and decisions are common. Participatory administration is gaining momentum among staff and clients.

Another change taking place in social service administration is interagency cooperation and the sharing of power and resources. More social service agencies than ever before are working together on common problems. The work that is being done with the homeless population is an excellent example of this coordinated effort. The homeless population has many needs, so many that there is not one social service agency that can provide all the needed services. Consequently, homeless shelters, mental health centers, employment agencies, and other social service programs are working together.

Homeless shelters are providing temporary housing, food, and clothing; mental health centers are assessing for mental illness and offering treatment and medications; and employment agencies are providing jobs and training opportunities. This coordinated effort by different social service agencies requires them to share power, decision making, and resources. Some social service agencies are also submitting joint grants to find additional resources for complicated social problems such as homelessness. Interagency cooperation will become even more important, even imperative, as we move further into the new century.

Research

Research is an enabling process in social work, one that is being stressed more in practice. Social workers are recognizing the need for scientific answers to numerous questions. They need to know why people behave as they do, particularly in their social functioning, and, also, what happens when various skills and techniques of the social worker are applied in helping disadvantaged people. Social workers recognize that they can ask many more questions than they can answer; thus research is needed as never before.

Definition

What is social research? Webster's *New International Dictionary* states that research is "careful or critical inquiry or examination in seeking facts or principles; diligent investigation in order to ascertain something." *The Encyclopedia of the Social Sciences* explains that research is "the manipulation of things, concepts or symbols for the purpose of generalizing to extend, correct, or verify knowledge, whether that knowledge aids in the construction of a theory or in the practice of an art." Stated briefly, social research is systematic inquiry regarding social situations and problems, the process of obtaining social facts, or methodical inquiry into social phenomena.

Social research is related to two or more people, or situations involving such people, and their interactions. Much social research is focused on social problems of people who live together.

There is a difference between pure research and applied research. Social workers are particularly interested in applied research, which is for utilitarian purposes contrasted with pure research, which is conducted for its own sake. Nevertheless, more social workers today are developing an interest and practice related to pure research as well as applied research.

As explained previously, social problems exist in society and cause pain, unhappiness, and difficulties to millions of people. Crime and delinquency, for example, cost the United States more than $300 billion each year. Even more important than the financial burdens are the individual and family heartaches and emotional scars that result. What causes crime? How can it be reduced? Can social work help to prevent it? These and related questions are open challenges to social workers on the present scene. Such problems as mental illness, physical disabilities, and many others open the door to similar questions and the need for research.

People have many false ideas and superstitions regarding the behavior of others, their social functioning, and their social problems. Millions of dollars are spent each year on charlatans who give questionable answers and guidance to people with personal and family difficulties. Scientific research is sorely needed to help provide data for social planning, improving society, and aiding people on an individual, family, and community basis.

Social Work and Research

Many social workers believe that "Common sense is enough in working with people." This is not so. Facts are needed if we are to accomplish the goals of professional social work.

Many values of research attach to social work. Accurate observation is basic to both research and other aspects of social work. Students and practitioners who develop abilities to do research enhance their abilities to work with people in other ways. A healthy skepticism of statistics is needed by social workers and is usually acquired by research study.

Social workers need to keep abreast of current investigations and to obtain access to the new facts, techniques, and skills that are developing. Social workers are more and more called on to participate in social research activities. Many of them are now hired on a full-time basis with their professional energies going into research. Social workers need to utilize the objective techniques of science and research in all that they do. This does not mean that they abolish or eradicate their personal warmth and interest in people, but it does mean that they bring into operation scientific attitudes and techniques that can help them come closer to the realities of life and to the solutions of problems.

Briar reaffirms the growing importance of research in the following statement:

Research is becoming accepted as an integral part of the social work profession. As we know, research was, of course, a part of our profession from its earliest beginnings, but more often than not we regarded research as a less than welcome intruder whose presence we ignored, avoided, and even openly rejected.

Such attitudes toward research stemmed, in part, from two beliefs. One idea was that research was somehow incompatible with the human elements central to our profession (especially social work practice)—the feelings, emotions, and intense relationships that are an inherent part of the social worker's daily practice. The other source was the belief that what social workers do, what their practice objectives are, and even the nature of problems

Administrative unit of a social service agency.

that social workers deal with are too complex and elusive to be studied and measured by "scientific research techniques." These beliefs were widespread among social workers until quite recently.

We have discovered that research can generate findings (knowledge) that have a direct and immediate use for us. The skepticism about research among social workers was not unfounded. Little of the social work research that had been conducted produced data that we could find useful in practice. In recent years an increasing number of research findings have appeared that have direct, useful, and constructive application to social work practice. As this trend continues, social workers can be expected to look to research findings (and actually engaging in research studies) for solutions to practice problems. Also, the emergence of research methods and techniques makes it more feasible for social workers to conduct research on their own practice and in their own agencies. This development, which makes possible the incorporation of research techniques into the normal routine of practice, provides the necessary foundation not only for the generation of a body of knowledge based on practice research but also for the use of research techniques by social workers to solve their practice problems.[18]

The CSWE 1992 Curriculum Policy Statement emphasizes the importance of research in social work education and practice. The curriculum guidelines for the MSW programs include the following:

M6.12 The foundation research curriculum must provide an understanding and appreciation of a scientific, analytic approach to building knowledge for practice and for evaluating service delivery in all areas of practice. Ethical standards of scientific inquiry must be included in the research content.

The research content must include qualitative and quantitative research methodologies; analysis of data, including statistical procedures; systematic evaluation of practice; analysis and evaluation of theoretical bases, research questions, methodologies, statistical procedures, and conclusions of research reports; and relevant technological advances.

M6.13 Each program must identify how the research curriculum contributes to the student's use of scientific knowledge for practice.

Grinnell has identified the following three research roles for social workers:

The Consumer of Research: The first professional role is that of the consumer of research. This role stems from the conviction that social workers have an obligation—to self, to society, and to the recipients of services—to base their efforts on knowledge in the field.

The Disseminator of Knowledge: The second professional role is that of a disseminator of knowledge. Social workers have a responsibility to initiate and participate in systematic efforts to determine effective practice methods for social work problems. The results of such efforts are then communicated to other social workers in ways that will be useful to them.

The Contributing Partner: The third professional role is that of a contributing partner. This means joining with others to broaden the knowledge base of our profession. This means joining with others who have similar tasks and problems to rank the importance of gaps in knowledge and to determine appropriate ways of filling them.[19]

Research plays a vital role in social work education. The knowledge of the research process enhances professional practice by helping the social worker become both a consumer and producer of research.

A current example of significant developments in social research in social work comes from the National Institute of Mental Health (NIMH), which in 1994 funded forty-nine research programs, nineteen of them new, with social work faculty and practitioners as directors or codirectors, with total funding amounting to $12.5 million. "These research projects rely on collaborations between practice settings and schools of social work. They produce knowledge to make a difference in people's lives. They provide a training ground for the investigators of the future."[20]

Major Steps in Research

Social workers need to have a knowledge of basic research technology. Because of the complexity of human problems, social workers often forget or neglect to utilize the scientific method in evaluating their own practice.

All research efforts, regardless of how complex they may seem, are—based on the scientific method—a logical guide to thinking that helps the scientist study and explain problems. The scientific method has been formulated into the following paradigm by Polansky.

1. A researchable problem is located, sharpened, and related to theory (conceptualized); because this is an applied field, its practical significance is also stated.
2. The logic by which conclusions will be drawn is specified (study design).
3. Potential subjects of the study are identified (sampling design).
4. Instruments for collecting information from or about the subjects are borrowed from others or created (method of data collection).
5. Data are collected (study execution).
6. The data are analyzed statistically and/or qualitatively (analysis of results).
7. Results are compared with the problem originally posed so that conclusions may be drawn.
8. Larger implications for theory and for practice are inferred.
9. The significant elements of the whole process are summarized into an intelligible report to be disseminated to colleagues.[21]

Actually, social workers apply the scientific method in all of their practice efforts. Both practice and research require an orderly thought process, beginning with a problem and working toward a solution. Social work practitioners base their conclusions on careful observation, experimentation, and intelligent analyses.

Main Kinds of Research for Social Workers

Several methods and techniques are utilized in social work research. *Experimental research* that encompasses statistical methodology is being used considerably and involves study of a number of cases. These cases are generally arranged and classified into two groups, a control group and an experimental group. The control group proceeds in normal fashion and the experimental group has some new facet or interactional relationship introduced, which theoretically will bring about the hypothesized change or alteration. Statistical techniques and procedures are utilized to show relationships and correlations between different sets of data. Most schools of social work require one or more classes in statistical knowledge and research procedures. They also specify the preparation of a thesis or participation in a research project, either individual or group or "research lab" experiences, which helps the student learn about the importance of research and provides a beginning knowledge regarding research methodology and techniques.

A second approach utilized by social workers is the *case study* method. This process is basically an intensive study of one or a few cases, keeping in mind that an understanding of a specific case may be helpful in acquiring knowledge of human behavior and social functioning. Case studies may be accomplished by the social worker through examining records or by interviewing a client or clients. They may be obtained through the *own story* technique, which provides an opportunity for a person to write about his or her experiences and his or her reactions to them. Not only are the details of a case important, but the feeling and implications are particularly significant to social work practice.

Another method utilized by social workers is the *social survey.* This is an attempt to study on a broad basis a given neighborhood or community and to attempt to understand the underlying foundations and principles related to social problems, the behavior of people within these localities, and the total social milieu. Ordinarily, control groups are not utilized but rather an attempt is made to give an overall descriptive view of a community or other segment of society. This kind of research has been sponsored in particular by community welfare councils and coordinating councils in an attempt to find out the facts of given communities descriptively.

The *human ecological* approach is also used in studying social phenomena. This emphasizes the spatial distribution of human behavior and attempts to explain why there are differentials, geographically speaking, in regard to social conditions and problems. An example of this would be a study in a given community that would result in a geographical map showing the actual distribution by residence of the homes of the delinquents handled by the police or courts. Generally, such a map depicts certain clusterings and concentrations. Using this information, social planners attempt to understand the differentials and to do something to prevent and control delinquency, particularly in the areas of high concentration of antisocial behavior.

Another useful method in social work is the *historical* approach. This attempts to give perspective from the past for understanding present issues, problems, and plans of action and to help in improving situations. Historical research can be accomplished through library study, interviews, viewing original documents of various kinds, and through objective study, comparison, and contrast of various materials.

One of the newer methods is *evaluation research.* This is an approach to assess program effectiveness—in social work, particularly social programs designed to improve the welfare of people. Weiss suggests that in evaluation research "the tools of research are pressed into service to make the judging process more accurate and objective. In its research guise, evaluation establishes clear and specific criteria for success. It collects evidence systematically from a representative sample of the units of concern. It usually translates the evidence into quantitative terms (23 percent of the audience, grades of 85 or better), and compares it with the criteria that were set. It then draws conclusions about the effectiveness, the merit, the success, of the phenomenon under study."[22]

Some researchers indicate a need to improve methodology in program evaluation. Grasso and Epstein observe that the traditional approach based on a retrospective quantitative focus is inadequate even though it may result in statistical indicators such as number of units of service delivered or the number of cases closed. They recommend a developmental approach that includes five primary stages of client–agency involvement which evaluation can address: referral, intake, intervention, program completion, and program follow-up. Grasso and Epstein conclude

> Developmental program evaluation relies on both qualitative and quantitative data for making future-oriented clinical and programmatic decisions. Using the individual case as the primary unit of analysis . . . not only guides future program decisions, but also helps direct service workers manage their cases. It provides a method for assessing client change across different stages of agency involvement and, as a result, helps workers focus their interventions more precisely on specific client needs.[23]

Another research development that has been gaining popularity in social work is *qualitative research*. Qualitative research is a general term that includes a number of nonquantitative research approaches. It has also been called naturalistic research, interpretive research, and field research. According to Grinnell, data sources can include (1) case studies, (2) personal experiences, (3) interviews, (4) life stories, and (5) historical texts.[24] Researchers who use qualitative methods study people in their natural settings, like their homes, and focus on the meaning that they give to personal life experiences. It is a research method that addresses the uniqueness of the individual and the importance of personal experience. It is likely that qualitative research will continue to be a viable alternative to more traditional quantitative research approaches.

Evidence-Based Practice

Many social work educators, practitioners, and researchers are now emphasizing evidence-based practice as a key component of the profession. According to Thomas O'Hare, evidence-based practice is "the planned use of empirically supported assessment and intervention methods combined with the judicious use of monitoring and evaluation strategies for the purpose of improving the psychosocial well-being of clients."[25] Evidence-based practice is a framework that utilizes current empirical information to support how social workers assess and intervene with clients to help them resolve their psychosocial problems. The framework emphasizes the use of valid and reliable assessment instruments, outcome-based intervention strategies, and empirically grounded evaluation methods. In summary, evidence-based practice focuses on assessment, intervention, and evaluation methods that work based on empirically supported research studies.

NIMH has been investigating for many years what assessment and treatment models work best in treating mental disorders. A case in point is the assessment and treatment of major depressive disorders. It is estimated that approximately 20 percent of the U.S. population will sometime during their lifetime suffer from a major depressive disorder. According to the *Diagnostic and Statistical Manual of Mental Disorders* (4th ed., text revision), a person who suffers from a major depressive disorder is either despondent all of the day or most of the day or has lost interest in all pleasurable activities. The person also suffers from four other symptoms such as a sleep disorder and suicidal thoughts. These symptoms must persist for at least two weeks before the person can be diagnosed with a major depressive disorder.[26]

After reviewing numerous empirical studies that focus on how to best treat clients with a major depressive disorder, NIMH reported three important findings. First, by themselves, antidepressants such as Zoloft, Prozac, and Wellbutrin help clients who are suffering from a major depressive disorder feel better when an outcome measure scale such as the Beck Depression Scale is used. Second, by themselves, different models of psychotherapy such as cognitive and behavioral therapy also help clients who are severely depressed feel better. The third NIMH finding emphasized that when antidepressants and psychotherapy are used together they are more effective than when used separately. This last finding has become a pivotal component of evidence-based practice in assessing and treating major depressive disorders. Evidence-based practice is now being used to assess and treat other mental disorders such as schizophrenia and anxiety disorders. The framework is also being used to improve the assessment and treatment of other psychosocial problems such as martial discord and parent–child relations.

Summary

Administration and research are essential to the profession of social work. Social work education is placing more and more emphasis in these areas.

Administration is one of the major social work methods; it involves the transformation of social policies into social services. It is a process receiving greater recognition in the totality of social work practice. This process involves many basic principles and skills, which are important for adequate agency functioning.

Essentially, *supervision* is a staff development process but it also carries administrative responsibility. Supervision has been the logical outgrowth of the complexity of the job workers have been asked to do. It is a response to workers' needs to receive help on matters that often are of a difficult nature, and the solution of which have long-range consequences for the client.

Principles of direct practice and supervision are used in *consultation.* Consultation, however, does not include responsibility for administration. It offers a service to workers that will make them more effective in working with clients.

The services of an agency can be extended by consultation. They are expanded when the worker is helped to become more skillful and knowledgeable in role performance.

Collaboration is a social invention for combining skills and knowledge of several helping professions and various community resources in the service of clients. The clinic team composed of the social worker, psychiatrist, psychologist, and nurse is one of the best-known arrangements of collaboration among the professions.

Research is being recognized as a critical element in the preparation of social work practitioners. The future of the profession is dependent on scientifically based research that adds to the social work knowledge base and answers practice questions.

The central theme of all research is the scientific method. This method can be stated in a paradigm that guides logical thinking. On a general level, steps in the research process include problem selection; problem identification and formulation; development of a strategy or methodology; data collection; processing, organizing, and analyzing data; conclusions and interpretation of results; and report and application of the research. Various research methods including the experimental, the historical, the social survey, the ecological, evaluation research, and the qualitative method are utilized to gain additional understanding about social functioning and the control and reduction of social problems.

Administrative and research knowledge and skills are essential for social workers. The two enabling processes strengthen the entire profession.

Selected References

Administration

BERNARD, JANINE M., and RODNEY K. GOODYEAR, *Fundamentals of Clinical Supervision,* 2nd ed. Boston: Allyn & Bacon, 1998.

FELT, MARVIN D., and PETER KWOK CHEI LI, *Financial Management in Human Services.* New York: Haworth Press, 1998.

GUTIÉRREZ, LORRAINE, LINNEA GLENMAYE, and KATE DELOIS, "The Organizational Context of Empowerment Practice: Implications for Social Work Administration," *Social Work,* 40 (March 1995), 249–258.

KUTTNER, PETER M. *Achieving Excellence in the Management of Human Service Organizations.* Boston: Allyn & Bacon, 2002.

MIZRAHI, TERRY, and JOHN MORRISON, eds., *Community Organization and Social Administration.* New York: Haworth Press, 1992.

PERLMUTTER, FELICE DAVIDSON, *Changing Hats: From Social Work Practice to Administration.* Silver Spring, MD: NASW Press, 1990.

ROTHMAN, JULIET C., *From the Front Lines: Student Cases in Social Work Ethics.* Boston: Allyn & Bacon, 1998.

SKIDMORE, REX A., "Administration Content for All Social Work Graduate Students," *Administration in Social Work,* 2 (Spring 1978), 59–73.

SKIDMORE, REX A., *Social Work Administration, Dynamic Management and Human Relationships,* 3rd ed. Boston: Allyn & Bacon, 1995.

Research

BERG, BRUCE L., *Qualitative Research Methods for the Social Sciences,* 5th ed. Boston: Allyn & Bacon, 2004.

EWALT, PATRICIA, "Research Questions," *Social Work,* 40 (January 1995), 5–6.

GIBBS, LEONARD E., *Scientific Reasoning for Social Workers.* New York: Macmillan, 1991.

GILGUN, JANE F., "A Case for Case Studies in Social Work Research," *Social Work,* 39 (July 1994), 371–380.

GILLESPIE, DAVID, and CHARLES GLISSON, eds., *Quantitative Methods in Social Work.* New York: Haworth Press, 1993.

GRINNELL, RICHARD M. JR., *Social Work Research & Evaluation: Quantitative and Qualitative Approaches.* Itasca, IL: F. E. Peacock, 1997.

KETTNER, PETER M., and LAWRENCE L. MARTIN, "Performance, Accountability, and Purchase of Service Contracting," *Administration in Social Work,* 17, no. 1 (1993), 61–79.

MARLOW, CHRISTINE, *Research Methods for Generalist Social Work.* Pacific Grove, CA: Brooks/Cole, 1993.

O'HARE, THOMAS. *Evidence-Based Practice for Social Workers.* Chicago: Lyceum Books, 2005.

RUBIN, ALLEN, and EARL BABBIE, *Research Methods for Social Work,* 4th ed. Belmont, CA: Wadsworth, 2001.

SCOTT, DOROTHY, "Practice Wisdom: The Neglected Source of Practice Research," *Social Work,* 35 (November 1990), 564–568.

VIDEKA-SHERMAN, LYNN, and WILLIAM J. REID, eds., *Advances in Clinical Social Work Research.* Silver Spring, MD: NASW, 1990.

WAGNER, DAVID, "Reviving the Action Research Model: Combining Case and Cause with Dislocated Workers," *Social Work,* 36 (November 1991), 477–482.

WITKIN, STANLEY L., "Whither Social Work Research? An Essay Review," *Social Work,* 40 (May 1995), 424–428.

YORK, REGINALD O., *Conducting Social Work Research: An Experiential Approach.* Boston: Allyn & Bacon, 1998.

Notes

1. Council on Social Work Education, *Statistics on Social Work Education in the United States: 1994* (Alexandria, VA: CSWE, 1995), p. 34.

2. Wayne A. Chess, Julia M. Norlin, and Srinika D. Jayaratne, "Social Work Administration, 1981–1985: Alive, Happy and Prospering," *Administration in Social Work,* 11 (Summer 1987), p. 68.

3. Ibid., p. 76.

4. John C. Kidneigh, "Social Work Administration, An Area of Social Work Practice?" *Social Work Journal,* 31 (April 1950), p. 58.

5. Herman Stein, "Social Work Administration," in Harry A. Schatz, ed., *Social Work Administration: A Resource Book,* (New York: CSWE, 1970), p. 7.

6. Robert L. Barker, *The Social Work Dictionary,* 3rd ed. (Washington, DC: NASW Press, 1995), p. 8.

7. Rex A. Skidmore, *Social Work Administration,* 3rd ed. (Boston: Allyn & Bacon, 1995), p. 3.

8. Council on Social Work Education, *Curriculum Policy for the Master's Degree and Baccalaureate Degree Programs in Social Work Education* (New York: CSWE, 1982), pp. 11–12.

9. Sue Spencer, *The Administration Method in Social Work Education, Curriculum Study,* Vol. 3 (New York: CSWE, 1959), pp. 26–32.

10. Edward Newman and Jerry Turem, "The Crisis of Accountability," *Social Work,* 19 (January 1974), 12.

11. Charles A. Rapp and John Poertner, "Moving Clients Center Stage Through the Use of Client Outcomes," *Administration in Social Work*, 11 (Fall/Winter 1987), 35.

12. Arthur G. Bedeian, *Management,* 3rd ed. (New York: Dryden Press, 1993), pp. 594–613.

13. Skidmore, *Social Work Administration,* pp. 168–169.

14. Stephen R. Covey, *The 7 Habits of Highly Effective People* (New York: Simon & Schuster, 1989), p. 46.

15. Ibid., pp. 42–62.

16. Barry Lenson, ed., *The Black Book of Executive Politics by Z.* (New York: National Institute of Business Management, n.d.), p. 2.

17. Spencer Johnson, *Who Moved My Cheese?* (New York: G. P. Putnam, 1998), p. 74.

18. Scott Briar, Foreword, in Richard M. Grinnell, Jr., *Social Work Research and Evaluation,* 2nd ed. (Itasca, IL: F. E. Peacock, 1985), pp. ix–x.

19. Richard M. Grinnell, Jr., *Social Work Research and Evaluation,* 2nd ed. (Itasca, IL: F. E. Peacock, 1985), pp. 3–5.

20. Patricia L. Ewalt, "Research Questions," *Social Work,* 40 (January 1995), 6.

21. Norman A. Polansky, ed., *Social Work Research* (Chicago: University of Chicago Press, 1975), p. 15.

22. Carol H. Weiss, *Evaluation Research* (Englewood Cliffs, NJ: Prentice Hall, 1972), pp. 1–2.

23. Anthony J. Grasso and Irwin Epstein, "Toward a Developmental Approach to Program Evaluation," *Administration in Social Work,* 16, nos. 3/4 (1992), pp. 199–200.

24. Richard M. Grinnell, Jr., *Social Work Research & Evaluation: Quantitative and Qualitative Approaches* (Itasca, IL: F. E. Peacock, 1997), p. 106.

25. Thomas O'Hare, *Evidence-Based Practice for Social Workers* (Chicago: Lyceum Books, 2005), p. 6.

26. *Diagnostic and Statistical Manual of Mental Disorders*, 4th ed., text revised (Washington, DC: American Psychiatric Association, 2000), pp. 375–376.

9

Mental Health Services

"Call the police. I've got to call the police now."
That thought kept beating out a rhythm in my
mind as I watched helplessly as my father made a
shambles of my living room—throwing books on
the floor, tipping over chairs and tables, smash-
ing a lamp against the fireplace.

I knew I had to have help to subdue him—
again. The officers came at my call, put him in
restraints, and carried him screaming out the door.
I committed him to the psychiatric ward of the hos-
pital once again. Then I came back home to com-
fort my sons. How do you explain to 5- and 7-year-
old boys that they are really not at fault, even
though it was their noisy playing that made grand-
father fly into a rage?

As usual, in three days he was back home,
under the influence of sedating drugs, quiet and
apologetic. Although he is very ill, the hospital
cannot keep him because he refuses to commit
himself. He is back because the issue has not
been resolved about whether mentally ill individ-
uals who are capable of harming themselves
and/or others can be involuntarily restrained
while receiving treatment.

My father is back with me, presumably
because his constitutional right to freedom is the
standard, not how desperately ill he is or how
much he needs long-term hospital care. It appears
to me that he is given the freedom to destroy
himself, to destroy me and my own little family, as
well as my home.

Are resources and social work services
available to help?

Mental health services have expanded and today Americans generally are able to talk about
mental health problems. They are so important that three presidents and one first lady, over
a span of less than twenty-five years, have focused the nation's attention on this problem.
In 1963 John F. Kennedy, in the first presidential message on mental health, highlighted
three tasks that have come to be an imperative:

1. Seek out the causes of mental illness and mental retardation and eradicate them.
2. Strengthen the underlying resources of knowledge and above all of skilled manpower, which are necessary to mount and sustain our attack on mental disability for
   many years to come.
3. Strengthen and improve the programs and facilities serving those who are mentally
   ill and the mentally retarded.

By Executive Order, Jimmy Carter established the President's Commission on Mental Health on February 17, 1977. The commission was charged to "conduct such public hearings, inquiries, and studies as may be necessary to identify the mental health needs of the nation and to submit a report to the President recommending how these needs can be met, and identifying the relative priority of those needs."[1]

In 1987 President Ronald Reagan signed legislation (P.L. 99-660) mandating states to develop a three-year statewide comprehensive plan of services for severely mentally ill persons to receive their share of federal funding for mental health services.

Nancy Reagan, during the presidency of Ronald Reagan, raised the consciousness of people everywhere to the growing need to attack the problems of drug abuse and alcoholism, stimulating interest among all levels of society. Public schools offer classes and workshops on drugs and structure peer counseling for students, teachers, and parents. Many services have been set up and people everywhere have been made aware of the growing menace and threat of drugs to scores of basic social institutions.

Ever since President Kennedy first mandated his three tasks, many billions of taxpayers' dollars have been spent in the struggle to "seek out the causes . . . and eradicate" mental illness. Some advances have been dramatic whereas others have been painfully slow. The treatment of chronic mental illnesses such as schizophrenia and major depression has significantly improved with the development of new medications such as Clozaril and Prozac. When these medications are used in conjunction with case management and other supportive services, such devastating mental illnesses have become more treatable. Even alcohol and drug dependence has started to lessen its grip on millions of Americans because of innovative treatment programs that utilize new medications along with supportive therapy. Progress is still needed in the field of prevention, especially in relation to children and the elderly. This unchartered field of prevention remains possibly the brightest hope for the future of mental health services.

Beginnings in Mental Health

Important changes were made in public opinion concerning mental illness that prepared the way for social work in the modern era. Exorcising, a barbaric and medieval method of treatment, made sense to those who believed that mentally ill people were possessed by demons, as did some means of cleansing and propitiation to those who saw sin as the cause of the malady. Such treatment methods seem absurd now in the light of physical, psychological, and social theories of causation.

Early attempts at care were crude and inhumane. Mentally ill individuals were housed in overcrowded insane asylums, in almshouses with criminals and degenerates, and, not infrequently, in jails and prisons. Bloodletting was one of the regular treatments along with starvation, blistering, purging, surprise baths, and whippings. For a small fee, curious visitors to the asylums were entertained by "baiting the madman."

Dorothea Lynde Dix, an outstanding crusader, worked to awaken public opinion to the suffering and the needs of those with mental illness; and many others have pioneered in the mental health movement. Study, diagnosis, and more humane treatment approaches began to be substituted for procedures based on superstition and ignorance of the needs of mentally ill people.

In the United States the first social workers in the mental health field worked in hospitals. Social work became a service in the Manhattan State Hospital in New York in 1906 and in the Boston Psychopathic Hospital in 1910. In 1919, after the end of World War I, the surgeon general asked the American Red Cross (ARC) to establish social work in federal hospitals. ARC assumed this responsibility and by January 1920, social service departments had been organized in forty-two hospitals. ARC was still in army hospitals until after World War II when social workers were first commissioned in the armed forces of the United States.

The Child Guidance Movement, and its work with juvenile delinquents by William Healy, included social work. This movement made its greatest advance when, under the support of the Commonwealth Fund, demonstration clinics were established in Norfolk and St. Louis in the 1920s. In the next twenty years social work expanded rapidly in mental health activities, and although the mental hospitals were the first to make use of social work, the practice in clinics expanded more fully.

World War II dramatically brought to the nation's attention the need for some program of treatment for veterans who were disabled because of mental illness. The Mental Health Act of 1946 supported personnel development and training for the disciplines of psychiatry, social work, psychology, and nursing and later for an expanded team of mental health specialists.

Today mental illness and emotional disturbances are recognized as major health problems. As a result of an extensive door-to-door survey in 1995, it was concluded that 20 percent of Americans suffer from at least one psychiatric disorder.[2] Thus, mental illness affects nearly twenty people in every hundred.

Where do people get help when in need of mental health services? A wide assortment of services has evolved. An estimated 4,000 to 5,000 thousand mental health facilities have been established, including such agencies as community mental health centers, state and county hospitals, private hospitals, VA psychiatric services, residential treatment centers for children, free-standing hospitals and clinics, and others.

Elements of the Mental Health Network

How a person or family gets into the mental health service network is illustrated graphically in Figure 9.1. Those who need counseling may be identified by workers in the major systems of our society, such as education, religion, corrections, welfare, health, or employment systems, or they may be self-referred. In Figure 9.1 the arrows of the referral process lead only to the periphery of the six-sided mental health network because there are so many possible referral points within the network that it is impossible to diagram them all. The large arrows on the side indicate the two basic services provided. The arrow on the left that moves from the clients to the network represents the mental health counseling service component, and the arrow on the right, moving from the network to its publics, represents the prevention component.

One of the most important elements of the mental health service network is the community mental health center (CMHC).

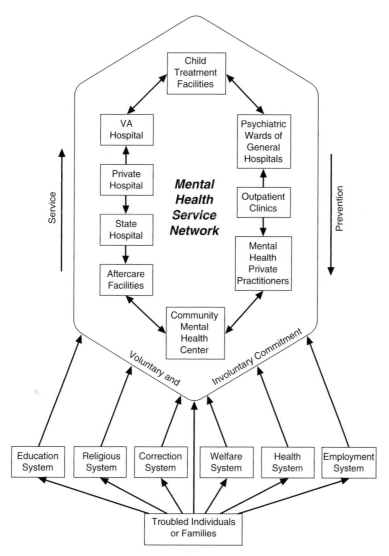

FIGURE 9.1   How the Troubled Individual or Family Gets Help from the Mental Health Service Network.

Source: Milton G. Thackeray, Rex A. Skidmore, and O. William Farley, *Introduction to Mental Health: Field and Practice* (Englewood Cliffs, NJ: Prentice Hall, 1979), p. 53.

Community Mental Health Centers

The center, a public support enterprise, provides comprehensive mental health services to citizens in every state of the country, including underserved minorities, elderly, some children, and to many living in sparsely populated, remote rural sectors of the country.

Centers, funded by federal grants to states, are mandated to provide:

1. Inpatient, outpatient, day care, and other partial hospitalization services and emergency services.
2. Programs of specialized services for the mental health of children and the elderly.
3. Consultation and education services for individuals and entities involved with mental health services (including health professions, schools, courts, law enforcement and correctional agencies, clergy, welfare agencies and health service agencies).
4. Screening services of individuals being considered for referral to a state mental health facility, and provision, where appropriate, of treatment for such individuals.
5. Follow-up care for residents discharged from a mental health facility.
6. Transitional halfway house services for those discharged from a mental health facility.
7. Provision . . . of services for prevention and treatment of alcoholism, drug addiction, and abuse and rehabilitation for alcoholics, drug addicts, and abusers.

In addition, the services of the center:

1. Must be coordinated with the provision of services by other health and social service agencies.
2. Must be available and accessible promptly.
3. When medically necessary, must be available and accessible twenty-four hours a day, seven days a week.[3]

In the late fifties and early sixties CMHCs were being planned. In the following thirty years more than 700 of the centers have been put into operation, but 2,000 are needed. Existing centers provide mental health care to millions of Americans.

Essential Elements of Comprehensive Mental Health

A public system is patterned to provide help in all areas for those who are in crisis, those who need short-term care, and those who have serious mental problems requiring care in a restrictive facility over a long period of time. This care includes locating those who need the help, and providing it, either in a mental health center or in their homes.

The treatment services include twenty-four-hour-a-day crisis services. This makes it possible for anyone in need to receive immediate help and access to medical care and placement in either a residential facility or a hospital.

All patients receive a complete diagnostic evaluation by an interdisciplinary team, with input from the family if possible. From this comes a treatment plan that considers psychological, social, rehabilitation, and medical needs. A medical evaluation is made, and follow-up care is given as necessary.

Case management services by a person or team provide long-term, caring, supportive relationships, using whatever community resources are appropriate. The case manager provides direct assistance in obtaining needed services and coordinates and monitors services within and outside the mental health system with all agencies providing service. (For more information on case management see Chapter 19.)

Therapeutic day treatment is provided four or five days a week, including either Saturday or Sunday. Clinical day treatment services are provided for short-term stabilization, and these individuals are referred to less intensive services when feasible. Psychosocial rehabilitation services are designed to help severely mentally ill persons gain or regain skills needed to live, work, and socialize successfully in the community, so that hospitalization is not needed. Patients are taught to cope with life's situations, to develop skills that make it possible for them to live independently and to be successful in the workplace. This includes prevocational assessment, transitional and supported employment, and long-term support as necessary to maintain themselves in the job market.

Outpatient treatment, including individual therapy, group therapy, and supportive counseling, is available to all who can benefit from these services. Individuals who need twenty-four-hour supervision are provided for in a residential treatment center where the focus is on stabilization. They are helped to make the transition back to community living.

Two types of hospitalization are available. Short-term intensive care is provided in the local hospital to those who need constant supervision. No severely mentally ill person is discharged from a hospital without an agreed-on place to go. For those who need longer care or a more secure setting, the state hospital is available to them. This option is selected only when less restrictive sources have been deemed to be inappropriate to the individual's needs.

Individuals with mental illness need a complete support system, and the public mental health facility provides this. As patients are able to move from residential settings to independent living, they may need to move through group homes with staff supervision to affordable, normal housing. Follow-up case management is needed to ensure that the skills they have practiced in day care or in the group home concerning hygiene and nutrition are being practiced. Support also comes from their peer groups and socialization groups, which may provide help with transportation, a meeting place, and activity planning.

Whenever possible, family support is encouraged so that family members can learn to handle crisis situations and behavioral problems. Mental health center staff see that the patient and the family learn about the nature of the illness and provide support in handling the problems arising from it. An important function of the center is to provide a period of respite services to the family members who care for severely mentally ill patients.

It is recognized that some of these elements are not now available in all centers. However, they are realistic, attainable, and very much in the planning and action stages for the future. The description that follows illustrates the struggle over a period of many years of one mentally ill person.

Diane, who first heard voices and saw hallucinations as a young teenager, moved into a two-room apartment in a quiet neighborhood. She had just been released from a mental hospital. Diagnosed as chronic paranoid schizophrenic, she had lived at the hospital most of the time during the last ten years.

Nearby her apartment was a neighborhood grocery store run by a couple who took a parental interest in Diane, and it was here that she got acquainted with other neighbors. Stabilized on medication and supervised by psychiatrists, social workers, and nurses at a nearby mental health center, Diane functioned adequately most of the time.

Although she was never employed, she got by on her Supplemental Security Income (SSI) payments and the generosity of her grocery store "parents" who also took over the daily dispensing of her medications because she so often couldn't remember whether or not she had taken her pills. This couple also provided daily conversation and in time a genuine caring for her.

When her fragile stability gave way to paranoia she feared for her own safety, and she was sure someone wanted to steal her meager possessions. Even with four locks on her door, she would call a neighbor at 3:00 A.M. to come to see if someone was prowling around her house.

Although she seldom attended church meetings, she had a high regard for the clergy and frequently sought their help when the "voices" became too insistent. Members of her church congregation became responsible for taking her shopping and to the laundromat and for calls on the phone to check on her and to chat. Some of the male members responded to her need for household repairs and periodically to put a new lock on her door. She often remarked that what kept her able to live alone and kept her out of the hospital were her friends and her religious faith.

Diane was one of the fortunate mentally ill because she had an extended network of support, mostly voluntary. She lived in a neighborhood where the people were able to reach out to her. In her good times she was friendly and during the bad times her neighbors were understanding. With this help, she lived alone for almost fifteen years.

Then her support system began to break down. Her little dog, a constant companion, had to be put to sleep because of old age. The grocery store went out of business and the proprietors both took full-time jobs. Her nurse at the mental health center transferred. Her landlord raised the rent beyond what she could pay. Her strongest support and best friends from her church moved away.

She was unable to cope with the changes in her life and with her feelings about these changes. As she deteriorated, she spent a few weeks in a psychiatric ward of a general hospital, and was counseled not to try to continue to live alone. She moved into a nursing home.

Mental Hospitals

Mental hospitals are an important part of the mental health service network and generally fall into three categories: (1) state and county hospitals, (2) Veterans Administration (VA) hospitals, and (3) private hospitals. Some hospitals are designated mental hospitals and all of their beds are used for psychiatric care, whereas other hospitals are a combination of both general and mental health care. Usually the VA hospitals and private hospitals have designated psychiatric wards.

Deinstitutionalization has had an impact on mental health hospitals. "In 1969 there were 468,831 inpatients in all facilities. By 1988, that figure had been cut to less than half, despite a growing population. The impact on state and county mental hospitals was even greater; their populations dropped from 387,629 to less than 100,000."[4]

The concept of the state mental hospital fell into disrepute in the later 1940s and early 1950s. The hope held out by people like Dorothea Lynde Dix had not been fulfilled. Rather than being a place of refuge with a healthy treatment atmosphere, the hospitals were too large, overcrowded, and understaffed. For example, one state hospital, built to house 250 patients, had a population of 1,400 patients in 1955. Many studies emphasize that large institutions have negative effects on patients. The final report of the Joint

Commission on Mental Illness and Health published in 1961 underscored this feeling about large state or county mental hospitals:

> No further state hospitals of more than 1000 beds should be built, and not one patient should be added to any existing mental hospital already housing 1000 or more patients. It is further recommended that all existing state hospitals of more than 1000 beds be gradually and progressively converted into centers for the long-term and combined care of chronic diseases, including mental illness.[5]

The Joint Commission report also recommended that smaller state hospitals of a thousand beds or less be converted into "intensive treatment centers for patients with major mental illness in the acute stages or, in the case of a more prolonged illness, those with a good prospect for improvement or recovery."[6]

During the 1960s the trend was to "keep the patient out of the hospital at all costs." The CMHC was seen as a vehicle to "get rid" of the state hospital. In the 1990s, however, specialists recognized that small, well-staffed, regional state hospitals are an important link in community mental health services. These hospitals provide the environment for skilled observation that aids diagnostic clarification, as well as special medical, nursing, and rehabilitative efforts. In addition to the patient-centered tasks, the hospital can protect society from the effects of suicidal or homicidal behavior.

Social Work in the Mental Hospital

The patient who is admitted to the hospital for the first time invariably possesses attitudes regarding the institution and the program of care that are inimical to his or her best interest. Furthermore, members of the family bring with them preconceived and distorted notions that seriously interfere with their efforts to assist in treatment plans. To many, the mental hospital is still the "end of the line." The idea persists that to hospitalize is to "put away" and that "once insane, always insane." For some, hospitalization means a loss of freedom. The denial to the patient of normal, simple pleasures is real. One patient said she disliked the hospital, not because she was mistreated or because the food was bad, but because she couldn't water her flowers or walk along the country lane. Many patients, hospitalized for the first time, fear other patients; they are apprehensive of attack, seduction, or lack of identity. The lonely and deprived patient feels rejection and a depth of loneliness deepened by the isolation of hospitalization. At admission, the social worker allays fears, helps the patient become oriented to the hospital, and eases the pain of separation. In similar ways, the social worker helps the family accept hospitalization and the patient's treatment program. Families thus assisted support treatment efforts and hasten the day when the patient can be discharged.

The ill individual is able to respond to treatment best when he or she has the assurance that the family continues to be involved. As the family is helped to mobilize its strengths, it can look ahead to reunion and the return to health of the ill member. The interaction within the family must be understood clearly before the problem can be resolved.

Social workers deal with all aspects of patient relationships in mental hospitals.

The importance of the family in rehabilitation is emphasized and families are increasingly involved in the treatment program. Treatment involving a family has many ramifications. Initially some families cannot bring themselves to think about the sick member's return home. For example, a wife who has been severely traumatized by her spouse may be reluctant to have him rejoin the family. A patient who hallucinates may not be welcomed by the family because she "hears voices" and talks to unseen audiences. A family and a neighborhood may need help to understand, accept, and live with hallucinatory behavior.

In one metropolitan community, citizens angrily protested when they learned that patients from a state hospital were to be placed in nursing homes in their area. They wrote letters to the local newspaper, circulated protest petitions among neighbors, held meetings with city officials, and forced reconsideration of the hospital's plan. Citizens need help to understand patients, their illnesses, and their capacity to lead normal lives in the community. In recent years nursing and foster home care of mental patients have become an important part of treatment. These programs are defeated, however, when patients are not given the freedom of the community or when the prevailing attitude of the neighborhood is one of mistrust, fear, and even hostility.

The social worker is concerned with all aspects of the patient's relationships within the hospital, as well as to his or her family and community. Patients respond to treatment best when they understand and cooperate with it and can trust the staff responsible for its administration. Rehabilitation can be achieved best when the patient's interest in family, employment, and the community is sustained while he or she is undergoing treatment. The social worker is often the key person to assist the patient in maintaining sound interpersonal relationships. It is also the social worker who assists the patient in using the family and community resources for protection and restoration to normal activities.

Aftercare Facilities

The mental health network provides aftercare services to assist in the resocialization of patients. Many of these facilities are operated as part of the hospital, community mental health center, or free-standing outpatient clinic.

One specialized aftercare facility is the halfway house providing living arrangements for people who have been hospitalized for mental illness and are trying to return to the community. It provides a transitional step for those who are not quite ready to participate in independent living. The halfway house, a nonmedical residential facility, provides for recovering patients to be a part of the community and to participate in regular activities. It provides opportunities for reestablishing work, family, and social relationships on a gradual basis under sheltered conditions. Many who leave institutions need a compassionate, warm, and empathic environment while they acquire skills and confidence to live in the community. Halfway houses that meet the highest standards provide for these needs.

Although the halfway house provides a viable link in the care of some mentally ill people, caution must be exercised in the control of these facilities. Many have become no more than holding tanks—understaffed and underprogrammed. Care needs to be taken to ensure that these facilities do provide the means for a recovering mentally ill person to reenter the community.

Therapeutic Clubs

Therapeutic clubs are one of the newer developments in aiding those who have been mentally ill. Fountain House, perhaps the first such facility, has been used as one model for others throughout the United States.

The Fountain House concept evolved from a group of former psychiatric patients who wanted to improve their chances of staying out of institutions. With the help of two community volunteers they sought other mental patients as *members* to join a *club*.

From this small beginning in the 1940s in New York City this one group has grown to more than a thousand members who attend club functions each month. The group has maintained these basic beliefs:

1. People with emotional disabilities, even severe ones, have productive potential. Every member has the ability to do something that is needed and will be valued by other club members.
2. Work is important for everyone. The club guarantees that each one will have the opportunity to work in the real world at regular, nonsubsidized jobs.
3. Everyone needs social relationships and the club provides opportunities for relaxing, social support on evenings every day of the year including weekends and holidays.
4. People need adequate housing. By leasing low-cost apartments, the club provides housing that is pleasant and affordable with congenial companions. Members pay their fair share of the cost.

From these basic concepts naturally evolved the work program that has members gaining skills by their working at needed tasks around the club—maintenance, cooking, clerical jobs, help with publishing a newsletter, answering telephones, and so on—which provide social effectiveness and preparation for outside jobs. As they are able to handle other work, they are put into the transitional employment program, which helps them find meaningful employment—often the biggest hurdle for mental patients. Jobs are secured in normal places of business where they are placed according to their skills and are paid the prevailing wage rate. These jobs are temporary, and a member may have several jobs before finding a permanent workplace.

Transitional employment is a part of almost all psychosocial rehabilitation programs. With the support of staff in easing members into the workplace, employers are guaranteed that the job will be done.

Viewed by both members and staff as one of the most important aspects of the program is the "reach out" feature. Members who do not come in for a time are sought out by staff and other members to let them know that they are missed, that they are cared about, and that the club wants to be of help. No one is forgotten just because he or she is absent. Regardless of how long it takes, each one is followed until the person is able to be completely independent.

Because Fountain House seems to be successful for many, similar programs have been set up based on this model. In 1980 there were 123 such programs, and by 1982 there were 456 employers in twenty-seven states involved in the transitional employment program.

By appealing to the basic human needs, this model emphasizes the cooperation between members and staff more as coworkers than client and superior, dignifies members' contributions, elevates their sense of self-worth, and improves their quality of life.

Outpatient Psychiatric Clinics

Outpatient clinics in many places have become a part of the community's comprehensive mental health program for children and adults. With the spread of the community centers, their function is changing as they become an integral part of the expanded health care system.

Outpatient clinics are widely used for the care of emotionally disturbed children, which illustrates this mode of mental health service. These clinics are often sponsored by voluntary contributions through such funding sources as the United Way, but they also may be a part of university medical centers, mental hospitals, or community mental health centers.

Through interviews and testing, a diagnosis is made. Treatment is planned that will alleviate the problems by modifying the child's unacceptable behavior. Treatment is usually given by psychiatrists, psychologists, and social workers, whose roles have become increasingly flexible in the recent past.

Difficulty in disciplining, temper tantrums, poor relationships with peers and siblings, and poor adaptation to school are the most frequently encountered problems in the children's clinics. Clinic staff members have been increasingly more willing to accept problems connected with severe childhood disorders as well as minor difficulties, such as behavior problems.

In conjunction with working with the child, the workers involve the parents in the treatment process, helping them understand the child's behavior and ways of dealing with it. Also, family conflicts are discussed in relation to their contributing to the situations causing the child to misbehave.

Mental health services for teenagers.

Residential Treatment Centers (RTCs) for Children

Residential treatment centers for children are another important element in the mental health service network. The RTC grew out of the child guidance movement, initiated in the early 1900s. The guidance clinics recognized that children needed to have special help with emotional problems and that early intervention could prevent more serious problems.

It is estimated that there are as many as 2 million children under the age of eighteen who have emotional problems severe enough to warrant urgent attention, and that there are 10 million to 15 million more who would benefit from psychiatric help of some kind.

The bulk of services to children is provided on an outpatient basis through private clinics and mental health professionals, but the RTC is an allied resource. In addition to the residential centers, state, county, and private hospitals care for emotionally disturbed children.

Although the importance of working with children has been recognized, the services have not been developed in a coordinated, effective fashion. As a society we need to move more aggressively toward establishing a total mental health system for children that will be preventive in nature and will help them develop their full potential.

Although we have an extensive mental health network, the needs of many go unmet. Mental disorders are pervasive in our society and are of concern to laypeople and professionals alike. What are a few of the areas of special concern?

Jails and Prisons

Two areas in desperate need of expanded mental health services are jails and prisons. In 1990, there were approximately 1.2 million men and women incarcerated in jails and prisons across the country. This figure jumped to 1.9 million in 2000 and reached 2.3 million in 2005.[7] Most jails and prisons have inadequate mental health services, especially for those inmates who suffer from alcohol and drug dependence. This is a severe limitation since it is estimated that one in two inmates has a serious alcohol or drug problem. A recent study completed at the Salt Lake County Jail in Salt Lake City, Utah, found that one-half of the women inmates were incarcerated for crimes related to drug use.[8]

In the Salt Lake County Jail, 1,800 inmates are incarcerated each month. Since 1984, mental health services have been provided by Valley Mental Health, a large private, non-profit community mental health center. This pattern of contracting with mental health centers has been followed by other jails across the country. With the support of these centers, jail personnel can assess the mental health needs of inmates when they are first incarcerated. This assessment can include screening for alcohol and drug dependence, chronic mental illness, and suicide risk. Inmates who need mental health services can be provided these services while they are in jail. Prisons are also contracting with mental health services although most prisons still operate their own alcohol and drug dependence programs as well as those programs for sexual offenders.

Special Problems and Issues in Mental Health

The plans in the 1960s were to create community mental health centers in 2,000 geographical areas. Today we have approximately 700 centers. Hospital beds have been emptied, but nothing was provided to take their place. When patients were discharged, the money did not follow them. Most of mental health funding still goes to mental institutions that house only a fraction of patients formerly housed there. More than 60 percent of chronically mentally ill persons are at large in the community.

Many of the "comprehensive" services are less than comprehensive. For instance, there are too few beds; hardly more than lip service is given to prevention; transitional housing is almost nonexistent, and specialized services for children, the elderly, and other underserved populations are in short supply where they exist at all.

Mental Illness and Homelessness

A problem currently being addressed is what to do with mentally ill people who are homeless. It is estimated that as many as one-third of all homeless Americans (350,000 to 3,000,000) are mentally ill. Their only asylum or place of refuge is the streets. An increasing number of these are children and women. Children are subjected to child abuse; many women are raped. Homeless men, women, and children are more often the victims of crime rather than the perpetrators. Some end up in overcrowded jails. Many are suicidal and take their own lives. Some are homicidal. Hunger, cold, and disease take a heavy toll.

Earl Ruth dramatically illustrates the plight of tens of thousands of mentally ill homeless people.

Earl Ruth is 47, partly deaf and schizophrenic. He heard voices for the first time at the age of six, spent most of his childhood in a foster home and an orphanage, and has lived much of his adult life in mental hospitals—sometimes voluntarily, sometimes not. Normally a gentle, apologetic man, Ruth is capable of violence: he once told a psychiatrist he was "fighting something evil, something powerful." He is both homeless and rootless. Although he spends most winters at church shelters in New York City, he usually heads across country each spring in a solitary and always fruitless search for a better life. This year, he says, he may take a trip to Houston.[9]

For homeless people there is a critical shortage of any kind of housing and employment opportunities. Income support channeled through a maze of bureaucratic organizations has decreased and is almost impossible to come by for those whose capacities are not impaired, much less for those who are mentally ill. Agencies tend to despair. They lack resources and find little reward in work that so much of the time is downside. In despair, some resort to the "Greyhound" therapy—one-way tickets to other parts of the country—for those expecting help. In winter "sunbirds" migrate to the sun belt.

Fortunately, chief executives and legislators are addressing the alarming and shocking problems of homeless mentally ill people. Many states are working to provide desperately needed housing. A Wisconsin project offers close supervision to those who have been deinstitutionalized. Maryland's Department of Mental Health has been mandated to supply appropriate services to women. In New Jersey, the Prevention and Homeless Act of 1984 affirms that "it is more socially desirable to place homeless people in suitable apartments, or to enable people to retain possession of their houses or apartments . . . than to house them in hotel rooms or other facilities intended for short-term occupancy." In Ohio, a concerted effort is being made to provide interest-free loans for low- or moderate-income housing developments.

New York is taking on the herculean task of finding shelters for this group. During the winter police are encouraged to pick up off the streets those individuals who appear mentally ill. If they refuse to go into a shelter, they are taken to a hospital for observation if the temperature is below freezing. California has embarked on an ambitious program to help those in ghetto areas, on the streets, and in the barrios. All across America, states and communities are reaching out to solve this problem, but the numbers are so overwhelming that it takes a lot of effort to make even a small impression.

Voluntary and Involuntary Commitment

In most states long-term commitment for mentally ill individuals has been abolished. Constitutional rights and liberty are deemed more important than the health of the patient or the protection of society. Unless a person has demonstrated that he or she is a threat to himself or herself or society, no one—not even family members—can take away the right to freedom. The fact that because of the nature of their illness many are unable to make rational decisions about their care is not considered by the courts.

Because of the uniqueness of emotional problems, there is a need to retain, in some form, the concept of involuntary commitment. Whereas some are aware of their needs and voluntarily ask for help, there are many who require involuntary commitment. All states have laws that govern commitment procedures. Because civil liberties have been reemphasized, states have acted to ensure the procedure of involuntary commitment and to protect the rights of individuals.

In one state an effort is being made to get a commitment law that will take the history of the patient into account. Performance or current behavior, taken in perspective, may be as important or more important than the current mental status examination.

Chronic Mental Illness

With the discovery and widespread use of psychoactive drugs and other therapies, hospital personnel found that fewer restraints were needed, bars and padded cells were removed, and amenities were added. Hospitals were becoming therapeutic communities and patients were beginning to participate in governing. They responded to the drugs and personal attention.

Moving patients out of state hospitals into communities was a logical next step. Professionals made plans that would provide (1) follow-up to make sure patients continued their medication, (2) professional help in communities through mental health centers, (3) support systems, (4) residential care as needed, (5) income for the patients' needs, and (6) help in getting and maintaining employment. Mentally ill people would be able to function in the community because the *community* would be therapeutic.

What happened? It was found that the "community" is not always therapeutic. Life on the outside is not protected or stress-free. Smaller hospitals were never built. The panacea of drugs collapsed when patients didn't have the supervision and care of those who monitored their medication.

Consequently, millions of mentally ill individuals were released to the streets. It is estimated by the National Institute of Mental Health (NIMH) that 2.4 million are chronically mentally ill. It will take a national commitment to address their needs.

It has been widely assumed that the community would learn to accept and live with those who are mentally ill. This hasn't happened. Angry citizens protest halfway houses and other mental health facilities planned for their neighborhoods. They write angry letters to local newspapers, circulate petitions, threaten lawsuits, hold meetings with officials. They are willing for a hospital or nursing home to be built as long as it is located somewhere else. "Not in my back yard" (NIMBY) is their plaint. Today, society still lives with the luxury of thinking that the responsibility for the care and treatment of those with mental illness belongs to someone else. This attitude continues to be a major deterrent to effective community-based programs.

Poverty

Sheafor and Horejsi provide guidelines for working with clients who are poor, a common challenge in the social service field. Being poor presents special problems other vulnerable groups do not always have to address such as food shortages, inadequate housing, minimal education, poor medical and dental care, and a host of other concerns. In working with poor clients, Sheafor and Horejsi offer the following suggestions:

1. When choosing an approach to work with clients who are poor, remember that once poverty exists clients encounter a multitude of forces and barriers that keep them poor. For example, in order to find employment, a person must have appropriate clothing, transportation, recent job experience, adequate education or training, and a

permanent address. These are things that a person living in poverty often does not have. To acquire these things that are necessary for employment, the person who is poor usually requires financial support and help of other empowering programs.

2. If you are working with poor clients, you must have a working knowledge of local, state, and federal programs that may be of assistance. In addition, you must be aware of the services that are provided by private agencies in your community. Also, helping poor individuals gain access to higher education and technical training is one of the most effective ways to address the problems of poverty.

3. Be aware that existing welfare policies, program rules, and eligibility standards often present formidable barriers or obstacles to people who are poor and in need of assistance. The social worker needs to be an advocate for them in removing these barriers or obstacles. This advocacy can also include urging the welfare institutions and bureaucracies to change and modify their programs for those who are poor.

4. Understand that the client's views about being poor are critical to the helping process. A person's response to the current situation, sense of hope for the future, and level of distress about being poor are shaped by his or her prior life experiences. For example, the individual who has always been poor will view living in poverty much differently than someone who has only recently become poor. Unless you understand clients and their backgrounds, you will not be able to make informed decisions regarding the best available options.

5. Try to understand the emotional and mental state of the person who is poor. Living in poverty is extremely stressful because so many aspects of a person's life are uncertain, unpredictable, and beyond control. This stress can lead to anxiety, fear, frustration, depression, helplessness, and hopelessness.

6. Empowerment strategies and strengths perspectives are especially important in helping people living in poverty. People who are poor need to be encouraged by those who have overcome their poverty. People who are poor need to build or rebuild their self-respect and self-esteem and learn to take control of their lives.

7. From a strengths perspective, encourage clients to share their knowledge for dealing with poverty. Have them explain to others how they have learned to be thrifty in shopping and stretching their limited resources. Sometimes they are using programs and community services that are overlooked by others. Many are cooperating with others and sharing what they have to help each other cope.

8. Reduce the social distance and power differential between yourself and the client. Talk about the ordinary aspects of life such as family, friends, interests, and hobbies. Meet with clients at times that are convenient for them. Invite them to share their music, art, and other creative skills.

9. Find opportunities for clients to shape and influence programs for low-income people by serving on agency boards and committees. Give them the opportunity to share with board members the impact the services they are receiving have on them and their families.

10. Understand that the person living in poverty often leads a life of desperation. Fear and worry over a lack of money and other resources can draw people into activities that are harmful to them including illegal activities. Although you cannot condone this behavior, you must understand the desperation and frustration that often triggers their harmful behavior.[10]

Teenage Suicide

Suicide among teenagers has reached epidemic proportions. In the past twenty-five years suicide has increased 300 percent in the United States and is the leading cause of death in the fifteen-to-twenty-four age group. The rate for this age group almost tripled from 4.5 per 100,000 in 1950 to 13.2 per 100,000 in 1990.[11] Many more suicides occur, but they are reported as "accidental deaths." Thousands of young people attempt suicide, but fortunately not all attempts are fatal.

Suicide in adolescence is correlated with sociological, psychological, and economic forces very much at the heart of the coping–social functioning dyad addressed by social workers. For example, there seems to be a correlation between suicide and high rates of youth unemployment. Unemployment, in turn, is associated with competition for jobs, and a sense of failure and loss of self-esteem to the unacceptably high number who don't find work. Feelings of helplessness and the inability to cope with problems or improve various life situations have been typically reported by depressed teenagers who are seriously suicidal.

Suicidal histories have been reported for teenagers who experience repeated school failures and who have long-standing behavioral problems. Youths who lack various kinds of social skills and handle stress situations poorly, if at all, are vulnerable.

Not having family support—no warmth, no security, and the message that they are expendable or unwanted—correlates with high numbers of youth suicides and suicide attempt rates. Hepworth, Farley, and Griffiths report

> Cohesiveness between parents and children is typically low in families of suicidal adolescents.
> Communication between adolescent suicide attempters and their parents is generally poor and conflict is high. In a study of adolescent drug overdosers, researchers found that about one-half of the group reported they felt unable to discuss problems with their mothers, and 89 percent felt similarly about communication with their fathers.[12]

The message of youth suicide is increasingly clear:

1. Employment opportunities for youth are imperative.
2. Success experiences will almost certainly reduce the risk of suicides.
3. All teaching–learning encounters need to emphasize the importance of good coping skills for youth.
4. Learning to deal with stress situations needs to be a high-priority educational objective for all youth.
5. Finally, as a nation we need to reaffirm the value and worth of good family support systems and the use of the nation's resources to strengthen the family.

Risk of Suicide

Approximately 30,000 deaths are reported each year in the United States that are attributed to suicide. Suicide rates increase with age. The suicide rate for men and women, for example, who are seventy-five years of age or older is three times the rate for those thirty years of age or younger.[13] The SAD PERSONS scale is an inventory used to assess the risk of suicide. The inventory focuses on ten factors often associated with suicide:

1. *Sex.* Males are more likely to complete suicide and choose more lethal means.
2. *Age.* Individuals under age eighteen and over age thirty-five are higher-risk groups.
3. *Depression.* Clients who are depressed are more likely to commit suicide, especially if they begin to feel better and have more energy after being severely depressed.
4. *Previous attempts.* Clients who have attempted suicide before may find it easier to attempt again.
5. *Ethanol.* The presence of alcohol/drugs is connected with suicide.
6. *Rational thinking loss.* If a person has thought disorders, he or she may not be able to find ways to cope with the crisis.
7. *Social supports lacking.* If a client feels isolated and does not have enough relationships of meaning, there is an increased chance of suicide.
8. *Organized plan.* If a client has an organized plan, this means that the lethality level is high.
9. *No spouse.* Single individuals are more likely to commit suicide.
10. *Sickness.* If a client has a serious physical illness, he or she is more prone to commit suicide.[14]

In *The Feeling Good Handbook,* Burns suggests asking the following questions if a family member or friend appears to be especially despondent or discouraged:

1. Have you been feeling sad or unhappy?
2. Do you ever feel hopeless? Does it seem as if things can never get better?
3. Do you have thoughts of death? Do you ever think you'd be better off dead?
4. Do you ever have any actual suicidal impulses? Do you have any urge to kill yourself?
5. Do you feel you can resist these impulses, or do they sometimes tempt you?
6. Do you have any actual plan to kill yourself?
7. When do you plan to kill yourself?
8. Is there anything that would hold you back, such as your family or your religious convictions?
9. Have you ever made a suicide attempt in the past?
10. Would you be willing to talk to someone or seek help if you felt desperate? Whom would you talk to?[15]

If a family member, friend, or client answers "yes" to any number of these questions, the threat of suicide may be imminent. Counselors and friends should always err on the side of caution and seek a thorough suicide evaluation if they believe a client or friend is at risk.

Suicide prevention is especially important with depressed teenagers.

Prevention

In the public health sector, prevention includes health promotion and protection. At the "primary" level, it is centered on health education and concerns the general health and well-being of the population and is not directed at any particular disease or disorder. Examples include immunization, sanitation, and sound nutrition. At the "secondary" level, prevention means early diagnosis and prompt treatment; the aim is to relieve distress and shorten duration. "Tertiary" prevention is focused on chronic and serious illness and includes attempts to reduce pain and suffering.

Two potentially fertile fields for prevention in mental illness are the public schools and the workplace. We know much about human behavior and the causation of mental disorders. There is much unused knowledge of human behavior that could be used to help youngsters before they drop out of school, take their own lives, abuse drugs, or turn to premature sex to relieve boredom.

One group that needs the help offered by the schools are the recent immigrants who come from Asia, Central America, Mexico, and many other countries. Our way of life to them is foreign, our culture strange, and often they are poor and without means of support. To adapt and develop their potential, the children as well as the parents need help. Schools can help and social workers can play a decisive role by helping these people relate to the human service system and by providing services both direct and system-oriented.

The workplace in America is another area rich with opportunity for a truly preventive approach. Here, employees under stress and about to be lost can be helped with counseling for themselves and families and to use the service network society has for them. Rehabilitation, once work is lost and the skills of the workplace atrophy from lack of use, is an example of secondary or even tertiary prevention.

Work as Therapy

A strong case has been made for the therapeutic value of work for mentally ill persons. Centers where work as therapy has been tried report that the days of care needed are greatly reduced. As with other workers, those with mental illness find daily meaning as well as daily bread in their employment, and they thrive on the recognition that comes from their fellow employees. Many of the nation's community centers and clubs have made finding nonsubsidized jobs for their people a top priority. Many become financially independent and are able to maintain themselves with minimal psychiatric supervision.

Because of the great gains made by those who have employment, NIMH has developed an approach to reduce discrimination by helping stimulate employment opportunities for them. Of the more than 2 million chronic and acute mental patients living in the community, between 70 to 85 percent are estimated to be unemployed. It is impossible to generalize on how many of these are potentially employable because of individual differences and capabilities.

The President's Committee on Employment of the Handicapped has set up affirmative action and nondiscrimination programs that apply to mentally restored persons as well as to those with physical disabilities. Affirmative action tries to ensure opportunities for work. However, applicants have to be "qualified"—capable of doing the work with reasonable accommodation. For mentally ill persons this may mean adjusting work schedules, restructuring jobs, and giving flexible leave. Many employers are making the necessary adjustments.

Research

Continuing research is needed. Even with all the scientific and technological achievements of our society, mysteries of the human mind abound. We have difficulty understanding why people behave as they do, and we are baffled with such diagnosed mental problems as manic depressive illness or schizophrenia—the most common serious mental illnesses. We need to know more about the genetics of human behavior and such biological factors as anatomy, physiology, morphology, and endocrinology. Little is known about the long-term effect of medical treatment. Many therapists report good results from planned, daily exercise including cycling, aerobics, jogging, hiking, and other physical exercise for depressed patients. Gene research offers hope in determining who may have mental health problems, and it may play a part in prevention and treatment.

Delegates to the White House Conference on Aging in 1995 passed a resolution on meeting basic mental health needs. In addition to support for providing affordable and quality mental health care, they asked for public and private long-term insurance plans to include mental disabilities. They supported expanded education and training programs for family and caregivers by faculty with clinical research expertise in mental health and aging.

The mental health needs of the elderly have been sorely neglected. This is a national tragedy, given the fact that by the year 2010 approximately 20 percent of the American population will be 65 years of age or older. In 1990, 32 million elderly lived in America; by the year 2030 that figure is expected to increase to 65 million.[16] The elderly have the fastest growing suicide rate of any group including adolescents. This unfortunate fact speaks to the despair, isolation, and neglect that many elderly experience in America. Our nation desperately needs a plan to address the growing mental health needs of our aging population.

Integration of Resources—Values

In this chapter significant developments have been outlined in the mental health field, particularly as these pertain to social work. Though modest compared to the challenges that lie ahead, they are nevertheless impressive. A network of services is clearly identified. In the main these are generally well known by consumers. Remaining are problems and issues relating to the interplay of mental health, other human services, and the corporate and professional community. Perhaps this is some of what Alice Mu-jung P. Lin had in mind when she wrote the following: "The challenges for the mental health system are to integrate mental health services with the housing, social, and economic needs of the population."[17]

Finally, the future may well need to focus more on values. Viktor Frankl postulates the survival values of meaning in life. Patients recover when they have a purpose. Neuroses are not only conflicted, instinctual forces, but also result from failure to connect with important values and action guided by a value system.

In the course of time the social work treatment approach has been subjected to a plethora of emphases, including environmental manipulation, external sociological forces, depth psychology, a combination of psychological social determinants, role theory, and cultural identifications. Cornett, along with others, believes "The time has come for social work to again broaden its perspective, this time to include the spiritual aspects of the physical, phenomenological individual in her or his environment."[18]

Clients often express concern about issues and problems that have spiritual and religious connotations. The meaning of life, purpose, and belief systems encompass the idea that help for everyday problems can come from forces outside themselves. Metaphysical factors figure prominently in the lives of many, if not most, of our clients who struggle to cope with the problems confronting them. Social workers, though somewhat silent about their observances of these behavioral determinants, have known clients who seem to get help from these sources. When we fail to consider this content, we miss an important opportunity to assist our clients and even impoverish our thinking and our practice.

Professionals need to look at what is good and right. Perhaps no example serves better to illustrate this assumption than the one coming from the addiction model, where the best results are reported from the invoking of prayer, faith, and religious experience. Spiritual forces help provide balance and fill dependency needs essential to self-sufficiency and independence.

The DSM in Mental Health

For thousands of years attempts have been made to classify mental disorders. Resulting from these attempts various diagnostic systems have evolved and been discarded. Since 1952 the American Psychiatric Association has made serious attempts to develop guidelines, which have evolved in what today is known as the Association's *Diagnostic and Statistical Manual of Mental Disorders* (4th ed., text revised). Called the *DSM-IV-TR*, this publication includes the names of disorders, various essential and associated features of disorders, and differential and diagnostic categories of mental illness. This classification is widely used in the practice of psychiatry and by many social workers, particularly those in the mental health field and in private practice.

There are differences of opinion among social workers regarding the use of the *DSM*. Some say that labels, names, or categories are unhelpful and also potentially harmful to some clients. They maintain it is harmful when labels are used to silence political dissidents, force sterilization, justify brain surgery, or as a device for getting clients on welfare rolls because, for example, they lack reading or writing skills.

A positive point of view is that categorization of mental disorders facilitates communication among social workers and between other mental health professionals—psychiatrists, psychologists, and nurses—and social workers. They suggest that the system can be used reliably by clinicians and research workers. Social workers in private practice often use the system for third-party payments for services.

The *DSM* uses a multiaxial approach to the categorization of mental disorders. Axis I and Axis II are used to identify each of the sixteen separate mental disorder categories, Axis III lists current medical conditions that may be impacting on the disorder, Axis IV reports psychosocial and environmental problems that may affect the disorder, and Axis V assesses the client's overall level of functioning. Each of the sixteen separate mental disorder categories (i.e, major depressive reaction, schizophrenia, etc.,) lists the cognitive, emotional, behavioral, and physical symptoms that characterize the disorder. The *DSM* also states how long the client must be experiencing these symptoms before a clinical diagnosis can be made. Statistics on the prevalence of the disorder along with the frequency of the disorder among first-degree biological relatives are also provided.

Summary

National attention has been focused on mentally ill individuals by three presidents and one first lady, indicating the scope and magnitude of the problem of mental illness in the United States.

Roots of the mental health movement are identified with such luminaries as Dorothea Lynde Dix, William White, Sigmund Freud, G. Stanley Hall, and Adolph Meyer. Resulting from great resolve and determination over decades of time, mental health networks and related systems can now be identified and are impressively serving tens of thousands of children and adults.

Efforts addressing the problems of those who are mentally ill clearly recognize the complexity and seriousness of the problem. Hospital services have been dramatically recast to take into account the use of psychedelic drugs, greater community awareness and effort, and the not-always-welcomed deinstitutionalization of people with mental illness.

Aftercare facilities help cushion the need for help when the patient is released from the hospital. Voluntary efforts such as Fountain House that engage patients in meaningful and productive work and other activities prove helpful in rehabilitation.

Problems of mentally ill people who are homeless are receiving greater understanding and help from state legislators and others in addressing this growing problem and blight.

More study, research, and a national commitment are required to solve the problems of chronic mental illness, the growing incidence of teen suicide, and the mental health needs of elderly people.

Becoming more prominent in the understanding and treatment of those with mental illness is the emphasis on values and the role and place of religion and spiritual components.

DSM-IV-TR is found to be useful to social workers in the mental health field and in private practice. However, different views exist and continue to surface about the usefulness of this major diagnostic tool for social workers.

Selected References

AUSTRIAN, SONIA G. *Mental Disorders, Medications, and Clinical Social Work.* New York: Columbia University Press, 1995.

BERK, LAURA E., *Development through the Lifespan,* 3rd ed. Boston: Allyn & Bacon, 2004.

BUTLER, ROBERT N., MYRNA I. LEWIS, and TREY SUNDERLAND, *Aging and Mental Health: Positive Psychosocial and Biomedical Approaches,* 5th ed. Boston: Allyn & Bacon, 1998.

Diagnostic and Statistical Manual of Mental Disorders, 4th ed., text revised. Washington, DC: American Psychiatric Association, 2000.

HOLT, BARBARA J., *The Practice of Generalist Case Management.* Boston: Allyn & Bacon, 2000.

KAPLAN, HAROLD I., and BENJAMIN J. SADOCK, *Concise Textbook of Clinical Psychiatry.* Baltimore: Williams & Wilkins, 1996.

MACIAS, CATHALEENE, RONALD KINNEY, O. WILLIAM FARLEY, ROBERT JACKSON, and BETTY VOS, "The Role of Case Management within a Community Support System: Partnership with Psychosocial Rehabilitation," *Community Mental Health Journal* 30 (August 1994), 323–339.

MCNEECE, C. AARON, and DIANA M. DINITTO, *Chemical Dependency: A Systems Approach,* 2nd ed. Boston: Allyn & Bacon, 1998.

MECHANIC, DAVID, *Mental Health and Social Policy: The Emergence of Managed Care,* 4th ed. Boston: Allyn & Bacon, 1999.

ROTHMAN, JACK, and JON SIMON SAGER, *Case Management: Integrating Individual and Community Practice,* 2nd ed. Boston: Allyn & Bacon, 1998.

SANDS, ROBERTA G., *Clinical Social Work Practice in Behavioral Mental Health,* 2nd ed. Boston: Allyn & Bacon, 2001.

SHEAFOR, BRADFORD W., and CHARLES R. HOREJSI, *Techniques and Guidelines for Social Work Practice,* 7th ed. Boston: Allyn & Bacon, 2006.

SMITH, TIMOTHY B., *Practicing Multiculturalism: Affirming Diversity in Counseling and Psychology.* Boston: Allyn & Bacon, 2004.

THACKERAY, MILTON G., REX A. SKIDMORE, and O. WILLIAM FARLEY, *Introduction to Mental Health: Field and Practice.* Englewood Cliffs, NJ: Prentice Hall, 1979.

WEISSMAN, HAROLD H., ed., *Serious Play: Creativity and Innovation in Social Work.* Silver Spring, MD: NASW Press, 1990.

ZIDE, MARILYN R., and SUSAN W. GRAY, *Psychopathology: A Competency-Based Assessment Model for Social Workers.* Belmont, CA: Brooks/Cole, 2001.

Notes

1. Presidential Executive Order 11973, signed February 17, 1977.

2. Adapted from materials compiled by the Social Research Institute, University of Utah.

3. Milton G. Thackeray, Rex A. Skidmore, and O. William Farley, *Introduction to Mental Health* (Englewood Cliffs, NJ: Prentice Hall, 1979), pp. 63–64.

4. Leon Ginsberg, *Social Work Almanac,* 2nd ed. Vol. 1 (Washington, DC: NASW Press, 1995), p. 258.

5. *Action for Mental Health, The Final Report of the Joint Commission on Mental Illness and Health* (New York: Basic Books, 1961), pp. xv–xvi.

6. Ibid.

7. "The Inmate Population Has Climbed," *USA Today,* Fri/Sat/Sun/, April 13–15, 2001, p. 1A.

8. Allan R. Rice, Larry L. Smith, and Fred V. Janzen, "Women Inmates, Drug Abuse, and the Salt Lake County Jail," *American Jails,* 13 (July/August 1999), p. 43.

9. *Newsweek,* January 6, 1986, p. 16.

10. Bradford W. Sheafor and Charles R. Horejsi, *Techniques and Guidelines for Social Work Practice,* 7th ed. (Boston: Allyn & Bacon, 2006), pp. 513–517.

11. Ginsberg, *Social Work Almanac,* p. 81.

12. Dean H. Hepworth, O. William Farley, and J. Kent Griffiths, "Suicidal Adolescents Correlates and Clinical Implications." Unpublished paper (January 1986).

13. Harold I. Kaplan and Benjamin J. Sadock, *Concise Textbook of Clinical Psychiatry* (Baltimore: Williams & Wilkins, 1996), p. 361.

14. W. M. Patterson, H. H. John, and G. A. Patterson, "Evaluation of Suicidal Patients: The SAD PERSONS Scale," *Psychosomatics,* 24 (1983), pp. 343–349.

15. David D. Burns, *The Feeling Good Handbook* (New York: Plume, 1990), pp. 40–41.

16. Ruth E. Dunkle and Theresa Norgard, "Aging Overview," in *Encyclopedia of Social Work,* 19th ed., Vol. 1 (Washington, DC: NASW Press, 1995), p. 142.

17. Alice Mu-jung P. Lin, "Mental Health Overview," in *Encyclopedia of Social Work*, 11th ed., Vol. 2 (Washington, DC: NASW Press, 1995), p. 1710.

18. Carlton Cornett, "Toward a More Comprehensive Personology: Integrating a Spiritual Perspective into Social Work Practice," *Social Work,* 37 (March 1992).

10

Social Work in Health Care

Mrs. M. was referred to the social worker because of her refusal to agree to an operation that would improve her hearing. She had been very hard-of-hearing since her birth. Mrs. M. had been hospitalized following an automobile accident. Doctors in the university hospital became confident that they could help her gain almost normal hearing.

Exploring Mrs. M.'s refusal of surgery, the social worker discovered a number of reasons for her reluctance. She was terrified of anesthesia and "being cut on"; she knew of persons who had not recovered from surgery. She had never been in a hospital until her accident—even her children had been born at home. She found the procedures confusing, painful, and frightening and wanted to go home as soon as possible. She was not sure which one of the doctors who came to see her was really her doctor. To this medically unsophisticated woman, the pressure for a quick decision was too much, and she felt that it would be better to say "no" than to take a chance.

What needs to be done so that Mrs. M. can understand the risks of surgery as weighed against the possible benefits? How would a greater understanding on the part of the doctors and nurses concerning Mrs. M.'s fear aid in her decision?[1]

In an era of tight money, the new intern, probing for ways to cut soaring costs for medical care, asked: "Why do we need social services in this hospital?" The administrator replied: "In the interest of quality health care, the hospital provides food, shelter and medication; why shouldn't it concern itself with the social and psychological needs of the patients? They, too, are important."

She further explained that social problems are basic to the understanding and total care and treatment of a patient; and if they are not considered, many times medical treatment fails.

What is social work in health care settings? What special knowledge and skill are required for practice in health services? Answers to these and related questions appear in this chapter.

Medicine and social work joined hands in 1905 with the establishment of medical social work at the Massachusetts General Hospital in Boston under the enthusiastic, able encouragement of Dr. Richard Cabot. He and others recognized the need to understand

176

more about social factors related to illness and its treatment and to utilize social and community resources in comprehensive patient care.

The introduction of social workers into hospital and other medical settings has been slow but steady, so today many hospitals have professional social workers on their staffs. Of the 5,000 hospitals reporting to the American Hospital Association in 1995, 75 percent indicated having social work services.

There is hardly any aspect of health care in which social and emotional factors can be ruled out for purposes of diagnosis, treatment, and in the work of prevention of illness. As the practice of medicine has grown more psychosocial the role of social workers, with their social functioning orientation, has increased in importance in the broad spectrum of health care delivery. Bracht, affirming his own known views and those of colleagues, attests to an overview of nationwide practice:

> There have been instances of the development of social work programs in virtually every type of primary health care setting—in prepaid group practices and health maintenance organizations; in fee-for-service practices and clinics, both solo and group; and in neighborhood and community health centers with outside funding. Some programs have provided social work practicum experiences. Many programs have enhanced physicians' residency experiences, especially in family medicine settings.[2]

A development that has affected social workers is the growth of corporate health care. Forty-five corporations in the United States with revenues greater than $10 million reported in 1984 that they provide health care services. In addition, it was expected that by 1990 the top thirty nursing home corporations would control all of the nursing home beds.[3] This meant that social workers in the health care field would be increasingly employed by the private sector.

The total number of social workers in the health field continues to increase. In 1960 there were 11,700 health care social workers, and it was estimated that for 1986 there were 50,000. The majority of social workers were practicing in long-term-care hospitals— 16,500 administer various aspects of the Medicare program in hospitals; 2,700 work in extended-care facilities; and 2,600 work in the Veterans Administration Hospital System.[4] Even with the large budget cuts in the health care funds, the role of social work in medicine is expected to expand.[5]

One of the greatest changes in the delivery of health care services in the 1990s was the growth of managed care programs. Managed care is a plan adopted by most health care providers to coordinate services and make health care more effective and efficient. Modeled somewhat after the earlier Medicare and Medicaid programs, managed care plans describe in detail how long patients will be hospitalized, the cost of care, the procedures and medications that will be administered, and the health care providers who will be utilized for most existing medical conditions. Since the inception of managed care, social workers have become an integral part of the plan especially as it relates to discharge planning and follow-up care and services. In these critical areas, the psychosocial expertise of social workers is used to help patients make the transition from hospital care, to home care, and hopefully to a full recovery.

Managed care programs have come under attack because of spiraling health care cost increases. Program directors have blamed the added costs primarily on prescription medication increases and the growth of our elderly population and their need for expanded medical services. Critics of managed care point to the growing bureaucracy of managed care and the inefficiency of their health care delivery system. In several areas across the country, physicians and other health care providers have abandoned managed care programs and started their own health care delivery systems. Whether or not these independent health care systems survive remains to be seen. Still, it is clear that managed care programs must be reformed, especially in how they offer services to our elderly population. Some managed care programs, in fact, have terminated health care services to the elderly and forced thousands of senior citizens to find other supplemental coverage to their existing Medicare program.

Definition of Social Work in Health Care

Social work in health care settings is practiced in collaboration with medicine and also with public health programs. It is the application of social work knowledge, skills, attitudes, and values to health care. Social work addresses itself to illness brought about by or related to social and environmental stresses that result in failures in social functioning and social relationships. It intervenes with medicine and related professions in the study, diagnosis, and treatment of illness at the point where social, psychological, and environmental forces impinge on role effectiveness.

Social work relates itself to the goals set by official health agencies, voluntary health agencies, rehabilitation centers, and medical care divisions of public welfare agencies.

Social workers practice in public health at the local, state, federal, and international levels; general medical hospitals; county and state health departments; children's hospitals; outpatient clinics; university teaching hospitals; nursing homes; neighborhood health centers; and private disease centers supported by such funding sources as March of Dimes and the heart and cancer associations. In addition, social workers are employed in the offices of private physicians and are meeting the challenge of showing that their skills can be cost-effective for private practice.

In the past, because of the nature of the practice of medicine, social work in health services emphasized understanding illness. Practice was focused on work with sick people and members of their families. Because of newer emphases in medical care, the scope of social work has been broadened and now encompasses the preservation and promotion of health and the prevention as well as cure of disease. Consideration is given to psychological factors in prevention of disability as well as in diagnosis and treatment. Using the team approach, medical social workers collaborate with physicians, nurses, and other health professionals for reciprocal sharing of ideas so that the skills of each are employed in the total care of the patients.

One of the most important developments for social workers in health care was the Health Maintenance Organization (HMO) Act of 1973. This act opened the door for an entirely new medical care delivery system. Keigher has defined managed care as an alternative to fee-for-service health care whereby the financing and delivery of medical care are integrated through contracts with selected physicians and hospitals furnishing a comprehensive set of services to enrolled members, usually for a predetermined monthly premium.

Managed care includes financial incentives for patients to use the services, and providers assume some financial risk as they try to balance the patient's health needs with the organization's cost-control efforts. Keigher further states

> Powerful commercial forces are quietly transforming the U.S. health care system with far more effect than policy discourse. Although policy agendas in 1993 and 1994 were focused on managed competition, regulations, and employer mandates, profound restrictions were already being placed on the health prospects of the employees, retirees, and public-aid recipients fortunate enough to have insurance. "Managed Care," a health care delivery enterprise that barely existed a few years ago, has been enjoying phenomenal growth facilitated by businesses' benefits offices, state Medicaid offices, the federal Health Care Financing Administration (HCFA), and insurance companies.
>
> The majority of citizens have been gradually and "voluntarily" relinquishing their right to choose their doctors in return for a promise of lower premiums. Their affiliations with health maintenance organizations (HMOs), preferred provider organizations (PPOs), and other capitated reimbursement plans have moved us light years toward total capitalistic corporatization of health care, delimiting the parameters of potential policy reform.[6]

Originally the HMO Act required the provision of social services in HMOs. Several consequent congressional actions blunted the effects of the original act and the mandates for social workers were eliminated. There has been a positive social work thrust in new home health care and rehabilitation laws that allow Medicaid funds to enhance the ability of persons with disabilities to live independently as family and community members. In 1983 Congress enacted one of the most radical changes in the history of Medicare. Until 1983 hospitals were reimbursed retroactively by Medicare, but as a result of the Social Security Amendments of 1983, hospitals are now paid prospectively by Medicare, based on prices determined by national averages of costs per diagnosis. This prospective pricing system (PPS) is the model for future health care reimbursement, both at the state and federal levels. Eventually the Department of Health and Human Services Health Care Financing Administration (HCFA) will include the PPS system to cover such problems as alcohol and drug abuse.[7] In nonprofit hospitals, social workers have been asked to do more work in the areas of preadmission and admission screening, but some proprietary hospitals have been cutting social workers in an attempt to maintain their profitability.

Health care costs are continuing to rise. In 1998 it was estimated that the United States would spend $1 trillion ($1,000 billion), or 15 percent of its gross national product, on health care. In 1994 it was estimated that there were 37 million Americans at or below the poverty level who experienced health risks associated with an inability to afford needed health care.[8] Health care reform was one of the major issues in the 1992 presidential campaign. The National Association of Social Workers played a key role in a major health care reform bill introduced in Congress on June 9,1992, by Senator Daniel K. Inouye. Senator Inouye stated: "The National Health Care Act of 1992 would significantly change the way our nation finances and delivers health care." The main elements of the bill included provisions to create a "single payer" health insurance plan that would be administered by the federal and state governments. Benefits would include primary, preventive hospital, dental and vision care, mental health and substance abuse treatment, rehabilitation services, prescription drugs, and long-term care for the elderly and for chronically ill people of all ages. The bill recommended that individuals would retain the freedom to choose their own physicians and other health care providers. Taxes would pay for the plan, but the bill's sponsors hoped that savings would occur by eliminating the duplicative costs and paperwork of thousands of insurance companies as well as utilizing negotiated fee structures for all care providers.[9]

The National Health Care Act of 1992 proposed by President Clinton was never really considered by the Congress. Health care reform was absent from the Capitol Hill agenda of the 1995 Congress. Instead of health care reform, the Republican "Contract with America" seemed to be moving to reduce many public programs that served as a safety net for millions of Americans. In 1995 NASW published a brief analyzing the direction Congress was moving. The brief included the following points:

> *Medicare.* The $160 billion Medicare program's size and its 10 percent per year growth rate make it vulnerable to budget cuts.

> *Medicaid.* The $125.2 billion Medicaid program will also be subjected to intense pressure as budget cuts are debated.

> *Supplemental Security Income (SSI).* A provision in the House welfare reform bill would deny SSI benefits and Medicaid to all people with drug and alcohol addictions who cannot qualify for SSI on the basis of other disabling conditions.[10]

The results of the congressional debates will not be known for some time, but the large number of American citizens without health care insurance is a national tragedy and probably, in the long term, will prove to be more expensive for our society. The country will have to solve the health care crisis in the next few years. Regardless of the ebb and flow of federal legislation, social workers will continue to be considered an important health care member because of their special knowledge and skill in the psychosocial aspects of illness.

Social work in the health services accepts the World Health Organization's (WHO) definition of health as "a state of complete physical, mental, and social well-being and not merely the absence of disease or infirmity."

Social workers in health care services use the problem-solving method in assisting individuals, groups, and communities in solving personal and family health problems. Social work is involved at various levels of prevention:

> *Primary*—health education, encouraging immunizations, good mental health practice in families, prenatal and postnatal care.

> *Secondary*—early screening programs for detection of disease, checkups, encouraging treatment.

> *Tertiary or rehabilitation*—preventing further deterioration of a disease or problem.

Social workers engage in research and add to a professional body of scientific knowledge. Through supervision and teaching, they assist paraprofessionals to develop scholarship and skill. They teach in schools of social work and serve in student-training units as field instructors.

Medical social work is shaped and guided by the attitudes, beliefs, knowledge, and acceptable ways of doing things by professionals serving in health care institutions and by the philosophy and practice of modern medicine. It requires a knowledge of illness and of the psychological and social impact of disease on the individual, the family, and the family interrelationships; it calls for the application and adaptation of social work concepts, principles, and ideas to the special needs of hospital and clinic clientele.

In the hospital social workers collaborate with medicine and a broad range of specialists, including nurses, dieticians, physical therapists, speech and hearing specialists, recreationists, and pharmacists. Outside the hospital they work with public health nurses and health educators.

As medicine has become highly technical and specialized, especially as practiced in the university hospital or complex rehabilitation setting, the social worker sometimes holds the process together, explaining the personnel and their functions to patients. If the patient moves from medicine to surgery, and back again, and changes in physicians occur, the social worker is the constant person.

Social work has a coordinate, rather than subordinate or ancillary, role to medicine and is responsible to the institution and the supporting public. The doctor is the clinical and medical authority and is held responsible under the law for medical practice. However, the doctor is only one member of the team in modern medical practice to whom the social worker relates.

The Meaning of Illness

Illness encompasses medical, social, economic, and even spiritual components. Illness affects people in many ways, directly and indirectly, and is of particular consequence to individuals, families, and communities. The social worker plays a major role in interpreting illness to people and in helping them muster their personal and social resources toward physical and mental well-being.

Webster's *International Dictionary* defines illness as a state of being ill or sick, bodily indisposition, disease. An ill person is one of "inferior quality, bad in condition, wretched, impolite, improper, incorrect, bad morally, evil in nature or character, malevolent, wicked, vicious, wrong." The word *disease* literally means want of ease, uneasiness. *Dis*, from the Latin prefix, means apart or asunder, and *ease* is a state of comfort or rest. The diseased person is a person wanting in ease. An invalid, on the other hand, is someone who is not valid, someone no longer able to bear the burdens of life or who, for temporary or prolonged periods of time, simply cannot function.

As defined by doctors, disease is objective. Causation relates to agents that can be stained, tested for chemical qualities, measured, and described. The laboratory procedures used by medical personnel in hospitals, clinics, and in doctors' offices are objective devices used to determine the degree of seriousness of disability or pathology resulting from disease processes. Determinations are made of organic states such as result from bacteria, viruses, trauma, cellular dysfunction, and various circulatory disturbances.

Broadly speaking, illness—impaired role function—may result from factors not wholly organic, but social, psychological, cultural, and economic. Anything affecting the total well-being of the patient may support the illness and render the patient incapable of normal role performance. It forces dependency and reduces usefulness to the family and other significant people. It cuts off the individual's access to normal enjoyment and satisfaction.

Social workers, in addressing themselves to other than organic factors, study and define illness in its cultural and environmental matrix and assist with the removal of barriers to health from these sources.

The increase in chronic disease among Americans has literally changed the meaning of illness for a great many people. In the 1940s infections such as tuberculosis, meningitis, and influenza were still major life threats. Polio was still maiming and killing people into the 1950s. Now, however, chronic diseases—heart disease, diabetes, emphysema, and stroke—are major threats.

The AIDS epidemic sweeping the world and the United States has strained health and psychosocial resources. Lloyd states

> Because of the long asymptomatic period, the number of AIDS cases at any given time reflects the level of HIV infection from 3 to 5 years ago or from an even earlier date. The World Health Organization Global Program on AIDS (WHO/GPA) reported on December 31, 1989, that a cumulative global total of 203,599 cases of AIDS had been reported from 152 countries. Of that number, 103,211 cumulative cases had been reported from the United States (WHO/GPA, 1989a). Because of significant underrecognition of the disease (especially in past years in many developing countries), underreporting, delays in reporting, and misdiagnosis, it is estimated that the actual cumulative global total of AIDS cases is nearly 500,000. This total is expected to double to more than 1.1 million cases by 1991.
>
> Reports to WHO/GPA in mid-1988 were the basis for estimates that at least 5 million to 10 million persons worldwide probably were infected with HIV. In mid-1989, WHO/GPA projected that new infections could double or triple during the 1990s. The near-term prospects for a vaccine or cure are slight, and the numbers of infected men, women, and children are increasing worldwide. Seroprevalance in children and transmission through drug injection are increasing.
>
> Given the epidemiology and demography of HIV and AIDS, it is doubtful that social workers can practice anywhere without being directly or indirectly involved with people affected by HIV infection and AIDS. Therefore, all social workers should be knowledgeable about HIV transmission and prevention, capable of adapting practice methods to needs of those affected by HIV or AIDS, and committed to applying social work values to ensure that people are not discriminated against in the workplace, social service agencies, or health care facilities because of their HIV status.[11]

People have to live with chronic disease, adjust to pain, change habits—diet, quit smoking, exercise, and change employment. With chronic conditions—arthritis, heart disease, AIDS, some cancers—the patient must be a partner in the care of the disease, in its prevention, and in its deterioration. Social work comes into the picture in helping the patient adjust, accept medical regimens, and relate to the health complex involved in the broadened care aspects of chronic disease.

Illness is always highly individual. For many, illness damages the self-image. Illness forces dependency on relatives and society, which may be difficult for the ill person to accept. The Essei Japanese man, for instance, whose rearing emphasizes the interdependence of family members, may develop symptoms, become immobilized, or resort to self-destruction when he can no longer count on a comfortable place of eminence within the family and is forced to accept relief or nursing home care.

Illness often minimizes the usefulness of the individual to his or her family and loved ones. When it interferes with the breadwinning function of the wage earner, illness can result in disorganization of the entire family, and for the wage earner in a loss of self-respect, feelings of helplessness, and despondency. The enjoyment of the normal functions of the individual is denied to the ill person, whose responses are often distorted and detrimental to normal social relationships.

The small child who is ill and who has to be hospitalized for extended periods of time may lose the feeling of closeness to parents and experience separation trauma. Some children who are separated even for short periods of time, particularly under unfavorable circumstances for which no preparation is made, carry a scar for many years, if not for a lifetime. Infants and young children who have been hospitalized and separated from their families for long durations, who lack the closeness of a vital tie to a parent or other significant person, may suffer irreversible physical and emotional damage, become autistic, distrustful of others, and encounter difficulties in relationships all their lives.

The adolescent who suffers from a prolonged illness, who is confined and obliged to curtail activities, may lose peer group support at a time when it is greatly needed in his or her struggle for autonomy and independence. A wage earner suffering from a "nervous breakdown" clings desperately to symptoms for fear that he will be asked to return to work and a job he cannot manage. He recovers only with skilled medical and social work help when he is assured that he will recover and be able to work again and support his family.

Aging individuals may use sickness as a method of forcing their children to give them care and attention. A mother, for example, who during her childbearing period was preoccupied with the task of rearing and educating her children, in middle age and retirement finds her usefulness often questioned, if not by others, by herself. Her children, long since established in their own homes, are independent and do not have the same need for her as when they were younger. She senses that her role in the family has changed. She choses illness as an escape from the feeling that she is no longer useful to force her children to live with and care for her. Unconscious regression to earlier states of dependency, helplessness, and illness are common reactions to stress. The ill person may be dependent, helpless, and under the care of others; nevertheless, the sick are also expected to cooperate with the hospital and other individuals who are responsible for assisting in their care and treatment.

The Role of Social Work in Health Care

Social workers in the health care field work in hospitals, with families, and in public health.

Social Work in Hospitals

Practice in hospitals is a major component of social work in health care. The functions of social work in the hospital include

1. Assess the patient's psychological and environmental strengths and weaknesses.
2. Collaborate with the team in the delivery of services to ensure the maximum utilization of the skill and knowledge of each team member.

3. Assist the family to cooperate with treatment and to support the patient's utilization of medical services.
4. Identify with a cadre of other professionals to improve the services of the hospital by an interdisciplinary sharing of knowledge.
5. Serve as a broker of community services, thus providing linkage of patient need with appropriate resources.
6. Participate in the policy-making process.
7. Engage in research to ensure a broadening of the knowledge base for successful practice.

Social work is illustrated by the following case of a patient admitted to the hospital for a renal (kidney) transplant.

At intake the social worker was responsible for obtaining the history of Paul's illness. She learned that he had an acute renal disorder at age 14. In the years following, he had lived with a fear of death, as well as anxiety over the problems of daily living. During a long period of remission, he married, became the father of a son, was employed in a small family-owned printing business, and lived a "normal" life.

When he was 26 his kidneys failed again and he was hospitalized. After lengthy examinations and consultations, he was scheduled for a renal transplant. The medical team, including the social worker, shared the responsibility for preparing Paul and his family for this operation. The social worker discussed the many ramifications of the operation with Paul's father, who was the donor. It was apparent that although the father was motivated to help, he was also frightened by the prospect of giving up one of his kidneys. He needed the reassurance and support offered by the worker to become comfortable in his lifesaving role and to dispel his feelings of guilt at his reluctance.

The social worker also was called on to be the broker for handling the costs of hospitalization, surgery, and medication. These costs are often more than a family can handle, and if outside help is not available, can lead to bankruptcy, loss of self-esteem, a lowered standard of living, and serious deprivation. In planning for money to pay for the transplant, Paul and his family decided to sell the printing business to meet part of the medical costs. Arrangements also were made with governmental and private agencies to pay the remaining expenses.

In addition to practical problems, Paul and his family had to be prepared for possible rejection of the transplant. The social worker supported and amplified the physician's explanation of rejection.

Two days before the scheduled operation, Paul became ill with a serious respiratory infection, necessitating a postponement. This was disappointing and frustrating.

Several weeks after he first entered the hospital the transplant finally was made, but it was not successful. Even though there had been lengthy discussions about the possible rejection, there was much for the social worker to do in helping Paul and his wife handle their extreme disappointment and fear for the future. Paul's father, too, needed reassurance that he had done all he could, that it was not his "fault" that the transplant had not been successful, and that he could live a normal life with just one kidney.

The social work effort concentrated on all members of the family in helping them sustain each other in this crisis and in introducing them to dialysis, the only means available for cleansing Paul's blood. Because the family lived some distance from a hospital with the necessary equipment for this treatment, it meant a 100-mile trip every other day, plus six hours for the dialysis. In addition, there were the constraints of living imposed by this necessity. All these problems necessitated constant support and help by the social worker.

A breakthrough came when a portable machine weighing forty-five pounds became available to Paul. This gave him mobility and greater independence.

As his health improved, and after he had resolved his hostile feelings about his dependency and had adjusted to his dialysis schedule, he decided to further his education. From the warm association and concrete assistance given by the social worker during his long illness, he decided to become a social worker. Encouraged and sustained by his family, the social work school, and the community, he completed his work to become a practicing social worker, feeling that his experience with disease and disability would give him insight into the feelings and problems of others facing death or other medical problems. He stated, "If people can't talk about their disabilities, they'll have a hard time living with them."

Individuals who are qualified to help with social factors are important members of the comprehensive treatment team. Their services are related to (1) direct help to the patient and (2) indirect aid through assistance to the family and/or others. Help to the patient is related to (a) intake, (b) hospitalization, (c) release, and (d) aftercare. The social worker can be most valuable at the time a patient is admitted to a medical setting. Through use of skills and knowledge, he or she can assist the patient to adjust better to the medical environment and treatment as well as offer help with financial arrangements when necessary. While the patient is in the hospital, the social worker can be of considerable assistance in providing an opportunity for the patient to talk to someone who will listen and who cares. This is usually therapeutically sound and helps in the total treatment plan. If a patient is worried about some problem, he or she is likely to feel better if the anxieties can be verbalized.

The following two cases illustrate other medical–social problems.

A 24-year-old woman was admitted to the emergency ward of a hospital after she attempted suicide for the third time. Because this was a hospital where there was no social service department, the administrator transferred her to another hospital where this service was provided. The main problem for this woman was familial, involving an alcoholic, mentally disturbed husband. It was only after the social worker gave help to the husband and family as a whole that the young woman could live with her situation.

A 15-year-old girl was hospitalized in the psychiatric ward of a general hospital. Part of her problem concerned her relationships with her mother and father. The psychiatrist worked with the girl in the hospital, and the social worker helped the mother and father understand their daughter better—her needs, their relationships, and what could be done to open the door for communication among them. Through joint guidance of the psychiatrist and social worker, the girl was able to leave the hospital and return to an emotional climate at home that was more conducive to satisfactory daily living than it had ever been before.

Social Work and Illness within the Family

A family is often controlled by its "sickest" member, with household activities revolving around the unhealthy individual. Small children are asked to curtail their natural exuberance when a parent or an elderly grandparent is ill, and older children are required to perform certain household tasks that previously may have been undertaken by the adults in the family. The family's entire way of life may be reorganized or drastically altered by the sickness of one of its members, and not infrequently, considerable family dysfunctioning results from the illness.

Mrs. Jones, an elderly mother, became disabled when she broke her hip. Following a short period of hospitalization a plan was made by her and her children for her to live in succession with several of her daughters. This plan was intended to provide variety for Mrs. Jones and to relieve the nursing care responsibility of any one of the daughters. A soft spot appeared in the arrangement when Mrs. Jones decided that she did not wish to be shunted from one home to another, that she wanted more permanency in her old age than this plan provided, and that her preference was to remain in one place. The children agreed, which meant that as Mrs. Jones became increasingly dependent and bedridden the full burden of nursing care had to be carried by one daughter. It was no longer a shared family experience.

Despite her illness and dependency, Mrs. Jones nevertheless continued to exercise the authority of a parent over the daughter, ordered her about, made demands on her, and made the other members of the household uncomfortable, creating an impasse with the grandchildren. The family was weakened and threatened with disorganization. Finally, with social work help, a plan was made for Mrs. Jones to move into a nursing home.

A social worker can help a family mobilize available resources.

Frequently, with the help of services within the community, it is possible for a family to mobilize its resources to care for a child or adult who is sick or disabled. Although it is true that illness can foster family disorganization, it can also result in a constructive use of the family to achieve family unity and goals. Social agencies are available for help. Many children with mental or physical disabilities can be cared for by their families, either by arranging the family's own resources, by using services within the community, or by a combination of family and community resources. Such resources as community mental health centers, visiting nurses associations, homemaker services, and family service agencies can be called on to strengthen and support the efforts of families. In his or her role, the social worker performs a function that supports the medical care given to a sick person and in so doing realistically appraises the needs of the family and the "assets and liabilities" within the family and community for meeting these needs.

One purpose of social work is to support and strengthen family life. In doing this the social worker makes use of existing services through referrals or assists in mobilizing the untapped potential of the community to prevent illness or to restore persons sick and disabled to health and usefulness.

The case of Peter Simpson illustrates the social and psychological components of illness and the function of the social worker in working with a young adolescent and his family.

Peter Simpson, a 13-year-old boy, was treated for stress at the outpatient clinic of a general hospital. His response to the usual medical regimen for ulcer patients was unsatisfactory. The medication and diet did not bring his ulcers under control, and when he began bleeding internally, a full investigation of his circumstances was ordered. The social worker determined in an interview with his mother that Peter was the only remaining child living at home and that his father had died three years previously. Left alone following the death of her husband and the move of the older children from her home, Mrs. Simpson turned to Peter for comfort and advice. She assuaged her loneliness by talking to him and consulted him about living expenses, budget, and the family income. She often referred to him as the "man of the house," and expected him to shoulder the responsibilities of husband and father. Her affectional demands on the boy were heavy and unusual. She had him sleep with her because alone she was "nervous and uneasy."

Medical care brought no relief of Peter's symptoms because of a totally unrealistic home situation. Catapulted into the head-of-a-family position and made the object of impossible affectional demands at age 13, Peter collapsed. The social worker arranged for Peter to live with an older married brother and sister-in-law and referred him to the child guidance clinic for treatment. His symptoms were relieved.

Mrs. Simpson was able to accept the plan for Peter as she was helped to form new affectional interests and secure her economic position. Her relationship with the social worker served as an introduction to an everwidening circle of friends and to financial independence. She surmounted an extremely difficult hurdle when, at age 53, with the help of social service, she decided to go to work. She had not been on the labor market at any time in her life and her decision was filled with apprehension and doubt. However, she was healthy and intelligent and able to complete training needed to qualify for work in a sportswear manufacturing

*Anger management is important
for personal and family health.*

*plant. Her beginning salary was double her AFDC check and the gains to her from employ-
ment of financial independence, association with others, and a growing self-actualization
opened an entirely new life for her.*

The medical care for Peter in this instance was aided by social services: first,
through study and diagnosis, which focused on the social and emotional components of
his illness; second, by a radical shift in living arrangements for Peter, which his mother
was helped to support; third, by referral to and use of child guidance; fourth, by job training and employment for Mrs. Simpson resulting in financial independence and greater
personal satisfaction.

Social Work in Public Health

A community is a society of individuals that plans for the welfare of its members for
mutual advantage. No community can afford to disregard the needs of people who are ill or
who might require medical care even if the family cannot bear the burden without help.
Recognizing various motives, the community must take steps to protect the health of its
members. The person who is sick or disabled who cannot get the care he or she needs
cannot be a healthy, contributing force within the community. Therefore, in its own self-
interest, the community provides hospitals, clinics, and other health services. Public health
services have been developed in most communities.

The following case illustrates the role of the social worker in public health services.

A social worker in the public health department was asked to accompany the public health nurse on a home visit to a young mother whose 6-month-old infant was failing to gain weight. Several times in the past month, the baby had been brought to the hospital's emergency room in a severely dehydrated condition.

The public health nurse was trying to help the mother, a 19-year-old woman of borderline intelligence, with the tasks of child rearing. The baby's 50-year-old father, formerly a truck driver, was homebound because of a back injury.

On her visit, the social worker noted that the mother seemed depressed and lethargic and, although fond of her child, seemed uncertain about how to care for him. When the baby cried, she became panicky. Her husband was demanding a great deal of her attention. In addition, the young mother was on bad terms with her own parents, who had disapproved of her marriage, and she did not want to involve them in her problems now.

The social worker found herself working with a family where multiple health problems were interacting. Consequently she referred the father to vocational rehabilitation for retraining in a skill compatible with his physical limitations and arranged for a homemaker to help the mother for several weeks so she could observe the details of child care and feeding from a competent model. The social worker also helped the mother reestablish a relationship with her own parents, who proved very interested in the progress of their new grandchild and helpful to their daughter.

Anger Management and Public Health

Anger can be a devastating emotion. It is often linked to a number of serious social problems including child abuse and domestic violence. Anger can also be a contributing factor in alcohol and drug abuse and a variety of criminal activities including assault and battery, road rage, and murder. Health care providers are investigating how anger affects a number of medical conditions such as hypertension, heart attack, and stroke. It appears that many Americans are becoming more angry and that their anger is adversely affecting their health. It has been suggested that this general increase in anger may have started shortly after the September 11 attacks. There are an increasing number of public service announcements on radio and television targeting anger and the role it plays in child abuse, domestic violence, road rage, hypertension, heart attack, and stroke. The message is clear: Uncontrolled anger is damaging the health and welfare of America.

Americans need to control their anger. To minimize anger in our lives, Alberti and Emmons offer the following suggestions:

1. Improve your relationships with others through community service, tolerance, forgiveness, even caring for a pet.
2. Adopt positive attitudes toward life through humor, religion, acting as if today is your last day.
3. Avoid overstimulation from chemicals, work stress, noise, and traffic.
4. Listen to others. Practice trusting others.

5. Have a confidant. Make a friend, and talk regularly, even before you feel stress building.
6. Laugh at yourself. You really are pretty funny, you know. (It goes with being human.)
7. Meditate. Calm yourself. Get in touch with your inner being.
8. Increase your empathy. Consider the possibility that the other person may be having a really bad day.
9. Be tolerant. Can you accept the infinite variety of being human?
10. Forgive. Let go of your need to blame somebody for everything that goes wrong in life.
11. Work toward resolution of problems with others in your life, not "victory."
12. Keep your life clear! Deal with issues when they arise, when you feel the feelings, not after hours/days/weeks of stewing about it. When you can't deal with it immediately, arrange a specific time when you can and will![12]

Clients with Disabilities

Clients with disabilities are a diverse group that often need special considerations and accommodations. The U.S. Census Bureau estimates that 49 million people living in the United States have a disability, or about one in five people.[13] Many of these disabled people become clients of social service agencies. As social work educators, we have worked with students who have been blind, deaf, paralyzed, recovering from mental disorders and strokes, and a myriad of other physical, mental, and emotional conditions. Social service agencies work with an even larger group of clients with disabilities. Providing social services to clients with disabilities is challenging and requires thoughtful consideration, planning, empathy, and creative solutions and programs.

In working with clients who have disabilities, Kirst-Ashman and Hull have compiled a "Do and Don't" list about how to communicate more effectively.

Do
- Refer to the person's disability only when it is relevant.
- Use the word *disability* instead of *handicap.*
- Refer to the person first and then the disability when needed.
- Ask a person with a disability before trying to help him or her.
- Follow the walking or talking pace of the person with the disability.
- Assume that a person with disabilities has other strengths and abilities.
- When meeting a person with a visual impairment, introduce yourself and anyone who is present.
- Continue to use terms such as *see, walk,* or *hear.* Avoiding these items is awkward and overemphasizes the disability.
- Use the term *accessible* to describe bathrooms and parking spaces.

Don't
- Use terms such as *crippled* or *defective* when referring to people.
- Refer to people with disabilities as "the disabled," "the mentally ill," "the blind."
- Employ terms that are unnecessarily derogatory such as *Mongoloid* or *spastic.*
- Use terms such as *invalid, victim of,* or *suffers from,* which are negative in application.
- Refer to the able-bodied population as "normal."

- Use terms such as *wheelchair-bound* or *confined to a wheelchair.*
- Assume that people with a communication disorder such as a speech impediment, hearing loss, or motor impairment have cognitive disabilities as well.
- Suggest that those with disabilities are special, heroes, or in some way out of the ordinary because they cope with their disability.
- Use the term *handicapped.*
- Lean on a wheelchair when talking; it is someone else's personal space.
- Use terms such as *dwarf* or *midget* to refer to people of small or short stature.[14]

Global Health Care Problems

Health care problems are not just confined to counties and states in America. Many of today's health care problems have crossed national borders and have become global concerns. AIDS, for example, is pandemic in much of Africa and threatens to become so in other third-world countries. It is estimated that one in four people in sub-Saharan Africa is infected with the AIDS virus.[15] Hundreds of millions of dollars have already been spent on AIDS research, but a cure has not been found.

The outbreak of foot-and-mouth disease in Britain in 2001 also demonstrates how health care problems can cross national borders and become global concerns. Although it appears that the deadly disease has been contained, millions of animals in Britain had to be slaughtered to stop the disease from spreading to Europe and other parts of the world. Even though a worldwide ban was imposed on British meat and livestock, isolated outbreaks of foot-and-mouth disease were still reported in France, Ireland, and the Netherlands. A global sigh of relief is being expressed now that foot-and-mouth disease appears to be controlled.

Although AIDS and foot-and-mouth disease have dominated the headlines in 2001, alcohol abuse continues to be a serious global problem. In fact, many health care experts believe that alcohol abuse is still America's and the world's number one health care problem. Billions of dollars are spent each year worldwide to treat alcohol abuse and related problems. In addition, billions of dollars of productivity are also lost because of accidents, illnesses, and lost workdays. Alcohol abuse costs America a staggering $185 billion a year, a figure greater than the cost of all illegal drugs combined.[16]

The Future of Social Work in the Health Care Services

The health care system of the United States is chaotic and costly. In 1989, health care spending averaged 40 percent more per person than health care in Canada, 90 percent more than in Germany, and twice as much as in Japan. One in five American children has no public or private health insurance coverage. One in four black children and one in three Hispanic children have no coverage.[17] These conditions continued into the late 1990s and have become even more dramatic. Today one out of every four American families is without health care coverage. This is without question a tragedy and a national embarrassment.

NASW, in preparing for the submission of the "single payer" bill (mentioned earlier in this chapter), developed a health care cost analysis. It states that the current cost of U.S. health care services is estimated to be $738 billion for 1991 and approximately $800 billion for 1992. Even more startling is the NASW projection that by the year 2002, if the current health care system remains unchanged, it is expected to cost $1.959 trillion, or 15.5 percent of the gross national product.[18]

It is reasonable to predict that social work will continue to have a function in the health services in the decades ahead. Care for the individual already is a widely recognized and accepted function of social work in acute care facilities. Numerous examples have been reported of social work's effectiveness in one-to-one arrangements in general hospitals, medical schools, clinics, and in mental health.

In addressing the future role of social work in health care, Rehr has developed the list of concerns shown in Figure 10.1.

The personal and social health problems represented in Figure 10.1 will require the services of social work. Physicians are not trained to develop social–health solutions. For instance, one study[19] reports that elderly patients account for 38 percent of all days in short-stay hospitals. The elderly are often faced with multiple readmissions, and the elderly person is especially vulnerable to the complex interaction of medical, psychological, and social factors. Social workers can play an important role in helping the elderly and their family members obtain appropriate medical services by preventing unnecessary hospitalizations, coordinating health planning, and doing discharge planning.

An important part of health care that will continue to grow in the future is home health care where the services of physicians, nurses, social workers, physical therapists, and other health care professionals are provided in the patient's home. Medicare, Medicaid, and most managed care programs already include home health care services as part of their

---

1. Chronic illnesses and their sequela in:
   the elderly
   infants and children
   persons who are retarded and developmentally disabled;
2. Social-psychological-emotional disorders, including family disequilibrium and
   interrelationship problems;
3. Social diseases resulting from lifestyle and environmental factors such as sclerosis,
   emphysema, hypertension, coronary disorders, and more recently, herpes and AIDS;
4. Social disorders:
   violence, substance abuse, accidents, suicides, person abuse, promiscuity, and excesses;
5. Stress anxiety, fear in the:
   worried well
   stabilized sick;
6. Minor ailments, self-limiting.

FIGURE 10.1   Major Personal and Social Health Problems in the Eighties.

Source: Adapted from Helen Rehr, "Health Care and Social Work Services: Present Concerns and Future Direction," *Social Work in Health Care,* 10 (Fall 1984), 71–83.

coverage plans. Social work has played a critical role in the delivery of home health care services from the beginning. Social workers are not only skilled in assessing individual needs, but they also organize, coordinate, and manage other community resources such as meals on wheels that augment home health care services. As home health care services expand, social workers will continue to be the linchpin in this vital service.

Prevention and Social Work

The social worker is in a unique and enviable position to contribute to prevention. Social work is health oriented, conceptually and philosophically. It addresses the strengths of the individual or family in a given situation.

As a go-between of services, the social worker is the linkage between the person and a system of support that maintains health, or that may be the means of detecting illness early, or of preventing deterioration of the problem.

Social work organizes and develops the community or mobilizes the resources for doing this. It is often the first to pinpoint needs and to engage in those activities designed to prevent breakdown for the person, the group, or for society. Social work has a resource and service focus and takes the position that no one can be healthy in a sick society.

Summary

Medical social work is social work in responsible collaboration with medicine. It is practiced in hospitals and clinics and in other settings that commonly are identified with the practice of medicine. The clientele of medical social work are those whose needs are social and psychological and whose functioning has been or is in danger of becoming impaired because of illness, disease, or disability.

The ill person, to the social worker, is one who is not performing adequately in the various social roles appropriate for him or her. There are many factors to illness and, in work with the ill person, social workers address themselves to those bearing directly on the person's performance in various roles—employee, employer, husband, wife, or child.

Illness has various and different meanings for the individual, family, and the community. The family's activities often are centered around the sick person, who is in a position to control the activities of the household.

Medical and health agencies within the community are established to assist the family in the performance of its role. The meaning of illness to the community lies largely in the need of the community to promote the health of its citizens. Social workers, particularly those in health care settings, are in strategic positions to give direction to the development of services in communities.

Selected References

BINSTOCK, ROBERT H., and STEPHEN G. PAST, eds., *Too Old for Health Care? Controversies in Medicine Law, Economics and Ethics*. Baltimore: Johns Hopkins University Press, 1991.

EPSTEIN, MAXINE W., and PATTI, ALDREDGE, *Good But Not Perfect: A Case Study of Managed Care*. Boston: Allyn & Bacon, 2000.

GINSBERG, LEON H., LARRY NACKERUD, and CHRISTOPHER R. LARRISON, *Human Biology for Social Workers: Development, Ecology, Genetics, and Health.* Boston: Allyn & Bacon, 2004.

KART, CARY S., and JENNIFER M. KINNEY, *The Realities of Aging: Introduction to Gerontology,* 6th ed. Boston: Allyn & Bacon, 2001.

KASTENBAUM, ROBERT J., *Death, Society, and the Human Experience,* 8th ed. Boston: Allyn & Bacon, 2004.

KAVANAGH, KATHRYN H., and PATRICIA H. KENNEDY, *Promoting Cultural Diversity: Strategies for Health Care Professionals.* Newberry Park, CA: Sage, 1992.

KIRST-ASHMAN, KAREN K., and GRAFTON H. HULL, JR., *Understanding Generalist Practice,* 4th ed. Belmont, CA: Thomson Brooks/Cole, 2006.

LINSK, NATHAN L., and REGGI E. MARDER, "Medical Social Work Long-Term Care Referral with HIV Infection," *Health and Social Work,* 17 (May 1992), 105–127.

LOVALLO, WILLIAM R., *Stress & Health: Biological and Psychological Interactions.* Thousand Oaks, CA: Sage, 1997.

LYNCH, VINCENT J., *HIV/AIDS at Year 2000: A Sourcebook for Social Workers.* Boston: Allyn & Bacon, 2000.

NEVID, JEFFERY A. *Choices: Sex in the Age of STD's,* 2nd ed. Boston: Allyn & Bacon, 1998.

REAMER, FREDERIC G., ed., *AIDS and Ethics.* New York: Columbia University Press, 1993.

TAPPEN, RUTH, *Interventions for Alzheimer's Disease: A Caregiver's Complete Reference.* Baltimore: Health Professions Press, 1997.

Notes

1. Adapted from the work of Rosalie A. Kane, former Associate Professor of Social Work, University of Utah, Graduate School of Social Work.

2. Neil F. Bracht, *Social Work in Health Care: A Guide to Professional Practice* (New York: Haworth Press, 1978), p. 212.

3. David Stoesz, "Corporate Health Care and Social Welfare," *Health and Social Work,* 11, no. 3 (Summer 1986), pp. 165–171.

4. Doman Lum, "Health Service System," in *Encyclopedia of Social Work,* 18th ed., Vol. 1 (Silver Spring, MD: NASW, 1987), pp. 720–731.

5. Thomas Owen Carlton, "Highlights of a Decade," *Health and Social Work,* 10 (Fall 1985), pp. 308–312.

6. Sharon M. Keigher, "Managed Care's Silent Seduction of America and the New Politics of Choice," *Health and Social Work,* 20, no. 2 (May 1995), pp. 146–147.

7. Terry Mizrahi, "Prospective Payments and Social Work: Obstacles and Opportunities," in John S. McNeil and Stanley E. Weinstein, eds., *Innovations in Health Care Practice* (Silver Spring, MD: NASW, 1988), pp. 1–13.

8. William J. Spitzer and Rachel Kuykendall, "Social Work Delivery of Hospital-Based Financial Assistance Services," *Health and Social Work,* 19, no. 4 (November 1994), pp. 295–297.

9. National Association of Social Workers, "NASW Health-Reform Bill Is Introduced," *NASW News,* 37 (July 1992), pp. 7.

10. National Association of Social Workers, "Health Reformers Skirmish with 'Deformers'," *NASW News,* 40 (June 1995), p. 9.

11. Gary A. Lloyd, "AIDS and HIV: The Syndrome," in *Encyclopedia of Social Work,* 18 ed. supplement (Silver Spring, MD: NASW, 1990), p. 13.

12. Robert Alberti and Michael L. Emmons, *Your Perfect Right* (Atascadero, CA: Impact, 2001), pp. 142–143.

13. Karla Krogsrud Miley, Michael O'Melia, and Brenda DuBois, *Generalist Social Work Practice,* 4th ed. (Boston: Pearson, 2004), p. 236.

14. Karen K. Kirst-Ashman and Grafton H. Hull, Jr., *Understanding Generalist Practice,* 4th ed. (Belmont, CA: Thomson Brooks/Cole, 2006), p. 419.

15. Rachel L. Swarns, "Free Aids Care Brings Hope to Botswana," *The New York Times,* Tuesday, May 8, 2001, p. 1A.

16. Claudia Kalb, "Can This Pill Stop You from Hitting the Bottle?" *Newsweek,* February 12, 2001, p. 48.

17. Youth Policy Institute, "National Health Care Reform: An Overview," *Youth Policy,* 14 (June/July 1992), p. 15.

18. Terry Mizrahi, "Toward a National Health Care System: Progress and Problems," *Health and Social Work,* 17 (August 1992), p. 169.

19. Barbara Berkman and Ruth D. Abrams, "Factors Related to Hospital Readmission of Elderly Cardiac Patients," *Social Work,* 31 (March/April 1986), pp. 99–103.

11

Social Work in the Schools

It's a long road to the White House from Marshall, a mountain hamlet in the Appalachians of western North Carolina. Few people make the trip. Fewer still are asked to hold forth once they get there.

But Regina Lynn, 23-year-old single mother of four, a former dropout, addressed the luncheon crowd in a firm, steady voice. Her smile was infectious.

"I can't believe I'm here," she told the gathering of foundation officers, convened in January 1990 by the Barbara Bush Foundation for Family Literacy. "Two years ago, I wouldn't even talk to the grocery store clerk when he gave me the wrong change."

But humor soon gave way to earnest talk.

The outlines of Ms. Lynn's story were familiar to many in the crowd. They knew her as Natalie, author of the poem "A Place to Start," popularized in a booklet of that name released by the National Center for Family Literacy in September 1989.

Ms. Lynn retold her story to the White House crowd—her past as a dropout, a single mother with no prospects for the future . . . her present as a GED diploma holder, a straight-A student at Mara Hill College, a mother aware and active in the education and the psycho-social development of her children . . . her future, yet to be discovered, but filled with promise beyond anything she dared to imagine before a social worker appeared at her door two years earlier.

The social worker, Regina explained, convinced her to enroll with her four-year-old son B.J. in a demonstration program of the Kenan Trust Family Literacy Project. There, she and B.J. found their place to start.

"I used to drive by the college as a kid, but I knew I'd never get there," she said. "The Kenan program gave me my dream."

Regina explained how the program inspired the change in her life—and the lives of her children.

"At first I wouldn't talk to the people in the class because I didn't think what I had to say was important," she said. "But they began to make me feel different about myself, and I started to ask questions." She also began to learn about building an atmosphere in her home that supports education: Evenings now, her older children line up for help with their homework; the younger ones look forward to sitting by as she reads a nighttime story.

The luncheon was a triumph for Regina. It was also a triumph for the expanding family literacy movement, a sign that finally, after years of obscurity, family literacy is taking its proper place at the top of the national agenda.

At the heart of this movement—its chief catalyst, advisor, and training and research center—is the National Center for Family Literacy in Louisville, Kentucky.

With the Center's support and guidance, model family literacy programs have been launched to serve:

—migrant workers in Oregon . . .
—welfare dependent families in West Philadelphia . . .
—mining and farm families in Eastern Kentucky . . .

—Eskimos in Alaska . . .
—and hundreds more throughout the nation.

The full harvest of family literacy is still some time off. But the National Center for Family Literacy is planting and nourishing the seeds.[1]

All, regardless of race or class or economic status, are entitled to a fair chance and to the tools for developing their individual powers of mind and spirit to the utmost. This promise means that all children by virtue of their own efforts, competently guided, can hope to attain the mature and informed judgment needed to secure gainful employment, and to manage their own lives, thereby serving not only their own interests, but also the progress of society itself.[2]

The American public school system always has been looked on as something everyone owned. Americans agree that all citizens are entitled to a fair chance to develop mind and spirit. All children guided by competent teachers can hope to become mature enough to secure employment and manage their own lives so that they can serve both themselves and society.

That is a lofty goal, but even as it was being written there were storm clouds over the education system, and T. H. Bell, secretary of education in 1983, called on the National Commission on Excellence in Education to assess American education and to make recommendations for creating excellence in our public schools.

After more than a decade of reform, our nation's schools are still at risk, and some are deteriorating further. All states have adopted some reforms, and several have made drastic changes in their systems; students are required to pass tests to graduate, teachers' salaries have increased, and competency tests are required of teachers in almost all states.

Yet high school dropout rates range from about 30 percent overall to as high as 50 percent in some urban areas, with minorities failing to graduate in even higher percentages in some cities. More than 25 million American adults are functionally illiterate. American students consistently score low in mathematics and science among industrialized nations, and American businesses spend billions of dollars annually in remedial training programs for new employees.

Perhaps the greatest good that has come is that the level of public consciousness concerning the tragic conditions of the schools has been raised. People have become aroused, angry, and determined to do something to make education more effective. The vocal proponents of change are being heard. There is much churning. Experiments on a wide scale are being tried. Social work has often been an important part of these experiments ever since school social work services were first provided independently in 1906 in New York, Boston, and Hartford.

Some of the programs that show promise are discussed in the sections that follow.

The Education Delivery System: New Approaches

The National Center for Family Literacy, which was started in Kentucky by Sharon Darling, seeks to end the intergenerational cycle of poverty and undereducation resulting in economic failure, hopelessness, and despair by fostering education where disadvantaged parents and children attend school together as partners in learning, partners in success. Funded largely by private industry, this concept has spread to many cities throughout the United States and has met with success in helping parents gain more self-confidence, get better jobs, and create a better home life for the entire family. They are able to change their lifestyle and learn to socialize. The children get a better start in their education; they expect and get help from their parents with their schoolwork, and they learn to communicate within the family and elsewhere.

Where there has been a high incidence of adult illiteracy it was found that 70 percent of the children did not graduate from high school. This created a never-ending cycle of dead-end jobs and welfare for parents, then for the children. Thus, parental involvement is crucial to student success.

Working within the public school system, the Alternative High School program has shown some promise. During the past decade 25 percent of all eighteen-year-olds have failed to graduate from high school. The alternative school program, designed to reach dropouts and potential dropouts, has been a solution for many. Creating an environment of learning involving all personnel, staff, and faculty in a caring and helpful atmosphere, teachers in small classes (usually five to ten students) are free to teach. Counselors, usually social workers, are available full time to provide in-depth discussion of personal and emotional problems, often involving the student's family or the community if the student is in trouble with the legal system.

Specific rules are made by each school district. Some allow a degree of freedom for habits the students may have—for instance, some may permit smoking, but not drinking alcohol or using drugs. Many admit older students who have been dropouts, teenage mothers, and those who are recovering alcoholics or drug abusers. Most encourage the student's taking responsibility for attendance and completion of schoolwork without involving the parents. Students, teachers, counselors, and staff become friends. Graduates receive a regular high school diploma.

One program gaining momentum is the Freedom to Choose plan, which allows parents to select their children's schools. Because this involves expenditure of public funds, it has become a hot political issue with sharply divided opinion. The basic plan is that public funds will be provided to pay part or all of the tuition for a student to attend a private school, including religious schools. Nearly 5 million school-age children were enrolled in private schools in 1991, with more than half in Roman Catholic schools and the rest enrolled in other religious schools or in nonsectarian private schools.

Those favoring this plan point out that private schools educate students for about half the cost of public schools, saving taxpayers about $2,000 per year per student. Private schools, according to proponents, do a better job of teaching than do public schools. Competition would force public schools to become better.

Opponents say freedom to choose will destroy the public school systems. They argue that schools always have been "free" and compulsory and should remain that way.

As an example of how troubled the public school system really is, many parents are opting to teach their children at home. Although this was a rarity in all but very isolated areas a few years back, large numbers of youngsters are now being taught by their parents, usually the mother. With the high rate of educated young parents, they are capable of teaching their children, and they can also teach religious and moral values as they choose. Parents find that life revolves around the family, not the school; they see their children excel scholastically and socially and develop good communication skills and discipline.

States have set up guidelines for home teaching, the number of days of instruction per year, and number of hours each day the student is to be taught. Parents are required to teach the same subjects as in the public schools and to give standardized tests.

Problems Plaguing the Public Schools

What are the problems in the schools that have turned the public against the system? Some of the most glaring will be discussed here.

Discipline

There is great emphasis today on an individual's "rights," from the unborn to the dying, and students don't want to be left out on this important issue. No longer does the teacher have authority over students, with the result that some teachers spend a lot of time trying to bring order to the classroom. This, of course, varies from school to school and among teachers; but one thing is certain: It is difficult to teach when students are disruptive. Students need structure and guidance, with clear, specific communication if they are to develop acceptable behavior and achieve academic success. An adult must be in charge to have a successful classroom.

Violence

With the relaxed discipline in many classrooms, the next step leads to violence. Students who are unable to control their emotions find themselves frustrated, angry, and combative, and they respond to the tension by attacking students or teachers. In the past we have said, "That only happens in the ghettos," but we are now faced with the reality that violence erupts on school playgrounds and in classrooms in all neighborhoods. Whereas it is true that these acts often identify students who need social workers to help them work through their problems, violent behavior creates an atmosphere that makes it difficult for others to learn or for teachers to teach.

School Shootings

On April 20, 1999, twelve students and one teacher were shot and killed by two students at Columbine High School in Littleton, Colorado. Twenty-three other students were wounded, some of them critically. This tragedy was the worst school shooting in America's history. Fatal shootings have also occurred in Jonesboro, Arkansas; Santee, California;

***Social workers often deal with
problems in the public schools.***

West Paducah, Kentucky; and Springfield, Oregon. America's public schools have not only
become violent, but some of them have also become deadly. School officials across the
country are trying frantically to find ways to prevent these deadly encounters.

In response to the Columbine school tragedy, school officials, school social workers, and other professionals are working to make our schools safer. Officials are developing profiles to help identify potentially dangerous students, armed guards are patrolling
the grounds, and metal detectors are being used to keep guns, knives, and other weapons
out of our schools. School social workers and other professionals are working with troubled students and their families to prevent further violence. Students are also being
encouraged to assume more responsibility themselves for making their schools safer.
Zero tolerance policies on violence and weapons possession are being adopted and
strictly enforced. We hope these and other programs will help our schools avoid another
Columbine disaster.

Drugs

"Drugs" are defined as anything that interferes with the healthy functioning of the user. In
addition to narcotics and other illegal substances, nicotine, alcohol, and anabolic steroids
are also included. Unfortunately, these are all found in the public schools, particularly in
high schools, but also in the lower grades. They not only interfere with a student's health
but also are detrimental to the student's capacity to learn and to the student's emotional and
mental health. Students who are using these substances make classroom teaching difficult.
Social workers know that just saying "no" will not keep youngsters off drugs. It takes more
than a warning to teach young people to cope with the pressures of adolescence.

The Supreme Court ruled in 1995 that public schools may randomly test their student athletes for drugs. Although this ruling (*Veronia School District* v. *Acton*) concerned
testing for marijuana, cocaine, and amphetamines in a sports program, lawyers predict that

it may be used as a first step toward testing entire student bodies if there is reason to suspect illegal drug use.

Gangs

Many experts believe that the growth of gangs is one reason why violence and substance abuse have increased so dramatically in public schools. Twenty years ago, gangs were seldom seen in most schools; now gangs are the rule rather than the exception. Gangs have created an even more hostile environment to learning that is infecting our schools. Today 57 percent of schools report crimes committed on school grounds to police. Many of these crimes are gang related. Money that is desperately needed to improve public education is now siphoned off to deal with gangs. Today many schools have security guards who patrol the halls and grounds. Some schools even have metal detectors and armed security guards to combat gang violence. Gangs in many public schools are holding the educational system hostage. If public education is to improve, gangs must be better monitored and controlled. School social workers have accepted this challenge and are increasing their involvement with gangs. By opening up a dialogue between gang members and school officials, school social workers are helping address this serious problem.

Cheating

With students from other industrialized nations excelling in science and math, along with other academic subjects, schools in America have sought ways to keep students competitive. To urge them to greater achievement, standardized tests were devised and required of students at various grade levels in virtually all public school systems. Teachers may feel threatened if their scholars don't meet certain standards; principals feel they have to have top performances from their schools; district officials get salary boosts and public recognition if their schools excel. Schools may receive financial bonuses if their students are in the top percentile; others are punished if their students score low. These may be some of the reasons for the rampant cheating that is found in many schools, but they are not excuses.

Why is widespread cheating common in many public schools? Students cheat so they can be the top in their class; teachers ignore the dishonesty or in some cases encourage it by focusing on the specific questions found on standardized tests, using the same tests year after year, or changing answers on tests for some students. Some principals have admitted altering test scores after being pressured by parents who want their children to be the best regardless of how they get there.

Many critics maintain that it is the entire educational system that fosters dishonesty. Until schools stress learning over grades, until universities and colleges look more to the whole individual rather than GPAs, and until parents are willing to send their children to good schools that may not be Ivy League, academic deceit is likely to continue.

Harassment

School officials are also concerned with the increasing incidence of harassment in our public schools. The harassment of students can take many forms. Physical harassment in which students push, shove, and physically intimidate others is just a small step away from more violent behavior. Verbal harassment damages the self-esteem of students and creates a hostile learning environment. Sexual harassment traumatizes students and makes the transition from childhood to adolescence even more difficult.

Students who are continually harassed and intimidated often become loners or misfits in the eyes of other students. There is reason to believe that some of these identified loners or misfits can become violent. In profiling students who act violently toward others in our public schools, one characteristic that stands out is that these students were often harassed and not accepted by other students. Other factors probably contributed to their violent behavior besides being harassed and made fun of by others. Even so, there is reason to believe that students who are continually harassed and made to feel different can become violent.

Teaching Values

There has been growing controversy about teaching values in the schools, with the big question: Whose values will be taught? Lawsuits and threats by parents and organizations have left teachers feeling it is easier to avoid the problems by ignoring values in their teaching. In practice, schools depend on value systems—they punish students who cheat on examinations, who steal textbooks, who assault other students and teachers. But most schools no longer give instruction in self-discipline, honesty, courage, good work habits, and being responsible.

William J. Bennett, secretary of education under President Reagan, advocates the teaching of moral education.

> Moral education—the training of heart and mind toward the good—*must* provide training in good habits.
> . . . If we want our children to possess the traits of character we most admire, we need to teach them what those traits are and why they deserve both admiration and allegiance. Children must learn to identify the forms and content of those traits. They must achieve at least a minimal level of moral literacy that will enable them to make sense of what they see in life, and, we may hope, help them live it well.[3]

Assessing the Risk of Violent Behavior

More than ever before, students are acting out in schools in violent, and often deadly, ways. It is essential that school administrators, teachers, psychologists, and social workers identify those students at risk for violence. Principles of crisis intervention theory and practice have been adapted to many areas of life. One especially important adaptation is using crisis principles to identify students at risk for violent behavior. In *Elements of Crisis Intervention,* Greenstone and Leviton present a checklist of "early warning signs" that can be used to identify students who might become violent. The more items that are checked, the greater the risk for violent acting-out behavior. Some of the items on the checklist include the following:

1. Expressing self-destructive or homicidal ideation
2. Articulating specific plans to harm self or others

3. Engaging in "bullying" other children
4. Engaging in substance abuse
5. Becoming involved in gangs
6. Harming small animals
7. Setting fires
8. Giving away possessions
9. Having been or being victims of child abuse
10. Having access to a firearm
11. Having brought a weapon to school
12. Exhibiting poor academic performance
13. Being truant from school frequently
14. Appearing withdrawn
15. Having experienced a significant loss[4]

The American Psychological Association and the American Academy of Child and Adolescent Psychiatry have also compiled a list of signs that indicate a child is likely to become violent. Their lists include some of the following:

1. Loss of temper on a daily basis
2. Frequent physical fighting
3. Significant vandalism or property damage
4. Increase in the use of drugs or alcohol
5. Increase in risk-taking behavior
6. Detailed plans to commits acts of violence
7. Threatening to hurt others
8. Enjoying hurting animals
9. Carrying a weapon
10. Previous aggressive or violent behavior
11. Being the victims of physical abuse, sexual abuse, or both
12. Exposure to violence in the home or in the community
13. Having a parent who is violent
14. Heavy exposure to violence on television or in movies
15. Brain damage from head injury[5]

Beginnings in School Social Work

Social work services have been a part of the public schools since 1906 when Boston, Hartford, and New York incorporated this help in their districts. It has evolved steadily with support from school boards, schools of social work, and publications until today many schools have social service workers available for their students. We recommend this service to all schools.

Through the years the place of the social worker in the schools has been one of child advocacy based on individual considerations. It has moved away from a "child problem" approach to one that recognizes that children learn in a milieu that supports learning.

Social Work Practice in the Schools

The Improving America's Schools Act of 1994 signed into law by President Clinton ensures a greater role for school social workers in improving educational opportunities for students. Although the goal of the act is to help all children succeed in school, it makes provisions for help in specific areas with vulnerable groups—minorities, limited-English students, and those who are disabled and economically disadvantaged. It also provides for social workers to receive interdisciplinary training with others on the professional helping team.

As the environment of schools changes, social workers may change their approach to specific problems, but the basic premises that have guided them over the years are still valid.

Social workers—brokers of services—facilitate the application of need and resource. Social workers help by working with the individual student, in group activities, and, in a larger sense, by working with the community to make it possible for learning to occur.

Along with school administrators, they may identify problem areas and possible solutions, as well as help formulate school policy that would address these concerns.

With parents, social workers help to bring about better lines of communication, helping both child and parent gain understanding and acceptance of each other. Through groups of other parents and students, problems often are solved. Community groups help identify the larger issues that may affect many in the school, and social workers act as agents of change in relation to the school and community.

Social workers need to maintain a liaison between social agencies and the legal practice and to become a catalyst in the evolving patterns of social structure.

The following examples involving social work with individuals and groups can be found in many schools.

Work with Individuals

A national problem impacting our schools is the high number of teenage pregnancies. Studies show that 70 percent of teenagers who become pregnant do not finish high school. Although a greater number than ever before are now opting to keep their babies, seldom is a teen ready for the responsibility of parenthood. The experience for her has negative emotional, social, and financial consequences. In some schools social work helps with the prevention of teen pregnancies. Sensitive to the pressures felt by some students, social workers can help them handle the pressures and not be pushed into relationships for which they are not yet ready.

Knowing that it is not the "norm" for teenagers to talk through feelings or to think about consequences, the social worker helps them look to themselves for answers. Good results have followed in reducing the number of pregnancies where school districts have a planned effort including groups, social workers, and teachers. Whereas much can be accomplished in the classroom or in small-group discussions, each pregnant teen presents an individual problem and needs one-on-one counseling. It is only through confidential discussions that all the options can be weighed and the choice that is right for her can be made.

In endeavoring to modify behavior in a child—either to accelerate, decelerate, or extinguish—cooperation and understanding of teachers and parents are very important. Through the help of the child's associates, positive reinforcement can be given during the treatment process and after the modification has taken place.

This treatment method can be effective and achieve the desired results in a short time, as illustrated in the following case.

Jan cried. She cried with tears, sobs, drippy nose, and red eyes. Sometimes she cried for forty-five minutes at a time, sometimes for all evening.

In school she cried when she could not answer a question, or when someone called her "crybaby," or for no reason at all. At home she cried when asked to clean her room, or wash the dishes, or for no reason at all.

Her junior high teachers constantly complained to Jan and the school counselor about the problem the crying caused in their classrooms. Her parents complained, too. The other students, even her old friends, avoided her because they were annoyed or embarrassed by her crying, so she spent most of her time alone.

In conference with Jan's parents, the counselor explained that he thought Jan cried because of the reinforcement (the increased attention) she received for this behavior. Jan's mother said, "There have been times when Jan was working and crying at the same time, and I told her to leave the work if she couldn't do it without crying." The counselor explained that this was placing more emphasis on negative behavior than on positive behavior.

He asked for permission to have Jan come to his office for two consecutive class periods a day (ninety minutes) until she modified this behavior. The parents agreed, and Jan was released from the classes for treatment.

When Jan came to the office the following Monday, the counselor assigned her a place to sit and then, looking at her with good eye to eye contact, said, "Now, Jan, I want you to cry, and don't stop until I tell you to." Jan gave a puzzled look and started crying. This continued every day for a week. At that time her crying started to weaken and she had to be reminded to cry.

The second Monday Jan knocked on the door and asked to talk. She said, "I haven't entered your office so I don't have to cry. Right?" The counselor said, "That's right, Jan." Then she said, "I don't want to cry any more. Will you let me stop?" He responded, "As soon as you enter my office, I want you to cry."

That day Jan cried for eighty minutes. Each day thereafter she cried less and less. On Friday of that week, the counselor told Jan she would not have to come to his office if she would stop crying at home and in her classes, even when she was asked to do something she did not want to do. She said she had not cried either at home or at school for several days. A check with the parents and teachers confirmed this.

Jan did not cry again for the rest of the thirty-day experimental period. Checks with teachers showed that she had made fantastic changes. Her parents, too, rejoiced at her improvement at home.

The parents and teachers were helped to see the need for positive reinforcement once the negative behavior had stopped and they learned how to provide this encouragement.

As the other students gradually accepted the new Jan, she became just another member of the group.[6]

Social Work Using a Group Approach

At a time when resources are at a minimum, social workers in some districts have mobilized an untapped resource in the schools—peer helpers. These individuals become assistants, facilitators, special friends to help others deal with adjustment problems. In groups, they are taught the important skills regarding the nature of helping, confidentiality, acceptance, understanding, trustworthiness, and caring.

Peer groups have proved particularly effective in preventing drug abuse among high-risk students. In one such group the social worker taught a group of students the basics of helping others. Then they identified high-risk students: new in school, racial minorities, underachievers scholastically, and so forth. The first group actively sought out the second group and included them in one-on-one activities and in larger group activities; they provided tutoring if needed with class assignments and became their friends.

Results of this activity were rated very good as a preventive measure, and it had some value when used with students who had previously acquired drug or alcohol problems.

Practice Related to the School System

Problems may arise because of certain dysfunctional influences within the school system itself. Such influences are suspect when a disproportionate number of students from a particular system are involved. When such factors as teacher perspectives or record systems are involved, a systems approach to solving the problem is suggested. For example, if the dropout rate is excessive, this says something about the school's failure to

A school social worker helps a student with special needs.

provide experiences that keep children in school and the failure of school experiences to compete with other influences in the child's life.

With a dropout rate of 28 percent (3 percent higher than the state average) in each of the Grades 10 through 12, the school superintendent in a rural district was alarmed. With a declining enrollment and state funds based on average daily attendance, important programs were being curtailed. In addition to the dropouts, much student unrest and dissatisfaction were extant. The social worker was asked to monitor the program, to find out what was wrong, and to suggest what might be done.

An example of what was done in this school follows.

A group consisting of two teachers, four students (two leaders, two nonachievers), their mothers, a counselor, and a social worker met weekly. Key administrators attended a few sessions.

Focusing on the dropout rate and student dissatisfaction, the group discussed other problems they were aware of. In a climate of trust, nonachievers and their mothers learned they could express their frustration and anger over their failure and the failure of the school to meet their needs. It became apparent that those who were not being served needed to be included in the planning if problems were to be solved.

The group recommended that students with poor attendance and low GPAs, who were excluded from participating in sports and other extracurricular activities, be actively recruited for the "fun" things with the expectation that school would be more appealing to them.

Students and parents who previously felt powerless in reaching school administration with their ideas and suggestions for changing policy were encouraged by the opportunity this group afforded them.

Teachers supported the students, who wanted to change some school policies, and concurred that the school should be a place of fulfillment for all students. They supported the final report recommending that the committee continue to discuss problems as they arose.

In still another school system the social worker became one of the decision makers in a small rural community.

The dropout rate over a period of three years had risen to 25 percent. Students were pushing and abusing drugs, and there was virtually no social life for them. Teacher morale had dropped to a low ebb. The principal of the high school was charged with misappropriating funds.

The director of mental health in the county, an MSW social worker, repeatedly unsuccessful in his efforts to help individual students, turned his attention to the school system. He discovered that some teachers were lacking in ability to handle pupils and were misassigned. One principal consistently blocked efforts to improve the climate of the school by punitive action against both pupils and teachers. The social worker was unsuccessful in gaining support from the district office. A recalcitrant school board did nothing to improve the operation of the schools except to hire and fire three superintendents in three years.

The social worker concluded he needed to be in a position of influence on the five-member school board. He ran for office. Getting elected was not difficult for the community was disillusioned and ripe for change. Within a year he was named chairman of the board. In a position to influence board decisions, he functioned as a community organizer. He influenced the system.

School Social Work and the Community

With the community as the target, one social work educator became involved in local government, ran for public office, and was elected city commissioner. She became involved in setting priorities for orderly development and in supporting government officials and the members of the community seeking to develop resources. She worked at planning, budgeting, and financing and engaged in formal and informal lobbying efforts at the local and state levels. Her role on boards, councils, and social service committees was a model for students in training. Observing her, students were able to understand the broadened concept of social work practice.

What were some of the gains of this community-centered effort? Giant strides were made in providing recreational facilities—municipal swimming pool, roller- and ice-skating rinks, tennis courts, and a golf course. Service organizations accepted responsibility for equipment for the recreational center and for scholarships, awards, and special recognition for school achievement. They also raised funds for medical and dental care for those in need.

Social workers on local boards, such as the community services council, mental health board, and planning boards, opened the door to the community by providing important linkage to the power structure of the community.[7]

Working with Minorities

Asians, Cubans, Koreans, Haitians, Mexicans, and countless children and adults from a great many countries are arriving in America, and our schools are being pressured by unprecedented numbers of people who are seeking to make a home here. It has been estimated that by the turn of the century the population of the United States will increase to more than 300 million—attributable not to a high birthrate, but to immigrants and refugees. The monumental effort it will take to acculturate and train these new arrivals has only begun. Excellence in our schools as called for by the National Commission on Excellence will make unimagined demands on us all. If new arrivals are to have a "fair chance" at developing their abilities and a chance to attain the mature and informed judgment needed to secure gainful employment, they will have to be trained.

Social work, concerned with the social functioning of individuals and youths in various group arrangements, will have a role in this effort. It has the expertise to help people adapt to their environment and develop their potential. It is particularly suited to help people cope with change. In instances where social work skills and methods have been applied in the schools to help minorities, satisfactory results have been reported. Certainly more is needed. We need more personnel and clearly defined roles for social work in schools for the benefit of administrators, teachers, and other school staff. There needs to be a broadening of social work practice beyond traditional methods to include a spectrum of direct and indirect practice. This is the challenge for social work in the schools for the remainder of this century and into the next.

Motivational Interviewing

Working with adolescents in school settings can be both challenging and frustrating. Adolescents often have problems with people whom they consider to be authority figures. They don't like to be told what to do and usually bristle at most people who offer them "motherly or fatherly" advice. In recent years, motivational interviewing has gained a considerable number of advocates among people who work with adolescents. According to Cormier and Nurius, "motivational interviewing is an interviewing style defined as direct yet client-centered helping style characterized by warmth, empathy, key questions, and reflective listening, designed to help clients explore and resolve ambivalence about change."[8] One goal of motivational interviewing is to demonstrate to adolescents how their problematic behavior opposes their own personal goals. Once this connection has been made, the treatment focuses on helping adolescents set and accomplish the goals they want.

Motivational interviewing focuses on five interviewing skills:

1. *Use empathy.* Use paraphrase and reflection to demonstrate to clients that you are interested in what they have to say. Demonstrate your interest by asking the clients to describe a typical day in their lives.
2. *Develop discrepancy.* When clients express a concern about their behavior, take this opportunity to point out the discrepancy between current behavior and the important goals they have set for themselves. Use a "pros" and "cons" approach and write down the advantages and disadvantages of the current behavior. Reflect back to clients at least two times the pros they have listed for changing their current behavior and the cons they have listed for not changing the behavior.
3. *Avoid argumentation.* Don't get into a power struggle. Don't push clients to accept or change a label about themselves (i.e., trouble maker, gang banger). Don't confront the client because confrontation usually leads to increased client resistance.
4. *Roll with resistance.* If the client is resistant to change, roll with it by acknowledging the client's reluctance to change. Don't dwell on a client's resistance but change the focus to some other issue he or she is more willing to discuss. When clients show less resistance, the more loaded topic can be discussed once again.
5. *Support self-efficacy.* Support clients regardless of what changes they choose to make in their lives even if you or someone else would have made other changes. Always give credit to the client for any shifts or changes that occur.[9]

When the System Fails

The dramatic, real-life story "Cipher in the Snow,"[10] written by a schoolteacher and counselor (see Chapter 1 for an explanation of the role of the school counselor as opposed to the social worker), was awarded first place in the National Education Association's teachers' writing contest in 1964. According to the author, the story is true except for such minor changes as were needed to protect the privacy and confidentiality of the characters in the story.

The story is a grim reminder of disturbing conditions in public schools. It suggests a role for social work when a lonely, insecure child who cannot ask for help falls prey to destructive social influences. This story applies to teachers, but it has been used by social work educators to teach systems theory.

Cipher in the Snow

It started with tragedy on a biting cold February morning. I was driving behind the Milford Corners bus as I did most snowy mornings on my way to school. It veered and stopped short at the hotel, which it had no business doing, and I was annoyed as I had to come to an unexpected stop. A boy lurched out of the bus, reeled, stumbled, and collapsed on the snowbank at the curb. The bus driver and I reached him at the same moment. His thin, hollow face was white even against the snow.

"He's dead," the driver whispered.

It didn't register for a minute. I glanced quickly at the scared young faces staring down at us from the school bus. "A doctor! Quick! I'll phone from the hotel . . . ."

"No use. I tell you he's dead." The driver looked down at the boy's still form. "He never even said he felt bad," he muttered, "just tapped me on the shoulder and said, real quiet, 'I'm sorry. I have to get off at the hotel.' That's all. Polite and apologizing like."

At school, the giggling, shuffling morning noise quieted as the news went down the halls. I passed a huddle of girls. "Who was it? Who dropped dead on the way to school?" I heard one of them half-whisper.

"Don't know his name; some kid from Milford Corners," was the reply.

It was like that in the faculty room and the principal's office. "I'd appreciate your going out to tell the parents," the principal told me. "They haven't a phone and, anyway, somebody from school should go there in person. I'll cover your classes."

"Why me?" I asked. "Wouldn't it be better if you did it?"

"I didn't know the boy," the principal admitted levelly. "And in last year's sophomore personalities column I note that you were listed as his favorite teacher."

I drove through the snow and cold down the bad canyon road to the Evans place and thought about the boy, Cliff Evans. His favorite teacher! I thought. He hasn't spoken two words to me in two years! I could see him in my mind's eye all right, sitting back there in the last seat in my afternoon literature class. He came in the room by himself and left by himself. "Cliff Evans," I muttered to myself, "a boy who never talked." I thought a minute. "A boy who never smiled. I never saw him smile once."

The big ranch kitchen was clean and warm. I blurted out my news somehow. Mrs. Evans reached blindly toward a chair. "He never said anything about bein' ailing."

His stepfather snorted. "He ain't said nothin' about anything since I moved in here."

Mrs. Evans pushed a pan to the back of the stove and began to untie her apron. "Now hold on," her husband snapped. "I got to have breakfast before I go to town. Nothin' we can do now anyway. If Cliff hadn't been so dumb, he'd have told us he didn't feel good."

After school I sat in the office and stared bleakly at the records spread out before me. I was to close the file and write the obituary for the school paper. The almost bare sheets mocked the effort. Cliff Evans, white, never legally adopted by stepfather, five young half brothers and sisters. These meager strands of information and the list of D grades were all the records had to offer.

Cliff Evans had silently come in the school door in the mornings and gone out the school door in the evenings, and that was all. He had never belonged to a club. He had never played on a team. He had never held an office. As far as I could tell, he had never done one happy, noisy kid thing. He had never been anybody at all.

How do you go about making a boy into a zero? The grade school records showed me. The first and second grade teachers' annotations read "sweet, shy child"; "timid but eager." Then the third grade note had opened the attack. Some teacher had written in a good, firm hand, "Cliff won't talk. Uncooperative. Slow learner." The other academic sheep had followed with "dull"; "slow-witted"; "low I.Q." They became correct. The boy's I.Q. score in the ninth grade was listed at 83. But his I.Q. in the third grade had been 106. The score didn't go under 100 until the seventh grade. Even shy, timid, sweet children have resilience. It takes time to break them.

I stomped to the typewriter and wrote a savage report pointing out what education had done to Cliff Evans. I slapped a copy on the principal's desk and another in the sad, dog-eared file. I banged the typewriter and slammed the file and crashed the door shut, but I didn't feel much better. A little boy kept walking after me, a little boy with a peaked, pale face; a skinny body in faded jeans; and big eyes that had looked and searched for a long time and then had become veiled.

I could guess how many times he'd been chosen last to play sides in a game, how many whispered child conversations had excluded him, how many times he hadn't been asked. I could see and hear the faces and voices that said over and over, "You're dumb. You're dumb. You're a nothing, Cliff Evans."

A child is a believing creature. Cliff undoubtedly believed them. Suddenly it seemed clear to me: When finally there was nothing left at all for Cliff Evans, he collapsed on a snowbank and went away. The doctor might list "heart failure" as the cause of death, but that wouldn't change my mind.

We couldn't find ten students in the school who had known Cliff well enough to attend the funeral as his friends. So the student body officers and a committee from the junior class went as a group to the church, being politely sad. I attended the services with them, and sat through it with a lump of cold lead in my chest and a big resolve growing through me.

I've never forgotten Cliff Evans nor that resolve. He has been my challenge year after year, class after class. I look up and down the rows carefully each September at the unfamiliar faces. I look for veiled eyes or bodies scrouged into a seat in an alien world. "Look, kids," I say silently, "I may not do anything else for you this year, but not one of you is going to come out of here a nobody. I'll work or fight to the bitter end doing battle with society and the school board, but I won't have one of you coming out of here thinking himself into a zero."

Most of the time—not always, but most of the time—I've succeeded.

The isolation felt by Cliff Evans was extreme but suggests problems not uncommon in public schools. Students commit suicide, "cop out" on drugs or alcohol, or vanish from school.

This story suggests the need for social study, individualizing needs, and the broker-mobilizer-coordinator role of social work. Community or school provisions obviously were not favorably impacting Cliff Evans or his family. A further implication for social work lies in the disturbing anonymity in the account, suggesting the need for a study of the system itself and, possibly, for the initiation of change.

Summary

School social work is embedded deeply in the roots of society's mandate to the schools to educate and train "all the children of all the people" to the maximum of their potentials and capacities. It is a corollary to compulsory school attendance, because not all children, unaided, are able to make profitable use of their formal learning experiences.

Specialists have been attached to the school to help the child achieve his or her potential in the academic setting. These specialists include social workers who relate themselves to the role performance of the child and his or her social and intellectual opportunities.

Social workers focus on social functioning and on the needs of the child to make the best possible use of the learning experience. They are concerned with the fact that forces within and outside the child, and often outside the school itself, may block the pupil's use of the school experience. They intervene to remove barriers to learning. In so doing, they may work with individuals, groups, and the school itself and ally themselves with the community in support of the school's purposes and objectives.

Social workers work with teachers, principals, pupils, or parents. Frequently they work with the teacher and the principal striving for greater understanding of the difficulty that confronts the pupil. One-to-one arrangements with students may be a treatment mode used by the workers or provided in their role of broker.

They may relate to families in helping them accept the purpose of school, the needs of the pupil, and in bringing the two together. Parents frequently function inadequately, simply because of their own needs and unsolved problems. School social workers help in solving problems that interfere directly or indirectly with the pupil's schooling. They work with the team—teachers and other specialists—to bring about the maximum educational benefits.

Selected References

ALLEN-MEARES, PAULA, *Social Work Services in Schools,* 4th ed. Boston: Allyn & Bacon, 2004.

BERK, LAURA E., *Infants, Children, and Adolescents,* 2nd ed. Boston: Allyn & Bacon, 1998.

BOTSTEIN, LEON, *Jefferson's Children: Education and the Creation of a Hopeful Culture.* New York: Doubleday Hardcover, 1997.

CONSTABLE, ROBERT, JOHN P. FLYNN, and SHIRLEY MCDONALD, eds., *School Social Work,* 3rd ed. Chicago: Lyceum Books, 1996.

CORMIER, SHERRY, and PAULA S. NURIUS, *Interviewing and Change Strategies for Helpers.* Belmont, CA: Thomson Brooks/Cole, 2003.

DOWNS, SUSAN WHITELAW, ERNESTINE MOORE, EMILY JEAN MCFADDEN, and LELA B. COSTIN, *Child Welfare and Family Services: Policies and Practice.* Boston: Allyn & Bacon, 2000.

EHRENKRANZ, SHIRLEY M., EDA G. GOLDSTEIN, LAWRENCE GOODMAN, and JEFFREY SEINFIELD, eds., *Clinical Social Work with Maltreated Children and Their Families: Introduction to Practice.* New York: New York University Press, 1989.

FISCHER, LOUIS, and GAIL PAULUS SORENSON, *School Law for Counselors, Psychologists, and Social Workers,* 3rd ed. Boston: Allyn & Bacon, 1996.

GLICKEN, MORLEY D., *Violent Young Children.* Boston: Allyn & Bacon, 2004.

ROSE, SHELDON D., *Group Therapy with Troubled Youth.* Thousand Oaks, CA: Sage, 1998.

STRAUSSNER, SHALAMITH LALA ASHENBERG, and NORMA KOLKO PHILLIPS, *Understanding Mass Violence: A Social Work Perspective.* Boston: Allyn & Bacon, 2004.

Notes

1. National Center for Family Literacy, *Spreading the Word, Planting the Seed* (Louisville, KY: National Center for Family Literacy, 1991), p. 5.

2. U.S. Department of Education, *A Nation at Risk: The Imperative for Educational Reform: A Report to the Nation and the Secretary of Education* (Washington, DC: U.S. Department of Education, April 1983), p. 4.

3. William J. Bennett, ed., *Book of Virtues, A Treasury of Great Moral Stories* (New York: Simon & Schuster, 1993), p. 11.

4. James L. Greenstone and Sharon C. Leviton, *Elements of Crisis Intervention,* 2nd ed. (Belmont, CA: Brooks/Cole, 2002), pp. 52–53.

5. Ibid., pp. 53–54.

6. Case material adapted from a presentation by Richard Johansen, behaviorist, Weber County Schools, Utah.

7. The leadership of Professor Phyllis C. Southwick, Graduate School of Social Work, University of Utah, is acknowledged in the development of this model.

8. Sherry Cormier and Paula S. Nurius, *Interviewing and Change Strategies for Helpers* (Belmont, CA: Thomson Brooks/Cole, 2003), p. 260.

9. Ibid., p. 216.

10. Jean E. Mizer Todhunter, "Cipher in the Snow," *National Education Association Journal* (November 1964), pp. 8–10. Reprinted by permission.

12

Social Security and Public Welfare

The 26-year-old mother of two little children was alone in the world as she arrived in a new city. She had left her husband of nine years because of abuse. He had been on drugs for a long time and when he started using cocaine she knew his attitude toward her would not improve and that there would never be enough money to support her, the children, and his drug habit.

With her two boys, ages 7 and 3, she settled in another state where she looked for a job. She had never had a paying job; she had married upon graduation from high school. When she could not find work she applied for welfare assistance and was put on AFDC.

Although it was not mandatory that she begin a program to become independent of welfare, she opted for "self-sufficiency" training. By placing her youngest child in day care (both children when there was no school) she was able to begin an educational program.

The "self-sufficiency" worker at the agency steered her into a program where she could learn a skill and become employable. She attended the state technical college to learn computer operation and office work.

Her AFDC allowance and food stamps met her basic needs. The welfare worker approved her application for subsidized housing, paid for child care and school expenses. She also was given "heat assistance" and paid a reduced amount for electricity. She was eligible for Medicaid. When she first arrived her youngest child was anemic and she received help from WIC, a program for women and children which gave basic instruction in nutrition and aid in providing a balanced diet.

At the end of her two-year course, she had excellent skills in office work and was placed with a large company. As her financial condition became stable, she was allowed to remain in her subsidized housing, but her rent increased with her ability to pay, and she continued to receive limited assistance until she became totally self-sufficient.

The two years had been lonely for her as she had no family support system near her. With her school classes, studying, and time with the children she had little time to make new friends. By turning again to the coordinator, who had been her advocate in school and during the early weeks on the job, she found the help needed to develop social skills and find new friends. Informal support systems also helped sustain her until the time when she could normalize her relationships and find the security of really belonging. Only by the linkage of many resources—workplace, welfare, new support systems—does it become possible to help women in poverty. Nothing short of total community effort can be expected to relieve this serious malaise. AFDC as provided under public welfare helped.[1]

What is public welfare? Public welfare means different things to many people, and what it means depends somewhat on who these people are and through what lens they view the picture.

To some, public welfare is the "garbage heap" for human wreckage—the idle, the shiftless, the unemployable, the sick and decrepit, the transient, loafers, malingerers, beggars, and certain ne'er-do-wells. In the minds of many, public welfare is income, medical and dental care, and commodities: public support to those who are widowed, blind, or disabled; dependent children with disabilities; and people who are sick and unable to cope without help in a complex, ever-changing society.

Individuals see public welfare in different ways. "Some, for example, see it as an aggregation of quite distinct programs, grouped together by most states and localities for administrative convenience in a public welfare department but quite independent from each other in purpose, origin, criteria of performance, and logic of development. Others by contrast . . . see public welfare evolving toward organic unity of function and purpose, a single whole in which the parts, however specialized in their functioning, derive their vitality and character from the parent body."[2]

Public welfare includes income and health maintenance programs for individuals who are aging, blind, or disabled; aid to families for care of dependent children; medical care to low-income and older persons; and various social rehabilitation services to eligible children, families, and single adults.

Government's Responsibility for Welfare

Basic responsibility of government for welfare was established in England with the Elizabethan Poor Laws, and relief under the provisions of those laws was a local matter, limited to specialized kinds of need and extending only to those whose claims of settlement could not be disputed legally.

Residual elements of relief in kind, means test approaches, public responsibility for only certain kinds of need, work and residence requirements, and characteristics of colonial relief still are found in various services and assistance provisions, particularly at the state and local levels of government. Although many of these measures are repressive and intended to discourage their use, remember that they do, nevertheless, affirm the principle of governmental responsibility.

The *federal* government's responsibility for welfare started in the earliest days of the republic when in 1785 Congress made grants of public lands to states for schools. Other responsibilities were extended when the people, through their elected representatives, added other agencies such as the Federal Office of Education, the Children's Bureau, and the Vocational Rehabilitation Administration; but a comprehensive plan for the protection of citizens against income risks did not become an *enduring* principle of federal responsibility for welfare until 1935 with the passage of the Social Security Act. Reinforcement of this principle has been a clear result of the many amendments to the act legislated by Congress.

The Department of Health, Education, and Welfare (HEW), created in 1953, with cabinet status, is an outgrowth of a widely held view that the federal government has a responsibility for the *general welfare*. In 1980, HEW was divided into two cabinet-level departments: The Department of Education and the Department of Health and Human Services.

The federal government now assumes responsibility to insure virtually all American workers and their families against the loss of income from retirement and disability. Survivors of insured workers also are protected. Risks to employed workers from unemployment for a specified period of time are assumed as a federal–state responsibility. A system is yet to be developed to protect workers for long periods of unemployment and various work stoppages.

An expanded health care system, the "largest human service system" in the history of the United States, further affirms the role of government as an instrument of social policy. Medical care under Social Security protects retired workers, their families, and certain persons with disabilities. A comprehensive national health plan has not been adopted but has been widely debated in congressional committees. The Clinton administration proposed a health care reform plan in 1993, but the plan was defeated by Congress a year later.

The federal government assumes financial responsibility for persons who are aging, blind, and disabled under the Supplemental Security Income (SSI) program, and in cooperation with the states it extends protection to families covered under the Aid to Families with Dependent Children (AFDC) program and to other citizens who qualify for assistance under other provisions of the Social Security Act as a statutory right, including medical care to indigent recipients of public assistance (Medicaid) and to older persons whose income is too low to provide this care.

With the presidency of Ronald Reagan there was a shift in the thinking about government's responsibility for welfare. It is sometimes asked, will the thinking of former President Reagan become a trend, implemented in policy and a new approach to welfare, or will the people and Congress resist more than cosmetic changes? This trend continued into the Bush presidency with even more emphasis placed on self-sufficiency programs. During the Clinton presidency, welfare reform again became a national priority although change was slow. Much of the national debate centered around the role federal and state government should play in welfare programs and the viability of self-sufficiency programs versus more traditional welfare assistance.

President Ronald Reagan's Ideology

Ronald Reagan "redrew the ideological landscape." His political and fiscal philosophy and his views on the role of government were in sharp contrast to Franklin Roosevelt's *New Deal* and Lyndon Johnson's *Great Society.*

As governor of California and as president, Reagan preached a limited role for government—it should do only what people could not do for themselves. He argued for fewer, not more, government regulations and for citizens to have greater freedom in the management of their lives and their money. He slashed taxes and urged the paring back of government programs, including those for poor and disadvantaged people, insisting that these should remain at the state and local levels. Reagan believed that people should get help when needed from families, neighborhoods, and local charitable, religious, and governmental entities; that power concentrated in Washington made serious inroads on individual freedom.

Reagan's philosophy impacted social legislation and continues to be debated in the halls of Congress. The jury, however, is still out and what to do about health and welfare is hotly debated. That these issues and problems are at the front of national concern where policy decisions are made is very much in the country's interest. It is hoped that individuals who are poor, disadvantaged, homeless, and are ill will be served by governmental and nongovernmental agencies seeking solutions to these most difficult social problems.

The Social Security Act

The cornerstone of public welfare in the United States is the Social Security Act, passed August 14, 1935. In general, this act, with its many amendments, is the chief means by which government at the local, state, and national levels provides income security to citizens.

Discussion in this chapter centers on provisions under old age, survivors, disability, and health insurance; unemployment compensation; old-age assistance; aid to families with dependent children; aid to blind persons; aid to disabled persons; temporary assistance to needy families; and social services.

Old Age, Survivors, Disability, and Health Insurance (OASDHI)

The national old-age, survivors, disability, and health insurance, popularly referred to as Social Security and administered by the federal government, is the largest and most important of the income and health insurance programs in the United States. Cash benefits from this program are designed to partially replace income lost when a worker retires or becomes disabled. Cash benefits also are paid to survivors of "insured" workers.

The program also provides partial health care benefits for old age and disability under Medicare. Amendments to the Social Security Act in 1965 set up a contributory health insurance plan for nearly all people aged sixty-five and over: a compulsory program of hospital insurance (HI) and a voluntary supplementary insurance (SMI) to pay for health services. Other amendments also extended coverage to certain severely disabled persons under age sixty-five, including disabled workers, disabled widows and widowers, and childhood disability beneficiaries.

Since its inception, Social Security has extended its benefits so old age, survivors, disability, and health insurance coverage approaches universal dimensions.

OASDHI is a contributory system. It is not to be confused with insurance in the private sector; it is *social* insurance. Payments to beneficiaries are based on previous earnings; equity can be claimed for the system. Beneficiaries of OASDHI are not subject to investigation or a test of means to establish eligibility. They do not have to prove they are poor to receive benefits. Records are maintained accurately and "claims" are processed and paid with technological efficiency. The system's administration is handled efficiently and nonjudgmentally. Other retirement income and that derived from interest on savings, stocks, and bonds, rental property, and annuities—regardless of the amount—do not limit payments. On the other hand, limits *are* placed on the amount of income retired workers can earn from employment while receiving Social Security payments.[3] To understand this

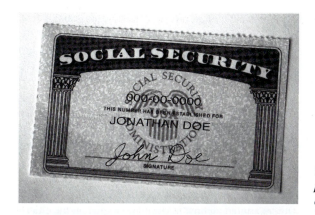

***The Social Security Program
provides benefits for elderly
and disabled persons.***

constraint it may be helpful to recall that the Social Security Act was passed in 1935 when the country was experiencing the Great Depression. Many workers were unemployed. Retirement was written into the law to encourage workers aged sixty-five and older to retire to make way on the labor market for younger, unemployed men and women. In times of high employment or labor shortage, the act might well have to be changed to induce workers not to retire but to continue in the labor force. Incentives for workers to continue employment now exist in the form of earning levels workers may attain without losing payment benefits.

Taxes, under the provision of the Federal Insurance Contribution Act (FICA), are collected from the employee and employer during the productive working life of the worker to pay for OASDHI. Self-employed workers pay the full amount of the tax. In 1935 the tax was 1 percent each for the employee and the employer on an income base of $3,000 per year. In 2005 the tax base has been raised to $90,000.

In adopting OASDHI, the United States radically departed from reliance on the family, the church, private philanthropy, local government, and unending emergency measures to provide a bulwark against want and income need. Many believe that such a departure was warranted and that for retired and disabled workers and survivors of insured workers, OASDHI offers greater security and financial independence than they previously knew. Five and one-half million persons were receiving Social Security in 1953.

At the end of August 1991, a total of $22 billion in monthly cash benefits was paid to 40,307,337 beneficiaries. Sixty-two percent of all OASDI beneficiaries were retired workers. Disabled worker beneficiaries numbered 3,124,129.

The concern raised about financing Social Security has to do with Medicare, not retirement and survivors' insurance. Authorities appear to be somewhat agreed that we can count on OASDHI being paid until 2020. To provide this assurance the tax on earnings has been increased on an income base of $90,000 in 2005 with provisions for further increases in the years ahead.

The spiralling costs of medical care pose a threat to the solvency of the system. This problem is being addressed, and we can be assured that steps will be taken such as caps on what the system will pay for medical procedures, limits the system will pay hospitals, higher costs to consumers in premiums, or some universal system of health care for everyone. Beginning in 1992 the base income taxed for Medicare had risen to $130,000. This is 1.45 percent for employers and employees each, and 2.9 percent for self-employed people.

When Social Security was enacted only workers in commerce and industry were covered. Since then major changes have been legislated, and today about 95 percent of the jobs in this country are covered. Medicare was expanded in 1972. The Medicare Catastrophic Coverage Act of 1988 is an example of government wanting to further reduce the financial risk on the elderly for prolonged health care and costly medical procedures; however, the major provisions of the act were repealed in 1989. The elderly themselves objected to the increase in their income taxes and lobbied Congress to repeal the legislation.

Under the provisions of this act, taxes on income of the nation's elderly would have paid for medical care. Some argued that the tax was fair, and that those receiving the benefits should pay for them. Others argued against it, using the logic that the elderly, who don't go to school, are nevertheless taxed to help pay the cost of educating youth. There seems to be a growing consensus that the costs of common human needs should be equitably shared and socially distributed. Additional expansion covering the health care field can be reasonably predicted in the years ahead.

In times of recession and high unemployment, the number of workers paying into Social Security is decreased, thus reducing the money available to pay beneficiaries. Also, inflation forces upward adjustments of payments, making heavier demands on the Social Security tax. The decline in the birth rate, not a major concern in the 1980s, may become so in the years ahead, when the retired population will be disproportionately large to the younger working population.

An alternative to government management would be to privatize the system in part or in full. Many believe that this would provide more generous retirement and cut back on the burden to the taxpayer. One objection to this approach is that those most likely to benefit would be the younger, more affluent, who also would not be contributing to the less affluent.

Basically, the system is a pay-as-you-go arrangement. Wage earners are taxed to pay benefits to retired and disabled workers and their dependents. Resistance to the system might be expected as taxes increase causing pay checks to shrink. Also, an increasing number of workers believe that the private sector can offer greater benefits than Social Security. Some experts are even suggesting that wage earners should be able to invest and manage their own social security taxes in various brokerage and financial accounts. Although this is undoubtedly true for some workers, for the vast majority of the population Social Security offers more income security for retired and disabled workers and their survivors. Social Security is a form of *social* insurance and a reasonably well-accepted mechanism for sharing costs and transferring income.

Congress appears unwilling to make the changes in Social Security that many believe necessary for the system to continue to be viable well into the next century. Scholars and analysts agree that the demographics of today are different from when the system was enacted and that the world for which it was designed no longer exists. For example, in 1950 there were sixteen workers paying taxes for every retiree. In 1995 only three taxpayers support each retiree. By 2030 two workers will support each person receiving benefits. Taxes on workers have increased from 3 percent on $3,000 in 1950 to 12.4 percent for workers and employers on $61,200 in 1995. It is estimated that for the system to remain solvent, taxes will have to be raised to 17 percent, a figure that appears to be unacceptable to the economy.

Most scholars and economists agree that changes can and should be made. For example:

1. An increase in the age of retirees to reflect the changes in demographics; men and women are living years longer.
2. The formula used today to increase benefits based on cost-of-living index should be more in line with private pensions.
3. Retirees independently wealthy and those with large incomes would receive less Social Security, if any.
4. Raise taxes.
5. A combination of the above, and possibly other changes as well.

Social work basically supports Social Security as a method of income transfer. It approaches universality in application. It is nondeterrent. It is a contributory system that makes it more acceptable to recipients as it is compatible with the ethic of "working for what you get." It is *social* as distinguished from regular insurance, suggesting a role of government in the welfare domain. Some central system of income maintenance for the retired and disabled workers and their survivors is essential.

Unemployment Insurance

OASDHI and unemployment insurance are the two insurance provisions of the Social Security Act. Unemployment insurance cushions workers whose income is interrupted by work stoppages and layoffs. Most states will pay unemployment compensation for a maximum of twenty-six weeks. In 1970 extended benefits became a "temporary" measure of a federal–state program for workers who had exhausted their entitlements in periods of high unemployment. The extended benefit provided for a 50 percent increase in benefit duration up to a maximum of thirteen weeks or a total of thirty-nine weeks of regular and extended benefits. Extensions of benefit periods were approved by Congress in 1974 and again in 1975. Extended benefits, in times of recession or periods of high rates of unemployment, may be "triggered" by the states or by the federal government up to an additional thirteen weeks, or for as many as two extended periods of thirteen weeks each. The maximum for which any insured worker has been covered is sixty-five weeks.

Unemployment insurance is no protection of income against strikes or long periods of unemployment resulting from economic recession and depression. The American system makes no income provisions for prolonged unemployment except to a few workers who can qualify for Aid to Families with Dependent Children or residual general assistance.

Unemployment compensation is a *nondeterrent*[4] *insurance* rather than a public assistance program. To be eligible to receive this compensation, in most states a person must

1. Demonstrate attachment to the labor force by a specified amount of recent work in covered employment.

2. Be ready, able, and willing to work.
3. Be registered for work in a public employment office and file a claim for benefits.
4. Not be disqualified for benefits by some act that would indicate he or she was responsible for his or her unemployment.
5. Demonstrate that unemployment is due to a lack of work for which the employee is qualified.
6. Not be unemployed because of a labor dispute or refusal to accept suitable employment.

Unemployment insurance is financed almost completely by a tax on employers. The employer pays the tax but to show a profit may pass this tax on to the consumer in higher costs of goods and services, or on to the employee in lower wages, or both. Workers, as consumers, also pay for unemployment insurance in higher costs of consumer goods and services. Extended benefits, those paid to workers beyond the period provided in their state plans, are financed equally by federal and state funds.

Public Assistance

Public assistance is an income-maintenance system that should not be confused with the insurance provisions of the Social Security Act. Four main categories of clients are classified under this system: aged, blind, disabled, and families of dependent children.

Supplemental Security Income

Under the Supplemental Security Income (SSI) program, the federal government pays monthly checks to people in need sixty-five years of age and older and to those in need at any age who are blind or disabled. People qualify for these payments who have little or no regular cash income, who own little, if any, property, or who have little cash or few assets that can be turned into cash, such as stocks and bonds, jewelry, or other valuables.

Payments under SSI, managed by the Social Security Administration, are based on the recipient's assets and income. States have the option of supplementing the payments. Financed from general revenues, not from Social Security contributions, SSI is not a contributory system; that is, no payments have been previously made by recipient or recipient's employer. Benefits are not presumed to have been "earned."

Aid to Families with Dependent Children

Income through Aid to Families with Dependent Children (AFDC) was available to those who qualified under provisions of the Social Security Act.

For example, AFDC families needed to satisfy such requirements as:

1. The child must have been under eighteen years of age (twenty-one if attending school or training full time).
2. The family had to reside in the United States and be citizens or otherwise permanently reside here under legal provisions.

3. No limits were placed on ownership of a home occupied by the family. Other personal and real property were limited to a net value of some specified amount.

AFDC was the most controversial of the welfare programs and was the concern of economists as well as politicians. It was a program that needed strong advocates, for the children involved were unable to speak for themselves. While it grew, it was clear that some changes needed to be made.

In January 1992, some 13.5 million Americans were on AFDC, up 2.2 million from two years earlier. Sixty percent of poor families with children were headed by women. The amount of money the recipients received varied by state. In addition to AFDC grants, recipients also received food stamps and Medicaid, which brought their total income higher than those who were working in low-paying jobs.

A major overhaul of the AFDC system was made in 1988 with the Family Support Act, which sought to modify the handling of grants. These new options were a step in the right direction. However, changes do not come quickly, and some of these needed more time and study.

Highlights of the reform were:

1. Beginning in January 1994, states were required to withhold court-ordered child-support payments.
2. States were required to meet federal standards in establishing paternity.
3. States were mandated to establish a Job Opportunities and Basic Skills (JOBS) program to provide education, training, and employment, with the objective of helping people leave the welfare rolls.
4. Most adult clients were enrolled in JOBS, with exemptions for parents with children under the age of three.
5. Child care, transportation, and work expenses were provided, and wage rates were not to be less than minimum rates.
6. Beginning in 1994 an unemployed parent was required to work a minimum of sixteen hours per week.

Although these work incentives sounded good, there was not a rush to enroll in JOBS. This program depended on state funds, and some states had not fully implemented the plan because of budget problems. Also, the definitions for "exemptions," "participation," and "able-bodied" were so imprecise that those who did not want to be a part of the program could easily find a way to circumvent it.

With the enormous financial drain on federal and state budgets, and the wasting of the young men and women in our country, there was clearly a need to replace or reform the welfare system. Politicians, economists, and other leaders suggested solutions to this problem. Some of their suggestions included:

1. All able-bodied recipients were to be off the AFDC rolls after two years. They were to be provided with child care, medical care, and job training while on the rolls.

2. To able-bodied recipients, 25 percent of the aid was to be cut after six months.

3. No additional money was to be given for any babies born while the mother was receiving AFDC.

4. Recipients were required to work toward self-sufficiency while receiving benefits.

5. Stricter discipline was to be set for those receiving aid: parents were to be in training, children in school.

6. Public-works-type jobs were to be available for those able to work.

President Clinton promised change. Among the changes proposed for AFDC were several of the previously mentioned and others: work requirements for the able-bodied, training and education for high-tech jobs, and public works for the homeless and those who might not be trainable.

In their Contract with America the House Republicans stated that their goal by 2003 was to have half the adults on AFDC—91 percent of whom were women—in the work-force, working a minimum of thirty-five hours per week.

Although all the suggested solutions sounded feasible, they do not take into account the reality of the situation of welfare clients. The reason that many AFDC parents could not be put to work and taken off welfare rolls was that they were not employable. They lacked education and aptitude. Two-thirds of recipients on the rolls for two years or more had not graduated from high school; their reading and math skills were so low that they could not solve even basic problems. The majority had no work experience and no work ethic. Because of low self-esteem many become depressed. One-third of AFDC mothers were disabled or had a disabled child. A large number of welfare mothers were in an abusive relationship with a spouse or boyfriend. Many of them refused to leave their children in day care because they feared the children would be abused.

A Health and Human Services study in 1994 found that 16 percent of welfare mothers had substance abuse problems that required treatment before they could succeed in the job market.

With more unwed teenage mothers keeping their babies, the welfare rolls continued to rise. The Contract with America would not provide money or housing for mothers under age eighteen if they had children out of wedlock. Yet often the parental home of the mother was unsuitable for the teenager and the baby. Teens, often without schooling or marketable skills and without family support, developed welfare dependency as a way of life. Special programs for them were indicated if the cycle of pregnancy and dependency on govern-ment support was to be broken.

The Family Support Act set up the Job Opportunities and Basic Skills (JOBS) pro-gram, which provided training for a place in the workforce. This, with various state-operated Job Club opportunities, began producing some results. It was possible to make some improvements. Some governors were asking for more leeway in administering the funds, stressing that at the state and local levels social workers could deal with their particular problems. They could work with individuals in job training and education to make the clients become employable. Programs in some states and communities showed progress, but it was slow.

It was a challenge to planners to find ways for single mothers to climb out of poverty so that they and their children would have sufficient means to live a decent life.[5]

The perfect solution has not yet been found, and there is not just one answer to this overwhelming problem. However, pilot programs in small areas both in inner-city ghettos and in middle-class communities have provided new insights into what works and what does not. People become dependent on welfare for many reasons, and they resist giving up the security of a regular paycheck to an unknown job where performance is a determining factor as to whether the money will continue to arrive.

Welfare Reform (TANF)

In 1996 President Clinton signed the Personal Responsibility and Work Opportunity Reconciliation Act, creating the program that provides temporary assistance to needy families (TANF). This new act replaces the former AFDC program that assisted children and families. This legislation ushered in dramatic changes to the nation's public welfare system. These changes included the loss of individual entitlement and the elimination of the economic safety net for children and their families. The act provided assistance to families in need with children by promoting job preparation, work, and marriage. States were required to develop programs to prevent out-of-wedlock pregnancies and encourage the formation of two-parent families. Adults in families receiving assistance were required to participate in work activities after receiving assistance for twenty-four months.

No state has embraced work and self-sufficiency programs more than the state of Wisconsin where the number of welfare recipients has been slashed by 85 percent since 1987. The state's approach has been simple—if you don't work, you don't get assistance. On April 1, 1998, Wisconsin became the first state to eliminate the old public welfare system that paid poor families to stay home. Instead, every adult able to work will be cut off welfare if he doesn't work. Only single mothers with children under twelve weeks will be given a reprieve. Other states will be implementing similar plans, although most are two to four years behind Wisconsin. Will work and self-sufficiency programs succeed in Wisconsin? Much of the nation is watching.[6]

On April 10, 1999, President Clinton announced that welfare caseloads made up of families with children on welfare had dropped by 50 percent or more in twenty-nine states and by about half nationwide.[7] This decline in welfare caseloads has permitted many states to reevaluate their welfare policies. States such as California and New York have rethought their long-term strategies and made some interesting changes.

In California, for example, working welfare recipients are now allowed to keep a larger portion of their welfare benefits as their earnings increase. This was necessary because the state offers relatively high welfare benefits to begin with and a higher adjustment was needed to increase participation in the program. The California experience with welfare reform also suggests that during a downturn in the economy the federal time limit for receiving welfare payments should be extended from twenty-four months to as many as sixty months.

It is also clear that welfare reform works best when states expand their employment and job training opportunities for welfare recipients. California and New York are now refocusing their long-term welfare plans and identifying those welfare recipients who have the greatest employment barriers. Once they are identified, then employment and job training opportunities and programs are implemented that will make them economically self-sufficient.

Poverty

Poverty continues to be a reality for many Americans. It has been reported that poverty rates in this country reached a seventeen-year high in the recession year of 1982. The Census Bureau reports increasing numbers of people below the poverty line. Income maintenance systems and such programs as work relief, food stamps, school lunches, and Medicaid haven't done the job. The rolls of poverty have not been reduced and there is no end in sight.

Many taxpayers are convinced that the system is ineffective and should be dismantled. Some say it provides too many disincentives, and that it favors those who don't work over those who can't. It is criticized because it is fragmented into a patchwork of overlapping out-of-control programs. While recognizing the cost to the country in a loss of productivity (people have little or no incentive to work because of the alternative—unemployment compensation, food stamps, etc.), some still believe the gains of the "welfare state" offset its losses.

Americans who address themselves seriously to the problems of poverty seem to agree on one thing: There are no easy victories where poverty and need are concerned. Perhaps offering as much hope as anything are those efforts that (1) recognize the existence of a problem of major proportions; (2) attempt to mobilize the talents of interested, capable men and women to work at the problem; and (3) recognize that a concerted, consistent, and independent pressure must be maintained to deal with the problems of poverty and material deprivation. Social work is one of the professions that, because of its value system, knowledge base, and methodology, helps find solutions to these serious problems. Increasingly, social work expects to provide some of the answers—both ameliorative and preventive—to problems resulting from poverty and economic deprivation.

The efforts and resources of the total community will have to be mobilized to make inroads on this problem. If the Great Society of the Lyndon Johnson administration proved anything, it was that resources alone will not do the job. Leadership is needed. Commitment and dedication are needed. Teamwork involving the sustained and united efforts of society's major institutions—political, educational, industrial, professional, governmental, religious—is the best hope for the prevention and "cure" of poverty.

Women in Poverty

In 1982 the number of persons living in poverty reached the highest level in this country since 1965. Although the economic recession of the early 1980s has pushed more working adults in general into poverty, the number of poor female-headed families has risen more rapidly than other segments of the poor. Since the late 1960s as the number of births to unmarried women and the divorce and separation rates have increased, the number of female-headed families has grown tremendously, and the rate of increase is greater for blacks than it is for whites. The number of female-headed families has more than doubled since 1970, and their proportion within the poverty population has also increased. Although more single mothers are entering the labor force, their earnings are far lower than those of single males. The substantial income gap between female-headed families and husband–wife families is greater than it was in 1960. The plight of female-headed families among the working poor, therefore, must be a major focus of national concern.[8]

Women who find themselves single after marriage—whether through death of a husband or through divorce—learn that being the "head of a household" brings with it a set of special problems. If there are children still living at home problems are compounded. In addition to the distress, loneliness, sense of loss, and often a loss of self-esteem, there are other problems such as facing financial obligations.

A woman who has been emotionally and financially dependent on a husband may be unable to cope with the heavy load of responsibility. Widows in their forties or fifties are too young for Social Security and may be left with mortgages, medical bills, and limited savings. Divorcees face similar circumstances and are often displaced from their homes and find that the courts have awarded inadequate child support payments and limited, often temporary, alimony. Divorce almost always has the greatest impact on women because it causes a bigger change in their lives than in the lives of the men involved. Women most often are given custody of the children, and although this attachment is satisfying, it also adds problems. These women must get jobs, but many do not have marketable skills or requisite knowledge.

As more and more women work in business, industry, and the professions and early in life become career-oriented, this will be less of a problem. But for the millions of women who face this problem now, it can be overwhelming. They need time to deal with their loss because until they come to grips with personal problems, they cannot cope with a job. Usually an employer will recognize the applicant who is not in control and will not trust her to perform. Mothers have to deal not only with their own personal problems, but also with the doubts of the children. Time, patience, and understanding are required.

Responding to the needs of these women, displaced homemaker centers are in operation in virtually every city. Here women, often with the help of social workers, are able to become independent. Through individual and group counseling they work through their

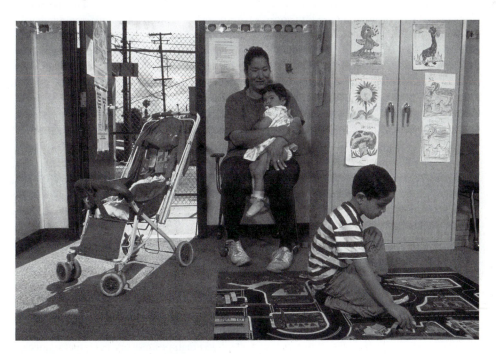

Welfare services provided to a family in need.

grief and sense of loss to find their true identity and to define their values. Through guidance, women learn to assess their potential and find self-confidence and self-worth.

Displaced homemaker services, operating under a variety of names, are sometimes associated with colleges and universities. Others are independently operated or are under city, county, or state support. They offer help in becoming independent and give women an opportunity to discuss their problems and vent their anger and feelings of hopelessness. They also act as referral agencies to those who need immediate psychological, financial, or legal advice. Often they are staffed with single women who have faced the problems their clients face and who have successfully made the transition from dependence to independence.

Usually the next big problem is to become employable. Wives and mothers who have efficiently cared for their homes and families and who have been involved in community activities may find that they have skills that lead them into employment without further training. Others need varying amounts of education or training. Counselors help them focus their energy toward a job and at the same time provide information where they can get the education they need.

Single women find that they can climb from the bottom to find a new life with its security and independence and on the way find new friends, new interests, skills, and self-confidence in learning to cope with their individual problems.

General Assistance

General Assistance (GA), residual to OASDHI, is intended to aid those who cannot qualify under the federally financed SSI program for aged, blind, or disabled persons, or AFDC, or who are not covered by social insurance. There were 1,221,625 recipients of GA reported in the United States in September 1990.

GA is not a popular program, from the standpoint of both the administration and the beneficiary. Because taxes for it must be raised at the state and local levels, the program usually is poorly funded because local taxes may not yield enough revenue. Payments tend to be minimal and grudgingly made to discourage people from applying or becoming dependent on welfare. Subject to such unpopular practices as voucher payments and giving assistance in kind, this form of aid carries with it the presumption that those who receive it are incapable of managing their own affairs. Other rules some states insist upon require the recipient to work for low wages at menial jobs, be reevaluated often, have payments so low it discourages applicants, and other requirements that are unacceptable to those who are in need. The GA program in some parts of the country is demoralizing, a disgrace to the community, and has much in common with the poor relief of the Elizabethan period.

Nondisabled employable men and women are sometimes found in the ranks of GA, and there exists a strong aversion to their receiving public "handouts." Also on GA are those whom Gladwin has labeled the "undeserving poor."

> It is not that these people are dirty, or dishonest, or unfaithful in marriage. We have no trouble in respecting the natives of other lands who never bathe, and at least some crooks, and the majority of movie stars. The real reason, in my opinion, is that they are unwilling to undertake responsibility on their own behalf. We like to help people who are trying to help themselves. However pitiful the individual, or unsavory his circumstances, if he is really trying to improve his lot we will help him, and we will respect him for trying.

The people with whom we are here concerned do not try. Some of us, certainly most social workers, may be able rationally to understand that in their unhappy environment these people have never learned to try; or, perhaps, even learned that it is better *not* to try. Nevertheless, our objective judgment that their apathy is not their fault seems to help even us professionals very little to persuade our subjective selves that we should accord them real respect. These are, in the immortal phrase of Alfred P. Doolittle in George Bernard Shaw's *Pygmalion,* the undeserving poor.[9]

Social work as a profession identifies with those in society who favor more constructive measures and interpretations, which include:

1. Providing an income floor for all citizens and the elimination of hunger and destitution, or their threat, as an instrument of social policy.
2. Extending relief to applicants who can qualify under eligibility requirements; that is, remove it from subjective, biased, and capricious considerations. Relief should be based on need as it is determined to exist by objective, rather than subjective, criteria and as a legally determined right.
3. It is assumed that workers, generally, prefer income from employment to public welfare and that motivations to work are built into the economy in the form of social, cultural, and economic advantages to the employed man or woman.
4. Psychological and social barriers sometimes stand in the way of rehabilitation and employment. Counseling and other services may be needed to restore certain individuals to economic and social self-sufficiency.
5. Preservation of the independence and self-respect of the applicant for assistance is a prime consideration in the administration of programs of relief.
6. A punitive approach defeats the purpose for which assistance is used, namely, the restoration of the individual to normal functioning; it deepens feelings of inadequacy and dependency, causes embarrassment and humiliation, and brings destructive psychological defenses into play.
7. There are many pulls in society that tend to make work more appealing than public welfare—a higher standard of living, the prestige and sense of importance one receives from work, tenure, the emoluments of society, and others.

Homelessness

Home! The word conjures up images of warmth, comfort, food, a bed, love—the American dream. But for a growing number of men, women, and children it is *only* a dream, for they are the homeless. Although experts argue over the number, estimates range from a low of 600,000 to a high of 3 million Americans who are without shelter in a place of their own.

Caring for these people takes more than just providing a house or apartment, for their problems are many and varied. Some are homeless because housing costs increased up to three times faster than income. Even though many of them have jobs, they are unable to find housing that they can pay for on their minimum wages. Each year as many as 2.5 million people are displaced by rent inflation, economic development plans, condominium development, abandonment, and arson. Although the waiting lists for new federally funded housing units are growing, the number of units available has decreased by nearly 90 percent since 1981.

Besides housing, many need much more help to solve their problems. Large numbers of homeless parents are minorities with few job skills and little experience in the work place. Many subsist on welfare.

A growing number of single parents, often in their teens or early twenties, with small children, are joining the ranks of the homeless. They, too, are without job training. Estimates place this group at about one-fourth of those in shelters or on the streets. Often they are driven from their homes by violence—which presents yet another special need.

School-age children (perhaps as many as 700,000) who move from shelter to shelter change schools frequently. They not only have a difficult time academically, they also have more chronic illnesses and need the services of mental health specialists more often than children who live in their own homes.

Homeless individuals often have serious personal problems. Approximately one-third of the adults are alcoholics, one-fourth are drug abusers, another one-fourth have had a felony conviction or have served time in a state or federal prison. A smaller number are mentally ill. (Many fit more than one category.)

In 1989 the NASW launched a campaign "There's No Place Like Home" designed to show how homelessness affects families and children. Their goal was to bring greater understanding to the American public of the magnitude of the problem and to suggest solutions through cooperation between the public and private sectors in providing better employment, better distribution of funds, and adequate housing. Through the efforts of social workers in their communities, services for the homeless, legislative reforms, and more involvement by volunteers have taken place.

Medicare

In 1965 Congress legislated health insurance for aged and disabled individuals under the provision of the Social Security Act, thus establishing the principle of a nonmeans test approach to health care.

Medicare is a compulsory hospital insurance (HI) plan and a voluntary supplementary medical insurance (SMI). HI, without the payment of monthly premiums, is for everyone aged sixty-five or over entitled to Social Security or railroad retirement. Others over age sixty-five may enroll for HI by paying monthly premiums. HI *helps* pay such costs as inpatient hospital care, nursing home care, and various services. SMI *helps* pay for physicians' services, outpatient hospital services, home "health" visits under certain conditions, outpatient physical therapy, and certain other prescribed services.

Title XVIII, an amendment to the Social Security Act, is the authority for Medicare. The action by Congress to provide Medicare hailed the beginning of what many leaders predict eventually will become a national health insurance program providing "coverage" for virtually all Americans. It can be assumed that some plan to underwrite some, if not most, of the cost of medical care and hospitalization will be legislated. Under Title XVIII the federal government has accepted in principle the centralized mechanism of support for medical care, by borrowing a funding arrangement—namely, the tax on payroll—from social security income maintenance.

Social Security as a "universal" income-maintenance program has been maturing as an enduring principle for workers and their families for more than fifty years. Social insurance appeals to Americans' sense of independence and justice. Provisions for health care should benefit from the nation's experience with social insurance. Nevertheless, it can be predicted that proponents and opponents will hotly debate the issues, with emerging patterns clearly showing the results of compromise.

Medicare was expanded by the 1972 amendments to extend the coverage to certain workers, widows, and widowers who are disabled, and childhood disability beneficiaries. Workers and their employers, including the self-employed, are taxed to pay for health insurance. As coverage is extended, the tax increases and results in the transfer of income from one group to another. How much and whose income will be transferred is a political issue. How much of the total cost will be paid from a payroll tax is also a political decision. Some leaders argue for general taxation and universal coverage, suggesting that eligibility should not be subjected to the payroll tax, which in the opinion of many fails to meet tests of equity or universality. Others argue that the payroll tax is more acceptable to vast numbers of Americans who want to "pay their own way." However, as benefits are extended and costs climb, a growing resistance to the payroll tax can be expected.

Congress is planning a rate of growth that is not to exceed the current rate of inflation. Proponents argue that it will not be possible to balance the budget unless proposed cuts are made in both Medicare and Medicaid. Opponents to cuts in these programs argue that proposals now being offered will be too painful, particularly to the elderly in case of Medicare and to the poor in case of Medicaid.

Medicare Reform

Senior citizens are anxiously awaiting a number of proposed reforms to the Medicare program. None is more anticipated or more debated than a universal Medicare prescription drug benefit that would be affordable to both taxpayers and beneficiaries. According to the Congressional Budget Office, $1.5 trillion will be spent on prescription drugs by the Medicare population over the next ten years.[10] The cost of prescription medications has become an onerous burden for many senior citizens, with some spending one-third or more of their disposal income on medications. Many senior citizens struggle each day with an unsolvable dilemma: either purchase the medications they need and cut back on food, clothing, and other necessities or go without prescription medications and risk serious medical complications. A prescription drug plan was passed by the Bush administration in 2004 as a stopgap measure. It has attempted to alleviate the problems of high drug costs but it has not done so. New prescription drug funding is being considered in 2006.

Another pressing issue that concerns senior citizens is the spiraling cost of nursing home care and the limited coverage provided by Medicare. At the present time, the Medicare program covers only the costs of skilled nursing home care and even that coverage is limited to so many nursing home days a year. Senior citizens who are being cared for in semiskilled or personal care nursing homes have no Medicare benefits. This poses significant personal expense to senior citizens who can't take care of themselves but who do not require skilled nursing home care. The cost of maintaining a senior citizen with Alzheimer's disease in a semiskilled nursing home can cost $4,000 or more a month. Because the senior citizen doesn't require skilled nursing home care, the costs must be assumed by the senior citizen and his or her family. This personal liability continues until the senior citizen has "paid down" his or her assets to a certain level, at which time he or she is then eligible for Medicaid benefits. Many senior citizen groups, including AARP, are lobbying Congress to close or at least modify this Medicare gap in nursing home coverage.

Medicare Drug Prescription Program

Beginning January 1, 2006, Medicare started providing insurance for prescription drugs. The Medicare Prescription Drug Program, known as Part D, emphasized the following: (1) everyone on Medicare can get drug coverage regardless of income or health; (2) you are not required to sign up; (3) to get drug coverage you must choose one of the many private drug companies Medicare has approved; (4) if you have limited income and can qualify for the "Extra Help" program, you will pay very little; (5) if your drug costs are high, Medicare will pay 95 percent of your costs beyond a certain amount in any one year; and (6) if you already have drug coverage, you won't need the new program unless you choose to enroll. If you wanted to participate in the Medicare drug program, people on Medicare had to apply by May 15, 2006. A late fee was charged for anyone who applied after that date. A premium of about $32 a month was charged for the Medicare drug program with a $250 annual deductible on drug costs before coverage began.[11]

Experts agree that the Medicare Prescription Drug Program has lowered the drug costs for most of the 23 million Americans who have enrolled in the program. The American Association of Retired People (AARP), a strong supporter of the program, believes that "prescription-drug coverage was an important benefit missing from Medicare."[12] To date, the greatest criticism of the program involves what is called "the doughnut hole." Under Part D, initial drug coverage is limited for most enrollees to $2,250 per year. After that amount is exceeded, the Medicare enrollee must pay $3,600 out-of-pocket drug expenses before the gap or doughnut hole is closed. After $3,600 in out-of-pocket expenses is paid, the Medicare coverage automatically returns to the catastrophic level with low copayments. Estimates suggest that from 24 to 38 percent of all enrollees fall into this gap or doughnut hole and are required to spend $3,600 in out-of-pocket expenses before the catastrophic level of Part D goes into effect.[13] Congress will no doubt look into this gap or doughnut hole and possibly change the law. Even with this setback, most Americans who have enrolled in Medicare Part D have seen their drug costs lowered.

Medicaid

Medical care for low-income people (Medicaid) is administered by the states. Direct payments are made to providers of services. Those persons who qualify for assistance under the federally financed income-maintenance program, SSI, are eligible for Medicaid. In addition, states have the option to include persons who are able to provide for their own daily living but whose income and resources are not sufficient to meet all of their medical costs.

Families who have larger incomes may be eligible for Medicaid provided their income, after they deduct for medical expenses, is within the limits set by the state for meeting maintenance expenses.

Under the 1972 amendments states are required to make family planning available on a confidential and voluntary basis to recipients of Medicaid.

Under provisions of both Medicare and Medicaid, hospital and nursing homes are required to use review committees and procedures (Peer Review Organization) established to provide assurance of appropriateness, necessity, and quality of medical and nursing care.

The main advantages of Medicaid are that it may be used to provide hospital and medical care for very-low-income people who have no regular income from employment, and it may be used for others whose income is so low that they are unable to pay the high cost of medical and health care for themselves and their families. The limitations are those of a means test system—namely, poverty has to be proved, the system lacks uniformity of application, availability to people in need depends on a wide range of interpretations of the law and its intent, and applicants for health care who have not "earned the right" to medical care may be made to feel they are objects of charity.

The Social Security Crisis

Every year the Social Security Administration sends a report to American workers advising them of what is happening to the social security program. On February 12, 2004, American workers enrolled in the Social Security program were sent the following ominous message:

> Social Security is a compact between generations. For more than 60 years, America has kept the promise of security for its workers and their families. But now, the Social Security system is facing serious future financial problems, and action is needed soon to make sure that the system is sound when today's younger workers are ready for retirement.
>
> Today there are almost 36 million Americans age 65 or older. Their Social Security retirement benefits are funded by today's workers and their employers who jointly pay Social Security taxes—just as the money they paid into Social Security was used to pay benefits to those who retired before them. Unless action is taken soon to strengthen Social Security, in just 15 years we will begin paying more in benefits than we collect in taxes. Without changes, by 2042 the Social Security Trust Fund will be exhausted. By then, the number of Americans 65 or older is expected to have doubled. There won't be enough younger people working to pay all of the benefits owed to those who are retiring. At that point, there will be enough money to pay only 73 cents for each dollar of scheduled benefits. We will need to resolve these issues soon to make sure Social Security continues to provide a foundation of protection for future generations as it has done in the past.[14]

This terse and blunt statement about the future of the Social Security program should cause alarm for all Americans, especially those who have not yet applied for retirement benefits. In a way, the problem is both simple and complex. Simple because our population growth is declining and fewer Americans are paying into the Social Security system, and complex because so many different "solutions" are being proposed to fix the problem. Some of these "solutions" include:

1. Gradually raising the retirement age from sixty-five to seventy as the number of American workers declines.

2. Increasing taxes on other retirement programs such as IRAs and 401(k)s.
3. Permitting Americans who are currently paying into the Social Security system to invest as much as 25 percent of their Social Security taxes into other equity programs such as stocks, bonds, and mutual funds.
4. Decreasing the monthly cash benefit currently being paid to retirees.
5. Reducing the benefits of other parts of the Social Security program (i.e., Medicare, Survivors, and Disability).
6. Reducing federal spending in other areas such as defense and education.

To complicate matters further, in December 2003 the Congress passed, and President George W. Bush signed, a new $400 billion Medicare drug legislation bill that will go into full effect in 2006. Critics and pundits alike are asking how America can afford such an expenditure and how this new $400 billion program can help an already faltering Social Security program. What concerns a lot of seniors is that one-third of the program's $400 billion cost will subsidize drugs for very-low-income people, with most seniors benefitting very little from the program.[15] Some critics are even saying the new Medicare drug program will bankrupt the Social Security system within ten years. Social Security reform continues to be a major political concern in the United States today. It will take our best minds and a united citizenry to fix what appears to be a problem that can't be fixed.

Social Services and Social Work

Public services, as distinguished from assistance payments, under the broad provisions of the Social Security Act, are available to certain categories of the population. These services provide for children, families, and certain adults.

Social workers play a major role in the administering of services and as providers. Service programs are financed under state–federal financial arrangements and are administered by the states and local communities. The particular service modality varies widely.

Until 1972 service and assistance were combined under one administration. Generally, it was assumed that services were needed for purposes of rehabilitation. In the minds of many, rehabilitation meant becoming independent of assistance. What has not been generally accepted is that assistance payments are made mainly for the benefit of dependent children, their parents (usually an unemployed mother), to persons who are aged, disabled, or blind, and to a few employable males and to mothers needed in the home to provide for their children.

Administered at the local level, service patterns are widely diverse. Nevertheless, services have received acceptance in many places as their need has been demonstrated, and although there is much criticism of service programs, studies in some places show that the public generally supports these services.

Under Title XX each state develops its own Comprehensive Annual Services Program Plan (CASP). The services to be provided are spelled out in each state plan. Fifty states and the District of Columbia listed 1,313 services reported in Social Services U.S.A.[16] Table 12.1 summarizes the kinds of services offered to children and adults for the quarter ending June 1978.

TABLE 12.1 *Services to Children and Adults*

Adoption Services	Foster Care—Children	Unmarried Parent Services
Case Management Services	Foster Care—Various	Socialization Services
Chore Services	Health-Related Services	Special Services—Alcohol
Counseling Services	Home Delivery Congregate	and Drug
Day Care—Adults	Meals	Special Services—Blind
Day Care—Children	Homemaker Services	Special Services—Child and
Day Care—Various	Home Management	Youth
Diagnostic and Evaluative	Housing Improvement	Special Services—Disabled
Services	Information and Referral	Special Services—Juvenile
Education and Training Services	Legal Services	Delinquents
Emergency Services	Placement Services	Transitional Services
Employment-Related Medical	Protective Services—Adults	Transportation
Services	Protective Services—Children	Vocational Rehabilitation
Employment Services	Protective Services—Various	Work Incentive (WIN) Medical
Family Planning	Recreational Services	Examinations
Foster Care—Adults	Residential, Care and Treatment	Other

Government and Public Welfare

There is a growing realization that government cannot solve all problems. Failures of the Great Society (President Lyndon Johnson's war on poverty) did not result entirely from a lack of resources. In some ways these failures resulted from a lack of leadership. Community action programs and the Model Cities program failed because power was given to some groups not ready to use it and because it was not recognized that great social changes cannot be mandated or brought about overnight. Change must be an extension of the past, and the war on poverty appeared to lack the impulse necessary for its survival.

The largest nondefense program, Social Security, expanded rapidly after 1965 into a set of programs. The question is raised: Has it promised too much to too many? It is a fallacy to assume (1) the nation has unlimited resources and (2) *only* money is needed to solve personal and family problems. The fact is that resources do not exist to provide all things for all people. Choices from alternatives will have to be made. A nation that invests in general health care may be unable to provide good pensions, and the assumption of resources that do not exist can lead to colossal failure in national policy.

With their vast experience in working with troubled families and individuals, social workers know that some problems defy complete solution and that money is needed, but so are understanding and compassionate regard. Money cannot provide these, nor is mere desire to help enough. Someone has described social work education as a "pasteurization process for taking the bugs out of the milk of human kindness." Robert Frost, speaking to the Israelis, justified education because it "raised human pain and suffering to a higher plane of regard." The solution to many human problems calls for widespread regard for the worth of the individual, and this cherished value cannot be legislated or purchased. Social work can help.

It is true that the voluntary field is experiencing some extremely difficult periods and that some national agencies are in trouble. However, voluntary agencies most likely will continue to play an important role in "public" welfare in the future. Some people have observed that centralized, computerized federal programs, including Social Security, often are not responsive to the special needs of individuals and localities. A tenet of social work is that the smaller private agencies have the edge on larger computerized governmental systems in regard to unmet, unplanned for, and unanticipated needs. Volunteerism in general is needed today as never before, particularly in the human service area.

Since 1935 and the passage of the Social Security Act the federal government has increasingly assumed responsibility for the protection of citizens against want as an *enduring* principle.

Fifty years later Ronald Reagan strongly argued for less government, greater local control of welfare, and a *market* economy. These sentiments have carried over to the Bush and Clinton administrations, especially in relation to welfare reform.

Summary

Government responsibility for welfare has become an *enduring* principle with passage of the Social Security Act of 1935.

A shift in thinking about welfare marked the administration of Ronald Reagan. It has been asked, will the Reagan views about welfare shape policy in the future and become a trend? Are the costs of state-funded welfare programs becoming greater than the country can bear or is willing to afford, and will Congress make the hard choices and reduce spending on such programs as income for the elderly, Medicare, and Medicaid? The debate continues into the George W. Bush administration.

Supplemental Security Income (SSI) and AFDC programs are the main *public assistance* programs. AFDC is criticized for the increasing numbers of young women who seem to rely on it as a way of life. Teenagers, becoming pregnant out of wedlock and unable to provide for themselves, are at the heart of the debate in Congress over what to do with our welfare system.

Poverty and the feminization of poverty continue to be major social problems, notwithstanding the gains that have been made toward the equalization of opportunities for women in industry and in the professions.

General Assistance is a public response to those in need who don't qualify for federally financed help. This assistance is paid for from taxes by local entities and is often barely adequate to provide for the needs of these recipients.

Medicare and Medicaid provide for the health care of the aged and others in need of doctor's care and hospitalization. Hospitals and doctors are available to covered workers under the provision of OASDHI. Medicaid provides care for low-income families who are not covered by the insurance provisions of Social Security.

Social services to children and adults, provided to certain categories of recipients, are generally seen as needed for purposes of rehabilitation.

Income needs are but a part of the problems people face. Values and ethics provide guidelines for practice, and a concerted effort of many elements of society is needed to solve complex social welfare problems.

Selected References

AXINN, JUNE, and MARK J. STERN,. *Social Welfare: A History of the American Response to Need*, 7th ed. Boston: Allyn & Bacon, 2008.

BESHAROV, DOUGLAS J., PETER GERMANIS, and PETER H. ROSSI, *Evaluating Welfare Reform.* College Park, MD: University of Maryland, 1997.

DAY, PHYLLIS J., *A History of Social Welfare,* 2nd ed. Boston: Allyn & Bacon, 1997.

DI NITTO, DIANA M., *Social Welfare: Politics and Public Policy,* 5th ed. Boston: Allyn & Bacon, 2003.

ELL, KATHLEEN, and HELEN NORTHERN, *Families and Health Care: Psychosocial Practice.* Hawthorne, NY: Aldine de Gruyter, 1990.

FUNICIELLO, THERESA, *Tyranny of Kindness: Dismantling the Welfare System to End Poverty in America.* New York: Atlantic Monthly Press, 1993.

GILBERT, NEIL, and PAUL TERRELL, *Dimensions of Social Welfare Policy,* 4th ed. Boston: Allyn & Bacon, 1998.

HARPER, KAREN V., and JIM LANTZ, *Cross-Cultural Practice: Social Work with Diverse Populations.* Chicago: Lyceum Books, 1996.

KARGER, HOWARD JACOB, *American Social Welfare Policy: A Pluralist Approach,* 4th ed. Boston: Allyn & Bacon, 2004.

KARGER, HOWARD JACOB, JAMES MIDGLEY, and C. BRENE BROWN, eds., *Controversial Issues in Social Policy,* 2nd ed. Boston: Allyn & Bacon, 2003.

KINGSON, ERIC R., and EDWARD D. BERKOWITZ, *Social Security and Medicare: A Policy Primer.* Westport, CT: Auburn House, 1993.

PARDECK, JOHN T., and JOHN W. MURPHY, eds., *Computers in Human Services: An Overview for Clinical and Welfare Services.* Chur, Switzerland: Harwood Academic, 1990.

PECORA, PETER J., and OTHERS. *The Child Welfare Challenge: Policy, Practice, and Research.* Hawthorne, NY: Aldine de Gruyter, 1992.

PILCHER, DONALD M., *Data Analysis for the Helping Professions: A Practical Guide.* Newbury Park, CA: Sage, 1990.

WHITEMAN, VICTOR L., *Social Security: What Every Human Services Professional Should Know.* Boston: Allyn & Bacon, 2001.

Notes

1. Case material provided by Phyllis N. Johnson, MSW, self-sufficiency coordinator at Utah Issues, a non-profit referral system advocacy for low-income people of Utah.

2. Elizabeth Wickenden and Winifred Bell, *Public Welfare, Time for Change,* a report of the Project on Public Services for Families and Children (New York: New York School of Social Work, Columbia University, 1961), p. 13.

3. No limits are placed on the income a person can earn after he or she turns 70.

4. Nondeterrent systems, as opposed to deterrent *means test* programs, eliminate tests of need. Beneficiaries are not "investigated," they do not have to be indigent to be eligible, and it is presumed that benefits are earned by the worker. Not only are repressive measures not employed, the OASDHI actively tries to locate workers eligible for benefits who have not filed claims.

5. David Whitman, Dorian Friedman, Mike Tharp, and Kate Griffin, "Welfare: The Myth of Reform," *U.S. News and World Report*, January 16, 1995, pp. 30–39.

6. Richard Wolf, "'Wisconsin Works'—or Else Gets Cut Off." *USA Today,* March 11, 1998, p. 9A.

7. Vicky N. Albert, "The Role of the Economy and Welfare Policies in Shaping Welfare Caseload: The California Experience," *Social Work Research,* 24 (December 2000), p. 197.

8. John S. Wodarski, T. M. Jim Parharm, Elizabeth W. Lindsey, and Barry W. Blackburn, "Reagan's AFDC Policy Changes: The Georgia Experience," *Social Work,* 31 (July/August 1986), p. 273.

9. Thomas Gladwin, "The Anthropologist's View of Poverty," in *The Social Welfare Forum, 1961* (New York: National Conference on Social Welfare, 1961), pp. 76–77.

10. Patricia Barry, "Costs, Politics Cloud Drug Benefit," *AARP Bulletin,* 42 (May 2001), p. 4.

11. Patricia Barry, "Medicare Drug Coverage: The Basics," *AARP The Magazine*, January/February 2006, pp. 61–63.

12. Erik D. Olsen, "Askerik," *AARP The Magazine*, September/October 2006, p. 156.

13. Patricia Barry, "In and Out of the Doughnut Hole," *AARP Bulletin*, 47 (June 2006), pp. 16–17.

14. "What Social Security Means to You," in *Your Social Security Statement* (Washington, DC: Social Security Administration, February 12, 2004), p. 1.

15. Jane Bryant Quinn, "The Drug Bill's Hidden Costs," *Newsweek*, December 22, 2003, p. 37.

16. *Social Services U.S.A.: Third Quarter Report, FY1978* (Washington, DC: U.S. Department of Health and Human Services, 1978), p. 38.

13

Family and Child Welfare Services

Sybil was a distraught young mother when her plane touched down in Denver. She had been fearful that when her fiance learned she had a child he would not marry her. So, she had decided to leave her home in the east to place her 1-year-old son, Tony, for adoption; once in Denver, she was advised by Traveler's Aid to seek help from a local child placing and adoption agency. After signing legal papers, she tearfully left on the next flight east. Tony was placed in foster care.

Two weeks later the agency received a telephone call from Sybil frantically seeking to have Tony returned to her. She had married, and when she could no longer bear the thought of living without her son, she confessed to her new husband. Wanting to be helpful and to make a home for young Tony, he supported her in getting her child back. In a few days, arrangements were completed for Sybil to fly west and pick up her son. For her, the children's agency was a temporary measure; it provided a home and protection for the child while she worked through personal problems.

In times of crises when forces assail the very foundation of society—the family—social agencies stand ready to give assistance; they serve as substitute families, if need be, but preferably shore up families who need their support.

The family is recognized as humanity's basic institution. Sociologists, social workers, psychiatrists, anthropologists, lay leaders, and average citizens agree that the family is fundamental to society. No other established pattern has been found more effective in molding the personality of children and adults. Social, personal, and emotional ties inhere more intimately in this relationship than in any other social dimension.

The family is the cradle for children, not only physically but psychologically. So powerful is its influence that some experts (psychodynamically oriented) indicate that a child's basic personality traits have been developed by the time he or she is four to five years of age, with the family playing the major role in their formation.

This book is family-focused, and much of it describes and illustrates the influence of the family on personal and group behavior. This chapter highlights some specifics in regard to family and children—especially those related to marriage and family counseling services and child welfare services available to strengthen families or to substitute for them.

Marriage and Family Counseling

If today is an average day in court in the United States, a judge's gavel will rise and fall and the words "divorce granted" will echo from the courtroom walls more than 4,000 times—adding up to more than 1 million divorces by the end of the year.

Before 1850, divorce statistics were practically unknown. In 1867 there were only about 10,000 divorces in the entire United States. However, since then there has been a steady increase—that has jumped at times—amounting to 613,000 in 1946 at the end of World War II, to an estimated total of 1 million in 2003. The trend was downward during the recession of the early eighties. Since the 1990s, an estimated one-half of all marriages have ended in divorce. This number continues to remain constant into the twenty-first century with an even higher percentage of divorces occurring with subsequent marriages.

When couples divorce, the income for a now single mother decreases by about two-thirds. The reduced income is felt not only by single parents but also by the children of divorced parents. For divorced mothers with children under the age of five, the picture is worse. These families have a more than double the chance of living in poverty because of the added expense of child care. Divorce has also been identified as a risk factor for children to be abused, to be involved in higher crime rates, to abuse drugs, and to have lower academic achievement.[1]

There are more than 100,000 desertions each year in which the husband walks out the door, never to return. In addition, desertions by wives are increasing at a startling rate. There are also thousands of separations in which husbands and wives agree to live apart, in addition to the thousands of "psychologically shattered" homes in which husband, wife, and children walk on the same carpets, eat at the same tables, but socially and emotionally live miles apart. They remain together only because of religious, economic, psychological, or other pressures. Such homes provide barren or meager emotional climates for children as well as adults.

In addition to the economic, interpersonal, and psychological difficulties experienced by single parents, studies have found that adults who are separated, divorced, or widowed report being sick and having health problems more often than their married counterparts. According to Ken Smith, professor of human development and family studies at the University of Utah, several theories have been presented to explain this occurrence. "One of the most prevalent theories attributes the increase in illness to an increase in stress and loss of physical and emotional support when a couple splits or a spouse dies."[2] Currently, research is pretty clear that there is a positive effect from marriage on one's health. In other words, some families are in trouble. What can be done about it? What is being done about it? Social work provides one answer. It is not the only answer, but it is an effective attempt that aids many marriages, families, partners, and children.

Historically, marriage counseling of a sort has taken place as long as families have existed. Early Hindu writings reflect a concern about the family and the usefulness of marriage counseling. In Old Testament days, the importance of counseling was illustrated by the statement from Proverbs (11:14): "Where no counsel is, the people fall: but in the multitude of counselors there is safety." St. Paul, in the early Christian era, attempted to safeguard the family in assuming the role of an authoritative counselor.

In modern times marriage counseling was instituted with the development of clinics, particularly premarital clinics, in Germany and Austria. In 1919 the Berlin Institute for the Study of Sex, a private agency directed by Magnus Hirshfeld, was established as a consultation center for advice and guidance regarding sex and marital problems. In 1922 in Vienna the first matrimonial health consultation center for marriage candidates was opened, sponsored by the Municipal Board of Health. Centers later were opened in other cities in Germany and Austria and in other European countries. Clients of these European marriage bureaus were essentially of three types: (1) those seeking premarital guidance, (2) spouses wanting advice on problems in their existing marriages, and (3) people in and out of marriage seeking guidance and help on sex and other personal problems.

In the United States the roots of professional marriage counseling are many and varied. Attempts to provide marital and family help came from the private welfare agencies, developed as a part of the charity organization movement more than a century ago. Particularly after the depression of 1873, an aftermath of the Civil War, there was a need for financial assistance to individuals and families. Within a few years, welfare agencies were organized in many cities throughout the East and Midwest. Although the main emphasis was on economic assistance, many families were helped to face other family problems and work through them.

Numerous agencies that have provided services directly or indirectly to strengthen families have emerged. The most significant one was the Family Welfare Association of America, established in 1911 to promote family agencies and services. In 1946, its name was changed to the Family Service Association of America to denote its changing role. It now has member agencies in the larger communities throughout the country. In 1983 the name was changed to Family Service America (FSA).

The first private "marriage consultation center" in the United States organized specifically for marriage counseling was the Marriage Counseling Center of the Community Church of New York. It was established originally in 1929 at the Labor Temple by Dr. Abraham Stone and his wife, Dr. Hannah Stone. The American Institute of Family Relations, initiated in 1930 by Dr. Paul Popenoe in Los Angeles, and the Marriage Counsel of Philadelphia, begun in 1932, were additional pioneer counseling agencies. In 1914 the Court of Domestic Relations operating in Cincinnati started to help reduce family problems and breakdown through counseling. Gradually, other private and public family counseling agencies have been developed.

On the professional level, the establishment of the National Council on Family Relations in 1938—with an emphasis on family values and their enhancement—was a significant development. In 1942 the American Association of Marriage Counselors was established. It has become an important professional body and changed its name to the American Association for Marriage and Family Therapy. Its membership includes social workers, psychiatrists, psychologists, lawyers, ministers, and others qualified to do marriage and family counseling.

In 1972, under the leadership of James J. Rue, the National Alliance for Family Life was founded to "promote and strengthen family life." One of its aims was to strengthen marriage and family life in America by improving the quantity and quality of marriage and family education and counseling.

Kinds of Services

Counseling in this service area may be divided into three kinds or levels: premarital, marriage, and family.

Premarital counseling is the assistance of a person or couple in regard to courtship and marital plans and problems. Couples preparing for marriage utilize it in making plans and in solving personal and courtship problems. In increased numbers, social workers participate in premarital counseling in family service associations, university and college settings, and numerous other private and public agencies. Their aim is to assist people in preparing for marriage and in moving toward or away from marriage (depending on the individual situation) in a mature manner.

Marriage counseling is concerned with husband–wife relationships, plans, and problems. Each year thousands of couples talk with social workers and seek help with their marriages. Most get the assistance they need; some do not. Most are helped to strengthen their marriages; some are assisted to separate and move toward other meaningful relationships.

Family counseling includes the husband–wife–children constellation. Problems relating to child discipline, money, education, communication, and so on may require assistance to a family by a trained counselor.

In addition to counseling with traditional nuclear family units, counselors today work with many new kinds of marital and family patterns; for example, stepfamilies, which by the year 2010 may outnumber all other types of families in the United States; gay or lesbian parents caring for children; one-parent households; and unmarried couples living together (2.9 million in 1990—up 80 percent from 1980).

Social workers use a variety of helping methods and approaches that include role theory, exchange theory, transactional analysis, Gestalt therapy, systems theory, family therapy, behavior modification, psychoanalytical approach, reality therapy, solution-focused therapy, and biologically based theories. Although most marriage counseling is done on an individual and couples basis, group process may also be used. Five or six couples meet regularly with a social worker to work on their problems. Single-parent families discuss their difficulties in groups where many methods of helping are used, including retreats, conjoint family therapy, family education, and behavioral techniques.

Kinds of Agencies

Social workers participate in marriage and family counseling through a variety of social and community agencies and are employed in both public and private settings. Much counseling is done by public social workers in county welfare or child and family services departments including work with families in the Temporary Assistance for Needy Families (TANF) program, foster care, adoptions, and family preservation programs. Many courts have social workers attached to them whose responsibility it is to provide services to families. Some play important roles in university and college counseling centers in providing marriage counseling, whereas others are employed at community mental health and drug and alcohol rehab programs.

Social workers also play important roles in private family counseling agencies, illustrated by the services of local affiliates of Family Service America. Social work practitioners in such agencies—whether they be for-profit or nonprofit—throughout North America help provide counseling services and strengthen families through family education and clinical work. Examples of the needs and problems of people with whom they work include the following: a marriage breaking up, premarital concerns, single-parent families, unwed parents, drug use, alcoholism, need for information about resources, help for neglected children, training, consultation, foster home placement, adoption, and numerous related community problems. Social workers in private practice in marriage and family counseling are employed both on a full-time and part-time basis.

Battered Women

In recent years a whole new segment of the population needing help has surfaced: battered women. A statement by the American Medical Association affirms that as many as a third of women's injuries coming into emergency rooms are not from accidents. "Most are the result of deliberate, premeditated acts of violence. And frequently they occur over and over until the woman is killed. Family violence is one of America's most critical health issues."[3] Whether this is an actual increase in the number of abused women or whether they are only recently becoming more visible is not entirely known. But they have captured the attention and sympathy of not only the helping professions but also of the general public.

In addition to the negative effects on women as victims of abuse, research focusing on children exposed to this behavior has determined that it has profound effects on them. Boys, for example, who witness interparental violence have higher rates of aggressive behavior and are at a higher risk of becoming batterers as adults.

As a result of the need and the visibility, social agencies in almost all cities have set up facilities to protect and care for those who are forced to leave their homes because of physical and/or emotional abuse. Funding for these projects is often shared by Family Services, United Way, Social Service departments, and philanthropic grants.

Victims—who come to the shelters after being beaten or stabbed, with broken bones and bruises, or who show no signs of physical abuse but have been put down so much that they may not even be able to recall their last names due to the effects of the traumatic stress experienced—receive a variety of services to meet their individual needs. Many agencies provide temporary housing where they may stay for anywhere from a few hours to several weeks or months until permanent facilities can be found. Counseling is provided in individual or group sessions, and support groups are available for continuing help. Often counseling is also made available for the abusers. Most of the agencies that have housing facilities for the women also care for young children of the family. U.S. Catholic bishops have declared that parishioners are not required by their religion "to submit to abusive husbands." Further, it is reported that violence is sinful in any form and parish priests should provide a "safe place" for women seeking help.

Who are the abusers? The vast majority are men from all walks of life, of every economic background. Often they are respected men in their communities, well educated, who hold high positions in business and professional circles. Many may choose not to accept help when it is offered. However, if there has been some contact with the court system, and the judge has mandated that they receive counseling as a condition of the court action, they are then more likely to participate in a program. In an attempt to protect themselves and their children, women often have a difficult time filing complaints against their husbands, so frequently there is no court involvement.

Regardless of whether the husband or partner gets help, agencies respond to the needs of the women and children. Women are helped to find housing, to get jobs, and to find adequate child care, and they are supported in their decisions. It is a needed service and a welcome one for those who are suffering.

Rape Crisis

Rape—a terrifying crime against women—has been brought into the open. More victims are seeking medical and legal help, and more are reporting the crime to police. Support and help are increasingly available to them by social workers.

Victims of rape are more often women who are vulnerable—hitchhikers, homeless women, aged women, young girls, and women in significant crisis situations. However, almost any woman is a potential target and should be considered a potential victim, most often because of the physical, but also the social, power differential that usually exists between the sexes.

Because of the need and demand, rape crisis centers offering twenty-four-hour help have been organized in almost all cities. These centers provide immediate crisis intervention, including information regarding availability of medical help and support in contacting the police. Later the centers sustain victims through the lengthy adjustment period that is usually needed to restore feelings of safety, self-worth, and freedom.

Women have complained that the police and courts have not been sympathetic to them when they report rape, and in the past many women refused to involve the police. It is true that the police have been most concerned with finding the criminal; the courts have sought to prosecute the rapist. The medical profession has served the victim's medical needs. Through an ongoing program, all who serve rape victims are being made aware of their deep emotional needs. The result is that doctors, police, and the courts now have a greater understanding of their problems and are able to care for them with more sensitivity.

It is the rape crisis centers, however, that primarily deal with the emotional problems women face after such an encounter. Workers help the victims rebuild their lives by sustaining and strengthening them with counseling and support groups. The women's movement is a strong supporter of rape crisis intervention and has helped in the education of the public. The result is that women are more aware of the help available, and more are asking for help when the need arises. Most come for immediate help at the time of the attack, but greater numbers of women who were molested years before but have not worked through their feelings and needs are coming to the centers to talk.

The majority of rape victims are attacked only once; however, those who continue in vulnerable situations may continue to be assaulted.

Changing Family Structures

A great many children live in homes with only one parent. A substantial number of children living in two-parent homes have a stepparent. By the year 2010 more than half of all families may be stepparent families. A current trend in divorce cases is for family or juvenile courts to award joint custody, with one parent having primary physical custody, so that both parents share in the rearing of children.

Whatever arrangement is worked out by the lawyers and the parents, divorce is never easy for anyone. Children, especially young ones, often blame themselves for the divorce. When they are pawns in the struggle between the parents and forced into alliances, their security is undermined and they are torn in their loyalties. The resulting problems and issues may be too difficult for them to handle without help.

A disproportionate number of children of divorced parents are dependent on public assistance. For these, the community's network of public services is often the first line of defense and its only organized support system.

Day care centers have mushroomed with the numbers of women seeking careers and/or helping financially support their families, along with the changes in family structures, and the implementation of the TANF program. Problems related to caring for babies and small children of working mothers or parents are important policy issues continually being addressed at multiple levels of government and by agencies that provide services.

Single parents shouldering the responsibility of two parents are often unable to provide the role models, parenting, or needed income found in households with both parents.

Many changes affecting the family have occurred in social roles and role expectations of individual members. In a relatively stable society, where social change is gradual, children learn the requirements of the group by imitation and observation. Their tasks tend

Day care services are crucial for working mothers.

to be simple and concrete rather than abstract. In America in 1850, when 85 percent of the total population lived in rural areas and only 5 percent in cities of 100,000 or more, children were deemed to be of great value and necessary for their work and productive effort. There was a radical change in the picture a century later, when about 60 percent of the total population was living in 168 metropolitan areas.

Few children in the United States and other Westernized societies today have the opportunity to learn vocational skills by working with their parents, and fewer children augment the family income by their employment. The variety of activities, roles, and the models from which youths may choose is infinite. But variety of choices and the rapidity of social change have, for some, resulted in bewilderment, loss of identity, and role confusion.

Roles have changed also for women who compete in industry and the professions and who often find themselves simultaneously in the dual major roles of caregiver and provider. In 1948, 11 percent of all married women in the United States with children six years of age or younger were in the workforce. In the year 1997, the numbers had risen to 63 percent. When the age of the children was extended to eighteen, the amount increased to 70 percent. For single mothers, 61 percent worked outside the home. The majority of all working mothers are employed full time.[4]

Child Abuse and Neglect

Family problems resulting in child abuse and neglect have become so vast as to result in new legislation in a nationwide attempt to do something. Child abuse—physical or mental injury, sexual abuse, negligent treatment, or maltreatment of a child under the age of eighteen by a person who is responsible for the child's welfare—was the focus of the 1974 Child Abuse Prevention and Treatment Act. Research showed that 60,000 children were being abused each year, but that little was being done for them or for their troubled families. This law was the outcome of investigation into the incidence, nature, and cause of child abuse and was aimed at prevention, identification, and treatment of this problem.

Prior to this act, no one at the federal government level was assigned to work on this problem full time. The limited funding of the existing child welfare programs through Social Security resulted in negligible work being accomplished on the state and local levels. The act provided funds to persons and agencies willing and able to take action, but who previously had been hampered in their efforts by lack of money.

Identifying child abuse and neglect as a social problem, along with educating people and the establishment of protective services, has positively influenced the general public to intervene where it had previously ignored a significant problem. Recent figures by the Department of Health and Human Services (DHHS; 2002)[5] estimate that approximately three million reports (including physical and sexual abuse, neglect, and psychological maltreatment) were received by social service agencies in 2000. The number of reports have steadily increased through the 1980s and the 1990s. Although children may be abused by anyone, parents of maltreated children have been found to be the majority of the perpetrators.[6]

Because of family problems, society has created services to help them. An example of a family problem with mental health overtones follows.

There sits a boy, eight or nine years old, in a chair that's too big for him. He's small for his age and thoroughly intimidated by the situation.

His mother and father sit to one side. They're obviously troubled. They speak earnestly and smile nervously at times.

A clinical social worker specializing in family problems at a community mental health center, sits on the edge of the desk. He has an open sort of posture, a friendly, now-what-seems-to-be-the-problem attitude.

In bits and pieces, hesitant at first and then more confident, the parents spill out their story:

> *Jon (the boy) has been suspended from school—for the third time. He beats up on smaller children. The principal won't let him come back to school until his behavior improves. They don't know what to do. He's always been a problem.*
>
> *Jon's parents are fed up, but they're trying not to show it. Jon doesn't say much.*
>
> *At this point, half an hour into an initial interview, our family specialist knows that there's something wrong. That's clear. Whatever it is, it may be inside the child or outside, perhaps both in greater or lesser amounts.*
>
> *He also knows that Jon has failed to live up to the expectations of those around him, notably his parents. Jon may or may not be emotionally disturbed. There's no way to be sure of that just yet.*
>
> *And he knows one thing more. Whatever is wrong, it's wrong with his family, not just with Jon. That's not to say that anyone is to blame. Our specialist isn't in the business of blaming; it's just not a very useful concept when you're trying to help people.*
>
> *The business at hand is to get this family unit back to the point where it can function reasonably well again. The odds? Pretty good, but with some big ifs:*
>
> *IF they can discover together the dynamics of the family structure: who does what to whom; who gets what from whom; what are the rules, the roles, the games; who is sabotaging what . . . and why?*
>
> *IF the family can realize that it's not just Jon's problem;*
>
> *IF they can work out ways to meet each other's needs more constructively, in a fashion that's less damaging to the whole family;*
>
> *IF they can, in short, open up communication. . . .*

Suppose we do begin to work with Jon in the mental health center's day care unit for children. There, specialists in behavior modification, people with an abiding love for children and a deep understanding of them, will tailor a program for Jon. They'll systematically encourage his more socially acceptable behavior and, just as systematically, they'll discourage his attacking behavior. They'll try to rechannel his energies. They'll be firm, but genuinely kind and concerned. They'll guide him and teach him. They'll accept him as a real person in his own right, a person with special, individual needs. They'll love him, in a way, no less than his parents do. And, in a few weeks, they'll work the minor miracle. . . . They can do it for nine Jons out of ten.[7]

Child Welfare Services

The comprehensive program of child welfare services consists of efforts to promote the physical, mental, and social well-being of all children and youth. Child welfare is (1) a field of service; (2) a social work practice area that encompasses a variety of child welfare activities; (3) a practice field that focuses attention on issues, problems, and policies related to the welfare of children; (4) the application of knowledge and skill to problems of children; and (5) the enhancement of social functioning of children.

Services to children are developed by various governmental agencies, religious institutions, and philanthropic organizations.

Child welfare services include provisions for children in their own homes, in substitute family homes, and in many institutions. Group living arrangements exist for unmarried mothers awaiting confinement, for abused and neglected children needing refuge and protection at a time of stress within a family, for children in detention waiting disposition or relocation into more permanent arrangements, and for children who have birth defects or who suffer from debilitating disabilities and illnesses. Short-term services exist for meeting emergencies within families resulting from illness or death. However, for many children such services as foster care or mental health may be needed throughout their childhood.

Statutory provisions in most states stipulate that except for the most compelling reasons, a child should not be deprived of a home or of the opportunity to be nurtured by his or her own parents.

Child welfare services.

Regardless of the kind of substitute care made for children, the entire arena of child welfare practice requires great sensitivity, maturity of judgment, extensive knowledge, and the finest skills of professional social work. They are needed to provide services for the children and their parents to maintain and strengthen their ties, and if separation takes place, to develop provisions for reuniting the family. When this is not possible, more permanent arrangements for the child must be made to have an acceptable substitute family. This could mean permanent foster care or adoption. Only in the event of major, irreparable breakdown in family life is it desirable to separate children permanently from their natural parents.

The program of Aid to Families with Dependent Children (AFDC), which in September 1990 provided financial aid to 4,092,876 families—11,794,968 children and their parents—was designed to make it possible for children to remain at home with their own parent or parents. With the passing of the Personal Responsibility and Work Opportunity Reconciliation Act of 1996 and the implementation of TANF, the philosophy of keeping families together will remain the same for social workers; however, an entitlement to aid will now be time limited. Chapter 12 of this text discusses more fully the AFDC and TANF programs.

Specifically in this chapter reference is made to such services as care of children in their own homes, foster care, group living, adoption, services for unmarried parents, and protective services.

In-Home Care of Children

Child welfare workers have long known that children are best nurtured in the care of loving parents who can offer food, clothing, shelter and the health care growing bodies and minds require. Permanency and stability are key policy objectives.

The Federal Adoption Assistance and Child Welfare Act of 1980 (P.L. 96-272) makes reasonable efforts to keep children in their own homes. This act has resulted in a shift of focus from child-centered care to family care and a further shift to a multisystems approach in the care of children. This approach can best be described as one that addresses several levels of care aimed at preserving the family entity. Cimmarusti identifies four important elements to be considered in preserving the family.

> The following four levels are generally important in each family preservation case: (1) *the family* includes all entities such as the members of the nuclear family (mother, father, and children). . . . (2) *the extended family* includes any significant relatives, grandparents, aunts, "play" parents, and partners. . . . (3) *the community* includes significant people from the neighborhood, peers, church, or school and. . . . (4) *the family preservation intervention group* includes the family preservation worker, supervisor, agency, public welfare agency, legal system, and other service providers.[8]

It is clearly recognized that parts of the surroundings include not only the child and mother (often the only parent in a home) but also the father and the extended family. Grandparents, aunts, uncles, and other relatives are pivotal to the kind of nurturing a

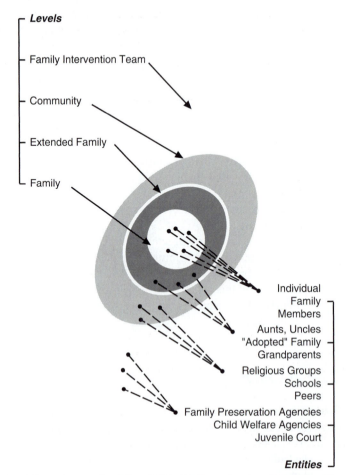

FIGURE 13.1   Multilevel Family Preservation System with Select Entities.

Source: Rocco A. Cimmarusti, "Family Preservation Practice Based upon a Multisystems Approach," *Child Welfare*, 71 (May–June 1992), 249.

child needs. With the rapid increase in one-parent families, the milieu includes a complex of babysitter, day care center, the playground, recreation and health care provisions, and other services. These all impact the growing child and must be addressed (see Figure 13.1).

The aim of care is to strengthen the family, to empower, and to build on existing resources. All families and the systems that may be arrayed to serve them have strengths. The preservation worker's task is to identify these and communicate them. People need to be pointed toward achievement and to experience success.

Social workers using a "variety of clinical methods, including parenting training, active listening, contracting, values clarification, cognitive-behavioral strategies, and problem management techniques" reported that Intensive Family Preservation Services (IFPS) "indicate that family-based programs, and IFPS programs in particular, are successful in preventing placement in 40% to 95% of the cases referred to them."

In studies in two states, Washington and Utah, Pecora, Fraser, and Haapala stated

Across all 581 children from 446 eligible families, the placement prevention rate at *case termination*—an outcome measure used by Nelson et al. (1988), Yuan et al. (1990), and others—was 92.9%. For Utah (*n* = 172), the rate was 90.7%, and for Washington (*n* = 409), it was 93.9%.[9]

More research is needed. However, the family preservation models are a promising trend toward keeping families together. We know that substitute family care is not the answer for many children. It is an option, usually for short periods of time when family weaknesses and problems are so overwhelming that intensive family preservation efforts simply don't suffice.

Foster Care of Children

Foster care is a residential arrangement for children outside their own homes. It includes care in foster homes or in a variety of institutions. For many it is of short duration, ending in adoption or return to the natural parents; for others it is a way of life, extending for long periods, perhaps ending only when the child establishes himself or herself by becoming financially independent.

It was hoped with the passage of P.L. 96-272 that temporary care would be virtually eliminated. The law has helped, but living with the natural parent or parents may not be desirable or even possible for some youngsters who are severely disabled or emotionally disturbed and who require specialized care or for those who are abused and neglected and whose parents are incapable of parenting. For these and for other children, substitute care provides the optimum of nurturing. Foster parents provide good family care, and the foster parent movement is one of the finest examples of volunteerism deserving public support and acclaim.

Foster care brings radical changes in a child's life; he or she must become a part of a new home group, may be enrolled in a new school, and must adapt to different living conditions. Since the mid-1980s, the number of children in foster care has risen to an estimated 520,000. This number has nearly doubled in the last twenty years. Children were found staying in foster care longer (five years or more) and more were entering foster care than were leaving.[10] In November of 1997, Congress passed the Adoption and Safe Families Act (ASFA) (P.L. 105-89) which amended the foster care provisions of the Social Security Act. It was the first sweeping overhaul of the nation's foster care system in more than a decade. The goal of the current changes is to speed up adoptions for children found to be abused and neglected. Where the 1980 federal law directed workers to make "reasonable efforts" to reunite foster children with their biological parents before going to court and terminating parental rights, the new law "clarifies that children's health and safety must be the child welfare agency's first priority and that 'reasonable efforts' are not required in all circumstances." Additionally, "the legislation requires states to have permanent plans for children within one year after placement in foster care. States must also begin parental rights termination proceedings after a child has been in foster care for 15 of the previous 22 months."[11] As a result of ASFA, foster care adoptions increased 78 percent from 1996 to 2000. This equated to an additional 34,000 adoptions from 1998 to 2000 that otherwise would not have happened.[12]

The social worker and the agency may be the only link to permanency for these children. The social worker studies the foster home and family, assesses strengths and limitations for a particular child, and makes and supervises the placement when it is made. The social worker is supportive of both the foster family and the child. Relating to the network of community services, and trained to know their organization and purposes, the social worker selectively brings need and resource together, and often over an extended period of time the social worker becomes the constant in the life of a child confronted with change.

Foster home care, usually preferable for babies and young children, is also the choice for older children able to benefit from individualized relationships with foster parents. To be successful in a home, the child must be able to adjust to the family and his or her behavior be such that the child is not dangerous to himself or herself or others. Helping the child and the foster family make this adjustment may be the most important contribution the social worker will make. This is a continuous process and invariably is needed as long as the child requires a substitute family.

Group living arrangements, substitutes for family care, are frequently recommended as a treatment mode for some children. They include agency-owned foster homes where the parent or parents are employees of the agency, residence clubs for older children, boys and girls "ranches," and congregate-type institutions for larger numbers of children. Children who act out excessively, who have serious conduct and behavior disorders, who steal, set fires, or who sexually "act out" ordinarily are not candidates for care in private homes. Furthermore, some children who have experienced prolonged emotional deprivations resulting in emotional stunting and who are unable to form close and satisfying relationships may not accept a family as a substitute for their own parents.

Some children benefit from the professional services that can be provided only in a group setting. Those who find it impossible to tolerate the demands of making attachments to new sets of parents are relieved in the group where such demands are minimized. For these and other children, group living experiences can, and often do, provide a healing experience.

A child living in a group home or institution can direct aggressive feelings against many more people safely. He or she is not under the same necessity to form close emotional ties and attachments. The child can move into the group at his or her own pace and is not traumatized by pressures to give or accept affection. The routine of the institution provides tangible security—meals at regular intervals, a place to sleep, school, and medical care. With planning on the part of administration it can offer privacy and a place for the child's personal belongings. Child- and adolescent-centered group living is a treatment resource for those with developmental and/or prominent psychological disorders as well as significant interpersonal and drug problems.

Gary, age 11, had lived in nine foster homes in three years. The only constant in his life was Child Protective Services, which supervised the homes. Foster parents had complained that Gary was disobedient, cruel to animals and small children, and lacking in manners and appreciation. For short periods of time they could "stand" him, but as his behavior lowered their level of tolerance they would demand that he be taken from their homes.

Gary was placed in a group home where houseparents, aided by social workers, provided continuity of care, a chance to relate to peers as he was ready for this experience, and professional help.

Reasons for Placement in Foster Care

Studies show many reasons for the placement of children in foster care. The following list is illustrative only and not comprehensive:

> Mental and/or emotional incapacity of caretaking parent
> Parent unwilling to care for the child
> Family problems, including family disorganization
> Environmental problems (inadequate housing, financial need)
> Specialized care the natural family cannot provide
> Death of the caretaking parent
> The child's behavioral or emotional problems
> Neglect and abuse
> Drug abuse by the parent(s)

Children may be placed in foster care by court commitments if they are dependent, neglected, or delinquent. The parents may make voluntary application for foster care.

When faced with a problem of seriously disturbed home situations, alternatives to foster care are considered to assist parents to keep their children at home. With help, parents are often able to improve the quality of care for their children and maintain an intact family.

If placement is inevitable, the question may arise about the type of foster care that will best meet the needs of the children. Today, family social workers' first choice for foster placement is most often in the home of a relative of the child that has been removed for safety purposes. Regardless of whether or not they are placed in a home of a relative, stranger, or group setting, children usually need counseling and other help to counteract physical and emotional deprivation.

If a foster home setting is chosen, care must be taken to match the children with parents who will be able to respond to their particular needs, to continue their support during periods of stress, and to be satisfied with the children's progress no matter how rapid or slow it might be.

Social Work with a Foster Child

The case of Angie, placed in foster care, shows what was done for an adolescent and her family by foster home placement.

Following a violent quarrel with her father, Angie, aged 16, went to a friend's home and hysterically declared she would kill herself if anyone attempted to send her home.

The oldest of five children in a middle-class family, Angie was an intelligent high school junior, but she could no longer cope with the beatings and abuse of her father. A psychiatrist on the staff of the social service agency that was called for help detected some psychotic tendencies such as mild delusions plus unreasonable guilt, severe depression, and a definite suicidal tendency. Angie related poorly to adults and her peers, but got along well with children. His recommendation was parental-substitute care, one-to-one counseling, and medication.

Foster home care was selected as the treatment of choice, and Angie was placed in a home of a couple with two young sons. The mother worked with a teenage organization of her church and felt she could get Angie involved with other young people. The father was easygoing, likable, and relaxed. They felt that they would be able to work out any problem with the help of the social worker. They lived near the high school Angie had been attending so there would be no interruption of her schoolwork.

Angie accepted the foster parents and was glad they had young children. She felt some ambivalence about seeing her own family; she wanted to see her mother and younger sisters, but was afraid of her father. Her parents accepted the placement, but refused to give financial aid, although they did send her personal belongings.

Problems apparent in the early relationship were Angie's lack of attention to personal care—bathing, changing into clean clothes, washing her hair—and her intense fear, amounting almost to panic, if she were in the room alone with the foster father.

Household chores assigned to her were carried out if she clearly understood what was wanted. However, she was unable to volunteer to help in any way, and was withdrawn, often spending long periods alone in her room.

Angie was conscientious in completing her schoolwork and showed a talent for creative writing. She had one friend, a girl from her old neighborhood, and they spent hours talking on the phone. She seldom went any place except to school, church, and an occasional outing with the foster family.

In counseling, she and her clinical social worker identified her pressing problems. They included her extreme hostility and fear of her father, her need for his approval, her pity for her mother, her concern and guilt for "deserting" her sisters and her role in her family's dynamics, her poor self-image, and her role identity.

After two months Angie had not communicated with her parents, and they had not initiated any inquiry about her. During this time they had sought counseling to help them resolve the difficulties that had been plaguing the family. They made some progress toward building a better relationship between husband and wife and with the children at home.

Gradually Angie became active in a group of girls in the neighborhood, but she could not express appreciation and did not take any initiative in doing tasks around the home. She learned to trust the foster father, and he became important to her.

Angie had many strengths. She was intelligent and worked hard at her studies. She felt responsible for her actions and wanted to help her mother and sisters. She was honest and had a high sense of personal morality.

As she gained understanding of herself, she became more attractive physically, being more careful of her dress and personal habits. Socially she made new friends and occasionally had a date. She learned to express her feelings and became more independent. She occasionally spent an afternoon with her mother.

Despite relapses of acute depression and withdrawal, Angie made steady progress. When her parents asked her to go to Disney World with them she spent a week of indecision before she decided to go. The trip was relatively successful and she came home with a more objective view of her parents.

With the support of the social worker's counseling, the parents and Angie decided she could return home. Her counseling continued and her family met with a mental health group. Her problems were many and did not disappear easily, but her strengths were able to compensate for them, and over time Angie was able to make a good adjustment.

For Angie, foster home placement was a good choice because of the intimacy and personal attention that were possible and the opportunity it provided for her to learn to trust those she shared a home with.[13]

The Foster Parent Movement

With the expansion of foster home care, increasing attention is given to this mode of providing for children. Much attention in the past focused on the foster child, the natural parents, and the social worker and their *use* of the foster family. Increasingly, attention is being paid to the foster parent as a *member of the team* with coordinate rights and responsibilities.

The foster parent movement is one of the newer developments in child welfare, with the first National Conference of Foster Parents being held in March 1971, with annual meetings since then. More than 150,000 foster families work with 2,000 social agencies.

Organizations of foster parents have a threefold purpose: (1) to strengthen and improve the quality of life for children in foster homes by sharing experiences, (2) to raise foster care to a higher plane of regard, and (3) to have an effect on legislation that concerns children and their natural parents. The movement recognizes the importance of foster parents in a triad of roles: parent surrogate, agency employee, and child advocate for all foster children. The organization has defined the substitute parent role and spelled out the elements of team relationships necessary for the effective nurturance of children whose biological natural parents for whatever reason do not, or cannot, function in the parental role. The organization addresses such questions as status for foster parents, salary and benefits, upgrading the quality of foster home care, permanency in arrangements for children, and participation in the decision-making processes affecting its own and the child's interest.

The movement seeks to remove the barriers to the sense of fulfillment that foster parents seek. In a special report reflecting views and attitudes of foster parents from the Greater Victoria Foster Parent Association, Tinney[14] makes a case for the reexamination of foster parent roles, responsibilities, and rights. Believing that traditional roles are too limited and inadequate, foster parents seek greater recognition and status. (See Figure 13.2.) It is apparent from this study that foster parents in Victoria, British Columbia, perceive aspects of what they do as being professional. Although their role as substitute

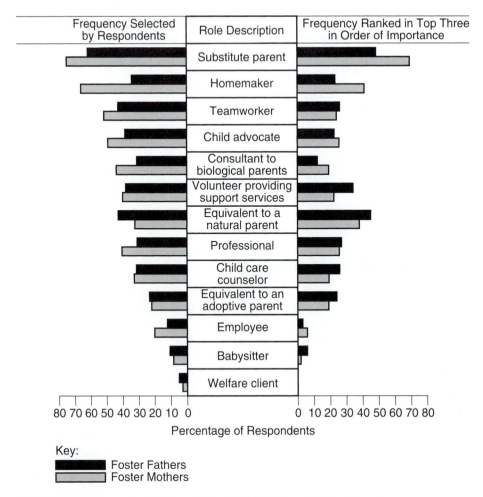

FIGURE 13.2   Respondents' Perceptions of Their Roles as Foster Parents.

Source: Mary-Anne Tinney, "Role Perceptions in Foster Parent Associations in British Columbia," *Child Welfare*, 64 (January–February 1985), 76. A publication of the Child Welfare League of America.

parents is frequently noted, high numbers list the role of teamworker, child advocate, consultant, child care counselor and professional with a high degree of frequency. Assuming this trend continues, as foster parents gain in knowledge and become even better organized, they might well aspire to be candidates for training in colleges and universities offering work in child welfare. Some elements of the work of foster parents is professional, and services to children in foster homes would benefit by formal community recognition and encouragement for foster parents to become better educated and trained.

Adoption Services

Adoption of children appears in the earliest recorded histories. The Babylonian Code of Hammurabi established adoption practices more than 4,000 years ago. The Bible refers to adoption; the ancient Romans practiced it as part of their civil law; adoption law was found among the remains of the early Spaniards; and the practice was known among Anglo-Saxon tribes.

The first legislation on adoption in the United States was enacted in 1851 in Massachusetts. Other states followed, and by 1867 Pennsylvania, Wisconsin, and Illinois had statutes on adoption. Today all states have legislation regarding adoption.

The number of children placed for adoption in the United States increased from 17,000 in 1937 to approximately 169,000 in 1971. This number was down from 175,000 in 1970, marking the first time since 1957 that there was no increase in adoption. In 1982 the total number of adoptions had dropped to 141,861, with 50,720 of these being unrelated; that is, neither of the adopting parents was related to the child adopted.[15] From the early eighties through the mid-nineties there were further declines in the number of adoptions. Of those young women in the United States who became pregnant between the ages of fifteen through nineteen, approximately 5 percent of their children were placed for adoption. This was equivalent to about 100,000 children in the United States being adopted each year. Since 1996, a slight but upward trend in adoptions has been recognized. The National Council for Adoption (NCFA) has reported an increase in the number of domestic adoptions from 108,463 in 1996 to 130,269 in 2002. The types of adoptions that have increased the most are intercountry adoptions (11,303 in 1996 to 21,063 in 2002) and foster care system adoptions (24,366 in 1996 to 42,942 in 2002).[16]

The number of infants available for adoption through agencies has decreased in the last decade because of (1) family planning; (2) legalization of abortions; (3) acceptance by society of the single-parent status; (4) an increase in the number of independent placements; (5) changes in values of society; (6) the Supreme Court's ruling that natural fathers in out-of-wedlock births have legal rights to their Offspring; (7) income-maintenance programs, food stamps, and subsidized housing for single-parent families; (8) the mandating of education for pregnant teenagers; and (9) the reduction in the number of maternity homes.

Children are placed in adoptive homes by one of two methods, either by social agencies licensed to place children or by interested, independent parties. *Independent placement* ranges from "selling" infants to other transactions involving intermediaries making placements independent of state-regulated agencies.

Independent placements lack protection and safeguards to all parties. Unwed mothers seen in social agencies years following the placement for adoption of their babies are still "suffering" because they didn't get the services they needed. With independent placements these services are not provided. Putative fathers often are completely ignored by the lawyers handling independent placements; in some cases, they do not even bother to ask who the father is.

Adoptive parents need preparation for adoption. Life for adopted children isn't the same as life for other children. Those parents not prepared for the differences in rearing adopted children may be ill-equipped to handle the demands adoptions will make on them which are greater and different from the demands made on the biological natural parents. This preparation isn't provided with independent placements; moreover, too many families adopting children independently of agencies possibly would not be accepted by agencies because they would not qualify under the standards of the licensed agency.

Independent placements are on the increase and likely will continue to increase. They are attractive because of the following reasons: the biological mother can more easily avoid the putative father or her own parents; and she may be offered money to pay boarding, medical, and confinement expenses; and she can usually elect to have a physician of her choice.

The attraction to adoptive parents is that they can have more control over the selection of a child, a child might be more readily available to them and they can sometimes avoid long waiting periods, and they might be able to get a child they could not qualify to get through an agency.

Social work supports agency placements because children, the adopting parents, and the natural parents are provided safeguards in agency arrangements not available in independent placements. It is a deeply held conviction that adoption is an appropriate concern of society and needs all the protection that legal, social, and other instrumentalities can provide.

It is estimated that fewer than half of all adoptions are nonrelative adoptions. More than half of the children are adopted by stepparents or other relatives.

Social agencies arrange for more than three-fourths of all nonrelative adoptions. However, as fewer babies become available for adoption, childless couples who cannot satisfy their desires for children through the licensed agency may turn to the "black market" and "gray market" for adoptions, and thus reverse the trend for adoptions to be arranged through socially sanctioned governmental and nongovernmental licensed agencies.

Black market adoptions are made "independent" of agencies and do not have social sanction; they are made for a financial consideration—literally sold for a price. With the electronic world creeping into all facets of our life, recently so-called facilitators have been found listing children for adoption on the Internet. Gray market placements are made by intermediaries (usually attorneys or physicians) on behalf of friends or acquaintances of people wanting to adopt or of a mother trying to find a suitable and permanent home for her child. Gray market placements are not made for financial gain. Babies are not sold in the marketplace, and the placement is usually viewed by the parties concerned as a favor or service, not a commercial transaction.

The first state laws on adoption required only a simple petition to the court of local jurisdiction by those wishing to adopt. If the parents were living, their consent was required. If the court was satisfied, the adoption was granted. Legislation has met with only indifferent success to require an investigation of the suitability of the proposed adoption home, provisions for a probationary period in the home of the applicants, safeguards of confidentiality of records, and other such measures as will best protect the welfare of the child.

In no particular is the adoptive applicant protected more than by what is done on behalf of the natural mother, who will be able to accept the decision to give up her child provided the following conditions are met:

1. The agency takes the release when she is ready to give it.
2. Her views and wishes (including religious beliefs) are respected.

3. Her doubts, uncertainties, and guilt are discussed and dealt with.
4. She has reason to believe that the best possible arrangement will be made for her child.

On the other hand, when the natural mother is not part of the process of relinquishment, when her release is taken under pressure, when practices are followed that do not recognize her rights and wishes, she may be unhappy, in doubt, and guilt-ridden, and later she may attempt to have the adoption set aside and regain parental control.

Over the past twenty years, the process of adopting a child has changed dramatically. Prior to the 1980s, birth parents and adopted children rarely knew of each other because the files containing the vital information on each were "closed." With societal changes on the value of having access to personal information and involvement in the decision-making process, adoptions have become "open." This means that contact is made between the birth parent(s) and adoptive families prior to and often following the placement of the child. The amount of contact varies between the two families, but generally it consists of the birth mother reviewing portfolios of potential adoptive parents and interviewing and selecting the couple with whom she wants her child to be placed. When possible, birth fathers are also involved in this process. After the birth of the child, the families exchange information (letters, phone calls, photos, gifts) by mail or by face-to-face contact, most often on birthdays and holidays. The type and frequency of contacts are decided on as part of the pre-placement arrangement. Allowing birth parents the option to be highly involved in the decision-making process appears to help them cope with this all-important decision.[17]

Many couples unable to find children to adopt from their own race turn to babies of other races or of mixed racial backgrounds as an alternative. In the past few decades children in countries ravaged by war have become increasingly available for adoption in the United States. These adoptions fill a twofold need: The parents want children to nurture, and the children need homes where love and affection are freely given. For many the alternative would be severe emotional and physical deprivation in their native lands.

Controversy continues among professionals and others toward interracial or biracial adoptions. Among whites there doesn't appear to be as much controversy, possibly because of their insensitivity to the meaning of loss of cultural identity and because of their insensitivity to ethnic minorities not being prepared by white families to compete in a society that practices racial discrimination.

Legislation prohibits biracial adoptions among Native Americans, and the National Association of Afro-American Social Workers opposes biracial adoptions. International placements continue to be a source of infants and small children for a large number of American families; however, here again the problem of ethnic and cultural identity is still to be resolved. Agencies are only beginning to move toward policies on adoption that are truly biracial, recognizing fully the rights and responsibilities alike of all ethnic groups.

Indian Child Welfare Act

In response to the identity and cultural needs of children, efforts have been initiated to better support children from varying backgrounds. Specifically, the needs of Native American children have been addressed. In 1978, Congress passed the Indian Child Welfare Act (ICWA), P.L. 95-608. In response to the high ratio of Native American children that were being adopted by non-Indian families, this law was established to help protect the identity and culture of both American Indian children and the tribes in the United States. The law reads

> The Congress hereby declares that it is the policy of this Nation to protect the best interests of Indian children and to promote the stability and security of Indian tribes and families by the establishment of minimum Federal standards for the removal of Indian children from their families and the placement of such children in foster or adoptive homes which will reflect the unique values of Indian culture, and by providing for assistance to Indian tribes in the operation of child and family service programs.

Therefore, if American Indian children are removed from their family, efforts must be made to place the child first with family members, second with tribal members, or, third, with an American Indian foster or adoptive family. As a result of this law, foster and adoptive services have improved for American Indian children. However, continued sensitivity and work in this area is needed, not only for this group of people, but also for members of all races, cultures, and religious backgrounds.

Applicants for Adoption

Adoption is one answer to the problem of (1) finding suitable homes for many children who might otherwise not know what it means to have parents, and (2) childless couples who long for children and to become parents. The following real-life situation, narrated with permission of the adopting parents, illustrates this point.

"She is so beautiful, so perfect; it is so wonderful to have her in our arms." These were our thoughts when we held little Dawn that first time in the agency room. As we examined her through our tears of joy, she really smiled at us.

Since the social worker called just a few hours earlier saying "I have a beautiful 6-week-old daughter for you. Can you come get her today?" my mind had been in such turmoil with questions and doubts, and feelings of unreality. Although our social worker had assured us that we would sometime get a baby, we had not expected one so soon. Our one-year waiting period had just elapsed, and he had repeatedly told us it would be several months before we could expect to have a child. To get one so soon seemed unreal. I asked myself if she were 6 weeks old, why had they not placed her, was something wrong with her, had others rejected her, if she were handicapped would we be able to accept her? Then, too, I had not told anyone at work that we were adopting. What would my boss say? How could I just not go to work anymore? All in all, it had been a long ride, those seventy miles from our home to the agency. But when we saw her, the questions vanished and we knew that she was meant for us.

It had been a long road from our happy wedding day to this joyful union nine years later. Both Don and I came from big families, and as we had just finished college we decided that having a family right away was what we wanted. But after eighteen months and I still wasn't pregnant we started looking for help at a fertility clinic. At that time we were in the Philippines where Don was in the Air Force, but as we moved seven times in three years we had little opportunity to complete the tests. When we returned to civilian life and Don was in law school, we were settled for three years and went through a lot of roller-coaster rides of excitement, hope, then crashing each month. Don had surgery for a minor difficulty they thought would raise his sperm count, then doctors discovered I had endometriosis and I had surgery. I kept temperature charts, our life became methodical, and we both did a lot of crying inside.

Our families were difficult and we began avoiding family gatherings with all the nieces and nephews playing about. My family blamed Don, and his family blamed me; they all offered lots of advice, but little understanding.

Our road eventually led us to Houston, Texas, where we found an excellent fertility clinic and the tests started all over again. Although we never gave up hope of having our own baby, we were advised to begin adoption proceedings. We had a social worker who knew how we felt, and it was a relief finally to talk with someone who understood. After the compatibility tests and all the paperwork were completed, he told us that it would be a year before we would be eligible to receive a baby, and that in reality it would probably be eighteen and possibly twenty-four months before we would get a child. We continued with the fertility clinic and I had surgery again.

So it was a shock when we got the call just one month after we became eligible. I had not prepared myself psychologically for this event, and I had made no preparation at my work to terminate. We had bought a crib and had it set up, and we had a few essentials, but not nearly enough. We were extremely busy during the next week getting organized into being parents, but it was such a happy time that nothing was too much for us to do. Six months later we went before a smiling judge who finalized the adoption.

Many people ask if there was any effort by the agency to match a baby to us. All I can think of is that the birth mother was very tall, as I am, and the worker may have thought that this physical characteristic could possibly play a part in the adjustment of our little girl as she grows up, if she, too, is tall.

One of the thoughtful things our social worker did was to write a detailed description of both the mother and father. This couple was married, but had decided to divorce, and neither felt they could care for a child. The agency had worked with them toward a reconciliation, and had placed the baby in a foster home for six weeks. Because the social worker knew both parents, he was able to give us details about them that we will be able to share with Dawn when she becomes interested in her birth parents.

As we watched her grow and we knew the joy she brought us, we realized that we wanted another child to grow up with her. We had moved again, and worked with a different agency, but when Dawn was not quite 3 years old we got another exciting call—"Come get a baby boy at 3:00 o'clock today." We were there and welcomed a biracial baby boy as a part of our family. Don has very dark hair and eyes and our newest addition seems to fit right in.

With greater insight the second time, I wrote a letter to the birth mother which was delivered by the agency, expressing my love for her child, and my deep respect for her, recognizing that she had made the supreme sacrifice in giving up her child for adoption. This letter, which was good therapy for me, gave me the opportunity to recognize her for bringing life into the world and having the courage to give him to us. I feel that women who give up their babies need to be recognized for their part in bringing great happiness to others although they feel a great sense of loss.

This couple's experience with adoption is somewhat typical of licensed agency placements. True, they were among the more fortunate few. Many couples desirous of adopting infants find it extremely difficult since there are far fewer babies than there are eligible couples who want them.

Older children and youngsters who are developmentally disabled may be the answer for some of these couples. However, adopting older children often presents the problem of dealing with the effects of long periods of neglect and abuse, the child care difficulties in the wake of prolonged trauma. Adopting children who are physically or mentally disabled, depending on the disability, may result in extra expenses—medical and/or surgical care, long periods of hospitalization, special education—that many families are unable to pay. Public and private agencies, eager to find homes for these children, sometimes are able to assist with these expenses, but the costs to the family still may be heavy.

The provisions made for the mother who legally surrenders her infant for adoption is a most vital part of sound placement. Adoption services can be no better than what is done for the natural parent.

Any parent faced with giving up a child most likely needs help. Although values are changing and society in general is now more accepting of the unmarried mother, she still may encounter public condemnation. Whatever the situation, the mother and to a lesser extent the father must make the important decision of whether or not to keep the child. The social worker can help.

It is almost axiomatic in child welfare that unless the natural mother, and increasingly the father as well, has accepted relinquishment (and acceptance in this sense is more than signing papers), adoptive parents cannot have the assurance that at some future date, when ties have been formed, the natural parent will not try to regain her or his parental rights. Lawsuits have been filed—some successful, others not—to recover a child, based on parental rights following questionable procedures of relinquishment.

Child Protective Services

In one sense, all child welfare work is protective work. Children are placed in day care centers while their parents work to protect them from neglect. Children who go into foster homes receive care they are unable to find in their own homes. Physical and emotional abuses are often the stark alternative.

Courts and law enforcement agencies give protection to children and to the community. Modern juvenile court philosophy stresses protection, treatment, and restoration.

Protective services are aimed at preventing abuse, neglect, and exploitation of children. Their aim is to preserve the family unit by assisting parents to develop the capacity for rearing children. Teenagers who become pregnant may not be ready for parenthood and frequently will need help with child care. The focus in protective care is on the family where unsolved problems have led to neglect and/or abuse and have become a hazard to the physical and emotional well-being of children.

Few services offered by social workers are demanding of greater skill and competence than those involved in seeking out neglect and abuse and in helping resistive parents accept the services of an agency in providing stability, nurturance, and love.

This service is usually initiated by the agency when a complaint is filed by a physician, school teacher, neighbor, or relative who is aware of the circumstances. The agency explores, studies, and evaluates the alleged nature of the neglect and abuse of the children. In accordance with policy, the court may be petitioned to constructively use its authority to secure protection for the child if his or her parents are unwilling to work in a voluntary relationship with the agency or the nature of the abuse is such that the child is in danger and placement outside the home is warranted to ensure the safety of the child.

Protective services have been greatly expanded and improved to ensure the prevention of abuse and neglect beyond those services provided to children who are victims of serious and continued mistreatment.

Demographics of children needing protective services and the type of mistreatment to which they have been exposed are capsulized in Figure 13.3. A few of the practices and issues of concern follow.

Issues and Practices in Protective Services

1. The *reporting* of abuse and neglect has been greatly improved and many states have strong reporting legislation. This is making it possible for children and for families to get help. Neighbors, relatives, the police, schools, juvenile courts, nurses, doctors, and many others are now reporting abuse and neglect practices that in the past went unnoticed.
2. The creation in the states of *child protective services (CPS)* has made it possible for people who need help to get it. Responsible citizens report abuse and neglect when they know that something can and will be done about it.
3. A *total service system* is at the disposal of the CPS worker who may initiate a process that will tie the family into the system. This includes an array of such services as assistance payments, day care, employment assistance, medical care, housing,

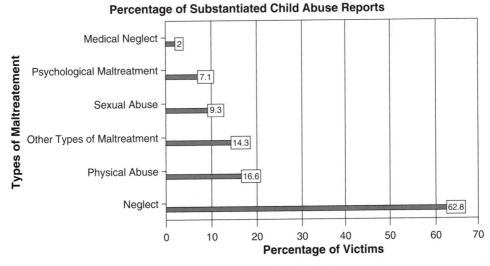

FIGURE 13.3　Percentages of Substantiated Child Abuse Reports

Source: Adapted from U.S. Department of Health and Human Services, Administration for Children and Families, Child Maltreatment 2005. Chapter 3, Children. *Types of Maltreatment*, 2002. Retrieved from http://acf.dhhs.gov/programs/cb/pubs/cm05/chapterthree.htm types.

testing services, child rearing and development classes, counseling services, home-making services, Big Brother and Big Sister services, and Share a Parent Services. Parents and other family members can be "pulled" into these services and often receive the help they need to handle their personal and family problems to aid in preventing abuse and neglect or to contain it.

4. The *needs of parents* are addressed by these services as well as the needs of the mis-treated children. Blaming or punishing parents is rapidly being discarded by the knowledge that their neglect and abuse are often symptomatic of a need for help. As help is made available they can often provide the parenting their children need. If it should be determined that for some reason parents cannot be rehabilitated or effec-tively trained as parents even with help, and that they cannot nurture and care for their children, substitute parental care may be arranged for the child or children.

5. The *courts are shifting* in their position and increasingly recognize that both parents and children have rights and should be protected alike under the law. Courts often work collaboratively with child protective agency workers and provide helpful and constructive use of authority.

6. *Medical care* is available as needed for children and parents and available to the CPS agency for help of its clients.

7. Personnel are *trained* to provide the services needed. The training social workers receive in schools of social work has been expanded greatly with the training and licensing of BSW social workers. In addition, ongoing training on the job is provided by agencies as new knowledge is developed and new skills required.

8. The issue of the CPS role in the public agency continues to be explored with result-ing refinement of practice.

9. Study of ways to make the CPS agency *increasingly functional* continues. Such study addresses such issues as workload standards, making creative use of personnel and resources, kinds of training needed for CPS workers, and how to coordinate ser-vices and to cooperate with other professional disciplines.

10. There is a growing concern that *national standards* for CPS agencies and workers be formulated and adopted.

11. Other critical issues include: legal aspects of CPS services and the training needed by the CPS worker to handle legal questions; the reciprocal responsibility of the courts and the CPS worker; training CPS personnel; what to do with "neglect of neglect" cases; enlisting community support for protective services.

Child Physical Abuse

Although child physical abuse has been evident throughout the history of the world, it remained a hidden problem in the United States until the 1960s, when an effort by a group of doctors brought the problem to light. During this time period, a number of physicians spear-headed by C. Henry Kempe believed that the only way to break the code of silence regarding indifference toward the problem was to mandate, by law, that physicians report this offense to the authorities. This group of doctors was able to influence the U.S. Children's Bureau to "publish a model law that required physicians to report children with a 'serious physical injury or injuries . . . other than by accidental means.'"[18] Within four years all fifty states had adopted some form of this model into law and it has since been expanded to include all professionals who work with children as well as reporting other forms of maltreatment.

"The Federal Child Abuse Prevention and Treatment Act (CAPTA), (42 U.S.C.A. 5106g), as amended by the Keep Children and Families Safe Act of 2003, defines child abuse and neglect as, at minimum:

- any recent act or failure to act on the part of a parent or caretaker which results in death, serious physical or emotional harm, sexual abuse or exploitation; or
- an act or failure to act which represents an imminent risk of serious harm."[19]

States develop their own definition of what constitutes child abuse and neglect, but most agree on four major types: child physical abuse, child sexual abuse, child neglect, and emotional maltreatment.

During fiscal year 2005, of all those who experienced some form of maltreatment, 16.6 percent were physically abused compared with 62.8 percent who were neglected, 9.3 percent who were sexually abused, 7.1 percent who experienced psychological maltreatment, and 2 percent who were medically neglected.[20] As sited earlier in this chapter, DHHS statistics for reports of any type of child maltreatment to child protective services (CPS) agencies in the United States in the year 2003 were approximately 3 million. Of these, about 900,000 were substantiated, equaling a rate of about 12 out of every 1,000 children. Of the 900,00, approximately 19 percent or roughly 168,000 were based on child physical abuse. In the same year, about 240 children died of physical abuse only whereas 255 died as a result of child physical abuse along with some other form of child maltreatment.[21]

Although it is difficult to determine exactly the effects of child physical abuse, due to its occurrence often in association with other problems, such as partner/marital violence, parental drug and alcohol abuse, or mental problems in caretakers, researchers have begun to identify some residual problems. The most obvious are those associated with *physical injuries* such as bruising, fractures, burns, punctures, or organ damage. *Cognitive deficits* are found in memory problems, problem solving, decreased math and reading skills, perceptual-motor skills, and poor academic achievement. *Behavioral effects* may include aggression (which is among the most common correlates), defiance, damage to others' property, fighting, and arrests. *Social-emotional deficits* include attachment problems, low self-esteem, peer relations, poor interpersonal skills, delay in play skills, and homelessness. An increase in *psychological disorders* may be found for depression (the most often experienced problem), oppositional defiant and conduct disorder, attention-deficit hyperactivity disorder (ADHD), borderline personality disorder, and posttraumatic stress disorder.[22]

The primary concern for CPS workers is for the immediate protection of the child or children. In the case of significant abuse, removal of the child to a safe environment is necessary while implementing a plan to restore safety to the home before reuniting the child with the parents. To help parents, CPS workers will develop a reunification plan that may require the parents to become involved in child management classes to learn behavior management skills that focus on appropriate reinforcement and punishment, and/or anger management groups where they learn to recognize angry thoughts and cues and how to control hostile responses. Included in the plan may be stress management classes to learn problem-solving skills, assertiveness, and calming techniques. Where finances and lack of employment are concerns that lead to increased stress in the lives of the adults, CPS workers may refer them to employment services or subsidized housing, along with aiding the family in obtaining medical insurance for physical and/or psychological problems experienced by the child, parent, or both.

CPS workers may also provide in-home services from professionals who act as models and coaches demonstrating, teaching, and encouraging the use of appropriate parenting skills, understanding the developmental needs of children, and improving the parent–child attachments. Included may be a family preservation worker who works intensively with one or two families to help create stability and provide counseling that focuses on changing those family interactions and dynamics that work in opposition to positive and healthy family interactions.

The following case illustrates how the unfortunate effects of child physical abuse are at times overlooked until a concerned citizen pays attention and is willing to get involved.

Examinations by the school nurse disclosed open sores on the scalps of the two girls and bruises on their bodies. The father, a teacher in the public schools, held status in the community that shielded his sadistic treatment of the girls. When the beatings were brought to the attention of the school nurse, she determined that no medical care had been provided, although the scalp wounds were deep and infected. The nurse brought the matter to the attention of child protective services, whose investigation disclosed gross neglect and abuse. The father was referred for treatment and determined unfit to have the children, who were placed by the court temporarily in a foster home while the father received counseling.

Child Sexual Abuse

Child sexual abuse is a horror story, a national disgrace. Tens of thousands of children, infants through adolescence, are the victims. The perpetrators—neighbors, acquaintances, "friends" of the family, extended family members, fathers—are mostly adult males.

The issue needs to be seriously addressed and social workers—protective service workers, mental health workers, and many others—may be the first in the network to learn about abuse and to see its ugly consequences. They have a responsibility. However, if the tide of abuse is to be stemmed the entire community needs to join forces in an unrelenting drive to stamp out the problem.

We know that convicting and imprisoning perpetrators, often leading to breakup of families, depriving them of the major source of support, and disrupting neighborhoods, may not always be the answer. Protracted court procedures with charges, countercharges, confessions followed by denials, and the gamut of feelings and behaviors surrounding abuse are not enough.

A modern civilized community can do better. We must find ways to check abuse without destroying people in the process. Victims who are invariably traumatized must be protected and offered the best possible treatment. Perpetrators who themselves may have been victims are invariably sick, and sick people need help. We need to know more about what causes this type of behavior. We need to determine the kind of help these people can use and address ourselves to treatment and rehabilitation appropriate to their diagnosed illnesses. More education is required. Research is needed, as is treatment. And community recognition of the ramifications of the problem is needed. Social work can help in a coordinate role with other helping professions and an educated and aroused public.

Summary

Humanity's basic institution, the family, is effective in shaping the lives of children and adults. But when the family is in trouble, clinical social workers may provide help through marriage and family counseling.

Husband–wife relationships and husband–wife–children constellations are the concern of various services established to assist families with problems and to strengthen the family unit. A variety of agencies have been established to provide these services.

The delivery of child welfare services for children remains focused on the protection and safety of the child with assistance given to parents. Whether the sweeping overhaul of welfare, with the implementation of the TANF program, will be effective in the long term in assisting families in need is yet to be determined. However, when professionally staffed, these programs are the means of preventing social breakdown or restoring the functioning of families where breakdown threatens or has occurred.

Services to children in their own homes has the highest priority. Empowering families is an objective of preservation systems, addressed to strengths, that make use of a variety of resources.

Strengthening the quality of life for children, raising foster care to a higher plane of regard, and favorably affecting legislation are purposes of the foster care movement.

For children who are unable to live with their natural parents, foster care, a residential living arrangement, is often recommended. Group living is also provided as a treatment of choice for certain children. Both of these may be temporary arrangements.

Adoptions provide a permanent arrangement for children whose natural parents relinquish their parental rights. Agencies offer a needed service to those who wish to adopt. The trend in the past twenty years is for birth parents to enter into an agreement for an "open adoption."

Child protective services provide support so that family strength is maintained and children are helped to adjust in their own homes. Child physical abuse, neglect, sexual abuse, medical neglect, and emotional maltreatment are a few of the concerns of child protective services. These services, established in state divisions of family services, take action to prevent abuse when it is reported.

Selected References

ANDERSON, GARY, ANGELA SHEN RYAN, and BOGART R. LEASHORE, eds., *The Challenge of Permanency Planning in Multicultural Society.* New York: Haworth Press, 1997.

BARTH, RICHARD P., JILL DUERR BERRICK, MARK COURTNEY, and VICKY ALBERT, *From Child Abuse to Permanency Planning: Child Welfare Services Pathways and Placements.* Hawthorne, NY: Aldine de Gruyter, 1994.

BARTH, RICHARD. P., JILL DUERR BERRICK, and NEIL GILBERT, eds., *Child Welfare Research Review,* Vol. 1, New York: Columbia University Press, 1994.

BERRY, MARIANNE, *Keeping Families Together.* New York: Garland, 1994.

COHEN, NEIL, *Child Welfare: A Multicultural Focus,* 2nd ed. Boston: Allyn & Bacon, 2000.

CRANE, RUSSELL D., *Fundamentals of Marital Therapy.* New York: Brunner/Mazel, 1996.

CROSSON-TOWER, CYNTHIA, *Exploring Child Welfare: A Practice Perspective,* 3rd ed. Boston: Allyn & Bacon, 2004.

EWALT, PATRICIA L., "Who Cares for the Children?" *Social Work,* 40 (March 1995), 149–150.

FILIP, JUDEE, PATRICIA SCHENE, and NANCY MCDANIEL, *Helping in Child Protective Services: A Casework*

Handbook. East Englewood, CO: American Humane Association, 1991.

FRASER, MARK W., PETER J. PECORA, and DAVID A. HAAPALA, *Families in Crisis: The Impact of Intensive Family Preservation Services.* Hawthorne, NY: Aldine de Gruyter, 1991.

GLADDING, SAMUEL, *Family Therapy: History, Therapy, and Practice,* 3rd ed. Englewood Cliffs, NJ: Prentice Hall, 2002.

MALUCCIO, ANTHONY, BARBARA PINE, and ELIZABETH M. TRACEY, *Social Work Practice with Families and Children.* New York: Columbia University Press, 2002.

MAUGANS, JOY GARLAND, *America's Forsaken Children: The Foster Care Dilemma,* 2nd ed. Charlotte, NC: John Russell, 1990.

OATES, R. KIM, *The Spectrum of Child Abuse. Assessment, Treatment, and Prevention.* New York: Brunner/Mazel, 1996.

ROSENFELD, ALVIN, and SAUL WASSERMAN, *Healing the Heart: A Therapeutic Approach to Disturbed Children in Group Care.* Washington DC: Child Welfare League of America, 1990.

SHIREMAN, JOAN, *Critical Issues in Child Welfare.* New York: Columbia University Press, 2003.

Notes

1. Adam C. Olson, "Divorce Hurts Children, Whole Society," *Davis County Clipper Today,* June 28, 2001, p. 1.

2. Ben Caballero, "Are Married Utahns Healthiest?" *Deseret Morning News* (Salt Lake City, UT), July 23, 2007, p. B4.

3. Kevin Fullin, "Battered Women Are Caught in a Cycle of Violence," *U.S. News and World Report,* October 12, 1992, p. 11.

4. U.S. Bureau of the Census, *Statistical Abstracts of the United States,* 118th ed. (Washington, DC: U.S. Government Printing Office, 1998).

5. U.S. Department of Health and Human Services, Administration for Children and Families, "HHS Reports New Child Abuse and Neglect Statistics," *HHS News* (Washington, DC, 2002).

6. Ola W. Barnett, Cindy L. Miller-Perrin, and Robin D. Perrin, *Family Violence Across the Lifespan*, 2nd ed. (Thousand Oaks, CA: Sage, 2005).

7. Nevada Division of Mental Hygiene and Mental Retardation, "Troubled Families," *People* (Spring 1973), pp. 8–9.

8. Rocco A. Cimmarusti, "Family Preservation Practice Based upon a Multisystems Approach," *Child Welfare,* 71 (May–June 1992), p. 248.

9. Peter J. Pecora, Mark W. Fraser, and David A. Haapala, "Intensive Home-Based Family Preservation Services: An Update from the FIT Project," *Child Welfare,* 71 (March/April 1992), p. 178.

10. United States General Accounting Office, *Foster Care: States' Early Experiences Implementing the Adoption and State Families Act* (Report to the Chairman, Subcommittee on Human Resources, Committee on Ways and Means, House of Representatives, December, 1999).

11. "Law Overhauls Foster Care," *NASW News,* 43, no.1 (January 1998), p. 6.

12. The Evan B. Donaldson Institute, *Foster Care Facts*, July 1, 2007. Retrieved from www.adoptioninstitute .org/FactOverview/foster.html.

13. Case material provided by Marah Grist, former Associate Professor of Social Work, University of Utah.

14. Mary-Anne Tinney, "Role Perceptions in Foster Parent Associations in British Columbia," *Child Welfare,* 64 (January/February 1985), pp. 73–79.

15. *Adoption Factbook, 1985, United States Data, Issues, Regulations and Resources.* Prepared by the National Committee for Adoptions, 2025 M Street, Suite 512, Washington, DC 20036.

16. U.S. Department of Health and Human Services, Administration for Children and Families, *National Child Abuse and Neglect Data System (NCANDS) Summary of Key Findings from Calendar Year 2000,* 2002. Retrieved from www.calib.com/nccanch/prevmnth/scope/ncands .cfm.

17. Harriet E. Gross, "Variants of Open Adoptions: The Early Years," *Marriage & Family Review*, 25, nos. 1–2, 1997, pp. 19–42.

18. Douglas J. Besharov, *Recognizing Child Abuse: A Guide for the Concerned* (New York: Free Press, 1990), p. 9.

19. U.S. Department of Health and Human Services, Administration for Children and Families, Child Abuse Prevention and Treatment Act as Amended by The Keeping Children and Families Safe Act of 2003. Sec. III: Definitions (2006). Retrieved from www.acf.hhs.gov/programs/cb/laws_policies/cblaws/capta03/Sec_I_111.htm.

20. Ibid., p. xiii.

21. Barnett, Miller-Perrin, and Perrin, *Family Violence Across the Lifespan.* p. 60.

22. Ibid.

14

Correctional Services

An 18-year-old senior stole a Cadillac from a wealthy family and was sentenced to 30 days in jail. During his first three years in high school he had worked well and had received excellent grades; then he began to fail his classes. His father had given him a car, money, everything he wanted—in fact, too much—and he had finally been arrested by the police for theft. A social worker attached to the Youth Bureau talked with the judge, who agreed to have the boy spend each night in jail, but have his father pick him up and take him to and from school each day. Prior to completion of the sentence, the social worker checked with the boy's teachers and found that he was doing very well.

What would be the possible influence of the following on the boy's behavior: the boy himself, the father, the social worker, the jail sentence, and peer pressures?

The Social Problems of Delinquency and Crime

Delinquency and crime are major social problems of modern society (see Figure 14.1). They are of concern not only to those who are involved directly as victims and otherwise but also to those who consider present and future implications of the increasing amount of antisocial behavior. In 2002, serious offenses amounted to 11,877,218 in the United States. Violent crimes—the kind that terrify people—had included 16,204 murders and nonnegligent manslaughters and 95,136 forcible rapes. In addition, there were 2,151,875 burglaries and 1,246,096 thefts of motor vehicles.[1]

Economically it is estimated that delinquency and crime cost the people of the United States today more than $500 billion annually.

On January 1, 1984, there were 419,820 prisoners under the jurisdiction of federal and state correctional institutions in the United States, 402,391 male and 17,429 female, more than double the number in 1970. At the same time the average daily population in the 3,500 jails in the United States exceeded 150,000 with more than 6 million commitments each year.[2] By 1993 there were more than 900,000 men and women incarcerated in state and federal prisons. In 2004 the prison population grew to 2.1 million inmates.

FIGURE 14.1   U.S. Crime Clock 2006.

Source: Crime in the United States—2006 (Washington, DC: FBI, U.S. Department of Justice, 2007), p. 6.

The National Center for Juvenile Justice[3] estimated that in 1977 there were 1,355,490 cases processed by courts with juvenile jurisdiction in the United States, of which 76.5 percent were male and 23.3 percent were female. At this rate it meant that in an average twenty-four-hour period about 11,000 boys and girls were handled by law enforcement officers, about 3,500 appeared before a juvenile court, and more than 300 spent the night in jail or lockup, most of which are unfit places for keeping children or youth. By 1993 the FBI indicated that arrests for serious crimes for those under eighteen reached 1,904,763, based on agency reports representing an estimated population of 200,200,000. The arrest figure grew to over 3 million in 2003.

Gang violence has become a major problem in the last two decades in cities of all sizes, especially in the larger urban areas. It involves youth and young adults of different ages, and their offenses include vandalism, fighting, violating of many laws, drug crimes,

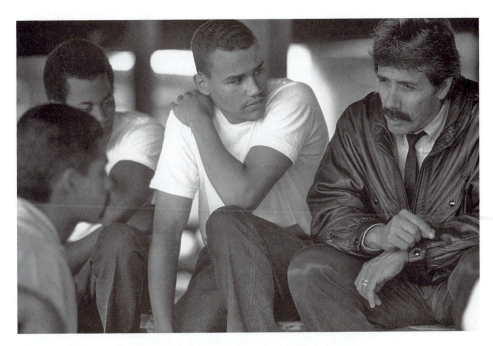

Social worker talking with youthful offenders in a correctional facility.

bodily injuries, and many homicides. In numerous neighborhoods many families are moving elsewhere because of concerns and fears related to these antisocial behaviors.

Social workers are employed by a variety of agencies including police departments, juvenile courts, prisons, schools, churches, and community service programs to help prevent and reduce the number of violations. It is clearly evident that we need more knowledge and improved skills to face these difficult situations. Regulus suggests that for effective gang intervention and violence reduction there must "be the inclusion of effective interpersonal engagement of gangs and gang memberships in the intervention process."[4]

The President's Commission on Law Enforcement and Administration of Justice, in its monumental report of 1967, summarized the challenging problems related to crime and delinquency as follows:

> Many Americans take comfort in the view that crime is the vice of a handful of people. This view is inaccurate. In the United States today, one boy in six is referred to the juvenile court. . . . Another Commission study suggests that about 40 percent of all male children now living in the United States will be arrested for a nontraffic offense during their lives. An independent survey of 1,700 persons found that 91 percent of the sample admitted they had committed acts for which they might have received jail or prison sentences.

In addition to the dollars and statistics, antisocial behavior rends the heartstrings of thousands of parents and loved ones. A single act of delinquency or crime may change the whole existence of a particular family; and as families are weakened and filled with tension, society is injured and threatened.

Social workers are playing prominent roles in administrative and practice positions in federal, state, and local correctional programs. Through the years social work also has provided a variety of services to help reduce and prevent delinquency and crime; today it is one answer to help with these perplexing and frightening social problems. Social workers are active in providing services in most correctional agencies and programs.

Social Work and Corrections

Throughout human history, punishments, especially corporal and capital, have often been offered in answer to antisocial behavior. Public hangings, floggings, mutilation, branding, banishment, the stocks and pillory, and many other physical penalties have been utilized to "punish the culprit and be a lesson to others." It was only toward the end of the eighteenth century, at the Walnut Street Prison in Philadelphia, in the shadows of Independence Hall, that the beginning of a new method—the use of time sentence in an institution—came into general usage. Enlightened humanitarians claimed that it was inhumane and unwise to torture offenders or put them to death. Instead the *penitentiary system* was developed, devised to give the offender a chance to think, have a "change of heart," and "mend his ways" through meditation in solitary confinement. Subsequently various kinds of penal institutions evolved to allow for incarceration. Eventually the use of probation came into being as a substitute for imprisonment through the efforts of John Augustus, a Boston shoemaker, and other benevolent reformers.

As offenders were sentenced to institutions and were placed on probation and parole, various professional groups became interested in making these efforts as effective as possible. Social work was one of these.

During the nineteenth century the roots of the emerging profession of social work were growing rapidly and a major area of focus involved the offender. For example, the *Proceedings of the National Conference of Charities and Correction* indicate that at the conference convened in 1885 a portion of the program was devoted to consideration of employment in reformatories, prison reforms, jails and police, and even to discussion of prevention of related social problems. During recent years there has been a revived interest in the field of corrections by social workers. This is epitomized in the Curriculum Study of the Council on Social Work Education.

> The modification of the penalty system did more than require a different kind of administrative structure and personnel. It made possible the idea of treatment. . . . With the increasing knowledge about the dynamics of human behavior and how it is modified, which has become available in the 20th century, it has become possible to give attention to the rehabilitation of the offender.[5]

Corrections is one of four social processes utilized in the administration of criminal justice. They include "(1) law enforcement, which is concerned with the collection of evidence about reported offenses and with the detection and arrest of suspected offenders; (2) prosecution and defense, or the preparation and presentation of criminal cases before the court; (3) judicial process, which is concerned with the legal determination of guilt and the assignment of penalties; (4) corrections, which is responsible for administering the assigned penalties."[6] The *Social Work Dictionary* defines corrections as "the legal specialty that seeks to change and improve the behaviors of convicted law offenders through *incarceration, parole, probation,* and ideally educational programs and *social services.*"[7]

Corrections, in one sense at least, is the total process of helping persons who have violated the law to be rehabilitated. The social worker plays a very important role in the total process. His or her basic goal is summarized as follows: "The correctional process has come to mean the administration of the penalty in such a way that the offender is 'corrected,' i.e., his current behavior is kept within acceptable limits at the same time that his general life adjustment is modified."[8]

The aim of the social worker in assisting boys and girls who are in trouble with the law is basically to rehabilitate rather than to punish them. The goal is to help them understand themselves, their relationships with others, and what is expected of them as members of the society in which they live. Corporal and physical punishment has been pushed aside, in the main relegated to history, and the emphasis is on trying to bring about positive change in behavior patterns. Reformation and rehabilitation are the key words today. These are all-important in working with persons in trouble, and, in particular, in attempting to help them adjust better to society.

The social worker's aim is to help the offender, not to retaliate or to punish. The goal is to utilize the knowledge and skills of the profession in a corrective manner, to rehabilitate individuals, to help them help themselves so that they can return to and become part of society, and to guide them toward becoming comfortable with themselves and their associates. "More than in any other social service, the correctional social worker's task is defined in terms of changing the values of the client so that they become congruent in action with the values of the community."[9]

The social worker aims to help the offender change patterns of behavior so that the offender can relate constructively to others and become socially acceptable. This is done through two avenues: (1) working with the individual to help him or her change through better understanding of self and by tapping the person's own strengths and resources, and (2) modification of environment to bring about a more healthy social climate in which to live.

Examples of individual problems of offenders with which the social worker helps are serious feelings of inferiority and inadequacy, inability to socialize, lack of status, negative feelings toward relatives, sibling rivalries, and family disorganization. The worker encourages the offender to talk about problems, feel about them, and come to an insightful understanding of self, accompanied by socially constructive behavior.

In regard to environmental problems, the worker may help the offender bolster his or her abilities to accept and withstand the pressures and/or assist in bringing about changes that alleviate such conditions as inadequate housing or diet, a family where no one cares, inadequate vocational training or job placement, and economic stresses.

In working with both individual and environmental situations, the social worker keeps close to the family unit; in fact, social work is family-centered.

Social Work Practice in Corrections

"Social Work practice," according to the 1967 Code of Ethics, National Association of Social Workers, "is a public trust that requires of its practitioners integrity, compassion, belief in the dignity and worth of human beings, respect for individual differences, a commitment to service, and a dedication to truth."

In working with offenders the social worker attempts to achieve socially desirable objectives within two kinds of settings: institutional and noninstitutional—probation or parole. Time is an influencing factor. For example, most juvenile delinquents who are placed on probation by the juvenile courts are given a sentence of three to nine months depending on their individual situations. During this time the social worker endeavors to establish a meaningful relationship with the individual and to help him or her alter behavior patterns in keeping with the values of society. Although inmates of reformatories and prisons receive longer sentences, most offenders return to society sooner than is generally supposed. Even murderers spend only a portion of their sentences in prisons. According to the U.S. Bureau of Justice Statistics the median time convicted murderers spend behind bars is only seven years, and one of every seven persons sentenced for "life" serves three years or less.

For inmates in prisons the social worker, where available, attempts to establish a relationship that, over a period of time, frees the individual to express feelings in a cathartic manner, muster ego strengths, change some personal values, and become a law-abiding citizen. This relationship is the essence of the social worker's contribution—along with the use of community resources. It means that the worker accepts the client, understands, and respects him or her and that the client develops feelings toward the worker and shares ideas, emotions, and problems. Then through a bond of warmth and support, changes may be effected. The social worker is nonjudgmental, sensitive to needs, and conveys a feeling of respect for the integrity and individuality of the client regardless of questionable conduct.

In institutions with social work staff, the worker may meet weekly with the client for about an hour and, through interviewing, help him or her to achieve goals. The pattern outside institutions is fundamentally the same and includes the periodic interviews that give support and assistance to the offender, focusing on treatment rather than punishment, reform rather than punitiveness.

The social work process consists of four parts: *social study* (finding the facts), *assessment* (defining and evaluating the problems), *treatment* (solving the problems), and *termination*. The first three ordinarily proceed simultaneously from the beginning, although in emphasis there is usually sequential order. Often the first interview, or two or three, is utilized for social study and assessment; then treatment entails varying numbers of interviews, depending on individual problems and environmental situations.

The number of interviews is significant. Many social workers leave the number open to the worker and client to ascertain as they move along together; others stipulate a specific number of interviews, so that termination goals and dynamics may be anticipated. Although a common pattern is for interviews to take place weekly, the number can be increased or decreased depending on the needs of the client in the rehabilitative process. During emergencies the social worker may be needed at once.

The social worker acts as a catalytic agent who makes it possible for an offender to gain self-understanding, to feel better, and in particular, to interact with others more constructively. The worker helps the offender tap his or her own strengths, bringing about better harmony within the person and in associations with others. Studies show that offenders often need help in learning to function adequately in interaction with others, particularly in close, personal relationships.

Although some problems may be eased by the social worker in an interview or two, most persons who are in legal trouble need assistance over a period of time and require guidance in making effective use of community services and resources.[10]

Timing is also important in the social worker's role. There are certain periods when he or she can be particularly effective, such as during intake, when emergencies occur, in preparing for release, and in aftercare treatment. A meaningful relationship between worker and client can make easier these time-bound experiences, resulting in desired change.

Eskridge raised some questions about training needed for probation officers—even though the American Bar Association in 1970 had reaffirmed a standard previously suggested that attainment of a master's degree be the preferred norm—and suggested that probation as a profession "should proceed cautiously before adopting any firm educational standards or inservice training programs."[11]

Since the mid-1960s, considerable efforts have been extended to develop training and hiring of paraprofessionals and those who have completed undergraduate training in social work or social welfare. Indigenous workers among paraprofessionals have been sought, particularly among some of the minority groups.

The President's Commission in 1967 stressed the need for more and better qualified staff when they stated: "The system of criminal justice must attract more people and better people—police, prosecutors, judges, defense attorneys, probation and parole officers, and corrections officials with more knowledge, expertise, initiative, and integrity." Social workers can fulfill significant roles in several of these positions.

Processes and Principles

What are the methods utilized by the social worker in assisting with antisocial behavior? Traditionally there have been three in particular: *direct practice, group work,* and *community organization.* Research and administration also bolster social work services both directly and indirectly.

A few of the key principles social workers keep in mind as they work with offenders and their families are (1) to utilize a *relationship* to help clients help themselves; (2) to not condemn or moralize, accepting clients as they are, and also their behavior, regardless of what has been in the past; (3) to respect their right of self-determination, that is, to assist them to think and feel through their problems and situations, but not to make basic decisions for them, helping to provide an emotional climate in which they can face their problems and work out appropriate solutions; (4) to recognize that one has to study and understand normal behavior as well as antisocial behavior in order to comprehend the *why* of delinquency and criminality and what should be done about them; (5) to provide a security-giving firmness, not physical punishment, but not "coddling," as some maintain, recognizing that in many ways a child is like a coil spring, and that the harder one pushes the farther he or she will be likely to spring back when an opportunity arises; and (6) to use authority in a positive manner to help offenders help themselves face their problems and readjust their thinking and behavior.

What are the specific functions of a social worker in relation to juvenile delinquency and crime? Some of the main functions are:

Helping to strengthen motivation is a primary function of the social worker. Many boys and girls, or adults, do not care much about what they do in life or what they do not do. The social worker, through talking with them sympathetically and understandingly, can usually be of aid. For a person to know that someone is interested, and will accept him or her as is, is a tremendously motivating factor. One delinquent, for example, who talked to a probation officer over a period of many weeks, said: "He was just like a hypnotist. I couldn't say no to him. To know that someone cared enough about me to spend time with me, to try to understand and help me, led me to where I am today." His desire to become a law-abiding citizen had been increased and supported.

Allowing for ventilation of feelings is a second service of the social worker. Most youths and adults who come to a probation officer need to share with someone, in confidence, their inner feelings, their fears and frustrations, as well as their hopes and aspirations. The importance of this is illustrated by the man who talked to a worker for more than sixty minutes, giving the listener only an opportunity to nod his head and acquiesce. At the end he stood up, greatly relieved, and said, "I feel much better. Thanks for all your wonderful advice!" Youths and adults have feelings well up within, and social workers provide a safe emotional climate in which they can express and verbalize them.

The *giving of information* is another important function of the social worker. Many youths and adults need help in understanding who they are, where they are going, and where they might go. Many times they do not comprehend the society to which they belong, and the social worker can help them to develop such an understanding and to acquire insights into their proper roles.

The probation officer's *helping offenders make decisions* is a fourth function. Probation officers do not make decisions for offenders, but help them to consider, rationally, their problems and the alternatives that face them. Should they obtain employment? Should they stay with their own family or move out? Should they continue to associate with their old friends? Should they return to school? How can they alter their behavioral patterns? These are some of the typical questions that arise.

The social worker helps the client in *defining the situation.* He or she assists the individual not only in *thinking* about a problem or a situation, but also in *feeling* about the situation. A positive illustration is the young boy who has serious feelings of inferiority and, as a result, is in legal trouble on a compensatory, acting-out basis. The social worker helps him to think and feel about himself and his behavior, and thereby to realize that his feelings of inferiority are not based on facts. This new understanding and insight can alter his whole pattern of living.

Assisting in modification of the environment is another major function. With knowledge of community resources, the social worker is able to help persons and families tap various financial and social resources to meet their individual needs. The social worker may help a boy who is on probation to get a part-time job. He or she may assist the individual in finding a place to live and may help him or her become enrolled in a vocational training program to prepare for worthwhile citizenship for the rest of his or her life.

Helping offenders reorganize behavior patterns is one of the most difficult functions of the social worker. This includes help for the chronic alcoholic, the drug abuser, and those with other personality problems. The social worker may refer such a person to another expert or talk to the individual personally, depending on his or her background, training, and experience. These kinds of cases usually require long periods of treatment and many never "make it."

Another major function is in *facilitating referral.* Sometimes the job is "helping Susie to get to the clinic." Often it is difficult for a person to take personal problems to another, and he or she needs support in so doing. Referral may be made to a psychiatrist, minister, internist, geneticist, or other person who may help with a particular situation. The social worker's comprehensive knowledge of community resources is used to advantage in making referrals.

Cognitive Therapy with Criminals

Cognitive therapy has emerged as a popular treatment model for working with criminals. In *The Criminal Personality,* Samenow and Yochelson describe in detail the thinking errors that criminals use to justify and sustain their criminal activities. Mottonen lists fourteen common thinking errors of criminals that have been adapted from Samenow and Yockelson's earlier work:

1. I have to look out for myself.
2. Force or cunning is the best way to get things done.
3. We live in a jungle and the strong person is the one who survives.
4. People will get at me if I don't get them first.
5. It is not important to keep promises or honor debts.
6. Lying and cheating are okay as long as you don't get caught.
7. I have been unfairly treated and am entitled to get my fair share by whatever means I can.
8. Other people are weak and deserve to be taken.
9. If I don't push other people, I will get pushed around.
10. I should do whatever I can get away with.
11. What others think of me doesn't really matter.
12. If I want something, I should do whatever is necessary to get it.
13. I can get away with things so I don't need to worry about bad consequences.
14. If people can't take care of themselves, that's their problem.[12]

In working with clients in the criminal justice system, the social worker focuses on these and other thinking errors or cognitive distortions and how they are used to justify and sustain criminal activity. Clients keep a log of their cognitive distortions, identify the specific thinking errors they use, and replace their cognitive distortions with more rational responses. Another cognitive approach used with clients in the criminal justice system is to encourage them to think more about their victims. By focusing on how people feel and behave after they have been victimized, criminals sometimes gain more empathy for the pain they caused their victims, and may become more reluctant to commit criminal acts. Only time will tell if a real change has taken place in the criminal's thinking and his subsequent behavior. In the words of Mottonen, if you are a criminal, "You only have three choices—change, keep doing the crime, or suicide. It's your lifestyle, think about it."[13]

Motivational Interviewing with Criminals

In recent years, motivational interviewing has gained a considerable number of advocates in the helping profession who work with criminals. Motivational interviewing is a direct yet client-centered interviewing style that focuses on warmth, empathy, key questions, and reflective listening. The main goal of motivational interviewing is to demonstrate to clients how their problematic behavior opposes their personal goals. In working with criminals, the main goal would be to demonstrate how their criminal behavior keeps them from accomplishing what they want to in life. Motivational interviewing seems to work especially well with involuntary clients like criminals who generally don't believe that they have a problem or who view someone else as the problem.

The traditional view of society toward the criminal is that society must get tough with offenders and treat them accordingly. Boot camps and scared straight programs reflect this get tough approach which utilizes confrontations and maximum control over the criminal. According to Miller and Rollnick, this adversarial stance creates a culture that leads to a "them versus us" situation.[14] This adversarial stance only adds to the ambivalence that many criminals have about changing their behavior, especially when the change is court ordered. When motivational interviewing is used with criminals, the focus shifts from what society wants to change in the criminal to what the criminal would like to focus on. By working to remove the external forces that binds the criminal, the focus shifts to what goals the criminal wishes to pursue and how these goals might be accomplished. Criminal justice research studies completed by Project Match "have begun to suggest that the authoritarian approach to prompting behavior changes is less effective than those approaches that target internal motivation."[15] Motivational interviewing focuses on targeting this internal motivation in criminals.

When criminals lack sufficient motivation to change or even to address troublesome behavior, Miller and Rollnick suggest that criminals ask themselves a series of questions that should encourage them to look at their lives more thoughtfully. A partial list of these questions include the following:

1. What worries you about your current situation?
2. What do you think will happen if you don't change anything?
3. How would you like for things to be different?
4. What would you like your life to be like five years from now?
5. What would be the advantage of making this change?
6. What are the main reasons you see for making a change?
7. What makes you think that if you decide to make a change, you could do it?
8. How confident are you that you can make things change?
9. Who could offer you helpful support in making these changes?
10. What options are you considering to help you make this change?[16]

Social Services and Case Examples

Police Departments and Youth Bureaus

Social workers are sometimes utilized in working with the police, particularly in their youth bureaus. In many larger cities professionally trained social workers are integral parts of police departments. They act as consultants to help the law enforcement officers better understand the boys and girls whom they apprehend. They help the total department to develop a rehabilitative attitude rather than a punitive one, and, in particular, to facilitate the rehabilitative processes. A new role for social workers is going on patrol with police officers on night duty, answering emergency calls, and assisting with serious family quarrels and other personal or family difficulties. In addition, they play an important role in trying to prevent antisocial behavior among children, youths, and adults. The social worker is in a strategic position to utilize existing community resources and to draw on whatever may be most needed to assist a particular offender to change hostile attitudes and behavior to those within societal standards.

To illustrate, young Rebecca, who was picked up on the street at 2 A.M., was interviewed by a social worker, who found that her family was "psychologically broken" and disorganized. The social worker, in cooperation with the police, accompanied the girl to her home. In the next several days, the worker interviewed the mother, father, and some of the neighbors. After several weeks, the mother and father, through the help of the social worker, were enabled to become more effective parents. Within a few months, the family constellation changed from one of constant bickering, trouble, and hostility to one on the pathway to becoming a solid, functioning family. The daughter, who had been in trouble with the police several times prior to her escapade, settled down and began to do well in school and otherwise.

Courts

Social workers are attached to juvenile courts, district courts, federal courts, and to some municipal courts, performing the role of probation officer. In this connection, they have several functions. The first is conducting investigations to find out the facts and the feelings involved in a particular violation of law. Because of their training, social workers can usually be objective yet sympathetic and can secure a picture of the total situation that is most helpful to the court. Judges are making decisions regarding disposition of cases based on facts and understandings supplied through the investigation of the social worker. Investigations are primarily related to the offender but nearly always involve the family, close relatives, and other key persons in the lives of the accused.

An example of this function is the case of a young man brought before a California judge on a charge of "stealing state property." The young man was handsome and appeared to be intelligent, but was a person who had been "kicked around from place to place." He had been born into a family where he was not wanted. He had run away from home many times, had been placed in foster care on several occasions, and for years had been "on the road." The judge took a personal interest in him and asked his social worker to make a careful investigation. The social worker reported the significant facts with his professional

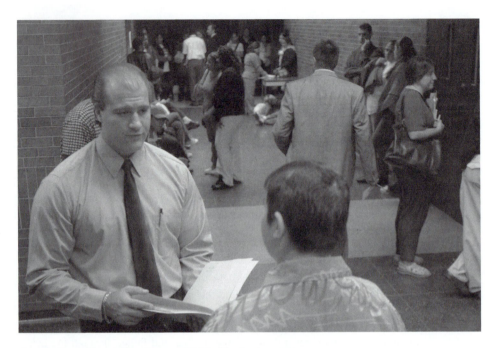

A probation officer talks with a youthful offender in court.

interpretations. On the basis of this investigation, the judge befriended the boy as no one had ever done before. The boy felt the sincere interest of this judge and social worker. The disposition was that the boy would be allowed to go into the service to perform his military obligation, which was mandatory at the time. When he filled in his papers, he asked the judge if he could put the judge's name down as the person "closest to him, who would always know his whereabouts." The judge said he would be complimented to be so designated. The boy was accepted into military service and adopted a mature pattern of living. His changed behavior was clear evidence of the need of one young man for understanding and interest from judges, social workers, and others who might supply these when they have not come through a regular channel.

A major function of the social worker is to represent the court after the judge has made a decision. Probation involves regular interviews and contacts between the probation officer and the offender. Again, the social worker attempts to use his or her best knowledge and skills to help bring about desired changes in the thinking, feeling, and behavior of those with whom he or she works. Many offenders for the first time in their lives have someone, the social worker, who really cares about them and is trying to help them to understand themselves and their relationships with others. The essence of this service is illustrated by the statement of Joe, age seventeen, who said, "For the first time in my life I was important to someone, and was wanted."

Another service, recent in appearance, is provided by the social worker as an expert witness in the courts. Gothard reports that before 1980 social workers rarely qualified as expert witnesses in legal proceedings.[17] Since the mid-1980s the profession has gained status, and individual social workers have been recognized as having sufficient expertise in several areas to qualify as experts in courts of law. This has placed social workers on a par with other professionals who have long been qualified as experts in the courts. Social workers are now invited to state their opinions and thereby influence the judgment or verdict. A recent development is the use of social workers as expert witnesses in child abuse cases.

Drug Courts

It is estimated that at least one-half of all the men and women incarcerated in jails and prisons in America have committed alcohol and drug offenses. A recent study at the Salt Lake County Jail in Salt Lake City, Utah, reported that 50 percent of all women inmates were imprisoned for alcohol and drug and related charges.[18] It also appears that many of our first-time and youthful offenders are mired in the criminal justice system because of alcohol and drug abuse. Many experts believe that these nonviolent drug offenders should be adjudicated differently from violent offenders. This has resulted in the development of drug courts across the country, many of which are modeled after a program started in Miami in 1989.

Instead of emphasizing imprisonment with nonviolent drug offenders, drug courts use long-term treatment along with intensive supervision and community service. The Orange County Drug Court in California focuses on the nonviolent drug offender who is willing to accept the responsibility for his or her drug behavior and cooperate with treatment services. After pleading guilty to drug charges, the offender is interviewed by probation officers and treatment counselors. A drug treatment program usually begins the day following the guilty plea. A jail sentence, usually averaging ninety days, is stayed pending successful completion of the treatment program which is implemented in three phases and usually lasts for eighteen months.

Participants graduate from the drug court after successfully completing all three phases of the program. Successful completion requires maintaining full-time employment, additional training or education during phase three, and achieving minimal periods of sobriety along with other requirements such as maintaining child support payments and clearing up all traffic cases. When the participants graduate from drug court, they are rewarded with dismissal of their cases. Reports from the Orange County Drug Court clearly show that drug court participants have better success rates and longer terms of sobriety than incarcerated offenders. In one study, 83 percent of the defendants had no new arrests following their drug court treatment whereas another study cited a 95 percent success rate.[19]

Social Work in Institutions

Although many youth development centers, detention homes, and prisons do not have trained social workers on their staffs, it is encouraging to note that the number that do is growing. Within such institutions, the social worker can play an extremely important role. He or she is usually assigned several inmates with whom to work on a face-to-face, individualized basis. The social worker ordinarily meets with them weekly, giving them an opportunity to talk over their problems in relation to society and life, especially in relation to their families. All kinds of cases exist indicating that thousands of boys and girls, youths, and adults are being helped by social workers who open the door for rehabilitation. Not only is social work with individuals used advantageously within these institutions, but the group approach is also more common.

That youths and adults need help in institutions is illustrated by the example of two seventeen-year-old boys who had been placed in a state prison for robbery. They were "ideal" prisoners. When they had served their time and were about to leave, the warden cautioned them to be truthful and law-abiding. They walked out of the prison gates with about $15 in their pockets. They located some stores, bought a few things they had not had for some time, and then began to look for jobs. When the applications were handed to them, they were faced with the question, "Have you ever been in prison?" They answered truthfully. No one would give them a job. Three nights later, about midnight, the two boys returned to the prison, rang the bell at the gate, and asked if the warden would give them a place to sleep. He, of course, granted their request. The next morning the guards passed a hat around, making a collection for the boys. More important, a social worker called employers and arranged for a job for each of them. Several years later, it was ascertained that these two young men had followed the warden's instructions, had lived law-abiding lives, and were respected citizens in their communities.

The 1973 Delegate Assembly of the National Association of Social Workers evidenced deep concern about delinquency and crime in this country and what social workers might do to combat and prevent them. They adopted a platform of fourteen objectives to help alleviate these devastating problems. Three of the salient ones were

1. NASW should work for greatly increased use of alternatives to incarceration to replace present excessive reliance on institutional commitment in the treatment of convicted offenders.
2. NASW should advocate that no new major large-scale institutions for either adults or juveniles be countenanced and that present large-scale juvenile institutions be phased out within a five-year period.
3. NASW should encourage greater emphasis on sound treatment programs within the community for most offenders.

With increased numbers of social workers being hired in correctional institutions comes the challenge to provide more effective services, a genuine challenge. Severson suggests that "providing social work services to the inmate and the institution concurrently requires that the social worker perform a balancing act. On one hand, incarcerated clients are entitled to the same protections that clients in mental health agencies or private practices are afforded. On the other hand, the institution has the need to know the forces that are affecting the population."[20]

Anyone who has worked in a correctional facility recognizes that inmates need mental health services. Anger management is a case in point. Most inmates would admit that uncontrolled anger has had a significant impact on their criminal behavior. Even so, an alarming number of correctional facilities lack mental health services that address problems like anger management. Social workers continue to advocate for improved mental health services in our prisons and jails. Recent studies show that when these services are provided, inmates learn to deal with destructive emotions such as anger in more appropriate ways.[21]

In recent years there has been a movement toward closing institutions for juveniles and/or decentralizing them, establishing smaller units in more communities. Massachusetts has closed down its correctional facilities for juveniles altogether and other states are looking carefully at this alternative. The basic premise is that too many juveniles are needlessly channeled through courts and institutions with scant regard for their offenses, civil liberties, and treatment. Additional emphasis is being given to the goals of diversion and rehabilitation rather than punishment.

Although "hard-core" violators of the law are maintained in most states in institutions, various "alternative programs" are also available, for example, residential care, proctor advocate programs, and residential treatment centers. Social workers may play significant roles in all of these.

In recent years there have been tough new laws passed to increase the punishment of offenders, particularly adults. New prisons and longer sentences are being introduced to try to combat increases in crime. Consequently, the number of inmates in U.S. prisons jumped by a record 7.3 percent during the first six months of 1989 to a total of 673,565, the highest rate of increase recorded during the sixty-four years the government has counted prisoners. As already stated, by 1993, over 900,000 men and women were being held in federal and state prisons in the United States. Most penologists and social workers have questions about these developments; they maintain that the certainty of punishment and rehabilitation are usually more effective than the severity of punishment.

Jails

Approximately 600,000 men and women were incarcerated in jails across the country in 2000. The mental health services that are provided to these inmates are severely limited in most jails. This is unfortunate because over one-half of all jail inmates have alcohol or drug dependence problems or suffer from mental illness. The Salt Lake County Jail in Salt Lake City, Utah, incarcerates over 1,800 each month in its two facilities. Since 1984, mental health services have been provided to the jail by Valley Mental Health, a large community mental health center.[22]

Inmates enter the Salt Lake County Jail at various times of the day. An inmate is seen immediately by a mental health worker if the inmate (1) exhibits unusual behavior, (2) has previously taken or is taking prescribed mental health medications, (3) makes a request, or (4) is referred by a family member or friend or a jail employee. If not seen by a mental health worker on entering the jail, every inmate receives a mandatory mental health assessment within fourteen days of incarceration. In assessing each inmate, the mental health worker follows a "Mental Health Intake Screening" form that evaluates (1) suicide potential, (2) mental health treatment, (3) substance abuse treatment, (4) observations, and (5) recommendations.

Once the mental health assessment is completed, the mental health worker makes one of two placements. If the inmate is expressing suicidal thoughts or engaging in self-destructive behaviors, the inmate is placed on the acute observation unit of the jail's mental health unit. Inmates who are not a suicide risk are placed with the general jail population. As part of the general jail population, inmates can participate in a drug counseling group treatment program contracted by the jail and administered by a community drug counseling center. Inmates can also participate in an alcohol/drug education group or an anger management education group offered by the mental health staff. On their release from jail, inmates can be referred to the community mental health center for follow-up services. These follow-up services are often mandated by the court as a condition of the inmate's release from jail.

Parole Activities

Most youths and adults who spend time in correctional institutions leave on parole. This means that they are released to a person who meets with them periodically and endeavors to help them. Social workers are used in this challenging position. Again, a social worker in such a position can be a most valuable anchor to a person who has an inadequate place to go or a family that really does not want him or her. A parole officer can not only support and sustain a person but also can work with the family, helping bring about changes in the total constellation that are helpful to all concerned.

Citizenry Involvement

Illustrative of the interest of leaders and responsible citizens in relation to the problems of crime and delinquency has been the effort extended by the Chamber of Commerce of the United States. In 1972 it issued a booklet titled *Marshaling Citizen Power to Modernize Corrections,* which made a strong plea for new programs "making use of community approaches to corrections as alternatives to incarceration, and also as a means of facilitating reintegration of the offender back into the community following a release from an institution."

The organization stressed that community corrections can be "cheaper and more humane." It described several types of community and traditional release programs that have demonstrated value in rehabilitating offenders and reducing social costs of recidivism, among which are pretrial intervention, probation, halfway houses, work release programs, prerelease centers, and parole.

Youth Services Systems

One of the 200 recommendations of the President's Commission on Law Enforcement and Administration of Justice related to the establishment of community correctional services. The President's Commission recommended that every community should consider establishing a Youth Service Bureau, "a community-based center to which juveniles could be referred by the police, the courts, parents, schools, and social agencies for counseling, education, work, or recreation programs and job placement" that would be "an agency to handle many troubled and troublesome young people outside the criminal system."

Gemignani discusses a national strategy for the prevention and reduction of juvenile delinquency. The broad plans of the strategy were developed at a meeting called by the

Youth Development Delinquency Prevention Administration in early 1970. Within the first two years twenty-three pilot programs were launched throughout the nation. The thrust was described as follows:

> The strategy calls for the establishment, nationwide, of youth services systems which will divert youth, insofar as possible, from the juvenile justice system by providing comprehensive, integrated, community-based programs designed to meet the needs of all youth, regardless of who they are or what their individual problems may be.[23]

A current example of an agency under this youth services system is a Youth Service Center (YSC) in a metropolitan area. It is an agency planned to be an advocate for youth and the family and is located in the city proper. It aims "to divert or offer alternative programs so the young people do not become involved with the juvenile justice system." The YSC provides coordination and cooperation with all social agencies in the county in an effort to offer opportunities for each young person or family to overcome their problems. The service is open to any young person or family on their request or from referral from law enforcement or other agencies; it is especially helpful for youth involved in status offenses. The agency does everything it can to help the child or the family in an informal, friendly manner. Social workers are on the staff. Action may result in any of the following: release with no follow-up, release with YSC counseling, referral to "cluster management," placement in a YSC receiving home, or detention placement. The service is open to youths and families twenty-four hours a day, seven days a week. YSC often helps young people gain employment.

Gemignani describes a typical example of how a youth services system may actually work in practice:

> In this case the mayor's office is the grantee agency. The boy is a school dropout with no job skills, and he is estranged from his family and is experiencing the effects of an overdose of LSD. He refuses traditional professional help. However, he comes in contact with the project when he calls its youth-manned Hotline, reporting that he is on LSD and wants to talk to someone about his problem. A sympathetic youth talks him into visiting the Hotline's adjunct drug crisis center. The center finds the youth to be under heavy influence of LSD. An ex-addict counselor is brought in to help the youth accept hospitalization. Within a few days of intensive contact with the ex-addict, the young man decides to accept some professional help.
>
> A plan is developed with him by the social worker at the center. It includes counseling for both him and his family; tutoring to prepare him for a GED (tests for general educational development); prevocational training; and the removal of now-unwanted tattoos from his hands. The counseling is rendered by the social worker at the center. The system's central information retrieval bank shows that the parents are already being seen by a local private agency and communication on the case is established with that agency. Tutorial services for the GED are supplied by a teacher from the local school assigned to work at the center. The prevocational training is rendered in the facilities of the local department of employment. The tattoo removal takes place in the plastic surgery clinic of a local private hospital, improving the youth's appearance and self-confidence.
>
> As a result of the counseling program, the young man is able to understand his problems and begin to do something about them. Although a reconciliation with his family is unsuccessful, a suitable independent living arrangement is made in a local boarding house. He is eventually awarded a GED. He gains some vocational skills and through the cooperation of

the local chapter of the Junior Chamber of Commerce is placed on a job. In this case, the young man continues his relationship with the program following his rehabilitation. He donates two nights a week to answering the Hotline telephone—a service to others that returns great satisfaction to him.[24]

The Halfway House

Since the 1960s a major surge has developed in providing halfway houses in the field of corrections for adults and youths, particularly for children and youths. A place "halfway" between the institution and the community, developed historically in the area of mental health, is being used in many communities, particularly in populated centers.

A halfway house in corrections, which often utilizes social workers as administrators or as staff workers, may be used in two ways: to help those about "halfway out" of an institution or to help those about "halfway in." A halfway house may be utilized for a youth or an adult who has been in a detention home, youth development center, or a prison as a major step toward the community and total freedom. It is also being used as a place for children to be housed in lieu of going to a formalized institution. It is a valid attempt to rehabilitate and prevent difficulties rather than to punish.

The philosophy of the halfway house is reflected by Rachin in the following:

> The Halfway House is intended to meet a need for client services between highly supervised, well structured, institutional programs and relatively free community living. In its popular function the halfway house has been a kind of decompression chamber through which institutional releases are helped to avoid the social-psychological bends of a too rapid reinvolvement in the real world.
>
> . . . The need for short-circuiting unnecessary institutional commitment has led to the development of the "halfway-in" house. Utilized primarily at this time for youth, treatment considerations and responsibility-oriented, reality-bound programming have been the hallmarks of these facilities. In addition to its traditional function, then, the halfway house can provide a means for diverting people from the institutional mill, which, as so many have pointed out, has more often harmed than helped.[25]

Prevention

Social workers are becoming more and more interested in preventive aspects of delinquency and crime. Philosophically, they believe that if more time and talent can be put into preventing antisocial behavior in the first place, society, as well as individuals and families, will be much better off. Prevention has many sides to it and involves all of the helping disciplines. Education is particularly important. Several studies show that there are many boys and girls in school who are near-delinquent and who will get into trouble if something is not done to help them solve their problems and adjust better to school, their families, and life in general. Marriage and family counseling, particularly premarital counseling, is another avenue that seems to be promising in preventing social ills.

Recreational activities and clubs can be utilized for prevention where there is proper leadership. An example was in the city of Battle Creek, Michigan, where in one dilapidated area the police arrested each year an average of 135 of the 450 boys and girls who called it home. Through the efforts of an energetic, enthusiastic police chief and other community and professional leaders, a clubhouse was built in this area. During the next twenty-two months not a single boy or girl from this poor neighborhood landed behind bars. There are many other kinds of challenging activities open to those who would like to work toward reducing and preventing antisocial behavior.

The President's Commission stressed the importance of prevention. In fact, it listed the following as the first objectives that need to be vigorously pursued:

> First, society must seek to prevent crime before it happens by assuring all Americans a stake in the benefits and responsibilities of American life, by strengthening law enforcement, and by reducing criminal opportunities.[26]

The President's Commission explained its position further:

> The prevention of crime covers a wide range of activities: eliminating social conditions closely associated with crime; improving the ability of the criminal justice system to detect, apprehend, judge, and reintegrate into their communities those who commit crimes; and reducing the situations in which crimes are most likely to be committed.
>
> Every effort must be made to strengthen the family, now often shattered by the grinding pressures of urban slums.
>
> Slum schools must be given enough resources to make them as good as schools elsewhere and to enable them to compensate for the various handicaps suffered by the slum child—to rescue him or her from his or her environment. . . .
>
> Employment opportunities must be enlarged and young people provided with more effective vocational training and individual job counseling.[27]

An encouraging example along the prevention path was the National Symposium on Addressing Violent Crime Through Community Involvement, which was sponsored by the FBI and held at the FBI Academy in Quantico, Virginia, October 16–17, 1991. This was the first such gathering of civic leaders and law enforcement officials by the FBI on a national level. It helped establish many important lines of communication essential to cooperative prevention and reduction of violent crime. Such statements as the following surfaced: "Using the combined resources of the police department and social agencies can go a long way in addressing crime" and "in order to get a handle on violence—the police must form working partnerships within the community.[28]

Summary

Juvenile delinquency and crime are major problems in modern society. Four social processes utilized in modern administration of criminal justice are law enforcement, prosecution and defense, judicial process, and corrections.

Social work has a major contribution to make in the control and prevention of juvenile delinquency and crime. Social work attempts to help the individual, family, and community face and solve delinquency and crime problems through utilization of individual, family, and community resources. The social worker in corrections works with individuals, groups, and communities. The social worker helps particularly with police departments and youth bureaus, courts, probation, institutions, parole, youth services systems, halfway houses, and prevention. The social worker is really just beginning to tap individual and community resources in the control and prevention of delinquency and crime. As alternatives to incarceration are developed and sound community treatment programs become common practice, more professional social workers will be asked to share the responsibility of providing improved professional service.

Selected References

"A Symposium on the Causes and Correlates of Juvenile Delinquency," *The Journal of Criminal Law and Criminology,* 82 (Spring 1991), 1–118.

COHEN, MONIQUE, *Counseling Addicted Women: A Practical Guide.* Thousand Oaks, CA: Sage, 1999.

CUMMINGS, SCOTT, and DANIEL J. MONTI, *Gangs: The Origins and Impacts of Contemporary Youth Gangs in the United States.* Albany: State University of New York Press, 1993.

KLEIN, MALCOLM W., *The American Street Gang: Its Nature, Prevalence, and Control.* New York: Oxford University Press, 1995.

LAHEY, BENJAMIN B., TERRIE E. MOFFITT, and AVSHALOM CASPI, eds., *Causes of Conduct Disorder and Juvenile Delinquency.* New York: Guilford Press, 2003.

LUNDMAN, RICHARD J., *Prevention and Control of Juvenile Delinquency,* 3rd ed. New York: Oxford University Press, 2001.

LYNCH, RUFUS SYLVESTER, and JACQUELYN MITCHELL, "Justice System Advocacy: A Must for NASW and the Social Work Community," *Social Work,* 40 (January 1995), 9–12.

MASON, MARY ANN, "Social Workers as Expert Witnesses in Child Sexual Abuse Cases," *Social Work,* 37 (January 1992), 30–34.

MASON, MARY ANN, "The McMartin Case Revisited: The Conflict between Social Work and Criminal Justice," *Social Work,* 36 (September 1991), 391–395.

MILLER, WILLIAM R., and STEPHEN ROLLNICK, *Motivational Interviewing,* 2nd ed. New York: Guilford Press, 2002.

MORRIS, NORVAL, and DAVID J. ROTHMAN, *The Oxford History of the Prison: The Practice of Punishment in Western Society.* New York: Oxford University Press, 1997.

RICE, ALLAN F., LARRY L. SMITH, and FRED V. JANZEN, "Mental Health Services and Women Inmates," *American Jails,* 14 (May/June 2000), 39–42.

RICE, ALLAN F., LARRY L. SMITH, and FRED V. JANZEN, "Women Inmates, Drug Abuse, and the Salt Lake County Jail," *American Jails,* 13 (July/August 1999), 43–47.

ROSSI, PETER H., and RICHARD A. BERK, *Just Punishment: Federal Guidelines and Public Views Compared.* Hawthorne, NY: Aldine de Gruyter, 1997.

SEVERSON, MARGARET M., "Adapting Social Work Values to the Corrections Environment," *Social Work,* 39 (July 1994), 451–456.

SMITH, LARRY L., JAMES N. SMITH, and BERYL M. BECKNER, "An Anger Management Workshop for Women Inmates," *Families in Society,* 75 (March 1994), 172–175.

TREGER, HARVEY, "Police Social Work," in *Encyclopedia of Social Work,* 19th ed., Vol. 3. Washington, DC: NASW Press, 1995, pp. 1843–1848.

UMBREIT, MARK S., "Crime Victims and Offenders in Mediation: An Emerging Area of Social Work Practice," *Social Work,* 38 (January 1993), 69–73.

WALLACE, HARVEY, *Family Violence: Legal, Medical, and Social Perspectives.* Boston: Allyn & Bacon, 1996.

Notes

1. *Crime in the United States—2002* (Washington, DC: FBI, U.S. Department of Justice, 2003), p. 58.

2. Dennis W. Nielsen, "U.S. Probation Officers as Jail Monitors: A New Responsibility on the Horizon," *Federal Probation,* 48 (September 1984), p. 29.

3. Daniel D. Smith, Terrence Finnegan, and Howard H. Snyder, *Delinquency 1977, United States Estimates of Cases Processed by Courts with Juvenile Jurisdiction* (Pittsburgh, PA: National Center for Juvenile Justice, 1980), p. 7.

4. Thomas A. Regulus, "Gang Violence," in *Encyclopedia of Social Work,* 19th ed., Vol. 2 (Washington, DC: NASW Press, 1995), p. 1050.

5. Elliot Studt, *Education for Social Workers in the Correctional Field,* Curriculum Study V (New York: CSWE, 1959), p. 7.

6. Ibid., p. 6.

7. Robert L. Barker, *The Social Work Dictionary,* 3rd ed. (Washington, DC: NASW Press, 1995), pp. 81–82.

8. Studt, *Education for Social Workers*, p. 7.

9. Ibid., p. 47.

10. For interesting analyses regarding short-term contacts, see Joseph R. Silver, "Social Case-work in Jail," *The Prison Journal,* 39 (October 1959), 51–55; also Harvey Treger, Doug Thomson, and Gordon Sloan Jaeck, "A Police-Social Work Team Model," *Crime and Delinquency,* 20 (July 1974), pp. 281–290.

11. Chris W. Eskridge, "Education and Training of Probation Officers: A Critical Assessment," *Federal Probation,* 43 (September 1979), p. 48.

12. Doug Mottonen, ed., *What Does Your Future Hold?* (Salt Lake City, UT: Valley Mental Health, 1987), p. 2.

13. Ibid., p. 18.

14. William R. Miller and Stephen Rollnick, *Motivational Interviewing*, 2nd ed. (New York: Guilford Press, 2002), p. 339.

15. Ibid.

16. Ibid., p. 79.

17. Sol Gothard, "Power in the Court: The Social Worker as an Expert Witness," *Social Work,* 34 (January 1989), p. 65.

18. Allan F. Rice, Larry L. Smith, and Fred V. Janzen, "Women Inmates, Drug Abuse, and the Salt Lake County Jail," *American Jails,* 13 (July/August 1999), p. 43.

19. Don E. Hallstrom, Ralph G. Rodgers, and David C. Velasquez, "Drug Court," *American Jails,* 14 (May/June 2000), pp. 27–31.

20. Margaret M. Severson, "Adapting Social Work Values to the Corrections Environment," *Social Work,* 39 (July 1994), p. 453.

21. Larry L. Smith, James N. Smith, and Beryl M. Beckner, "An Anger Management Workshop for Women Inmates," *Families in Society,* 75 (March 1994), 172–175; Larry L. Smith and Beryl M. Beckner, "An Anger Management Workshop for Inmates in a Medium Security Facility," *Journal of Offender Rehabilitation,* 19, (nos. 3/4, 1993), pp. 103–112.

22. Allan F. Rice, Larry L. Smith, and Fred V. Janzen, "Mental Health Services & Women Inmates," *American Jails,* 14 (May/June 2000), pp. 39–42.

23. Robert J. Gemignani, "Youth Services System," *Federal Probation,* 36 (December 1972), p. 48.

24. Ibid., p. 51.

25. Richard L. Rachin, "So You Want to Open a Halfway House," *Federal Probation,* 36 (March 1972), p. 30.

26. *The Challenge of Crime in a Free Society* (Washington, DC: U.S. Government Printing Office, 1967), p. vi.

27. Ibid.

28. Lee P. Brown, "Violent Crime and Community Involvement," *FBI Law Enforcement Bulletin,* 61 (May 1992), 2–5; and "Focus on Community Partnerships," *FBI Law Enforcement Bulletin,* 61 (May 1992), pp. 12–13.

15

Services for Older Americans

"What have you fed your immortal soul today?" was a question my father repeatedly asked me when I was young. I adored my father and wanted to please him, so I always tried to learn something worthwhile during the day. As I grew older I would think of that question as I got into bed each night and recall what I had read that day. If I had read nothing of value, I would get up and read from the Scriptures or passages from my literature books, often memorizing the lines. The values and standards I learned from my books have been a guide all my life and have helped me understand myself and my associates.

Now that I am nearing my 90th year, the infirmities of age have overtaken me, and my eyes no longer let me read books I love so much. My hearing is so poor that I cannot listen to them on records. I have to depend on what I learned earlier. I think of the characters in literature and the ideas and concepts expressed in the Scriptures; they are part of me and sustain me as I live alone, giving me the support I need to live at peace with myself. Although I no longer can give to others I try to maintain a serene attitude, for I remember the teachings of Plato: "He who is of a calm and happy nature will hardly feel the pressure of age, but to him who is of an opposite disposition, youth and age are equally a burden."

Governmental agencies, universities, and private organizations have been studying older citizens to learn everything about them. Who are these people? What are their sources of income? Where do they live? What occupies their time? What is their state of health? Who cares for them? What is the role of social work in the provision of services for the elderly?

These older Americans are mothers and fathers, brothers and sisters, grandparents and great-grandparents. The great majority of them do not fit the stereotype of rocking-chair sitters, slow and poor and sick elderly people. Today, those over 65 have better health because of an awareness of the benefits of a moderate lifestyle, better nutrition, increased physical activity, and better care from the medical profession. They are becoming better educated, with many attending universities and colleges to pursue degrees or just to learn. They are active in political parties, both as candidates for office and as workers. They have more money to spend as they follow the sun in the winter and seek the cool northern breezes in summer in their mobile homes. They are survivors. They have lived through the Great Depression of the 1930s, a world war, and a lifetime of sacrifice and struggle to become financially independent. A few are wealthy, and most are able to care for their financial needs.

Although the majority function independently or with the aid of their families, the requirements of those who are in need of services are often so great that they cannot continue to live without help. Some need financial assistance. However, the poverty rate for seniors has been dropping. In the 50s the poverty rate for those over 65 was 35.2 percent; by 1995 it was reduced to 10.3 percent.[1] The 10.3 percent still represents a significant number of seniors who need financial help. Others need health and personal care. There are 25,000 centenarians in the United States today, and the Census Bureau estimates that by the year 2050 there will be one million people over the age of 100.

As people pass the age of 85, it becomes increasingly difficult for them to care for themselves. Although many are cared for by family, it is often 75-year-old "kids" caring for 95-year-old parents. As it becomes increasingly difficult to cope with the problems—whether they are physical, mental, emotional, or financial—it may be necessary for the elderly person to be placed in a nursing home. Although only about 5 percent of the elderly are in institutions at any one time, those who are there need to be watched over and provided with constant care.

They live in all states and in all levels of society. Because the elderly make up a large percentage of our population, and because many have special needs and many others are potentially "needy," their problems become the problems of society. The solutions are a challenge to science, government, industry, education, and especially to the helping professions, including social work.

The "pyramids" in Figure 15.1 show the increase in the population of the United States projected to the year 2030 and the dramatic rise in the number of people over age 65.

In 1900 there were approximately 3 million people 65 and older in the United States. In 1950 there were approximately 12.4 million, and projections made by the Bureau of the Census place the number in the year 2000 at 35 million. By 2030 there will be 8 million Americans in the 85+ population, the ones most in need of health care and social programs.

The 1950 figure resembles a Christmas tree with a young population of 152 million people. Bars representing recent births are wider at the base, and bars representing older ages gradually narrow as mortality depletes the population.

The 1989 figure is larger because the population had grown to 249 million. Life expectancy was 75.2 years. Declining mortality rates cause bars at the top to widen.

By 2030 the shape is almost a rectangle with a projected population of 301 million. The number of deaths outnumber births, and life expectancy will be about 79 years.

Older Americans Act of 1965

The first White House Conference on Aging, in January 1961, was a nationwide citizens' forum designed to focus public attention on the problems and potentials of older Americans. At this conference, delegates made recommendations on research, training,

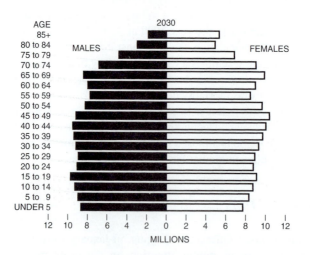

FIGURE 15.1 The Graying of America.

Source: Donald G. Fowles, "The Numbers Game: Pyramid Power," *Aging,* 362 (Washington, DC: Administration of Aging, 1991), pp. 58–59.

federal organization, and other aspects of aging that prepared the way for the passing of P.L. 89-73, known as the Older Americans Act of 1965.[2]

This legislation and subsequent amendments to the act provide assistance to older persons through grants to the states for community planning and services; training and research; and to establish within the Department of Health and Human Services an operating agency designated as the "Administration on Aging."

This law and its amendments are the basis for financial aid given by the federal government to assist older people. Ten objectives of the act are to secure

1. an adequate income;
2. best possible physical and mental health;
3. suitable housing;
4. restorative services for those who require institutional care;
5. opportunity for employment;
6. retirement in health, honor, dignity;
7. pursuit of meaningful activity;
8. efficient community services;
9. immediate benefit from research knowledge to sustain and improve health and happiness; and
10. freedom, independence, and the free exercise of individual initiative in planning and managing their own lives.[3]

Appropriations are made to the states and communities for their programs on aging. Monies are allocated for (1) planning and coordination of programs, (2) activities valuable in reaching the goals, (3) training of personnel, and (4) establishment of new or expansion of existing programs.

Anyone working with the older population needs to be fully aware of the provisions of the Older Americans Act, including the current conditions attached to the appropriations and the many changes made and projected because of Gramm-Rudman legislation and shifts in funding patterns from federal to state and local structures.

White House Conference on Aging, 1971

Delegates to the second White House Conference on Aging, held in 1971, were asked to formulate a comprehensive plan to meet the needs of older people.

In preconference meetings thousands of individuals who had contributed to the building of the country expressed their desire to continue to be a part of future plans. Representatives of all states and ethnic groups, all economic levels and social organizations, set four goals for making life more rewarding for the elderly:

1. An adequate income
2. Appropriate living arrangements

3. Institutional responsiveness and a new attitude toward aging
4. Independence and dignity

Adequate Income

In 1980 about one-third of the older population was living at or below the poverty level. In 1995 the number was down to approximately 10.3 percent. Americans over eighty-five—believed to be the fastest-growing segment of the population—are far more likely to be poor than those sixty-five to eighty years old. Many live in apartments or hotels in the urban inner cities with inadequate living conditions. Their neighborhoods are frequently a threat to their peace of mind because drug addicts, thieves, and alcoholics surround them.

Inflation is unacceptably high for those on meager, fixed incomes. In the early 1990s there are still some people who were wage earners in the Great Depression years of the 1930s. Although wages for most did increase dramatically, there were many, because of lack of education or other reasons, who were unable to move upward with the economic times and were unable to save adequately for their old age.

Recognizing the need for additional income for retired workers, Congress passed the Social Security Act, which has been repeatedly changed to increase monthly payments, to give wider coverage to workers, and to make retired workers independent. The "automatic escalator" clause was included in 1974, providing an increase in payments when the Consumer Price Index increased.

Those who also have sufficient assets in savings, home ownership, life insurance, and pensions are able to care for themselves through their retirement years. Those who have only Social Security find this inadequate. A Supplemental Security Income program for those without social security provides eligible recipients cash payments each month. Important considerations of this program are that recipients are not required to give a lien on their homes, and children are not forced to contribute to their support. Also, the older person may own life insurance and property in a limited amount.

It is readily apparent that Congress cannot assure every person a monthly income equal to his or her preretirement level. Many people need help in planning during their productive years to prepare for the loss of income that comes at retirement.

In the latter part of 1999, Congress moved unanimously to reduce all limitations on earnings for individuals over sixty-five. This means that individuals over sixty-five can receive full Social Security benefits and maintain full-time jobs. This new law encourages seniors to work full time longer, which, in turn will contribute to society.

It is apparent that with the aging of baby boomers, the Social Security system as we now know it will be bankrupt if nothing new is done. President Clinton made a speech in Kansas City, Missouri, where he stated that after 2029, if no action is taken, the trust fund will only be enough to cover 75 cents on the dollar of current benefits.[4] Much work has to be done if this important safety net for seniors is to be preserved. In 2001, President George W. Bush appointed a high-level task force to study the problems of Social Security and make recommendations to ensure the viability of the program.

Appropriate Living Arrangements

The goal for housing the elderly population has been greatly broadened from the old concept of providing a quiet place in the country to providing a variety of choices from which older persons can select one suited to their needs. For most, the preferable way to live is to remain in their own homes or to live with their children or relatives. Public and private housing developments are being built in answer to the needs of the large number of elderly persons who are looking for a place to live. Some promote independent living facilities with recreational and activity programs; others provide such services as congregate meals and personal services; others have facilities providing limited medical care, food, and homemaker services.

The Department of Housing and Urban Development (HUD) is constantly reviewing and changing its program to provide better housing for the elderly. Crises often develop in inner-city areas when new industrial developments necessitate the removal of buildings used to house the elderly poor. Many times these facilities are inadequate living quarters, but to those being displaced, they are "home." Legislation has been passed to assure tenants that adequate housing will be available before they are displaced.

For those older persons who are well enough to stay at home, but need some help, a variety of social and health services have been started. As their value becomes more apparent, they probably will be more widely available. These include homemaker services, "Meals on Wheels," visiting nurses, shopping, and counseling.

Several hospitals in the Chicago area have designed Mobile Medical Care Units (MMCU) to provide in-home health care to seniors. These mobile units consist of physicians,

Appropriate living arrangements for the elderly are important.

nurses, nurse practitioners, physician assistants, and social workers who have expertise in gerontology and understand the medical needs of older adults and their caregivers. This service essentially brings back the practice of the physician housecall. These mobile home-care units may develop into an important system that may allow seniors to live out their lives in their own homes with dignity and respect.[5]

Institutional Responsiveness and a New Attitude toward Aging

No one ever dies of "old age"; there is no such disease, according to the American Medical Association. Yet, almost invariably, aging results in physical changes in the individual. About 75 percent of the elderly have suffered one or more chronic illnesses by age seventy-five. Among the more common ailments are the same diseases that affect younger people: cardiac disease, hypertension, asthma, diabetes, arthritis, as well as the disabilities usually associated with old age—loss of hearing, impaired eyesight, mental disorders including senility, and disabilities resulting from accidents, particularly falling, which accounts for the hospitalization of 11 percent of the elderly.

Medicare pays some of the costs for hospitalization and various medical services. However, those who thought it would be the answer to all medical care needs have been disappointed. Some of the most frequently mentioned shortcomings are that it does not pay for long-term care in nursing homes, prescription drugs, eyeglasses, dental expense, or hearing aids. Prescribed medicines are often the largest medical expense for chronically ill persons. Medicaid, a federal state-administered welfare medical program, may pay medical bills not covered by Medicare for the elderly poor, those with a low income and few assets who cannot afford the cost of private health care insurance.

Some of the difficulty in securing proper medical care lies with older persons themselves. They often neglect to seek help until it is too late because they fear cancer or other terminal illnesses or because they have lost their regular physicians. Many have not been educated to the need for regular checkups, the dangers of self-doctoring, or accident prevention. Some are afraid of hospitals and others resist seeking help because they cannot afford to pay. Furthermore, families dismiss early symptoms as a part of growing old.

Older people have nearly twice as many home accidents as the average adult and three times as many fatal accidents. Their illnesses last longer and if hospitalization occurs, the stay is, on the average, twice as long as for younger people. Nearly half of the older citizens with arthritis, rheumatism, hernias, or who have trouble seeing or hearing are not now under care. One out of seven with a heart condition is not receiving medical attention.

In the recent past there were only a few members of medical school faculties who were identified primarily with aging, but this is changing. Older people are becoming organized and by their sheer numbers they are gaining political and economic clout. They are being recognized for their power, and gradually changes are taking place in medical schools to give more emphasis to the needs of this large segment of our population.

Defining "old" as anyone over the age of sixty-five, approximately three-fourths of them function independently of their families or institutions. This is true because of the large numbers of the younger old people, those aged sixty-five to seventy-five.

Although both husband and wife are alive they often continue to live on their own, caring for each other. Because most women have longer life expectancies and marry men who are older than themselves, they are much more likely than their husbands to assume the role of caregiver for a spouse. Research indicates that

> in old age men generally depend more on their wives than women depend on their husbands. Studies have shown that even when an aged wife becomes ill due to stress and the burden of caregiving and needs assistance, she will neglect her health and continue to care for her disabled husband. . . . Because of their nurturing skills and sensitivity to human interactions, women are considered more responsive to pain and suffering and more willing to take on arduous and often unrewarded personal duties. Performing stressful and often painful duties without pay is assumed to be a labor of love, an activity that is taken for granted for the female population. . . . Many elderly wives believe that, for better or for worse, they must respond to the needs of their disabled spouses without regard for their own unheralded personal and emotional sacrifices.[6]

A married couple may get along well especially if they live in close proximity to some of their children. The population has become more mobile, but most people still live close enough to some of their kin to be able to have some assistance when needed. In the beginning this assistance may be just for transportation, shopping, and emotional support, but as health deteriorates additional duties are added such as help in making social contacts, phoning, visiting, decision making, participation in family events, listening, and having someone to rely on, someone who cares.

If a spouse dies and the survivor is unable to live alone, it may be necessary to take the second best option—to live with one's children.

Where it is feasible an elderly parent looks to the daughters for support. When sons are called on to become the major caregiver to their parents, it is usually the daughter-in-law who provides the day-to-day personal care because this is perceived as women's work. Sons play a role in providing money management and are helpful in decision making, for these are perceived as men's work.

In her research, Elaine M. Brody, head of the Department of Human Services at the Philadelphia Geriatrics Center, found that

> families have reacted responsibly—even heroically—to the vastly increased demand for parent and parent-in-law care. It is the women in the family—wives, daughters, and daughters-in-law—who provide the vast majority of services needed by dependent older people, with daughters predominating in helping those elderly who are the most severely disabled. The needs of the disabled older people have exceeded the capacities of many caregiving women. In addition, societal values about women's roles have been changing so that the different values they hold may pull them in opposite directions. . . .
>
> To put the matter in perspective, it is emphasized that the vast majority of women *want* to care for elderly parents and *do so willingly.* They derive many positive benefits from parent care such as satisfaction from fulfilling what they see as their responsibilities, adhering to religious and cultural values, expressing their feelings of affection, seeing to it that the parent is well cared for, reciprocating help the parent had given them in the past, and feeling that they are serving as a good model for their own children to follow.[7]

Whereas social workers in the past have focused mainly on the elderly patient, more and more they are considering the younger caregiver as also being in need of support and help. With the added responsibility of caring for someone who is ill or disabled, a woman who may still have children of her own at home, who has a place in the working world, has hobbies and social commitments, and who may be slowing down herself may find that her energy level is too low for all that needs to be done.

It becomes increasingly difficult if the elderly parent has Alzheimer's disease or related mental disorders. If it is an inherited disease the caregiver may think, "Will this happen to me?" Where an older member of the family is depressed or has other mental disabilities, it is more damaging to the relationships of other family members than when the older person is physically impaired.

As greater numbers of people live to old age, caring for parents will become a universal experience and problem. Ways will be found to address this problem more adequately. Such efforts as reported by the American Association of Retired Persons (AARP)[8] may be a milestone and one of the answers.

Case Management Applied

"Aging in place" is a concept used to denote a program for elderly Americans. Iowa has tried this program. According to the 1990 Census, Iowa was the state with the most "old old" people (eighty-five and older) in proportion to the population. Keeping these people in their own homes as long as possible, helping them remain independent, and reducing inappropriate use of long-term nursing home care are goals set by Iowa.

By the year 2010 the percentage of "old old" Americans in other states will catch up with Iowa. But Iowa, which did not have the luxury of waiting until then, has the problem now. What Iowa is now doing may well be a bellwether for the rest of the country.

A top priority is keeping the elderly in their own homes. In Cedar Rapids, Iowa, 110 old people live at home who would otherwise be living in long-term nursing homes, affording them more dignity and saving their own money and that of the taxpayer. This is achieved in large part by implementing a "case management" concept. Case management works by orchestration of a multiple number of services (thirty-two in Cedar Rapids) used in the delivery of vitally needed assistance and tailored to fit individual needs. Iowa has pulled together disparate elements: family service professionals, public and private agencies, and volunteers.

Ninety-two-year-old Harold Mills is an example.

Nancy Hanson cleans his house, gives him a back rub (to alleviate a painful rash), takes him grocery shopping or runs errands. Other aides bring hot meals at noon and do yard work and snow shoveling. A social worker drives by to see how he is doing. . . .[9]

Nancy Hanson, the home-health aide. . . , comes from the Linn County Department of Human Resources Management. The aide who cuts his grass is sent by Aging Services, Inc., a private nonprofit firm that also provides a visiting social worker. His meals are delivered courtesy of Family Service Agency, a private nonprofit group. And he gets an emergency response hookup from Mercy Medical Center.[10]

Thirty-two agencies work in a consortium. The agency providing the greatest number of services is designated case manager and client advocate. Eighty thousand volunteers, mostly over age sixty, provide a wide range of services coordinated by the case manager. In addition to case management more than a dozen programs have sprung up since 1980. Despite all that is done by professionals, paraprofessionals, and organized services, the family, neighbors, and friends continue to provide the lion's share of elder care. After family resources have been exhausted, or when the elderly parent's life is so precarious that twenty-four-hour nursing care is needed, they then turn to the next option—nursing homes.

Nursing Homes

More than any other group, except perhaps the very young, the elderly are in need of the helping services offered by the social work profession. This is particularly true of those in institutions who are infirm or have disabilities that make them incompetent—who are ill as well as old.

Fortunately, nursing homes billing Medicare and Medicaid are now mandated by law to provide psychological and social services; some networking of services is offered. However, the 1997 Balanced Budget Act specified that clinical social workers could not bill Medicare directly for services to skilled-nursing facilities' residents. The National Association of Social Workers is working to eliminate this provision in the act so that social work providers are not subject to the whims of for-profit nursing home administrators.[11]

Prior to 1966 there were comparatively few nursing homes in America. As the need increased, and after Medicare and Medicaid were introduced, government and private money was channeled into the building of facilities for the care of those with long-term illnesses. Because of the genuine need for nursing home care for those unable to be cared for in any other place, it is important that the quality of care be improved. About 5 percent of the 30 million Americans sixty-five and older live in nursing homes on a long-term basis. In addition about one of five older people will spend some time in a nursing home for short-term medical care or physical therapy.

In addition 1.3 million receive home health care. Another 1.1 million live in congregate living facilities where they receive some help. Many of these 2.4 million would be unable to maintain themselves outside a nursing home without these supportive services.

Old people look on nursing homes with fear and hostility; they believe that going into a home is a prelude to death. Higher death rates are recorded among those in nursing homes, and some experts charge that the shock of uprooting is the cause. But many go to a nursing home only when their physical condition is so precarious that life cannot be sustained without constant medical supervision.

There is a popular belief that families use nursing homes to get rid of elderly relatives, but studies reveal that this is not true. Brody and others have reported that as many as 14 million elderly live with their spouses and 4 million with other relatives.

Although the rest live on their own, about 80 percent have children, and about 55 percent of those who don't live with their adult children do live within 30 minutes distance from them. A recent survey showed that more than three quarters of those surveyed had seen at least one of their children within the previous week. Moreover, as much as 50 percent of home-help services received by the elderly are provided by family and friends. A great deal of care is provided by social workers and other health and mental health professionals outside the family.[12]

Nursing homes employing professionally trained social workers provide essential services such as interpreting the program to patient and family, explaining the nature of the illness, discussing ways of coping with the problem, providing the opportunity for the family to share their grief and to express guilt and concerns, and assisting with the mobilization by the family of resources needed to sustain the family and the patient.

Educational programs have demonstrated that a group relationship is one therapeutic way of resolving feelings of anxiety, guilt, and hostility, as well as for sharing experiences and thereby gaining the reassurance to be able to move toward a positive resolution of one's problems. Adult children who participate feel relief of guilt when they understand the process of aging, feel the support of the social workers, and know that their experiences are shared by others whose problems parallel their own.

The depressing situation families found as they looked for nursing homes before the passage of the Older Americans Act is changing. The care and services in many homes have improved. Confronted with the frustration and dissatisfaction of families and the standards mandated by state and federal authorities, nursing home owners have moved ahead to upgrade services and meet the standards people are demanding. Society has also created the mechanism needed with Social Security, Medicare, and Medicaid to pay for these improvements. Experimental programs, started to prove the feasibility of providing social work and other services in nursing homes, have proved their relevance.

Social worker assisting elderly man.

Alternatives to Nursing Home Care

Most older people would prefer to remain in their own homes or homes of relatives. When home health care, meal, and homemaker services are available, such care may not only postpone, but possibly prevent, more costly institutional care.

Home health services include visiting nursing, laboratory services, physical therapy, drugs, and sick room equipment supplied by members of the medical profession.

Food service programs have been greatly expanded and are basically of two types: the delivery of meals to the home six days a week or the serving of meals in a common dining room.

Homemaker services have been developed to provide for the needs of those who are not ill, but who are dependent on someone to perform the tasks that they are no longer able to do for themselves. Thousands who would have to depend on government money to maintain them in nursing homes have adequate income and savings to maintain themselves with these services. With imagination a community may hit on the answer to a difficult social problem as reported in the following incident.

The Utah Department of Health became concerned about the quality of life of seniors living in nursing homes. They were determined to utilize Medicaid funds in a more flexible way, hence, the name "flex care" was coined. Prior to this time Medicaid money was spent only for nursing home care, and the agency set about to develop a new program that allowed Medicaid money to be used to meet individualized needs. Administrators of this new program began to assess the needs of seniors referred to them and to determine if they like to be placed in assisted-living centers, group homes, nursing homes, or, in fact, remain in their own homes. This program is in its infancy, but this more flexible use of Medicaid money might signal a new era for seniors in the state of Utah.

Fifty people who had been receiving homemaker services under the Division of Family Services were declared ineligible because they were receiving Social Security payments above the welfare-grant level. Some were receiving help only a few hours a week for such essential services as grocery shopping and being taken for medical care. The homemaker had helped them to remain in their own homes. For many the alternative seemed to be the much more expensive solution of going into a nursing home.

The director of the family service program sought help through the daily newspaper. An appealing feature story picturing one elderly woman told the plight of all. In one day offers to help came from 80 individuals as well as numerous church and civic groups.

Although the director had at first appealed for help on a temporary basis until other funds could be arranged, the overwhelming public response made him turn to the community's volunteer program as a permanent solution.

Day Care Centers

Many individuals who live at home require some of the services offered by an institution. The high cost of nursing home care and the desire of the individuals and their families for them to remain in the community have brought about the development of day care centers.

They are designed primarily to provide a protective environment and emotional support during the daytime hours. Social workers are generally utilized to act as liaison between the families and the program and between other agencies and the center. Because the program is new, there is a need to educate the public and, more particularly, the older people and their families to the opportunities provided by these facilities. The activities are determined by the needs of the group and help those who participate to function adequately in their social groups.

This service gives the family some relief from twenty-four-hour-a-day care, prevents or postpones institutional care, and provides a program designed to maintain maximum functioning, both physical and emotional.

Mental Health

Between 15 and 25 percent of the elderly living in the community are said to have moderate to severe psychiatric impairment. They are able to remain in the community because they are able to carry out the activities necessary to keep themselves functioning, even though it may be in a limited way, and they are cared for and protected by their families.

A growing number of severely ill older persons who will not accept commitment to public hospitals are found among the homeless wanderers who live on the streets in our larger cities.

A cliche states that the old are set in their ways—"they are too old to change." Yet at no other time in life are so many drastic changes thrust on one. Included in these changes are loss of spouse; loss of a job with its accompanying role in the community; loss of accustomed income often necessitating changes in activities and sometimes changes in living accommodations; poorer health; and loss of friends and relatives through death or moving.

People who have adjusted to changes in earlier life usually are able to accept these losses and make the necessary changes in attitudes and activities. Others unable to cope with the new situations are unable to find suitable substitutes.

For those who cannot adjust, it is only a short step to becoming isolated, lonely, fearful, suspicious, hypochondriacal, and depressed. The depression is frequently expressed by somatic symptoms. When seen by their physicians, these people are treated for bodily aches and pains and not the underlying depression. In a recent study of seventy-nine elderly clients who were judged to be of risk for nursing home placement, it was discovered that depressive symptomatology was present among 29 percent of the sample.[13]

At the conclusion of an eleven-year study, the National Institute of Mental Health identified two major sociopsychological barriers to good mental health in the later years: (1) the inability to bounce back from psychosocial losses and (2) failure to maintain "meaningful" life goals.

Because withdrawal symptoms are common among the aging population, many families feel it is just a part of "growing old." These conditions do not necessarily have to go uncorrected, for there are mental health organizations that offer services. Social workers, teaming with other professions, work with these individuals to keep them in touch with reality, compensating for their losses in acceptable ways and providing emotional support.

Zoroaster, a Persian prophet of the sixth century B.C., wrote of good mental health:

Nobody grows old merely by living a number of years; people grow old by deserting their ideals. Years wrinkle the skin, but giving up enthusiasm wrinkles the soul. Worry, doubt, self-distrust, fear, and despair—these are the long years that bow the head and turn the growing spirit back to dust. You are as young as your faith, and as old as your doubts, as young as your self-confidence, as old as your fears, as young as your hope, as old as your despair.

The Growing Suicide Rate among the Elderly

In the *Concise Textbook of Clinical Psychiatry,* Kaplan and Sadock offer this information about suicide and the elderly:

Suicide rates increase with age. The significance of the midlife crisis is underscored by suicide rates. Among men, suicides peak after age 45; among women, the greatest number of completed suicides occur after age 55. Rates of 40 per 100,000 population are found in men aged 65 and older. The elderly attempt suicide less often than do younger people but are successful more often. The elderly account for 25 percent of suicides, although they make up only 10 percent of the total population. The rate for those 75 or older is more than three times the rate among the young.[14]

In *The Feeling Good Handbook,* Burns suggests asking the following questions if an elderly family member or friend appears to be especially despondent or discouraged:

1. Have you been feeling sad or unhappy?
2. Do you ever feel hopeless? Does it seem as if things can never get better?
3. Do you have thoughts of death? Do you ever think you'd be better off dead?
4. Do you ever have any actual suicide impulses? Do you have any urge to kill yourself?
5. Do you feel you can resist these impulses, or do they sometimes tempt you?
6. Do you have any actual plan to kill yourself?
7. When do you plan to kill yourself?
8. Is there anything that would hold you back, such as your family or your religious convictions?
9. Have you ever made a suicide attempt in the past?
10. Would you be willing to talk to someone or seek help if you felt desperate? Whom would you talk to?[15]

If an elderly family member or friend answers "yes" to any number of these questions, the threat of suicide may not only be real but imminent. When an elderly person answers "yes" to either question 6 (Do you have any actual plan to kill yourself?) or question 7 (When do you plan to kill yourself?), the threat of suicide may be imminent and appropriate action should be taken. For example, if an elderly person says he has a revolver in the dresser by his bed and most nights he takes the gun out and thinks about shooting himself, the threat of suicide is imminent. A concerned family member may choose to talk the elderly person out of the suicide attempt and his concern may persuade the elderly person not to kill himself. In our opinion, this is putting too much faith in the ability of a family member to talk an elderly person out of suicide. A more prudent approach would be for the family member to express his concern to the elderly person for the emotional pain he must be feeling and strongly encourage him to go with him to the nearest hospital emergency room for professional help. If the elderly person refuses to go, the family member may insist and even add that if the elderly person doesn't go to the hospital with him the family member will call the police and request their assistance. Although this will probably strain the relationship, it is almost always better to err in the name of caution and concern.

If the elderly person answers "no" to both questions 6 and 7, then the threat of suicide is probably not imminent. Even so, multiple "yes" answers to any of the remaining questions in the suicide inventory suggest that the elderly person is probably depressed and could benefit from professional help. Numerous empirical studies have shown that depressed people generally respond very well to medications and talk therapy. The concerned family member should share this fact with the elderly person and encourage him to seek professional help. The family member may take this a step further and let the elderly person know that he will find out about the professional services that are available in the community and talk with him as soon as possible. Often it is wise to be a strong advocate for an elderly person who is depressed. Because of depression, the elderly person often doesn't have the energy or motivation to seek help for himself. A concerned family member is often needed to bridge this gap so the elderly person can receive the professional help he requires.

Independence and Dignity

Senior citizens need to maintain a high degree of independence and self-mastery resulting in self-respect and dignity. As they grow older, people need the reward of a secure place in the world where they have a serene sense of belonging and of adding significantly to society. Dignity and self-worth are qualities the majority of older people are able to maintain.

A retired person must remain an individual, not a statistic, or an anonymous member of the group called "aged." With the power of his or her judgment, knowledge, and skill acquired over the years, he or she has the opportunity to display dynamic maturity, to continue to contribute to society, and to live a satisfying life.

Employment—Retirement

Some gerontologists feel that the changes in one's life at retirement constitute the most critical major adjustment an older person has to make. Even with pensions, individuals too often feel they are being eased out of a job that others think they are no longer capable of performing. Accompanying the loss of a job is the loss of social status that employment gives.

Common mistakes that many people make related to retirement are lack of planning on what to do with time, failure to consider alternative plans, and lack of planning in relation to reduced buying power.

Individuals in their sixties are not old. Many people are urged to retire at a time when they are most valuable to their company or organization. Wisdom that accompanies years of experience cannot be replaced by younger workers who possibly move a little faster.

For those who want to continue working, two factors must be considered: who wants to earn money and who wants to give of their time in public service.

With an increasing number of older people looking for ways to be gainfully employed, some employers are realizing that experienced workers bring skills, knowledge, good judgment, and dependability to their organizations. The Commerce Department estimates that 11 percent of people sixty-five or over are employed either full or part time.

Governmental agencies help older, low-income persons find work. Foster Grandparents help children in institutions who need individual care and love. Green Thumb, Inc. employees work to beautify highways, build parks, and work with conservation programs. Senior Aides provide home health services and homemaker services. Senior Community Service workers help in community action programs.

Two national organizations that offer opportunities for people of any age or financial status are the Peace Corps and Volunteers in Service to America (VISTA). Peace Corps members work overseas in education, agriculture, health, housing, public works, and community development programs, serving a minimum of two years. VISTA members serve in institutions and in impoverished urban and rural communities in the United States.

Bertrand Russell wrote: "It is the great reward of losing youth that one finds oneself able to be of use." For many, retirement brings the first opportunity to spend freely large blocks of time serving others. This can be an exciting adventure to the worker, and his or her contribution may be more valuable than money.

Volunteer work with veterans hospitals, the Red Cross, and welfare and social agencies is largely under the direction of social workers, who maintain active recruiting and training programs for volunteers. Social agencies use volunteers for a wide variety of agency functions, including transportation for clients, entertainment of patients in hospitals and other institutions, shopping for the homebound, tutoring, maintenance work, and various professional and semiprofessional services. Social workers interpret the need for services, develop programs, and direct the activities.

Volunteers are concerned people who want to be busy. They make friends easily, have empathy and sympathy for others, and have a religious conviction of love for their neighbors.

An innovative volunteer program has been developed in the Salt Lake City area by the School of Social Work at the University of Utah and a private businessman. Wilford and Dorothy Goodwill were concerned that many senior citizens were not receiving proper care from agencies in the area because of sheer numbers and lack of proper funding. They were determined to create a cadre of senior volunteers in one specific catchment area of the city who were to become the "eyes and ears" of the neighborhood. These volunteers report problems to social work students who then assess the problems and try to find solutions. The problems range from assigning volunteers to a specific person for friendly visiting to having volunteers paint houses. Senior volunteers from the neighborhood are utilized whenever possible; but if the job becomes too large, volunteers from the university or other segments of the community are recruited.

The social work students who direct this project are well aware of all the resources available, and they link seniors to these services whenever possible. When seniors in the project are not eligible for county or state help, the Goodwill Family Foundation provides the funds to purchase such items as furnaces, roofs, and house paint.

This project is called "Neighbor to Neighbor" and is a culmination of several years of grassroots work and a unique partnership between a state-funded university and a private businessman. The project is still in its infancy, but it holds great potential. Seniors working in this project feel validated as they actively serve others.

George Black, A Peace Corps Volunteer

At retirement, George Black did not abandon his interests and activities, but changed the emphasis and reassessed his values. The sharing of his skills brought satisfaction to him and help to another country.

For more than 80 years, this man has been making bricks by hand in Winston-Salem, North Carolina, his own special way of doing it. He is a master craftsman.

When he came in to see me, he didn't look it but he told me he was 93 years old. But his productive years were not over. So our government, under one of the programs that we fortunately had, sent this remarkable man to a country that needed to learn about that almost forgotten skill of making bricks by hand. George Black went to Guyana, in South America, so that he could share his skills with the people of that less developed country.

When I asked him about his trip, this is what he said: "I have always asked the Lord to let my last days be my best days. I feel like He is answering my prayers."

George Black's prayer is the prayer of millions of Americans—"to let my last days be my best days." And for them, as for him, its answer depends not only on what they are given, but on what they continue to give.

Older Americans have much to give to this country. The best thing this country can give to them is the chance to be a part of it, a chance to play a continuing role in the great American adventure.[16]

Many older persons have discovered that education just for the sake of learning is rewarding. They accept the counsel of Seneca who wrote, "As long as you live, keep learning how to live." Men and women of all educational backgrounds enroll in classes in art, music, foreign languages, and other cultural subjects or in crafts, or sewing or carpentry, or woodworking. Community schools, colleges, and universities beckon with a wide variety of subjects to those interested. Some offer free or reduced tuition to those over sixty-five.

White House Conference on Aging, 1995

Delegates to the White House Conference on Aging in 1995 gave approval for the reauthorization of the Older American's Act with its broad concern for the health and welfare of older citizens.

Reflecting the national debate, delegates focused on the financial and health needs, passing a resolution to preserve Social Security for now and into the future. They opposed arbitrary cuts in Medicare and voted for a resolution that opposes block granting of the Medicaid program. Universal health care and expanded development of home- and community-based long-term-care services were high priorities, as also was medical research into diseases, both mental and physical, of the aging.

For the first time in White House Conference history, they adopted a resolution to provide assistance to grandparents who are primary caregivers for their grandchildren.

Affordable housing in safe neighborhoods was addressed. Resolutions were also passed concerning assuring the dignity and worth of individuals including the right of personal choice and right for education or training for employment if needed.[17]

Older People Are Individuals Too

An increasing number of healthy, competent men and women are joining the ranks of older people in the United States every day. In addition to the basic needs of good housing, adequate income, and medical care, they need to be independent to choose the kinds of activities they pursue. They need to make decisions concerning their lives. Social workers have the responsibility to see that older people are given these opportunities. The more responsibility they take for themselves and the direction of their lives, the longer they will remain interested and be competent to do productive work.

Social workers help. They support the established trend among the elderly to organize and become strong consumer groups. They support their ongoing efforts to maintain and strengthen the income base that provides economic security and financial independence. Schools of social work ally themselves with interdisciplinary efforts to educate and train professionals to address the issues and problems of the elderly. They provide curriculum emphases that will sensitize and assist their graduates in overcoming myths and biases and acquire the expertise that will make it possible for them to shape social policy. The family is the basic institution for helping the elderly population, and the social work role is ancillary to the family. In the words of Elaine Brody,

> Today's adult children provide more care and more difficult care to more elderly parents over longer periods of time than ever before. . . . Most do so willingly. Some go beyond the limits of endurance. . . .
>
> The vast majority of helping services to the aged are provided by the family, not by government, professionals, or agencies . . . only 4 percent of those receiving help with activities of daily living (an intense level of caregiving) received subsidized assistance from the formal system. In fact, all formal services together accounted for less than 15 percent of all "helper days of care. . . ."
>
> Services given by professionals, government, and agencies do not reduce family services; rather, they complement and supplement the family's helping activities. Moreover, when formal services are offered, families are extremely modest in their requests. . . .
>
> The family mobilizes, coordinates, and monitors informal and formal services—which professionals characterize as "case management" and like to think of as their own discovery. . . .
>
> Adult daughters, the main filial caregivers, deal with the multiple demands on their time and energy. . . .
>
> Families do not dump older people into nursing homes. Most often, institutional placement is preceded by prolonged, strenuous, and exhausting efforts to keep the older person in the community.[18]

Joy in Working with Older People

David Soyer, who had extensive experience working with older people, reports the joy and satisfaction received from meeting the needs of these people.

> There is a certain purity about working with the aged, especially those who are beyond the productive years. One does not justify this work on the basis of crime prevention or helping to develop untapped, potentially productive forces or freeing the oppressed so as to ward off summer insurrection or any other instrumental value. One justifies it only on the basis that each human being has value—intrinsic value, the meaning and dignity of being human. So many of our clients we serve for this reason alone. That is why social work is concerned about those in whom our society loses interest.
>
> I believe that working with the aged is one of those fields in social work that, by setting forth the issue so clearly, gives the worker a chance to test, temper, and affirm this core value of our profession. . . .
>
> When one works with younger people and the world is open and one is looking ahead, there can be a terrible striving to make one's client normal within whatever definition the worker has of that concept. In work with the aged the perspective is different. There is a look backward. No longer is there the dream of what life may become, but there is a stark look at what it was. There is a search for the things that gave life meaning. Sometimes they have been big: the coming to America, the founding of a labor union or of a family. Sometimes they are smaller: memories of old baseball stars, of neighborhoods or countrysides as they were long ago, bittersweet thoughts of old business ventures with high hopes and small returns.[19]

Summary

Science, government, industry, education, and the helping professions focus their attention on the 30 million older Americans and their needs. What are their special needs?

1. An adequate income to ensure physical necessities
2. The best possible physical and mental health
3. Suitable housing, whether they live alone or with others
4. Opportunity for employment if they wish to work
5. Retirement in honor and dignity
6. Restorative services for those in institutions
7. Pursuit of meaningful activity
8. Efficient community services for special needs
9. Benefits from research to sustain and improve their health and happiness
10. Freedom, independence, and the free exercise of individual initiative in planning and managing their own lives

Social workers individualize problems and administer the services that preserve the respect and dignity of the older individuals who receive them.

Selected References

BRODY, ELAINE M., *Women in the Middle: Their Parent-Care Years.* New York: Springer, 1990.

BROWNE, COLETTE, V., "Empowerment in Social Work Practice with Older Women," *Social Work,* 40 (May 1995), 358–364.

BUMAGIN, VICTORIA E., and KATHRYN F. HIRN, *Helping the Aging Family: A Guide for Professionals.* Glenview IL: Scott, Foresman, 1990.

COX, ENID O., and RUTH J. PERSONS, *Empowerment-Oriented Social Work Practice with the Elderly.* Pacific Grove, CA: Brooks/Cole, 1993.

DITTRICH, KATHLEEN MCINNIS, *Social Work with Elders: A Biopsychosocial Approach in Assessment and Intervention.* Boston: Allyn & Bacon, 2002.

HOOYMAN, NANCY, and H. AUSMAN KIYAK, *Social Gerontology: A Multidisciplinary Perspective*, 8th ed. Boston: Allyn & Bacon, 2008.

KARGER, HOWARD JACOB, and DAVID STOESZ, *American Social Welfare Policy.* New York: Addison-Wesley Longman, 1998.

MOTENKO, ALUMA KOPITO, and SARAH GREENBERG, "Reframing Dependence in Old Age: A Positive Transition for Families," *Social Work,* 40 (May 1995), 382–390.

Older Americans Act of 1965, as Amended, Text and History. Washington, DC: U.S. Department of Health, Education, and Welfare, 1970.

OZAWA, MARTHA N., "The Economic Well-Being of Elderly People and Children in a Changing Society," *Social Work,* 44 (January 1999), 9–19.

SMITH, ELIZABETH D., "Addressing the Psychospiritual Distress of Death as Reality: A Transpersonal Approach," *Social Work,* 40 (May 1995), 402–413.

YEO, GWEN, and DOLORES GALLAGHER-THOMPSON, eds., *Ethnicity and the Dementias.* Washington, DC: Taylor and Francis, 1996.

Notes

1. Howard Jacob Karger and David Stoesz, *American Social Welfare Policy* (New York: Addison-Wesley Longman, 1998), p. 130.

2. *Older Americans Act of 1965, as Amended, Text and History* (Washington, DC: U.S. Department of Health, Education, and Welfare, 1970).

3. Ibid., p. 2.

4. Elliot Carlson, "We Must Act—And Act Now," *AARP Bulletin* (May 1998), pp. 1, 5, 6.

5. Nancy Kelley, "Keeping Frail, Homebound Elderly in the Community Using an Innovative Approach: Mobile Medical Care Units" (Salt Lake City: University of Utah, unpublished paper, 2000), p. 7.

6. Vanessa Wilson, "The Consequences of Elderly Wives Caring for Disabled Husbands: Implications for Practice," *Social Work,* 35 (September 1990), p. 85.

7. Elaine M. Brody, *Women in the Middle: Their Parent-Care Years* (New York: Springer, 1990), pp. 40–41.

8. Robert Lewis, "Iowa Back to the Future," *AARP Bulletin* (November 1992), pp. 1, 16, 17.

9. Ibid., p. 1.

10. Ibid., p. 16.

11. *NASW News,* 43 (May 1998), p. 1.

12. *NASW News,* 31 (January 1986), p. 3.

13. Anissa Taun Rogers, "Factors Associated with Depression and Low Life Satisfaction in the Low-Income, Frail Elderly" (Salt Lake City: University of Utah, Doctoral Dissertation 1997), p. IV.

14. Harold I. Kaplan and Benjamin J. Sadock, *Concise Textbook of Clinical Psychiatry* (Baltimore: Williams & Wilkins, 1996), p. 361.

15. David D. Burns, *The Feeling Good Handbook* (New York: Plume, 1989), pp. 40–42.

16. *Toward a National Policy on Aging, Proceedings of the 1971 White House Conference on Aging,* Vol. 1 (Washington, DC: U.S. Government Printing Office, 1971), p. 143.

17. *Official 1995 White House Conference on Aging, Adopted Resolutions* (Washington, DC: U.S. Government Printing Office, May 2–5, 1995), pp. 1–3.

18. *NASW News,* 31 (March 1986), p. 9.

19. David Soyer, "Reverie on Working with the Aged," *Social Casework,* 50 (May 1969), pp. 292–294.

16

Drug Abuse and Social Work

Bill was brought to the attention of school social workers when he was 10 years old because he had been caught sniffing glue. He was reprimanded, and he stopped for a time. He moved on to tobacco and occasionally drank beer in junior high. Social workers were again asked to help, but there was no in-depth effort to work through his problems.

During his junior year in high school, Bill discovered marijuana, continued using alcohol, and became engrossed in the use of amphetamines, which were easy to obtain from dealers at the school or by occasionally burglarizing a drugstore.

At the beginning of Bill's senior year the school social worker sought to help him and several others in his group by involving their parents. With individual counseling sessions and regular group therapy meetings with the students alone, parents alone, and all together, they slowly worked their way through problems in communication and relationships. The parents, who were concerned about their children, were able to offer better home relationships, understanding, and support in the boys' efforts to get off the drugs.

There were relapses at test time and when disappointments came from school activities, but the group made progress. At the end of the school year, the group was disbanded, with the social worker expressing confidence that the boys would be able to remain drug free.

During the summer Bill worked and saved his money so that he could go to the local junior college. He was often restless, and his leisure time posed problems for him. But he was determined that he was not going to slip back into his old habits.

As fall approached he showed some signs of anxiety over facing the new school situation, but his parents were not particularly concerned for it had been about five months since his last relapse.

The night before he was to begin classes at the college, he was restless and went out quite late for a walk to relax before going to bed. He never returned. A few blocks from his home was a small drugstore. He climbed the roof, removed a skylight, and was trying to enter the store through a narrow air vent.

He was found dead the next day. His head was hanging down from the ceiling. He had become trapped and ultimately suffocated in his fateful attempt to get high one more time.

Drugs! No other word in the American language has caused more concern to the American people in recent times. All America watched as drugs spilled over the nation in the 1960s. Drugs had long been a problem for large inner cities but have since spread to the suburbs, to high schools, and university campuses in epidemic proportions, affecting all ethnic groups and classes of society.

What was the cause of this "sudden" eruption? There are many hypotheses. The psychological shock caused by unprecedented technological advances, rapid societal changes, and in some cases wealth and in other cases poverty. Each has been reported to have had an impact on attitudes and lifestyles. Mobility and affluence took social activities out of the home and neighborhoods and into the community.

Television advertised pills and remedies for every body ailment, stressing that no one need to be uncomfortable even for a moment. Sponsors wanted one to believe that there was a ready solution to all problems in the home medicine cabinet or at the pharmacy. No one suggested that there were other, lasting solutions to inner stress.

Tranquilizers were prescribed to help the anxious feel calm and stimulants were given to help the depressed become more active. Drugs became the panacea for coping with all of life's stresses. Soon, the illegal manufacturing and distribution of these drugs made their way into the hands of dealers and into the lives of weight-conscious adults and teens, long-haul truck drivers, college students cramming for exams, struggling executives, harried homemakers, and young people looking to "party" after a boring day at school or home.

Disillusioned by the hypocrisy and deceit of some adult leaders, young people in the 1960s and 1970s protested the Vietnam War, political involvement in faraway places, their parents, the police, the "Establishment," and what they perceived as inequality in the laws. Many adopted drugs as a means of refocusing attention and to make themselves heard. The "hippie" culture developed with long hair, beards, dirty jeans, communal living, and "doing one's own thing" attitudes. Marijuana and LSD became the symbol of dissatisfied American youth, and their use quickly spread from communes to young people all across the country.

A leader for the drug culture arose. The articulate Timothy Leary wrote and preached the gospel of drugs. He not only advocated the unrestricted use of drugs, but actively recruited dealers. Blum quotes from an underground press article of 1969 written by Leary:

> I think that this is the noblest of all human professions and would certainly like to urge any creative young person sincerely interested in evolving himself and helping society to grow to consider this ancient and honorable profession. . . . The righteous dealer is . . . selling you the celestial dream . . . he is peddling . . . freedom and joy.[1]

A number of powerful forces continue to influence increasing numbers of youth toward the use and abuse of drugs. Many today use drugs because they do not want to be left out of their peer group. For years, advertising has portrayed the use of recreational drugs (tobacco, alcohol) as pleasurable and socially rewarding. They have been associated with the "good life." Growing up can be difficult and painful and drugs have been found, by many, as a way to temporarily relieve the confusion.

In addition to peer pressure and advertisements, the American society seems to be producing more stress for youth, adults, and families. With the rapid changes being felt by families, due to the increase in divorce rates and blending of families plus the mobility created by an industrialized and technologically based economy, young people and adults have often been led to feel disconnected. Because of these internal and external pressures, many people turn to drugs as a way of coping.

In recent years, cocaine and performance-enhancing steroids have received national attention because they have been linked to the deaths and achievements of young and promising athletes and actors. In fact, the entire world of athletics has struggled with the problems of increased steroid use.

In pursuit of perfection and to gain an advantage, steroids have created problems for many athletes, as was evidenced by the disqualification of a gold-medal winner in the 1988 Olympics. Since then commentators have been referring to more sophisticated methods of using steroids. The concern is raised that athletes are using steroids in training but stopping the practice just in time so that the drug is not detected at the time of drug testing prior to the sporting event.

More recently, it has been found that researchers have been able to change, alter, or develop new types of steroids in order to avoid detection through current methods of drug screening. When better screening methods are introduced, new drugs have already been developed that go undetected. This may be the case with major league baseball in the years leading up to and including 2007 when Barry Bonds broke one of the game's most coveted records, Hank Aaron's lifetime number of home runs, 755. Bonds had been suspected of knowingly using performance enhancing drugs to increase his body mass and strength. If he achieved this milestone aided by the use of steroids many believe at the least he should not be recognized as the all-time home run leader, but at most he should be banned from the game and his records stripped.

Various musical groups also seem to condone the use of drugs through song lyrics and by presenting themselves as individuals who have achieved success while abusing drugs. Both athletes and musicians can provide young people with strong role models that subtly encourage drug abuse.

During the 1980s, First Lady Nancy Reagan championed the "just say no" program. The emphasis was placed on prevention and abstinence beginning with our nation's school-aged children. President Bush tried to combat the problem of drugs by appointing a "drug czar" to coordinate all drug prevention programs as well as oversee the enforcement of drug laws. The effects of their work seemed to have a positive influence on the nation's youth.

President Clinton tried to prevent drug abuse by funding programs for children and youth. He believed that programs such as Headstart would assist children to have a better self-esteem, which in turn would prevent drug abuse. The Clinton administration also allocated money to create employment for teenagers all over the country which it hoped would ameliorate drug abuse. But the positive trends noted with the two previous administrations appeared to slip through most of the 1990s.

Under President George W. Bush, a three-pronged approach has been implemented to combat the national drug problem. Known as *The President's National Drug Control Strategy*,[2] it seeks to help prevent youth from initiating illicit drug use through community antidrug coalitions and antidrug education campaigns; to help with recovery by expanding access to drug treatment programs, increasing drug court programs, and research on addictions and recovery; and to disrupt, dismantle, and prosecute those organizations and persons involved in trafficking illegal drugs.

There were indications that the many programs designed to eliminate drug abuse had been having a positive effect. In December 1990, Louis W. Sullivan, secretary of health and human services, released results of the department's 1990 National Household Survey on Drug Abuse. He stated that the study showed declining use of most illicit drugs by Americans, including a dramatic 45 percent drop in "current" cocaine use (used at least once in the past month). The 1990 survey also found a 44 percent reduction in current use of any illicit drug in the past five years, down from 23 million users in 1985 to 12.9 million in 1990. Secretary Sullivan was pleased to report progress, but he also warned that many pockets of serious drug abuse remain.

In their 1993 National Survey Results on Drug Use, Johnston, O'Malley, and Bachman recognized the fact that even though there had been appreciable declines in the use of a number of the illicit drugs among seniors in high school, college students, and young adults, worrying new data signaled problems ahead. They wrote

> While the general decline resumed in 1986 and, most importantly, was joined by the start of a decline in cocaine use in 1987 and crack use in 1988, in 1992 we heard a number of alarm bells sounding. While the seniors continued to show improvement on a number of measures in 1992, the college students and young adults did not. Further, the attitudes and beliefs of seniors regarding drug use began to soften. Perhaps of greatest importance, the eighth graders exhibited a significant increase in marijuana, cocaine, LSD, and hallucinogens other than LSD, as well as a not-quite significant increase in inhalant use.[3]

By 1995, the National Survey Results found further discouraging evidence of an increase in the use of a number of illicit drugs among secondary students and some reversals with regard to key attitudes and beliefs. Illicit drug use rose sharply again in 1995 in all three grade levels (eighth, tenth, and twelfth). Further, negative attitudes and beliefs about drugs continued to erode. These recent findings on illicit drug use signified a continuation of the 1993 and 1994 surveys, with marijuana rising sharply among secondary students and a more gradual rise noted with other illicit drugs.[4]

The late 1990s survey results found that the use of marijuana peaked for eighth graders in 1996. It was a year later for tenth and twelfth graders. The use of marijuana has declined for eighth graders since 1996, but no significant reduction has been noted in tenth and twelfth graders. Whereas the use of some drugs remained at a constant rate, more recent data showed a rise in others. MDMA (ecstasy) had the highest increase of all drugs. Often referred to as the "club drug" and used at "raves," its greatest use is found among older teens. It is now more prevalent than cocaine among American youths. The other drugs found to be on the rise were steroids (sharp increase in younger males in 1999) and heroin (increased in twelfth graders). Drugs on the decline since the mid-1990s were inhalants, LSD, crystal meth, and Rohypnol.[5]

The surveys of eighth-, tenth-, and twelfth-grade students in the United States, beginning with the new millennium again began showing positive signs. The surveys "in

2002 and 2003 generated a more positive picture than was seen in recent years. Quite a number of illicit drugs showed broad declines this year—most notably marijuana and ecstasy . . . of the illicit drugs, perhaps the most significant change in 2003 was the drop in use of ecstasy in all three grades."[6] The researchers believed that efforts at the national level helped bring about these improvements. "The Partnership for a Drug-Free America, in conjunction with the Office of National Drug Control Policy, launched an anti-ecstasy advertising campaign in January 2002. In addition to normal news coverage of some consequences of ecstasy use by young people, this campaign may well have contributed to the important downturn in use of the drug."[7]

In the findings reported in 2006, a number of drugs held steady whereas a number of others showed modest one-year declines. The declines were not statistically significant, yet they continued to follow the pattern that began after 1995. Only four classes of drugs showed any increases in the previous year. They were inhalants, Vicodin, OxyContin, and ecstasy. Further, these increases were found in only one or two grades, not across all groups (see Table 16.1).[8]

Misused Drugs and What They Do

By affecting the central nervous system, drugs produce a change in the behavior, emotional responses, and thought processes of the abuser. Repeated use may develop into an addiction (the compulsive use of a drug or substance despite the negative consequences). Addiction is characterized by physical dependence (when the body tissues require the presence of the drug to function normally) and psychological dependence (when a person believes he or she needs the chemical in the body in order to feel and think normally). All psychoactive drugs have an element of psychological dependence, but not all have the capacity to develop physical dependence, as is the case with LSD.

The major classes of drugs that have the potential for abuse are broadly categorized as narcotics, stimulants, depressants, hallucinogens, marijuana, inhalants, and steroids.

Narcotics

Narcotics are used medically to kill pain and suppress coughs. Opium, heroin, morphine, codeine, synthetic opiates, OxyContin Vicodin, Dilaudid, Percodan, methadone, Darvon, Demerol, and Talwin are classified as narcotics. In addition to their medical uses, these drugs have a euphoric effect which is why they are used as recreational drugs. They also have a sedating effect. Prolonged or incorrect use can lead to physical and psychological dependence and tolerance.

Stimulants

Stimulants, principally amphetamines (methedrine, methamphetamine, dexedrine, and dextromethamphetamine) cocaine (crack, coke), Ritalin and Cylert, and the over-the-counter products containing caffeine (NoDoz, Alert, Vivarin), along with coffee, tea, and

TABLE 16.1   Trends in Lifetime Prevalence of Use of Various Drugs for Eighth, Tenth, and Twelfth Graders (Entries are percentages)

	Lifetime																'05–'06 CHANGE
	1991	1992	1993	1994	1995	1996	1997	1998	1999	2000	2001	2002	2003	2004	2005	2006	
Any Illicit Drug																	
8th Grade	18.7	20.6	22.5	25.7	28.5	31.2	29.4	29.0	28.3	26.8	26.8	24.5	22.8	21.5	21.4	20.9	−0.5
10th Grade	30.6	29.8	32.8	37.4	40.9	45.4	47.3	44.9	46.2	45.6	45.6	44.6	41.4	39.8	38.2	36.1	−2.1
12th Grade	44.1	40.7	42.9	45.6	48.4	50.8	54.3	54.1	54.7	54.0	53.9	53.0	51.1	51.1	50.4	48.2	−2.2
Any Illicit Drug Other Than Marijuana																	
8th Grade	14.3	15.6	16.8	17.5	18.8	19.2	17.7	16.9	16.3	15.8‡	17.0	13.7	13.6	12.2	12.1	12.2	+0.1
10th Grade	19.1	19.2	20.9	21.7	24.3	25.5	25.0	23.6	24.0	23.1‡	23.6	22.1	19.7	18.8	18.0	17.5	−0.5
12th Grade	26.9	25.1	26.7	27.6	28.1	28.5	30.0	29.4	29.4	29.0‡	30.7	29.5	27.7	28.7	27.4	26.9	−0.4
Any Illicit Drug Including Inhalants																	
8th Grade	28.5	29.6	32.3	35.1	38.1	39.4	38.1	37.8	37.2	35.1	34.5	31.6	30.3	30.2	30.0	29.2	−0.7
10th Grade	36.1	36.2	38.7	42.7	45.9	49.8	50.9	49.3	49.9	49.3	48.8	47.7	44.9	43.1	42.1	40.1	−2.0
12th Grade	47.6	44.4	46.6	49.1	51.5	53.5	56.3	56.1	56.3	57.0	56.0	54.6	52.8	53.0	53.5	51.2	−2.4
Marijuana/Hashish																	
8th Grade	10.2	11.2	12.6	16.7	19.9	23.1	22.6	22.2	22.0	20.3	20.4	19.2	17.5	16.3	16.5	15.7	−0.8
10th Grade	23.4	21.4	24.4	30.4	34.1	39.8	42.3	39.6	40.9	40.3	40.1	38.7	36.4	35.1	34.1	31.8	−2.3 s
12th Grade	36.7	32.6	35.3	38.2	41.7	44.9	49.6	49.1	49.7	48.8	49.0	47.8	46.1	45.7	44.8	42.3	−2.5
Inhalants																	
8th Grade	17.6	17.4	19.4	19.9	21.6	21.2	21.0	20.5	19.7	17.9	17.1	15.2	15.8	17.3	17.1	16.1	−0.9
10th Grade	15.7	16.6	17.5	18.0	19.0	19.3	18.3	18.3	17.0	16.6	15.2	13.5	12.7	12.4	13.1	13.3	+0.3
12th Grade	17.6	16.6	17.4	17.7	17.4	16.6	16.1	15.2	15.4	14.2	13.0	11.7	11.2	10.9	11.4	11.1	−0.2
Nitrites																	
8th Grade	—	—	—	—	—	—	—	—	—	—	—	—	—	—	—	—	—
10th Grade	—	—	—	—	—	—	—	—	—	—	—	—	—	—	—	—	—
12th Grade	1.6	1.5	1.4	1.7	1.5	1.8	2.0	2.7	1.7	0.8	1.9	1.5	1.6	1.3	1.1	1.2	0.0

(Continued)

TABLE 16.1 Continued

| | | | | | | | | | | Lifetime | | | | | | | | '05–'06 |
	1991	1992	1993	1994	1995	1996	1997	1998	1999	2000	2001	2002	2003	2004	2005	2006	CHANGE
Hallucinogens																	
8th Grade	3.2	3.8	3.9	4.3	5.2	5.9	5.4	4.9	4.8	4.6‡	5.2	4.1	4.0	3.5	3.8	3.4	−0.4
10th Grade	6.1	6.4	6.8	8.1	9.3	10.5	10.5	9.8	9.7	8.9‡	8.9	7.8	6.9	6.4	5.8	6.1	+0.3
12th Grade	9.6	9.2	10.9	11.4	12.7	14.0	15.1	14.1	13.7	13.0‡	14.7	12.0	10.6	9.7	8.8	8.3	−0.5
LSD																	
8th Grade	2.7	3.2	3.5	3.7	4.4	5.1	4.7	4.1	4.1	3.9	3.4	2.5	2.1	1.8	1.9	1.6	−0.3
10th Grade	5.6	5.8	6.2	7.2	8.4	9.4	9.5	8.5	8.5	7.6	6.3	5.0	3.5	2.8	2.5	2.7	+0.3
12th Grade	8.8	8.6	10.3	10.5	11.7	12.6	13.6	12.6	12.2	11.1	10.9	8.4	5.9	4.6	3.5	3.3	−0.2
Hallucinogens Other Than LSD																	
8th Grade	1.4	1.7	1.7	2.2	2.5	3.0	2.6	2.5	2.4	2.3‡	3.9	3.3	3.2	3.0	3.3	2.8	−0.4
10th Grade	2.2	2.5	2.8	3.8	3.9	4.7	4.8	5.0	4.7	4.8‡	6.6	6.3	5.9	5.8	5.2	5.5	+0.2
12th Grade	3.7	3.3	3.9	4.9	5.4	6.8	7.5	7.1	6.7	6.9‡	10.4	9.2	9.0	8.7	8.1	7.8	−0.4
PCP																	
8th Grade	—	—	—	—	—	—	—	—	—	—	—	—	—	—	—	—	—
10th Grade	—	—	—	—	—	—	—	—	—	—	—	—	—	—	—	—	—
12th Grade	2.9	2.4	2.9	2.8	2.7	4.0	3.9	3.9	3.4	3.4	3.5	3.1	2.5	1.6	2.4	2.2	−0.2
MDMA (Ecstasy)																	
8th Grade	—	—	—	—	—	3.4	3.2	2.7	2.7	4.3	5.2	4.3	3.2	2.8	2.8	2.5	−0.3
10th Grade	—	—	—	—	—	5.6	5.7	5.1	6.0	7.3	8.0	6.6	5.4	4.3	4.0	4.5	+0.5
12th Grade	—	—	—	—	—	6.1	6.9	5.8	8.0	11.0	11.7	10.5	8.3	7.5	5.4	6.5	+1.1
Cocaine																	
8th Grade	2.3	2.9	2.9	3.6	4.2	4.5	4.4	4.6	4.7	4.5	4.3	3.6	3.6	3.4	3.7	3.4	−0.3
10th Grade	4.1	3.3	3.6	4.3	5.0	6.5	7.1	7.2	7.7	6.9	5.7	6.1	5.1	5.4	5.2	4.8	−0.4
12th Grade	7.8	6.1	6.1	5.9	6.0	7.1	8.7	9.3	9.8	8.6	8.2	7.8	7.7	8.1	8.0	8.5	+0.5

TABLE 16.1 *Continued*

									Lifetime								
	1991	1992	1993	1994	1995	1996	1997	1998	1999	2000	2001	2002	2003	2004	2005	2006	'05–'06 CHANGE
Crack																	
8th Grade	1.3	1.6	1.7	2.4	2.7	2.9	2.7	3.2	3.1	3.1	3.0	2.5	2.5	2.4	2.4	2.3	−0.2
10th Grade	1.7	1.5	1.8	2.1	2.8	3.3	3.6	3.9	4.0	3.7	3.1	3.6	2.7	2.6	2.5	2.2	−0.3
12th Grade	3.1	2.6	2.6	3.0	3.0	3.3	3.9	4.4	4.6	3.9	3.7	3.8	3.6	3.9	3.5	3.5	+0.1
Other Cocaine																	
8th Grade	2.0	2.4	2.4	3.0	3.4	3.8	3.5	3.7	3.8	3.5	3.3	2.8	2.7	2.6	2.9	2.7	−0.3
10th Grade	3.8	3.0	3.3	3.8	4.4	5.5	6.1	6.4	6.8	6.0	5.0	5.2	4.5	4.8	4.6	4.3	−0.2
12th Grade	7.0	5.3	5.4	5.2	5.1	6.4	8.2	8.4	8.8	7.7	7.4	7.0	6.7	7.3	7.1	7.9	+0.8
Heroin																	
8th Grade	1.2	1.4	1.4	2.0	2.3	2.4	2.1	2.3	2.3	1.9	1.7	1.6	1.6	1.6	1.5	1.4	0.0
10th Grade	1.2	1.2	1.3	1.5	1.7	2.1	2.1	2.3	2.3	2.2	1.7	1.8	1.5	1.5	1.5	1.4	−0.1
12th Grade	0.9	1.2	1.1	1.2	1.6	1.8	2.1	2.0	2.0	2.4	1.8	1.7	1.5	1.5	1.5	1.4	−0.1
With a Needle																	
8th Grade	—	—	—	—	1.5	1.6	1.3	1.4	1.6	1.1	1.2	1.0	1.0	1.1	1.0	1.0	0.0
10th Grade	—	—	—	—	1.0	1.1	1.1	1.2	1.3	1.0	0.8	1.0	0.9	0.8	0.8	0.9	0.0
12th Grade	—	—	—	—	0.7	0.8	0.9	0.8	0.9	0.8	0.7	0.8	0.7	0.7	0.9	0.8	−0.1
Without a Needle																	
8th Grade	—	—	—	—	1.5	1.6	1.4	1.5	1.4	1.3	1.1	1.0	1.1	1.0	0.9	0.9	0.0
10th Grade	—	—	—	—	1.1	1.7	1.7	1.7	1.6	1.7	1.3	1.3	1.0	1.1	1.1	1.0	−0.1
12th Grade	—	—	—	—	1.4	1.7	2.1	1.6	1.8	2.4	1.5	1.6	1.8	1.4	1.3	1.1	−0.2
Other Narcotics																	
8th Grade	—	—	—	—	—	—	—	—	—	—	—	—	—	—	—	—	—
10th Grade	—	—	—	—	—	—	—	—	—	—	—	—	—	—	—	—	—
12th Grade	6.6	6.1	6.4	6.6	7.2	8.2	9.7	9.8	10.2	10.6	9.9‡	13.5	13.2	13.5	12.8	13.4	+0.6
Amphetamines																	
8th Grade	10.5	10.8	11.8	12.3	13.1	13.5	12.3	11.3	10.7	9.9	10.2	8.7	8.4	7.5	7.4	7.3	−0.2
10th Grade	13.2	13.1	14.9	15.1	17.4	17.7	17.0	16.0	15.7	15.7	16.0	14.9	13.1	11.9	11.1	11.2	+0.1
12th Grade	15.4	13.9	15.1	15.7	15.3	15.3	16.5	16.4	16.3	15.6	16.2	16.8	14.4	15.0	13.1	12.4	−0.6

(Continued)

TABLE 16.1 *Continued*

									Lifetime									
	1991	1992	1993	1994	1995	1996	1997	1998	1999	2000	2001	2002	2003	2004	2005	2006	'05–'06 CHANGE
Methamphetamine																	
8th Grade	—	—	—	—	—	—	—	—	4.5	4.2	4.4	3.5	3.9	2.5	3.1	2.7	−0.3
10th Grade	—	—	—	—	—	—	—	—	7.3	6.9	6.4	6.1	5.2	5.3	4.1	3.2	−0.8
12th Grade	—	—	—	—	—	—	—	—	8.2	7.9	6.9	6.7	6.2	6.2	4.5	4.4	−0.1
Ice																	
8th Grade	—	—	—	—	—	—	—	—	—	—	—	—	—	—	—	—	—
10th Grade	—	—	—	—	—	—	—	—	—	—	—	—	—	—	—	—	—
12th Grade	3.3	2.9	3.1	3.4	3.9	4.4	4.4	5.3	4.8	4.0	4.1	4.7	3.9	4.0	4.0	3.4	−0.6
Sedatives (Barbiturates)																	
8th Grade	—	—	—	—	—	—	—	—	—	—	—	—	—	—	—	—	—
10th Grade	—	—	—	—	—	—	—	—	—	—	—	—	—	—	—	—	—
12th Grade	6.2	5.5	6.3	7.0	7.4	7.6	8.1	8.7	8.9	9.2	8.7	9.5	8.8	9.9	10.5	10.2	−0.3
Methaqualone																	
8th Grade	—	—	—	—	—	—	—	—	—	—	—	—	—	—	—	—	—
10th Grade	—	—	—	—	—	—	—	—	—	—	—	—	—	—	—	—	—
12th Grade	1.3	1.6	0.8	1.4	1.2	2.0	1.7	1.6	1.8	0.8	1.1	1.5	1.0	1.3	1.3	1.2	−0.1
Tranquilizers																	
8th Grade	3.8	4.1	4.4	4.6	4.5	5.3	4.8	4.6	4.4	4.4‡	5.0	4.3	4.4	4.0	4.1	4.3	+0.3
10th Grade	5.8	5.9	5.7	5.4	6.0	7.1	7.3	7.8	7.9	8.0‡	9.2	8.8	7.8	7.3	7.1	7.2	+0.2
12th Grade	7.2	6.0	6.4	6.6	7.1	7.2	7.8	8.5	9.3	8.9‡	10.3	11.4	10.2	10.6	9.9	10.3	+0.4
Rohypnol																	
8th Grade	—	—	—	—	—	1.5	1.1	1.4	1.3	1.0	1.1	0.8	1.0	1.0	1.1	1.0	0.0
10th Grade	—	—	—	—	—	1.5	1.7	2.0	1.8	1.3	1.5	1.3	1.0	1.2	1.0	0.8	−0.2
12th Grade	—	—	—	—	—	1.2	1.8	3.0	2.0	1.5	1.7	—	—	—	—	—	—

TABLE 16.1 *Continued*

									Lifetime									'05–'06 CHANGE
	1991	1992	1993	1994	1995	1996	1997	1998	1999	2000	2001	2002	2003	2004	2005	2006	
Alcohol Any Use																	
8th Grade	70.1	69.3‡	55.7	55.8	54.5	55.3	53.8	52.5	52.1	51.7	50.5	47.0	45.6	43.9	41.0	40.5	−0.6
10th Grade	83.8	82.3‡	71.6	71.1	70.5	71.8	72.0	69.8	70.6	71.4	70.1	66.9	66.0	64.2	63.2	61.5	−1.7
12th Grade	88.0	87.5‡	80.0	80.4	80.7	79.2	81.7	81.4	80.0	80.3	79.7	78.4	76.6	76.8	75.1	72.7	−2.4 s
Been Drunk																	
8th Grade	26.7	26.8	26.4	25.9	25.3	26.8	25.2	24.8	24.8	25.1	23.4	21.3	20.3	19.9	19.5	19.5	0.0
10th Grade	50.0	47.7	47.9	47.2	46.9	48.5	49.4	46.7	48.9	49.3	48.2	44.0	42.4	42.3	42.1	41.4	−0.7
12th Grade	65.4	63.4	62.5	62.9	63.2	61.8	64.2	62.4	62.3	62.3	63.9	61.6	58.1	60.3	57.5	56.4	−1.0
Flavored Alcoholic Beverages																	
8th Grade	—	—	—	—	—	—	—	—	—	—	—	—	—	37.9	35.5	35.5	0.0
10th Grade	—	—	—	—	—	—	—	—	—	—	—	—	—	58.6	58.8	58.1	−0.7
12th Grade	—	—	—	—	—	—	—	—	—	—	—	—	—	71.0	73.6	69.9	−3.7
Cigarettes Any Use																	
8th Grade	44.0	45.2	45.3	46.1	46.4	49.2	47.3	45.7	44.1	40.5	36.6	31.4	28.4	27.9	25.9	24.6	−1.3
10th Grade	55.1	53.5	56.3	56.9	57.6	61.2	60.2	57.7	57.6	55.1	52.8	47.4	43.0	40.7	38.9	36.1	−2.8 ss
12th Grade	63.1	61.8	61.9	62.0	64.2	63.5	65.4	65.3	64.6	62.5	61.0	57.2	53.7	52.8	50.0	47.1	−2.9 s
Smokeless Tobacco																	
8th Grade	22.2	20.7	18.7	19.9	20.0	20.4	16.8	15.0	14.4	12.8	11.7	11.2	11.3	11.0	10.1	10.2	+0.1
10th Grade	28.2	26.6	28.1	29.2	27.6	27.4	26.3	22.7	20.4	19.1	19.5	16.9	14.6	13.8	14.5	15.0	+0.6
12th Grade	—	32.4	31.0	30.7	30.9	29.8	25.3	26.2	23.4	23.1	19.7	18.3	17.0	16.7	17.5	15.2	−2.3
Steroids																	
8th Grade	1.9	1.7	1.6	2.0	2.0	1.8	1.8	2.3	2.7	3.0	2.8	2.5	2.5	1.9	1.7	1.6	−0.1
10th Grade	1.8	1.7	1.7	1.8	2.0	1.8	2.0	2.0	2.7	3.5	3.5	3.5	3.0	2.4	2.0	1.8	−0.3
12th Grade	2.1	2.1	2.0	2.4	2.3	1.9	2.4	2.7	2.9	2.5	3.7	4.0	3.5	3.4	2.6	2.7	+0.1

Source: The Monitoring the Future Study, the University of Michigan.

Notes: Level of significance of difference between the two most recent classes: s = .05, ss = .01, sss = .001

'—' indicates data not available.

‡ indicates some change in the question.

Any apparent inconsistency between the change estimate and the prevalence of use estimates for the two most recent classes is due to rounding error.

Drug abuse paraphernalia.

some soda drinks (colas), are central nervous system stimulants. Users will experience an increase in heart rate, blood pressure, alertness, respiration, and motor activity (speech, arms, hands, and leg movement). Almost all the drugs in this class are taken for recreational use because they give a feeling of energy and euphoria plus a sense of self-confidence. Side effects of these drugs are the loss of appetite and an increase in energy. For this reason, people wishing to lose weight or stay up for long periods take amphetamines.

Tobacco is one of the most abused of all drugs. Nicotine, an active ingredient of tobacco, is a stimulant. When tobacco smoke is inhaled, it causes the heart to beat faster and blood pressure to elevate. Tar in smoke causes cancer and such respiratory disorders as shortness of breath, coughing, and cardiovascular difficulties. The agents in smoke are a cause of serious health problems such as arteriosclerosis, emphysema, chronic bronchitis, heart disease, lung cancer, and cancer to other parts of the body. Women who smoke during pregnancy run the risk of having babies who weigh less, and they more frequently lose the offspring through stillbirth or death soon after birth.

Depressants—Sedatives—Hypnotics

Depressants act as a tranquilizing or calming agent. They induce sedation and drowsiness and may cause a coma. This class of drugs is the most commonly abused and include alcohol, antianxiety drugs (also referred to as benzodiazepines—Valium, Librium, Xanax, Ativan, Dalmane, and Halcion), sleeping medications (also referred to as barbiturates—Seconal,

Nembutal, Tuinal, Amytal, and Phenobarbital), nonbarbiturates (Doriden, Quaalude, Miltown, and Equinil), and over-the-counter sleep aids (Nytol and Sominex).

Low doses cause muscle relaxation, calmness, and a reduction in anxiety. At high doses one will experience a staggering gait, slurred speech, and drowsiness. Taken in large quantities, they may also cause death.

Recently, the drug Rohypnol (Roofies), a benzodiazepine, has been in the news. It is also known as the "date rape" drug. It is given to unknowing women in their drinks. Combined with alcohol, it produces disinhibition and amnesia.[9]

Alcohol is generally socially accepted, even though alcoholism is one of the most prevalent addictions and a major health problem in this country. Some of the long-term effects of alcoholism include:

- Liver damage, especially cirrhosis (scarring of the liver); alcoholic hepatitis (symptoms include fever, jaundice, and abdominal pain); cancer of the liver.
- Heart problems including high blood pressure, congestive heart failure.
- Ulcers and gastritis, due to irritation of the stomach lining by alcohol.
- Malnutrition, because alcohol has no food value. Alcohol robs the body of some vitamins and minerals and interferes with digestion of food.
- "DTs" (delirium tremens), resulting from alcohol withdrawal, characterized by disorientation, memory impairment, and sometimes hallucinations.
- Pancreatitis (inflamation of the pancreas).
- Cancer of the mouth, esophagus, throat, voice box, colon, and rectum. Women are at a slight risk for breast cancer.
- Brain damage, some types of strokes leading to dementia.
- Damage to developing fetus when mother drinks while she is pregnant (fetal alcohol syndrome). [10,11]

One of the findings resulting from research on the effects of alcohol has to do with fetal alcohol syndrome and fetal alcohol effects. These conditions are characterized by physical deformity and abnormality, impulsiveness, and mental retardation; it results when the mother drinks during pregnancy. Some authorities believe that the effects of alcohol on the fetus are more damaging than thalidomide. The surgeon general's office advises women to abstain from any alcohol during pregnancy.

Hallucinogens

Hallucinogens are mind-altering drugs that affect sensory perception (visual, auditory, olfactory, gustatory, and/or tactile). People also report having an altered awareness of their thoughts and impulses (depersonalization, delusions, and hallucinations). Drugs in this category include LSD, psilocybin (magic mushrooms), mescaline, STP (serenity, tranquility, peace), MDMA (ecstasy), Ketamine (Special K, Vitamin K), and PCP (angel dust).

It is well known that users of LSD may experience "flashbacks." They may be experienced many years after the drug has no longer been ingested. "Bad trips" resulting from flashbacks may result in the person's harming himself or herself or others.

Marijuana

The most controversial drug in use is marijuana, known to humans for nearly 5,000 years, but one of the least understood of all natural drugs. The dried flowers and leaves of the cannabis plant when smoked affect the user's mood and thinking.

Marijuana has been classified by itself because of the variation in effects experienced by those who use it. Under different doses and conditions the user may experience hallucinogenic, sedative, or stimulant effects. Use interferes with a person's reaction time and motor skills that can impede the ability to handle vehicles and machines. Users report experiencing a dreamlike effect and a sense of feeling detached. It has also been reported to cause amotivation (apathy or lack of having goals).

The psychoactive ingredient of marijuana is the chemical THC. The amount of THC that a person ingests determines the potency. THC is fat-soluable (it binds to fat in the body) and may take one to three months to be completely eliminated from the body.[12]

Over the years, research has found that in some people marijuana use can develop into dependence and it is also believed to cause symptoms associated with withdrawal. However, because marijuana is slowly eliminated from the body the effects from withdrawal are experienced to a lesser degree when compared to other drugs and alcohol. This is something past researchers believed to not have happened. In addition to dependence, the following short- and long-term effects have been identified:

Short-term
- Problems with memory and learning
- Distorted perceptions (sights, sounds, time, and touch)
- Trouble thinking and problem solving
- Loss of motor coordination
- Increased heart rate

Long-term
- Impaired lung function similar to that found in cigarette smokers (with more serious effects following extended use)
- Decreased sperm count and sperm motility
- Interference with ovulation and prenatal development
- Impaired immune response
- Cancer
- Possible adverse effects on heart function
- By-products of marijuana remain in the body fat for several weeks with unknown consequences [13,14]

Inhalants

Inhalants come in the form of aerosol sprays, petroleum, and solvents (gasoline, kerosene, airplane glue, aerosols contained in some spray cans, paint thinner and paint remover, metallic paints, nail polish remover, and some typewriter correction fluids, to name but a few). Nitrites (amyl nitrite, butyl, and isobutyl) and nitrous oxide are also included in this class of drugs.

These products are inhaled and create a feeling of euphoria, slurred speech, and dizziness. An overdose can cause hallucinations, irregular heartbeat, headaches, coma, and ultimately death.

Steroids

Steroids are synthetic drugs used to increase muscle and athletic performance. They mimic the male hormone testosterone. In 1990, Congress enacted the Anabolic Steroids Act which regulates the use of this drug. Some steroids are approved for medical use. Those approved in the United States are Halotestin, Danocrine, Depo-Testosterone, and Durabolin.[15] Some individuals are willing to use steroids produced for animals.

Negative side effects include atrophy of the testicles, decrease in sperm production, early baldness, acne, and enlarged breasts in males. Females find an increase in facial and body hair, irregular or absence of menses, and lowered voice. There is the risk of coronary heart disease and mood swings including anger and rage.

Extent and Cost of Drug Abuse

It is extremely difficult to estimate the number of persons who are abusing drugs. Through controlled surveys it is estimated that there are as many as 20 million users of marijuana in this country. Marijuana is used much more than any other drug except alcohol. Surveys in schools show that between 20 and 30 percent of the students have used marijuana at least once and indicate varying rates of use of other drugs. Many reporting use in college started in high school, and an increasing number reported starting in junior high.

Estimates are that 10 percent of the 66 million children under eighteen live in homes that abuse drugs. Two-thirds of child abuse and neglect deaths are related to substance abuse. A Boston hospital reported that 69 percent of babies born to mothers who were chronic drinkers are born with one or more mental or physical deformities. Fetal alcohol syndrome (deformities of infants born to drinking mothers) is a major and growing health problem.

Many people involved in drug abuse are lost as productive members of society. They often suffer poor health, and their families endure emotional conflicts and financial loss. In addition, drug abuse pours millions of dollars into organized crime, society loses hundreds of thousands of dollars' worth of property, and the taxpayer pays to reclaim the abusers. The impact on the U.S. economy for alcohol and drug abuse in 1992 was estimated to be $245.7 billion. Included in this estimate were the costs for treatment, prevention, loss of job productivity, as well as crime and related health care. Of this total, $97.7 billion was believed to be directly related to drug abuse.[16]

More deaths and accidents occur as the result of alcohol than from other drugs. Half of all highway fatalities, nearly half of all arrests, half of all homicides, and one out of three suicides are alcohol-related. The suffering of families is not measurable.

Opium, marijuana, alcohol, and cocaine have been known since the earliest recorded times. More than 600 new drugs have been put on the market since 1940, many of them with abuse potential.

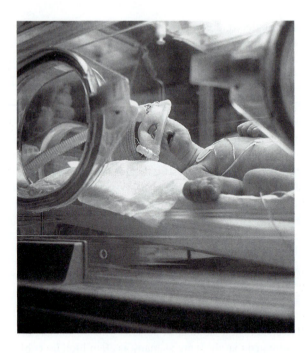

*Drug abuse in pregnancy can
cause serious birth defects.*

Research has found that a person abusing one drug is likely to abuse others, because he or she may be exposed to a variety through other abusers and sellers, and because of the potential for addiction.

Table 16.1 shows the trends in drug use among junior and senior high school students over the past decade. Generally, illicit drug use increased throughout the 1990s and has begun to decline since the year 1996.

Programs for Control, Prevention, Treatment

Before the 1960s the problems connected with drugs mainly concerned law enforcement officers. There was little effort to cure or rehabilitate addicts, for their numbers were few and it was believed that once a person was addicted there was little that could be done for him or her.

But when the problem assumed epidemic proportions, and especially when it reached the suburbs, a now concerned public began to look for ways of stopping the spread of drug use, of salvaging the victims, and of restoring the families. To accomplish this task takes the combined efforts of a concerned community—law enforcement, the medical profession, schools, legislators, and social agencies—all working toward a common goal.

Government Agencies

The Bureau of Narcotics and Dangerous Drugs (BNDD) was established in 1968 to control the illicit use of narcotics and dangerous drugs through law enforcement, education, training, and research. It supports the efforts of state and local governments and gives aid to industry, universities, and others concerned with drug abuse. It is responsible for the enforcement of laws relating to narcotics, marijuana, depressants, stimulants, and hallucinogens. It also controls the legal trade in narcotics but ensures an adequate supply for medicinal purposes and research.[17]

As mentioned previously in this chapter, the first President Bush designated William Bennett as a "drug czar" with wide-ranging powers to coordinate the prevention, treatment, and law enforcement aspects of drug abuse. The 1989 Congress passed a bill allocating $9.4 billion to fund all aspects of the struggle against drugs. It was hoped that the high visibility of this cabinet position, the extra money, the president's sanction, and an aroused society would produce positive results. The Clinton administration continued the effort to address drug abuse by increased funding for drug prevention programs and by giving an economic boost to families in poverty and their children in the form of new job opportunities. President Clinton also tried to develop a sense of hope and self-esteem in vulnerable families throughout the country. He believed that this plan would address the causes of substance abuse. President George W. Bush, along with John P. Walters, director of National Drug Policy, have continued to support efforts to reduce drug use by implementing a balanced approach in national policy. Efforts are being made to increase access to treatment, to prevent drug abuse through community action and advertising, and to disrupt those people and organizations involved in the trafficking of illegal drugs.

Facilities already established—schools, social services, health organizations, and law enforcement agencies—form the basis for a community's program. Special clinics that focus on drug treatment are necessary and are described later in this chapter.

Programs involving social work can be classified according to the following general categories: (1) to head off abuse before it begins, (2) to treat the victims and their families, and (3) to alleviate social conditions that breed abuse.

Education

To solve the drug problem, emphasis must be given to prevention. Social workers in schools and social agencies need to be alert to conditions that make for potential drug abuse and take necessary steps to correct these circumstances.

Social workers help in the prevention and education program that includes, but is not limited to, the following:

- Teaching about drug abuse in the classroom, beginning in elementary grades
- Arranging for groups to hear credible speakers
- Sponsoring adult education classes
- Helping business and industry take advantage of educational opportunities
- Training professionals and paraprofessionals who work with drug abusers
- Making information readily available to the public

Changes that might be made in high schools to make schooling more appealing than drugs include providing credit for students who work on community projects, promoting greater involvement in their own learning and school administration, making vocational education programs relevant, and providing recreational facilities for leisure time. An effective preventive tool used in many high schools is the work of peer self-help groups. Students from a wide range of social and economic groups are taught how to reach all the students—with emphasis on those who appear to be vulnerable—to help them remain drug free.

Recognizing that drug abusers are people with personal problems, and that these problems often originate in the family interaction, many school districts are developing family life education programs that extend from kindergarten through high school. Successful programs relate drug abuse to self-understanding, interpersonal and family relationships, and the role of the family in society.

Just as young people like to talk with their peers, so do parents appreciate opportunities for talking with other parents. In groups they learn about drugs and also have the supportive contact of other parents who may have problems similar to their own. With imagination, leaders, who are often social workers, use role playing, small discussion groups, films, and lectures.

Treatment

Community programs generally give high priority to treatment facilities for drug abusers. Social and psychiatric services have been combined with medicine in treatment. Therapeutic services include psychotherapy, family therapy, medical and chemical treatment, and individual and group counseling.

Because there are differences in the treatment approach to the different drugs used, a variety of modalities have been developed for abusers. A method of treatment that works well for one may not be effective for another. Treatment centers for drug abusers include emergency care, inpatient services, outpatient clinics, chemical therapy, therapeutic communities, and referral services. Social workers are important members of the teams of professionals who staff these services.

Emergency Care

Provisions for emergency medical and nonmedical help need to be provided. Social workers in drug crisis centers and hotlines, maintained on a twenty-four-hour basis, deal with many emergencies.

Inpatient Services

An essential element of any drug treatment program is a facility to detoxify those who are in crisis situations. Individuals who have become dependent on certain drugs or who may have serious illnesses connected with their drug use need hospital care. Because of potential psychotic and paranoid reactions by users who have become toxic on a drug or are coming off from chronic use of alcohol or barbiturates, it is usually preferable to admit them on an inpatient basis. Withdrawal from these drugs requires constant care because of the many physical, behavioral, and psychological complications that may arise. The potential for death is also a concern for those who are detoxifying from alcohol and barbiturates.

Outpatient Services

Many agencies provide outpatient therapy, including established mental health centers and social agencies in addition to the clinics or treatment centers established exclusively for drug abusers. They may offer short- or long-term therapy, combine methadone or other chemical therapy, or offer group sessions. Outpatient clinics are often the first contact an abuser has when seeking help.

Individual and group psychotherapy, vocational and educational assistance, and help in solving personal problems are services that are available to support addicts who have been detoxified and are seeking help on an outpatient basis.

Methadone Maintenance

The use of methadone to "treat" heroin addiction is a controversial solution to the problem. Those who oppose its use maintain that methadone itself is addictive and should not be used to treat narcotic addiction. Those who favor its use say it is orally effective, nontoxic, and safe to use over a long period of time. It is used in both residential and outpatient clinics where the staff usually includes a psychiatrist, a physician, nurses, social workers, and paraprofessionals.

After a patient has worked through personal, family, and employment problems, and is successfully living a normal life, the methadone is gradually decreased until he or she is drug free or on as low a dosage as possible for maintenance. The time involved varies but many are able to achieve a drug-free state in about nine months. This method has helped thousands of hardcore addicts become law-abiding citizens.

Narcotic Antagonists

Narcotic antagonists are drugs that work against opiates, and when they are used, narcotics cannot be felt. Two antagonists commonly used are cyclazocine and naloxone. They have been effective with well-motivated and well-integrated persons and are also used with younger users.

Therapeutic Communities

Self-help therapeutic communities have generated great interest. Across the nation hundreds of facilities offer residential experiences, small-group therapy, and participation in vocational rehabilitation preparatory to living "outside" again.

Admission requirements and living rules generally stress the need for the user to come to grips with his or her problem and accept the help offered. Many depend heavily on paraprofessionals, usually ex-addicts who serve as counselors and role models. Long-term surveillance and aftercare attention, plus the closeness of the group, are basic ingredients of the treatment program.

Therapeutic Communities for Young Users

Because many young abusers are unable to get the help they need from outpatient facilities, some workers in the drug abuse field recommend therapeutic communities especially adapted to youth. They often need vocational and on-the-job training as well as high school classes needed for graduation. Work with their families is often indicated.

Treatment for Alcohol Abuse

Alcoholics Anonymous (AA), using the self-help approach, has been the outstanding source of help for alcoholics in the past. Its auxiliaries, Al-Anon and Alateen, have helped spouses and children. Alcoholics, as other addicts, show a history of emotional deprivation, feelings of inferiority, depression, anxiety, and difficulties with parents and family. Social workers are seeing more alcoholics and their families in mental health clinics, family counseling centers, and in industry-sponsored clinics.

Integrating Approaches to Treatment

Having a number of approaches to treatment makes it possible for drug abusers to choose the type of treatment best suited to their needs. Outpatient services are the least expensive. Long-term inpatient services are expensive, and many are not able to commit themselves to staying on the program long enough to be rehabilitated.

In making plans with an individual for treatment, social and family ties, job opportunities, and personal strengths need to be assessed before deciding which facility would best suit his or her needs. With their knowledge of community resources, social workers are helpful in providing information to patients of the types of facilities available. They also aid in coordinating the efforts of those who work with this problem.

To combat this widespread use and abuse of drugs, it would help to (1) strengthen parent–child relationships, (2) stress positive aspects of the parent role in the home, (3) make clear and articulate to children the value system of parents, (4) make the school experience socially and emotionally rewarding and supportive for youth, and (5) program all social institutions in their efforts on behalf of youth to achieve a growth-promoting, psychological, therapeutic, and educational experience.

The teen years may be difficult for some. Those who have not had strong relationships with their parents and have no close family ties, who have had difficulties in school, or who have had conflict with the law may turn to drugs for relief of emotional problems, to help them acquire status with a group, to achieve sociability, or to defy authority. Social work is one of the professions that can help. Teenagers often seek help from social workers when life is threatening and difficult.

Preventing Alcohol and Other Drug Abuse

Treatment and rehabilitation of drug or alcohol abuse and dependence is expensive as well as unpredictable as to its ultimate success. Therefore, programs to alleviate conditions that breed drug abuse should be given high priority.

Although drug abuse most often starts in adolescence, the climate that precipitates it may start many years earlier. Teachers and social workers in schools can be alert for problems of youths in elementary and secondary grades along with those in counseling.

Adolescents who have a variety of interests and ways of using their leisure time are less likely to become involved in the drug culture. A community drug abuse council can generate action to provide alternatives and new and appealing programs for youth.

Over the past 25 years, drug abuse prevention has focused on peer resistance and education. However, research findings on the effectiveness of these programs came up with less than positive results. In 1998, a new direction was unveiled by Kumpfer, the director of the federal agency for the Center for Substance Abuse Prevention. She focused on a family-centered approach that has been found to be successful. The approach includes the following components: parent and family skills training, in-home support services, and family therapy.[18]

Since 1998, the National Institute on Drugs and Alcohol (NIDA) has identified sixteen principles recommended for inclusion in prevention programs. "The principles listed below are the result of long-term research studies on the origins for drug abuse behaviors and the common elements of effective prevention."[19] The following is a summary of the principles.

- Programs should direct efforts at reducing risk factors and increasing protective factors (risk factors include deviant behaviors and attitudes exhibited by youths whereas protective factors include parental support).
- Programs need to address all forms of substance abuse including over-the-counter drugs, legal drugs, along with illegal drugs.
- Programs ought to target those drugs of prominent use/abuse and target those risk factors that can be altered.
- Programs need to be designed to address the risk factors associated with the gender, age, and ethnicity of the target group.
- Programs that are family-based need to strengthen the bonds among parent(s) and child(ren) with the inclusion of parenting skills; strengthen the development, discussion, and enforcement of family rules around substance abuse; and provide education on drugs and their effects.
- Programs may begin as early as preschool in addressing high-risk behaviors (aggression, academic problems, poor socialization).
- Programs provided in elementary schools need to focus on development in the following areas: self-control, emotional awareness, communication, problem solving, and academic aid especially in the area of reading.
- Programs conducted in the middle, junior high, or high schools need to focus on the following areas: communication, study habits, peer relationships, assertiveness and self-efficacy, resistence of drugs, reinforcement of antidrug attitudes, and support of personal commitments to not use drugs.
- Programs that target general populations during key transition times (elementary to middle school) have been found to produce positive effects, even for those youths at high risk.
- Programs that combine two or more programs that have been deemed effective have been more effective than any single program (family-based with a school-based program).

- Those programs that reach out to populations in multiple settings are most effective when they present messages in each of the settings (schools, boys/girls clubs, churches, etc.).
- When programs adjust/adapt to community norms, cultures, and needs they also need to retain the core elements of research-based interventions.
- Programs need to be long term with booster sessions to continually reinforce the prevention goals. If not, the gains youths make diminish in high school.
- Programs ought to include training teachers on classroom management that reinforces positive behavior, student achievement, bonding with the school, and academic achievement.
- Programs do best when they use interactive teaching techniques (role plays, discussion groups).
- Prevention programs have been found to be cost-effective. For each dollar spent, it is predicted that $10 will be saved.

Research

Research is being conducted covering many phases of drug abuse, including models for treatment, medical factors such as the role of genetics, law enforcement problems, industrial losses, and social implications. Research plays an important part in the understanding of this problem and likely will continue.

"Regardless of the model of addiction one adheres to, the use patterns and attitudes about alcohol and other drugs of family members and peers is highly related to addiction."[20] Children whose parents are alcoholics have a 30 percent chance of also becoming alcoholics in their lifetime as compared with 10 percent of children whose parents abstain and 5 percent whose parents drink alcoholic beverages in moderation.[21] Also, having friends who use alcohol or illicit drugs is a primary predictor of substance abuse among adolescents.[22]

Parents, as role models for their children, need to examine the effect of their own use of legal and illegal drugs. Parents who use legal psychoactive or mood-altering drugs (such as sedatives, depressants, stimulants, or sleeping pills) should examine honestly their reasons for doing so. In consultation with their spouses, adult friends, and physicians, they should decide whether they can do without these prescription drugs; if they cannot, they should be extremely cautious not to abuse medical permission to use them. Parents also should tell their children why they use the drug, that it is a legally controlled substance, that it should never be mixed with other drugs or alcohol, and that it should never be used "for fun." It is medicine, not a "recreational drug."

Parents who use illegal drugs must reevaluate their behavior. Not to use legal or illegal drugs may not prevent their children from using them. It will, however, increase their credibility when trying to intervene or prevent their children's abuse of drugs.

Most young people learn about illicit drug use from their peers. Blum conducted a lengthy study to find out why some youngsters become drug users and others do not.[23] This study has significance to social workers. Blum and associates studied 101 white middle-class families, classified according to the drug use of their children. All families lived in the same area, both parents lived at home, one child was in college, and younger children were at home. All members of the families participated.

Conclusions from this study are that children from homes where parental love and concern are evident, where teachings against use of mind- or mood-altering substances are stressed, and where emotional needs are met are less likely to become drug users.

The families in this study where there was no drug abuse were alert, flexible, firm, polite, self-confident, honest, and forgiving. These qualities can be learned, and if they are not learned through the family, they can be learned through other group experiences. Priority needs to be given to action programs that help families develop responsible citizens. Peer groups will become the primary force in a young person's life only if parents relinquish their position as head of the family.

Blum's research points to an association between drug abuse and home influences. Other studies reveal similar associations between drug abuse and the school, employment, the widespread use of prescription drugs, and the drug culture. As with most major social problems, there are many influences within and outside the individual that contribute to the misuse and abuse of drugs.

Harrison, Boyle, and Farley evaluated an alcohol- and other drug-prevention demonstration project that was funded by the National Office for Substance Abuse Prevention.[24] The project was designed to reduce risk factors for alcohol and other drug abuse by improving family communication skills.

Their study found that families who participated in the project significantly increased family cohesion, family time together, and decreased family conflicts. The parents showed increases in their parenting abilities and mental health, and the youth exhibited fewer problem behaviors, better social skills, and more appropriate behavior.

The Johnston et al. study had indicated that after several years of significant increase in illicit drug use, junior and senior high school students have been using fewer drugs. The 2000 study suggested that a small but positive trend was beginning to occur in some areas, but there was still much work to be done. With the more significant results of the 2006 study, highlighted below, the current findings indicate that the positive trends are continuing for many illicit and licit drugs. Although the exact reason for the declines are uncertain, it may be that the ad campaigns conducted nationally are having a positive effect on youth.

- In 2006 a number of drugs showed modest yet statistically insignificant yearly reductions, showing a continuation of earlier declines.
- A number of other drugs stayed steady, but had declined in previous years.
- Four classes of drugs (ecstasy, OxyContin, Vicodin, and inhalants) showed signs of increase, yet the increases were not across all grades.
- Since the peak of drug use in 1996 for eighth graders and 1997 for tenth and twelfth graders, any illicit drugs use is down by more than one-third among eighth graders, one-fourth among tenth graders, and about 14 percent in twelfth graders.
- Whereas gradual declines continue in all grades, none of the 2005 to 2006 declines were found to be statistically significant.
- The 2006 lifetime prevalence rates for any illicit drug use by eighth, tenth, and twelfth graders were 21 percent, 36 percent, and 48 percent respectively, suggesting that by the time students graduate from high school in the United States, almost half have tried illicit drugs at some time.

- A number of classes of drugs showed declines in at least one grade. They were marijuana, any illicit drug other than marijuana, hallucinogens other than LSD, amphetamines, methamphetamine, alcohol, and cigarettes.
- The classes of drugs holding steady in all grade levels for 2006 were LSD, power cocaine, crystal methamphetamine ("ice"), heroin, narcotics other than heroin, tranquilizers, three "club drugs" (Ketamine, Rohypnol, and GHB), and steroids.
- Just four classes of drugs were found to have any increase and those were modest and confined to one or more grades.[25]

The following recommendations supporting the need for the continuation of prevention of substance abuse among our youth were presented by Johnson et al. in the 2006 report. They include the following:

- New drugs and older ones (i.e., LSD, methamphetamine) are being reintroduced and are continuing to show up among our young people. Drugs that have made a resurgence do so because it is believed that the adverse consequences known about them in the past have faded. This is referred to as "generational forgetting."
- The attempts at containing the use of new drugs lag behind because of the time it takes to identify the adverse consequences and to disseminate that information.
- To a significant degree, prevention of drug abuse needs to occur for each specific drug. Young people seem not to generalize the negative consequences of one drug to another. Among many young people their attitudes about drugs are specific to the particular drug and the trends of use for any particular drug change over time.[26]

Role of Social Work in Treatment

Social work is becoming more involved in the treatment of drug abusers. As in the case with the abuse of alcohol, the families of drug abusers are almost always affected; they need help to understand the problem, to allay fears, anxieties, and guilt feelings; to help solidify the family unit; and at the same time learn to give support to the abuser.

Social workers are called on to help in a variety of traditional social work settings—juvenile courts, adult probation and parole, mental health clinics, hospitals, family counseling centers, schools, university health and counseling centers, and in private practice. In addition, drug treatment centers are employing social workers. In many, social workers are the administrators as well as the therapists, and they work with the psychiatrist, physician, psychologist, and often ex-addicts who may, or may not, have had professional training as drug abuse counselors.

Some drug dependent and abusing persons have serious personality problems, suffer from social maladjustment, or have disruptive home influences before they start using drugs. Treatment cannot be complete until these earlier problems are faced and worked through. Social workers provide these services.

Working with drug abuse and dependency presents many problems that social workers have not heretofore encountered, and new methods of approach and new thinking are needed to cope with the situations they are facing.

One of the big problems in clinical social work is that attempting to substitute acceptable satisfactions for drugs does not appeal to the addict because there is nothing else that creates the euphoria, with its accompanying feeling of "all's right with the world." Clinical work should not be abandoned, but must become flexible enough to bend with the client, who possibly has little motivation to give up drugs. Drug users seek help if they are financially unable to support the habit, if they are worn out from evading the police, their family or friends have stopped supporting or denying their addictive behaviors and problems, are physically ill, if they have had a close friend die of an overdose, or if they have to choose between going to jail or seeking treatment.

For some drug dependent persons, it may be unrealistic to assume that the only goal is to be drug free. With the use of chemotherapy many who have been unable to continue in drug-free treatment centers are finding their way back into productivity. Social workers may set the ultimate goal of total abstinence, but must realize that this may be achieved only after numerous relapses, if at all. It is important for workers to realize that any period of abstinence is a step forward and has important aspects to the user, family, and to the community. Addicts often return to the use of drugs when crises occur.

Some of the ways that social workers are involved in the treatment of drug and alcohol abusers and their families are illustrated by the following examples.

Treating Preaddictive Adolescents

Treating preaddictive adolescents is difficult. The results of most studies indicate that a total-family approach is necessary. Parents and adolescents have to agree to a set of ground rules. There should he no drugs available in the home, and the parents have to be committed to this condition. Parents have to enforce the rules by providing constant vigilance, parental prohibition, and love.

Most parents have an underlying concern to be good parents. Through the enforcement of the rules, parents begin to feel respected. Parents also begin to see themselves as positive forces in the lives of their children. Many times adolescents will respond to the more positive atmosphere in the family and feel that their parents really do care about their successes and about them.

When the family atmosphere begins to improve, the social worker should give both the parents and adolescent positive feedback and reinforcement. The worker can play an important role in sustaining the family improvement.

Social Work with Alcoholics

In the past social work had been slow to reach out to alcohol-dependent persons to offer therapy, leaving this large group to get help from Alcoholics Anonymous and Salvation Army programs. With an estimated annual increase of 200,000, alcoholics and their families are greatly in need of the service of social workers, who have much to offer with traditional and new methods of therapy. As with other substance-dependent persons, no one method of treatment is successful with all, and a variety of approaches greatly increases the likelihood that one will find the treatment that fits his or her particular needs. Treatment centers and trained personnel have not kept pace with the demands.

Social workers must increase their knowledge and skills in working with alcoholics. As Kane states

> For social workers in alcoholism clinics, inpatient alcoholism treatment centers, halfway houses, court-affiliated "drunk driving" programs, the prevention and treatment of alcohol problems in some form or other are the primary focus of their work. But for many other social workers (and perhaps, unfortunately, to a greater extent than they appreciate) some form of problem drinking is an intervening variable complicating the achievement of professional goals with a client. Problem drinking, for instance, often contributes to child and wife abuse, delinquent behavior, marital friction, economic dependence, and noncompliance with medical regimens. As one article illustrates, alcohol abuse by one or more parents may even be an unsuspected contributor to the poor performance in school of children in the caseload of a school social worker. Taken together, we social workers are in frontline positions to identify problem drinking in a family constellation and to make appropriate referrals for special help or to incorporate goals on drinking practices into our own work with clients.[27]

Working with the alcoholic presents different problems from working with other clients and requires understanding of the disease as well as of the individual. Workers who reject people with addictive disorders will not be successful with them, for they may be very sensitive people with low self-esteem and, having experienced rejection by their families, friends, and employers, look for it in social workers. It is important for the worker to understand that clients will have relapses, but this does not mean failure.

It is important to understand that family support is essential in the treatment of substance abuse. In almost all families, there is disorganization and distress over the dependent person's problems. The extent to which families suffer from the effects of alcoholism is difficult to describe. Not only do they often suffer monetary privations, but also have to endure rejection by neighbors and friends; anxiety and guilt feelings; and humiliation, abuse, neglect, and failure. Clearly, the problem of alcoholism in one individual cannot be separated from its effect on all the members of a family. The whole family needs to recover from this family disease.

Treating a Heroin Addict on an Outpatient Basis

Charles, a person addicted to heroin, was successful in becoming drug free by the use of methadone, coupled with intensive therapy and vocational assistance.

Charles came into the clinic every morning at 6:45 to be checked and to drink his daily supply of methadone on his way to work. He chatted amiably with the fellow in back of him in line, commented to his social worker on the music at the symphony concert he had attended the night before, and went whistling out the door.

Eleven months earlier when Charles first dragged into the clinic, he was burned out, in poor health, and in the depths of despair. He had been caught in a burglary, and the judge had given him the alternative of seeking help or going to jail.

In his early twenties, Charles was married and had one son. He was always broke, had mountains of unpaid bills, was suspicious and depressed. In the home there was constant conflict over his addiction, lack of respect, indifference to his family obligations, and unlawful activities. He spent most of his time hustling money to buy a fix and often turned to burglarizing to obtain cash or property to pawn to supply his heroin.

At the clinic, he was made to feel comfortable and helped to accept the treatment offered. He suffered during the first few weeks and would certainly have dropped out if he could have done so without going to jail. But after he had been stabilized on methadone he was helped to find a job as a bricklayer, which he enjoyed.

He was given help with his personal problems in therapy sessions during the evening, and his wife came with him for group therapy where they both were given support and understanding of the drug problem.

Several times conflicts, anxieties, and feelings of helplessness made him reach out for the euphoria of heroin. But he would start over again. To help him through the evening hours, the clinic frequently provided him with tickets to symphony concerts, plays, and ballets, which afforded new experiences for him. During the summer one of the counselors, a former addict, took him hiking and fishing on weekends.

After seven months of treatment, Charles and his wife had paid off their most pressing debts and were able to move into their own apartment, being alone for the first time in four years. When family life became more stable, his job secure, and his finances adequate, the team of workers at the clinic decided to cut down on his daily doses of methadone, a little at a time, until he was drug free.

Charles was one of the relatively few who did become drug free. Unfortunately, all cases are not this successful.

Social Work with Drug- and Alcohol-Dependent Persons in a Residential Facility

Some heroin addicts have such serious personal problems that they are unable to maintain themselves or benefit from help offered in outpatient clinics. For them, residential services are needed. Linda, who needed constant support on a twenty-four-hour basis, is a case study in a community-sponsored facility.

Linda, age 23 and pregnant, voluntarily came to the clinic optimistic about kicking her drug dependence. She had tried a drug-free therapeutic community but had been unable to maintain their strict requirements.

She had started using marijuana at age 18 and had tried barbiturates, amphetamines, and tranquilizers. She had been dependent on heroin for about three years. Those years had been permeated with a succession of affairs, a brief marriage, the births of two infants, and continual involvement with the criminal justice system for theft, prostitution, drugs, and traffic violations.

Linda was bright, resourceful, manipulative, and highly motivated to become drug free one day, but lacking in motivation another day. Her two children had been placed in foster care, and the judge had decreed that she could not have them back unless she was totally drug free within six months. She wanted to have her children, and this was the chief source of motivation.

In therapy she was rarely able to handle insightful kinds of efforts, fleeing either mentally, physically, or both from any attempt to examine the thinking style associated with abuse. She related only to crisis intervention or task-centered therapeutic approaches. Her only concern was with immediate solutions to currently pressing problems directly affecting her. She responded to such problems with a sense of panic, despair, or urgency. Avoidance was typically preferable to having to deal with the problem. Once a problem was solved, she saw no value in learning how it had developed or how it could have been handled in less anxiety-provoking ways.

By virtue of her membership in the drug culture, she had successfully learned habits, values, attitudes, and lifestyle modes of behavior with which she could function well in that environment. She could efficiently function in aspects of the larger social system that were important to her lifestyle, for example, the criminal justice system and the social welfare system. When necessary, she could function in the drug-free labor market to meet her immediate needs.

In a therapeutic-helping relationship the social worker set a specific goal to build a foundation of trust and confidence that would enable Linda to feel comfortable in asking for help with her day-to-day problems. A longer range goal was to deepen that trust and confidence.

She was able initially to communicate that she recognized her emotional difficulties, but had previously discovered that the fear of risking oftentimes had become too great to handle, so that she felt unable or unwilling to delve into her feelings any further than just the initial cry for help. She withdrew from the risk, hurt, and fear of explaining her feelings by running away, either physically, mentally, or both. She would curl up, face away, leave the room, go to sleep, or decline to talk.

Several weeks before the birth of her child, she became completely drug free, hoping the baby would not show signs of dependence. But three days after birth, the infant began to show withdrawal symptoms. This necessitated finding a foster home where the foster parents would have the patience and understanding and stamina necessary for the close vigilance of this child. Having the baby drug dependent was defeating to Linda, who felt she had tried hard to save it from this difficulty. She was very depressed and in the next few weeks needed constant support.

In seeking support and then not being able to utilize it fully, Linda nevertheless received valuable reinforcement through the meaningful testing of loyalties that she felt capable of initiating. She learned that help was really there, that promises were fulfilled, and that the relationship remained intact regardless of the problems encountered. The decision of the judge that she be drug free within six months was not realistic in terms of her extremely precarious history. It was apparent that he was imposing his values on her, and that she would not be able to respond, not within the time limit he set. Many people lead a "normal" life, maintain a home, and work steadily on methadone maintenance. Perhaps using these guidelines, a more realistic goal could have been set for Linda, one that she possibly could have attained.

Summary

Narcotics, marijuana, and alcohol have been used from the earliest recorded times and are likely to be used for years to come. Add the enormous number of new drugs that have been put on the market since World War II, and it is easy to see that the drug-abuse problem is one that will not easily be eradicated. Almost daily it is discovered that another drug has the potential for abuse.

Most drug abuse begins with teenagers who are influenced by their peers to try something new and exciting. Some of them continue to experiment until it is too late to turn back without help. The extent of drug abuse and dependence is enormous and extremely costly both in terms of personal loss and the monetary loss to society as a whole.

No single agency or small group of agencies can handle this problem. A total community effort is necessary, using education, preventive measures, various treatment modalities, and rehabilitative services to those who are the victims of drugs.

Because of the almost insurmountable difficulties to treatment of many addicts, emphasis needs to be given to programs of prevention among the coming generations. Factual information alone will not do this. Efforts are needed to strengthen the family and to make family relationships a dominant force in the lives of young people, to help children develop positive attitudes and communication skills, and to provide satisfying experiences in their school activities. It is important to find recreational and leisure time activities that will turn young people to worthwhile endeavors, instead of having them turn to drugs.

A herculean task is presented by drug abuse, and it is becoming increasingly clear that little short of a total community effort is needed to make inroads into what was once considered hopeless. Social work can help.

Selected References

BECK, AARON T., *Cognitive Therapy of Substance Abuse.* New York: Guilford Press, 1993.

BENSHOFF, JOHN J., and TIMOTHY P. JANIKOWSKI, *The Rehabilitation Model of Substance Abuse Counseling.* Pacific Grove, CA: Brooks/Cole, 2000.

CHASNOFF, IRA, "Cocaine, Pregnancy and the Growing Child," *Current Problems in Pediatrics,* August 1992.

FISHER, GARY L., and THOMAS C. HARRISON, *Substance Abuse: Information for School Counselors, Social Workers, Therapists, and Counselors,* 2nd ed. Boston: Allyn & Bacon, 2000.

GRANT, MARCUS, and BRUCE PITSON, *Alcohol: The Prevention Debate.* New York: St. Martin's Press, 1983.

HOGAN, JULIE, KRISTEN GABRIELSEN, NORA LUNA, and DENISE GROTHAUS, *Substance Abuse Prevention: The Intersection of Science and Practice.* Boston: Allyn & Bacon, 2003.

JOHNSTON, LLOYD D., PATRICK M. O'MALLEY, and JERALD G. BACHMAN, *Monitoring the Future National Results on Adolescent Drug Use: Overview of Key Findings, 2002.* (NIH Publication No. 03–5374). Bethesda, MD: National Institute on Drug Abuse, 2003.

KINNEY, JEAN, and GWEN LEATON, *Loosening the Grip*, 5th ed. St. Louis, MO: Mosby, 1995.

LOWINSON, JOYCE H., PEDRO RUIZ, ROBERT B. MILLMAN, and JOHN G. LANGROD, eds., *Substance Abuse: A Comprehensive Textbook,* 3rd ed. Baltimore: Williams & Wilkins, 1997.

MCNEECE, C. AARON, and DIANA M. DINITTO, *Chemical Dependency: A Systems Approach,* 2nd ed. Boston: Allyn & Bacon, 1998.

NATIONAL INSTITUTE ON DRUG ABUSE, *Drug Abuse and Drug Abuse Research: The Third Triennial Report to Congress.* Washington, DC: U.S. Department of Health and Human Services, 1991.

NATIONAL INSTITUTE ON DRUG ABUSE, National Institutes of Health, Department of Health and Human Services, Bethesda, MD. Available at www.nida.nih.gov/.

PHILLEO, JOANNE, and FRANCES LARRY BRISBANE, eds., *Cultural Competence for Social Workers: A Guide for Alcohol and Other Drug Abuse Prevention. Professionals Working with Ethnic/Racial Communities.* Special Collaborative NASW/CSAP Monograph no. 4, Washington, DC: U.S. Department of Health and Human Services, 1995.

STEPHENS, RICHARD C., *The Street Addict Role: A Theory of Heroin Addiction.* Ithaca: New York State University Press, 1991.

WASHTON, ARNOLD M., ed., *Psychotherapy and Substance Abuse: A Practitioner's Handbook.* New York: Guilford Press, 1995.

Notes

1. Richard H. Blum and Associates, *The Dream Sellers* (San Francisco: Jossey-Bass, 1972), p. 4.

2. Office of National Drug Control Policy, *The President's National Drug Control Strategy,* 2004. Retrieved from www.whitehousedrugpolicy.gov/publications/policy/ndcs04/national_priorities.html.

3. Lloyd D. Johnston, Patrick M. O'Malley, and Jerald G. Bachman, *National Survey Results on Drug Use from the Monitoring the Future Study,* 1975–1993 (Washington, DC: National Institute on Drug Abuse, NIH Publication No. 94-3809, 1994), pp. 23–24.

4. Lloyd D. Johnston, Patrick M. O'Malley, and Jerald G. Bachman, *National Survey Results on Drug Use from the Monitoring the Future Study, 1975–1995* (Washington, DC: National Institute on Drug Abuse, NIH Publication No. 94-4139, 1996), pp. 28–29.

5. Lloyd D. Johnston, Patrick M. O'Malley, and Jerald G. Bachman, *Monitoring the Future. National Results on Adolescent Drug Use: Overview of Key Findings, 2000* (Bethesda, MD: National Institute on Drug Abuse, NIH Publication No. 01-4923, 2001).

6. Lloyd D. Johnston, Patrick M. O'Malley, Jerald G. Bachman, and John E. Schulenberg, *Monitoring the Future National Results on Adolescent Drug Use: Overview of Key Findings, 2003* (Bethesda, MD: National Institute on Drug Abuse, NIH Publication No. 07-6202).

7. Ibid., p. 4.

8. Lloyd D. Johnston, Patrick M. O'Malley, Jerald G. Bachman, and John E. Schulenberg, *Monitoring the Future: National Survey Results on Drug Use, 1975–2006,* Vol. 1. National Institute on Drug Abuse. Retrieved from http://www.monitoringthefuture.org/pubs/monographs/vol1_2006.pdf.

9. Gary L. Fisher and Thomas C. Harrison, *Substance Abuse,* 2nd ed. (Boston: Allyn & Bacon, 2000).

10. Channing L. Bete Co., Inc., "What Everyone Should Know about Alcoholism," a scriptographic booklet (South Deerfield, MA: 1985), p. 5.

11. U.S. Department of Health and Human Services and SAMHSA's National Clearinghouse for Alcohol & Drug Information, *Alcohol: What You Don't Know Can Harm You—Alcohol-Related Birth Defects, Long-Term Health Problems, 2007.* Retrieved from http://ncadi.samhsa.gov/govpubs/ph326x/#ABD.

12. Richard G. Schlaadt and Peter T. Shannon, *Drugs: Use, Misuse, and Abuse,* 4th ed. (Upper Saddle River, NJ: Prentice Hall, 1994), p. 288.

13. C. Everett Koop, *Marijuana and Health,* Ninth Report to the U.S. Congress by the Secretary of Health and Human Services (Rockville MD: National Institute on Drug Abuse, 1982).

14. National Institute on Drug Abuse, *Marijuana: Facts for Teens, What Are the Short-Term Effects of Marijuana Use? What Are the Long-Term Effects of Marijuana Use?,* 2007. Retrieved from www.nida.nih.gov/MarijBroch/Marijteenstxt.html#short.

15. Gary L. Fisher and Thomas C. Harrison, *Substance Abuse,* 2nd ed. (Boston: Allyn & Bacon, 2000).

16. National Institute on Drug Abuse, *Info Facts, Costs to Society.* National Institutes of Health, U.S. Department of Health and Human Services. Retrieved from http://www.nida.gov/infofax/costs.html.

17. Bureau of Narcotics and Dangerous Drugs, *Fact Sheets* (Washington, DC: U.S. Department of Justice, n.d.), pp. 1-1, 1-2.

18. Karol L. Kumpfer, "Prevention Approaches to Adolescent Substance Use/Abuse," presentation to the American Academy of Child Psychiatry Institute on Substance Abuse and Adolescence (San Antonio, TX: October 23, 1985).

19. National Institute on Drug Abuse, *NIDA InfoFacts: Lessons from Prevention Research*, Revised 2004. Retrieved from http://drugabuse.gov/Infofacts/lessons.html.

20. G. L. Fisher and T. C. Harrison, *Substance Abuse: Information for School Counselors, Social Workers, Therapists, and Counselors* (Boston: Allyn & Bacon, 2000), p. 38.

21. G. W. Lawson, J. S. Peterson, and A. W. Lawson, *Alcoholism and the Family: A Guide to Treatment and Prevention* (Gaithersburg, MD: Aspen, 1983).

22. J. D. Hawkins, D. M. Lishner, R. F. Catalano, and M. O. Howard, "Childhood Predictors of Adolescent Substance Abuse: Toward an Empirically Grounded Theory." [Special Issue, *Childhood and Chemical Abuse: Prevention and Intervention*]. *Journal of Children in Contemporary Society,* 18 (1985), pp. 11–48.

23. Richard H. Blum and Associates, *Horatio Alger's Children* (San Francisco: Jossey-Bass, 1972).

24. Steven R. Harrison, Scott W. Boyle, and O. William Farley, "Evaluating the Outcomes of Family-Based Intervention for Troubled Children: A Pretest-Posttest Study," *Research on Social Work Practice,* 9, no. 6 (1999), pp. 640–655.

25. Johnston, O'Malley, Bachman, and Schulenberg, *Monitoring the Future National Results*, (2007) pp. 5–10.

26. Ibid.

27. Rosalie Kane, "To Our Health! . . . Social Work and Alcohol Problems," *Health and Social Work,* 4 (November 1979), pp. 6–7.

17

Services with Minorities

Jawan and Ron, 17-year-old high school seniors, celebrated graduation by participating in drinking parties that resulted in each stealing a car. Both were picked up by the police the next day, but Ron was released to his parents; Jawan, who is black, was put in jail. Although they had both *been in trouble with the law a few times, when they were brought before the juvenile court judge, Jawan was sent to the Youth Development Center and Ron was placed on probation. People who knew them both observed that they should have been treated the same.*

Social work has a deep tradition in social reform. Part of that early effort was in working with minorities and addressing such issues as immigration laws, relocation, and work with individuals.

With the civil rights movements of the 1960s, social work became more sensitive to the pressing problems of minorities as affected by various social institutions. Social work is attempting to strengthen and broaden its approach in its effort to bring about institutional change that will benefit minorities in America. At the present time many new forces are appearing that may change the direction of the country in addressing the social structures needed to deal with minority problems. In 1994 California voted for Proposition 187, which denied most public services to illegal immigrants. *NASW News* reported

> Six states—California, Texas and Florida among them—have sued the federal government to recoup billions the states contend they have spent for public services, education, health care and prison costs for illegal immigrants. In 1993, Florida started denying foster care to illegal immigrant children, a policy that also is being challenged in court, according to news reports.[1]

In November of 1996, Proposition 209 was adopted by the voters of California and became part of the state's constitution. The key operative of the proposition states

> The state shall not discriminate against, or grant preferential treatment to any individual or group on the basis of race, sex, color, ethnicity, or national origin in the operation of public employment, public education, or public contracting.

With the passage of this measure, affirmative action, as it had been known and implemented, had come to an end. Many fear that African Americans, as well as other minorities, will no longer be protected from discrimination in public education, employment, and contracting.

It has become clear that if social work is to assist minorities effectively, it must mediate the strong forces that seem to be returning the blame of minority problems to the victims themselves. Social workers must not forget both the subtle and overt discrimination in our society that deprives minority groups from accessing rewarding social roles such as good jobs and good education.

Minority Problems

Racial discrimination is real. A vivid example is given in the *Autobiography of Malcolm X*. When Malcolm told his eighth-grade teacher that he wanted to be a lawyer, she advised him:

> Malcolm, one of life's first needs is for us to be realistic. . . . A lawyer, that's no realistic goal for a nigger. . . . You are good with your hands—making things. . . . Why don't you plan to become a carpenter?[2]

Racism is the word used to reflect prejudices and mistreatment of those from minority groups, particularly African Americans, American Indians, and Spanish-speaking Americans. Two kinds of racism—individual and institutional—are described by Carmichael and Hamilton:

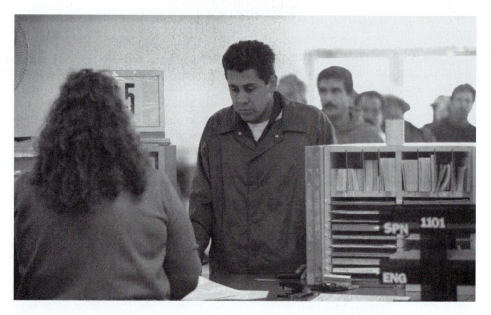

Unemployment is often a particularly difficult problem in minority populations.

Racism is both overt and covert. It takes two closely related forms: individual whites acting against individual blacks, and acts by the total white community against the black community. We call these individual racism and institutional racism. The first consists of overt acts by individuals, which cause death, injury, or the violent destruction of property. This type can be recorded by television cameras; it can frequently be observed in the process of commission. The second type is less overt, far more subtle, less identifiable in terms of *specific* individuals committing the acts. But it is no less destructive of human life. The second type originates in the operation of established and respected forces in the society, and thus receives far less public condemnation than the first type.

When white terrorists bomb a black church and kill five black children, that is an act of individual racism, widely deplored by most segments of the society. But when in the same city—Birmingham, Alabama—500 black babies die each year because of the lack of proper food, shelter, and medical facilities, and thousands more are destroyed and maimed physically, emotionally, and intellectually because of conditions of poverty and discrimination in the black community, that is a function of institutional racism.[3]

Jones underlined the potency of racism when he wrote: "Institutional racism is comparable to a runaway vine. Often it is difficult to find its root. And as with the vine, you can kill as many branches as you choose, but if you fail to destroy the root, the vine continues to grow."[4]

There have been important gains in the lifestyles of minorities since the Civil Rights Act was passed on June 29, 1964. No longer would a public school teacher suggest openly that "a lawyer, that's no realistic goal for a nigger."

According to the 2000 U.S. Census, estimates suggest that minorities made up 49 million (17.8 percent) of the total population of 276 million. Of those ethnic groups cited, blacks made up 35.4 million (12.8 percent), Asian Americans accounted for 24.5 million (9 percent), and those of Hispanic origin, who may be of any race, made up 32.8 million (11.9 percent) of the population. These U.S. Census projections for the year 2000 suggest that the white population has declined from 84 percent to 82 percent, with increases being found for blacks (12 to 12.8 percent), for Asian and Pacific Islanders (3 to 4 percent), and with the most significant increase, from 9 to 11.9 percent of the total population, for Hispanics.[5]

The structure and culture of the United States are continually attempting to accommodate and assimilate people from all over the world. Historically the "melting-pot" theory was established as the answer for new immigrants coming to the United States. This theory suggests that all kinds of people are brought together, and a melding of races and cultures results from the assimilation of the new members. Glasgow suggests that "the melting-pot ideal was never viewed as encompassing black Americans or any other non-whites."[6] Many believe that cultural diversity and ethnic reaffirmation are important and enriching aspects of the American way of life, that values and opportunities are inherent in multiethnic diversities.

Even though gains have been made by ethnic minorities in this country, discrimination is still a real problem. Minority groups have never been offered the full scope of the reward structures of our society. Wilson states

It is no secret that the social problems of urban life in the United States are, in great measure, associated with race.

While rising rates of crime, drug addiction, out-of-wedlock births, female-headed families, and welfare dependency have afflicted American society generally in recent years, the increases have been most dramatic among what has become a large and seemingly permanent black underclass inhabiting the cores of the nation's major cities.

And yet, liberal journalists, social scientists, policy makers, and civil-rights leaders for almost two decades have been reluctant to face this fact. Often, analysts of such issues as violent crime or teenage pregnancy deliberately make no reference to race at all, unless to emphasize the deleterious consequences of racial discrimination or the institutionalized inequality of American society.[7]

Although gains are being made, minority families in general still lag behind economically. According to the 1999 U.S. Census reports, the median family income (in constant dollars) for all families in 1999 was $40,816. However, when income for families is examined by race, a different picture emerges. For the same year (1999), the median family income for whites was $44,366 compared with blacks at $27,910 and those of Hispanic origin, at $30,735, whereas Asian and Pacific Islander households had the highest ever recorded income for their group at $51,205. When the amount of family income is reviewed by percentages of the population within a given category, approximately 60 percent of the white families earn incomes of $35,000 and above. This figure has remained constant for 15 years. When compared with blacks, 41.3 percent were in the same category, up 4 percent in the last ten years, whereas Hispanic families earning $35,000 and above rose to nearly 44 percent in the same period.[8]

In addition to blacks, Hispanics, Asian Americans, American Indians, and other minority groups display a scenario of both continuing problems and progress. However, anyone looking at the total picture must admit to the critical, growing gap between the majority and minority populations.

Two years before the racially motivated riots in Los Angeles, one author, Hugh Davis Graham, warned

> As the United States approaches the year 2000, special studies are accumulating that describe our entry into the 21st century with a tone of alarm. In *LA 2000: A City for the Future,* a blue ribbon panel of civic leaders assisted by the Rand Corporation warned that "Los Angeles is rapidly becoming a bimodal city." The city's high school class of 2000, which was just entering kindergarten when *LA 2000* was released was more than 72% minority (51.4% Hispanic, 12.4% Black, 6.9% Asian). In 1988, 38% of these students were classified as limited-English proficient (LEP), and a third of them (approximately 25% of the Black students and 40% of the Latino students) were expected to drop out of school. Almost half of the applicants for entry-level jobs in Los Angeles County, the report observed, were currently rejected because of inadequate skills in reading, writing, and basic computations.[9]

Social workers responded quickly to the 1992 Los Angeles rioting by going "into schools, disaster centers, and communities, offering crisis counseling, delivering food and clothing, and confronting ethnic tensions, racism and bigotry."[10] Hiratsuka states:

> Few were surprised by the violence that exploded this spring after a jury acquitted four white police officers of nearly all charges in the beating of Rodney King, a black motorist whose ordeal was captured on videotape.

Social workers traced the roots of the crisis to a society that refuses to acknowledge race and class division, denies opportunities to those at the bottom and often pits struggling ethnic groups against each other. Many despaired of making U.S. leaders understand the seriousness of the problems that led to the nation's deadliest riot—and could do so again.[11]

More than any other profession, social work has tried to address the problems of discrimination. In 1978 the Council on Social Work Education published *The Dual Perspective: Inclusion of Ethnic Minority Content in the Social Work Curriculum.* The Dual Perspective model was actually mandated by the social work profession to sensitize both social work faculty and students to the special problems and needs of minorities. G. De Hoyos, A. De Hoyos, and Anderson describe the dual perspective model as follows:

The model suggests that individuals develop two self-images: a personal self-image (through the individual's family and immediate community—the nurturing system) and a social self-image (through the society's political, economic, and educational systems—the sustaining system). It further suggests that whether minority group members acquire a good or poor self-image within the family unit, they usually develop a poor "social," or "major," self-image because of the prejudice and discrimination typically found in social institutions.[12]

De Hoyos and colleagues further state that although the dual perspective has been an important sensitizing tool in social work, they believe that two other perspectives are utilized much more in social work literature to explain the problems of minorities. These two perspectives are cultural dissonance and institutional racism.[13] Traditionally, cultural dissonance has been thought to be created by the differences between the culture of the minority group and the culture of the majority group. Cultural dissonance can be illustrated by the following case history.

Juanita was an 18-year-old Native American girl who finished her high school education on one of the larger southwest reservations. She went to college in another state. She had a struggle in getting registered and getting adjusted to the large impersonal college system. Three weeks into the semester one of Juanita's aunts died unexpectedly and, as was the custom or culture of her family, Juanita immediately left for the reservation. She did not think it was appropriate to mention her family situation to any of her teachers. When she returned to school, she was critically behind in much of her work. A few of her teachers were understanding, but most of them required her to make up the class work quickly and under pressure. Juanita panicked and left the college without even taking the time to withdraw formally.

The culture of Juanita's family had required her to leave to attend her aunt's funeral. The college culture required her to get her work in on time and to produce even though she was under stress. The cultural dissonance created so many problems that she could not cope and left abruptly for home.

The second perspective of institutional racism was popularized in the mid-1960s. Institutional racism deals with minority problems in terms of discrimination practiced in social structures. The most glaring institutional racism is found in the employment structures of the United States. There are far fewer employment opportunities for minorities. The following case history illustrates the impact of institutional racism.

Jamal, a 17-year-old black high school junior, moved from the west coast to a midwestern semi-rural community. He needed a job, and so he made applications all over the community. He was constantly turned down by the local businessmen and went the whole summer without a job. His divorced mother was working at a dry-cleaning establishment and tried to give him some spending money, but it was a continual strain on the family.

Jamal began to interact with other boys who were defined by the community as undesirables. Soon he was picked up for stealing clothes and gas. The juvenile authorities established a record on him, and by the time he entered school for his senior year, he had been labeled as a "gangbanger." Jamal had never been a top student, but now his grades really began to suffer. The combination of his increased truancy and more involvement with his "gang" caused the school officials to ask him to leave. They sent him to an alternative program which he did not complete. After three more arrests he was placed in a juvenile correction facility.

Jamal's case history illustrates how subtly institutional racism works. Although no one can predict what would have happened to Jamal if he had been given a good summer job, the chances of his making it in our society seemingly would have been much better. Society has to reward its members, and the economic system is unfortunately one of the most powerful reward systems.

Social Work Intervention with Minorities

Social work practice with people of color has been referred to by a number of different terms including *ethnic-sensitive practice, ethnic competence, ethnic minority practice, cross-cultural* or *cross-racial practice,* and *multicultural counseling.*[14] Thus, recognizing the need for an expanded definition of culturally competent social work practice to meet the needs of diverse individuals and groups, NASW published standards on this topic in 2001. Following is a summary of the ten standards:

- Values and ethics—we are to work within the values, ethics, and standards of the profession, yet there is a need to examine how our values (professional and personal) may conflict with or accommodate the needs of people from diverse backgrounds.
- Self-awareness—we look to understand our own personal and cultural values as a way of appreciating the multicultural identities found in others.
- Cross-cultural knowledge—we continually seek to gain advanced knowledge of diverse groups regarding their history, values, traditions, expressions, and family systems.
- Cross-cultural skills—we apply appropriate skills, methods, and techniques that demonstrate an awareness of the role that one's culture has in the helping relationship.
- Service delivery—we are knowledgeable about services in the community so that we can make appropriate referrals.

- Empowerment and advocacy—when appropriate, we advocate for and with clients for change in programs and policies.
- Diverse workforce—we advocate for the recruitment, hiring, and retention of persons that ensure diversity in programs and agencies.
- Professional education—we participate in educational programs that promote cultural competence.
- Language and diversity—we advocate for services, information, and referrals to agencies and programs that provide services in a language appropriate for clients.
- Cross-cultural leadership—we advance information about diverse clients to other professionals.[15]

As far back as 1989, Cross et al.[16] recommended developing five basic skills to aid in the provision of competent cross-cultural services. Whereas advances have been made in the field, their recommendations continue to be applicable today. They are as follows: First is the development of an awareness and acceptance of differences, especially when those differences may interfere with the helping process. For example, one's values, the concept of time, how people are shown respect, the meaning of family, and how children are disciplined may differ significantly. The helper needs to seek to understand and respect differences in an effort to help. Second is the need for heightened self-awareness. This is becoming aware of the influence of one's own culture and how it shapes values, customs, traditions, and ways of living. As social workers become cross-culturally competent, they come to realize that there are qualities about one's own culture as well as other cultures that are negative as well as positive. Further, an awareness develops that conflicts between people from different cultures can arise and, out of respect for both, compromises will need to be negotiated. Third is the acknowledgement of differences that are introduced into the dynamics of the relationship. As the social worker's self-awareness increases, he or she realizes that, at some point, misinterpretations of verbal communication, nonverbal communication, or both will likely occur. Being aware of potential miscommunications is evidence that the social worker has reached a level of cross-cultural competence, as well as gaining an understanding of how to effectively deal with miscommunications as they occur. The fourth skill is the increase in specialized knowledge of clients' cultures. Becoming familiar with differing values, norms, customs, and traditions is important in developing an understanding of clients and their behaviors. This knowledge will enable the practitioner to avoiding making mistakes that may offend the client as well as his or her family and community. Finally, the adaptation of skills by the helper is the ability to adjust one's methods of practice in response to the differences found between cultures. For example, instead of holding to fixed hourly appointments, the worker may need to set flexible times in order to meet the needs of his or her clients.

Two theoretical models seem to hold promise for systematic social work intervention into the problems of minority groups. The first model is a three-stage model proposed by De Hoyos et al.[17] and others, who utilize the stages of (1) individual intervention, (2) interactional intervention, and (3) social-cultural intervention as their basic framework (see Figure 17.1). They make the point that social workers have utilized stages 1 and 2 with both nonminority and minority clients rather effectively. However, they state that "Although this two-level approach may be sufficient with nonminority clients a third stage of intervention—the sociocultural approach—is needed."[18]

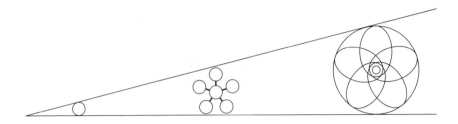

Individual Intervention	Interactional Intervention	Sociocultural Intervention
Neo-Freudian theory, Cognitive theory, etc.	Ecological systems, General systems, etc.	Structural functionalism
Psychoanalysis, Traditional casework, Existential therapy, etc.	Structural, functional, family, ecological, and communication therapies, etc.	Sociocultural therapy

FIGURE 17.1   Three-Stage Model.

Source: Genevieve De Hoyos, Arturo De Hoyos, and Christian B. Anderson. "Sociocultural Dislocation, Beyond the Dual Perspective," *Social Work*, 31 (January/February 1986), 63.

At the sociocultural level, social workers know that without conditionally rewarding roles individuals can only remain forever unrewarded, marginal, and alienated. On the basis of this understanding, professionals can objectively and openly help minority clients to identify goals by choosing to

- accommodate to the majority structure so as to share in its social rewards;
- reject the accommodation to the majority structure and build separate majority institutions; and
- strike a compromise between accommodation to and rejection of the majority structure.

The authors suggest that, by using sociocultural intervention skills with minority clients, social workers can be

- more objective and insightful in their assessment of cases;
- more understanding, supportive, and nonjudgmental;
- better informed regarding sociocultural issues;
- more effective in problem solving;
- more effective in interpreting and teaching middle-class values and behavior;
- more effective in interpreting and teaching values and behavior of minority groups;
- better negotiators between majority and minority persons, as advocates, and as peacemakers; and
- more realistic, rational, and pragmatic in their role as sounding boards.[19]

By utilizing this three-stage model, social workers can conceptualize their practice with minorities in a more meaningful way. The social worker can be effective with minority clients by methodically considering each of the three stages to see where intervention needs to take place. Perhaps intervention in only one of the stages can be helpful, but more often than not, intervention needs to occur in two or three of the stages at the same time. For instance, a client's self-image (stage 1) problem can be helped immensely if the social worker can arrange a job (stage 2). However, the social worker who can help the client begin to negotiate between his or her minority value system and the majority value system (stage 3) will be helping the client learn to deal with both cultural dissonance and institutional racism. It should be obvious that stage 3 also requires social workers to try to intervene in the structure of society to ensure that minorities can seek out and find rewarding roles to prevent a sense of hopelessness and alienation.

The second model entitled biculturalism was effectively presented by de Anda in 1984.[20] Her thrust was to propose a model that would help social workers conceptualize minority people living and being socialized in two cultures simultaneously. De Anda proposed that dual socialization is made possible because there is, generally speaking, an overlap between the minority and majority cultures that provides for shared values and norms. De Anda's model of biculturalism is illustrated in Figures 17.2 and 17.3.

De Anda further addressed six factors that play an important role in helping a member of an ethnic minority group to become bicultural. These six factors are seminal for the social work profession. De Anda states

> To foster the development of behavioral repertoires for dealing with the demands of both the majority and minority cultures, the worker needs to examine the impact of the six factors previously discussed to determine whether they are serving to facilitate or impede the process of bicultural socialization for the client. The components of this complex task include:
>
> **1.** Determining areas of interface between the two cultures that can serve as "doorways" between them.
> **2.** Noting the major points of conflict between the two cultures and the negative consequences for the client.

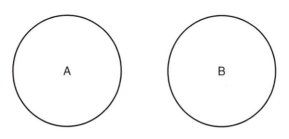

A = Majority Culture
B = Minority Culture

FIGURE 17.2 Two Separate Cultures.

Source: Diane de Anda, "Bicultural Socialization: Factors Affecting the Minority Experience," *Social Work,* 29 (March/April 1984), 102.

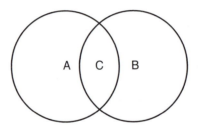

A = Majority Culture
B = Minority Culture
C = Shared Values and Norms

FIGURE 17.3   Biculturalism.

Source: de Anda, p. 102.

3. Searching out and providing translators, mediators, and models who can offer guidelines for dealing with such conflicts and offer critical experiential information.
4. Arranging when possible for increased corrective feedback for the client in the environment.
5. Working to expand the client's repertoire of problem-solving skills, particularly those that are the least context bound, and helping to develop a larger repertoire of context-specific problem-solving skills.
6. Educating people of the majority culture about the significant characteristics, values, and needs of minority cultures, as well as serving as an advocate of greater flexibility and adjustment in the mainstream culture's institutions.[21]

The biculturalism framework provides another conceptual tool for the profession of social work to continue to help minority clients realize their full potential in the American culture.

Social Services

A controversial issue is whether or not social workers need to be of the same color and race to be effective in working with clients and their problems. Numerous differing opinions and positions exist. Some claim it is essential for blacks to work with blacks; others disagree and propose that individual problems and competencies, not race, are the important factors.

Harper and Lantz view cross-cultural social work as both potentially damaging and useful. Those critical of such practice voice concern that efforts by a majority person social worker, serving minorities, may be directed toward helping them adjust to the status-quo and keeping them satisfied with their impoverished living condition.

Critics have pointed to a number of variables that become barriers to the helping relationship. These variables include "language differences, class-bound value differences between social worker and client." Although barriers to cross-culture practice exist, it is possible for social workers to accept and respect human differences and similarities. "Only by respecting the sameness of our common human needs and the uniqueness of our different cultural methods of meeting those needs can a person begin to become a competent cross-cultural social work practitioner."[22]

Kadushin reports various studies indicating that social workers can cross color boundaries effectively in some situations, although in others racial similarity is definitely advantageous. He concludes that

> although nonwhite workers may be necessary for nonwhite clients in some instances and therapeutically desirable in others, white workers can work and have worked effectively with nonwhite clients. They seem to say that although race is important, the nature of the interpersonal relationship established between two people is more important than skin color and that although there are disadvantages to racially mixed worker-client contacts, there are special advantages. Conversely, there are special advantages to racial similarity and there are countervailing disadvantages. In other words, the problem is not as clear-cut as might be supposed.[23]

In providing services for and with persons of a different ethnicity, two factors seem to be particularly important. One is the need for the workers to understand the differences, culturally and otherwise, that exist and be accepting of these. The other is to be selective in regard to who does what; in other words, in working with some individuals and problems it would be essential for the worker to be of the same race; in other situations it might make no difference or could even be advantageous to have a worker of a different ethnic group.

Social work services with minority populations.

Illustrative of cultural differences that need to be kept in mind are those listed by Locklear regarding the American Indian:

1. Generosity is still the paramount virtue among most Indians.
2. Many Indians continue to hold the old concepts of time. For them, time is circular rather than horizontal. Past, present, and future are all one.
3. For most Indians, work must be more than a steady job.
4. Family and interpersonal relationships have priority over all else.
5. The extended family system continues to operate in many tribes, thus providing an enlarged sphere of family relationships as well as family responsibilities.
6. Many Indians are basically noncompetitive in their relationships to non-Indians.[24]

Because of language barriers and cultural differences, it is maintained by many that Chicanos, for example, should work with Chicanos. Others suggest that non-Chicanos may be just as effective if they understand the cultural differences and have language skills. Mizio agrees that oftentimes a person of the same ethnic origin may be most effective; then adds, "But it is also true that some white workers can establish viable working relationships with minority clients, some minority workers do not work well with minority clients, and the majority of social workers are white."[25]

Van Soest has suggested several seminal guidelines for social work practitioners who work in our multicultural society. The guidelines are

- Honor each person's value, dignity, and right to self-determination.
- Use effective communication, listening, empathy, and negotiating skills.
- Avoid attacking others and their views as a way of validating one's own position.
- Recognize the pervasiveness of oppression in society, and encourage examination of the residues of racism, sexism, and homophobia on both individual and organization levels.
- Maintain the interests and welfare of clients as the priority.[26]

In recent years, professionals have begun debating whether or not there are counseling principles and techniques that are common to all cultures or principles and techniques that are unique to differing cultures and need to be implemented. Fischer, Jome, and Atkinson concluded that there needs to be a combination of the two perspectives. Social workers and other helpers need to apply principles based on an understanding of the individual's families or group's culture but that general principles also apply across all cultures. The four common principles identified by these authors are

- Client–counselor relationship. Characteristics of warmth, genuineness, and empathy as well as the ability to put the client at ease are essential to the success of any relationship.
- Shared worldview. Refers to the beliefs about values and reality that are held in common by people of a particular group or culture. The helper needs to understand the client's worldview and treat it with respect.

- Expectation of positive outcome. This principle is concerned with the client's expectation about a positive outcome from the helping relationship. The shared worldview, the strength of the relationship, and the credibility of the helper contribute to raising the expectations of the client.
- Interventions. Cultures differ in the types of interventions which they will tolerate. Helpers need to be sensitive and flexible to the differences and adapt accordingly. The intervention may not be as important as the belief that it will be helpful.[27]

Educational Developments

The history of social work reflects differential services, often limited or isolated, for ethnic and racial groups. Individuals and families from minority groups have been assisted by social workers in various ways. Concomitant with these services have been attempts to provide special emphasis and direction in the training of social workers so they could become more sensitive and effective in providing these services. Across the past several decades only a minimum of effort has been expended in this direction. Since the 1960s numerous thrusts have emerged, pinpointing the need for more understanding of ethnic differences and special needs in working with minority clients.

Schools of social work and undergraduate social work programs have inaugurated, in various degrees and ways, programs and curricula tooled to improve services to minority peoples. These efforts have gained in momentum, culminating, at least standardwise, with the official pronouncement of the accreditation standard approved by the Council on Social Work Education that schools of social work must demonstrate in a positive manner a program to recruit more minority students and faculty and to change and alter their curricula to incorporate more understanding and training for working with minorities.

Three important parts of the educational venture relevant to minorities are students, faculty, and curriculum. Positive movements regarding all three are taking place in most schools of social work and in undergraduate social work programs.

Minority Students

Minority student enrollments are on the upswing. In the 1950s many schools of social work enrolled no minority students and the numbers in the other schools were minimal. Since the late 1960s enrollments of minority students have increased considerably. Social work educators have conscientiously recruited minority students. In 1999, 32.7 percent of a total of 24,475 juniors and seniors in baccalaureate social work programs were ethnic minority students, up 1.7 percent in three years. In 2004, that percentage had risen further to 37.3 or 9,583 minority students from an overall enrollment of 25,715. Minorities comprised 29 percent of the 22,936 full-time MSW students and 32 percent of the 13,539 part-time students (both were increases—2.9 percent from 1999 to 2004). Minorities comprised 34 percent of the 1,808 full-time doctoral students and 28.9 percent of the 1009 part-time students in 2004.

Most schools of social work have adopted specific recruitment and training programs, which usually offer scholarships and other financial aid to increase the number of minority students in training, who may then become available to provide services for their own people and others. For example, one western school, through several grants and planned emphasis, has sponsored special programs to aid American Indian students.

In addition to financial assistance needed for minority students, other assistance is often provided to offset educational and cultural limitations experienced by some minority students wishing to enter schools of social work. Many schools have faculty and others who provide special counseling and assistance for minority students before coming to school, and while there, to ensure competency on graduation.

Substantial efforts are in operation to recruit and train more minority students in the undergraduate social work programs. The standards for accreditation for baccalaureate degree programs in social work, which have as their primary stated educational objective "preparation for beginning professional social work practice," state that major positive efforts are to be carried out in recruiting and training of minority students, encompassing additional minority faculty and significant alterations in curricula. The standards are explicit: "Preparation for effective social work practice requires curriculum content that develops in the student an understanding of and appreciation for ethnic, racial, and cultural diversity in a pluralistic society."

Minority Faculty

A second major thrust has been in relation to the increase of minority faculty. In November 1967, fifty-nine schools of social work in the United States reported[28] a total of 212 full-time minority group faculty members for all ranks, which amounted to 12.3 percent of the total of 1,718 faculty. By 1999, a significant and positive trend emerged. Of the 417 BSW programs reporting their statistics to the CSWE, 25.4 percent of the faculty members were ethnic minorities. However, through 2004 the percentage of minority faculty in baccalaureate programs essentially remained the same (25.8 percent). Further, 25.1 percent of the faculty in graduate programs in this same year were minorities. It is also important to note that back in 1999, 64.8 percent of the full-time faculty members were women and minorities. Social work education is, however, committed to opening its system to women. In 2004, the percentage had declined to 50.7.

Not only has there been considerable increase in the number of minority faculty in schools of social work, but there has been a major development toward helping other faculty members understand more about minorities and increase their abilities to teach minority content and practice. Workshops, classes, consultations, and other staff development activities have been inaugurated to increase knowledge and teaching skills and improve attitudes toward minorities.

Turner suggests there are two major issues confronting social work education in relation to minorities: "(1) how to equip social workers with the knowledge, skills, and attitudes that will enable them to improve the status of minorities and (2) how to attract more minority-group students into social work education."[29]

Turner also proposes that schools of social work respond with the following, specifically:

1. Developmental recruitment.
2. Willingness to pay a significant part of the cost of preparing teachers.

3. Willingness to employ minority persons at senior as well as junior levels.
4. Employment of more than token numbers of minority faculty.
5. Reeducation of existing faculty members about their roles.
6. Development of university administration support for hiring of minority persons.[30]

Curriculum Minority Content

In addition to increasing the number of minority students and faculty, it is imperative that the curricula of the schools of social work be altered and enriched to include pertinent materials regarding content, attitudes, and skills of practice. The current standards of the CSWE state that positive attempts must be made in this direction for accreditation to be approved, both on undergraduate and graduate levels.

Turner suggests that the curriculum must deal with three distinct educational needs:

(1) the need of the minority student to have a systematic and in-depth knowledge of his own group, (2) the need for all students to have basic information about the major ethnic and racial groups in America today, and (3) the need of the minority-majority problem specialist for more in-depth knowledge about any minority group he expects to work with.[31]

It is clearly apparent that there is a bona fide need to incorporate into the curricula of graduate and undergraduate programs the knowledge, attitudes, and skills that bring the minority peoples, their problems, and solutions within the scope of social work practice. Turner suggests that these developments are tied in with social justice:

Tradition and history have made problems of ethnic and racial justice an inextricable part of the more general problem of social justice. The curriculum must make this connection clear to the student, for he who fights for one must be committed to fight for both.[32]

Turner summarizes action all social workers should be able to perform in the minority arena:

1. Recognize racist policies and acts, individual or institutional.
2. Bring racist practices to the attention of those who have responsibility and power to stop them.
3. Commit resources they have to change or redesign policies that are racist.
4. Respond constructively to efforts to eliminate racism.[33]

Summary

From this brief presentation it is apparent that social work is in the process of developing an increased interest in minorities and enriched services that cope with some of the problems related to ethnic and racial diversity. That many debilitating and unfair racial prejudices exist is obvious; that attempts are being made to meet some of these problems is encouraging.

Minority persons are aided by social workers in nearly all of the traditional social agencies; in fact, they constitute unduly large clientele percentages in public welfare, corrections, and other community services. Two major concepts used to define minority problems are cultural dissonance and institutional racism. The social work profession is acutely aware of these phenomena and is working to mitigate them in our society.

Two new major theoretical concepts of sociocultural intervention and biculturalism are adding new insights to the practice of social work. These models give specific guidelines for working with minorities.

A beginning has been made in recruiting and training more minority students, to provide more minority social workers. Increased numbers of minority faculty are teaching in graduate and undergraduate educational programs. Curricula of schools of social work and undergraduate social work programs have been and are being altered to help all students understand more about working with minority clients, and to give special emphasis to many in becoming more competent in providing professional services to all ethnic groups.

Selected References

BALGOPAL, PALLASSANA, ed., *Social Work Practice with Immigrants and Refugees.* New York: Columbia University Press, 2000.

CONER-EDWARDS, ALICE F., and JEANNE SPURLOCK, *Black Families in Crisis: The Middle Class.* Bristol, PA: Brunner/Mazel, 1998.

DE ANDA, DIANE, *Controversial Issues in Multiculturalism.* Boston: Allyn & Bacon, 1997.

DEVORE, WYNETTA, and ELFREDIA G. SCHLESINGER, *Ethnic-Sensitive Social Work Practice,* 4th ed. Boston: Allyn & Bacon, 1996.

GIL, DAVID G., *Confronting Injustice and Oppression.* New York: Columbia University Press, 1998.

GITTERMAN, ALEX, ed., *Handbook of Social Work Practice with Vulnerable Populations.* New York: Columbia University Press, 1991.

GRAHAM, HUGH DAVIS, "Race, Language, and Social Policy: Comparing the Black and Hispanic Experience in the U.S.," *Population and Environment,* 12, no. 1 (Fall 1990), 43–58.

GREEN, JAMES W., *Cultural Awareness in the Human Services: A Multi-Ethnic Approach,* 2nd ed. Boston: Allyn & Bacon, 1995.

LONGRES, JOHN F., *Human Behavior in the Social Environment,* 3rd ed. Itasca, IL: F. E. Peacock, 2000.

LUM, DOMAN, *Cultural Competence, Practice Stages, and Client Systems: A Case Study Approach.* Pacific Grove, CA: Brooks/Cole, 2005.

MARTIN, ELMER P., and JOANNE MITCHELL MARTIN, *Social Work and the Black Experience.* Annapolis JCT, MD: NASW Press, 1995.

PROCTOR, ENOLA K., and LARRY E. DAVID, "The Challenge of Racial Difference: Skills for Clinical Practice," *Social Work,* 39 (May 1994), 314–323.

QUERALT, MAGALY, *Social Environment and Human Behavior: A Diversity Perspective.* Boston: Allyn & Bacon, 1996.

SCHRIVER, JOE M., *Human Behavior and the Social Environment: Shifting Paradigms in Essential Knowledge for Social Work Practice,* 2nd ed. Boston: Allyn & Bacon, 1998.

SUE, DERALD WING, and DAVID SUE, *Counseling the Culturally Different: Theory and Practice,* 2nd ed. New York: Wiley, 1990.

Notes

1. John Hiratsuka, "Immigration Cost, Compassion Collide," *NASW News,* 40 (January 1995), p. 3.

2. Quoted in William G. Mayfield, "Mental Health in the Black Community," *Social Work,* 17 (May 1972), p. 110.

3. Stokely Carmichael and Charles V. Hamilton, *Black Power: The Politics of Liberation in America* (New York: Random House, 1967), p. 4.

4. Terry Jones, "Institutional Racism in the United States," *Social Work,* 19 (March 1974), p. 221.

5. U.S. Department of Commerce, *U.S. Census Bureau, Population Estimates Program, Population Division* (Washington, DC, Internet release date January 2, 2001). Retrieved from www.census.gov/population/estimates/nation.

6. Douglas Glasgow, "Black Power through Community Control," *Social Work,* 17 (May 1972), p. 61.

7. William Julius Wilson, "The Black Underclass," *Wilson Quarterly,* 7, no. 2 (Spring 1984), p. 88.

8. U.S. Department of Commerce, U.S. Census Bureau, *Money Income in the United States, Current Population Reports, 1999* (issued September 2000). Retrieved from www.census.gov/prod/2000pubs/p60-209.pdf.

9. Hugh Davis Graham, "Race, Language and Social Policy: Comparing the Black and Hispanic Experience in the U.S.," *Population and Environment,* 12, no. 1 (Fall 1990), p. 44.

10. John Hiratsuka, "L.A. Burning: Social Workers Respond," *NASW News,* 37 (July 1992), p. 3.

11. Ibid., p. 3.

12. Genevieve De Hoyos, Arturo De Hoyos, and Christian B. Anderson, "Sociocultural Dislocation: Beyond the Dual Perspective," *Social Work,* 31 (January/February 1986), p. 61.

13. Ibid., p. 61.

14. Jerry V. Diller, *Cultural Diversity: A Primer for the Human Services* (Belmont, CA: Brooks/Cole, 1999).

15. National Association of Social Workers, *NASW Standards for Cultural Competence in Social Work Practice,* 2001. Retrieved from www.socialworkers.org/practice/Standards/NASWCulturalStandards.pdf.

16. T. L. Cross, B. J. Bazron, K. W. Dennis, and M. R. Isaacs, *Towards a Culturally Competent System of Care* (Washington, DC: Georgetown University Child Development Center, 1989).

17. Genevieve De Hoyos, Arturo De Hoyos, and Christian B. Anderson, "Sociocultural Dislocation: Beyond the Dual Perspective," *Social Work,* 31 (January/February 1986), p. 62.

18. Ibid., p. 62.

19. Ibid., p. 65.

20. Diane de Anda, "Bicultural Socialization: Factors Affecting the Minority Experience," *Social Work,* 29 (March/April 1984), pp. 101–107.

21. Ibid., pp. 106–107.

22. Karen V. Harper and Jim Lantz, *Cross-Cultural Practice. Social Work with Diverse Populations* (Chicago: Lyceum Books, 1996), p. 2.

23. Alfred Kadushin, "The Racial Factor in the Interview," *Social Work,* 17 (May 1972), p. 98.

24. Herbert H. Locklear, "American Indian Myths," *Social Work,* 17 (May 1972), pp. 77–78.

25. Emelicia Mizio, "White Worker-Minority Client," *Social Work,* 17 (May 1972), p. 83.

26. Dorothy Van Soest, "Multiculturalism and Social Work Education: The Non-Debate about Competing Perspectives," *Social Work Education,* 31 (Winter 1995), p. 64.

27. A. R. Fischer, L. M. Jome, and D. R. Atkinson, "Reconceptualizing Multicultural Counseling: Universal Healing Conditions in a Culturally Specific Context," *Counseling Psychologist,* 26, no. 4, 1998).

28. Carl Scott, ed., *Ethnic Minorities in Social Work Education* (New York: CSWE, 1970), pp. 45–46.

29. John B. Turner, "Education for Practice with Minorities," *Social Work,* 17 (May 1972), 112. Reprinted with permission of the National Association of Social Workers.

30. Ibid., p. 113.

31. Ibid., p. 117.

32. Ibid., p. 116.

33. Ibid., p. 115.

18

Social Work in Rural Areas

John sat, quiet and withdrawn, gazing out the car window as they traveled the country road toward the county seat. The "voices" were calling to him, as they so often did, and he became increasingly restless, which was also happening more and more frequently. In the two years since he graduated from high school, things just hadn't been going well. He had imagined as he grew up that he would be a help to his dad on the farm, but now he could do little because of the insistent "voices."

His parents watched in disbelief as he changed. They tried to understand what was happening. They had never known anyone to behave as he did. He became agitated over nothing. He couldn't concentrate for more than a few minutes. They knew he needed help, and it was for this help that they

were making this trip to town. They had an appointment for him to see the traveling mental health professionals who came only once a month to their remote area.

As they drove on, they wondered what the recommendations would be. They feared he would need to be hospitalized, which would mean he would be 240 miles from home. Now that the haying season was here, it would be almost impossible for them to visit the hospital. They hoped they would be able to care for him at home and that his medication would not be too complicated for them to manage. But most of all, they hoped their son would be able to get some help so he could be a normal, happy person who could lead a productive life again.

Social work services are needed in the rural areas of the United States. Ginsberg states that "the social and economic problems faced by the people of nonmetropolitan America are often as severe or even more serious than those faced by their metropolitan fellow citizens."[1] The rural population of the United States is difficult to define, but demographic experts place the rural population between 55 and 87 million, depending on the definition that is used for rural. Ginsberg graphically makes the point that "it is larger than the populations of all but a few of the world's nations and nearly equals the population of France or England."[2] A study by the National Center for Social Policy and Practice found a shortage of mental health professionals in the rural areas of six selected states.[3] The report graphically outlines the difficulty rural people have in obtaining services. The shortages found in mental health workers is only a tip of the iceberg. Professional social work services are lacking in many rural social service delivery systems.

In addition to a lack of rural social work services and personnel, rural areas are under tremendous stress. In the past thirty years some rural communities have been emptied of most of their people and are now faced with a crumbling social infrastructure. Other small communities have had to withstand the effects of proportionately enormous growth when a manufacturing plant has located nearby. In addition to these major population shifts, rural communities are in the throes of economic recession. The "farm crisis" is real, as across the nation farmers and their families are uprooted by bankruptcy.

All of these combined forces have taken their toll on the traditionally stable farm family. One rural study identified urgently needed services in the following areas: (1) job and economic problems; (2) alcohol and drug problems of adults and youth; (3) lack of constructive leisure-time programs and facilities; (4) marriage and family problems; and (5) personal stress, anxiety, and depression.[4]

At a hearing of the House Select Committee on Children, Youth, and Families in April 1989, it was noted that 16.9 percent of the population living in rural areas had incomes below the poverty line.[5] The poverty line was defined as $9,056 annual income for a family of three. The 16.9 percent in rural areas is almost equal to the 18.6 percent poverty rate found in the central city areas of our large cities. It is alarming to note that between the years 1978 and 1987 poverty rates rose from 13.5 to 16.9 percent. The report also indicates that rural poor families are more likely than urban families to live in households headed by two parents who both work. Rural poor are somewhat more likely to be elderly and white.

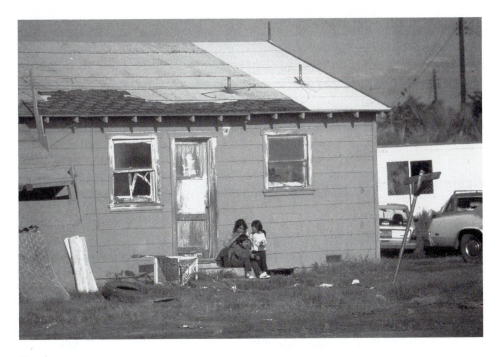

Rural poverty.

In the 1980s and 1990s, rural communities have continued to change. Ruff contends that some rural communities have combined "rural" and "urban" to become "rurban."[6] She states that a rurban community is somewhere on a continuum between rural and urban and meets the following four criteria:

1. *Population size.* The U.S. Census Bureau uses 2,500 or less as a population size to define rural. The author suggests a population between 2,500 and 10,000 to define a rurban community.
2. *Economic base.* Moving from dependence on a primary source of occupational income to a diversity of occupations causes the community to shift from rural into a rurban status. Some residents may live in the rurban community and work outside, but the community does not necessarily become a suburb or a purely residential area.
3. *Availability of services.* The rurban community moves from being isolated or completely removed from services to a situation where services become more accessible either because of improved transportation, or because services physically move into the geographic area.
4. *Homogeneous cultural mores.* In the traditional rural community, the majority of the population is in tune with communally accepted mores and behavior. As populations grow and newcomers move in, these dynamics change and diverse groups with different expectations and social behavior mores appear, and the community moves to a rurban status as opposed to a rural status.[7]

Regardless of whether a community is a traditional rural community or a rurban transition community, it is frequently underserved by human service professionals. As Human and Windle (as cited in Wagenfield et al.) state:

> Rural areas are often neglected in health care planning because it is easier and more economical to rely on existing urban models than to gather new information and to plan systems specifically suited for rural communities. As a result, rural communities are often forced to use or adapt service systems or service support mechanisms designed for conditions that differ greatly from those in most rural areas.[8]

Beginnings in Rural Social Work

The beginnings of rural social work practice can be traced to the Country Life Commission of 1908 appointed by President Theodore Roosevelt and the National Conference of Charities and Correction of the same year. The Great Depression and New Deal philosophy of the 1930s gave impetus and a broadening to the practice of rural social work.

Interest in rural social work waned during World War II and the 1950s. A resurgence of interest began to develop in the late 1960s as a result of the War on Poverty philosophy and also important social work leadership by Leon Ginsberg and others. In 1969 Ginsberg, dean of the West Virginia School of Social Work, delivered a major address on rural social work at the Council on Social Work Education Annual Program Meeting. Other leaders joined the rural social work movement and created organizations and meetings called the

Rural Caucus and the Annual Institute of Rural Social Work. A professional journal called *Human Services in the Rural Environment* was initiated in 1976 at the University of Wisconsin at Madison.

At the Tenth National Institute on Social Work in Rural Areas held in 1985, one of the presenters, Mike Jacobsen, observed

> It has been demonstrated that the years 1969 to 1985 mark a rapid growth in the scholarly activities of rural social work educators and practitioners in the United States. A qualitative analysis of this development suggests that this scholarly productivity has had the effect of providing a history for rural social work in the United States, specified useful arrangements for field and continuing rural education, detailed many professional and community changes in rural human services, demonstrated the nature of competence in rural practice, and provided the context for further scholarly development of rural social work topics.[9]

Rural Social Work Practice

A rural social worker is described as a generalist who brings to bear a broad range of methodologies and skills in practice. The generalist rural social worker must have a good background in community development and organization and must also be able to work with individuals or groups. He or she must have the skills to analyze community systems and decide on effective intervention levels within the total system. The rural social worker also needs to be a good administrator and a resource specialist. Rural social work requires a strong sense of independence and the ability to work in an unstructured environment. Ginsberg states

> The special characteristics of rural settings require most workers to practice in ways that differ from their urban counterparts. Social workers in rural communities require skills in all the social work methods and must be able to use themselves effectively with social institutions of all sizes—from the individual and his family to the total community. The need for social workers who are generalists in rural communities is confirmed by social work theoreticians and practitioners of both the past and the present.[10]

The rural social worker needs to understand both the positives and negatives of working in small rural communities. Some important positive elements include (1) open communication systems, (2) interagency cooperation, and (3) a sense of community. The rural community has perhaps the most open communication system in our society today. News travels quickly, and residents can respond readily. Even though services are minimal in many areas, the positive interagency cooperation can help to mitigate the lack of resources. Agency personnel reach out to one another on a personal, informal level to provide resources to clients. The sense of community is pervasive, and community residents are willing to take care of "their own." An example of this sense of community was demonstrated recently in a rural community when a large barn filled with hay burned down. Before the embers were completely cooled, neighbors came with their equipment and had the mess cleaned up within hours. Many brought loads of baled hay to enable the burned-out family to feed their stock until other arrangements could be made.

Some negative elements of working in a rural area are (1) geographic isolation, (2) personnel isolation, and (3) service isolation. When a client who lives 150 miles away calls for an appointment, care must be taken to coordinate times and efforts so that valuable time and energy will not be wasted. Geographic isolation is also demonstrated when it takes a rural social worker two or three hours to return children to their homes following an after-school self-esteem group session. Personnel and service isolation can cause the rural social worker to feel great pressure of being the "only one" available. The rural social worker needs to be able to reach out frequently for consultation and support systems to prevent worker burnout.

Two authors have developed the argument for the need to develop a curriculum for "advanced generalist" in social work education. They acknowledge that there continues to be a disparity between social work education and rural social work practice. They believe that MSW programs should allow for a rural advanced generalist concentration that includes the following:

> This program attempts to build upon the generic core of social work education essential to students training to be rural practitioners. In developing practitioners who can work with all segments and institutions of the rural community and who are prepared to adopt a variety of roles, this disparity between the promise of social work and its practice can be reached.
>
> Students must both be prepared with the technical expertise of micro, mezzo, and macro intervention skills, and instilled with a guiding philosophy which leads them to look for opportunities to intervene at multiple levels.
>
> The task of preparing advanced generalist practitioners who are able to intervene with individuals suffering from the effects of social problems, as well as the systems from which the social problems themselves are generated, is not simple. This, however, is the task to which rural social work educators must commit themselves.[11]

In *The Practice of Social Work*, Zastrow offers this timely advice about rural social work practice:

> Workers who practice in a basically rural environment must also be aware of a multiplicity of factors that impinge on effectiveness. . . . Seemingly innocuous factors like style of dress, hair length, and model of car can set the social worker in a rural area apart. In addition, the worker in a rural area may discover that events of the past still affect the behavior of the residents today. Long-standing family and church conflicts may exist and create barriers to getting community members to work on a problem or issue. The fact that many rural social workers lack exposure to the rural environment before beginning their practice creates additional difficulties. The worker's attitudes and ideas regarding rural communities may be outdated or even quite negative. This can affect interactions with residents just as strongly as racial bias in a minority community. The struggle to survive in a rural setting under these conditions may explain the burnout commonly experienced by in-migrant practitioners.[12]

The preceding paragraph that offers timely advice about rural social work practice rings clear for the state of Utah. With a population of over 3 million people, most of the state's population is concentrated in a narrow ninety-mile corridor from Ogden to Salt Lake to Provo. The rest of the state is more rural than urban and takes up approximately

80 percent of the land area. Social workers who practice in the rural areas of Utah must respond to a number of issues that are not as prominent in the urban centers. Dress is more casual and western in the rural areas and social workers who wear suits and ties are often seen as outsiders who want to force their big-city ideas on rural Utah. There is also a general misgiving and even mistrust of federal and state government in the rural areas. Rural citizens would rather have their county and municipal representatives help them with their local concerns rather than be dictated to by federal and state officers. Yet when it comes to food stamps, protective services, drug and alcohol programs, and other human services, the counties and municipalities don't have the resources to provide the needed services and must rely on federal and state programs for assistance. Another unique factor in rural Utah is religion with more than 90 percent of the rural citizens members of the Church of Jesus Christ of Latter-day Saints (LDS) or Mormon religion. Social workers who are not members of the LDS Church must attend to the beliefs and family perspectives of their rural LDS clients when they are providing social services. Similar rural concerns also occur in other western states such as Idaho, Wyoming, Montana, Nevada, Arizona, and New Mexico.

Roles of the Rural Social Worker

As mentioned earlier, the rural social worker is a generalist who must have the ability to work with individuals, families, and groups, as well as with the total community. A more specific listing of roles follows:

> *Direct Service Role—with Individuals, Couples, Families and Groups:* Rural social workers need to convey to the community the fact that social work is a valuable resource to every community member. Working directly with individuals and families to help them function more effectively is central to rural social work practice.
>
> Rural communities that are faced with population change or economic downturn require increased social work services to individuals and families. With these additional stresses comes an increase in problems such as family violence, substance abuse, and depression. Many rural social service agencies have established twenty-four-hour-a-day crisis lines where individuals and families can call for help.
>
> *Resource Specialist:* One of the most difficult roles the rural social worker assumes is that of assisting in the optimal utilization of the limited resources available in many rural areas. It requires imagination and creativity to put resources together in a different configuration in order to serve human needs effectively.
>
> The rural social worker must find ways to keep up with all the programs being funded through the states and federal government. For instance, if a couple has a newborn child who is blind, the social worker needs to know what resources are available and how the couple can make proper contact with the appropriate program. Because programs are continually changing, the rural social worker must keep up with the changes.
>
> *Social Service Administrator and Community Organizer:* Most rural communities have few professional people, and rural social workers usually find themselves in the role of trying to coordinate all the social services in the community. For instance, one rural social worker initiated monthly meetings with the public health nurse, school teachers,

probation officer, and several local church leaders to insure that community social service activities were coordinated and effective.

The rural social worker may also be called on to develop new funding sources to meet unmet needs in the community. The administrative function of raising money can be a real challenge to a social worker who wants to serve the community well.

The rural social worker needs to be able to relate to the power structure of the community. Rural communities have an informal power structure of leaders who operate unofficially but often have greater power than elected officials. These leaders reflect local values and may play an important role in determining how money is spent and whether or not the community will give new programs their support. Local government officials and funding sources must also be informed about the total agency operation. Rural social work agencies get into trouble when they fail to develop meaningful linkages with their governing bodies. Rural social workers need to be able to relate to both the informal and the formal power structure of the community and to orchestrate agency support, which in turn facilitates important services to rural clients.

The following case is an example of the work done by a rural social worker that incorporates all of the roles described previously.

The social worker was informed of a problem that was developing in a rural junior high school. A group of popular, well-known girls were making it difficult for new students to be accepted in the school. They went out of their way to make newcomers feel they were not wanted. The situation was exacerbated when the group of girls began to victimize a brain-damaged youngster.

The social worker decided to mobilize the school system and the PTA to remedy the situation. The social worker, the principal, and the president of the PTA planned a series of five lectures entitled "A Community That Cares" to be given at the PTA meetings during the school year. The lectures were developed around the themes, "Individualizing and Accepting Each Child" and "Understanding the Feelings of New People Moving into the Community."

The community accepted the lecture series very well. The PTA president had strong ties with the dominant religious group and received the backing of the community from several different power bases.

The initial meeting was cordial, and PTA members were pleased to consider problems of new and different children. The second meeting turned out to be the key meeting. The social worker talked of the importance of individualizing each child and the constant need to reinforce the child's feeling of self-worth.

A newcomer to the community, a father, asked if he could tell his story. He, his wife, and a daughter who had been brain-damaged at birth had purposely moved into a rural community so that their child would have greater opportunities to interact with other children and the school system. With some feeling, he said that they had been extremely disappointed because this community had rejected them. The hardest thing they had to deal with was the rejection of their daughter by other children, some teachers, and even adults in the community. In a parent-teacher conference, one teacher had insisted that the only thing wrong with their daughter was that they had spoiled her so that she acted like a baby. He related incidents where the "in" group of girls seemed to delight in hitting her every time they passed her. And perhaps hardest of all was that he had heard some parents actually told their children not to play with her because she was different.

As the parents and teachers listened to the father, they could sense the beginning of an atti-tude change in the community. The social worker quickly followed up with interviews with involved teachers and PTA officers to keep the lines of communication open.

The remainder of the lecture series reinforced important attitude changes in a community that was willing to listen. There was marked improvement in the system. The community became more sensitive to the needs of the newcomers. Some of the children invited the brain-damaged girl to their homes. The social worker continued to work with the family and the girl throughout the school year. Relationships became much more positive.[13]

Positive Aspects of Social Work Roles in Rural Communities

Even though rural social work is challenging, there are many positive aspects of serving in smaller communities. Ginsberg has identified five areas that offer the rural social worker significant rewards:

- *Independence.* Social workers in metropolitan areas frequently are responsible to a fairly complex administrative and supervisory structure. They may find their work closely monitored. They may have extensive reporting requirements in the organiza-tion. Social workers in rural communities are more likely to be autonomous and to work with little or no supervision because there are simply fewer social workers in the agency. A metropolitan social services agency, for example, might have hundreds of social work employees. The rural office of the same agency might have only a handful of workers. Therefore, those who are ambitious to work independently or prefer setting their own courses and critiquing their own performances may find it much more satisfying to work in a smaller community.
- *Rapid Advancement.* Social workers in smaller communities can often expect rela-tively rapid advancement. Workers may move from direct worker to supervisor and to administrator or manager in a relatively short time because other workers find smaller communities to be unattractive locations for their work. The competition for promotion or other opportunities is often not nearly as great in smaller communities as it is in metropolitan areas.

  Most American social workers, like most other Americans, come from metro-politan areas. Their family and social ties are in such communities, and, therefore, many are reluctant to relocate in rural communities. Such attitudes and behaviors only enhance the opportunities for workers who enjoy life in smaller communities.
- *Tangible Results.* Social workers in smaller communities often find that they can see tangible results from their efforts. That is, they can see the impact of their efforts on the lives of the people in the community. Being able to see the difference one makes is one of social work's rewards in all settings and in communities of all sizes. In a rural community, one can make a difference at the micro as well as the macro level. One can see changes made in individuals and families, as well as changes made in the larger community and in the social system.
- *Personal Rewards.* Great personal rewards are possible for human services profes-sionals in many small communities. Because they are independent and can make a difference in the lives of many people, rural workers may find themselves being

thanked for the work they do. A small-community physician, Dr. Michael Watson (1992), reported at a recent meeting that some of his clients tell him they "love" him for what he has done to help them. A nurse practitioner, who serves with him and who performs some of the primary health care tasks that might be done by physicians in larger communities, receives similar kinds of comments from her patients. Another nurse, who is also a midwife in Dr. Watson's community, has delivered many of the children in that small community. This nurse-midwife is a good example of what can happen to the rural professional. She is relatively autonomous and works under the direction of only one physician, who provides her with consultation more than supervision. She practices a skill that is not as frequently used by nurses in metropolitan communities. She has special relationships with her clients and has won their respect and affection.

- *Recognition.* While many people prefer anonymity, there is a special joy for many in being well-known and recognized in the community. The social worker who is known to everyone, who is spoken to by everyone on the street, in the grocery store, and in the post office, has the special satisfaction of being an important person in the rural community. Rarely are social workers in metropolitan areas accorded the same kinds of respect that social workers are often given in nonmetropolitan communities. The social worker may be a frequent speaker at major civic clubs or a consultant to local government who is quoted regularly in the local newspaper. In many ways, rural social workers establish stronger and broader relationships than their metropolitan counterparts might have.[14]

Rural Social Service Agencies

Rural social service agencies are going to play an important role as the United States tries to redirect some of its resources to meet the growing needs of rural areas. This will result in opportunities for new social workers to begin their professional careers in rural agencies.

The rural agencies are unique in the social welfare system. They are usually small, informal, and have a strong personal, direct link to the community they serve. The typical agency has one to three workers plus an agency director, who often doubles as a supervisor. The agency's service area is likely to include several small towns as well as isolated residents distributed over hundreds of square miles.

In the last few years the National Institute of Mental Health has encouraged the development of community mental health centers in rural areas. These centers and the public welfare agencies provide most of the services to individuals and families. Other service providers such as corrections, substance abuse, vocational rehabilitation, and education may establish a one- or two-person agency in a rural county.

Whatever system the state employs to deliver social services to its rural residents, the social worker actually "becomes the agency." The personal visibility of rural practitioners is so great that residents will quickly equate both their professional and personal behavior with the agency. In one rural area the mental health agency was highly respected because of the work of one social worker who was sincerely committed to his clients. People in the area made use of the agency because they knew and respected the social work practitioner.

Distance Learning for Rural Social Work

In the early 1990s the University of Utah's Graduate School of Social Work received numerous requests from individuals living in rural areas to find a way to bring an MSW program to these communities. Many of the individuals making these requests had received undergraduate degrees in sociology or psychology from small colleges located in their communities.

The individuals who were interested in distance social work education tended to be older, had families to support, and could not afford the time or expenses of moving 300 to 400 miles to attend school in Salt Lake City. Many times, these potential students had their own small farming operations and were settled into their communities.

Social service agencies operating in rural areas of the state were always trying to recruit MSW personnel. All of these forces came together, and the GSSW established a distance learning program by recruiting campus faculty who were willing to travel 250 to 300 miles to teach in centralized locations where the rural students would gather from their small rural towns. From the original cohort of twenty-five students, twenty-three graduated and began filling MSW personnel needs of rural agencies.

It was determined that the program was a success but that it demanded too much from both the faculty and the students with the long drives often in bad weather. The GSSW was determined to support rural social work and was fortunate to join forces with the Utah Education Network (EDNET) that is located on the University of Utah campus and is an interactive video/audio system operating through a system of television monitors, video cameras, microphones, telephones, fiber optics, and microwave links. Because this system is interactive, students and faculty at several different sites can see, hear, and speak to the instructors and also to students at other sites. Although distance learning is not a perfect system, the GSSW has been able to institute supportive structures such as on-site trainers, special examination procedures, and field work structures. Also, faculty have undergone extensive training to be effective on the interactive television.

Another group of rural social workers has graduated and again most of them have remained in rural areas to work. The GSSW will continue to offer its MSW through the EDNET system because it is, perhaps, the only way that rural citizens can earn their degrees. Extensive evaluation of the program has ascertained that the rural distance learning program is comparable to the campus program and that it truly serves the needs of rural areas to recruit and retain professional social workers.[15]

It is expected that EDNET and even more sophisticated technology will be developed so that rural social workers can continually update their practice. Further, the technological linkage may assist statewide social service agencies to share resources and more efficiently serve rural citizens.

Summary

Rural areas of the United States are facing difficult times. Boom and bust cycles—coupled with high inflation and lower land prices—have created a great deal of stress and unhappiness for rural residents. Rural social workers are actively attempting to mitigate the problems of individuals, families, and communities.

Rural social work practice requires skills in all social work methods, and individual social workers must be able to adapt themselves effectively to social institutions of all sizes, from the individual to the total community. Rural social workers also need to understand the functioning of a rural community and must be able to work within the values and structures of that community. There are many positive rewards for social workers choosing to practice in rural areas.

Social work education is an ideal curriculum for rural practice. The emphasis on the interaction of the individual and the environment prepares the rural social worker to provide important leadership in the area of social services. Although social workers may not be able to effect an upturn in the rural economy or create new jobs, they can help cushion the negative effects and help individuals, families, and communities cope with the problems and find workable solutions.

Suggested References

ALLEN, BARBARA, and THOMAS J. SCHLERETH, eds., *Sense of Place: American Regional Cultures.* Lexington: University Press of Kentucky, 1990.

COWARD, RAYMOND T., and JOHN A. KRAUT, eds., *Aging in Rural Settings: Life Circumstances and Distinctive Features.* New York: Springer, 1998.

DAVIS, SHARON, SCOTT MEYER, and MARGARET TERRASI, "The Whole Village Center: A Model for Promoting Client Access to Services in Rural Areas," *Human Services in the Rural Environment,* 19 (Winter 1996), 25–28.

FARLEY, O. WILLIAM, KENNETH A. GRIFFITHS, REX A. SKIDMORE, and MILTON G. THACKERAY, *Rural Social Work Practice.* New York: Free Press, 1982.

FITCHEN, J. M., *Endangered Spaces, Enduring Places: Change, Identity and Survival in Rural America.* Boulder, CO: Westview Press, 1991.

GINSBERG, LEON, *Social Work Almanac.* Washington, DC: National Association of Social Workers, 1992.

GINSBERG, LEON H., ed., *Social Work in Rural Communities,* 2nd ed. Alexandria, VA: CSWE, 1993.

PATTERSON, SHIRLEY L., JAY L. MEMMOTT, and CAREL G. GERMAIN, "Old Wine in New Bottles: Utilizing Gender-Specific Natural Helping Capacities in Rural Social Work," *Human Services in the Rural Environment,* 18 (Spring 1995), 42–47.

ROWLES, GRAHAM D., JOYCE E. BEAULIEU, and WAYNE W. MYERS, *Long-Term Care for the Rural Elderly.* New York: Springer, 1997.

Notes

1. Leon H. Ginsberg, ed., *Social Work in Rural Communities,* 2nd ed. (Alexandria, VA: CSWE, 1993), p. 4. Reprinted with the permission of the Council on Social Work Education.

2. Ibid., p. 4.

3. *NASW News,* 8 (September 1988), p. 1.

4. O. William Farley, Kenneth A. Griffiths, Mark Fraser, and Lou Ann Jorgensen, "Rural Social Work: Addressing the Crisis of Rural America," in John S. McNeil and Stanley E. Weinstein, eds., *Innovations in Health Care Practices* (Washington, DC: NASW, 1988), p. 64.

5. Kathryn H. Porter, *Poverty in Rural America: A National Overview* (Washington DC: Center on Budget and Policy Priorities, 1989), p. 3.

6. Elizabeth Ruff, "The Community as Client in Rural Social Work," *Human Services in the Rural Environment,* 14 (Spring 1991), p. 21.

7. Ibid., p. 21.

8. Morton O. Wagenfeld, J. Dennis Murray, Dennis F. Mohatt, and Jeanne C. DeBruyn, *Mental Health and Rural America 1980–1993* (Washington, DC: National Institute of Mental Health, 1994), p. iii.

9. Mike Jacobsen, "Scholarship and the Rural Social Work Movement," in Anne Summers, Joe M. Schriner, Paul Sundet, and Roland Meinert, eds., *Social Work in Rural Areas: Proceedings of the Tenth National Institute on Social Work in Rural Areas,* (Batesville: Arkansas College, 1987), p. 21.

10. Leon H. Ginsberg, "Social Work in Rural Areas," in Ronald K. Green and Stephen Webster, eds., *Social Work in Rural Areas: Preparation and Practice,* (Knoxville: University of Tennessee, 1977), p. 7.

11. James A. Campbell and Melanie Shepart, "Social Work Education for Rural Practice: The Advanced Generalist," *Human Services in the Rural Environment,* 14 (Summer 1990), p. 24.

12. Charles H. Zastrow, *The Practice of Social Work: Applications of Generalist and Advanced Content,* 7th ed. (Pacific Grove, CA: Brooks/Cole, 2003), p. 279.

13. O. William Farley, Kenneth A. Griffiths, Rex A. Skidmore, and Milton G. Thackeray, *Rural Social Work Practice* (New York: Free Press, 1982), pp. 227–228.

14. Ginsberg, *Social Work in Rural Communities,* pp. 12–13.

15. Sandra L. Kikuchi and Scott R. Sorensen, "Reach Out and Teach Someone: Experience of the Rural Off-Campus MSW Program, Graduate School of Social Work, University of Utah" (unpublished paper presented at the Information Technologies for Social Work Education Conference, Charleston, South Carolina, 1997).

19

Case Management

Joyce is a 33-year-old white married female who spent the majority of her life between the ages of 16 and 27 in state mental hospitals. During her late teenage years she was diagnosed as having paranoid-type schizophrenia. In addition to her psychosis, Joyce also struggled with substance abuse. Staff from a rural community mental health center responded to requests from Joyce's family to see if she could be released from the hospital and returned to the community where she would have a better quality of life. State hospital personnel were worried about discharging Joyce and predicted dire consequences.

Joyce returned to the community, and the mental health center initiated case management to assist her in being able to live out of the hospital. Even though Joyce suffered from hallucinations and suicidal ideation, the case management staff helped her through these episodes. Joyce also had a family that was interested and supportive of her. A year later Joyce and another mental health client were married.

Joyce worked at numerous jobs but always tried to do more than she was capable of doing, which resulted in her becoming overwhelmed and unable to work. The rural community was also limited in job opportunities, and Joyce usually ended up in menial cleaning jobs. Joyce continued to need short hospitalization periods to keep herself under control. However, the short periods of hospitalization were in the community where she lived and where she could receive continuous support from her case manager, husband, and family. With this support she could return to independent living within a few days.

Even though Joyce continues to struggle with recurring episodes of illness, the case management intervention has helped sustain her in an environment where she has the opportunity to develop independence and a quality lifestyle. Joyce is adamant that case management services were very important in her attempt to adjust to the community. She has remained out of long-term state hospitalization for six years.

Case management is a newly emerging human service designed to deliver services to individuals and their families with complex, multiple problems or disabilities. Social work and other helping professions have often utilized case management as part of their service delivery systems, but now it is becoming a discrete, independently reimbursed, primary service. Barker has defined the general parameters of case management as a procedure to plan, seek, and monitor services from different social agencies and staff on behalf of a client. Usually one agency takes primary responsibility for the client and assigns a case manager, who coordinates services, advocates for the client and sometimes controls resources and purchases services for the client. The procedure makes it possible for many social workers in the agency, or different agencies, to coordinate their efforts to serve a given client through professional teamwork, thus expanding the range of needed services offered. Case management may involve monitoring the progress of a client whose needs require the services of several professionals, agencies, health care facilities, and human services programs. It typically involves case finding, comprehensive multidimensional assessment, and frequent reassessment. Case management can occur within a single large organization or within a community program that coordinates services among agencies.[1]

Renewal of interest in case management as a separate service delivery system has been brought about by our increasingly complex and diverse society, which has created a fragmented, complicated, and depersonalized social service system. Many of the most vulnerable people—who need services the most—do not receive timely, meaningful, and preventive assistance because they cannot effectively apply for needed services or negotiate the conflicting eligibility requirements of social service agencies. The purpose of case management is to assist clients to receive the services they need by linking clients to both the formal and informal helping-service networks within a community and then to follow up to ensure that the client has actually received the resources and social services required.

The new appeal of case management has also been based on the belief that this service could assist with cost-effectiveness and cost-control. The skyrocketing costs of health care have provided the impetus for much of the case management movement. Winn and Sierra address case management in the health care context as follows:

> Medical cost containment, of which case management is a part, is estimated to be a $7 billion industry in the United States. While case management provides no direct care, it serves to facilitate appropriate, cost-effective access to finite health care resources. Private, state, and federal payers are ever vigilant to find creative ways to coordinate care and contain costs for high-risk populations.
>
> Case managers act as gatekeepers, resource managers and decision makers for billions of dollars worth of care annually. Various professions vie for leadership because case management is such a growing and important function due to increased demand for services and the need to reduce and manage costs. Each discipline perceives theirs as uniquely suited to manage complex cases. Those professions include physicians, social workers, nurses, and vocational rehabilitation specialists.[2]

Whether case management will be able to fulfill its mandate of being able both to personalize and coordinate services and to make them cost-effective is yet to be determined. However, the following case history illustrates that case management can be effective.

Mrs. J. is a 35-year-old divorced woman with two children (ages 7 and 10). Her husband left her six years ago. For the first four years she was supported by the Aid to Families with Dependent Children (AFDC) program of the state welfare department. During those four years, her life was spent trying to find housing, obtaining food stamps, trying to get medical care for

A case management team meeting.

her children or mental health counseling for herself. Much of her energy was spent in going from agency to agency filling out forms and meeting with workers from different agencies. She had no direction and little hope.

Two years ago she was assigned a case manager in a pilot project developed by the state welfare department. The case manager was assigned a very small caseload of twenty clients, which allowed her the opportunity of making contact with each of her clients on a weekly basis. After making an assessment of Mrs. J.'s total situation, the case manager and Mrs. J. developed, jointly, a treatment plan that was workable. During this process, the case manager used counseling skills to help Mrs. J. resolve some painful emotional dilemmas that had in the past impeded her from making sound decisions.

Mrs. J.'s treatment plan was focused on her obtaining a marketable job skill. Before being able to obtain any training, Mrs. J.'s family needs had to be addressed. The case manager assisted Mrs. J. in obtaining public housing and child care for her children. In addition, the case manager helped Mrs. J. obtain special funding to pay for tuition at a local community college.

The first year of college work was not easy for Mrs. J., and the case manager had to be very supportive; however, the second year was much less traumatic. Mrs. J. is now in her third year of schooling and is looking forward to fulfilling her prenursing requirements.

The case history of Mrs. J. illustrates that case managers must deal with both "concrete" services such as finding a client a place to live, making sure clients have food and proper medical care, and "counseling" services to help individuals resolve emotional blocks to making effective decisions. The luxury of a small caseload allowed the case manager to individualize the treatment plan for Mrs. J. and to conduct follow-up when personal problems emerged from time to time. Mrs. J.'s continuing therapeutic relationship with the case manager allowed her to obtain a sense of hope, which in turn motivated her to develop a more satisfying, functional, and productive lifestyle.

The profession of social work has been in the forefront of designing case management systems throughout its history. Case management is one of the most important treatment interventions that social workers have at their disposal. The entire profession of social work is based on "person-in-the-environment" interaction. Most schools of social work have utilized an ecosystems approach to help students conceptualize the interaction between society and the individual and to assess problems based on that interaction. From this assessment, the treatment plan is formulated and includes both individual counseling and attempts to impact the social system—which may be part of the problem.

Professional social workers are entering a job market in the new millennium that is clamoring for case management expertise. Almost all social service agencies are designing case management systems to help long-term clients who are dysfunctional because of problems in such areas as health, child welfare, juvenile justice, mental health, aging, and developmental disabilities. Many patterns of case management are developing throughout the country, but regardless of the pattern chosen, the social work profession needs to play a major role in this treatment intervention. Social workers are professionally well equipped to design, manage, and provide case management services.

Historical Developments

Case management was identified as early as 1863 when the commonwealth of Massachusetts established programs under the Board of Charities to coordinate public services as well as to conserve public funds.[3] Case management has also been linked to the Mary Richmond era and the early settlement house developments.

Much of the focus of the current case management had its origins in the rehabilitation-focused workers' compensation programs of the 1940s. Case management programs did not receive a lot of attention until the early 1970s when the federal government identified social service coordination and service integration as a priority and began funding demonstration projects of service coordination systems. Various federal laws were passed between 1970 and 1987 that included components of case management services. The Consolidated Omnibus Budget Reconciliation Act (COBRA), which was passed in 1985, encouraged states to provide case management as an optional Medicaid service. The Special Education Legislation of 1987 (P.L. 99-457) and the Family Support Act of 1988 (P.L. 100-485) included case management provisions. These laws expanded the use of case management in many social service areas.[4]

The Family Support Act (FSA) of 1988 also provided new impetus for case management. The Job Opportunities and Basic Skills (JOBS) training program by which the FSA seeks to increase the economic self-sufficiency of AFDC recipients contains provisions for case management. The goal of case management under this program is to ensure that needy families with children obtain education, training, and employment to help them avoid long-term welfare dependence. Hagen observed

> The most obvious direct practice role for social work is in case management provided for by the JOBS legislation. States have the option of using case managers to assist recipients in

participating in the JOBS program. The models for case management and roles of case managers will be developed at the state and local levels. Social work could have an instrumental role in developing models that build on the participants' strengths, empower AFDC mothers, and broker services and advocate on the client's behalf for necessary support services. These services may extend beyond the education and training provision of JOBS to include the other social services that families may need.[5]

Various case management models are currently in use. In some instances, case management is viewed as monitoring of client progress on paper only, a function sometimes performed by specially trained clerical staff. In other instances, personnel are drawn from other vocational education and training programs. In Iowa's program to serve multiproblem families, family development specialists are used. To date, there is not much social work presence in the development of case management models.

The JOBS program also requires state welfare agencies to develop individualized employment plans and services for participants based on an initial assessment of their education, work experience, employment skills, family circumstances, and supportive services needs including child care. At state option, the assessment may also include the needs of the children. To develop meaningful employability plans, these assessments must be comprehensive and must involve the client as a mutual partner. Complex decisions must be made about such issues as child care arrangements and what family circumstances will constitute deferral from the JOBS program. Social workers are well prepared to conduct a thorough psychosocial assessment.

Derezotes has defined the key elements of the case management paradigm as follows:

Focus. The focus is on improving the quality and accessibility of resources and opportunities that support individual client development and the collective welfare of all diverse populations.

Developmental dimensions. Although there may be a focus on the furthering of all dimensions of human development, social development is particularly emphasized (e.g., social skills that empower client to develop and use resources in equitable and sustainable ways).

View of health. There is a focus on the ability of the client/system to provide the diversity of individuals, families, and communities with equal access to resources, political power, and opportunities for individual development. Self-sufficiency is maximized, and there is a focus on strategies that support sustainable resources.

View of pathology. The unhealthy client/system does not provide the diversity of individuals with equal access to resources, political power, and opportunities for individual development. Human and natural resources are depleted rather than kept sustainable, and maximum self-sufficiency is not encouraged.

Art and science. Although social science has tested the efficacy of some case management strategies, we still do not know enough about how the availability and use of resources and opportunities in the environment influence bio-psycho-social-spiritual well-being and multidimensional human development. Practioners can thus select case management interventions based on empirical research, theory, and worker and client intuition.

Relationship. Although some traditional case management forms have taken approaches that appeared quite vertical to clients, the social worker can take a horizontal or vertical relationship with the client and client/system, depending on the development ability of the client(s) to share in responsibility for creating and implementing intervention strategies.[6]

There are many professions involved with case management. In addition to social workers, nurses, medical assistants, occupational therapists, and nutritionists may also act as case managers. In 1990 the National Association of Case Management (NACM) was founded. The purpose of the organization is to provide case managers with opportunities for professional growth. Also the *Journal of Case Management* is published quarterly as a forum for case management issues and practices.[7]

Case Management Defined

Obviously, the profession of social work is vitally interested in the case management movement. In 1984 the board of directors of the National Association of Social Workers (NASW) published *Standards and Guidelines for Social Work Case Management for the Functionally Impaired.* In June 1992 NASW's board of directors approved new standards for social work case management, which described the intervention as "a method of providing services whereby a professional social worker assesses the needs of the client and the client's family, when appropriate, and arranges, coordinates, monitors, evaluates and advocates for a package of multiple services to meet the specific client's complex needs."[8]

Greene defines the key elements of case management practice, which are shown in Table 19.1.[9]

TABLE 19.1 *Key Features of Social Work Case Management Practice*

Social Work Case Management Practice
• is a process based on a trusting and enabling client–social worker relationship
• utilizes the social work dual focus of understanding the person in the environment in working with populations at risk
• aims to ensure a continuum of care to clients with complex, multiple problems and disabilities
• attempts to intervene clinically to ameliorate the emotional problems accompanying illness or loss of function
• utilizes the social work skills of brokering and advocacy as a boundary-spanning approach to service delivery
• targets clients who require a range of community-based or long-term-care services, encompassing economic, health/medical, social, and personal care needs
• aims to provide services in the least restrictive environment
• requires the use of assessment of the client's functional capacity and support network in determining the level of care
• affirms the traditional social work values of self-determination and the worth and dignity of the individual and the concept of mutual responsibility in decision making

Rothman suggests that case management basically incorporates two central functions: "(1) providing individualized advice, counseling, and therapy to clients in the community and (2) linking clients to needed services and supports in community agencies and informal helping networks."[10]

Vourlekis and Greene define case management by describing the following practice functions:

CLIENT IDENTIFICATION AND OUTREACH

In this initial stage of the case management process, consultation with potential consumers provides information on potential barriers and obstacles to service utilization and access. . . .

At the service system or community level, the case manager provides input into policy and program plans, helping to define the scope and shape of services. . . .

INDIVIDUAL AND FAMILY ASSESSMENT AND DIAGNOSIS

The case manager uses systematic data-gathering skills to answer critical questions about needed improvements in the fit between the person and family, and the relevant environment. . . . The case manager assesses the service system resources and deficits at the same time. . . .

PLANNING AND RESOURCE IDENTIFICATION

The case manager mobilizes client problem-solving capacity to develop jointly a care plan that is workable. Negotiation—requiring contracting skills—among client, family, and other providers concerning goals and expectations may be necessary before a realistic plan can be determined. . . .

At the service system level, the case manager searches for appropriate resources, including those that are culturally sensitive. Resource gaps are identified as well. . . .

LINKING CLIENTS TO NEEDED RESOURCES

At this point, accessing, acquiring, and even creating needed resources is a central concern. In working with the client, the case manager addresses any of the client's specific concerns or perceived obstacles to using a resource. . . .

SERVICE IMPLEMENTATION AND COORDINATION

With some clients, the case manager must draw upon advanced clinical skills to assist the client throughout the process of using services to reach desired goals. . . .

Clients may need practical assistance from the case manager as well. Emergency transportation, assistance with making a move, coffee and danish, and a chance to get outside—these requests might be made of a case manager. . . .

MONITORING SERVICE DELIVERY

It is at the case level that the case manager makes sure that the system is accountable to the client, and that the client meets agreed-upon expectations. The case manager works actively to make things go as they should, and reports and intervenes when things go wrong. . . .

ADVOCACY TO OBTAIN SERVICES

This function involves the case manager in implementing a planned strategy of power to obtain specific services or resources for a client (case advocacy) or perhaps for the total group of clients (cause advocacy). . . .

EVALUATION

The involvement of the direct-practitioner case manager in evaluating the quality, appropriateness, and effectiveness of the case management services provided takes place on two levels as well . . . at the level of the individual client . . . at the delivery system level.[11]

The eight "practice key skills" developed by Vourlekis and Greene are included because they represent a comprehensive definitional statement and explanation of social work case management. However, all of these helping skills are to little avail if the case manager is asked to work with more than fifteen or twenty clients at one time. Case management intervention is only effective when caseloads are kept small. Again, it should be noted that the case management movement has been created to individualize the treatment process and to empower dysfunctional individuals by being able to assist them to better utilize resources that are available to them.

Rothman developed an empirically based model of case management after reviewing the literature and interviewing many case managers. His model recognizes the complexities of case management and the many different roles that case managers must assume in working with clients. In *Direct Social Work Practice: Theory and Skills,* Hepworth, Rooney, and Larsen summarize Rothman's case management model:

1. *Access to agency.* Case managers need to arrange agency appointments for clients as soon as possible. This often requires the case manager to be an advocate for the client.
2. *Intake.* During intake, care must be taken to develop rapport with the client. Building a strong relationship with the client will help the case manager guide the client through the system.
3. *Assessment.* Case managers must also talk to family members and friends in determining what the clients needs. These outside assessments will also help the case manager evaluate the client's potential for change.
4. *Goal setting.* Case managers must involve the client in setting clear and reasonable goals. These goals should be both short-term and long-term goals.
5. *Planning intervention.* Case managers often have to use outside resources to help clients reach their short-term and long-term goals. This is especially true in regard to housing and employment training.
6. *Linking clients.* Case managers need to coordinate the client's work with other resources. This linkage is an important part of helping the client successfully use services once they are provided.
7. *Monitoring and assessing.* Case managers must monitor and assess the daily, weekly, and monthly progress of clients. This constant monitoring is especially valuable in dealing in a timely way with crisis situations when they occur.
8. *Outcome evaluation.* Case managers need to help the client assess the extent to which short-term and long-term goals were accomplished. Using baseline measures in the beginning of the case management can help facilitate these outcome evaluations.[12]

Case Management Research

More research is needed in case management. Regardless of its growing acceptance, case management is not a well-defined service intervention. Almost every agency tailors the intervention to meet its own needs. The measure of outcome is especially troublesome in many case management projects. Rothman states that the major foci in case management measurement attempts are "(1) social functioning or quality of life, (2) intrapsychic status, and (3) behavioral indicators of experience with key institutions."[13] All three of the measurement foci are rather difficult to put into operation. In addition to measurement problems, case management takes place in service environments that "are turbulent, with shifting funding levels, policies, and client priorities, as well as turnover of staff, cross-professional rivalries, and political pressures."[14]

Regardless of the many methodological problems, researchers continue to try to validate the intervention of case management. For example, one recent study of a semirural community mental health center in Utah has produced some significant findings on case management effectiveness. Funded by the National Institute of Mental Health, this research project was actually able to maintain an experimental design that included a control and experimental group over a two-year period. Also, the case management team was well trained in the Strengths case management model advocated by Rapp and Wintersteen.[15] The following research report summarizes the effective work accomplished by case managers:

> A year after full implementation of an experimental case management program in Logan, Utah, case management consumers reported significantly better mental and physical health, fewer problems with mood or thinking, greater competence in daily living, and higher psychological well-being in comparison to a control group of consumers who received only psychosocial rehabilitation services. Case management family members also reported lower consumer psychiatric symptomatology and felt less burdened by their consumer's illness than the control group's family members. In addition, primary care providers assessed case management consumers as less depressed, more rational, and more productive than control group consumers. These group differences in consumer, family member, and service provider reports were obtained in spite of group equivalence in pre-intervention level of functioning, level of help received, social support, family cohesiveness, and a variety of personal liabilities (e.g., chronic pain or poor work history).
>
> A 36-month longitudinal analysis of hospitalization and crisis center records substantiated these interview reports. Following full program implementation, case management consumers showed a decrease in rate of hospitalization and frequency of crisis center contacts; control group consumers did not. The co-occurrence within the case management group of fewer hospitalizations and crises, together with family member reports of lower emotional burden, is of particular relevance to mental health policy. Although researchers warn that planned reductions in consumer hospitalization often increase family burden (e.g., Olfson, 1990), family member reports in Logan suggest that case management can simultaneously reduce hospitalizations and lower family burden by providing continuous emotional support to consumers and consultation to family members. That is, when a reduction in hospitalization is brought about through a decrease in consumer symptomatology, reductions in family burden can accompany consumer community retention.[16]

Continued research efforts must be made to define case management empirically and to test its effectiveness as a social work intervention. Social service personnel who have worked in the case management arena are convinced that the intervention works and that individuals are helped to be more functional.

Summary

The emphasis being placed on case management at the present time is the result of a number of forces in our society. There has been a recognition that many people cannot negotiate our complicated and fragmented social service systems without help. The federal government has recognized this need and has legislated requirements for case managers for various programs.

The profession of social work has traditionally been concerned with the interaction of the individual and society and is in an excellent position to provide leadership in this field. Professional social workers are entering a job market in the new millennium that is clamoring for case management expertise. Social workers are well-equipped professionals with the skill and competency to design, manage, and provide case management.

The definition of case management is still rather unclear. However, researchers are continuing to define and measure case management tasks in an empirical fashion. Some studies have demonstrated impressive results, but many questions remain regarding research methodologies.

The key roles that case managers accomplish are (1) client identification and outreach; (2) individual and family assessment and diagnosis; (3) planning and resource identification; (4) linking clients to needed resources; (5) service implementation and coordination; (6) monitoring service delivery; (7) advocacy to obtain services; and (8) evaluation.

The renewed interest of case management in social work has been created by a recognition that social service systems must return to an individualized, coordinated, follow-up approach if we are to help and empower dysfunctional individuals in our society. This renewed interest in case management has also made it important to evaluate the impact and effectiveness of these services. The social work profession, like all helping professions, has become concerned with best practice issues and case management is no exception. Because case management has become such an important part of our social service system, there is a pressing need to conduct research on what aspects of case management work and what aspects are not as effective as they should be. Best practice concerns will continue to shape case management services and in the end, agencies and the clients they serve will all benefit.

Selected References _____

BIGELOW, D. A., and D. J. YOUNG, "Effectiveness of a Case Management Program," *Community Mental Health Journal,* 25 (1991), 115–123.

CHAMBERLAIN, R., and C. A. RAPP, "A Decade of Case Management: A Methodological Review of Outcome Research," *Community Mental Health Journal,* 27 (1991), 171–188.

DEREZOTES, DAVID S., *Advanced Generalist Social Work Practice.* Thousand Oaks, CA: Sage, 2000.

FRANKEL, ARTHUR J., and SHELDON R. GELMAN, *Case Management.* Chicago: Lyceum Books, 1998.

HOLT, BARBARA J., *The Practice of Generalist Case Management.* Boston: Allyn & Bacon, 2000.

MACIAS, CATHALEENE, O. WILLIAM FARLEY, ROBERT JACKSON, and RONALD KINNEY, "Case Management in the Context of Capitation Financing: An Evaluation of the Strengths Model," *Administration and Policy in Mental Health,* 24, no. 6 (1997), 535–543.

MACIAS, CATHALEENE, RONALD KINNEY, O. WILLIAM FARLEY, ROBERT JACKSON, and BETTY VOS, "The Role of Case Management within a Community Support System: Partnership with Psychosocial Rehabilitation," *Community Mental Health Journal,* 30, no. 4 (1994), 323–339.

MOORE, STEPHEN, "Case Management and the Integration of Services: How Service Delivery Systems Shape Case Management," *Social Work,* 37 (September 1992), 418–423.

ROTHMAN, JACK, *Guidelines for Case Management.* Itasca, IL: F.E. Peacock, 1992.

ROTHMAN, JACK, and JON SIMON SAEGER, *Case Management: Integrating Individual and Community Practice,* 2nd ed. Boston: Allyn & Bacon, 1998.

SOLOMON, P., "The Efficacy of Case Management Services for Severely Mentally Disabled Clients," *Community Mental Health Journal,* 28, no. 3 (1992), 163–180.

VOURLEKIS, BETSY S., and ROBERTA R. GREENE, eds., *Social Work Case Management.* Hawthorne, NY: Aldine de Gruyter, 1992.

Notes

1. Robert L. Barker, *The Social Work Dictionary,* 3rd ed. (Washington, DC: NASW Press, 1995), p. 33.

2. Judy Winn and Ramona Sierra, "Case Management: Cooperation Among Disciplines," *Journal of Insurance Medicine,* 28 (Winter 1991), p. 258.

3. Karen Orloss Kaplan, "Recent Trends in Case Management," in Leon Ginsberg et al., *Encyclopedia of Social Work,* 18th ed., 1990 supplement (Silver Spring, MD: NASW, 1990), p. 61.

4. Ibid., p. 61.

5. Jan L. Hagen, "Women, Work and Welfare: Is There a Role for Social Work?," *Social Work,* 37 (January 1992), p. 11.

6. David S. Derezotes, *Advanced Generalist Social Work Practice* (Thousand Oaks, CA: Sage, 2000), pp. 145–146.

7. Arthur J. Frankel and Sheldon R. Gilman, *Case Management* (Chicago: Lyceum Books, 1998), p. 9.

8. National Association of Social Workers, "Case Manager's Role Clarified by Guidelines," *NASW News,* 37 (September 1992), p. 7.

9. Roberta R. Greene, "Case Management: An Arena for Social Work Practice," in Betsy S. Vourlekis and Roberta R. Greene, eds., *Social Work Case Management* (Hawthorne, NY: Aldine de Gruyter, 1992), p. 3.

10. Jack Rothman, *Guidelines for Case Management* (Itasca, IL: F. E. Peacock, 1992), p. 3.

11. Betsy S. Vourlekis and Roberta R. Greene, eds., *Social Work Case Management* (Hawthorne, NY: Aldine de Gruyter, 1992), pp. 183–188.

12. Dean H. Hepworth, Ronald H. Rooney, and Jo Ann Larsen, *Direct Social Work Practice: Theory and Skills,* 6th ed. (Pacific Grove, CA: Brooks/Cole, 2002), pp. 472–473.

13. Rothman, *Guidelines for Case Management,* p. 11.

14. Ibid., p. 11.

15. Charles A. Rapp and R. Wintersteen, "The Strengths Model of Case Management: Results from Twelve Demonstrations," *Psychosocial Rehabilitation Journal,* 13 (1989), pp. 23–32.

16. Cathaleene Macias, Ronald Kinney, O. William Farley, Robert Jackson, and Betty Vos, "The Role of Case Management within a Community Support System: Partnership with Psychosocial Rehabilitation," *Community Mental Health Journal,* 30, no. 4 (1994), pp. 335–337.

Social Work:
A Maturing Profession

Two college students were discussing their goals in life. One turned to his friend and queried, "When I'm all through working and about to retire, I wonder what I will have accomplished in life?"

He and his friend talked about various professions and jobs, and then the first student

observed, "I've decided to become a social worker. As I've thought about it, I feel I can make a great contribution to people, as well as obtain real satisfactions for myself."

Social work is regarded by most people as a profession. Many say it is a recognized profession; others believe it is an emerging one. The U.S. Census Bureau includes, among others, the following as professions: accountant, architect, artist, attorney, clergy, college professor, dentist, engineer, journalist, judge, librarian, natural scientist, optometrist, pharmacist, physician, social scientist, social worker, surgeon, and teacher. Is social work really a profession? Has it emerged or is it still maturing? What are the characteristics of a profession? These and related questions are considered in this chapter.

Criteria of a Profession

William Wickenden, while president of Case School of Applied Science, gave a pioneering address before the Engineering Institute of Canada in which he described the characteristics of the professional person. He mentioned four distinctive marks. The first is a "*type of activity,* which carries high individual responsibility and which applies special skill to problems on a distinctly intellectual plane." Second, he said "is a *motive of service,* associated with limited rewards as distinct from profit." The third is "the *motive of self-expression,* which implies joy and pride in one's work and a self-imposed standard of excellence." And fourth is "a conscious *recognition of social duty* to be fulfilled among other means by guarding the ideals and standards of one's profession, by advancing it in public understanding and esteem, by sharing advances in technical knowledge, and by rendering gratuitous public service, in addition to that for ordinary compensation, as a return to society for special advantages of education and status."

Wickenden went on to describe the attributes that mark off the corporate life of a group of persons as professional in character:

> We may place first a *body of knowledge* (science) and of *art* (skill) held as a common possession and to be extended by united effort. Next is *an educational process* based on this body of knowledge and art, in ordering which the professional group has a recognized responsibility. Third is a *standard* of personal qualifications for admission to the professional group, based on character, training, and proved competence. Next follows *a standard of conduct* based on courtesy, honor, and ethics, which guides the practitioner in his relations with clients, colleagues, and the public. Fifth, we may place a more or less formal *recognition of status,* either by one's colleagues or by the state, as a basis for good standing. And finally, there is usually *an organization* of the professional group, devoted to its common advancement and its social duty, rather than to the maintenance of an economic monopoly.[1]

Greenwood[2] canvassed the sociological literature on occupations and came to the conclusion that there are five distinguishing attributes of a profession: (1) systematic theory, (2) authority, (3) community sanction, (4) ethical codes, and (5) a culture. He discusses each of these characteristics and then concludes

> Social work is already a profession; it has too many points of congruence with the model to be classifiable otherwise. Social work is, however, seeking to rise within the professional hierarchy, so that it, too, might enjoy maximum prestige, authority, and monopoly, which presently belong to a few top professions.[3]

In regard to a systematic body of knowledge or theory, social work is getting a good start. In comparison to some professions it has a long way to go. Nevertheless, if one studies carefully the research being accomplished and the theories now extant in social work, it is clearly evident that there is a beginning systematic body of knowledge that serves as a foundation for this helping profession.

The social worker today possesses a professional authority. He or she is respected by other disciplines and, in the main, by clients who come for help. Although the social worker honors the freedom of choice and the right of self-determination of the client, he or she possesses an authoritative demeanor that builds confidence in the client and helps, through the use of a relationship, to bring about desired changes. The client derives a sense of security from this assumption of authority by the professional social worker.

As Greenwood points out, the social worker also has the sanction of the community. It is evident that society in general approves of social work and respects it—as indicated by the number of social workers who are hired for positions in public and private agencies. More and more people are asking, "Where can I find a social worker?"

In 1960 the social work profession developed a code of ethics that replaced earlier preliminary codes sponsored by local and national groups in social welfare. The code was revised in 1967, in 1979, and again in 1990 by the Delegate Assembly of NASW.

The fifth characteristic, that of a professional culture, is certainly existent in social work today. Social work has its own professional organizations, such as the National Association of Social Workers and the Council on Social Work Education. It has a characteristic jargon and has a unique focus on certain values, norms, and symbols. It stresses the importance of social work as a career and the necessity of dedication and interest in humankind and society as personal prerequisites for the individual who plans to go into this field.

If we look at some of the distinguishing characteristics of social work, we find amplification of the uniqueness of social work as a profession. Social work considers the total person in the total social environment, and is usually within an agency that has structure. It sponsors the use of direct practice, group work, community organization, social research, and administration in unique combinations of problem-solving methodologies. It places particular stress on self-determination and helping the client to help himself or herself, adhering particularly to the democratic process. Social workers are the only persons in the professions who are called *workers*. They use and coordinate agency and community resources. All of these factors—and others—set social work apart from the other helping professions.

Historical Background

A profession includes an approved training program, a professional organization, related organizations and activities, and a body of skilled workers. If we turn the pages of history, we find social work has substantial professional underpinning.

Schools of Social Work

Within the past several decades social work has been developing rapidly, and the importance of the training process is evident. Its roots go far back, particularly in relation to the efforts in England and the United States of more than a century ago when welfare agencies were created to help families and individuals, especially financially, and also to provide some psychological support. As these services began to increase and become formalized, the need for training became apparent.

By 1898 the New York Charity Organization Society "took the initial steps in the direction of a professional school by holding a six weeks' training course, designed primarily to increase the efficiency of social workers already in the field."[4] This was the beginning of the New York School of Social Work. (The name was changed in 1963 to Columbia University School of Social Work.) Soon other training centers were established in different parts of the country. Before 1910 there were schools of social work in the five largest cities in the United States.

Professional schools of social work increased in number so that by 2004 there were 143 programs in the United States offering appropriate master's education. Most of these programs are integral parts of universities and have become recognized as important centers for providing graduate, professional training in higher education. Many universities also offer undergraduate training programs in social work.

Enrollments in these schools, involving only a few persons at the turn of the century, have increased so that in 1961–62 there were 6,666 full-time students enrolled in graduate schools of social work, and in June 1962, a total of 2,476 students graduated with the Master of Social Work degree.

In November 1996, there were 22,832 full-time students in the social work master's program, along with 12,636 part-time students, based on data provided by CSWE. For the academic year 1995–96, there were 14,484 master's degrees awarded by these programs, an all-time high. In 1995–96, degrees in baccalaureate social work education were awarded to 12,356 students.

Council on Social Work Education

Established in 1952 through a merger of three organizations with related functions, the Council on Social Work Education (CSWE) gives leadership in the United States and throughout the world to the efforts of the "total social work profession and to citizens interested in the welfare of their own families and their communities to increase the number of professionally qualified social workers, and at the same time improve the quality of their education for social work." The basic aims of the council are to support, strengthen, and improve social work education and to increase the number of qualified social workers.

The CSWE sponsors a unique partnership of citizens, social work practitioners, agency executives, and educators who work together.

A council brochure explains that it is responsible for ensuring the quality of social work education and is the only accrediting body for social work education in the United States. It is authorized by the Department of Education and by the National Commission on Accrediting.

Membership is open to institutional members, which include graduate and undergraduate programs of social work in the United States, major public and voluntary national state and local social agencies, the National Federation of Student Social Workers, and professional membership organizations. Individual members include practitioners, educators, and anyone interested in social work education.

The council sponsors or assists with the following: standards, curriculum development, continuing education, research, services to minority groups, fellowships, consultation services, publications, and an annual program meeting.

The 1995 annual program meeting of CSWE was held in San Diego, California, with the underlying goal of improving the quality of social work education and practice, and with a general theme of "Empowerment: Building for Strength." The 42nd annual program meeting of CSWE was held in Washington, DC, in 1996 with the theme "Public Policy Challenges for Social Work Education." The 1997 meeting was held in Chicago, Illinois, and in Orlando, Florida, in 1998 where the theme was "Launching into the Future."

The Commission on Accreditation, authorized by the council, accredits new schools of social work, as well as periodically conducts on-campus reviews of all the graduate schools of social work with the goal of improving social work training and strengthening academic standards. Also, since 1974 the commission has had the authority and responsibility to accredit undergraduate social work programs.

One of the most valuable services of the council is to provide publications that help schools of social work, agencies, and individuals improve educational facilities and social work practice. Current catalogs include pages of available publications related to the social work educational endeavor.

National Association of Social Workers

For a discipline to become a profession, it is imperative that a professional organization be established. This has happened in social work. The first basic professional organization was the American Association of Social Workers, established in 1921, and which by 1954 had a membership of about 13,500 located in 132 local chapters. Six other professional organizations, built around social work specialties and with memberships totaling more than 7,500, had also furthered the profession. In the 1950s representatives of these seven organizations met and established a single integrated organization, the National Association of Social Workers, which is open to all trained and qualified social workers. This association was officially organized on July 7, 1955, at a special meeting of representatives of the seven predecessor organizations.

NASW has grown in numbers and prestige so that by 2004 it had a membership of 145,000 and is respected among professionally trained people in the various helping disciplines. The association has a code of ethics and has issued policy statements on salaries, on the goals of public social policy, and on standards for social work personnel practices. It has made tremendous strides in helping with the recruitment of qualified personnel for social work training and practice. In 1986 NASW had fifty-five chapters (each state, plus New York City, Los Angeles, Puerto Rico, the Virgin Islands, and Europe). By 1998, a few changes had taken place with fifty-five chapters remaining.

The seven associations that participated in the formation of the NASW were the American Association of Group Workers, American Association of Medical Social Workers, American Association of Psychiatric Social Workers, American Association of Social Workers, Association for the Study of Community Organization, National Association of School Social Workers, and the Social Work Research Group. Actually, the main activities of most of these groups have been absorbed by NASW. The various group members have been able to maintain some of their specialized interests, at the same time fusing into a united organization that is benefiting all social workers, social work education, and social work practice.

According to its bylaws, amended in August 1990, the association, to achieve its aims, "shall at all times recognize and carry out a threefold responsibility: (1) to promote activities appropriate to strengthening and unifying the social work profession as a whole, (2) to promote the sound and continuous development of the various areas of social work practice whereby the profession contributes to the meeting of particular aspects of human need, and (3) to promote efforts in behalf of human well-being by methods of social action."

A major development sponsored by NASW has been the establishment of the Academy of Certified Social Workers (ACSW). Through careful planning and good public relations, 18,500 social workers became certified on December 1, 1961, when this program officially began. Today there are more than 58,000. This is a significant step in raising the status of social workers and, in particular, in improving standards of practice in this field. Moreover, a new NASW credential has been established for social workers who have bachelor's degrees—the Academy of Certified Baccalaureate Social Worker (ACBSW). More than 2,000 qualified by passing the first BSW credential exam, which was given in June 1991.[5]

A new development in professional social work has been the emergence of the NASW Diplomate Exam,[6] which may lead to a credential properly referred to as the

NASW Diplomate in Clinical Social Work, the NASW Diplomate, or the DCSW. Some 2,000 social workers in November 1994 completed the first examination administered in the new NASW Diplomate in Clinical Social Work credential program.

The NASW has a delegate assembly that meets every three years to consider issues, policies, and social action. The Delegate Assembly is the ultimate policy-making body. In February 1995 its president, Ann A. Abbott, issued a call to launch the process that would culminate August 14–18, 1996, in convening this assembly, comprising 300 elected delegates who would represent NASW's members, and who "will determine organizational policy, set program priorities and take stands on social and professional issues to guide NASW for three years."[7]

Another area of interest to NASW is licensing. Certification and licensing in social work began with the legal regulation of the profession of social work in Puerto Rico in 1934, by an act that established compulsory certification, or licensing. In 1945 in California the first voluntary registration for MSWs in social work was enacted. In the 1960s, eight state laws were passed to expand legal regulation of the profession. Additional laws were passed in three states in 1972 and two more in 1974, bringing the total to fourteen states with some form of legal regulation. By 1985 there were thirty-six states and U.S. territories with social work licensure or registration laws.[8]

In 1969 the delegate assembly adopted a position favoring licensure, and since then NASW has given considerable guidance and support for licensing.

In 1973 NASW, according to a news release, "incorporated the requirement for ACSW certification—the MSW degree plus two years' experience, together with a written examination—into its model licensing statute. This statute is being used as a guideline in promoting state licensing and regulation of social work practice. NASW is negotiating with states that have licensing laws to accept ACSW membership as an alternative to the states examination processes."

By 1988, forty-four states, the District of Columbia, the Virgin Islands, and Puerto Rico had some form of regulation, such as licensure or certification. This meant there were only six remaining states without social work regulations. It was anticipated that by the 1990 Delegate Assembly there would likely be at least an initial form of regulation in all states.[9] Through the efforts of NASW and others the social work profession gained its goal of legal regulation throughout the United States when, in April 1992, Governor Tommy Thompson of Wisconsin signed a social work certification act for that state.

NASW plays an active role in establishing and maintaining standards for social work practice. Illustrative of this function are the standards for the practice of clinical social work, approved by the NASW board of directors, June 1984, revised April 1989, which state that clinical social workers shall:

Function in accordance with the ethics and the stated standards of the profession, including its accountability procedures.

Have and continue to develop specialized knowledge and understanding of individuals, families, and groups and of therapeutic and preventive interventions.

Respond in a professional manner to all persons who seek their assistance.

Be knowledgeable about the services available in the community and make appropriate referrals for their clients.

Maintain their accessibility to clients.

Safeguard the confidential nature of the treatment relationship and of the information obtained within that relationship.

Maintain access to professional case consultation.

Establish and maintain professional offices and procedures.

Represent themselves to the public with accuracy.

Engage in the independent private practice of clinical social work only when qualified to do so.

Have the right to establish an independent private practice.

Another indication of the professional vitality of NASW was the plan announced in 1988 for a new building to house the association. It was to be located in the nation's capital and would likely cost about $36 million when completed.[10] NASW moved into its new headquarters in February 1992 at 750 First St. N.E., Washington, DC.

Social Work Today

Another way to view the maturing of social work as a profession is to consider some of the major characteristics and activities of social work and social workers in the present era.

Code of Ethics

A major breakthrough in the development of social work as a profession occurred when the delegate assembly of the NASW adopted an official code of ethics for the association on October 13, 1960, and amended on April 11, 1967, with a philosophical introduction as follows:

> Social work is based on humanitarian, democratic ideals. Professional social workers are dedicated to service for the welfare of mankind, to the disciplined use of a recognized body of knowledge about human beings and their interactions, and to the marshaling of community resources to promote the well-being of all without discrimination.
>
> Social work practice is a public trust that requires of its practitioners integrity, compassion, belief in the dignity and worth of human beings, respect for individual differences, a commitment to service, and a dedication to truth. It requires mastery of a body of knowledge and skill gained through professional education and experience. It requires also recognition of the limitations of present knowledge and skill and of the services we are now equipped to give. The end sought is the performance of a service with integrity and competence.

Each member of the profession carries responsibility to maintain and improve social work service; constantly to examine, use, and increase the knowledge on which practice and social policy are based; and to develop further the philosophy and skills of the profession.

The 1997 Delegate Assembly revised the Code of Ethics adapted by the 1979 Delegate Assembly and specified the professional relationships and standards as follows:

1997 NASW Code of Ethics: Summary of Major Principles[11]

I. SOCIAL WORKERS' ETHICAL RESPONSIBILITIES TO CLIENTS
   A. *Commitment to Clients.* Social workers' primary responsibility is to promote the well-being of clients.
   B. *Self-Determination.* Social workers respect and promote the right of self-determination and assist clients in their efforts to identify and clarify their goals.
   C. *Informed Consent.* Social workers should provide services to clients only in the context of a professional relationship based on valid informed consent.
   D. *Competence.* Social workers should provide services and represent themselves only within the boundaries of their education, training, license, certification, etc.
   E. *Cultural Competence and Social Diversity.* Social workers should understand culture and its function in human behavior and society.
   F. *Conflicts of Interest.* Social workers should be alert to and avoid conflicts of interest that interfere with the exercise of professional discretion and impartial judgment.
   G. *Privacy and Confidentiality.* Social workers should respect clients' right to privacy.
   H. *Access to Records.* Social workers should provide clients with reasonable access to their records.
   I. *Sexual Relationships.* Social workers should under no circumstances engage in sexual activities or sexual contact with current clients, whether such contact is consensual or forced.
   J. *Payment for Services.* When setting fees, social workers should ensure that the fees are fair, reasonable, and commensurate with the services performed.
   K. *Termination of Services.* Social workers should terminate services to clients when such services are no longer required or no longer serve the clients' needs or interests.

II. SOCIAL WORKERS' ETHICAL RESPONSIBILITIES TO COLLEAGUES
   A. *Respect.* Social workers should treat colleagues with respect and should represent accurately and fairly the qualifications, views, and obligations of colleagues.
   B. *Confidentiality.* Social workers should respect confidential information shared by colleagues.
   C. *Interdisciplinary Collaboration.* Social workers who are members of an interdisciplinary team should participate in and contribute to decisions that affect the well-being of clients.
   D. *Consultation.* Social workers should seek the advice and counsel of colleagues whenever such consultation is in the best interests of clients.

E. *Sexual Relationships.* Social workers who function as supervisors or educators should not engage in sexual activities or contact with supervisees, students, trainees, or other colleagues over whom they exercise professional authority.

F. *Unethical Conduct of Colleagues.* Social workers should take adequate measures to discourage, prevent, expose, and correct the unethical conduct of colleagues.

III. SOCIAL WORKERS' ETHICAL RESPONSIBILITIES IN PRACTICE SETTINGS

A. *Supervision and Consultation.* Social workers should have the necessary knowledge and skill to supervise or consult appropriately.

B. *Education and Training.* Social workers should provide instruction only within their areas of knowledge and competence.

C. *Client Records.* Social workers should take reasonable steps to ensure that documentation in records is accurate and reflects the services provided.

D. *Billing.* Social workers should establish and maintain billing practices that accurately reflect the nature and extent of services provided.

E. *Administration.* Social work administrators should advocate within and outside their agencies for adequate resources to meet clients' needs.

F. *Commitment to Employers.* Social workers generally should adhere to commitments made to employers and employing organizations.

IV. SOCIAL WORKERS' ETHICAL RESPONSIBILITIES AS PROFESSIONALS

A. *Competence.* Social workers should accept responsibility or employment only on the basis of existing competence.

B. *Discrimination.* Social workers should not practice, condone, facilitate, or collaborate with any form of discrimination.

C. *Dishonesty, Fraud, and Deception.* Social workers should not participate in, condone, or be associated with dishonesty, fraud, or deception.

D. *Solicitations.* Social workers should not engage in uninvited solicitation of potential clients who, because of their circumstances, are vulnerable to undue influence, manipulation, or coercion.

V. SOCIAL WORKERS' ETHICAL RESPONSIBILITIES TO THE SOCIAL WORK PROFESSION

A. *Integrity of the Profession.* Social workers should work toward the maintenance of high standards of practice.

B. *Evaluation and Research.* Social workers should monitor and evaluate policies, the implementation of programs, and practice interventions.

VI. SOCIAL WORKERS' ETHICAL RESPONSIBILITIES TO THE BROADER SOCIETY

A. *Social Welfare.* Social workers should promote the general welfare of society, from local to global levels, and the development of people, their communities, and their environments.

B. *Public Participation.* Social workers should facilitate informed participation by the public in shaping social policies and institutions.

C. *Public Emergencies.* Social workers should provide appropriate professional services in public emergencies to the greatest extent possible.

D. *Social and Political Action.* Social workers should engage in social and political action that seeks to ensure that all people have equal access to the resources, employment, services, and opportunities they require to meet their basic human needs and to develop fully.

This code of ethics gives the social worker a societal compass. It helps the worker realize that he or she is a person who should have responsible interest and compassion regarding people, their problems, and their relationships with others.

A bright light on the ethical horizon is the introduction of ethics committees in social work. Reamer suggests that this movement is bringing significant changes in human service agencies, and that such committees assist in educating staff, formulating policies, and reviewing cases that contain complex ethical issues.[12]

Schools of Social Work

Social work education is provided on both undergraduate and graduate levels. The Council on Social Work Education by 2004 had accredited the programs of 422 undergraduate departments of colleges and universities offering social work training. Many persons who complete their undergraduate training go on to graduate social work schools or take social work positions in agencies. Another aim of this program is to provide social welfare content in the liberal education of students to aid in promoting good citizenship.

The 143 graduate training programs for the master's degree in the United States ordinarily take two years and combine classes in instruction with actual fieldwork practice in agencies. Since 1971 the council has authorized "advanced standing" for students who have completed approved undergraduate social work programs, and some schools of social

Interviewing for social work program.

work have established various plans that make it possible for such students to obtain their master's degrees in less than two years, some requiring only one year of graduate work.

Most graduate schools operate on the concurrent plan wherein they offer academic classes and field work training simultaneously. Several schools use the *block* plan, which provides for academic training at the beginning of the total program, followed by intensive five-day-a-week field instruction for several months, and finally culminates in additional academic seminars and other integrative instructional activities. Nearly all of the health and welfare agencies are utilized for field instruction, including psychiatric, medical, school, correctional, settlement, public welfare, child welfare, and group work agencies.

The basic program for the master's degree includes the three core areas of human behavior and social environment, social services and social policies, and the methods courses. Earlier, considerable emphasis was placed on *specialization* in certain fields such as psychiatric social work, medical social work, and school social work. Since the 1960s the training has been mainly on a generic base, with students taking the two-year training program to become social workers qualified to work in various agencies. In addition to the three core areas there is considerable work offered in research, and schools require either an individual or group thesis, a research project or completion of research classes for graduation. Elective courses provide a well-rounded program for the person who is going to practice as a professional social worker.

There is again a focus and emphasis on "specialization." Schools of social work have one or more "concentrations" involving methods and/or fields or problems for practice—casework, group work, micro or macro approach, social planning, drug abuse, health care. In addition, most schools have one or more "special emphases," which again bring added support to cope with specific problems in specific ways.

Some schools offer a third-year program, which provides for a deepening and intensification of study regarding casework, group work, administration, research, community organization, or some other aspect of the total service program.

Fifty-one graduate schools have introduced doctoral programs. In 1962 there were seventeen schools (two in Canada) offering post-master's programs, either a third-year or doctoral program, or both. Enrollment during 1962–63 amounted to 176 full-time students. In November 1987 there were 703 full-time and 820 part-time students enrolled in doctoral programs, based on data provided by CSWE from forty-two of the forty-seven existing programs. For the academic year 1995–96, doctoral degrees were awarded to 258 students by fifty-five graduate programs. A current movement exists to change DSW programs to Ph.D. programs.

Research

Since the 1960s social work has blossomed in the area of research, which is basic to professional development. Most schools of social work have one or more research projects or grants they are sponsoring. Grants are awarded not only from federal and state government sources, but also from foundations and from private business and other corporations. More and more people are coming to social workers requesting help to study human social behavior, the helping processes, and related activities.

A development that is augmenting research in social work is that many agencies, public and private, are sponsoring research projects of their own. Various kinds of studies are being financed from regular agency budgets to ferret out facts regarding social problems and what might be done about them. A concrete example of this trend is the allocation of $17,000 by one state welfare department to a community services council to conduct a study of working mothers—with the aim of ascertaining the pertinent facts and implications related to family problems and their solutions.

Another contribution, as it applies to research, is the work being done by the more than 14,000 students who graduate each year with their MSW degrees. Many participate in a research study, individually or in groups. About 250 doctoral dissertations are being completed each year. These studies are making contributions toward new knowledge about human behavior and social work education and practice.

Private Practice

One of the key developments in recent years has been the increase in the amount of private practice by persons with training in social work. Many social workers have joined forces with doctors or psychiatrists in providing services for patients. Others have set up their "shingles" in offices by themselves. Numerous questions have arisen and some leaders in social work have wondered about this development. However, the fact is that many qualified social workers are in private practice, and recent articles and studies reflect that this development seems to be another move toward professionalism. A study in 1968 of NASW members indicated fewer than 1,000 full-time private practitioners, with an estimated 15,000 doing some private counseling on a part-time basis.[13]

In 1975 a review of the NASW Data Bank indicated 8,500 members were in full-time or part-time private practice. Gabriel estimated, using these data and adding those not reporting and those not members of NASW, that there were from 10,000 to 20,000 social workers in private practice.[14] In 1992 Barker reported it is likely "there are more than 28,000 social workers in private practice."[15] He also suggested that private social work is growing not only in the United States but in many other countries, especially in Australia, India, Israel, Great Britain, and Canada.

Since then there has been a considerable and gradual increase in private practice, both full time and part time, so that today social work students are seriously considering these career choices. In fact, in a study of students in a New York State Master's of Social Work program, two-thirds (63 percent) thought they would enter private practice sometime during their careers.[16]

In December 1962, a workshop on private practice was held in Cleveland, Ohio, immediately prior to the 1962 NASW delegate assembly. Considerable difference of opinion was presented, but the overall conclusion was that, with certain safeguards, private practice does seem to fit into the total realm of professional social work. Following hours of debate, the delegate assembly adopted interim minimum standards for NASW members engaged in private practice of social work. They agreed that no NASW member may enter private practice unless:

1. He [or she] is a graduate of a school of social work accredited by the Council on Social Work Education or its predecessor organizations.
2. He [or she] is a member of the Academy of Certified Social Workers.

3. He [or she] has five years of acceptable full-time experience in agencies providing supervision by professionally trained social workers, of which two years were in one agency consecutively under such supervision, while giving direct service and using the method or methods to be used in the practice contemplated.[17]

The assembly, in adopting these standards and recommendations, pointed out that the qualifications should "not be construed as an endorsement of the competence of any individual member who meets the standards but rather be viewed as minimum criteria under which the form of practice would be sanctioned." The NASW board of directors modified these standards in 1971[18] stipulating that membership in ACSW was the profession's sole standard for self-regulated practice, in agency or private practice.

Social workers differ about the desirability of private practice. Of course, there are advantages and disadvantages in this challenging endeavor. Barker[19] suggests that the actual and anticipated rewards of private practice are: freedom from bureaucratic limitations found in agency employment, flexibility in work, opportunity to remain in direct practice, financial considerations, the challenge, opportunity to work with more motivated clients, and greater control over one's own work environment. He also suggests there are three main hazards in private practice: financial difficulties facing most private practitioners; malpractice and other legal difficulties; and problems centering in professional and public accountability, licensing, and qualifications for practice.

Numerous attempts have been made, some successfully, in the past few years to gain status for social workers for third-party payments for their services. NASW, many local chapters, and many individuals are working to gain further recognition in this regard. Acceptance of third-party payments for social workers is a step that will undoubtedly greatly strengthen and increase private social work practice. The 1984–85 annual report of NASW highlights its philosophy and current developments regarding third-party payments, as follows:

> Vendorship, the term sometimes applied to the practice of payment by a third party (an insurance carrier) to an individual who has provided services to another (the first and second parties), is an important issue for the profession. Only 15 states now have laws that require insurance carriers to extend vendorship rights to clinical social workers. While it seems illogical and unjust to deny such rights to the profession that provides the bulk of mental health services in the United States, the chief impact of such a policy is to deny millions of citizens access to the services of qualified practitioners, who generally charge less for the same services than other mental health professionals granted vendorship rights.
>
> Universal vendorship is one of the organization's highest priorities. Through arduous work by chapter leaders, two states, Montana and Tennessee, passed vendorship bills in the fiscal year 1985.[20]

Reimbursement demands and treatment decisions related to vendorship and third-party payments, according to Strom in 1992, are producing a growing dilemma for social workers. Strom reports that as "health costs have increased, so have the number of restrictions placed by insurers on reimbursement for mental health services" and "with the growth in vendorship for social workers, professionals in the mental health field are increasingly challenged to provide appropriate services within the parameters of what will be reimbursed by the third party."[21]

Kelley and Alexander made a questionnaire study of clinical social workers and concluded that private practice has become an accepted form of social work in recent years, and that most who conduct private practice provide services on a part-time basis.[22] The advantages of such private practice included the following: provides a professional independence for agency practitioners, additional income, and contact for supervisors and administrators with clients; educators can maintain skills and enrich teaching; and social workers who are parents can keep their schedules flexible and choose hours of work. The disadvantages related to these broad areas are generating of referrals, practical business issues, time management, professional development and quality control, and interaction between the agency and the private practitioner.

Publications

Another criterion of a profession is that it produces professional publications. *Social Work,* introduced in 1955, is published bimonthly by NASW and is recognized as a respectable professional journal. It has a current circulation of more than 160,000. This same organization publishes *NASW News*, a monthly that keeps professional social workers up-to-date on current developments, and includes personnel information, which lists job openings. NASW also publishes the *Encyclopedia of Social Work*, which has become the standard reference work for social work education and practice.

In addition, NASW publishes *Social Work Abstracts,* a quarterly that has brief descriptions of current articles and other materials relevant to social work practice, research, and education. Three newer quarterly journals, *Health and Social Work, Social Work in Education*, and *Social Work Research*, are offered for health care practitioners, school social workers, and those interested in research, respectively.

The Council on Social Work Education publishes the *Journal of Social Work Education,* which first appeared in July 1965 and is published three times a year. It is concerned with education for the fields of social work and social welfare, which includes materials on trends, new developments, issues, and problems at the undergraduate, master's, and postmaster's levels.

Salaries and Jobs

One of the first official activities of NASW was to establish a policy regarding salaries. The association recommended in 1957 that the beginning salary be a minimum of $5,400 per annum and suggested that social workers should be able to look forward to receiving $10,000 per annum after ten years' experience. In 1974 NASW recommended that the graduate of an approved baccalaureate social work program should receive $10,000 annually and the inexperienced master's graduate should receive a minimum of $12,500. Since then salaries have increased considerably. Present salaries for most MSW graduates would be in the range of $30,000 to $35,000 a year and for those who have been in practice about ten years, $40,000 to $60,000. Some social workers in private practice now make $75,000 to $150,000 annually. The 1995 *Social Work Almanac* reports an NASW sample study of its members which showed that in 1993 the average salary of those in direct service was $31,729 and the median salary was $29,000.

An NASW study in 1987 indicated that the average salary earned by social workers amounted to $27,800. This was based on salaries of administrators, direct service workers, experienced therapists, and the new BSW, and those in private practice as well as salaried workers.[23]

One of the fascinating aspects of social work practice is that it can take place in a variety of settings or agencies. Job opportunities are available in almost every kind of endeavor for helping people individually or on a family or community basis. Positions are offered in settings such as comprehensive mental health centers, medical hospitals, business and industry, schools, prisons, YMCAs, public welfare, child welfare, suicide prevention centers, and adoption agencies.

The contributions of social work as a profession are being recognized in today's world. For the first time in history the U.S. Congress, in 1984, declared March as National Social Work Month. President Reagan signed the resolution, P.L. 98-232, which affirmed appreciation to the many thousands of social workers who dedicate their lives to helping those in need. The resolution recognized that "professional social workers are in the vanguard of the forces working to provide protection for children and the aged, the reduction of racism and sexism, and the prevention of the social and emotional disintegration of individuals and families."

Alice Stratton, deputy assistant secretary of the Navy, was an example of a social worker making significant contributions in a high position in government. In 1988 she was making policies on issues affecting the quality of life of Navy and Marine Corps families throughout the nation and abroad, especially about 400,000 active-duty personnel who were married or single parents.[24]

In addition, social worker Patricia A. E. Rodgers, in 1990, was director of VISTA, guiding the efforts of more than 3,000 volunteers in this "domestic Peace Corps." In 1993 five social workers were nominated by President Clinton to fill high-level posts as assistant secretaries[25] directly under cabinet members who were heads of federal departments, as follows: Fernando Torres-Gill, assistant secretary for aging at the Department of Health and Human Services; Wardell Townsend, assistant secretary of agriculture at the Department of Agriculture; Wendy Sherman, assistant secretary for legislative affairs at the Department of State; Ada Deer, assistant secretary for Indian Affairs at the Department of the Interior; and Augusta Kappner, assistant secretary for vocational and adult education at the Department of Education. Prior to these appointments only one social worker had served as an assistant secretary in the federal government at any one time. Currently, social workers serve in the U.S. Congress, in numerous state legislatures, and in other important government and community positions.

Elective Offices

A final measure of the growth of social work as a profession is the number of social workers serving in elective offices across the United States. In 1996, NASW identified the recruitment, training, and promotion of social workers as candidates for elective office as a goal for the profession. This goal reflects the growing recognition within the profession for social workers to contribute directly to the democratic process as elected public officials. In 1997, there were five social workers serving in the U.S. House of Representatives: Barbara A. Mikulski (D), Maryland; Ronald V. Dellums (D), California, 9th District; Edolphus "Ed"

Towns (D), New York, 10th District; Debbie Stabenow (D), Michigan, 8th District; and Ciro D. Rodrequez (D), Texas, 28th District. At the state, county, and city level, 204 social workers were serving in elective offices in 1997. This figure not only reflects the profession's commitment to public service through elective office but also the confidence the American electorate has in social workers to represent their interests.[26]

The Changing Nature of Work

Social work practice and education have been influenced by changes in America's economy, especially in terms of patterns of employment and unemployment. In their article "Nature of Work and Future of the Social Work Profession," Reisch and Gorin assess how changes in work might affect the social work profession.[27] Some of their conclusions are disturbing. According to some experts, the U.S. economy is shifting to "the new, ruthless economy" characterized by more inequality, a shift in power from labor to capital, and the proliferation of low-wage employment. Some believe this will lead to "severe poverty" because it will be more difficult for low-income people to move into the middle class while the chances of middle-class Americans moving into poverty will increase.

A second factor affecting social work in the twenty-first century is the reorganization and transformation of work. After years of anticipation, new computer and communication technologies are throwing the world into a third great revolution, the technological revolution. Unlike earlier decades, however, millions of people will be thrown into unemployment because new industries have not been developed to hire these displaced workers.

Social work as a profession must be ready to address this anticipated increase in poverty and unemployment. According to Reisch and Gorin, it would be important for the profession to begin a serious debate about what constitutes "work" in a postmodern, technological world. This debate would include discussion around (1) the number of hours per week individuals are expected to work in order to earn a "living wage," (2) the types of activities considered useful or productive in this new technological world, (3) what is considered to be adequate compensation for labor, and (4) the importance of social supports (i.e., child care, health care, housing, etc.) in helping individuals reach their greatest potential.[28]

The Path Ahead

Although we live in difficult times, the path ahead for the social work profession is very promising as we move further into the twenty-first century. This is especially true in the areas of aging, mental health, and public welfare. It is estimated that by the year 2020 the elderly population in the United States will nearly double. Social work has already made a significant contribution to the area of aging and this contribution will continue to grow. Dating back to the 1930s, social workers have worked tirelessly for Social Security and the later amendments to the Social Security Act of 1933. The profession has been particularly involved with the Medicare and Medicaid programs and their subsequent reforms. Social workers have been actively involved in the development and growth of various hospice programs and associations and with the current proposals regarding prescription medications benefits and expanded nursing home coverage. Social work as a profession remains committed to America's aging population.

The social work profession remains very active in the field of mental health. Since the early 1960s, social workers have advocated for the rights of individuals with mental illness. Today, every comprehensive mental health center in the country is staffed, in part, with professional social workers who often are the primary therapists and advocates for those who are mentally ill and their families. The 1990s saw the profession refocus its efforts on the prevention and treatment of mental illness. The case management approach to the treatment of mental illness was championed by the social work profession and has become the treatment of choice across America.

Some of the greatest achievements of the social work profession have been made in the field of public welfare. From the early days of the "friendly visitor," social workers and the profession have been the primary advocates for children in America. Since the late 1800s, the profession has continued to advocate for the rights of children. The results have led to prenatal care and early child development programs, various Headstart alliances, foster care, child protection services, and countless other programs designed to improve the quality of life for America's children. To be sure, the social work profession will continue to be the gatekeeper for America's children.

What Does the Future Hold?

In the years to come, the social work profession must continue to evaluate the effectiveness of its treatment and service programs. "Evidence-based practice" is one of the important buzz words in the profession and the importance of evaluating the impact of social work practice and service will continue to mount. Americans are more cost-efficient than ever before. This has occurred, in part, because of the decline of financial and business markets following the September 11 attacks. There is a growing emphasis in American society on making business and government more lean and efficient and this emphasis is already impacting the social welfare system. A case in point is how to rescue the social security system before too much damage is done by our dwindling workforce.

Another concern that the profession will have to address is the growing disparity between the "haves and the have-nots" in American society. The gap between the rich and the poor continues to grow. Although the growth in service-oriented jobs continues, many of these jobs provide incomes little above the poverty level. The American middle class, the bulwark of our society, is under attack as never before. As corporations downsize and as jobs move outside the United States, we are weakening the very segment of American society that has been our greatest strength. As the middle class weakens, more people move dangerously close to the poverty level. International social work will continue to grow in importance as terrorism continues to plague our world. The September 11 attacks demonstrated how a nation can almost be brought to its knees by terrorists. The deaths of over 200 killed by terrorists' bombs on March 11, 2004, in Madrid reinforces how small our planet is and how vulnerable every country can be. Social workers around the world will be asked by their nation-states to help fight terrorism and to aid the victims of these callous and hateful attacks.

Another trend we can expect to continue is social workers teaming up with other professional groups and promoting interdisciplinary training and service. Interdisciplinary training and service has already been an important part of the health care industry in America. Interdisciplinary health care teams of physicians, nurses, nutritionists, social workers, psychologists, and other health care providers are already providing training and service for sub-Saharan Africa in the fight against AIDS. This interdisciplinary focus will also impact other service areas such as corrections and child welfare. It is clear that no one profession can continue to act on its own. The problems that nations and our world face are too complex for that kind of myopic thinking to continue. In summary, the future for the social work profession is both exciting and challenging as the world's problems become even more complex and difficult to manage.

The war in Afghanistan and Iraq has divided America. As we move into 2008, some elected leaders want us to stay the course whereas others are urging us to move out of both countries as soon as possible. What role should the profession of social work play in this unfolding drama? Some social workers are urging the profession to take a stand against the war in Afghanistan and Iraq. They believe both wars have wasted valuable resources that our country could use to address growing domestic problems including the rebuilding of New Orleans following Hurricane Katrina. They add that the war is damaging our relationships with other countries and compromising our humanitarian programs throughout the world. Other social workers believe bringing democracy to both countries is worth the price our country is paying. Whatever argument is proposed, one role that the social work profession will continue to play is helping the troops who are returning from both battlefields. As in previous conflicts, many troops are returning with serious mental health problems such as posttraumatic stress, substance abuse, and depression. Other troops must recover from the physical trauma of war that has left many of them blind, paralyzed, or missing arms and legs. Social workers will continue to offer services to these returning troops in a variety of public, private, and military settings. By doing so, we continue our century-old tradition of helping America's military men and women who are returning home from war.

Summary

Social work is a rapidly developing profession. Its charity and social welfare roots reach back for many centuries. The history of civilization reflects a sincere attempt to provide welfare services for people, families, and communities with problems. Particularly since the turn of the twentieth century, there have been more formalized programs to professionalize the social welfare helping process.

To train qualified social workers, many schools of social work and related programs have been established, providing appropriate social work degrees at the baccalaureate, master's, and doctoral levels. Professional organizations were created to help dedicated, welfare-minded individuals to join forces and support each other in providing humanitarian services. These associations provided effective services over a period of years. In 1955 came the unity and integration of seven professional social work organizations into the unified National Association of Social Workers. This organization has made significant contributions within its years of existence.

In the field of education, the Council on Social Work Education, established in 1952, has likewise made important strides in upgrading standards of education, in furthering recruitment, in offering consultation services, and in interpreting to the public what social work really is and can be.

Research, publications, and private practice all point to an ongoing, significant profession of social work. The code of ethics outlines the "right" goals of this helping profession and presents worthwhile guidelines for the dedicated persons who join. Advanced educational programs beyond the master's degree are on the increase, and they are providing opportunities for further education, greater knowledge, better skills, and mature professional attitudes.

Selected References

ABBOTT, ANN A., "Professional Conduct," in *Encyclopedia of Social Work,* 19th ed., Vol. 3. Washington, DC: NASW Press, 1995, pp. 1916–1921.

ARCHES, JOAN, "Social Structure, Burnout, and Job Satisfaction," *Social Work,* 36 (May 1991), 202–206.

BARKER, ROBERT L., "Private Practice," in *Encyclopedia of Social Work,* 19th ed., Vol. 3. Washington, DC: NASW Press, 1995, pp. 1905–1910.

BARKER, ROBERT L., *Social Work in Private Practice,* 2nd ed. Silver Spring, MD: NASW Press, 1992.

BUTLER, AMY C., "The Attractions of Private Practice," *Journal of Social Work Education,* 28 (Winter 1992), 47–60.

FARLEY, O. WILLIAM, BOYD E. OVIATT, REX A. SKIDMORE, and MILTON G. THACKERAY, "Social Work—Professional Mediocrity or Maturation," *Social Casework,* 58 (April 1977), 236–242.

GINSBERG, LEON, *Careers in Social Work,* 2nd ed. Boston: Allyn & Bacon, 2001.

HAYNES, KAREN, and JAMES S. MICKELSON, *Affecting Change: Social Workers in the Political Arena,* 5th ed. Boston: Allyn & Bacon, 2003.

HICK, STEVEN, and JOHN G. MCNUTT, eds., *Advocacy, Activism, and the Internet.* Chicago: Lyceum Books, 2002.

HOLLAND, THOMAS P., and ALLIE C. KILPATRICK, "Ethical Issues in Social Work: Toward a Grounded Theory of Professional Ethics," *Social Work,* 36 (March 1991), 138–143.

HOPPS, JUNE GARY, and PAULINE M. COLLINS, "Social Work Profession Overview," in *Encyclopedia of Social Work,* 19th ed., Vol. 3. Washington, DC: NASW Press, 1995, pp. 2266–2282.

JAYARATNE, SRINIKA, MARY LOU DAVIS-SACKS, and WAYNE A. CHESS, "Private Practice May Be Good for Your Health and Well-being," *Social Work,* 36 (May 1991), 224–229.

LECROY, CRAIG, *The Call of Social Work: Life Stories.* Thousand Oaks, CA: Sage, 2002.

MIRINGOFF, MARC, and MARQUE-LUISA MARINGOFF, *The Social Health of the Nation.* New York: Oxford University Press, 1999.

MORALES, ARMANDO, and BRADFORD W. SHEAFOR, *Social Work: A Profession of Many Faces,* 10th ed. Boston: Allyn & Bacon, 2004.

NORTHHOUSE, PETER G., *Leadership: Theory and Practice,* 3rd ed. Thousand Oaks, CA: Sage, 2003.

RAFFOUL, PAUL R., and AARON MCNEECE, *Future Issues for Social Work Practice.* Boston: Allyn & Bacon, 1996.

SKOLNICK, JEROME H., and ELLIOT CURRIE, *Crisis in American Institutions,* 12th ed. Boston: Allyn & Bacon, 2004.

Notes

1. William E. Wickenden, "The Second Mile," address delivered before the Engineering Institute of Canada, 1941.

2. Ernest Greenwood, "Attributes of a Profession," *Social Work,* 2 (July 1957), pp. 45–55.

3. Ibid., p. 54.

4. Esther Lucile Brown, *Social Work as a Profession* (New York: Russell Sage Foundation, 1942), p. 29.

5. *NASW News,* 36 (July 1991), p. 7.

6. NASW *News,* 40 (March 1995), p. 11.

7. "Call to Delegate Assembly," *NASW News,* 40 (March 1995), p. 2.

8. "In Retrospect: Three Decades of Progress," *NASW News,* 30 (October 1985), p. 16.

9. "Social Work Regulation Gaining Support in Six Remaining States," *NASW News,* 33 (October 1988), 11; *NASW News,* 37 (June 1992), p. 10.

10. *NASW News,* 33 (November 1988), p. 1.

11. *Code of Ethics* (Silver Spring, MD: NASW, n.d.), pp. 1–16.

12. Frederic G. Reamer, "Ethics Committees in Social Work," *Social Work,* 32 (May/June 1987), p. 188.

13. Patricia W. Soyka, "Unlocking Human Resources: A Career in Social Work," *Public Affairs Pamphlet* No. 458 (1973), p. 10.

14. Estelle Gabriel, "Private Practice in Social Work," in *Encyclopedia of Social Work,* Vol. 2 (Washington, DC: NASW, 1977), p. 1056.

15. Robert L. Barker, *Social Work in Private Practice,* 2nd ed. (Washington, DC: NASW, 1992), p. 13.

16. Amy C. Butler, "The Attractions of Private Practice," *Journal of Social Work Education,* 28 (Winter 1992), p. 52.

17. *NASW News,* 8 (February 1963), p. 5.

18. Gabriel, *Encyclopedia of Social Work,* p. 1055.

19. Robert Barker, *Social Work in Private Practice*, pp. 28, 38.

20. National Association of Social Workers, *Annual Report, 1984–85,* p. 6.

21. Kimberly Strom, "Reimbursement Demands and Treatment Decisions: A Growing Dilemma for Social Workers," *Social Work,* 37 (September 1992), pp. 398–403.

22. Patricia Kelley and Paul Alexander, "Part-time Private Practice: Practical and Ethical Considerations," *Social Work,* 30 (May/June 1985), pp. 254–257.

23. *Salaries in Social Work* (Silver Spring, MD: NASW, 1987), p. 3.

24. "Social Worker Carves Niche at Pentagon," *NASW News,* 33 (April 1988), p. 5.

25. *NASW News,* 38 (September 1993), pp. 1, 14.

26. *Social Workers Serving in Elective Offices: 1997* (Washington, DC: NASW, 1997), pp. 1–5, 16.

27. Michael Reisch and Stephen H. Gorin, "Nature of Work and Future of the Social Work Profession," *Social Work,* 46 (January 2001), pp. 9–19.

28. Ibid., p. 15.

21

Social Work Prevention and Enrichment

Police officials report that most automobiles that are stolen by teenagers have the keys in the ignition and a few even have the engines running. If something were done to educate adults to remove the keys from their automobiles and to lock their cars when they park, the number of auto thefts would likely decrease. In thinking about human behavior, and especially about social problems, *is it not possible to reduce and prevent problems? Social work is very much interested in this approach. For example, social work now provides "home-based family care" in which a social worker may be attached to a family in crisis with its children for twenty-four hours a day, helping prevent family breakup or other problems.*

Prevention is a word used in many different ways. It indicates action that staves off something from happening. Stated positively, it is the process of action taken so that biological, psychological, behaviorial, interpersonal, personal, family, or community problems are minimized or do not arise at all. Theoretically, it means the doing of something so that personal and social pathology will not develop. The National Commission on Social Work Practice of the National Association of Social Workers defined prevention in social work as "activities which have merit in averting, or discouraging the development of, specific social problems, or in delaying or controlling the growth of such problems after they have presented beginning symptoms."

Broadly speaking, prevention in relation to social work may be regarded in two ways: first, proper action taken so that the personal, family, or community problems do not arise at all; and second, action taken so that personal, family, and community problems are not repeated even though such problems existed at the outset. Prevention is concerned with keeping the vase intact, rather than trying to repair the broken pieces. It is interested in keeping human personalities and human interrelationships operating on an integrated and mature level, rather than in gluing together human parts that may have been cracked, broken apart, or splintered.

The field of public health in medicine has offered many helpful concepts and specific terminology in regard to prevention, and social workers have borrowed from this field several ideas and principles. Five levels of prevention in public health, commonly accepted in preventive medicine, are (1) health promotion, (2) specific protection, (3) early diagnosis and treatment, (4) disability limitation, and (5) rehabilitation.[1]

The field of public health also describes the levels of prevention as primary, secondary, and tertiary. Leavell and Clark[2] explain that primary prevention includes health promotion and specific protection, that secondary prevention encompasses early diagnosis and prompt treatment, and that tertiary prevention includes disability limitation and rehabilitation. Health promotion concerns the general health and well-being of the population and is not directed at any particular disease or disorder. Health education and motivation are particularly important on this level of prevention. Examples of this level would include promotion of adequate housing, selective periodic health examinations, and health promotional activities that aim toward the realization of optimal personality development. Specific protection would include such measures as immunization, sanitation, and sound nutrition.

In regard to secondary prevention, early diagnosis and prompt treatment are particularly important. This level stresses case findings and handling of disruptive problems. The aim, of course, is to relieve distress and to shorten duration of the illness, minimize contagion, and reduce symptoms. Tertiary prevention is focused mainly on the chronic and serious illnesses and includes attempts to reduce pain and suffering. Disability limitation includes delaying the consequences of clinically advanced diseases. The preventive measures are primarily therapeutic and are directed toward the patient in order to arrest the disease process and to prevent further complications.

Rapoport claims that the concept of prevention, evolved largely from the public health field, is often used in "a distorted and confusing manner in the social work framework."[3] Wittman, a pioneer in social work prevention, observed that we are devoting our main effort to areas of secondary and tertiary prevention and are doing very little on the primary level.[4] We need to become more interested in and focused on enhancing the well-being of individuals, families, and communities and helping bring about an enrichment in daily living. Social workers need to look at the socially healthy people as well as those who are disabled. To assist on the broad basis of health promotion, we need to do more on the positive side by working with nondisabled people and increasing the long-range values of social work to the community. We need to consider the "points of entry" where preventive social work may be particularly effective. Social work may help especially in relation to obstetrics, the nursery school, kindergarten, with adolescence, and at time of marriage. "All can provide points of departure for constructive preventive social services."[5]

Wittman suggests that until there is some extension of service coverage to the total population, rather than to the present social work clientele as we now know it, we must remain committed mainly to the secondary and tertiary levels of prevention. The major concern for the near future should be "to develop adaptations of current practice which will reach more of the healthy segment of the population and may thereby retard the rising incidence of social pathology."[6]

Dr. Stephen Goldston, at a pilot national conference on primary prevention in mental health in April 1976, presented the following definition, which also has meaning for social work:

> Primary prevention encompasses those activities directed to specifically identified vulnerable high-risk groups within the community who have not been labeled as psychiatrically ill

and for whom measures can be undertaken to avoid the onset of emotional disturbance and/or to enhance their level of positive mental health. Programs for the promotion of mental health are primarily educational rather than clinical in conception and operation with their ultimate goal being to increase people's capacities for dealing with crises and for taking steps to improve their own lives.[7]

Hazelkorn recognizes that social work has a long way to go in regard to prevention both in relation to training and practice. She concludes, however, that "there is the obligation to prepare graduates for a future that will undoubtedly include preventive social work alongside preventive medicine and preventive psychiatry."[8] She also indicated many approaches being experimented with by social workers that have a preventive emphasis, such as genetic counseling, activities in family planning, prenatal and well-baby clinics, family life education, work with tenant groups, and epidemiological approaches in public assistance.

A general, current definition of prevention is found in *The Social Work Dictionary:*

> Actions taken by social workers and others to minimize and eliminate those social, psychological, or other conditions known to cause or contribute to physical and emotional illness and sometimes socioeconomic problems. Prevention includes establishing those conditions in society that enhance the opportunities for individuals, families, and communities to achieve positive fulfillment.[9]

Social Work Focus on Prevention

At present there is considerable interest in prevention in social work practice, and this interest is filtering into the educational process. Some individuals think this emphasis is entirely new to social welfare and social work; history shows otherwise.

At the Twelfth Annual Session of the National Conference of Charities and Correction, held in Washington, DC, in June 1885, a considerable amount of the conference was devoted to *preventive work.* In fact, more than sixty pages of the proceedings were concerned with various papers and discussions in this area, which included such topics as "Thirty Years' Experience in Nursery and Child Hospital Work," "The Shady Side of the 'Placing-Out System'," "Methods of Industrial Training for Girls," "The Kindergarten as a Character Builder," and "Compulsory Education." Indicative of pioneer thinking was a report of one discussion in this field.

> Mr. Caldwell thought the method of trying to get rid of crime by attacking the adult criminal was like trying to restore a tree to health by binding up the branches, when the real trouble was in the root. The way to get rid of pauperism and crime is to take care of the children, and to begin with them as early as possible. As John Plowman says about breaking a colt, "The work will thrive, if you start before he's five." Not only the children, but the homes need reforming.[10]

Within more recent years social work educators and practitioners have developed considerable interest in prevention and have conceptualized some of their ideas. Boehm, in a paper on the nature of social work, describes the functions of social work as threefold: (1) *restoration*—which seeks to identify, control, or eliminate factors in the interactional process that cause breakdown or impairment of social relationships; (2) *provision of resources*—which is concerned with the creation, enrichment, improvement, and coordination of social resources; and (3) *prevention*—which consists of early discovery, control, and elimination of conditions that could hamper effective social functioning.[11]

This same classification was presented in the Curriculum Study by the Council on Social Work Education, which gives emphasis to the importance of prevention in the total field of social work.

The NASW has been very much interested in the whole area and process of prevention. In 1962, a pioneering report "Prevention and Treatment" contained a pertinent statement with an introduction as follows:

> The basic concern of social work with prevention arises out of the profession's service commitment. If the social pathology with which most social workers deal could be prevented, then many individuals would be spared destructive experiences and society would benefit. This in itself is important enough to justify greater efforts toward the further development of effective prevention. If, for example, it is possible to prevent the disintegration of families rather than merely aiding members of the disintegrated family group to deal with affects of separation, who would deny the worthiness of the preventative effort?[12]

After considerable discussion of some of the issues and problems related to prevention, the report concluded that "NASW, as the single professional membership association with the authority and responsibility to speak for social work, needs, through the democratic process, to evolve its position concerning the issue of prevention and then implement that position in communities throughout the nation."[13]

Wittman recalls that the 1960s was the period for the emergence of beginning theory dealing with prevention in social work and that the 1970s produced demonstrations in class and field experiences.[14] In February 1980, there were four schools offering concentrations in prevention and eight schools with elective courses in preventive social work. The four schools offering a concentration in prevention with a combination of class and field experiences were George Warren Brown School of Social Work, Simmons College, University of North Carolina, and University of Connecticut.

Several developments on the political and economic scene have given additional interest and emphasis to the area of prevention. President John F. Kennedy, in the first presidential message wholly on the subject of welfare, in 1962 told Congress, "Public welfare must be more than a salvage operation, picking up debris from the wreckage of human lives. Its emphasis must be directed increasingly toward prevention and rehabilitation." In 1961, the U.S. Congress passed a law for the prevention and control of juvenile delinquency, which provided $10 million annually to encourage demonstrations, experimentations, and training activities that would help meet this problem and prevent it. Twenty years later seven cabinet-level departments and two federal agencies provided direct financial assistance to forty-five delinquency-related programs. Olson-Raymer suggests that today's practitioners and theorists question the effectiveness of individualized treatment in preventing delinquency but "they have good reasons to believe preventive school, family, community, and peer group programs aimed at modifying negative institutional policies and practices may help prevent juvenile crime."[15]

In February 1963, President Kennedy, in the first presidential address to Congress specifically on mental health, asked lawmakers to consider this disastrous national problem and to appropriate money to increase facilities, particularly community mental health centers for reducing and preventing mental illness. He suggested that we must first "seek out the causes of mental illness and of mental retardation and eradicate them." He warned that we need to prevent thousands of new cases of mental illness and mental retardation, and he recommended appropriations of several millions of dollars to help establish additional community mental health centers and provide staff and other activities that would help in this total preventive and rehabilitative movement.

The 1962 amendments to the Social Security Act included a new emphasis on prevention as well as protection and rehabilitation. Legislation and proposals by the Johnson, Nixon, Ford, Carter, Reagan, Bush, Clinton, and Bush administrations have emphasized reduction and prevention of many social problems, such as delinquency, drug abuse, alcoholism, and child abuse.

Both social work education and practice are putting more emphasis on primary prevention. For example, the CSWE project on Prevention in Social Work Education held a two-day conference in Louisville, Kentucky, in October 1979, with a major focus on primary prevention for curriculum development. It was the "first major forum for faculty development in primary prevention in social work education."[16]

In December 1985, a Governor's Conference was held in New York on "Healthy People." Steven E. Katz, state commissioner of mental health, said, "The theme of this conference reinforces the conviction that Governor Cuomo shares with us: Prevention is a critical element in human services and as such deserves serious attention."[17] Topics covered at the three-day conference represented some of the most critical prevention problems facing health and human services today, including Alzheimer's disease, depression, teenage suicide, developmental disabilities, alcohol abuse, substance abuse, rural mental health, child abuse, sex abuse, family violence, stress, and emotional problems in children.

The federal government's ongoing commitment to the prevention of child abuse and neglect, into the twenty-first century, continues to be evidenced by the passage of P.L. 108-36. In June of 2003, "President George W. Bush signed into law the Keeping Children and Families Safe Act of 2003 (P.L. 108-36). The Act reauthorizes the Child Abuse Prevention and Treatment Act (CAPTA), the Adoptions Opportunities program, the Abandoned Infant Assistance Act, and the Family Violence Prevention and Services Act, authorizing funding for fiscal year 2004 through 2008."[18] In addition to the number of grants provided by the act supporting, among many things, the hiring and training of CPS workers and the linking of community resources, it also established that a focus be maintained on the prevention of child abuse. This is to be accomplished by providing monies to states to support community-based services and programs for families relating directly to the prevention and treatment of child abuse and neglect.

Another indication of the importance of prevention to the profession of social work and related services was the introduction of a journal in this area of study and practice, *Prevention in Human Services*. This journal began publication in 1982 and is published biannually.

Problems Involved

Several factors cloud the preventive scene. First is the complexity of human behavior. Final answers have not been acquired regarding what causes social problems or the best solutions. Thus, it is very difficult to plan action and to predict what the outcome will be in regard to a specific personal or social situation. A legitimate question arises: If we do not know the precise causes of a social problem, can we prevent the problem? In medicine and other fields, even though we do not know the exact causal relationships of phenomena, we are able to produce situations that seem to bring about desired results. We do not know for sure what electricity is, but we are able to control it. In medicine, for example we are not always aware of the exact cause of illness, but there are precautions and activities practiced that seem to prevent them and reduce their numbers. Specifically, handwashing helped prevent surgical deaths before anyone knew about germ theory.

Unlike the medical field, where causes of an illness may be reduced to a single virus, specific bacteria, gene, or chromosome, the causes or sources of problems in the field of human behavior likely stem from multiple and/or combinations of factors. Knowledge and skills in relation to human behavior and social functioning are just in the beginning stages. We can ask many more questions than we can answer. Thus, it becomes a genuine challenge to increase and utilize knowledge and skills in the prevention of social malfunctioning.

For example, McMurtry reviewed the literature and research studies about the effectiveness of prevention related to child maltreatment. He suggested that secondary prevention of child maltreatment involves identifying potential abusers and treating them before the abuse takes place. He concluded that although accurate identification of parents at risk may eventually be possible, more research is needed to establish identifying criteria and to determine effective means of intervention to prevent abuse.[19]

Another problem is the difficulty of evaluation. How do we know for sure that the action we have taken has brought the results we desired? With so many factors involved in human behavior, it is especially difficult to be objective in evaluating what takes place and why.

Examples of Prevention

Several examples of prevention are presented to illustrate some of the possibilities and potentialities involving social work.

Premarital Counseling

Premarital counseling is illustrative of an attempt at primary prevention on the part of social workers and other counselors. With approximately one-half of all first marriages ending in divorce and the potentially negative impact it has on individuals, families, and society, many have sought to understand why this occurs when people starting out have such hopeful expectations. In studying the problem, psychologist Neil Warren has found that the choice of who one marries is the most crucial decision.[20] Premarital counseling to assist individuals in making this all-important decision is one example of how helping professionals can reduce the painful effects associated with divorce. A record taken from a university setting illustrates some aspects of this process.

Mr. C., age 26, majoring in biology, and Ms. T., age 23, majoring in English, came to the clinic in the spring of the academic year and stated that they planned to marry in June, after Mr. C. had received his master's degree and Ms. T. had completed her undergraduate studies. They said they had come to the clinic because they had heard that marriage counseling would provide an opportunity for them to learn more about each other and about marriage. They had no major problems. Although they had differed on many things during the two years of courtship, they had been able to work through their disagreements to the satisfaction of each.

A clinical social worker interviewed each of them three times and then saw them together for one final interview. Each was given an opportunity to take the Marriage Prediction and the Personality Inventory tests. The results of these tests were favorable and indicated that each had a mature personality.

In the individual interviews with the social worker, Ms. T. discussed a few of her fears about marriage, particularly in relation to childbearing. She also indicated some concern about the differences in religious belief and activity between herself and Mr. C., although both belonged to the same denomination. She had many other questions related to courtship and the future marital relationship. She talked about how she and Mr. C. might improve their ability to communicate with each other and to solve differences that seemed to arise. Mr. C. also raised several questions that he seemed anxious to discuss with the worker. He, too, was worried about religious differences, but felt that these could be worked out satisfactorily. He was concerned about money management, and he wondered whether he was being fair and realistic in going ahead with marriage at this time in view of his desire to continue graduate work.

In the joint interview, Ms. T. and Mr. C.'s religious differences, their financial planning, and other matters were discussed, and the couple seemed to develop greater understanding of each other and some helpful insights regarding their relationship. They felt definitely that they would like to go ahead with their plans for marriage. At the close of this interview Mr. C. said, "I feel that counseling has helped us to understand ourselves, each other, and what marriage is all about as we never have before." Ms. T. added, "Talking to the worker has removed some fears I have had. I think it has opened the door for us to know each other better, to communicate with each other better, and to learn how to solve problems that are bound to come up in marriage."

A summary of functions by three marriage counselors who work in a university agency further describes the emphasis on and the methods of prevention through premarital counseling:

1. Through interviewing, providing an opportunity for prospective marriage partners to discuss concerns regarding their approaching marriage. Questions frequently focus on personality differences, wedding plans, the honeymoon, physical adjustment, housing plans, religious differences, money and its management, emancipation from family, adjustment to new friendships, and in-laws.
2. By giving factual information directly or by suggesting appropriate reading material.

3. Through the use of personality tests, inventories, and other tools.

4. By giving counselees an opportunity to vent fears, doubts, and wishes regarding marriage and each other, so that they recognize how important inner feelings are in a marital relationship.

5. By encouraging the couple to go to a physician for medical examination and conference, which includes a pelvic examination for the woman.

6. By referring, if indicated, to other specialists or agencies for needed assistance.

7. Through the counselor's conferring, if the situation warrants, with other counselors or consultants in his own agency, or with other specialists in the community regarding the problems of the counselees.

8. By acquainting the couple with the resources of marriage counseling so if later they are confronted with problems they feel unable to handle alone they will seek professional help.

9. By assisting the couple to build and strengthen a realistic, positive philosophy toward marriage. The counselor encourages the couple to discuss their basic goals and values; he or she aids them to realize that no marriage is perfect, all have conflicts, and all require effort, compromise, and adjustment. The clinical social worker helps the couple to leave the counseling situation with "eyes open" to the somewhat uncertain path ahead but with a firm conviction that a happy and successful marriage is worth working for.

In Family Service Societies, many activities are sponsored to assist on a preventive level. Staff members give talks before service clubs, PTA groups, Family Life Institutes, and other groups of people. Their purpose is to help members of society understand marriage and family relationships better and adjust more adequately in these relationships.

Preventive Mental Health

From 1964 to 1968 a pioneering demonstration-research project, supported in part by the Department of Health, Education, and Welfare in cooperation with both labor and management, took place in the men's garment industry in New York City.[21] The project involved several hundred blue-collar workers with mental health problems.

During the life of the project, 718 persons (from about 20,000 workers) were referred to the program, of which 442 were evaluated and serviced, mainly on a short-term basis. The initial interview was shared by a psychiatrist and a social worker.

Probably the most significant conclusion of this mental health program was that mentally ill individuals can work and produce on the job successfully if the total work community, bolstered by professional workers, understands, accepts, and utilizes mental health care and its benefits.

An innovative example of preventive services is the InstaCare Center, sponsored by a local hospital in a suburb of a metropolitan area. A licensed clinical social worker in 1998 was providing individual and marital counseling services, with considerable emphasis on prevention of personal, emotional, and social problems. The worker also was teaching classes, again in the preventive realm, on Pain and Stress Management, Imaging and Weight Management, Creating Your Own Self-Esteem, and Saying What You Really Mean.

With greater emphasis on accountability for outcomes based on monies spent for programs, in both private and public sectors, it will be of vital importance for social workers to demonstrate that prevention programs are achieving their desired goals. For example, a significant amount of research has been undertaken on the efficiency of the popular DARE (Drug Abuse Resistance Education) program. Data has consistently found that those who attended the program were just as likely to have used drugs and alcohol in the past year as those students who did not attend.[22] This does not imply that drug prevention programs are of no value, but that data on the outcomes of such programs will assist professionals in identifying what works and what does not. For example, early results of a family-based drug prevention program appear to demonstrate positive outcomes. Harrison, Boyle, and Farley[23] conducted a study on nine- to twelve-year old children who were identified as being at risk for substance abuse. These children, along with their parents, were included in a skills training program developed by Kumpfer titled "Strengthening the Families Program." Both parents and young people were brought together at the local community mental health center. Parents and their children were together for the first half-hour to interact and to eat a meal. The next hour, parents and youth separated into groups for skills training. They reconvened as an entire group for the last half hour to discuss what they had learned. During the twelve-week course, families were also invited to attend a recreation activity to assist families in learning how to better spend leisure time together. Data from the study found positive gains at the end of the study for both parents and the youth (both males and females). The question posed by the researchers was whether or not the positive gains will be maintained. The answer to this question will be of vital importance to the future planning and implementation of prevention programs.

Family Counseling

An additional example of the preventive aspects of social work comes from the files of the Family Service Association of America. The following case glimpse was presented in an interpretive publication to illustrate its procedures and services and was taken from the files of a southern family service agency.

Mr. Wilson, an airline pilot, came to Family Service stating he was at the end of his rope. For the last six months he had been struggling to find a way to help his wife control her drinking. He felt she was becoming an alcoholic and he feared not only what she was doing to herself, but also what might happen to their son. He found himself, he said, "pushing his plane on the home journey."

There had been no apparent problem for either of the Wilsons until about a year before. The trouble started when Mrs. Wilson always wanted "just one more" at parties and "just one more" after she got home. Mr. Wilson began to lose his temper because she didn't stop drinking until she passed out. He wasn't sure how much drinking she did while he was away, but she was almost always in a bad state when he arrived home. When he tried to talk to her about it, she just became quieter and more depressed. Then she would say, "get the divorce you want and leave me alone." He couldn't get across to her that he didn't want a divorce—he wanted her as his wife—the wife she had been—not the one she was now. Both Mr. and Mrs. Wilson received family counseling for a period of six months.

Strangely enough, Mrs. Wilson's pattern of drinking was related to her husband's presence in the home. While he was away—she did not drink—but as his return became imminent, she began to drink heavily. This pattern was further related to a major source of friction— Mrs. Wilson's almost irrational involvement with her younger brother and sister, their resentment of her, and their dislike and criticism of Mr. Wilson.

Mrs. Wilson was the oldest of the three children in her family. The parents had died when the children were quite young and the family was divided. Mrs. Wilson had tried desperately to meet her own needs for a family by attempting to care for the other children. As soon as she began working, she had sent money to the next oldest. She assumed more responsibility than was appreciated, and her strivings and ambitions for her brother and sister were not met by them. Currently, Mrs. Wilson's superior financial, educational, and social status, and her constant effort to "help" them achieve more, were further irritants to them.

They felt that Mr. Wilson, too, saw himself as better off than they were. They were openly critical and suspicious of him, and they insinuated to Mrs. Wilson that her husband probably was paying attention to other women on his trips out of town. She began to believe this.

Mr. Wilson was impatient and concerned about the way in which Mrs. Wilson was continually frustrated in her attempts to "mother" her younger brother and sister, because they were irritated rather than appreciative of her help. He had been openly critical about this and he had been increasingly critical of Mrs. Wilson's housekeeping, her care of their child, and her unwillingness to be his wife. He said if she didn't straighten out—the marriage couldn't continue.

In the course of family counseling, Mrs. Wilson was helped to give up her attempted control over her brother and sister. She became more independent of them and allowed them to be themselves. As she was able to separate herself from her assumed "mother role," she was better able to view her own marriage and her role as a wife and mother.

When Mr. Wilson was able to face the fact that her drinking was related to the relationship between himself, his wife, and her relatives, and to realize that it did not represent a hopeless alcoholic pattern, he was able to relax some of the pressures he had placed on Mrs. Wilson.

Although the beginning of success in talking together and listening to each other came in the caseworker's office, later on they were more truly "communicating" with each other when they were alone, and at home. Mr. Wilson became more accepting of his wife's need to talk out her frustrations about her brother and sister, and he was better able to let her manage his life in little ways. Mrs. Wilson, who has gained a better understanding of herself and a truer self-concept, doesn't need to escape by drinking.[24]

Religious Leaders

A social worker was invited to meet with religious leaders in a rural community. He talked for some time about understanding parent–child relationships and behavior of people. Questions were invited to help the people gain understanding and some insights regarding what causes personal and social problems and what might be done about them. The whole focus was to assist these people in a positive manner to understand more about human relationships and how they can assist in preventing problems. The first session was considered to be so profitable by all the participants that they agreed to hold a series of six more meetings in which the social worker was the facilitator, assisting these religious leaders to increase their knowledge and skills and, consequently, to aid them in working with their clientele to prevent personal and social problems.

Delinquency Prevention

In a metropolitan community in the eastern United States was a dilapidated area with poor housing and a high degree of social disorganization. Delinquency rates were very high. Some enterprising, dedicated community leaders decided to take action. Through the efforts of public-spirited citizens and professional helpers who involved the youth, a recreational center was established. In the next year, only three arrests were made among the teenagers in comparison with more than 150 the year before. What had happened? Had this concerted action helped prevent delinquency? The answer is yes. The introduction of a recreational center brought about a significant change in this innercity community. It was staffed by trained and interested personnel providing services, including counseling and group involvement of the youth in this part of the city.

In 1993 there were numerous attempts by police officers, aided by social workers, to prevent "runaway children" (about 10,000 daily in the United States) and to reduce child abuse from relatives and others, which has become a major personal and social problem in our high-tech society. Experience reflects that most victimized children are uneducated on methods of self-protection and that positive programs for child education and parental education can make a difference. Numerous programs are being established, with the assistance of social workers, to help prevent and reduce both runaways and child abuse.

Families in Crisis

A very exciting prevention idea that has appeared recently is called family preservation services (FPS). Its purpose is to have social workers or other FPS workers provide immediate and intense services to families in crisis. The workers carry small caseloads of two to six families and are on call at all times, providing twenty-four-hour-a-day coverage. All services are provided in the family's natural environment—primarily the home—and are directed toward maintaining children in their own homes. The workers provide a wide range of counseling, advocacy, training, and concrete assistance.

The theory behind this comprehensive family approach is basically prevention. If a chaotic family environment can be modified, then parents and children may have a chance to increase their level of functioning and prevent critical problems that result from family breakdown. The following case illustrates the preventive efforts of family preservation services.

The Clark family was referred to an FPS worker when their infant daughter was released from the hospital. A nurse had referred the Clarks because she was concerned with the family situation. The Clarks' three-year-old son had recently been diagnosed as hyperactive, and Childrens Protective Services was concerned about three concussions the boy had been treated for over the last year.

When the FPS worker arrived at the home, she found complete chaos. It was filthy and had a strong odor of gas. Ms. Clark was thin, pale, and weak. She had lost her front teeth due to poor health. Mr. Clark worked as an insurance salesman but had not sold a policy for five months. Ms. Clark told the worker that they had many conflicts. She did not know how to handle her three-year-old son and expressed total frustration.

The FPS worker helped Ms. Clark deal with the gas leak. Together they called the landlord and had the furnace repaired. Each day the worker concentrated on concrete ways to help this family, which eventually built a strong relationship between both Mr. and Ms. Clark and the worker. The worker assisted Ms. Clark with her dental problems and encouraged Mr. Clark to enroll in a job training program. During this time the worker helped both parents learn to treat their children in a less abusive manner.

This treatment intervention took place over several weeks, with the FPS worker seeing the family each day. Toward the end of the intervention the worker helped the family move to a better apartment and arranged marital counseling for Mr. and Ms. Clark. The parents were feeling better about themselves and had not hurt their two children in any way. The intense day-to-day intervention of an FPS worker had prevented major problems and had offered the Clark family a sense of hope.[25]

Suicide Prevention

In most populous centers throughout the United States, social workers are playing significant roles in suicide prevention centers. Their understanding and skills have helped "save" lives of many men, women, and youths.

Many "hotline" calls have helped disturbed or distraught persons handle personal crisis situations and make contact with people or agencies that can make a difference in their lives. Rape crisis and domestic violence centers are now available in many cities to assist with this difficult problem and its damaging results. Social workers are helping provide treatment and preventive services on a twenty-four-hour basis.

Social Work Practice in the Workplace

Social work practice in the workplace is emerging on the cutting edge of prevention. Within the past two decades innovative developments have appeared on the industrial scene involving social workers. Enough demonstrations have taken place to indicate that preventive social work can make a difference in human problems and their solutions in business and in labor unions.

An example of a positive preventive program took place in a large telephone company in a metropolitan city that invited a school of social work to train students in their head office. Counseling was provided and a series of bimonthly noon-day lectures were presented to employees who wished to attend. The voluntary response was substantial and many who attended observed that the lectures had been helpful. Sample topics, presented by experts, were "Family Patterns of Communication," "Human Sexuality," "Stress Management," and " The Empty Nest Syndrome."

Anderson and Stark[26] suggest another service for social work prevention, related to employment and geographic relocation. They recommend that employment assistance programs (EAPs) be increased in industry to reduce stress-related problems for workers and their families as they move from one position to another area.

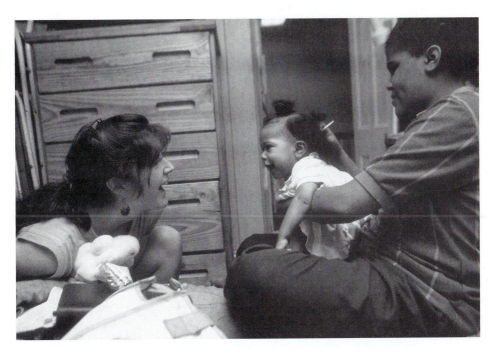

Social worker helping young mother and baby.

Relapse Prevention

Originally developed as part of treatment for substance abuse, relapse prevention has found its way into the treatment of other disorders. The purpose of the technique is to increase the length of the positive outcome of treatment and to prevent a return to the problematic behavior. It is accomplished by helping individuals set up conditions where they might fall back into old behaviors and then practice new behaviors that would prevent this from occurring. It has been successfully implemented in weight loss, exercise, smoking cessation, and pain management programs. Recently, Huber and Kragh adapted the model to extend the positive results accomplished from family therapy.[27]

Implications of Prevention

With the current interest and emphasis on social work, it is apparent that considerable time and talents must be spent in thinking through the relationship of professional social work to the preventive process. Several implications stand out.

If social workers are really going to tap the resources of prevention, they must spend more time and effort in creative thinking and activity. They will need to go beyond and extend the present boundaries and activities of practice. What can be done by social workers to prevent personal, family, and community problems is one of the great challenges of today.

It is apparent that practice in working with individuals, groups, and communities will need to be utilized, as well as the process of research and administration, if prevention is to become more effective. Social workers employed as case managers, clinical social workers, administrators, or community organizers can all play important roles in the preventive process. Through working together, they can assist each other in accomplishing desired goals. One challenge seems to be a closer cooperation and coordination among workers who are skilled in different techniques and methodologies.

One great need is for objective research and evaluation of activities and projects related to prevention. We need to quantify and objectify procedures. We need to know in advance what we are doing, what we hope to accomplish, and then to be able to measure afterward what has actually taken place.

A step forward came with the appearance of Bloom's *Primary Prevention: The Possible Science.*[28] He studies primary prevention theoretically and also presents illustrations of empirical studies of preventive programs in social work and related areas. He presents selected examples, related to a developmental framework, such as school dropout, substance abuse, delinquency, divorce, child abuse, heart disease, and widowhood. He suggests that complete preventive solutions have not been achieved in any of these areas, but illustrates important advances in each. He views "primary prevention of many social and medical problems as possible, not as a dream, but as a possible science, a systematic and creative enterprise that identifies probable future states among currently neutral events and acts to promote desired configuration among them while at the same time attempting to obviate undesired combinations."

There should be special focus on the *before* in relation to prevention. In other words, if social workers can utilize professional knowledge and skills to prevent problems from arising on the horizon of daily living, this seems to be particularly important. The educational and consultation processes are especially significant in this area of social work.

To anticipate problems that might arise in advance of their occurrence calls for greater understanding of human behavior, interrelationships, and social phenomena.

Experimentation is needed as never before. Social workers must try new techniques, skills, and plans to see if they will work in preventing personal and social problems. In the educational field, additional interest in prevention will necessitate increased offerings regarding this process in the curriculum of the professional schools. Principles regarding prevention and case examples will need to be introduced into the core areas and specific classes, and probably diffused directly and indirectly throughout the total curriculum. A few schools already offer separate classes on prevention, and there will undoubtedly be more in the future.

Social work practice needs to be broadened to include more emphasis on consultation, family life education, and related activities. Social workers must become more community-minded and more family-minded. They need to ferret out the principles and knowledge that will help families and communities to anticipate problems and to prevent them. They need to broaden their skills so that they can utilize a variety of techniques and methods to help bring about desired prevention-based results.

Social Work Enrichment

The newest process utilized by social workers is enrichment. Traditionally social work has provided services for individuals, families, and communities; offered counseling/therapy for persons and families in trouble; and advanced its interest and services with prevention. All these processes are relevant to relationship problems or the reduction or prevention of them. Enrichment has a different focus, aimed especially at the quality of life. It encompasses attempts to help people go on from where they are, to add positive experiences and values to living.

Enrichment includes working not only with individuals who are disabled or disadvantaged but all people, recognizing that all people have problems in human relationships and also have room for growth and improvement of their abilities and activities.

Most of the materials in this chapter relate to the enrichment process, directly or indirectly. Solving relationship problems may not only relieve pain and tension, but also can enhance satisfactions in living.

Social work enrichment is the process of helping people improve their relationships with others, bringing increased satisfactions and enjoyments. For example, a married couple may be getting along satisfactorily, but with increased knowledge and improved abilities in their relationship they may be able to taste of life in positive ways they have never experienced before. The social worker helps couples increase their knowledge and improve abilities to move ahead. All of the social work methods may be utilized in enrichment: clinical work, group work, and community organization. Research may provide evaluative data on what is effective. Administration may be used in staff development and in providing community enrichment programs.

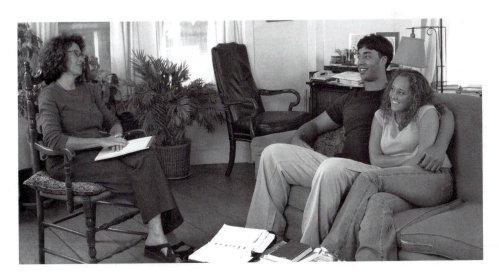

Young couple receiving counseling from a social worker.

Premarital counseling is an example of enrichment that can make a difference. Couples with no major problems may talk with a social worker and gain increased knowledge and improved abilities to benefit from marital relationships on a higher level of satisfaction. They may gain insights about self-esteem, decision making, communication, solving conflicts, and the loving process that can deepen their life together in many ways. They may learn how to build each other rather than psychologically bruise each other, resulting in a genuine maturity of living.

Classes taught by social workers on parenting for the general public are another example of the enrichment process. Discussion of various topics can bring deeper meanings and satisfactions for parent–child relationships, such as accepting your children, loving your children, building self-esteem, and listening to your children.

The whole area of enrichment has hardly been touched, even though some social workers question it. Creative social workers may encourage all kinds of positive developments in this innovative, qualitative arena.

Summary

The old adage of "An ounce of prevention is worth a pound of cure" is emphasized as never before in the helping professions. In particular, medicine has led with its public health programs.

Within the past few years, prevention has come to the fore in social work and is now recognized as a major function. There is still considerable uncertainty and lack of clarity regarding the roles of social work in relation to prevention. Nevertheless, various demonstrations and experiments indicate that the social worker can anticipate social problems and can help to avert them. Additional study, experimentation, and research are much needed in this area.

The enrichment process is just beginning to take hold in social work. Almost unlimited potentials seem available for introducing practical services that will increase knowledge of people about human relationships and enhance their social abilities, bringing deeper, positive satisfactions.

Selected References _____

BARKER, ROBERT L., *Social Work in Private Practice,* 2nd ed. Washington, DC: NASW, 1992.

BRACHT, NEIL, "Prevention and Wellness," in *Encyclopedia of Social Work,* 19th ed., Vol. 3. Washington, DC: NASW Press, 1994, pp. 1879–1887.

CAREY, WILLIAM B., and SEAN McDEVILL, *Prevention and Early Intervention.* Philadelphia: Brunner/Mazel, 1994.

COOMBS, ROBERT H., and DOUGLAS ZIEDONIS, *Handbook on Drug Abuse Prevention.* Boston: Allyn & Bacon, 1995.

GITTERMAN, ALEX, ed., *Handbook of Social Work Practice with Vulnerable and Resilient Populations,* 2nd ed. New York: Columbia University Press, 2001.

HARRISON, W. DAVID, "Community Development," in *Encyclopedia of Social Work,* 19th ed., Vol. 1. Washington, DC: NASW Press, 1995, pp. 555–562.

HOGAN, JULIE, KRISTEN GABRIELSEN, NORA LUNA, and DENISE GROTHAUS, *Substance Abuse Prevention: The Intersection of Science and Practice.* Boston: Allyn & Bacon, 2003.

Mostofsky, David I., and David H. Barlow, eds., *The Management of Stress and Anxiety in Medical Disorders.* Boston: Allyn & Bacon, 2000.

Oates, R. Kim, *The Spectrum of Child Abuse: Assessment, Treatment, and Prevention.* Philadelphia: Brunner/Mazel, 1996.

Peters, Ray D., Kelly Petrunka, and Robert Arnold, "The Better Beginnings, Better Futures Project: A Universal, Comprehensive, Community-Based Prevention Approach for Primary School Children and Their Families," *Journal of Clinical Child & Adolescent Psychology,* 32, no. 2 (June 2003), 215–227.

Quinsey, Vernon L., Tracey A. Skilling, Martin L. Lalumiere, and Wendy W. Craig, *Juvenile Delinquency: Understanding the Origins of Individual Differences.* Washington, DC: American Psychological Association, 2003.

Reamer, Frederic G., *Social Work Malpractice and Liability Stages for Prevention.* New York: Columbia University Press, 2001.

Schwartz, Ira M., "Delinquency Prevention: Where's the Beef?" *The Journal of Criminal Law and Criminology,* 82 (Spring 1991), 132–140.

Notes

1. Hugh R. Leavell and E. Gurney Clark, *Preventive Medicine—For the Doctor in His Community* (New York: McGraw-Hill, 1958), p. 31.

2. Ibid., pp. 21–39.

3. Lydia Rapoport, "The Concept of Prevention in Social Work," *Social Work,* 6 (January 1961), p. 3.

4. Milton Wittman, "Preventive Social Work: A Goal for Practice and Education," *Social Work,* 6 (January 1961), p. 23.

5. Ibid., p. 24.

6. Ibid., p. 27.

7. Donald C. Klein and Stephen E. Goldston, eds., *Primary Prevention: An Idea Whose Time Has Come* (Rockville, MD: National Institute of Mental Health, 1977), p. 27.

8. Florence Hazelkorn, "An Ounce of Prevention . . .," *Journal of Education for Social Work,* 3 (Fall 1967), p. 70.

9. Robert L. Barker, *The Social Work Dictionary,* 4th ed. (Washington, DC: NASW Press, 1999), p. 375.

10. *Proceedings of the National Conference of Charities and Correction,* Twelfth Annual Session, held in Washington, DC, June 4–10, 1885 (Boston: Press of George H. Ellis, 1885), p. 462.

11. Werner W. Boehm, "The Nature of Social Work," *Social Work,* 3 (April 1958), pp. 16–17.

12. Bertram M. Beck, "Prevention and Treatment," based on the work of the subcommittee on Trends, Issues, and Priorities of the NASW National Commission on Social Work Practice, 1962, p. 1 (mimeographed).

13. Ibid., p. 31.

14. Milton Wittman, "Preventive Social Work: What? How? Where?" Educational Symposium, Preventive Social Work, Graduate School of Social Work, University of Utah, Salt Lake City, April 17–18, 1980.

15. Gayle Olson-Raymer, "The Role of the Federal Government in Juvenile Delinquency Prevention," *The Journal of Criminal Law and Criminology,* 74 (Summer 1983), p. 600.

16. "National Conference on Primary Prevention in Mental Health Convened," *Social Work Reporter* 28 (January 1980), p. 7.

17. New York State Office of Mental Health, *This Month in Mental Health,* 9 (January 1986), pp. 1, 3.

18. U.S. Department of Health and Human Services, Administration for Children and Families, Children's Bureau Express, *Keeping Children & Families Safe Act of 2003 Signed Into Law,* August 1, 2003. Retrieved from http://cbexpress.acf.hhs.gov/articles.cfm?&issue_id=2003-08&article_id=685.

19. Steven L. McMurtry, "Secondary Prevention of Child Maltreatment: A Review," *Social Work,* 30 (January/February 1985), p. 42.

20. Neil Clark Warren, *Finding the Love of Your Life: Ten Principles for Choosing the Right Marriage Partner* (Colorado Springs, CO: Focus on the Family Publishing, 1992), p. 3.

21. J. Weiner Hyman, Sheila H. Akabas, and John J. Sommer, *Mental Health Care in the World of Work* (New York: Association Press, 1973).

22. Miriam P. Kluger and Noelle Gallant, "What Works in School-Based Substance Abuse Prevention: Interactive or Peer Programs" in Miriam P. Kluger, Gina Alexander, and Patrick A. Curtis, eds., *What Works in Child Welfare* (Washington, DC: Child Welfare League of America, 2000).

23. Steven Harrison, Scott W. Boyle, and O. William Farley, "Evaluating the Outcomes of Family-Based Intervention for Troubled Children: A Pretest-Posttest

Study," *Research on Social Work Practice,* 9, no. 6 (1999), pp. 640–655.

24. "An Airline Pilot Who Was Pushing His Plane," *Family Service Highlights,* Family Service Association of America, 21 (September/November 1960), pp. 114–115.

25. This case was shared by Dr. Mark Fraser, former Professor of Social Work, University of Utah.

26. Charlene Anderson and Carolyn Stark, "Psychosocial Problems of Job Relocation: Preventive Roles in Industry," *Social Work,* 33 (January/February 1988), pp. 38–41.

27. Charles H. Huber and Jeffery Kragh, "Relapse Prevention: Extending Treatment Results in Family Counseling," *The Family Journal: Counseling and Therapy for Couples and Families,* 3 (1995), pp. 239–241.

28. Martin Bloom, *Primary Prevention: The Possible Science* (Upper Saddle River, NJ: Prentice Hall, 1981).

22

Social Work and the Future

Naisbitt and Aburdene, in their challenging book Megatrends 2000 *(1990), forecasted that the year 2000 should be "operating like a powerful magnet on humanity, reaching down into the 1990s and intensifying the decade. It is amplifying emotions, accelerating change, heightening awareness, and compelling us to reexamine ourselves, our values, and our institutions."[1] They discussed ten likely new directions for the 1990s, which included a global economic boom, women in leadership, global lifestyles and cultural nationalism, and triumph of the individual.*

Their predictions turned out to be quite accurate. The United States, as well as other countries, sustained significant economic growth throughout the 1990s and into the twenty-first century. The numbers of women, although not yet equal to that of men, increased in positions of leadership and the trend continues, and one's culture and national pride are now being recognized as positive qualities to be celebrated. But, where do we go from here as we look to the twenty-first century? How will the anticipated developments and discoveries influence the lives of human beings at large and the profession of social work in particular?

In J. Naisbitt, N. Naisbitt, and Philips's more recent book *High Tech, High Touch* (1999) the current state of our society, one that is filled with technology, is examined. According to the authors, we have gone from using technology as a means of reducing labor to a "Technologically Intoxicated Zone." This zone, with all of its enticements to produce wealth and pleasure, also has its consequences. "The Intoxicated Zone is spiritually empty, dissatisfying and dangerous, and impossible to climb out of *unless* we recognize that we're in it . . . at its best, technology supports and improves human life, and at its worst, it alienates, isolates, distorts, and destroys."[2]

To support their hypothesis, they came up with six symptoms of a society that is intoxicated:

1. We look for quick fixes or solutions to deal with problems or obstacles that face us in life.

2. We look to technology as the solution to our problems, yet we fear that it will cause us harm such as people having more and more access to our personal lives.
3. The line between what is real and what is fake has become blurred. Copies and imitations look so much like the real thing that it is difficult to distinguish between the two.
4. Violence has become accepted within our culture. It is continually in our homes through the media (news, movies, computer games, and television shows).
5. Technology is seen as being a toy and seeking to have the newest, fanciest, most up-to-date version, whether it is a cell phone, car, computer, exercise machine, or radio-controlled model airplane, is necessary to sustain our cravings. "Consumer technologies have evolved from luxury to necessity to toy."
6. Although we are highly connected through the Internet and by cell phones, we are more distracted and physically removed from people through the increase in technology. Further, technology distracts us so that we miss out on opportunities to connect with others.[3]

High tech and high touch is "recognizing that technology is an integral part of the evolution of culture. The creative product of our imaginations, our dreams and aspirations and the desire to create new technologies is fundamentally instinctive. But it is also recognizing that art, story, play, religion, nature, and time are equal partners in the evolution of technology because they nourish the soul and fulfil its yearnings."[4] As it specifically applies to social work, we must remember that the human connection we have with a client is the most important aspect of the helping relationship. It cannot be replaced by technology (computers, TV, stereos, palm pilots, CDs, etc.), because its products lack the important quality that can only be found in human beings, the soul that each one of us carries within and the human connections that we need to sustain us. It is the human touch that can never be replaced by technology.

Indicative of the prospects of the future and the rapidly changing world was a suggestion of Mortimer Adler that the most important cabinet position in the United States government in the future could well be the "Secretary of the Future."[5] He then suggested that two major problems face future generations. First, "Can the masses obtain the intellectual, cultural, and comfortable levels which in the past were held only by a few aristocrats?" Second, "Could it be that man isn't up to enjoying too much free time, power, comfort, and wealth, which technological advances will undoubtedly realize in the next thousand years?"

In 1970 Toffler's startling book, *Future Shock,*[6] was published, in which he dramatically described ways in which people are becoming overwhelmed in responding to change. He claimed that future shock is no longer "a distantly potential danger, but a real sickness from which increasingly large numbers already suffer," and he also suggested that "unless man quickly learns to control the rate of change in his personal affairs as well as in society at large, we are doomed to a massive adaptational breakdown."[7]

Although Toffler describes realistically some of the specific effects of drastic, accelerated change on individuals, families, and communities, he is basically optimistic that we can do something about these things, illustrated by his concluding statement, "by making imaginative use of change to channel change, we cannot only spare ourselves the trauma of future shock, we can reach out and humanize distant tomorrows."[8]

In *Megatrends 2000,* Naisbitt outlined where our sophisticated technology is taking us, stressing that we are moving from an industrial society to an economy based on the creation and distribution of information. He described basic trends affecting our political, social, and economic life that will shape our future. He suggested that while we are moving in dual directions of high tech/high touch, matching each new technology with a human response, human relations are becoming even more important. In conclusion he observed that "as we move from an industrial to an information society, we will use our brainpower to create instead of our physical power, and the technology of the day will extend and enhance our mental ability. . . . Yet the most formidable challenge will be to train people to work in the information society."[9]

In this fast-moving uncertain age, where is social work likely to find itself? In the years ahead, how will social work fit into the total scheme?

If it were possible to look into a crystal ball and to see exactly what is ahead, we would likely be surprised in many ways. Because this is impossible, the next best action is to look at the past and the present and to make projections and predictions based upon available knowledge regarding what is likely to happen. This chapter is an attempt to consider some of the likely developments in social work in the years ahead.

Professional Maturation

Social work educators and practitioners see our profession as vibrant and maturing as we move into the twenty-first century. Our influence is being felt in many fields of practice, and growth continues to occur not only at the state and national levels but also internationally, with schools of social work adding components, even concentrations, at the master's level that address international practice. For example, Josephine V. A. Allen, NASW president in 1998, was clearly hopeful about our future and sees opportunities for growth and influence on both the national and international scenes.

> It is critical that we enhance our skills in order to deliver culturally competent services. These are factors that support the presidential initiative on international social work whose purpose is to strengthen NASW's position and work on such global issues as facilitating international social development, advocating for human rights, social justice, and a more humane and equitable immigration policy. Similarly, the profession's attention to related issues on the domestic scene must reflect its outreach to the international community.[10]

Most social workers feel that although there are critical problems and pressures, numerous opportunities are available for the social work profession to move ahead on a sound basis, strengthening current delivery of services and innovating services that have been partially untouched to date. An example is the growth of social work in private counseling, which is being accepted and accelerated by insurance companies and employee assistance programs (EAPs) where clinical social workers provide much needed services for individuals, families, and employees, relating to individual and interpersonal problems.

Social work is still considered, by some, to be a relatively new profession, having been recognized only since the end of the nineteenth century. Therefore, it is bound to face some critical problems. When one realizes it is only since the 1950s that the National

Association of Social Workers and the Council on Social Work Education came into existence, it seems almost phenomenal what has happened in the development of social work. Many leaders anticipate that the current divergencies of opinion regarding training and practice are healthy and will bring about a balanced combination of generic principles and skills in practice, accompanied by specializations providing skills and knowledge for working with various social problems and with groups of people with particular needs. Another positive factor is America's service commitment for competent personnel for its institutions. What happens in the years ahead will depend on the leaders in social work education and practice and how they act and react with other social workers, related professions, and political leaders. Philosophically, social workers would agree with the Chinese, who have two definitions for the word *crisis*—danger and opportunity.

Increase in Services

Based on data supplied by the U.S. Department of Labor, it was estimated there were 385,000 social workers in the United States in 1978. Since then there has been a steady increase in social workers (more than 600,000 in 1996). The U.S. Department of Labor Statistics reported in May 2006 that national estimates for the number of people employed in community and social service occupations was 1,749,210. Whereas social workers make up a large portion of persons in this category, these statistics do not give the complete picture as some positions are filled by those trained in other, yet related, professions such as substance abuse and behavioral disorder counselors, probation officers, and marriage and family therapists. The annual income reported for all these combined jobs was $39,000 with a median hourly wage of $17.21. There was a 4 percent rise in employment over the previous year.[11] New services continue to be developed, both in public and private sectors, requiring the skills and knowledge of qualified social workers. Also, private practice continues to expand.

Problems found in human relationships and in many other areas are reaching for social workers. Drug abuse is of great concern in the sports world, and social workers are being hired to help. For example, all four major sports (football, baseball, basketball, and hockey) now have leaguewide policies prohibiting use of drugs by athletes. The National Football League and the NFL Players Association have involved the Hazelden Foundation in Minnesota, since 1982, to operate a program to help players end their drug problems, including alcohol. *NASW News* reported that "Tim Plant, a social worker who counsels football players at Hazelden, says services include outpatient and inpatient care or a combination. An aftercare program also is provided to support the work done during initial counseling."[12]

Symour and Marston report an innovative development in social work practice, evolving in a vision care clinic, where optometric students and graduate and undergraduate social work students in field placements are working together offering opportunities in interdisciplinary cooperation. The social workers help with understanding of psychosocial factors and in assisting patients to make effective use of treatment and rehabilitation programs that are available. The authors conclude: "The relationship between visual functioning and nonvisual factors such as stress offers opportunities for a new role for social workers in the field of vision care."[13]

Other doors are opening for social work. The knowledge and skills gleaned from the profession are considered vital to other academic fields, and cooperative programs or dual degrees are being sought in areas such as public administration and the law. Students are entering graduate schools and combining both areas of study in preparation for employment with the underprivileged and underserved of our society.

Professional Identification and Visibility

One of the challenging problems of the emerging profession of social work has been the need to develop a stronger professional identification. A few decades ago there were many dedicated social workers and several independent, semiprofessional associations, all of which at times seemed to be striking out in different directions. A significant step took place in 1955 with the creation of the National Association of Social Workers, which has made major contributions to the development of professional interest and identification. Through its staff and various committees, it has helped practitioners, educators, lay citizens, and students to realize that social work is an important profession calling for the best in people, including integrity, maturity of personality, and specific professional training. The association has helped considerably to assist social workers to identify with their profession, and to interpret to nonsocial workers the role of social work.

In an effort to be forward thinking and to reunify the various professional organizations affiliated with social work, Elvira Craig de Silva, MSW president, and Elizabeth J. Clark, MSW executive director, spearheaded a meeting in June of 2007. Included were ten various groups or organizations within the profession. One of the goals of the gathering was to find ways to improve collaboration within the profession in order to become more unified. A similar occurrence happened back in 1955 when seven different social work organizations came together. That gathering ultimately produced NASW, the creation of which did result in a more unified profession. Although the results of the 2007 meeting were not as dramatic, it did result in the Wingspread resolution on social work unification that stated

> Leaders of 10 professional social work organizations convened at Wingspread to address the future of the profession. Participants signed a resolution: We resolve to create a unified profession with one social work organization by 2012. . . . The social work profession requires a strong unified voice to enhance its ability, to serve, to education, to develop research and to influence social service, social policy and social change. But the challenges of the 21st century, identified by the Social Work Congress of 2005, compel a vibrant, proactive, nimble, flexible organizational structure that reflects collective vision and ensures impact.[14]

Whether or not a new organization is ultimately created from this resolution is yet to be determined. What is recognized, however, is the need for the profession to continue to be unified in its mission and purpose in order to meet the demands of a rapidly changing national and global society in the twenty-first century. This resolution also works to ensure that the profession continues to be inclusive of all its vital components in working toward common goals.

Graduate and undergraduate students are encouraged to become members in NASW and to identify with its purposes and activities prior to embarking on a career in the field. Through their course work, students have an opportunity to study the code of ethics and to understand its professional implications. They also have opportunities for association with professional persons, self-expression, and professional identification. In 1997, nearly 3,000 social workers gathered at the annual NASW meeting in Baltimore, Maryland. The focus, in part, was concerning human rights, the blurring of boundaries between public and private practice, and the direction taken by managed care. As participants join together each year, they do so with the intent of addressing current policies, practices, and trends pertinent to the profession of social work.

On a local chapter basis, it is probable that members of NASW will devote more of their time and talents to strengthening their profession, improving practice, expanding recruitment, and participating in other professional activities. Local chapters are more aware of the specific needs of professionals within a particular state. The state's executive director will often work closely with legislators and lobbyists concerning political and professional issues that directly impact social workers' values and/or practice. For example, when legislators seek to change licensure laws, local NASW members rally to provide input to help ensure that accurate information is received and to see that the integrity of the profession as well as those services rendered by trained professionals remains intact.

The Council on Social Work Education, with its special emphasis on training, has been another major force in leading social workers to a stronger professional identification. Its annual conference has increased in stature in the past few years. For the 1989 conference in Chicago participants came from colleges and universities with graduate training programs in social work, from undergraduate programs in preparation for social work, as well as from various fields of practice. More than 3,500 participants joined together with serious intent to understand social work better and to improve the training programs resulting in more effective practice in social work. The 1999 and 2004 CSWE statistics identify approximately 6,900 faculty in social work programs who join together in advancing the values and skills of the profession. Various projects and activities of the council are providing many opportunities for strengthening the total profession at all levels—paraprofessional, undergraduate, master's, and doctoral.

Some questions have been raised, over the years, about the effectiveness of social work practice, particularly in relation to the one-to-one method. Research studies differ somewhat on outcomes. However, Rubin reviewed twelve research studies with controlled experimentation between July 1978 and June 1983 and reported that the overall conclusion was, "Recent experiments have provided more grounds for optimism regarding the development of effective forms of direct social work practice."[15] He also suggested we need more methodologically credible experimental research evaluating effectiveness of social work direct practice. More recently, Asay and Lambert's review of the effects of counseling over the past forty-plus years reported positive findings. They concluded that clients who participate in therapy/counseling are better off than 80 percent of those who do not receive help.[16]

Certification and Licensing

Since the 1960s several steps have been made toward licensing in social work. For a field to become a full-fledged profession, it is almost imperative that some kind of official control and licensing be in operation. Doctors must pass examinations and be issued licenses in the states in which they practice. Lawyers qualify by taking state bar examinations to become properly licensed. Until a few years ago, there was little attempt to control social work standards and practice. However, there have been assertive activities in several states related to certification or licensing.

In 1961 NASW inaugurated a movement to strengthen social work practice. Provision was made for a voluntary system of registration, resulting in *certified social workers*. An Academy of Certified Social Workers (ACSW) was established and practicing workers were invited to apply for membership. Membership was contingent upon a person's having had two years of paid social work employment and two years of NASW membership. Stipulations were that future applicants must not only have a master's degree in social work, but also at least two years of experience in social work under qualified supervision by a member of ACSW. This plan has been approved with considerable enthusiasm by professional social workers as a major step toward licensing. In 1963 there were more than 20,000 persons who had applied for certification and who had been awarded membership in the academy; in 1980 the number had increased to 46,300 and today there are more than 58,000. As a result of this movement, many social workers now add *ACSW* after their names, just as those of other professions give designations that display professional meaning.

To date, licensure or certification is found in all fifty states and Puerto Rico. *Licensure* or *certification* are the terms most frequently used and usually refer to authorization by a state board of professional licensure to practice in the profession. Whereas states may have multiple levels of licensure or certification, to become licensed as an independent practitioner in any state it is generally necessary for the applicant to meet the following minimum requirements:

- Graduate from a CSWE-accredited MSW program.
- Complete a minimum of 4,000 clock hours—equivalent to two years' full-time employment.
- Work in a setting where psychotherapeutic services are rendered (assessment, planning, and treatment on individual, family, and/or group levels).
- Receive a minimum of 100 clock hours of supervision—one hour minimum per week of face-to-face supervision from a licensed clinical social worker.
- Pass a required examination approved by the licensure board. The examination may also include a separate section on ethics.
- Pass an oral examination, as required in some states.

Spirituality in Social Work Practice

In keeping with social work's philosophy of working with the total person in the total environment, a current development is the increased consideration of spiritual factors in social work education and practice. A significant event related to the spiritual component, as part of human behavior, and social work's inclusion of it in practice was the First National Conference for the Society for Spirituality and Social Work held in Salt Lake City, Utah, July 7–11, 1995. More than 400 participants were present. Since that conference, we have further recognized that spiritual components may be a vital component and necessary for inclusion when working with someone who may be experiencing intrapersonal or interpersonal problems.

Spirituality, according to *The Social Work Dictionary*, is "devotion to the immaterial part of humanity and nature rather then worldly things such as possessions; an orientation to people's religious, moral, or emotional nature."[17] Derezotes and Hoffman identify six arguments for the inclusion of spirituality into the practice of social work. They are as follows:

- As a country, the people of the United States are highly religious.
- Spiritual/religious aspects of a person's or community's life are a part of the ecological environment.
- The roots of social work stem from religious-based charitable organizations.
- One of social work's values focuses on human diversity. This includes one's religious and/or spiritual beliefs.
- There is a correlation between psychosocial well-being and religiosity/spirituality.
- Most social work professionals already consider religious and spiritual content in their work with clients.[18]

Sermabeikian suggests that "the spiritual perspective is an important but relatively unexplored area in social work practice."[19] Obviously, we need more research to understand

Spiritual factors must be considered in social work practice.

its significance in human behavior, especially as it relates to meeting basic needs of clients. We also need to improve our skills in utilizing spiritual resources in bringing positive behavioral changes.

Changing Continuum in Social Work Education

Social work education is churning; changes are developing rapidly. There is, however, an emphasis on a "social work continuum," which encompasses training on the paraprofessional, undergraduate, master's, and doctoral levels.

CSWE has assumed leadership in providing guidance and direction for community colleges and other educational institutions offering training for paraprofessionals (many of whom are indigenous persons) on the first- and second-year or special levels of education not involving regular college work. The number of such programs is on the increase.

On the undergraduate level there is a major thrust toward strengthening the social work curriculum, in moving toward the BSW degree, or providing a substantive major on the undergraduate level. In 1971 the council authorized the establishment of undergraduate programs that could be approved by the council (which now may be accredited by the council) and provide the "first professional level of practice," for its graduates. Since that time, social work education has continued to evolve. The most recent Educational Policy and Accreditation Standards (EPAS) approved by CSWE in 2001 require programs offering baccalaureate degrees to prepare undergraduates for generalist professional practice. In addition, curriculum standards also require accredited programs to include the following foundation content as both the undergraduate level and first year of graduate studies: values and ethics, diversity, populations-at-risk and social economic justice, human behavior and the social environment (HBSE), social welfare and policy, social work practice, research, and field practicum.

MSW programs provide a professional course of study at two levels. As is emphasized at the undergraduate level, the first-year MSW curriculum also concentrates on generalist practice. However, as students further their professional development in the second year of study they receive advanced knowledge and skills in one or more areas of concentration. Concentrations generally focus on fields of practice (mental health, medical social work, administration, or public services) or populations (children, elderly, or families). Often, the advanced learning centers around the five basic content areas: HBSE, policy, practice, research, and field practicum. Students may also be encouraged to take elective courses to increase their level of expertise in areas of special interest.

A development in social work education that will likely increase is the doctoral program. These programs vary considerably, and so far there have been no specific standards established by CSWE regarding them. However, within a few years there will probably be some recommendations and minimum requirements formulated.

In all probability, most of those who obtain a doctoral degree will go into schools of social work and become teachers and researchers. Some will enter practice in key administrative positions in hospitals, community mental health centers, county and state welfare departments, or other social work agencies; others will accept exclusive research positions.

A current trend is to replace the DSW degree with the PhD degree with the goal of strengthening academic research and advanced graduate study.

Development of the Role of Consultant

Within the past years, social workers have not only used consultants from the disciplines of psychiatry, psychology, medicine, and other areas, but have become consultants themselves. Many social workers spend full time in the role of the consultant. For example, in one school district in California, two social workers spend their entire working day, every day, in a consultative capacity. They talk with teachers, principals, counselors, and other professional people about their problems in working with the boys and girls and their families. The basic aim is to help teachers, counselors, and others understand themselves better and what they are doing in relation to assisting the youngsters with personal or family troubles.

Social workers are used as consultants in a variety of settings and are likely in the future to be used by additional agencies. They are hired as consultants not only in schools and in comprehensive mental health centers, but also in family service societies, in YWCAs and YMCAs, in Girl Scout groups, in hospitals, in business enterprises, and in numerous other kinds of agencies or settings.

In the role of consultant, the social worker acts mainly as a catalyst who unlocks the door to bring about better understanding, information, and procedures that may be helpful to other professional people. In this capacity the social worker does not instruct the others as to what to do, but helps them understand what different lines of action are possible and then leaves the choices to them. As a consultant, the social worker does not have authority over those with whom he or she consults. The social worker acts as an advisor and one who assists them to understand more about social dysfunctioning and what can be done about it.

Status of the Social Worker

The future portends higher status for social workers than in the past. When social work was coming into its own during the early decades of the twentieth century, many people were very critical of it. Some claimed social work was all wrong because it abolished independence. Others declared social work was synonymous with socialism. A minority thought of social work as merely the process of handing out a dole to the poor and transient.

In the last few decades major shifts in attitudes have taken place. Whereas community leaders were sometimes critical of social work and its practices, today many of these same leaders are referring members of their families and close friends to social work agencies. The general attitude has changed so that most citizens today look on social work as a profession with many *solid* services to perform. These changes are evident in the demand for social workers, not only in regard to well-established social work services, but in the creation of new agencies and services.

A major reason for the favorable shift in attitude has been that millions of individuals, families, and numerous communities have benefited from social work services.

As people have been helped with their personal and family problems, to face them, work them through, and go on to an enrichment of living, they have usually become exponents of social work and its services.

Although according to some studies there are several professions that have higher prestige and status ratings than does social work, movement seems to be gradual and substantial toward an elevation of its position. Increased salaries and improved working conditions, along with fringe benefits, are indicative of this development. In the last two decades salaries for social workers have increased considerably, so that current salaries for most MSW graduates are in the range of $30,000 a year or more, and for those with practice experience of about ten years, $30,000 to $50,000. Higher incomes will likely attract more men and women of excellent backgrounds and dedicated interests in people. This, again, will provide an effective chain reaction for improving the status and prestige of the profession. As salaries increase, better people apply for training, which results in more effective social work services. More effective services help to bring about increases in income. From nearly every direction the prospect looks encouraging for higher salaries in social work.

Today social workers are being appointed to key administrative positions in government, education, business, and private endeavors, adding to their status. Another example of the increased status of social work is that since the middle of the 1980s social workers have been invited to appear in court hearings as expert witnesses. They are asked to state their opinions and often influence the judgment or verdict. Their professional understanding of people and their behavior is respected as never before.

Private Practice

In the years ahead there is likely to be an increase in private practice. Because NASW has given its approval to private practice, more practitioners are moving into this area, either on a full-time or part-time basis. Economic emoluments, clinical challenges, and opportunities for service seem to be primary motivating factors. In 1968 a study of NASW members revealed fewer than 1,000 full-time private practitioners, with an estimated 15,000 doing part-time private counseling.[20] By 1995 there were more than 28,000 social workers in private practice.

Currently, private practice has become a major component of social work practice, involving both full-time and part-time patterns. A study of students in a New York State Master's of Social Work program indicated that more than half of them (57 percent) said they thought they would enter private practice within ten years after obtaining their MSW degree.[21]

With the boon of managed care companies in the United States, there is a growing demand for less expensive, cost-saving services. Hospitals and outpatient service agencies are making every attempt to reduce costs. Much of a company's costs are tied up in employee wages and benefits. In the 90s, a significant trend has emerged toward hiring independent social work contractors to deliver services. This may free up to 25 percent of the expenses paid in salaries to employees. Though some may find it very attractive to work independently, they must also invest in their own retirement, health care, malpractice, paid vacations, and sick leave, which may be very costly. This trend is, however, expected to continue for the next several years.

The Aging of Our Population

The aging of our population is one of the public health's major concerns leading to the twenty-first century. The U.S. Administration on Aging has predicted that by the year 2030 roughly 70 million citizens will be sixty-five years of age or older, or about 20 percent of the total population. This number will more than double from the year 2000. With the dramatic increase in persons in this age range, it is also projected that health care spending will go up by 25 percent.[22]

With this segment of the population growing at such a significant rate, it will necessarily call for an increase in both private and public services. Social workers have been called on to assist with the social, emotional, health, and financial needs of elderly persons as well as assisting their families through this important phase of the life cycle. Tasks in aiding this group may include counseling for psychological problems (anxiety and depression), aiding in the decision process regarding assisted living for those not able to manage on their own, assisting in the provision of nursing care for those who are severely ill, arranging hospice care for those who are dying, providing supportive counseling for family members of elderly clients, and assisting in locating needed community services. These needs do not come without concern. NASW's Workforce Center recently reported that the number of professionals in our field is expected to decrease over the next two years. This, in turn, may result in a void of trained social workers who are prepared to adequately deliver services and meet the needs and demands of this segment of our population.

Advocacy Role

Numerous social workers and agencies employing social workers assume a social action role encompassing advocacy for their clients. It is likely in the future that this role will be increased. Social workers assume the role of helping individuals, alone and in groups, but also help them in relation to the societal context in which they live.

On a broad base, more social workers are becoming active in political movements and politics and are sharing their goals and ideas with others to help bring about changes in the political, social, and economic arenas, as well as to assist clients clinically.

Improved Public Relations

Many believe that one of the major weaknesses of social work is its inadequate public relations. Especially in the past, social work has done very little to paint a favorable public image. Today there is considerable interest in this kind of activity, and many social workers and agencies are spending time and energy in improving their public relations policies and activities.

The strengthening of public relations is arising through two main avenues. The first involves increased interest and activity among the social workers themselves. There is additional interest in studying knowledge and skills of public relations in the graduate schools of social work. There are also more social workers "on the firing line" who feel that they must take more interest and participate more fully in improving their public image.

A second approach is one that will probably be tapped more in the future. This is the hiring of public relations experts as consultants to social work agencies and social workers. Social workers are beginning to recognize that they are not experts in public relations and that if they are going to obtain the best professional services available, they will need to pay for these services and employ those who are especially trained. Why should not social workers hire experts in public relations just as they hire consultants in psychiatry, psychology, and other related disciplines? There are many examples to indicate that this procedure has been most effective in improving the public image of social work and social work agencies and programs. This trend likely will continue in the future.

Lobbying is being recognized as another important development in social work. CSWE and NASW have full-time lobbyists in Washington, DC, who have become highly effective in helping influence federal legislation relevant to social work education and practice. Mahaffey maintains that social workers need to understand the lobbying process and suggests actions and techniques that might be utilized. She quotes the late Whitney M. Young, Jr., who said in his closing remarks to the 1969 NASW delegate assembly: "I think that social work is uniquely equipped to play a major role in the social and human renaissance of our society," and then concluded, "There *are* social workers who are successfully influencing the political process. The profession needs more of them."[23]

Rural Social Work

In recent years, movement has brought more social work services to the sparsely populated areas of the United States.

Two major efforts have been taking place in bringing social work services to less populated communities: (1) traveling teams of professional workers, including social workers, have made regular visits to outlying areas, offering nearly the whole gamut of health and welfare services; (2) individual social workers with inclination toward the rural way of life have accepted positions and moved to smaller communities.

Rural social work has many limitations, but also many advantages. Professional isolation, limited resources, and minimal cultural opportunities exemplify the limitations. Positives include an openness and a personal and informal way of life, along with many opportunities for recreational and social activities. Rural social work services are likely to increase in the years ahead.

Technology

Technology is beginning to play a part in the profession. Already, social workers and other helping professionals are using the Internet to interact with clients. Services may range from a one-time question and answer chat to a weekly group-counseling session. This may offer much needed help for the homebound person with small children, someone with a debilitating illness, or for people in rural locations. The down side is that nonverbal communication is eliminated and total confidentiality cannot be guaranteed. This is an emerging area of practice and many questions are yet being asked.

Technology is playing an ever-increasing role in social work.

With the output of information in recent years, social workers must also keep abreast of current research in their field of practice. Many are turning to the Internet to find information fast. This allows people to work from their home or office and is an attractive alternative to finding needed resources.

Technology is also entering the field of education. In the past, social workers desiring to increase their skills and marketability, yet living a significant distance from a university having an MSW or doctoral program, had to leave their families or homes and employment to return to school. With the advent of technology, MSW and doctoral programs in social work are being offered through Ednet, an interactive audio and visual telecommunications system that connects faculty with students in remote sites. Social workers are able to continue working in their rural or distant communities while achieving their goal of continuing their education. Ednet is a benefit to the rural community because the graduate is more likely to remain in the community upon graduation than one who has already removed him or herself and has a sense of having "moved on." The Ednet system is also a means of helping social workers obtain continuing education hours toward relicensure or recertification, a requirement now mandated in most states for those licensed at the MSW level who perform "clinical" work.

As technology is further utilized in the profession, it is likely to be incorporated into the development of self-help practice interventions. Areas most likely to be developed are those relating to psychological problems, relationship problems, and areas of self-improvement.

Expansion of Leadership Roles

During the past few decades social workers have been rather quiescent in terms of leadership. Today the situation is changing, and tomorrow augurs well for increased leadership positions for social workers.

Social workers are gaining positions as directors of mental health centers, state hospitals, state training schools, youth development centers, and in many other agencies and organizations. It is recognized that social workers have a breadth of knowledge and skill in regard to the larger community that is positive and can be meaningful in leadership positions. Also, more social workers are playing leadership roles in agencies in directing staff development for all professionals and in acting as team coordinators and planners.

On the political scene social workers are moving into elected positions and are gaining status in governmental councils and legislative bodies. In recent years social workers have been elected to the United States Senate and House of Representatives as well as to state legislatures and many other governmental positions. In educational circles social workers are beginning to become presidents of colleges and universities, vice presidents, and deans for student affairs. It is likely these trends will continue.

An example of a top educational appointment was that of Leon H. Ginsberg, former social work dean and commissioner of the West Virginia Human Services Department, who in 1984 was named chancellor of the West Virginia Board of Regents, which administers the state's sixteen colleges and universities.

According to Brilliant, insufficient attention has been given to training in leadership for students in schools of social work. She recommends the following:

> Students should study theories of leadership and the role of social work leadership; they should be given practice in leadership role playing and in field situations; and they should be presented with stimulating models of leadership behavior by teachers and mentors in school and in fieldwork.[24]

Increase in International Social Work

Social work knowledge and skills have little concern for national boundaries. Numerous social workers are traveling to countries around the world, acting as consultants for government agencies and social work leaders, both public and private. This movement is a two-way process with social workers in countries abroad being used as consultants in the United States and in other New World countries.

An example of active international cooperation and collaboration in human relations is the Alliance of Universities for Democracy, a consortium of ninety-four universities from central and eastern Europe and the United States. It was established in 1990 to enhance the role of universities in promoting democratic institutions, economic development, education, philanthropy, and human rights in the newly established democracies of central and eastern Europe. The alliance promotes collaborative work among universities, drawing on social workers for expert participation.

The International Federation of Social Workers is an organization that is doing much to further the cause of social work throughout the world. NASW president Ann A. Abbott attended the meeting in Sri Lanka on July 4, 1994, and reported that more than seventy countries sent representatives to this biennial conference with the challenging theme "The Social Work Profession: A Family United in Troubled Times." She recalled that half a world away she "experienced in a highly personal way the power of social work's commitment to embrace rather than reject diversity."[25]

Prevention

CSWE's Curriculum Study of 1959 stressed prevention as one of the three basic functions of social work practice, which gave added impetus to the preventive movement. Recent professional conferences and meetings have nearly all included one or more papers and discussions on the importance of prevention in social work.

Certainly in the years ahead there will be more stress placed on prevention. Is it not really better to try to prevent personal, family, and community problems from happening in the first place, rather than to cure or treat them? Is it not more effective to spend time and talents in action that will prevent problem situations from taking place? Many believe that the intrinsic powers and contributions of social work in the years ahead lie in preventive approaches.

Enrichment

Traditionally, social work has been concerned with helping the poor and the handicapped, working with emergency and long-range problems in human relationships. Two decades ago a major thrust appeared on the helping scene to prevent social problems for both individuals and society. Social work moved ahead with a variety of programs and methods to meet this challenge. In more recent years, another social focus has come to the fore—enrichment in living.

Enrichment in living involves working with all classes of people, the rich, middle class, or poor—with the aim of assisting them to experience a fuller, more meaningful life. Millions of individuals, couples, and families are getting along satisfactorily but are not tapping positive resources that are inherent in them and their relationships. They may enrich their lives by utilizing qualitative resources, knowledge, and skills that are available. Marriage enrichment groups are an example of a pattern that is developing rapidly. Social workers often act as leaders of such groups and assist seven or eight couples to look at who they are, where they are, where they would like to be, and help them reach their goals. Many such programs call for couples to attend a weekend retreat for group sessions, individual discussions, and other activities that help extend their paths to fuller living. The future is wide open for expansion of enrichment programs.

Movement for Higher Quality

Traditionally, social work has provided services for the disadvantaged and others with inadequate social relationships. In the past, report after report has been collected to emphasize numbers of interviews, group conferences, testing, and other indicators of work accomplished. Efficiency and effectiveness have been tabulated in many different ways to reflect agency services. Today there is a growing emphasis to provide not only quantity of services, but, in particular, to reach for quality.

According to Martin, top-quality management (TQM) is rapidly shaping up as today's new managerial wave. Many corporations have initiated TQM programs in recent years. Martin also suggests that it is just a matter of time "before this new management wave washes over human service organizations. In anticipation of this eventuality, human service administrators may find it in their best interest to begin exploring the concept of TQM."[26] A major element in this new approach is its emphasis on quality as a primary organizational goal.

Summary

We live in a fast-changing world, which has many implications for the rapidly developing profession of social work. In the years ahead, what pathways will social work be likely to follow?

Several trends and developments are emerging as projections are made into the future of social work: innovative services, increased status, higher salaries, growth of private practice, spirituality considerations in practice, curriculum modification, greater use of case management, increased advocacy role, improved public relations, growth in international social work, more leadership roles, additional emphasis on prevention and enrichment, use of technology, and movement for higher quality in social work education and practice.

The potentialities seem generally favorable for social work and social workers. Some rough spots lie ahead, but professional training and services are likely to be consolidated, increased, and improved.

Selected References

CORNETT, CARLTON, "Toward a More Comprehensive Personology: Integrating a Spiritual Perspective into Social Work Practice," *Social Work,* 37 (March 1992), 101–102.

COWLEY, AU-DEANE S., "Transpersonal Social Work: A Theory for the 1990s," *Social Work,* 38 (September 1993), 527–534.

GINSBERG, LEON, *Careers in Social Work.* Boston: Allyn & Bacon, 1998.

HOKENSTAD, M. C., and JAMES MIDGLEY, eds., *Issues in International Social Work: Global Challenges for a New Century.* Annapolis JCT, MD: NASW Press, 1997.

HOKENSTAD, M. C., S. K. KHINDUKA, and JAMES MIDGLEY, eds., *Profiles in International Social Work.* Washington, DC: National Association of Social Workers, 1992.

MACAROV, DAVID, *Certain Change: Social Work Practice in the Future.* Silver Spring, MD: National Association of Social Workers, 1991.

PROCTOR, ENOLA K., and LARRY E. DAVIS, "The Challenge of Racial Difference: Skills for Clinical Practice," *Social Work,* 39 (May 1994), 314–323.

RAFFOUL, PAUL R., and AARON MCNEECE, *Future Issues for Social Work Practice.* Boston: Allyn & Bacon, 1996.

REESER, LINDA CHERREY, and IRWIN EPSTEIN, *Professionalization and Activism in Social Work: The 60's, the 80's, and the Future.* New York: Columbia University Press, 1990.

REISCH, MICHAEL, and LILY JARMAN-ROHDE, "The Future of Social Work in the United States: Implications for Field Education," *Journal of Social Work Education,* 36, no. 2 (Spring/Summer 2000), 201–215.

SERMABEIKIAN, PATRICIA, "Our Clients, Ourselves: The Spiritual Perspective and Social Work Practice," *Social Work,* 39 (March 1994), 178–182.

SOWERS, KAREN M., and RODNEY A. ELLIS, "Steering Currents for the Future of Social Work," *Research on Social Work Practice,* 11, no. 2 (March 2001), 245–253.

Notes

1. John Naisbitt and Patricia Aburdene, *Megatrends 2000, Ten New Directions for the 1990's* (New York: William Morrow, 1990), p. 11.

2. John Naisbitt, Nana Naisbitt, and Douglas Philips, *High Tech, High Touch* (New York: Broadway Books, 1999), p. 3.

3. Ibid., p. 17

4. Ibid., p. 26.

5. Lecture by Dr. Mortimer Adler at the University of Utah, February 18, 1963.

6. Alvin Toffler, *Future Shock* (New York: Random House, 1970).

7. Ibid., p. 2.

8. Ibid., p. 487.

9. John Naisbitt, *Megatrends, Ten New Directions Transforming Our Lives* (New York: Warner Books, 1982), pp. 249–250.

10. Josephine A. V. Allen, "International Focus Key for Future," *NASW News,* 43, no. 4 (April 1998), p. 2.

11. U.S. Department of Labor, Bureau of Labor Statistics, *Occupational Employment and Wages, Community and Social Service Occupations (Major Group), Social Workers, All Other*, May 2006. Retrieved from www.bls.gov/oes/current/oes210000.htm.

12. "Therapists Tackle Drug Abuse in Sports," *NASW News,* 30 (September 1985), p. 7.

13. B. J. Symour and Beverly Marston, "Social Work and Optometry: A New Partnership," *Social Work,* 29 (November/December 1984), p. 540.

14. Elvira Craig de Silva and Elizabeth J. Clark, National Association of Social Workers, *Re-Engineering Our Structure for the Future*, September 2007, p. 1. Retrieved from www.socialworkers.org/pubs/news/2007/09/deSilva.asp.

15. Allen Rubin, "Practice Effectiveness: More Grounds for Optimism," *Social Work,* 30 (November/December 1985), p. 469.

16. Ted P. Asay and Michael J. Lambert, "The Empirical Case for the Common Factors in Therapy: Quantitative Factors," in Mark Hubble and Barry L. Duncan, eds., *The Heart and Soul of Change: What Works in Therapy* (Washington, DC: American Psychological Association, 1999), pp. 23–55.

17. Robert L. Barker, *The Social Work Dictionary,* 5th ed. (Washington, DC: NASW Press, 2003), p. 414.

18. David Derezotes and Tracie Hoffman, "Spiritual Issues in Practice with Vulnerable Children and Families" in Alvin L. Sallee, Hal A. Lawson, and Katherine Briar-Lawson, eds., *Innovative Practices with Vulnerable Children and Families* (Dubuque, IA: Eddie Bower, 2001).

19. Patricia Sermabeikian, "Our Clients, Ourselves: The Spiritual Perspective and Social Work Practice," *Social Work,* 39 (March 1994), p. 178.

20. Patricia W. Soyka, *Unlocking Human Resources: A Career in Social Work* (New York: Public Affairs Committee, 1971), p. 10.

21. Amy C. Butler, "The Attractions of Private Practice," *Journal of Social Work Education,* 28 (Winter 1992), p. 52.

22. Centers for Disease Control and Prevention and the Merck Company Foundation, *The State of Aging and Health in America 2007,* March 2007. Retrieved from www.cdc.gov/aging/saha.htm.

23. Maryann Mahaffey, "Lobbying and Social Work," *Social Work,* 17 (January 1972), p. 11.

24. Eleanor L. Brilliant, "Social Work Leadership: A Missing Ingredient?" *Social Work,* 31 (September/October 1986), p. 329.

25. *NASW News,* 39 (September 1994), p. 2.

26. Lawrence L. Martin, "Total Quality Management: The New Managerial Wave," *Administration in Social Work,* 17, no. 2 (1993), pp. 1–2.

Name Index

Abbott, Ann A., 429
Ackerman, 69
Addams, Jane, 24–25
Adler, Mortimer, 69, 416
Alberti, Robert, 189
Anderson, Christian B., 341
Arnold, Matthew, 88
Atkinson, D.R., 348
Augustus, John, 270

Bachman, Jerald G., 311
Barker, Robert L., 93, 113, 366, 388, 389
Bartlett, Harriet, 6, 76
Beck, 69
Bennett, William J., 201, 323
Bloom, Martin, 410
Blum, Richard H., 328
Bonds, Barry, 310
Boyle, Scott W., 329, 405
Bracht, Neil F., 177
Brager, George, 114
Briar, Scott, 144–145
Brilliant, Eleanor L., 429
Brody, Elaine M., 295, 297, 305
Burns, David D., 170, 301
Bush, George, 401
Bush, George W., 18, 19, 232, 292, 310–311, 323, 401

Cabot, Richard, 176
Carter, Jimmy, 153, 401
Chess, Wayne A., 130
Clark, E. Gurney, 398
Clark, Elizabeth J., 419
Clinton, Bill, 18, 180, 222, 223, 292, 310, 391
Cnaan, Ram, 18–19

Cormier, Sherry, 208
Cornett, Carlton, 172
Covey, Stephen, 141
Cross, T.L., 343
Cuomo, Mario, 401

Daley, John M., 114
de Anda, Diane, 345
De Hoyos, A., 341, 343
De Hoyos, G., 341
De Silva, Elvira Craig, 419
Deer, Ada, 391
Dellums, Ronald V., 391
Denison, Edward, 22
Derezotes, David S., 49, 422
Dix, Dorothea Lynde, 22, 153, 158
DuBois, Brenda, 63
Dunham, Arthur, 113

Elizabeth II (queen), 21
Ellis, 69
Emerson, 135
Emmons, Michael L., 189
Epstein, Irwin, 148
Erikson, Erik, 58, 69
Erlich, John L., 115
Eskridge, Chris W., 273
Evans, Cliff, 209–210

Farley, O. William, 168, 329, 405
Fischer, A.R., 348
Ford, Gerald, 401
Frank, Anne, 88
Frankl, Viktor, 172
Fraser, Mark, 249
Freud, Anna, 69

Freud, Sigmund, 58, 69
Friedlander, Walter A., 3
Frost, Robert, 233

Gemignani, Robert, 282–283
Gide, André, 45
Ginsberg, Leon, 354, 357, 361, 429
Gitterman, Alex, 94
Glasgow, Douglas, 339
Goldston, Stephen, 398
Goodwill, Dorothy, 303
Goodwill, Wilford, 303
Gorin, Stephen H., 392
Gothard, Sol, 278
Graham, Hugh Davis, 340
Grasso, Anthony J., 148
Greene, Roberta R., 371, 372, 373
Greenstone, James L., 201–202
Greenwood, Ernest, 378
Griffiths, J. Kent, 168
Grinnell, Richard M., 145

Haapala, David A., 249
Hagen, Jan L., 369
Haley, 69
Hall, G. Stanley, 69
Hamilton, Gordon, 75
Harper, Karen V., 346
Harrison, Stephen R., 329, 405
Hazelkorn, Florence, 399
Healy, William, 154
Hepworth, Dean H., 168, 373
Hill, Octavia, 22
Hiratsuka, John, 340
Hirshfeld, Magnus, 239
Hoffman, Tracie, 422

Huber, Charles H., 409
Hull, Grafton H., Jr., 50, 114, 190
Human, 356

Inuoye, Daniel K., 179

Jackson, Aurora P., 67
Jacobsen, Mike, 357
Jayaratne, Srinika D., 130
Jefferson, Thomas, 88
Johnson, Lyndon, 215, 224, 233
Johnson, Spencer, 141–142
Johnston, Lloyd D., 311, 329
Jome, L.M., 348
Jones, Terry, 339

Kadushin, Alfred, 347
Kane, Rosalie, 332
Kaplan, Harold I., 301
Kappner, Augusta, 391
Katz, Steven E., 401
Keigher, Sharon M., 179
Kempe, C. Henry, 262
Kennedy, John F., 17, 26, 152, 400–401
Kettner, Peter M., 114, 118
Kidneigh, John, 131
King, Rodney, 340–341
Kirst-Ashman, Karen K., 50, 113, 114, 190
Konopka, Gisela, 92
Kragh, Jeffrey, 409
Kumpfer, Karol L., 327, 405

Lantz, Jim, 346
Laotse, 130
Larsen, Ann, 373
Leary, Timothy, 309
Leavell, Hugh R., 398
Lenson, Z., 141
Leviton, Sharon C., 201–202
Lin, Alice Mu-jung P., 172
Lloyd, Gary A., 182
Locklear, Herbert H., 348

Malcolm X, 338
Marston, Beverly, 418
Martin, Lawrence L., 431

McKlean, Frances H., 68
McMurty, Steven L., 118, 402
McNeil, C.F., 120
Mikulski, Barbara A., 391
Miley, Karla Krosgrud, 49, 51
Miller, William R., 276
Minuchin, 69
Mizio, Emelicia, 348
Mottonen, Doug, 276

Naisbitt, J., 415
Naisbitt, N., 415
Netting, F. Ellen, 118
Newman, Edward, 133
Nichols, Ann Weaver, 114
Nixon, Richard, 401
Norlin, Julia M., 130
Northern, Helen, 91
Nurius, Paula S., 208

O'Hare, Thomas, 148
Olson-Raymer, Gayle, 400
O'Malley, Patrick M., 311
O'Melia, Michael, 49
Ozawa, Martha N., 27

Papell, Catherine P., 94
Paul, St., 239
Pavlov, Ivan Petrovich, 69, 75
Pearls, 69
Pecora, Peter J., 249
Perlman, Helen, 70, 75
Philips, Douglas, 415
Plant, Tim, 418
Poertner, John, 133
Popenoe, Paul, 239

Rachin, Richard L., 284
Rank, Otto, 75
Rapoport, Lydia, 398
Rapp, Charles A., 133, 374
Reagan, Nancy, 153, 215–216, 310
Reagan, Ronald, 18, 153, 201, 234, 391, 401
Reamer, Frederic G., 386
Regulus, Thomas A., 269
Rehr, Helen, 192
Reisch, Michael, 392

Richmond, Mary, 68
Rivas, Robert F., 89, 105
Rivera, Feliz G., 115
Rodgers, Patricia A.E., 391
Rodrequez, Ciro D., 392
Rogers, 69
Rollnick, Stephen, 276
Rooney, Ronald H., 373
Roosevelt, Franklin, 215
Roosevelt, Theodore, 356
Ross, Murray G., 120
Rothman, 114, 372–373, 374
Rue, James J., 239
Russell, Bertrand, 303
Ruth, Earl, 164

Sadock, Benjamin J., 301
Samenow, 275
Seneca, 304
Sermabeikian, Patricia, 422–423
Severson, Margaret M., 280
Shaw, George Bernard, 227
Sherman, Wendy, 391
Shulman, Lawrence, 94
Sierra, Ramona, 367
Simpson, Peter, 187
Sinkovitch, Mary K., 66
Skidmore, 131, 140
Skinner, B.F., 69, 75
Smith, Ken, 238
Soyer, David, 306
Specht, Harry, 114
Spencer, 132
Stabenow, Debbie, 392
Stone, Abraham, 239
Stone, Hannah, 239
Strom, Kimberly, 389
Sullivan, Louis W., 311
Symour, B.J., 418

Thompson, Tommy, 382
Tinney, Mary-Anne, 253
Toffler, Alvin, 416
Torres-Gill, Fernando, 391
Toseland, Ronald W., 89, 105
Towns, Edolphus, 391–392
Townsend, Wardell, 391
Turem, Terry, 133

Turner, John B., 350, 351

Van Soest, Dorothy, 348
Vourlekis, Betsy S., 372, 373

Walters, John P., 323
Warren, Neil, 402

Watson, Michael, 362
White, William, 69
Wickenden, William, 377–378
Wilson, William Julius,
   339–340
Windle, 356
Winn, Judy, 367

Wintersteen, R., 374
Wittman, Milton, 400

Yochelson, 275

Zastrow, Charles H., 92, 113, 358
Zoroaster, 301

Subject Index

AA. *See* Alcoholics Anonymous

AARP. *See* American Association of Retired People

AASSW. *See* American Association of Schools of Social Work

AASWG. *See* Association for the Advancement of Social Work Groups

Abandoned Infant Assistance Act, 401

Academy of Certified Baccalaureate Social Worker (ACBSW), 381

Academy of Certified Social Workers (ACSW), 13, 381, 421

ACBSW. *See* Academy of Certified Baccalaureate Social Worker

ACSW. *See* Academy of Certified Social Workers

ADHD. *See* Attention-deficit hyperactivity disorder

Administration, 123, 130–142, 144, 149
  basic principles, 132–133
  collaboration and, 138–141
  consultation and, 136–138
  definition of, 131–132
  life management strategies and, 141–142
  shifting power in, 142
  supervision, 133

Administration in Social Work (journal), 132

Adoption and Safe Families Act (ASFA), 249, 250

Adoption services, 255–257
  applicants, 258–260

Adult socialization, 76

Advocacy, 124, 426

AFDC. *See* Aid to Families with Dependent Children

Afghanistan, 394

Aftercare facilities, 161

Age, 99, 183

Agency goals, 97–98

Aging population, 288–289, 426
  case management in, 296–297
  in day care centers, 299–300
  dignity of, 302–306
  health of, 294–296
  independence of, 302–306
  living arrangements of, 293–294
  mental health in, 300–301
  nursing home alternatives for, 299
  in nursing homes, 297–298
  poverty amongst, 292
  retirement and, 302–304

AICP. *See* Association for Improving the Conditions of the Poor

Aid to Families with Dependent Children (AFDC), 215, 219, 220–223, 247, 367, 369

AIDS, 182, 191, 394

Alcohol abuse, 191, 318–319, 326–328
  social work with, 331–332

Alcoholics Anonymous (AA), 326, 331

Allen, Josephine V.A., 417

Alms, 20

Almshouses, 22

Alternative High School program, 197

Alzheimer's disease, 229

American Academy of Child and Adolescent Psychiatry, 202

American Association for Marriage and Family Therapy, 239

American Association of Group Workers, 90, 381

American Association of Medical Social Workers, 381

American Association of Psychiatric Social Workers, 381

American Association of Retired People (AARP), 230, 296

American Association of Schools of Social Work (AASSW), 90, 381

American Association of Social Workers, 29, 34

American Bar Association, 273

American Medical Association, 241, 294

American Psychiatric Association (APA), 11, 172

American Psychological Association, 202

American Red Cross, 14, 154
American University of
    Bulgaria, 14
Amphetamines, 312
Anger management, 189–190
Annual Program Meeting, 356
Antianxiety drugs, 318–319
APA. *See* American Psychiatric
    Association
ASFA. *See* Adoption and Safe
    Families Act
Assessment phase, 78–79
Associated Charities in Denver,
    23, 116
Association for Improving the
    Conditions of the Poor
    (AICP), 68
Association for the
    Advancement of Social
    Work Groups (AASWG),
    91
Association of Medical
    Superintendents of
    American Institutions for
    the Insane, 11
Atlantic City, 117
Attention-deficit hyperactivity
    disorder (ADHD), 263
Autobiography of Malcolm X,
    338

Baby boomers, 26
Bachelor of Social Work
    (BSW), 9, 29, 35, 42–43,
    76, 350
    admissions, 43
Balanced Budget Act, 297
Battered women, 241–242
Beck Depression Scale, 149
Behavior modification, 41
    in clinical social work,
    84–85
Behavioral effects, 263
Behavioral model, 75
Behavioral psychology, 69
Bell, T.H., 196
Berlin Institute for the Study
    of Sex, 239
Biculturalism, 346

Biology, 74
*Black Book of Executive
    Politics* (Lenson), 141
Block plans, 387
BNDD. *See* Bureau of
    Narcotics and Dangerous
    Drugs
Board of Guardians, 21
Book of Tao (Laotse), 130
Boot camps, 276
Boston Psychopathic
    Hospital, 154
Boundaries, 53
Boys' Clubs of America, 107
BSW. *See* Bachelor of Social
    Work
Buddha, 20
Buffalo, 23, 117
Bureau of Narcotics and
    Dangerous Drugs
    (BNDD), 322–323

Camp Fire Girls, 107
CAPTA. *See* Child Abuse
    Prevention and Treatment
    Act
Case management, 366–369
    defined, 371–373
    historical developments,
    369–371
    models, 373–374
    research, 374–375
Case School of Applied
    Science, 377
Case study method, 147
CASP. *See* Comprehensive
    Annual Services Program
    Plan
Catholic Youth Organizations,
    107
CCC. *See* Civilian
    Conservation Corps
CE. *See* Continuing education
Center for Substance Abuse
    Prevention, 327
Certification, 420–421
Chamber of Commerce, 282
Charity, 20
    scientific, 68

Charity Organization Society
    (COS), 22, 23, 29, 33–34,
    52, 68
Cheating, 200
Chicago, 24
Child abuse, 244–245
    physical, 262–264
    reports, 261
    sexual, 264
Child Abuse Prevention and
    Treatment Act (CAPTA),
    244, 263, 401
Child Guidance Movement,
    154
Child protective services,
    260–264
    issues and practices in,
    261–262
Child Welfare Division, 127
Child welfare services,
    246–247
Children's Bureau, 214
China, 20
Christian Church, 4
Church, 20
Church of Jesus Christ of
    Latter-day Saints, 359
"Cipher in the Snow," 208–210
Civil Rights Act, 339
Civil rights movement, 41, 124
Civil War, 23, 239
Civilian Conservation Corps
    (CCC), 25, 70
Clinical work, 9
    assessment phase of, 78–79
    behavior modification model
    of, 84–85
    defined, 66–67
    history of, 67–69
    intervention phase of, 79–80
    knowledge and, 73–74
    methods of, 74–76
    multisystems approach, 85
    practice framework, 71–74
    process of, 76–85
    psychosocial model in,
    81–82
    purpose, 71
    sanctions, 72–73

social work values, 71
study phase of, 76–78
task-centered model in, 82–84
termination phase of, 80–81
trends in, 69–71
Clozaril, 153
CMHC. *See* Community mental health center
COBRA. *See* Consolidated Omnibus Budget Reconciliation Act
Cocaine, 311, 312
Code of Ethics, 271, 383–386
Code of Hammurabi, 255
Codeine, 312
Cognitive movement, 69
Cognitive therapy, 41
  with criminals, 275–276
Collaboration, 138–141, 149
  teamwork concepts, 139–141
Collectivism, 20
Columbia University School of Social Work, 34, 75, 379
Commission on Accreditation, 380
Commitment, 165–166
Committee operation, 123
Common problems, 100
Community Chests, 24, 116
Community mental health center (CMHC), 154, 155–156, 159
Community organization, 9, 113–116
  case summaries, 126–127
  correctional services and, 273–275
  roles in, 125
  underlying principles in, 119–121
Community resources, 7
Community Services Council, 6, 126
Community social work administration, 123
  beginnings of, 116–119
  committee operation, 123–124

coordination, 121–122
financing, 123
organization, 122–123
planning, 121
processes, 121–124
research, 121
school and, 207
Comprehensive Annual Services Program Plan (CASP), 232
Comprehensive Mental Health Centers, 27
Concise Textbook of Clinical Psychiatry (Kaplan and Sadock), 301–302
Congress, 17
Congressional Budget Office, 229
Consolidated Omnibus Budget Reconciliation Act (COBRA), 369
Consultants, 424
Consultation, 136–138, 149
  principles of, 137–138
Consumer of research, 145
Continuing education (CE), 44–45
Contract with America, 180
Contributing partners, 145
Cooperative Committee on Administration, 131
Coordination, 121–122
Correctional services, 270–273. *See also* Crime
  case examples, 277–279
  cognitive therapy and, 275–276
  community organization and, 273–275
  direct practice, 273–275
  group work and, 273–275
  in institutions, 279–285
  motivational interviewing and, 276
  prevention and, 284–285
  principles, 273–275
  processes, 273–275
COS. *See* Charity Organization Society

Council on Social Work Education (CSWE), 4, 5, 9, 29, 35, 38, 45–49, 52, 73, 91, 130, 132, 341, 349, 351, 380, 418, 420, 427. *See also* Curriculum Policy Statements
  Annual Program Meeting, 356
  minority content, 351
Councils of Social Agencies, 23, 116
Counseling, 13
County Recreation Department, 126
Court of Domestic Relations, 239
Courts, 277–278
  drug, 279
Crime, 267–270. *See also* Correctional services
Criminal Personality (Samenow and Yochelson), 275
Crisis intervention, 76
CSWE. *See* Council on Social Work Education
Culture, 67
Curriculum Committee, 131
Curriculum Policy Statements, 6–7, 48, 117, 131, 145
Curriculum Studies, 5, 400
Curriculum Study (Spencer), 132
Cylert, 312

DARE, 405
Darvon, 312
Day care, 243
  for aging population, 299–300
Daydreaming, 58–59
Deinstitutionalization, 158
Delegate Assembly, 280, 378, 384
Demerol, 312
Democracy and Social Ethics (Addams), 25
Department of Education, 215

Department of Health and
    Human Services (DHHS),
    27, 215, 222, 244, 263
Department of Health,
    Education, and Welfare
    (HEW), 27, 214
Department of Housing and
    Urban Development
    (HUD), 293
Department of Labor, 27
Depressants, 318–319
Depression, 149, 301–302
Depth psychology, 70
Developmental aspects, 6
DHHS. *See* Department of
    Health and Human
    Services
*Diagnostic and Statistical
    Manual of Mental
    Disorders(DSM),* 149,
    172–173
*Diagnostic and Statistical
    Manual of Mental
    Disorders,* mental disorder
    categorization in, 173
Dignity, 302–306
Dilaudid, 312
Direct practice, 76–85
    correctional services
    and, 273–275
*Direct Social Work Practice:
    Theory and Skills*
    (Hepworth, Rooney, and
    Larsen), 373
Disabilities, 190–191
Discipline, 198
Disease, 181
Disseminator of knowledge, 145
Distance learning, 363
Distribution, 119
Diversity, 36
Division of Child and Family
    Services, 124
Divorce, 238
Doctoral programs, 44–46
    continuing education and,
    44–45
    curriculum, 44
    scholarships, 46

stipends, 46
    student participation in, 45
Drama, 54
Dream analysis, 69
Dropout rates, 196, 206
Drugs, 199–200, 309–312, 418.
    See also specific types
    abuse of, 321–322
    commonly abused, 312–321
    control, 322–330
    courts, 279
    education, 323–324
    emergency, 324
    government agencies,
    322–323
    inpatient services, 324
    outpatient services, 325
    prevalence of, 313–317
    prevention of, 322–330
    research, 328–330
    social work and, 330–334
    therapeutic communities,
    325–326
    therapy, 12
    treatment, 324
*DSM. See Diagnostic and
    Statistical Manual of
    Mental Disorders*
*Dual Perspective: Inclusion of
    Ethnic Minority Content in
    the Social Work
    Curriculum,* 341
Dynamic psychology, 68, 69

EAPs. *See* Employment
    assistance programs
Ecological theory, 53
Ednet system, 428
Education, 9. *See also* Public
    school
    delivery system, 197–198
    minorities and, 349–351
Educational aspects, 6
Educational Policy and
    Accreditation Standards
    (EPAS), 35, 36, 37–38, 52,
    118, 423
Ego strengths, 101
Elderly. *See* Aging population

Elective offices, 391–392
Elements of Crisis Intervention
    (Greenstone and Leviton),
    201–202
Elizabethan Poor Laws, 4, 21,
    30, 214
Employment agencies, 142
Employment assistance
    programs (EAPs), 408, 417
Empowerment, 51
Encyclopedia of Social Work
    (journal), 390
Engineering Institute of
    Canada, 377
England, 21, 23
English Poor Laws, 20–21, 68
Enjoyment patterns, 100
Enrichment, 411, 430
EPAS. *See* Educational Policy
    and Accreditation
    Standards
ERA. *See* Federal Emergency
    Relief Administration
Essential theory, 93
Ethics, 36. *See also* Code of
    Ethics
Ethnicity, 67
Europe, 20–22
Every Child Matters Education
    Fund, 19
Evidence-based practice,
    148–149, 393

Faith-based social service,
    18–19, 31
Family, 237–238
    in crisis, 407–408
    illness within, 186–188
    interaction, 7, 70
    preservation, 76
    structure, 242–244
    therapies, 69
Family counseling, 238–239,
    405–406
    agencies, 240–241
    kinds of, 240
Family Life Institutes, 404
Family preservation services
    (FPS), 407–408

Family Service America, 240
Family Service Association, 68, 405
Family Service Societies, 6
Family Social Societies, 404
Family Support Act, 221, 222, 369
Family Violence Prevention and Services Act, 401
Family Welfare Association, 131, 239
Farming out, 22
FBI. *See* Federal Bureau of Investigation
Federal Adoption Assistance and Child Welfare Act, 247
Federal Bureau of Investigation (FBI), 285
Federal Emergency Relief Act, 70
Federal Emergency Relief Administration (ERA), 25
Federal Insurance Contribution Act (FICA), 217
Federal Office of Education, 214
Feeling Good Handbook (Burns), 170, 301
FICA. *See* Federal Insurance Contribution Act
Field education, 37
Field theory, 96
Financing, 123
Foot-and-mouth disease, 191
Foster children, 251–253
Foster homes, 250, 251
Foster parents, 253–254
Fountain House, 161, 162
FPS. *See* Family preservation services
Free association, 69
Freedom, 19
Freedom to Choose plan, 197
Functional model, 75
Fundraising agencies, 116–117
Future Shock (Toffler), 416

GA. *See* General Assistance
Gangs, 200, 268–269

GDP. *See* Gross domestic product
General Assistance (GA), 226–227
Generalist social work practice, 9, 48–63, 76
  base for, 61–62
  with individuals, 64–66
  roles in, 51
  systems in, 50–51
  theoretical framework, 52–53
George Warren Brown School of Social Work, 400
Girl Scouts, 107, 424
Girls' Clubs of America, 107
Global health care problems, 191
Goodwill Family Foundation, 303
Government responsibility, 18
Gramm-Rudman Legislation, 291
Great Depression, 34, 70, 131, 217, 289
Greater Victoria Foster Parent Association, 253
Greeks, 20
Grey Panthers, 124
Gross domestic product (GDP), 3
Group psychotherapy, 93
Group work, 9, 87–89
  agency goals in, 97–98
  beginning, 105
  closed, 103
  correctional services and, 273–275
  defined, 91–93
  end, 106
  female groups in, 103
  formation of groups in, 97–101
  goal attainment in, 104–105
  group goals in, 98
  historical developments in, 89–91
  leadership in, 104
  long-term, 103
  male groups in, 103

  meeting days and times, 103
  member goals in, 98
  member selection in, 99–101
  middle, 105
  mixed groups in, 103
  models, 93–97
  open, 103
  preparation of members in, 101
  reciprocal goals model, 95–97
  remedial goals model of, 94
  rules, 102
  in schools, 205–206
  setting of, 102, 106–109
  short-term, 103
  size of groups in, 102
  social goals model of, 94
  stages of, 105–106
  structuring, 102–105
  worker goals in, 98

Halfway houses, 284
Hallucinogens, 319
Harassment, 200–201
Hartland Partnership Center, 14
Hazeldon Foundation, 418
HBSE. *See* Human behavior and social environment
HCFA. *See* Health Care Financing Administration
Headstart alliances, 393
Health and Social Work (journal), 390
Health care, 176–178
  definition of, 178–181
  global, 191
  public, 188–189
  roles in, 183–191
  social work in, 178–181
  universal, 304–305
Health Care Financing Administration (HCFA), 179–180
Health Maintenance Organization (HMO), 178–179
Hebrews, 20
Heroin, 312, 325
  addiction, 332–333

HEW. *See* Department of Health, Education, and Welfare
HI. *See* Hospital insurance
High Tech, High Touch (Naisbitt, Naisbitt, and Philips), 415
Hinduism, 238
Historical approach, 147
HIV, 182
HMO. *See* Health Maintenance Organization
Homeless, 50, 227–228
mental health and, 164–165
shelters, 142
Hospital insurance (HI), 216, 228
Hospitalization, 157, 159
Hospitals, 108
social work in, 183–186
Host agencies, 108–109
House of Delegates, 45
House Select Committee on Children, Youth, and Families, 355
HUD. *See* Department of Housing and Urban Development
Hull House, 24
Human behavior, 36, 41
forces in shaping, 54–56
social environment and, 52–53
Human behavior and social environment (HBSE), 423
Human biology, 69
Human ecological approach, 147
Human relations, 89
Human Services in the Rural Environment (journal), 357
Humanistic psychology, 69
Hurricane Katrina, 394

ICWA. *See* Indian Child Welfare Act
IFPS. *See* Intensive Family Preservation Services
Illiteracy, 197

Illness, 61
defining, 181–183
familial, 186–188
Incarceration, 271
Independence, 302–306
India, 20
Indian Child Welfare Act (ICWA), 257–258
Individual worth, 71–72
Individualism, 20
Individuals, 64–66
Indoor relief, 22
Industrial Revolution, 89
Infants, 88
Influenza, 182
Inhalants, 311, 320–321, 329
In-home care of children, 247–249
Inner and outer forces paradigm, 53–56
life cycle and, 57–60
social functioning and, 60
systems in, 56–57
Inpatient services, 324
InstaCare Center, 404
Institute of Social Science, 34
Institutions, 279–285
Insurance. *See also* Old Age, Survivors, Disability, and Health Insurance
Integration of resources, 172
Integrative model, 74–75
Intelligence, 101
Intensive Family Preservation Services (IFPS), 249
International Federation of Social Workers, 429
International Red Cross, 14
International social work, 14–15, 429–430
Intervention phase, 79–80
Invalids, 181
Iowa, 296
Iraq War, 2, 394
Isolation, 88
Ivy League, 200

Jails, 22–23, 163–164, 281–282
Jewish Community Centers, 107

Job Opportunities and Basic Skills (JOBS), 222, 369–370
JOBS. *See* Job Opportunities and Basic Skills
Joint Commission on Mental Illness and Health, 158–159
Journal of Case Management, 371
Justice, 36
Juvenile delinquents, 23, 108, 267–270
prevention of, 407

Keeping Children and Families Safe Act, 263, 401
Ketamine, 319
Knowledge, 73–74

Labor Temple, 239
Leadership, 130, 428–429
Learning theory, 74, 93
Less eligibility, 67
Licensing laws, 136, 420–421
Life cycle, 57–60
Life management strategies, 141–142
Liverpool, 23, 116
Lobbying, 427
Locality development, 114
London, 90
"London Society for Organizing Charitable Relief and Repressing Mendicancy," 22
Loneliness, 88
Los Angeles riots, 1, 115, 340–341
LSD, 309, 311, 319, 330

Macro practice, 113, 118–119
Macro systems, 53, 56–57, 62, 65
Madrid, 393
Manhattan State Hospital, 154
March of Dimes, 178

Marijuana, 309, 320
Marriage counseling, 13,
   238–239. *See also*
   Premarital counseling
  agencies, 240–241
  kinds of, 240
Marshaling Citizen Power to
   Modernize Corrections,
  282
Maryland, 165
Massachusetts, 22
Massachusetts General
   Hospital, 176
Master of Social Work (MSW),
  9, 29, 35, 38–42, 44, 76,
  136, 145, 349, 388, 425
  admission to, 40
  evaluating programs, 40–42
  students enrolled in, 38–39
MDMA, 311, 319
Media, 2
Medicaid, 26, 30, 177, 179,
  180, 192, 230–231, 234,
  294, 298, 304
  flex care, 299
Medicare, 26, 30, 177, 179,
  180, 192, 217, 218,
  228–229, 294, 298, 304
  drug prescription program,
   230
  reform, 229–230
Medicare Catastrophic
   Coverage Act, 218
Medieval period, 20
Megatrends 2000 (Naisbitt),
  417
Member goals, 98
Meningitis, 182
Mental health, 152–153
  aftercare facilities, 161
  in aging population, 300–301
  beginnings in, 153–154
  chronic illness, 166
  DSM in, 172–173
  elements of comprehensive,
   156–158
  homelessness and, 164–165
  jails and prisons and,
   163–164

  network, 154–156
  outpatient clinics, 162
  prevention of problems, 170
  preventive, 404–405
  research, 171
  special problems and issues
   in, 164–173
  teenagers and, 163
  workplace and, 171
Mental Health Act of
   1946, 154
Mental health centers, 142
Mental hospitals, 158–159
Mental illness, 23
  poverty and, 166–167
Methadone, 312, 325
Mezzo systems, 53, 56–57, 62,
  65
Micro practice, 118–119
Micro systems, 53, 56–57, 62,
  65
Milwaukee, 23, 116
Minorities, 337–338
  educational developments
   and, 349–351
  problems, 338–346
  school social work and, 207
  social work intervention
   with, 342–346
  students, 349–350
  theoretical work models,
   343–345
MMCU. *See* Mobile Medical
   Care Units
Mobile Medical Care Units
   (MMCU), 293
Mormon religion, 359
Morphine, 312
Motivational interviewing,
  208
  with criminals, 276–277
MSW. *See* Master of Social
   Work
Multidimensional models, 74
Multisystems approach, 85
Municipal Board of Health,
  239
Mutual aid, 20
Mutual support, 119

NACM. *See* National
   Association of Case
   Management
NAMI. *See* National
   Association for the
   Mentally Ill
Narcotics, 312, 325
NASW. *See* National
   Association of Social
   Workers
National Alliance for Family
   Life, 239
National Association for the
   Mentally Ill (NAMI), 123
National Association for the
   Study of Group Work, 90
National Association of Case
   Management (NACM),
   371
National Association of Social
   Workers (NASW), 4, 9, 13,
   18, 67, 90, 130, 192, 271,
   381–383, 417, 419, 421,
   425, 427. *See also*
   Delegate Assembly
  institutional work and, 280
  Workforce Center, 426
National Center for Family
   Literacy, 197
National Center for Juvenile
   Justice, 268
National Center for Social
   Policy, 354
National Commission on
   Excellence in Education,
   196, 207
National Commission on Social
   Work Practice, 397
National Conference of
   Charities and Corrections,
   68, 117, 399
National Conference of Foster
   Parents, 253
National Conference of Social
   Work at Atlantic City, 117
National Conference of Social
   Work in Buffalo, 117
National Conference on Social
   Work, 90, 131

National Council for Adoption
(NCFA), 255
National Council on Family
of Relations, 239
National Drug Policy, 323
National Education
Association, 208
National Football League, 418
National Health Care Act, 179
National Household Survey on
Drug Abuse, 311
National Institute of Mental
Health (NIMH), 146, 148,
166, 171, 300, 362, 374
National Institute on Drugs and
Alcohol (NIDA), 327
National Institute on Social
Work in Rural Areas, 357
National Office for Substance
Abuse Prevention, 329
National Social Work Month,
391
National Survey Results, 311
National Symposium on
Addressing Violent Crime
Through Community
Involvement, 285
Native Americans, 257–258,
350
NCFA. *See* National Council
for Adoption
Neglect, 244–245
Neighborhood Team, 124
Nervous exhaustion, 61
New Orleans, 22, 394
New York Charity Organization
Society, 379
New York City, 161
New York School of
Philanthropy, 29, 34
New York School of Social
Work, 75
New York Times, 4–5
Nicotine, 318
NIDA. *See* National Institute
on Drugs and Alcohol
NIMH. *See* National Institute
of Mental Health
Nitrites, 320

Nobel Prize, 45
Nondeterrent insurance, 219
North American Association
of Christian Social
Workers, 19
Nursing homes, 297–298
alternatives to, 299

OASDHI. *See* Old Age,
Survivors, Disability, and
Health Insurance
Office of National Drug
Control Policy, 312
Old Age, Survivors, Disability,
and Health Insurance
(OASDHI), 3, 25, 216–219
Old Testament, 238–239
Older Americans Act of 1965,
289–291, 298
Older Citizens' Center, 126
Olympics, 310
Opiates, 312
Orange County Drug Court,
279
Orient, 20
Orphans, 20, 22
Outdoor relief, 22
Outer forces, 54
Outpatient treatment, 157, 162,
332–333
for drugs, 325
OxyContin, 312, 329

Parole, 271, 282
Participation of Residents, 120
Partnership for a Drug-Free
America, 312
PCP, 319
Peace Corps, 26, 303
Peer groups, 205
Penitentiary system, 270
Pennsylvania School of Social
Work, 75
Pennsylvania System, 23
Percodan, 312
Personal Responsibility and
Work Opportunity
Reconciliation Act of
1996, 18, 27, 31, 223, 247

Philadelphia Geriatrics Center,
295
Physical injuries, 263
Pittsburgh, 23, 116
Police departments, 277
Polio, 182
Poor, classifications of, 21
Poor Law Commissioners, 21
Poor Law of 1834, 21
Poor taxes, 20, 21
Populations-at-risk, 36
Poverty
in aging population, 292
mental illness and, 166–167
rural, 355
welfare and, 223–226
women in, 224–226
PPOs. *See* Preferred provider
organizations
Practice of Social Work
(Zastrow), 358
Preaddictive adolescents,
331
Preferred provider
organizations (PPOs), 179
Premarital counseling, 6, 240,
402–404, 412. *See also*
Marriage counseling
President's Commission on
Law Enforcement and
Administration of Justice,
269, 282, 285
President's Commission on
Mental Health, 153
President's Committee on
Employment of the
Handicapped, 171
President's National Drug
Control Strategy, 310–311
Prevention, 56, 397–398, 430
delinquency, 407
examples of, 402–409
focusing on, 399–401
implications of, 409–410
mental health, 404–405
problems involved in, 402
relapse, 409
religious leaders and,
406–407

social work and, 193
suicide, 408
Prevention and Homeless
Act, 165
*Prevention in Human
Services,* 401
*Primary Prevention: The
Possible Science*
(Bloom), 410
Primitive societies, 20
Prisons, 163–164
Private practices, 388–390, 425
Probation, 271
Problem-solving method, 75
*Proceedings of the National
Conference of Charities
and Correction,* 270
Production, 119
Profession of social work,
377–379
changing nature of, 392
code of ethics, 383–386
contemporary, 383–394
elective offices, 391–392
future developments in,
392–394
historical background,
379–383
identification and visibility
in, 419–420
jobs and, 390–391
maturation of, 417–418
private practices, 388–390
publications, 390
research, 387–388
salaries, 390–391
schools of, 379–380
Project Match, 276
Proposition 187, 337–338
Proposition 209, 337
Protective services, 126
Provisional Council on Clinical
Social Work, 69
Prozac, 149, 153
Psychiatry, 11–12, 69
Psychoanalysis, 70, 74
Psychoanalytic theory, 93
Psychological disorders, 263
Psychology, 12–13, 69

behavioral, 69
depth, 70
dynamic, 68, 69
humanistic, 69
Psychosocial model, 75
in clinical social work,
81–82
Public assistance, 220
social welfare and, 25–27
Public health, 188–190
anger management
and, 188–189
Public relations, 426–427
Public school, 197–198. *See
also* Education
assessing risks in, 201–202
cheating in, 200
discipline in, 198
drugs in, 199–200
gangs in, 200
harassment in, 200–201
problems in, 198–202
school shootings, 198–199
teaching values in, 201
violence in, 198
Public welfare, 17–18,
233–234, 393, 400
Public Welfare Amendments,
25
Punishment, 271
Pygmalion (Shaw), 227

Race, 67
Racism, 338
Rape, 242
Reach out features, 162
Reciprocal goals model, 95–97
Referrals, 8
Reformation, 271
Rehabilitation counselors, 13
Relapses, 409
Relationship, 9–10
Religious leaders, 406–407
Remedial goals model, 94–95
Research, 143–149
applied, 143
case study method of, 147
definition, 143
evaluation, 147–148

evidence-based practices,
148
experimental, 146
historical, 147
human ecological, 147
main kinds of, 146–147
major steps in, 146
mental health, 171
professional, 387–388
pure, 143
qualitative, 148
roles in, 145–146
social survey, 147
social work, 37, 143–146
Residential treatment centers
(RTCs), 163
Retirement, 302–304
Riots, Los Angeles, 1, 115,
340–341
Ritalin, 312
Rohypnol, 311, 319
Role function, 60–61
RTCs. *See* Residential
treatment centers
Runaway children, 407
Rural areas, 354–355
poverty, 355
Rural social work, 427
beginnings of, 356–357
distance learning for, 363
positive aspects of, 361–362
practice, 357–359
roles, 359–361
service agencies, 362

SAD PERSONS scale, 169
Salt Lake County Jail,
164, 281
Salvation Army, 331
Sanctions, 72–73
Scared straight programs, 276
Schizophrenia, 157
Scholarships, 46
School counselors, 13
School of Applied Social
Sciences, 90
School of Social Service
Administration, 130
School shootings, 198–199

School social work
  beginnings of, 202
  community and, 207
  group, 205–206
  with individuals, 203–204
  minorities and, 207
  motivational interviewing
    in, 208
  practice, 203–204
Science, 88
Scientific charity, 68
Self-determination, 72
September 11, 2001, 189, 393
Settlement House Movement
  (SHM), 52
*The Seven Habits of Highly
  Effective People* (Covey),
  141
Sex, 101
Sexual abuse, 264
SHM. *See* Settlement House
  Movement
Simmons College, 400
Single mothers, 238
Single payer bill, 192
Sleeping medications,
  318–319
SMI. *See* Supplementary
  insurance
Social action, 114, 124
Social agency, 131
Social casework, 66, 117
  history of, 67–69
  process, 77
  trends in, 69–71
Social Casework (journal), 68
Social Casework (Perlman), 75
Social control, 119
Social dysfunction, 5, 6
Social environment, human
  behavior and, 52–53
Social exchange theory, 93
Social functioning
  inner and outer forces
    paradigm and, 60
  levels of, 60–61
Social goals model, 94
Social interaction, 88

Social planning, 114
Social Security Act, 26, 30, 70,
  214, 216–220, 228,
  233–234, 249, 292, 392
  amendments to, 401
  crisis, 231–232
Social Security Administration,
  26
Social Security Bulletin, 3
Social service, 89
  minorities and, 346–349
Social surveys, 147
Social systems theory, 93
Social welfare, 3–4, 17–18
  European roots of, 20–22
  expenditures, 3
  policy, 36–37
  premises of, 2–3
  public assistance and, 25–27
  social work, 4
  in United States, 22–25
Social work. *See also*
  Community organization;
  Generalist social work
  practice; Group work;
  International social work;
  Profession of social work;
  Rural social work
  with alcoholics, 331–332
  appearance of, 28–30
  basic functions of, 6
  certification, 420–421
  continuum in, 423–424
  corrections and, 270–271
  counseling and, 13
  curriculum content, 37–38
  defining, 4–5, 7, 8
  distinguishing characteristics
    of, 7–11
  education in, 29–30, 35–46
  enrichment, 411–412
  field education, 37
  with foster children,
    251–253
  higher quality, 430–431
  in hospitals, 183–186
  increase in services, 418–419
  in institutions, 279–285

  licensing, 420–421
  master's program, 38–42
  in mental hospitals, 159–160
  with minorities, 342–346
  practice, 37, 72
  premises of, 2–3
  prevention and, 193
  professional bodies, 9
  psychiatry and, 11–12
  research, 37, 143–146
  schools of, 386–387
  social welfare, 4
  sociology and, 11
  spirituality and, 421–423
  status, 424–425
  student participation in, 45
  training, 4
  underlying assumptions of,
    5–6
  values, 71–72
  in workplace, 408–409
  in world, 13–15
Social Work Abstracts (journal),
  390
Social Work Almanac, 390
Social Work Dictionary, 7, 19,
  93, 131, 270, 399, 422
Social Work in Education
  (journal), 390
Social Work Research (journal),
  390
Social Work Research Group,
  381
Social-emotional deficits, 263
Socialization, 119
Sociology, 11, 69, 74
Special Education Legislation
  of 1987, 369
Specialization, 387
Spirituality, 421–423
Sri Lanka, 429
SSI. *See* Supplementary
  Security Income
*Standards and Guidelines for
  Social Work Case
  Management for the
  Functionally Impaired,* 371
Steroids, 310, 321

Stimulants, 312
Stipends, 46
Study phase, 76–78
Suicide, 185
  in aging population,
    301–302
  prevention, 408
  risks of, 168–169
  teenage, 168
Supervision, 8–9, 133–134, 149
  licensing laws and, 136
  as teaching, 134–135
Supplementary insurance
    (SMI), 216, 228
Supplementary Security
    Income (SSI), 158, 180,
    215, 220, 292
Supreme Court, 199
Systems theory, 41, 53, 65, 96.
    See also Macro systems;
    Mezzo systems; Micro
    systems

Talwin, 312
TANF. *See* Temporary
    Assistance for Needy
    Families
Task-centered casework, 75
  in clinical social work,
    82–84
Tax cuts, 18
Teaching
  supervision and, 134–135
  values, 201
Teamship, 140
Teamwork concepts, 139–141
Technology, 2, 427–428
Teenage suicide, 168
Teenagers, mental health
    services for, 163
Temporary Assistance for
    Needy Families (TANF),
    240, 243
Termination phase, 80–81
Terrorism, 2, 393
Therapeutic clubs, 161–162
  for drugs, 325–326
Tobacco, 318

Top-quality management
    (TQM), 431
Toynbee Hall, 24, 90
TQM. *See* Top-quality
    management
Tranquilizers, 309
Transplants, 184
Treatment groups, 93
Tribal customs, 20
Tuberculosis, 182

Undergraduate programs,
    42–43
Unemployment insurance,
    219–220
Uniqueness, 72
United States, 19
  insurance programs in, 3
  social welfare in, 22–25
United Way, 24, 28, 117, 123,
    241
University of Chicago, 75, 130
University of Connecticut, 400
University of North Carolina,
    400
University of Pennsylvania
    School of Social Work, 18
University of Utah, 14, 30
Ursuline Sisters, 22
U.S. Bureau of Justice
    Statistics, 272
U.S. Bureau of the Census, 4,
    190, 289
U.S. Children's Bureau, 262
Utah, 136, 358–359
Utah Education Network, 363

VA. *See* Veterans
    Administration
Valley Mental Health, 164
Value systems, 99
Values, 36
Vendorship, 389
*Veronia School District v.
    Acton,* 199
Veterans Administration
    (VA), 135, 158
Vicodin, 312, 329

Violence, 198
  risks of, 201–202
  towards women, 241–242
Visitors in training, 68
VISTA. *See* Volunteers in
    Service to America
Vocational Rehabilitation
    Administration, 214
Volunteers, 27–28
Volunteers in Service to
    America (VISTA), 26,
    303

Walnut Street Prison, 270
Welfare, 214. *See also* Public
    welfare; Social welfare
  government's responsibility
    for, 214–215
  poverty and, 223–226
  reform, 223
Wellbutrin, 149
West Virginia Human Services
    Department, 429
White House Conference on
    Aging, 171, 289, 291–292,
    304–305
WHO. *See* World Health
    Organization
Who Moved My Cheese?
    (Johnson), 141–142
Wholeness of individuals, 7, 60
Women
  battered, 241–242
  in poverty, 224–226
  rape and, 242
Worker goals, 98
Worker-client relationship, 80
Workforce Center, 426
Workhouse test, 67
Workplace, 170
  mental health and, 171
  social work in, 408–409
Works Progress Administration
    (WPA), 25
World Health Organization
    (WHO), 180, 182
World War I, 69, 116, 131, 154
World War II, 131, 154

Worth values, 71–72
WPA. *See* Works Progress
    Administration

YMCA. *See* Young Men's
    Christian Association
YMHA. *See* Young Men's
    Hebrew Association
Young Men's Christian
    Association (YMCA), 89,
    106–107, 424

Young Men's Hebrew
    Association (YMHA),
    107
Young, Whitney M., Jr., 427
Young Women's Christian
    Association (YWCA), 89,
    106–107, 424
Young Women's Hebrew
    Association (YWHA),
    107
Youth bureaus, 277

Youth Development
    Delinquency Prevention
    Administration, 283
Youth service systems,
    282–283
YWCA. *See* Young Women's
    Christian Association
YWHA. *See* Young Women's
    Hebrew Association

Zoloft, 149

Photo Credits

Page 5: Charles Gupton/Stone/Getty Images
15: Hazir Reka/Corbis/Reuters
24: Underwood & Underwood/Corbis
28: Myrleen Ferguson Cate/PhotoEdit
34: John A. Rizzo/Photodisc/Getty Images
41: Michael Newman/PhotoEdit
50: Jeff Greenberg/The Image Works
54: David Young-Wolff/PhotoEdit
78: Michael Newman/PhotoEdit
83: Jeff Greenberg/PhotoEdit
91: Michael Newman/PhotoEdit
104: Mary Kate Denny/PhotoEdit
115: Michael Newman/PhotoEdit
119: Richard Lord/The Image Works
134: Jeff Greenberg/PhotoEdit
144: Will Hart
160: David Young-Wolff/PhotoEdit
163: Mary Kate Denny/PhotoEdit
170: Ellen Senisi/The Image Works
186: Robin Nelson/PhotoEdit
188: Lon C. Diehl/PhotoEdit

199: Dann Tardif/Corbis
205: Will Faller
217: David Young-Wolff/PhotoEdit
225: Will Hart
243: Ellen Senisi/The Image Works
246: Robert Harbison
269: Mark Richards/PhotoEdit
278: AP Images
293: Julia Cumes/The Image Works
298: Robert Harbison
318: Doug Menuez/Photodisc/Getty Images
322: Steven Rubin/The Image Works
338: AP Images
347: Bob Daemmrich/The Image Works
355: Wolfgang Spunbarg/PhotoEdit
368: Michael Newman/PhotoEdit
386: Will Hart
409: Robert Harbison
411: Nancy Sheehan/PhotoEdit
422: Kathy McLaughlin/The Image Works
428: Bill Aron/PhotoEdit